Learning to Become a BSD Guru

The Best of FreeBSD® Basics

By Dru Lavigne

Title: The Best of FreeBSD Basics
Subtitle: Learning to Become a BSD Guru
Author: Dru Lavigne

December 2007
Publisher: Reed Media Services
Editor: Jeremy C. Reed

ISBN: 0-9790342-2-1
ISBN-13: 978-0-9790342-2-0

Contents

List of Figures

List of Tables

Foreword

Software documentation has always been a sore point, but nowhere more than with free software. Traditionally people write free software to "scratch an itch". This causes two problems: firstly, since people have written the software themselves, they already understand it and don't need documentation. Secondly, because the itch has gone away, they see no reason to write documentation. Those that do write the documentation write it from their own perspective, and others have difficulty understanding it.

What happens? People who like the idea of the software, but can't quite understand it, write *HOWTO*s, which effectively describe how they got the software to work. This approach is very popular in the Linux world, but you only need to google for combinations like `+mythtv +HOWTO` to realize that this approach is frequently a case of the one-eyed leading the blind.

But what's the real problem with HOWTOs? Many people write them – I do too. The problem is that it's another case of scratching an itch. Getting the software to work is complicated enough that you write down the steps you took to make things work. Once it works, the job of the HOWTO is done, at least for you. But it only describes part of the issue, the part that interested you, and other people who find the HOWTO on the web get hopelessly confused.

Dru Lavigne has taken the professional approach: she didn't give up when it worked for her. Instead, she polished each HOWTO until it was intelligible, and then she published it.

Publishing things on the web is great, but it's still relatively easy for the reader to lose the plot. Where's the best HOWTO? Despite all advances in online technology, well-prepared books have lost none of their popularity. So the next step is this book, for which Dru has polished the articles *again*..

The proof of the pudding is in the eating, of course. I've taken a look at a couple of drafts, and I'm impressed. The nice thing about this sort of book is that you can always find something interesting, even if you have a lot of experience in the area. I've found interesting ideas; I hope you will too.

Greg Lehey
Dereel, Victoria, Australia, October 2007

Preface

In early 2000, Chris Coleman sent an email to a FreeBSD mailing list asking for articles on performing common tasks on FreeBSD. Being the meticulous sort, I had a journal of all of the attempts, error messages, and successes I had encountered since stumbling upon freebsd.org through an Internet search. I went through these notes and decided that nine of the tasks were significant enough to warrant an article and sent that list of nine tasks back to Chris. As it turned out, I was the only one who responded, and even luckier for me, the articles were to be published by O'Reilly. And thus, the FreeBSD Basics column was born.

I don't think anyone foresaw that that column would still be around seven years later or that an entire generation (in Internet terms) of new BSD users would cut their teeth on its contents. As the years went by it was always in the back of my mind to some day review the content and to update the crusty bits.

Regular readers of the column should note that the content has been organized into chapters and that everything has been written for and tested on FreeBSD 6.2. Some articles were significantly reworked; for example, some tasks that used to take 1000 words to describe and accomplish are now either automatic or can be achieved with one or two commands. A few of the utilities have gone the way of the dodo bird while others have been replaced with better equivalents. It is also interesting to note that some articles required no to very little change, especially those dealing with principles.

Each reworked article contains an *Additional Resources* section which includes the URL to the original article as well as the still existing websites referenced in the original article. Those of you who like to track historical changes like I do will have the opportunity to compare what has changed between the original and the reworked writing.

Some changes are due to my own growth since the column started. For example, there is less emphasis on the ports collection and more on **pkg_add** and you'll rarely be advised to reboot or enter single-user mode.

I'd like to thank Chris Coleman for introducing me to O'Reilly. I'd like to thank Jeremy C. Reed for being a top-notch editor who recognizes the value of using subversion and vi to write a book, has a good eye for catching my mistakes, and has the patience to put up with my formatting glitches. I'd like to thank all of the readers of the FreeBSD Basics column, especially those who took the time and the courage to email me or introduce themselves at conferences and events.

–Dru Lavigne

Typographical Conventions

The following are the typographical conventions used in this book:

`Constant Width Teletype Font` is used for computer interaction examples and for output from commands.

In examples, **`bold fixed width`** is used to show input typed by the user (or reader). Examples that mix user input and command output have the user input printed in bold. These are commands or text that should be typed in literally.

Options that vary or are chosen by the user (or reader) are shown in *`slanted fixed width text`*. This content should be substituted with an actual appropriate value.

Bold text is used for program names, Unix utilities, commands that can be ran, command line switches, and keyboard keys.

A `fixed face` is also used for file and device names, directory paths, URIs, variable names, and configuration parameters.

Slanted text is used for host and domain names, email addresses, user names and group names. *Emphasis in italics* is for new concepts and important terminology.

A Sans serif face is used for menu choices, window buttons, and GUI elements.

In long command line examples, a trailing backslash can be used literally to mean the following line is part of same command line. Long lines that end with ⇓ (down arrow) mean that the following line in the book should be read (or used) as being on the same line.

Licenses

This book uses a few examples from open source documentation included with FreeBSD or installed via FreeBSD ports. The following are the copyright statements.

Redistribution and use in source and binary forms, with or without modification, are permitted provided that the following conditions are met:

1. Redistributions of source code must retain the above copyright notice, this list of conditions and the following disclaimer.

2. Redistributions in binary form must reproduce the above copyright notice, this list of conditions and the following disclaimer in the documentation and/or other materials provided with the distribution.

4. Neither the name of the University nor the names of its contributors may be used to endorse or promote products derived from this software without specific prior written permission.

THIS SOFTWARE IS PROVIDED BY THE REGENTS AND CONTRIBUTORS "AS IS" AND ANY EX-PRESS OR IMPLIED WARRANTIES, INCLUDING, BUT NOT LIMITED TO, THE IMPLIED WAR-RANTIES OF MERCHANTABILITY AND FITNESS FOR A PARTICULAR PURPOSE ARE DISCLAIMED. IN NO EVENT SHALL THE REGENTS OR CONTRIBUTORS BE LIABLE FOR ANY DIRECT, INDI-RECT, INCIDENTAL, SPECIAL, EXEMPLARY, OR CONSEQUENTIAL DAMAGES (INCLUDING, BUT NOT LIMITED TO, PROCUREMENT OF SUBSTITUTE GOODS OR SERVICES; LOSS OF USE, DATA, OR PROFITS; OR BUSINESS INTERRUPTION) HOWEVER CAUSED AND ON ANY THEORY OF LI-ABILITY, WHETHER IN CONTRACT, STRICT LIABILITY, OR TORT (INCLUDING NEGLIGENCE OR OTHERWISE) ARISING IN ANY WAY OUT OF THE USE OF THIS SOFTWARE, EVEN IF ADVISED OF THE POSSIBILITY OF SUCH DAMAGE.

1 Becoming Familiar with FreeBSD

1.1 Building an X Server and a Window Manager

One of the first tasks most users accomplish on their FreeBSD system is setting up X and a window manager. If you prefer to have the install do this for you, consider installing PC-BSD or DesktopBSD instead.[1]

While configuring X has improved significantly since the original FreeBSD Basics article from 2000, it still is not an exact science; there are a lot of video cards out there and some are supported better than others.

Configuring X

To configure X, you'll need to have the X.org distribution installed. If you're not sure whether you installed this when you installed FreeBSD, type:

```
# pkg_info | grep xorg
```

If you receive output from this command it will show the version of **xorg** installed. If you just get your prompt back, you can install **xorg** as the superuser with this command:

```
# pkg_add -r xorg
```

Once installed, this command will probe your video card and automagically configure X for you:

```
# rehash
# Xorg -configure
```

Note: When you install a new command on a FreeBSD system it won't be found until you type **rehash**. This is because the superuser's shell is **tcsh** and **tcsh** only looks for new binaries when you start your shell. Typing **rehash** tells **tcsh** that you want it to look for new binaries now without having to first exit and reenter your shell.

A sample configuration file will be created for you in /root/xorg.conf.new. This file won't be used until you copy it to /etc/X11/xorg.conf.

---

[1]PC-BSD and DesktopBSD are introduced in sections 1.3 and 1.4 respectively.

Configuring a Window Manager

Once you have configured X, you'll want to start customizing your desktop environment. If I type **startx** as a regular user immediately after configuring X the resulting GUI may prove functional, but it looks awful. If you're unsure which window manager to install, `http://xwinman.org/` is an excellent resource that provides screenshots of the most popular window managers and desktops.

If you like simplicity, configurability, and a clean look to a desktop, Windowmaker and Xfce are good choices. They also perform well on older video cards and computers with as little as 16MB of RAM.

If you have a new video card and lots of RAM and like a desktop with the works, KDE or Gnome are meant for you.

The hardest part of installing a window manager is deciding which to install. I like to install a new one every month, which gives me time to become acquainted with its features so I can rate it on looks, configurability, and performance. Every window manager has its own unique features you'll find you can't live without, as well as some irritating glitches you wish someone would fix.

If you are in a GUI, you can return to your other virtual terminals using **Ctrl-Alt-Fx** where *x* is the number of the terminal you wish to access. To return to your GUI, use **Ctrl-Alt-F9**. If you have two GUIs running, you'll find the second one hiding at **Ctrl-Alt-F10**.

The file that contains the command to execute your window manager is `~/.xinitrc`. As a regular user you will have to create this file initially and change it if you change your window manager. The file will need a line to start your window manager — the line itself varies by window manager. Here are some examples to get you started:

- For Windowmaker, you'll need the line: `exec wmaker`

- For Gnome with Afterstep, use: `gnome-session & exec afterstep`

- For Xfce, use: `exec xfce`

- For KDE, use: `exec startkde`

Additional Resources

Original Article:

`http://www.onlamp.com/pub/a/bsd/2000/06/21/FreeBSD_Basics.html`

X section of FreeBSD Handbook:

`http://www.freebsd.org/doc/en_US.ISO8859-1/books/handbook/x11.html`

1.2 Customizing Your Desktop Environment

One of the most addictive activities a computer geek can engage in is tweaking his desktop settings to reflect his own taste and personality. Most of the window managers that run on the X Window System allow you to customize your menu options and wallpaper. Unfortunately, you'll also find that most window managers aren't ready to use as-is, since they come with shortcuts to applications that haven't been installed yet and don't necessarily have shortcuts to your favorite applications. And unless you've used a specific window manager before, you may spend a lot of time figuring out how to change the defaults. This section will help you get started on the Xfce Window Manager.

Getting Started

Let's assume you've just installed Xfce by typing this command as superuser:

```
# pkg_add -r xfce
```

To launch Xfce, type **exit** to leave the superuser account and go back to your regular user, then type:

```
% startx xfce
```

Later on, if you decide you like Xfce, you can save yourself future keystrokes by editing (or creating) the .xinitrc file located in your home directory so that it only contains these lines:

```
exec xfce
```

Now you'll just have to type:

```
% startx
```

A program named **xinit** will read the .xinitrc configuration file in your home directory and start Xfce for you.

Once you've launched Xfce, start looking around. OK, boring gray zigzag wallpaper, and a menu bar with some icons. If you start clicking on icons, some will execute applications, while others won't seem to do anything. If you click on the arrow above an icon, you'll discover a pop-up menu with shortcuts to other applications; if you click on all eight arrows, you'll end up with eight pop-up menus. It might take a couple of minutes to figure out you have to click the arrow again to close the pop-up menu. If you start clicking on applications in the pop-up menus, usually nothing happens. It's time to start customizing.

Mounting Devices using the Menu

Let's start with the arrow on the far left. It has entries to mount and unmount floppies and CD-ROMs; unfortunately, the commands are incorrect for your FreeBSD system.

Open up an **xterm** by clicking on the icon that has a monitor with a red check mark in it. You'll notice that you can only type in this **xterm** if your mouse is hovering somewhere within the white box.

Hint: in X terminology, this is known as giving that window focus.

Create two empty directories in your home directory to use as mount points for the floppy and the CD-ROM:

```
% mkdir ~/cdrom
% mkdir ~/floppy
```

When you are finished, type **exit** to close the **xterm**.

Let's return to the pop-up menu; right-click on the Mount CDROM option to enter its configuration screen. Notice that the entry in the Command Line: section is incorrect. Use your mouse to highlight /mnt and your delete key to delete that text. Change it to read:

```
mount ~/cdrom
```

Click OK to save your changes.

Repeat this process for Unmount CDROM, Mount Floppy, and Unmount Floppy. The corrected Command Line: entries should be:

```
umount ~/cdrom
mount ~/floppy
umount ~/floppy
```

Make sure you have a floppy in the floppy drive and a data CD-ROM in the CD-ROM drive before testing your new menu commands.

If you're *root*, the floppy and CD-ROM should mount successfully. If you open an **xterm** and type:

```
% ls /floppy
% ls /cdrom
```

you should be able to see the contents of the floppy and the CD-ROM. If you type **df**, the output should show both as mounted.

However, if you're not *root*, neither will mount. You may have issued the command from Xfce's menu option, but a window manager must still abide by the rules of the Unix system it is installed on.

"No problem," you might think to yourself, "if that user is a member of the group *wheel*, I'll just open an **xterm** and **su** to *root*." However, if you try that, you'll still have the same error whenever you try to use the menu option to mount the floppy or CD-ROM.

To change this default so you can use your menu options to mount and unmount as a regular user, type this as the superuser:

```
# sysctl -w vfs.usermount=1
# chmod 666 /dev/fd0 /dev/cd0
```

(For an example of using a group instead, see the FreeBSD Handbook at http://www.freebsd.org/doc/en_ US.ISO8859-1/books/faq/disks.html#USER-FLOPPYMOUNT.)

To ensure these changes remain after a reboot, you'll need to carefully edit two files as superuser. Add this line to /etc/sysctl.conf:

```
vfs.usermount=1
```

Add these two lines to /etc/devfs.conf:

```
perm cd0 0666
perm fd0 0666
```

The other two options in this pop-up menu are installed and work by default. You can remove them if you don't like them, change their default icon by right-clicking on the option and browsing through the Icon File: list, or change the text that appears in the menu by editing the Label: section.

Adding Applications to Menus

Now it's time to start installing packages as superuser and adding them to the pop-up menus as a regular user. Remember, only *root* can install software, but any user can customize his or her own desktop by adding a pre-installed application to the desired menu screen.

If you are new to the packages collection, you may be unsure of which packages to try first. Spend some time at http://freshports.org which provides a search engine for FreeBSD software as well as descriptions for each application.

As an example, let's add GIMP, the image manipulation program:

```
# pkg_add -r gimp
```

Once installed, click on the desired menu's arrow, and click on the Add icon. In the Command Line: section, use the browse button to find the application. If it is not listed in /usr/X11R6/bin, it is probably in /usr/local/bin. When in doubt, open up an **xterm** and ask the **which** command for the path to the binary or **pkg_info** to list which binaries were installed:

```
% which gimp
/usr/local/bin/gimp
% pkg_info -Lx gimp | grep bin
/usr/local/bin/gimp
/usr/local/bin/gimp-2.2
/usr/local/bin/gimp-remote
/usr/local/bin/gimp-remote-2.2
/usr/local/bin/gimptool-2.0
```

Hint: the **which** command is used to locate the full path to applications, which are usually called binaries in Unix.

In this example, **gimp** is located in /usr/local/bin, so locate it in the files section and double-click. Now browse for an icon. **gimp** has its own; if you don't like it, try another one. Finally, type in the Label: section the text you want to appear in your menu screen. Click OK and you are done.

gimp will now appear as a menu option. If you click on it, you should see **gimp** load for the first time. Press continue as you are prompted to accept the defaults.

You may find yourself spending inordinate amounts of time building packages and adding and deleting items from your menus as you become more comfortable with customizing your desktop.

Configuring Wallpaper

The last customization we'll discuss is wallpaper. The second menu from the right has an option labeled Backdrop. Click Backdrop, then Browse. You'll see that Xfce comes with quite a few built-in wallpapers. If you select one that sounds interesting, you'll see a preview; if you like it, press Apply.

If you're like me, you accumulate your own collection of backgrounds. In your home directory, make a directory to store your images:

```
% mkdir ~/pictures
```

Hint: in Unix, ~ is a shortcut to your home directory. Alternately, typing **cd** will always take you back to your home directory.

If you find an interesting image on the Web while using your browser, right-click on the image, choose Save This Image As, and save it to your `pictures` directory. To turn it into wallpaper, open up your Backdrop menu option and browse to your `pictures` directory to locate the image.

These tips should get you started on personalizing Xfce.

1.2.1 Additional Resources

Original Article:

`http://www.onlamp.com/pub/a/bsd/2000/06/28/FreeBSD_Basics.html`

1.3 Using PC-BSD

The next two sections demonstrate the features of two desktop operating systems that are based on FreeBSD. Both PC-BSD and DesktopBSD[2] provide an easy to install and easy to use desktop environment suited for the corporate desktop user as well as the home user with no previous Unix experience.

While much of this section provides an introduction to what a novice BSD user can expect if they install PC-BSD, users already familiar with FreeBSD and the KDE desktop will still find some interesting features for dealing with ports, **csup**, and updates.

Getting and Installing PC-BSD

PC-BSD is available from the PC-BSD download page[3], from where you can download and then burn the ISO. Alternately, if you don't have access to a burner or wish to support the project, you can purchase a two-CD set for $15.

Hint: power users may enjoy downloading and trying the new PC-BSD vmware image, which is also available from the download site.

Once you have the CD, insert it into the CD drive as you start your computer. Most systems should already be configured to boot from CD, meaning the install program will automatically begin. The PC-BSD website has screenshots of everything you'll see during the install.

Some text messages will go by and then you'll see the PC-BSD splash screen. When you see the Installation menu, press enter to start the graphical install.

You'll have the option to choose your language, keyboard layout and timezone. Click the Next button to proceed. You'll be prompted to choose a system installation type and to agree to the BSD license. Press Next to continue.

The installer will then ask you to set the *root* (administrative) password and make a login account. Be careful when you pick your username, as it is case-sensitive. You may want to keep your username lowercase, and spell your full name correctly under Real Name, which is just a description.

---

[2]DesktopBSD is introduced in section 1.4.
[3]http://www.pcbsd.org/?p=download

The installer will then show you your hard drive(s) and ask you to select where to install PC-BSD. If you only have one hard drive and only want PC-BSD on your computer, click on the box that says Use entire disk. You also have the opportunity to "install the PC-BSD bootloader". You won't need to select this box if PC-BSD will be the only operating system on your computer. Click Next to continue then Next again. You can now watch as PC-BSD installs on your computer.

When finished, you'll receive a message indicating that the install is complete. Click Finish to reboot into the new system to eject the CD.

Becoming Familiar with the Desktop

The first time you reboot into PC-BSD, you should hear the KDE theme, if you have a working soundcard. Then you'll go through prompts to customize KDE. You'll also receive a KTip that gives tips on using KDE; if you prefer not to see these whenever you start your system, uncheck the Show tips on startup box.

Click on the FreeBSD logo (the red icon on the far left of the task bar) to access the KDE menu, which is somewhat like the Windows Start menu. Here you can Log Out, which allows you to End Current Session (log off), Turn Off Computer, Restart Computer, or Cancel if you've changed your mind. If you have a fairly recent computer, the Turn Off Computer option should do just that without you having to push the power button yourself.

The Lock Session button will save what you are doing and go into a locked screensaver. If you click your mouse button, you will see a password prompt to unlock the screensaver. This is a good option if you want to leave your computer and don't want anyone else using it or seeing what you were doing.

Run Command is similar to the Windows run command. If you already know the name of the command, you can type it in. If you click the Options button, you can also check the box for Run as a different user, which is similar to the Windows runas command.

Accessing Media and Sharing Files

Next in the KDE menu system is the System menu, which provides a quick way to access your Home Folder, Storage Media, Remote Places (similar to My Network Places on Windows), Trash, and Users Folders.

Start with Storage Media. This will open up the Konqueror browser in a view that shows your CD-ROM, floppy, and hard disk. It will also show supported removable media such as USB thumb drives. By default, CDs should auto-mount when you insert them, meaning you can just double-click the CD-ROM icon to see its contents. When you finish, right-click the icon to Eject the CD. If you right-click the floppy icon, you'll see options to Format or Mount the floppy. The format utility can do a quick or full DOS format that Windows systems will understand. You can also choose to format with UFS, which only Unix systems will understand. If you do mount a floppy to view its contents, don't forget to right-click and Unmount it when you finish but before you physically eject the floppy. This lets the operating system know that you have finished using the floppy.

PC-BSD comes with a SMB client, which makes it easy to access shared folders on Windows systems, other PC-BSD systems, and any other Unix-like system that provides a SMB server. If you go into Remote Places and double-click Samba Shares, you should be able to see all of the aforementioned systems on your network. If you double-click a system, you should be able to access its shares. Note: XP systems running SP2 have a firewall automatically enabled, so you may have to (carefully) configure an XP system's firewall before you can access its shares inside your own network.

Here is an easy method to configure your own shares: from Remote Places, right-click the word Desktop that appears in the left-hand pane and select Create Folder. Select your new folder, and then right-click in the right pane and Create New –> Text File. Double-click the file to edit it and then save your changes. Now, right-click your folder and choose Properties –> Share and click the Configure File Sharing button. You must then type in the *root* password. (Note: Whenever you're prompted for the *root* password, if you select the Keep password box, you won't be prompted again the next time you run that specific utility.) If you keep the default of Simple sharing, users can share any of their own files without knowing the *root* password.

Customizing Your Desktop

Next in the menu is the Settings section, which is similar to Windows Control Panel. If you plan on viewing or changing several settings, use Control Center, which provides an interface for each section in this menu. Alternately, you can navigate the Settings menu, which contains Appearance & Themes, Desktop, Internet & Network, KDE Components, Peripherals, Regional & Accessibility, Security & Privacy, Sound & Multimedia, and System Administration. This is where you can customize your operating system to your tastes. I recommend you spend some time trying out all of the various options for yourself. There is a lot here, so you might want to try out a few things every time you use your computer.

Hint: if you like to use keyboard shortcuts, check out Regional & Accessibility –> Keyboard Shortcuts to view and change the default shortcuts.

The KDE menu also provides a quick way to access Home (Personal Files), the KDE Help system, the Find Files/Folders utility, and the Control Center.

KDE Programs is similar to the Windows Programs menu. Here you will find all of the KDE applications categorized into Games, Graphics, Internet, Multimedia, Office, Settings, System, and Utilities. Again, there is a lot here, so make a point to discover at least one new utility whenever you use your computer.

The final option on the KDE menu is unique to PC-BSD: Computer. It provides another way to access your Drives and the Local Network. There is also the PC-BSD Settings menu, where you can Add User, configure your Display, configure your Keyboard, and configure your Mouse, as well as access Network Manager, Online Update, PBI Update Check, Printer Manager, Remove Programs, Sound Mixer, and System.

Network Manager is similar to Windows Network Connections as it allows you to view your network adapters and modify their TCP/IP settings. I want to spend some more time on a few of the other menu items.

Hint: if you use your numlock key, go into the Keyboard menu and select Turn on under the NumLock on KDE Startup section.

The System Menu

System is somewhat like the Windows System icon, but with a BSD twist. The General tab indicates both the version of PC-BSD and the FreeBSD version it is based upon. For example, mine says:

```
PC-BSD Version: 1.0rc2
Base Version: 6.0-RELEASE-p3
```

The -p3 indicates it is FreeBSD 6.0 at the third patch level.

This tab also contains a Generate button, which is a very convenient way to generate a diagnostics report. More advanced users will appreciate having /var/run/dmesg.boot, /etc/rc.conf, /boot/loader.conf, and the outputs of **dmesg**, **df**, and **ps** in one written report. Less advanced users can send a generated report to their nearest guru or support person.

The Kernel tab allows you to select from a single processor or multi-processor kernel. It also provides check boxes to enable a splash screen or ATAPI DMA Mode. You can also select the boot delay number of seconds in this tab.

The Services tab allows you to select whether to start the SSH, NFS, Samba, and CUPS daemons at boot time.

The Tasks menu is the real jewel of this utility (see Figure 1.1). Click on Fetch System Source to connect to a **cvsup** server and fetch src. Note that this will take a while the first time you run it, as you'll be downloading over 400MB of src. However, subsequent **cvsup** runs will go quickly, as the utility needs to download only the src that has changed since your last fetch. Power users who wish to modify the default cvs-supfile will find it in /root/standard-supfile.

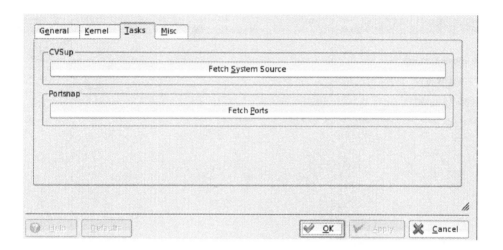

Figure 1.1: The Tasks menu

The Tasks tab also contains a button to Fetch Ports using **portsnap**. The first time you run this utility, be patient, as it will take a while to download and extract the entire ports tree. Even if it seems nothing is happening for a very long time, it is working — simply go do something else until it says it is finished. The next time you run this utility, it will be very quick, as it needs to download only the changes to the ports collection.

Adding and Removing Programs

On a PC-BSD system, there are three built-in mechanisms for installing software. You can use the ports collection, meaning you **cd** into the desired ports subdirectory and type **make install clean**. You can also use the packages collection, meaning you type **pkg_add -r** *name_of_package*.

The easiest way for new users to install software is to download a PBI (Push Button Installer) to the Desktop, and double-click the PBI to start its installer. PBI is the file format for the PC-BSD Installer. The PC-BSD site has plenty of PBI screenshots.

The advantage to PBI is that the installer offers to create shortcuts both on the Desktop and in the Programs menu of the KDE menu. This makes it easy to find your applications and remember which applications you have installed.

PBIs also come with their own de-installers, in Computer –> PC-BSD Settings –> Remove Programs. Simply highlight the desired program and click the Remove button. Note: This will not work for programs installed through the ports or packages collections; for these, you need to type **pkg_delete -x** *name_of_program*.

Keeping Up To Date

The Online Update in Computer –> PC-BSD Settings is one of the slickest utilities that comes with this operating system (Figure 1.2). Similar to Windows Update, it can check your operating system and programs for both security vulnerabilities and new features. Once instructed to do so, it will download and apply any missing patches for you. You can also use this utility to safely upgrade your operating system when a new version becomes available.

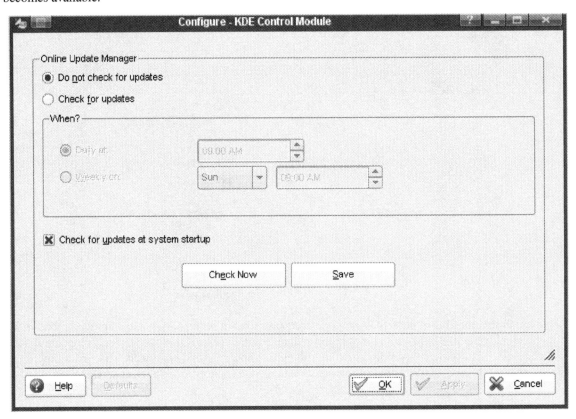

Figure 1.2: Online Update

If you select Check for updates, you have the option to automatically schedule the process on a daily or weekly basis.

If you prefer to manually watch the process, instead click the Check Now button. When I tested my version of PC-BSD, it was only nine days old, so I received a "Your system is up-to-date" message. However, when I tried this on an older version, I saw Figure 1.3. By highlighting one of the entries and clicking on the More info button, I was able to get more detailed information about a given feature or security vulnerability. When I clicked Next, the patches were applied.

Note that patches that affect the kernel will require a reboot. The computer will automatically do this for you.

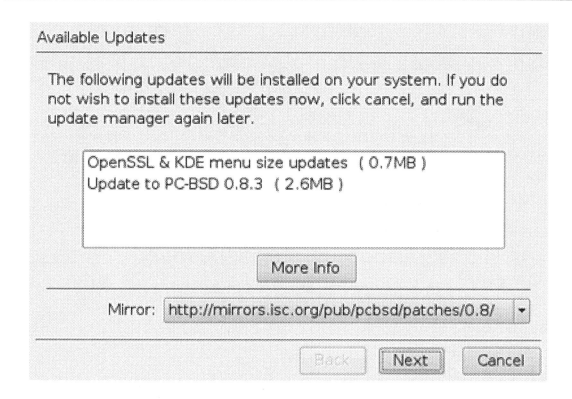

Figure 1.3: Update Now!

Configuring Flash and Java

For novice users, there are currently three available web browsers: Konqueror, which comes installed with KDE, and Firefox and Opera, which are available for download as PBIs.

To install browser Java support, download and run the PBI for the Java Runtime (you can find this easily if you search the PBI directory for "java"). During installation, you will be prompted to accept the Sun licensing agreement. Once installed, you can verify Java support in Konqueror or Firefox by typing **about:plugins** into the Location bar. In Opera, type **opera:about**.

Note: At the time of this writing, there is a bug that prevents Firefox from correctly seeing Java support. Hopefully it has been corrected by the time you read this.

Hint: a good site to test your browser is http://www.privacy.net. Click on the hyperlink for Analyzer at the bottom of the page.

To install Flash support, download the Flash PBI. If Flash doesn't immediately show up in Konqueror when you type **about:plugins**, go to Settings –> Configure Konqueror –> Plugins. Click on the Scan for New Plugins button and it will enable Flash support.

For Firefox, go to Programs menu –> Firefox –> Install Flash Plugin, which will prompt you for the *root* password. When finished, Flash support will now show in about:plugins.

For Opera, simply download the PBI for Opera with Flash and enjoy.

Conclusion

If you haven't had a chance to try out PC-BSD, take some time to install and poke about this user-friendly operating system. If you're looking for a free and stable operating system for friends or family, burn them an ISO and have them give it a test drive.

The PC-BSD engineering team appreciates all feedback and suggestions for improving the operating system from a user perspective. The email address for the project lead is available from the PC-BSD contact page. Don't be surprised if you see one of your feature requests implemented in a later version of PC-BSD.

Additional Resources

Original Article:

`http://www.onlamp.com/pub/a/bsd/2006/05/11/FreeBSD_Basics.html`

PC-BSD Website:

`http://www.pcbsd.org`

PBI Website:

`http://www.pbidir.com`

1.4 Using DesktopBSD

Like PC-BSD, DesktopBSD provides many features that will allow a complete Unix novice to start using the operating system immediately. Those already familiar with FreeBSD and the KDE desktop will recognize the tools underlying the GUI conveniences.

Installation

DesktopBSD is available for download as either a CD or DVD ISO. The DesktopBSD Release Notes describe the extras that are available in the DVD version. If you're downloading the ISO, take a look at the DesktopBSD screenshots while you are waiting. They will give you a good idea of what to expect during the installation.

I find the installation routine to be very self-explanatory, even for beginners. For example, the DesktopBSD Bootloader screen explains when it is appropriate to pick each option.

If you only want to have DesktopBSD on your disk, choose Use entire disk in the Disk partitioning screen. If you wish to run multiple operating systems, you need to have some empty disk space available. Assuming this is the case, click the New Partition button to specify how much of the empty space to use. Once you have selected either the entire disk or created a new partition, highlight it with your mouse and click the Install into selected partition button. Once you confirm your choice, the installer will start copying files to the hard disk.

When finished, the installer will ask you to reboot and will then enter the Initial Configuration Wizard. You will receive the option to insert the Language Packages CD for additional language support; the default is to support only the language you chose at the very beginning of the install.

The Users dialog won't let you continue until you add at least one user and set the system password. You can then select your language so you can read the Getting Started tutorial in one of 10 languages. Although you can instead click on the Finish button, I highly recommend you go through the tutorial during your first install as it will explain how to mount file systems using the GUI Mounter, how to view and configure your network settings, how to use the KDE Control center, and how to access the system Documentations.

Click the Finish button, then log in as the user you created. The very first time you log in, the KPersonalizer will run so you can customize your KDE desktop.

Desktop Icons

A newly installed DesktopBSD system provides several desktop icons to get you started. If you are attached to a network of Windows systems, clicking on the Browse the Network icon should allow you to browse network shares, much like the behavior of My Network Places in Windows.

Many new users to FreeBSD don't realize that the operating system and its applications include a lot of documentation. The Documentation icon provides an easy shortcut to /usr/local/share/doc which contains the documentation installed with applications. Similarly, the Documentation (X11) icon points to the location of documentation installed with X11 applications.

Note: As you learn more about the operating system, take a look at the contents of /usr/share/examples.

The Getting Started icon opens up Konqueror, giving quick access to your Home Folder, Network Folders, Applications, Storage Media, Trash, and Settings, as well as a link to Next: An Introduction to Konqueror. That last link provides some handy tips and tricks.

The desktop also contains a Home icon so you can quickly access the files in your home directory. A Trash icon provides features similar to the Windows Recycle Bin, allowing you to restore deleted files or to delete them permanently.

The two remaining desktop icons, Software and System, deserve more attention.

Dealing with Software

DesktopBSD's Software icon allows you to easily install and uninstall applications, as well as view known security vulnerabilities and upgrade to newer software versions. You should be attached to the Internet if you want to install or upgrade any software.

When you click on the Software icon, you must enter the *root* password; if you check the Keep password box, you will not receive a prompt the next time you click this icon.

The very first time you click the Software icon, you'll see a message:

> In DesktopBSD, software is bundled in so-called packages. These packages can be applications or components shared between different applications. Most applications reuse features of other software to avoid duplications, so they depend on other packages. The package list contains available packages. You should update it regularly to know about security upgrades and new program versions. You can open this introduction from the Help menu later.

Depending on how old the operating system is, you may also receive a message similar to:

> CRITICAL WARNING: Security information is 72 days old! Please update it and check for new security issues in installed software.

or:

> DesktopBSD maintains a package list that contains available packages, their versions, and dependencies between them. An up-to-date list is necessary to be able to install and upgrade software on this computer. This list doesn't exist on your system, so it has to be downloaded from the internet first. Please ensure you are connected to the internet and click Proceed to download the package list. If you don't want to do this now, click Quit to exit the package manager.

If you click the Proceed button (or Update List if you didn't receive that message), the system will ask you to "Please specify an update server." Click on OK to see Figure 1.4. Click on Find fastest server which will automatically fill in the server URLs for you. Clicking on OK opens a terminal that shows **cvsup** running and downloading ports-all. This initial download is quite large, so wait the half hour or so (depending on the speed of your Internet connection) for it to finish. Subsequent downloads will be very quick, as they need only download the ports which have changed since your most recent update.

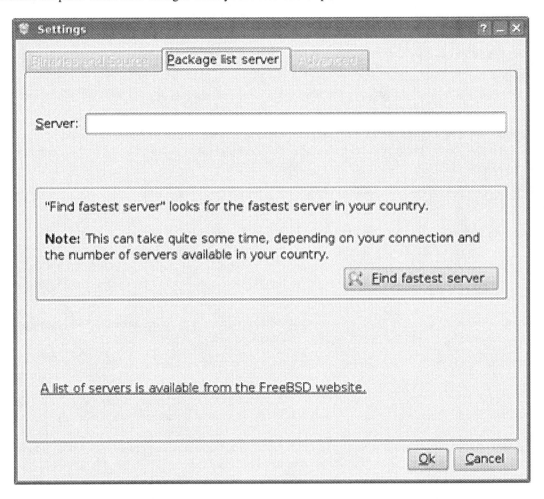

Figure 1.4: Choosing an update server

When this finishes, you will see something like Figure 1.5. If you click on the Installed Packages screen then click the Upgrade all outdated packages button, the names of those outdated packages will be added to the Pending Operations window.

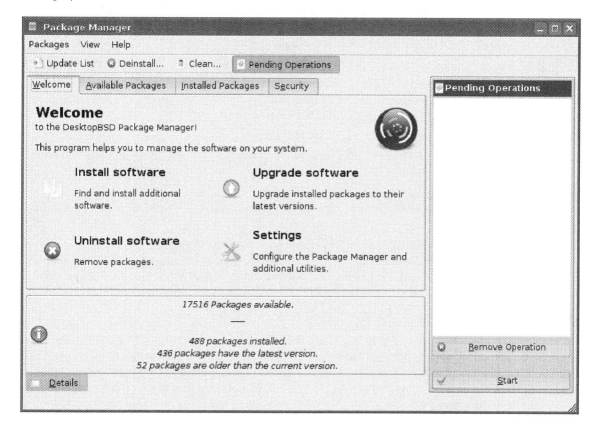

Figure 1.5: Upgrading packages

If there is a package you don't want to upgrade, highlight it and click the Remove Operation button. Otherwise, click Start which will bring up another menu:

> You selected packages to upgrade. Do you want to read the update notes first?

Complete novices may wish to say No and proceed. Otherwise, it is a good idea to say Yes and skim through this file as it will tell you if there are any gotchas when upgrading your software. At the end of the process, it will ask you:

> Now that you've read the update notes, do you want to continue installing and upgrading packages?

If you chose Yes, a terminal will open so you can watch the upgrade process.

It's useful to know what happens behind the scenes so you can understand the results of your upgrade. FreeBSD provides two methods for installing software. The first is the packages system, where a package is similar to a Windows installer program: it downloads the executable, documentation, and everything the program needs to run. Packages are really quick to install, but aren't always available for the latest version of software as someone has to create the package. The second method is the ports system; a port is the instructions needed to build a program. Ports tend to be available before packages but it can take a long time for a port to build the application. A long time can be anywhere from a few minutes to a few hours (and sometimes a few days) depending upon the size of the application and the speed of your CPU. For example, KDE and OpenOffice are very large applications and can take a very long time to build.

The default upgrade method for DesktopBSD's Package Manager is to upgrade packages. This means your upgrades will be very quick, but you will most likely receive some errors as not every application will have a new package available. If you receive an error, you have two choices. You can either try again in a week or so to see if there is a new package, or you can try to build the port.

If you decide to try building the port, go into the Packages menu –> Settings –> Binaries and Source. Change Binary packages only to Binary packages whenever possible. Then, in Advanced, check (at least) two options:

```
[x]Always upgrade the packages required by the specified packages as well.
[x]Always upgrade the packages depending on the specified packages as well.
```

Repeat your upgrade, which will take a while. You should check on it every now and then as sometimes it will pause and wait for you to select from a menu of options. Also be aware that sometimes a port will fail to build. The reason for the failure often pertains to something you should have read in the file which appeared before starting the upgrade.

Note: If you're curious, the name of that file is /usr/ports/UPDATING.

You can do much more than upgrade your software using this utility. To see what software is installed, select the Group by...None button under Installed Packages. To install software, click on the Available Packages tab. Here you will find a search utility where you can search by package name or by description. Alternately, click on the x to clear the search and bring up the categories to browse manually. If you select an application, it will give a short description and the latest version. Other buttons allow you to see the long description, view the website for the application, and install the application. When you click install, the application will be added to the Pending Operations pane. This allows you to select multiple applications; the installations will occur when you click the Start button.

After the install, you will have the opportunity to add menu entries for the new applications. If you say Yes, click the Scan button when Kappfinder opens. I've found Kappfinder to be a bit flaky, so it may or may not find the application you just installed. I prefer to click on K menu (the red DesktopBSD icon in the far left of the taskbar), then Settings –> Menu Editor to review and modify the K menu.

Should you wish to uninstall an application, the safest way is to click the Deinstall button. You will see the message:

> Welcome to the deinstallation wizard! Most packages need other software to work properly. When you deinstall such packages, previously required software may remain on the system and consume disk space unnecessarily. This wizard guides you through the deinstallation of packages and no longer required software.

When you select the application(s) you wish to deinstall, you may need to select other applications which came with that application. Clicking on the Calculate button will tell you how much disk space this operation will free and clicking Finish will perform the deinstallation(s).

Note: This utility won't let you uninstall software that other applications require. This allows novices to safely uninstall applications without messing up the system.

The Security tab will show known vulnerabilities for applications you can install using Package Manager, allowing you to decide if you wish to install or keep already installed applications with known outstanding security issues.

Finally, the Clean button will start another wizard:

> Welcome to the cleaning wizard! When you install new software, installation files remain on your system. They can be useful for later reinstallations and upgrades, but in most cases they unnecessarily consume disk space. This wizard helps you to remove such files from your system.

If disk space is an issue, its not a bad idea to periodically run this wizard as it can free up some disk space.

Configuring Remote Places

The System icon provides another method for accessing your Home Folder and Trash. It also provides shortcuts to Storage Media and Users Folders. I'd like to spend some time on the Add a Network Folder wizard found within its final shortcut: Remote Places. Double-clicking that shortcut will allow you to make shortcuts to FTP, Windows network drive, and SSH connections.

For example, I configured an SSH shortcut to a SSH server running inside my network as follows:

```
Name: server
User: dru
Server: 192.168.2.98
Port: 22
Folder: /usr/home/dru
[x] Create an icon for this remote folder
```

When I pressed Save & Connect, a SSH Authorization menu prompted me for my password and gave an option to Keep password. Because I asked to save password, KWallet opened:

> Welcome to KWallet, the KDE Wallet System. KWallet allows you to store your passwords and other personal information on disk in an encrypted file, preventing others from viewing the information. This wizard will tell you about KWallet and help you configure it for the first time.

I pressed Next to enter Basic setup (recommended) and received another message:

> Various applications may attempt to use the KDE wallet to store passwords or other information such as web form data and cookies. If you would like these applications to use the wallet, you must enable it now and choose a password. The password you choose cannot be recovered if it is lost, and will allow anyone who knows it to obtain all the information contained in the wallet.

I checked [x] Yes, I wish to use the KDE wallet to store my personal information and entered a password. It prompted me to enter that password to access the wallet. It then finished connecting to the SSH server and opened my home directory on that system in Konqueror.

The next time I wish to connect to server, I can simply double-click its icon in Remote Places.

Hint: If you prefer to make a desktop icon, right-click the icon in Remote Places, select to copy and right-click on the Desktop and choose Paste URL.

Once you start creating and using your connection shortcuts, your Recent Connections will show in the drop-down menu in the Network Folder Wizard.

System Tray Icons

There are several convenient icons in the right side of the system tray, next to the clock. Klipper keeps track of your copy operations, making it easy to paste text between applications. Mixer gives quick access to sound volume. Korganizer is a full-featured personal calendar — spend some time poking about its Events and Settings menus. Right-clicking the Mounted Devices icon gives quick access to CDs, DVDs, floppies, and file systems. If you right-click Network Control and select Configure, you can view the status of your NICs, customize your TCP/IP settings and scan for wireless networks.

I'll leave it to you to explore the KDE menu on your own as there is much there to see. There is one last note to mention: if you decide to Switch User and Start a New Session, find your first session at **Alt-F9** and your new session at **Alt-F10**.

If you have been hesitant to try FreeBSD because you heard the install was difficult or were afraid you would have problems configuring the GUI or sound or networking, now is a great time to take the plunge. Both PC-BSD and DesktopBSD provide you with a fully configured, ready to use system so you can be up and running in under half an hour. Both include features to help you install software and keep up to date. I recommend you try both to see which one you prefer for yourself. Since both provide FreeBSD under the hood, all of the documentation at the FreeBSD website as well as the many tutorials and howtos on the internet will apply to your desktop operating system.

Additional Resources

Original Article:

`http://www.onlamp.com/pub/a/bsd/2006/07/13/FreeBSDBasics.html`

DesktopBSD Website:

`http://www.desktopbsd.net/`

1.5 Fun with X.org

The FreeBSD Handbook provides an excellent overview for understanding and configuring the X Window System. This section goes beyond the Handbook to demonstrate some of the cool things you can do with your FreeBSD system and other systems running X.

Getting the Most out of your Video Card

While **Xorg -configure** does a good job of configuring video cards, the X drivers don't provide automatic support for DRI (Direct Rendering Interface), DRM (Direct Rendering Manager), or OpenGL (OPEN Graphics Library) – meaning you're probably not getting the most out of your video hardware.

The **dri** and **linux_dri** packages provide these missing features by installing FreeBSD kernel loadable modules for several cards (see Table 1.1).

Note: If you have a NVidia card and want to use the binary-only driver, you need to compile the nvidia-driver port against your kernel. The superuser can do this with this command:

```
# cd /usr/ports/x11/nvidia-driver && make install clean
```

Table 1.1: Kernel Modules for Video

Card/Chipset	Module Name
Intel i810	i810
Intel i915	i915
Intel i965	i965
ATI Mach64	mach64
Matrox Gxxx	mga
ATI Rage128	r128
ATI Rage200	r200
ATI Rage300	r300
ATI Radeon	radeon
S3 Savage	savage
SiS 3xx	sis
Voodoo 3dfx	tdfx

Depending upon the software you have installed, these DRI modules may already be on your system. Check with the command:

```
# pkg_info | grep dri
```

If you receive your prompt back with no output, or the output mentions only **linux_dri**, install the **dri** package:

```
# pkg_add -r dri
```

Once you have it installed, add a few lines to the end of /etc/X11/xorg.conf:

```
Section "DRI"
    Mode 0666
EndSection
```

Note: If that file doesn't exist, then:

```
# cp /root/xorg.conf.new /etc/X11/xorg.conf
```

Finally, double-check that X.org will load DRI and GLX (OpenGL Extension to the X Window System); if these lines don't exist, add them to the Section "Module" portion of /etc/X11/xorg.conf:

```
# grep dri /etc/X11/xorg.conf
Load "dri"
# grep glx /etc/X11/xorg.conf
Load "glx"
```

Loading and Testing the Kernel Module

Now you're ready to determine which kernel module to load. First, figure out which video card X.org wants to use:

```
# grep Name /etc/X11/xorg.conf
VendorName "IBM"
ModelName "IBM G72"
VendorName "ATI Technologies Inc"
BoardName "Rage 128 Pro Ultra TF"
```

Compare that output to the earlier table. This system needs to use the r128 module. If I issue this command at **Alt-F1** (the console), a successful driver load will display as bright white text:

```
# kldload r128
drm0:  <ATI Rage 128 Pro Ultra TF (AGP)> port 0xd000-0xd0ff mem 0xf4000000-0xf7ff
ffff,0xfbefffff irq 10 at device 0.0 on pci1
info:  [drm] AGP at 0xf0000000 64MB
info:  [drm] Initialized r128 2.5.0 20030725
```

Once your driver successfully loads, start an X session as a regular user and check the OpenGL rendering capabilities from within the GUI:

```
% glxinfo | grep rendering
direct rendering:  Yes
```

Once you have rendering enabled, add a line to /boot/loader.conf as the superuser so the driver automatically loads when the system boots. My line looks like:

```
r128_load="YES"
```

Replace r128 with the module name for your video card and double-check the file for typos.

3d-Desktop is an XGL-ish[4] desktop switcher and a cool way to test your DRI:

```
# pkg_add -r 3ddesktop
```

Once installed, run it from the GUI as a regular user:

```
% 3ddesk
```

Use your arrow keys to rotate the cube of desktops and **Enter** or **Space** to bring a desktop into the foreground.

---

[4]XGL is a layer to the X protocol which takes advantage of modern graphics cards via OpenGL which supports 3D effects and hardware acceleration.

Nesting Xservers

When you install X, you get a whole suite of interesting utilities, many of which you may not be aware of. One of these is **Xnest**, which allows you to run multiple window managers simultaneously. Confirm that you have **Xnest** installed with:

```
# pkg_info | grep nest
xorg-nestserver-6.9.0_1 Nesting X server from X.org
```

If you just get your prompt back, install the program with the command:

```
# pkg_add -r xorg-nestserver
```

Here is an example of how to use **Xnest**. On a system already configured for KDE, I installed three additional window managers:

```
# pkg_add -r windowmaker
# pkg_add -r xfce
# pkg_add -r fluxbox
```

Note: On FreeBSD, you can see which window managers are available at the Freshports X11 window managers listing at http://www.freshports.org/x11-wm/.

Once installed, start the GUI as a regular user. In my case, I see the KDE desktop. I can use **Xnest** to start **windowmaker**, which will appear as just another window with "Windowmaker" in the title bar:

```
% Xnest :1 -ac -name Windowmaker & wmaker -display :1
```

Note: X assigns the first window manager you start (in my case, KDE) a display number of *:0*. In this example, **windowmaker** gets the second display, *:1*, which **Xnest** nests within the original display.

To start two more window managers, bump up the display number and specify the name of the window manager:

```
% Xnest :2 -ac -name Xfce & xfce -display :2
% Xnest :3 -ac -name Fluxbox & fluxbox -display :3
```

Figure 1.6 shows all four window managers running simultaneously.

Distributed Multihead

One of X's design goals was to work in a networked environment, so there are several cool things you can do if you have access to multiple systems running X. It is remarkably easy for X systems to share display information, so I recommend performing these experiments within a home LAN behind an internet firewall.

One experiment allows you to spread a single display across multiple monitors using DMX (Distributed Multihead X). Start by installing the package on all the systems that will share the display:

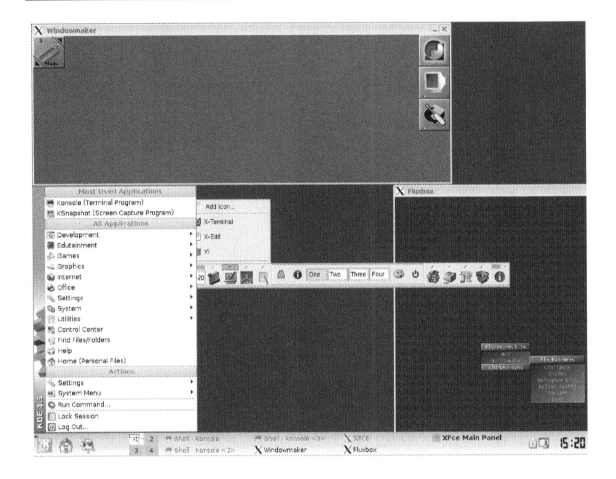

Figure 1.6: Four window managers running simultaneously through Xnest

```
# pkg_add -r xorg-dmx
```

For security reasons, FreeBSD systems don't participate on an X network by default, so temporarily change this behavior. Close any open X sessions and restart X with the option:

```
% startx -listen_tcp
```

The **sockstat** command can be used to determine if X is listening on the network. If the following command just returns your command prompt, X is not listening. However, if you receive output, X is ready to accept incoming connections.

```
% sockstat -4 | grep Xorg
root    Xorg    33811 1  tcp4    *.6000    *.*
```

Now that X is listening, you have to tell it to accept incoming connections. The lazy approach is to run on all the systems:

```
% xhost +
access control disabled, clients can connect from any host
```

This message means exactly that; anyone can connect to your X display, which is why a firewall between you and the Internet is important. It makes more sense to allow only the specific IP(s) of the systems you are experimenting with:

```
% xhost -
access control enabled, only authorized clients can connect
% xhost +192.168.1.1
192.168.1.1 being added to access control list
% xhost
access control enabled, only authorized clients can connect
INET:192.168.1.1
```

A good place to start is with an example of sharing a display between two monitors. 192.168.1.1 has the desktop I wish to display and 192.168.1.2 is the second system. I have configured both systems to accept X connections from each other.

From the GUI on 192.168.1.1, I run the command:

```
% startx -- /usr/X11R6/bin/Xdmx :1 -display 192.168.1.1:0 \
    -display 192.168.1.2:0 +xinerama -noglxproxy
```

Note that this is one long command. Don't include the \ when you type it in. You'll also receive an error if you don't give the full path name to **Xdmx**.

This command starts a new shared display (*:1*) that overrides the current display on both systems. The server will accept keyboard and mouse input from the first IP address, but it will work on either monitor. If you move your mouse, it can move onto the second monitor. While there, you can right-click on the second monitor and change the wallpaper for the entire display. When you wish to go back to your original displays, press **Ctrl-Alt-Backspace**. Any changes that you made in the shared display won't affect the two original displays.

man Xdmx provides many options for experimentation. See the Developer Works article in Additional Resources for instructions on adding monitors vertically, as well as some good troubleshooting tips.

Monitor Other Systems

Once you've configured systems to allow X connections from each other, it is trivial to monitor activity on other systems. I installed a watcher program on 192.168.1.1:

```
# pkg_add -r xwatchwin
```

Every time a window (or window manager) opens in X, it receives a window ID. In order to watch another system, you need to know the ID of the window you wish to view. As an example, if I want to watch 192.168.1.2's KDE session, from 192.168.1.2's GUI, I can determine the window ID by typing:

```
% xwininfo
xwininfo:  Please select the window about which you
would like information by clicking the
mouse in that window.
```

If I click the desktop, this is the first line of output:

```
xwininfo:  Window id:  0x1200008 "KDE Desktop"
```

In this case, "KDE Desktop" is the window ID. It is worth noting that the default window ID names are easily guessable. This is the reason why we use firewalls and why X shouldn't listen on the network by default.

I can watch everything that happens during that remote KDE session by typing one command on 192.168.1.1:

```
% xwatchwin -u 1 192.168.1.2 KDE Session
```

The update switch (**-u 1**) will refresh the display every second. Figure 1.7 shows the result.

Figure 1.7: Watching a remote window

If you found this section interesting, read **man X** (note the capital X), which details many of the programs that come with the X window system. Each of these will run easily on your own system, but you may have to delve a bit deeper into **man Xsecurity** if you want to experiment with other systems within your firewall-protected network.

Additional Resources

Original Article:

`http://www.onlamp.com/pub/a/bsd/2006/12/07/freebsd_basicsg.html`

X Section of FreeBSD Handbook:

`http://www.freebsd.org/doc/en_US.ISO8859-1/books/handbook/x11.html`

Distributed multihead support with Linux and Xdmx

`http://www-128.ibm.com/developerworks/linux/library/os-mltihed/index.html`

1.6 Configuring Java and Flash

I purchased a shiny new PC and decided to turn it into a multimedia desktop. I spend far too much time in research and networking; I figured it was time to delve deeper into the world of Flash, DVD, and mp3s.

FreeBSD still seems to get a bad rap as a desktop. The impression is still out there that sure, it's a rock-solid server, but you need a master's degree in rocket science in order to get a sound card or Java to work. Hogwash. Granted, you still have to take the time to build and configure the components you desire, but that is the beauty of FreeBSD. No company is deciding for you what you want in your desktop, and you have the satisfaction of knowing you built your system your way. Not to mention the literally hundreds of multimedia applications to choose from, some which put their commercial counterparts to shame.

Note: Since this was originally written, PC-BSD and DesktopBSD were developed to automagically provide much of the functionality described in this section.[5]

This section concentrates on integrating Java, Flash, and streaming multimedia into a browser.

Configuring Java and Flash

If you don't have a browser yet, start by installing **firefox**:

```
# pkg_add -r firefox
```

The FreeBSD Foundation `http://www.freebsdfoundation.org/downloads/java.shtml` provides packages for JDK (Development Kit) and JRE (Runtime Environment) for 32 bit (i386) and 64 bit architectures. Download the two *.tbz* files which match your architecture and FreeBSD version, **cd** as the superuser to the directory you downloaded the files to, then install as in this example:

```
# pkg_add diablo-jdk-freebsd5.i386.1.5.0.07.01.tbz
# pkg_add diablo-jre-freebsd5.i386.1.5.0.07.01.tbz
```

---

[5]PC-BSD and DesktopBSD are introduced in sections 1.3 and 1.4 respectively.

If you receive a message stating that **javavmwrapper** is missing, install the wrapper script for Java Virtual Machines and try again:

pkg_add -r javavmwrapper

Note: PC-BSD users may prefer to use the Java PBIs from http://www.pbidir.com.

When finished, double-check that it worked. As a regular user, restart **firefox** and go to Help –> About Plug-ins. You should get about a page's worth of Java plugins. A short trip to http://javaboutique.internet.com should convince you that Java is indeed functional.

Next comes streaming multimedia:

pkg_add -r plugger

This package installs MPEG, AVI, QuickTime, MIDI, and PDF support into your browser; you'll see the full list once you re-check your Help –> About Plug-ins. You can test your setup at the plugger testing grounds at http://fredrik.hubbe.net/plugger/test.html.[6]

Finally, the Flash plugin:

pkg_add -r flashplugin-mozilla

Before installing this plugin, be advised that Flash is a registered trademark and it was "designed solely for the Windows PC and Macintosh desktop operating systems." There are also redistribution issues, which means that the GPL version does not support full Flash functionality. This means that some Flash sites will work, some will hang, some will crash your browser.

Note: Some users prefer to **cd /usr/ports/www/linux-flashplugin7 && make install** – you may wish to experiment with different browsers and Flash players to find the one that works best for you.[7] PC-BSD users can also install the Flash PBI from http://www.pbidir.com. As of this writing, a FreeBSD native Flash version is being negotiated; it may be available by the time you read this book.

For example, if you install the Flash plugin, don't bother heading over to http://www.shockwave.com unless you want to watch your browser crash. And I've found that it depends upon the phase of the moon and a certain combination of mojo whether or not the Flash ecards at Hallmark will show me anything other than a grey screen. However, my browser seems to have no problems displaying those annoying Flash introductions that are becoming increasingly popular on Web sites. Go figure.

Configuring Firefox Skins

Now that the plugins are enabled for **firefox**, I'll move on to installing some skins. Go to the Tools menu –> Add-ons –> Themes, then click on the hyperlink Get Themes.

If you find a theme that looks interesing, simply click its Install Now button. The installer may prompt you to Restart Firefox – if so, return to the Themes menu. Your new theme will appear and you can start using it if you click on Use Theme and restart **firefox**. You can download as many themes as you like; to switch a theme, select it and restart **firefox**.

---

[6]More details on plugger are covered in section 1.9.

[7]Also see /usr/ports/www/linux-flashplugin9.

KDE Background

Now that my browser looks pretty awesome, I'll check out my KDE wallpapers.

To change the wallpaper in KDE, right click the desktop and choose Configure Desktop. Click on the Background icon and browse for your favorite wallpaper. If you have some time to kill, click on the Get New Wallpaper button to browse a large collection of user donated wallpapers.

Additional Resources

Original Article:

```
http://www.onlamp.com/pub/a/bsd/2002/09/05/FreeBSD_Basics.html
```

1.7 Configuring Sound Applications

If you're running PC-BSD or DesktopBSD, your soundcard probably just works as sound has already been configured for you. Fortunately, it is an easy matter to locate and load the correct driver for your sound card.

Loading the Sound Driver

If sound is not working on your FreeBSD system, load the all-in-one sound driver then probe the `sndstat` device for the name of your particular driver:

```
# kldload snd_driver
# more /dev/sndstat
FreeBSD Audio Driver (newpcm)
Installed devices:
pcm0:  <Creative CT5880-C> at io 0xb800 irq 5 kld snd_es137x (1p/1r/0v
channels duplex default)
```

The name of the FreeBSD driver will be after the *kld* keyword — in this example it is `snd_es137x`. To tell FreeBSD to load your particular sound driver at every boot, carefully add the line for your driver to `/boot/loader.conf`:

```
snd_es137x_load="YES"
```

Replace *snd_es137x* with the name of your sound driver. Double-check for typos when you save your changes to this file.

There are several **sysctl** values that can be tweaked to improve your sound and multimedia performance. Two of them are read-only, meaning that you must place these values in the file `/boot/loader.conf`, like so:

```
hw.ata.atapi_dma="1"
hw.ata.ata_dma="1"
```

The other four values are placed in the file /etc/sysctl.conf. Note that, unlike the previous file, you don't use quotations around the values in this file:

```
kern.ipc.shmmax=67108864
kern.ipc.shmall=32768
hw.snd.pcm0.vchans=4
hw.snd.maxautovchans=4
```

If your output from **more /dev/sndstat** indicates that your soundcard doesn't use the pcm device, don't include that third **sysctl** value dealing with pcm0. If it indicated that you use pcm1 instead of pcm0, change the *0* to a *1* when you add that **sysctl** value. Also note that you will need to reboot in order for the read-only changes to take effect.

If you would like to be able to play audio CD-ROMs as a regular user, instead of having to become the superuser, change the permissions of the CD-ROM device file:

```
# chmod 666 /dev/cd0
```

To make this change permanent across a reboot, carefully add this line to /etc/devfs.conf:

```
perm cd0 0666
```

(You could also use a *cdrom* group — see the example in **man devfs.conf**.)

Playing with XMMS

Now I can start building some sound applications. I've tried most of the applications in the audio section of the ports collection, and I can honestly say that you'll be hard pressed to find a sweeter sound-playing utility than **xmms**. It is skinnable, even though it looks great by default; it has dozens of audio, visualization, and other plugins; it plays MP3s, MPEGs, WAVs, and SHOUTcast, as well as CDs, and supports the use of CDDB (Compact Disc Database) servers. Thorough documentation of how to use its features, along with screenshots, plugins, and skins can be found at the XMMS website.

To install this utility:

```
# pkg_add -r xmms
```

I also installed and tried out all of the available plugins from the ports collection. You can view the description for each by doing a search for *xmms-* at http://www.freshports.org.

To configure installed plugins, right-click in **xmms**, select Options then Preferences. Here you'll find tabs for Effects Plugins, General Plugins and Visualization Plugins. You'll want to set aside an afternoon to check out each plugin's configuration options and what happens when you enable it.

Note: If you install **xmms-gdancer** you will get a message telling you where to download the themes which are required to get dancing characters. If you miss the message, you can read it again with **pkg_info -Dx dancer**.

Now, let's take a quick tour of **xmms**. Instead of repeating the basic usage that is already well-documented in the XMMS User Manual at the XMMS website, I'll instead give some first-hand tips to get you started.

I'll assume that your CD-ROM and sound card are installed properly and that you were successful in getting FreeBSD to recognize your particular sound card.

Let's start with a music CD-ROM. From your Window Manager, start **xmms** and press **Ctrl-P** to bring up the Preferences screen. You'll note the various plugins tabs that I referred to earlier, and you'll recognize the plugins that you chose to install.

In the Audio I/O Plugins tab, click on CD Audio Player, then the Configure button. Under the Device tab, ensure your device is set to /dev/cd0 and the directory to /cdrom. Then, click on the CD Info tab if you would like to configure a CDDB server. CDDB servers are great, as they contain information regarding audio CDs, such as the names of the CD and artist, and the names of the songs on the CD. However, they do require you to be attached to the Internet when you first load an audio CD so that you can download that information. If you'd like that feature, click on Use CDDB and type in the name of your favorite CDDB server in the CDDB server type-in section. I use the default of freedb.freedb.org.

Save your changes, insert an audio CD into your CD-ROM drive, and wait for the light to stop flashing. Then, click on the eject icon in XMMS. Instead of ejecting the CD, XMMS will give you a pop-up window, where you can choose which files to load. Navigate to /cdrom and you should see all of the CD's tracks in the file section. (If you don't, you probably forgot to change the permissions on /dev/cd0.) Click on Add all files in directory. If you chose to use a CDDB server and this is the first time you've played this CD, be patient; it takes a minute or two to download the details. Once the files are added, click on Close and you should see the name of each track in your playlist. If you don't see a playlist, click on the PL button to open up the playlist editor window. If the various XMMS icons for playing, stopping, and moving through the tracks aren't intuitive to you, spend a bit of time to familiarize yourself with the available features.

The **xmms** utility can play more than CDs. I tend to have eclectic music tastes, which means the CDs I like are rarely in stock in my community. Fortunately, the Internet is a great resource for discovering new artists. How else would I have known that I enjoy Jewish reggae, Middle Eastern pop, East Indian blues, electronica remixes of the classics, and even the occasional gothic rock? My spare time is usually spent finding and listening to new MP3s, so I always have a list of CDs to order when I visit my favorite music shop.

I've configured **firefox** to use **xmms** to play MP3s by going to its Edit menu –> Preferences and clicking on Content and then the Manage button. Note that if MP3 isn't listed in your actions menu, **firefox** will ask you what you would like to do the first time you try to play an MP3 from your browser. If you change your mind, this is the menu that allows you to change the action.

In my home directory, I've created a directory called mp3s to store the MP3s I'd like to listen to while my CDs are on order. To tell XMMS to play these MP3s, I press **Shift-L** and double-click on the directory where the MP3s are stored.

If you've installed the **xmms-liveice** plugin, you can also listen to SHOUTcast streaming audio. Head over to http://www.shoutcast.com, find something interesting, and click on the Tune In! button. If your browser asks you what to do with this type of file, indicate that you would like to use **xmms**.

If you like to be visually entertained while listening to music, press **Ctrl-P** to open up the Preferences and click on Visualization Plugins. Highlight one of the plugins you installed, then click on Enable plugin. I liked **xmms-jess** the best, with **xmms-goom** a close second. If you get tired of being entertained, re-click the enable button to toggle off the plugin. Depending upon your hardware, you may find that your screen freezes if you try to enable more than two visualization plugins at once.

XMMS Skins

While we're on visualization, let's take a look at skins. The first time you ran **xmms**, a skins directory called .xmms/Skins was created for you in your home directory. Head over to http://www.xmms.org/skins.php

and if you see a skin you like, download it to your `Skins` directory. To apply the new skin, press **Alt-S** and highlight the new skin to get an instant preview.

I also found that `http://www.spacefem.com/xmms.shtml` had a very nice collection of skins. If you're into skins, you'll find that most of the skins on the Internet are advertised as Winamp skins. Don't let that deter you; save them to your `Skins` directory and like magic they'll work on XMMS. For example, I did an Internet search for the popular "mooamp" skin and now my XMMS has its own "ecowlizer." Don't let the extension of the skin scare you off; my `Skins` directory has *tar.gz*, *zip*, *wsz* and *png* files all coexisting nicely together. So, feel free to spend some time browsing through `http://www.winamp.com/skins`.

If you've installed **smpeg-xmms**, you can also watch movies with an *MPG* extension. Simply press **l** (the letter ell) to select the previously saved movie file. This plugin can be configured to display the movie in a centered window, in doublesize mode, or in fullscreen mode. To get you started, the Library of Congress has an extensive movie collection at `http://lcweb.loc.gov/rr/mopic/ndlmps.html`.

One of my favorite features is the alarm that gets installed with the **xmms-alarm** plugin. Use **Ctrl-P** to open up Preferences and click on the General Plugins tab. Highlight Alarm and go into the Configure button to set the alarm time and days. Unless you like to be jolted out of bed, don't set the volume to 100%. If you don't set a Playlist in the Options tab, you'll wake up to whatever song happens to be selected on your playlist. Just make sure **xmms** is started before going to bed, if you want it to wake you up in the morning.

Additional Resources

Original Article:

`http://www.onlamp.com/pub/a/bsd/2002/09/19/FreeBSD_Basics.html`

Sound Section of FreeBSD Handbook

`http://www.freebsd.org/doc/en_US.ISO8859-1/books/handbook/sound-setup.html`

XMMS Website

`http://www.xmms.org`

1.8 DVD Playback on FreeBSD

This section is on DVD playback, and I'll be demonstrating four applications from the ports collection which can be used for this purpose.

Some Terminology

There are two terms you should be aware of as they deal with DVD playback on a computer. The first is region codes. Nearly every DVD you purchase has a burnt-in region code indicating the distribution area for that DVD release. You'll find the DVD's region code on the rear jacket; it is usually towards the bottom next to the other symbols for Dolby Digital, the name of the studio, and the movie rating. Since movies are released at different times in different areas of the world, region codes are used to discourage the sale of DVDs before a region's official release date. Typically this isn't an issue unless, for example, you purchase a DVD while abroad only to discover you can't play it when you return home.

Table 1.2: DVD Region Codes

Region Code	Geographic Area
1	Canada, US, US territories
2	Japan, Europe, South Africa, Middle East, Egypt
3	Southeast Asia, East Asia
4	Australia, New Zealand, Pacific Islands, Central America, Mexico, South America, Caribbean
5	Russia, India, Pakistan, Africa (except Egypt), North Korea, Mongolia
6	China
7	Reserved
8	Airplanes, cruise ships

I'll list the region codes in Table 1.2 since some of the DVD ports default to region code 1, meaning you may need to reconfigure the DVD application with the region code for your geographic area.

The other term is CSS, or the Content Scrambling System. Almost all DVDs (usually the ones with region codes) are encrypted to prevent users from creating illegal copies, meaning that in order to actually view the DVD, the hardware DVD player needs the necessary software to unscramble the DVD. This is where things get murky and downright ugly. Since this issue is still before the courts and I'm not a lawyer, I'll leave it to you to do your own research on the subject and decide whether or not you want to play encrypted DVDs on your computer. A Google search of "dvd css" will definitely give lots of food for thought. Again, not all DVDs are encrypted. When I went through my DVD collection, I discovered that about 75 percent of them were.

DVD playback on a computer is still an emerging science, meaning that your mileage will definitely vary depending upon your CPU, video card, and resolution settings. It is quite possible that your results will be very different than mine, so read the section with a grain of salt and leave yourself some time for experimentation. I would strongly suggest that you run the latest version of FreeBSD and the latest version of X.

You'll also want to become the superuser and create the following links:

```
# ln -s /dev/cd0 /dev/dvd
# ln -s /dev/cd0 /dev/rdvd
```

One of the first things I discovered when I started playing DVDs on my computer is that most of my DVDs are scrambled by CSS, but a few aren't. As chance would have it, the very first DVD I tried playing just happened to not be scrambled. The second DVD I tried to play was encrypted, which left me wondering why something that had seemed so easy had suddenly become so difficult. As I demonstrate each port, I'll show the differences between playing an unencrypted and an encrypted DVD.

Fortunately for you, DVD players have improved considerably since I first wrote this. Each should now work out-of-the-box, meaning you only have to select the application which appeals to you.

DVD Players

I tested four ports that deal with DVD playback: **vlc**, **xine**, **mplayer**, and **ogle**. My criteria for evaluating each was, in order of importance:

1. No choppiness in audio or video

2. Works "out-of-the-box" without having to read tons of documentation

3. Skinnable, nice-looking interface

vlc

OK, enough prep. Let's start with **vlc**:

```
# pkg_add -r vlc
```

Note: Powerusers may prefer to build the port as it provides a menu of options for selecting which supported formats to compile into the application.

vlc is skinnable with skins and instructions for installing available at `http://www.videolan.org/vlc/skins.php`. To start a DVD, click on the eject button and select the Disc tab. Under Device name type in **/dev/cd0**. Your DVD will start and you'll be presented with the DVD menu to select which portion of the DVD to view.

If you find when you play a DVD that you're only seeing the top two-thirds of the movie, your resolution is set too high. Press **Ctrl-Alt -** (use the - on the **Num Lock** portion of the keyboard on the far right). This will allow you to scroll through your resolutions until you find the best one for playing DVDs.

I had no problems playing either encrypted or non-encrypted DVDs.

xine

Next, I tried **xine**:

```
# pkg_add -r xine
```

Note: **xine** used to require separate plugins in order to play encrypted DVDs and to use all of a DVD's menu features. This is no longer the case.

xine is skinnable with skins available at `http://xinehq.de/index.php/skins`. If you find a skin you like:

```
% mkdir ~/.xine/skins
```

Then, download the skin to your skins directory. The **xine** skins were a real strain on my sanity. Each skin moved the buttons to a different place, renamed the buttons to something else, and changed the configuration options. Some of the skins were non-intuitive. I had no idea what would happen if I pressed a certain button.

Trying to start DVDs turned into an even more frustrating experience. Sometimes, clicking on the DVD button, then the play button, would start playing a DVD. Sometimes, clicking on the MRL browser button, then clicking on its DVD button, then clicking on play did it. Sometimes I clicked all over, waited forever, and only froze up the GUI.

However, once I could get a DVD started, I had good luck playing both unencrypted and encrypted DVDs with excellent audio and video with no choppiness.

MPlayer

Next, I tried MPlayer. If you are using the KDE desktop, **pkg_add -r kmplayer** will build this player and integrate a GUI into your KDE menu. If you just **pkg_add -r mplayer**, only the command-line version will be installed. If you prefer a GUI on a non-KDE desktop, you'll want to install the **mplayer** port instead and ensure the GUI option is selected when you are presented with the menu of options. Power users may prefer to build the port so they can pick and choose from the codecs in the port's options menu.

To build the port (and receive that menu of options):

```
# cd /usr/ports/graphics/mplayer
# make install clean
```

The MPlayer GUI is skinnable, so I also installed the skins:

```
# pkg_add -r mplayer-skins
```

To start the GUI, use **gmplayer** instead of **mplayer** which starts the command-line interface.

A right-click anywhere on the GUI allowed me to change skins, set preferences, and open a DVD disc. Before trying to start a DVD, you'll need to go into Preferences and click on the Misc tab. Change the DVD device: to point to /dev/cd0.

To start a DVD, right-click on the interface, choose DVD then Open disc. Rather than showing the DVD menu, it will start playing at the first title. Once it starts, you can return to the DVD menu to select an alternate title or chapter.

This utility should be able to play both non-encrypted and encrypted DVDs. Depending upon your system, you may have to fiddle about with the Preferences menu. Power-users may prefer the command-line interface and spend an afternoon or so experimenting with the literally hundreds of configuration possibilities.

ogle

Finally, I tried **ogle**. By default, **ogle**'s engine is command-line based, but there is a package that will also install a simple GUI:

```
# pkg_add -r ogle-gui
```

The non-skinnable interface isn't anything to write home about, but it is clean and intuitive. To play a DVD, go to the File menu –> Open and browse to /dev/cd0. You can use your mouse to select the desired menu option once the movie starts.

I've found that unencrypted DVDs play very well. However it can be hit and miss with encrypted DVDs. Some play perfectly, while others lack sound and the video races along at double-speed. Hopefully future versions of **ogle** will fix this issue.

Additional Resources

Original Article:

`http://www.onlamp.com/pub/a/bsd/2002/10/03/FreeBSD_Basics.html`

Video Playback Section of FreeBSD Handbook:

`http://www.freebsd.org/doc/en_US.ISO8859-1/books/handbook/video-playback.html`

MPlayer Documentation:

`http://www.mplayerhq.hu/DOCS/HTML/en/index.html`

Xine FAQ:

`http://xinehq.de/index.php/faq`

VLC Website:

`http://www.videolan.org/`

Ogle Website:

`http://www.dtek.chalmers.se/groups/dvd/`

1.9 Playing Audio and Video Files with FreeBSD

One of the first things you'll notice if you're new to surfing the web from a Unix system is the lack of automagic support for the various audio and video formats splattered throughout the pages of Cyberspace. Do keep in mind that Unix is designed for the roll-your-own crowd who like to do their own customizations. Over time, I've configured my browser to display just about anything I come across on the Net. I've even learned a few things about multimedia and MIME types along the way.

If, like myself, you're using **firefox** as your browser, follow along as I demonstrate the configurations.

In section 1.6, I installed the **plugger** port which integrates plugin support into the **firefox** browser. In practice, I've found that this allows **firefox** to play just about every audio format I've come across on the Web: *mid*, *midi*, *mod*, *mp2*, *mp3*, *mpa*, *sid*, *au*, *snd*, and *wav*. It also adds support for text formats, meaning I can display *pdf*, *rtf*, and *doc* files, which is very handy as I do a lot of research on the Internet and constantly come across tech papers in these formats.

Video Formats

The **plugger** port also supports several audio/video formats, but not all of them. This is where things get a little more interesting. Many of these formats are proprietary and the codecs (and even the extensions for the files) tend to change every time the vendor releases a new, improved player.

For example, here are some popular formats and the extensions you could expect to find with each:

- Windows media: asf, asx, wax, wma, wmv, wvx, wmp, wmx

- QuickTime: mov, qt, avi

- MPEG: mpg, mpeg, m1v, mp2, mp3, mpa, mpe, mpvw, m3u

- Real: ra, rm, ram

- DivX: divx, avi, mp4

An interesting oddity is the avi extension which is shared by three different formats. An *avi* file might be a QuickTime video or a DivX video. While both of these formats deliver high quality video, they use very different and proprietary compression methods. It's also possible that an avi file might simply be a lower quality video using the Microsoft avi standard. In the case of avi, it isn't the extension that is important, but rather what the file purports to be. If it is QuickTime, it will say so and will require a viewer capable of playing the QuickTime standard. If it is DivX, it will say so and will require a viewer capable of playing the DivX standard.

The Windows media formats are yet another exercise in fun. As Microsoft improves on its video technologies, it releases new compression methods using new file extensions. New file formats require new versions of a proprietary player which understands those new formats.

Other Players

Confused yet? Let's compare the capabilities of some of the applications which are available for your FreeBSD system. Table 1.3 compares **plugger** to two media players discussed earlier for DVD playback, **vlc** and **mplayer**.

Note: Sometimes you'll come across zipped movies. You won't be able to play a zipped movie directly from the browser, and you'll have to unzip it before you can play it with a player that supports the file format of the unzipped file. For any file with a *zip* extension, you can unzip it from your FreeBSD system using the **unzip** utility. You may already have this utility if you've installed a port that uses it. To see if you do, use this command:

```
% pkg_info | grep unzip
unzip-5.52_3 List, test and extract compressed files in a ZIP archive
```

If you don't get any results back, install the utility like so:

```
# pkg_add -r unzip
```

Now, whenever you need to unzip a file with a zip extension, simply do this:

```
% unzip name_of_file.zip
```

MIME Types

Now, let's take a look at MIME types. In order to configure any browser to call another application to play a file, you need to know which MIME type is associated with which file extension. Table 1.4 shows the MIME types for the video formats **vlc** and **mplayer** are capable of playing, but doesn't include those already configured by **plugger**.

To configure firefox, go to the Edit menu –> Preferences –> Helper Applications, then click on the New Type button. In my case, I'll create three new types, one for each line in the above chart.

When creating your own types, choose a description that is useful to you, then fill in the remaining fields using the information from the above chart. By default, firefox will prompt to open using your specified application whenever you encounter an associated file type. If you don't want to receive that prompt, highlight your type, then go into Edit and uncheck the ask me before opening option.

Table 1.3: Video Player Capabilities

Format	plugger	vlc	mplayer
.3gp		video only	video only
.aiff (audio)		X	X
.asx		X	
.au (audio)		X	
.avi (divx)	X	X	X
.m3u	X	X	
.mov	X		
.mp3 (audio)	X	X	X
.mp4		video only	X
.mpg	X	X	X
.ogg (audio)	X	X	X
.ram	X		video only
.rm	X		X
.wav (audio)	X	X	X
.wma (audio)		X	X
.wmv	X	X	X

Additional Resources

Original Article:

http://www.onlamp.com/pub/a/bsd/2002/10/17/FreeBSD_Basics.html

Windows Multimedia File Formats

http://support.microsoft.com/default.aspx?scid=kb;[LN];316992

1.10 Tips and Tricks

At least once a year, I like to comb through the files on my FreeBSD system to see if there are any new docs, scripts, or manpages that I've missed. I started my search in /usr/share/examples, and the first thing that caught my eye was a subdirectory called BSD_daemon:

```
% ls /usr/share/examples/BSD_daemon
FreeBSD.pfa    beastie.eps    eps.patch
README         beastie.fig    poster.sh
```

Table 1.4: Video MIME Types

MIME type	File Extension	Application to use
video/avi	.3gp	vlc or mplayer
video/x-ms-asf	.asx	vlc
video/mp4	.mp4	mplayer

The README explains each of the files in this directory, created by Poul-Henning Kamp and protected by the Beerware license (also explained in the README).[8]

The README also gives the instructions for creating a GIF and PNG using the **fig2dev** utility. That utility wasn't on my system, but a quick Google search indicated that it is part of the **transfig** suite of tools. I installed that package then ran the commands required to generate the images:

```
# pkg_add -r transfig
# fig2dev -L gif -g '#f0f0f0' -t '#f0f0f0' \
  beastie.fig beastie.gif
# fig2dev -L png beastie.fig beastie.png
```

The resulting images are a nice rendering of Beastie. If you like experimenting with images, **man fig2dev** is well worth reading.

Adding Interaction to Scripts

Next, I checked out the dialog subdirectory:

```
% ls /usr/share/examples/dialog
README        infobox        msgbox        textbox
checklist     inputbox       prgbox        treebox
ftreebox      menubox        radiolist     yesno
```

Earlier in the year I had experimented with **dialog**, which allows you to add interactive menus to your shell scripts. At the time, I scoured the Internet for some working examples but was disappointed. I could only find a few that demonstrated creating a menubox, which is only one of **dialog**'s box options. While **man dialog** does a pretty good job of explaining each option, I find it easier to have a working example to refer to when I'm learning something new.

For your benefit, this directory contains examples for each type of **dialog** box. These are Bourne shell scripts, so you can easily read each script and use it as a template for creating your own interactive scripts. To test each script, first set them as executable:

```
# chmod +x [a-z]*
```

---

[8]The BSD Daemon figure is copyrighted by Marshall Kirk McKusick; details are at http://www.mckusick.com/beastie/mainpage/copyright.html.

Notice that I used filename globbing with my **chmod** command. I didn't want to set the README file as executable (**+x**), but I wanted to match all of the other files in this directory. The files I wanted to match all have lowercase names, and the **[a-z]** before the * wildcard means to match all files with lowercase letters.

Also, because the scripts are in /usr/share/examples and that directory isn't in the default path, you must give the full path to each script in order to execute it. Alternately, you can **cd** into that directory and put a ./ before the script's name, like this:

```
# cd /usr/share/examples
# ./yesno
```

In Case of Emergency

It's rare that things go wrong once you pass the initial learning phase, where it seems that you're reinstalling your system from scratch every second day. However, it's always good to be aware of the various emergency exits just in case something does go wrong.

If you're running FreeBSD 5.2 or higher, check out **man rescue**, then take a look through **ls /rescue**. It's reassuring to know there is a safety net of utilities available in the unlikely event that you can't access /bin or /sbin. The manpage also gives step-by-step instructions on how to proceed in such an emergency. It's well worth printing and storing with your offline documentation.

Have you ever really screwed up a configuration file, or worse, accidentally deleted it from your system? If that file was in /etc, all isn't lost. Your system should have copies of the originals safely tucked away in /usr/share/examples/etc/.

Finally, the one place you don't want to be when you're playing with the **rm** command is /dev. Have you ever noticed that a long listing in this directory includes two extra fields not seen elsewhere on your file system? A long listing is used to see the permissions, size, and last modification time of files. For example, compare these two listings:

```
% ls  -l /etc/rc.conf
-rw-r--r--  1 root  wheel  230 Jul  4 08:52 /etc/rc.conf
% ls -l /dev/fd0
crw-r-----  1 root  operator    0,  76 Aug 17 09:21 /dev/fd0
```

Instead of showing the size of the file in bytes, a long listing of a device file shows the major number followed by the minor number. These numbers represent the type of device so that the kernel knows how to interact with the device. This means that if you were to accidentally delete /dev/fd0, simply issuing the command **touch /dev/fd0** wouldn't fix it. Instead, use the **mknod** command, which uses this syntax:

```
# mknod fd0 c 0 76
```

The **c** indicates that this is a character device; note the c was in the long listing as the first letter next to the permissions set. What does all of this mean? If you accidentally delete a device, you need to know three things in order to recreate it: whether it is a block or character device, its major number, and its minor number. If you have another FreeBSD system available, you can retrieve that information by doing a long listing for the missing device. If you know you don't have access to another system, consider backing up /dev or printing out a copy of **ls -l /dev**.

Note: Newer versions of FreeBSD use the device file system, devfs(5). **man mknod** and **man devfs** explains this in further detail.

Reading Material

I was pleasantly surprised by the increase in FreeBSD articles this past year. Many of these are available in `/usr/share/doc/en/articles`.

Hack #89 of BSD Hacks[9] demonstrates how to update your offline documentation with newly posted articles. Ensure that this line is in your CVS `supfile`:

```
doc-all tag=.
```

Because the sources are SGML, you'll need this port to convert them to HTML:

```
# pkg_add -r docproj-nojadetex
```

I script my up-to-date processes. The part of the script that converts the documentation is:

```
echo "Updating docs"
cd /usr/doc
cp Makefile.orig Makefile
make install > /dev/null
```

Some of the articles are ideal for new users, and, even if you're not a new user, they are well worth pointing out to your novice friends. In `/usr/share/doc/en/articles`, check out `new-users` and `freebsd-questions`. For those who feel at a loss when asked to explain what FreeBSD is, see `explaining-bsd`. If you have a hankering to contribute to the project but feel you can't because you don't write code, read through `contributing`.

Have you ever wanted a visual map of how the BSDs integrate into the Unix family tree? Take a look at **more /usr/share/misc/bsd-family-tree**. .

Perhaps you've had a hankering to create a manpage. You'll find templates called `man.template` and `mdoc.template` in `/usr/share/misc`. Even better, `/usr/share/examples/mdoc` contains the formatting for three well-commented sample manpages.

A GUI `rc.conf`

Whenever I can, I like to take a long perusal through the ports collection while installing and trying out interesting sounding ports on my test system. I had been meaning to try out **thefish** for a while. I started by installing the package:

```
# pkg_add -r thefish
```

However, when I ran **thefish**, it ran the ncurses version. You know that blue screen you see when you type **sysinstall**, where your mouse doesn't work and you have to use your arrow and tab keys to navigate? That type of screen uses the ncurses library to provide a quasi-GUI at a console. This is great on a system that doesn't have X installed. However, if you're using a GUI and want a nice-looking menu, you should instead use the widget set appropriate to your windowing environment.

What do I mean? Once I uninstalled the console-only binary of **thefish**, I built the port instead:

---

[9]`http://www.oreilly.com/catalog/bsdhks/`

```
# pkg_delete -x thefish
# cd /usr/ports/sysutils/thefish
# make install clean
```

It presented me with this menu:

```
[ ] CONSOLE      Disable X11 support
[x] GTK          Use GTK+ for the X11 interface
[ ] QT           Use Qt for the X11 interface
```

GTK+ and QT are the possible widget sets. A widget set controls how a window looks; for example, where the minimize and maximize controls are, and how they look. If you use the Gnome desktop, you're using the GTK+ widget set. If you use KDE, you're using QT. I prefer the look of QT windows, so I built my version of **thefish** with QT. If you take a closer look at the screenshots at the web site for **thefish**, you'll see that the buttons on the QT menu are different from the second screenshot for the GTK+ version of the program.

Once you have **thefish**, you have an easy-to-use interface for changing /etc/rc.conf parameters with brief descriptions regarding each parameter. You also have the ability to add other parameters if you've installed an application that comes with its own rc.conf knobs.

Changing Your Mind

Have you ever built a port, seen its menu of options, and then changed your mind? For example, after building the QT version of **thefish**, I had the urge to uninstall it to try the GTK+ version. However, when I issued my **make** command, it didn't present the options menu. I instead noticed a one-liner stating that my configuration had been saved, followed by **make** happily recreating the QT version.

After a bit of poking around, I found this:

```
# more /var/db/ports/thefish/options
 This file generated by 'make config'.
# No user-servicable parts inside!
# Options for thefish-0.6.5_2
_OPTIONS_READ=thefish-0.6.5_2
WITHOUT_CONSOLE=true
WITHOUT_GTK=true
WITH_QT=true
```

I removed that file, restarted **make**, and voila, again saw the options menu so that I could choose GTK. On your own system, use **ls /var/db/ports** to see which of your ports have saved options.

Note: Another method is to type **make rmconfig** in the directory for the port you wish to make.

RSS

I have a list of web sites that I visit on a daily basis to keep up with news, weather, articles, and blogs. I was aware of RSS Web feeds, but up to now hadn't had the time to check out the various RSS clients. A search through the ports collection showed a dozen or so clients, each of which I tried. I wanted an attractive GUI interface that was easy to configure. In my book, `/usr/ports/www/akregator` is the clear winner.

Some of the other RSS clients came with pre-defined lists. While it was convenient to pick out some of the more common sites, such as Slashdot and FreeBSDDiary, often the URLs were outdated and I still had to go to the web site and hunt for the proper RSS URL.

Out of the clients, **akregator** was the easiest to use to add a feed. Most other clients don't check the URL until you try to download a feed; if there is a typo, or you don't specify the full path to the RSS feed, this step will fail.

With **akregator**, I can type `slashdot.org` and it will connect to Slashdot, locate the feed, and correctly save the URL as `http://slashdot.org/index.rss`. This worked for all of the sites I tried, making it pretty goof-proof.

On a side note, I also use **firefox**, which supports adding RSS feeds as live bookmarks. The `http://www.mozilla.com/en-US/firefox/live-bookmarks` website gives screenshots and explains the basics of RSS and how to use live bookmarks. It also hyperlinks to `http://del.icio.us`, a site you don't want to visit unless you have some spare time to kill. While it's convenient to have RSS feeds integrated into the browser, I prefer **akregator**'s interface.

Now that I've joined the RSS generation, I don't know how I lived without it. I'm informed whenever a new blog/article is posted, the weather has changed (hey, I don't always remember to look outside), or a port has been added or modified.

For example, I found out about `/usr/ports/ports-mgmt/pkg_rmleaves` from the Freshports feed[10] approximately eight minutes after its commit. Having used `/usr/ports/ports-mgmt/pkg_cutleaves` in the past to prune unwanted ports, I was intrigued.

Because the port was just committed, I ran **csup** to grab the sources in order to build the port. When I ran **pkg_rmleaves**, it presented me with a checklist **dialog** menu where I could easily pick and choose which ports to uninstall. This port offers a very convenient way to manage orphaned (and possibly no longer required) ports.

Additional Resources

Original Article:

`http://www.onlamp.com/pub/a/bsd/2005/02/17/FreeBSD_Basics.html`

Dialog: An Introductory Tutorial:

`http://www.linuxjournal.com/node/2807/print`

The Fish Website:

`http://www.energyhq.es.eu.org/thefish.html`

1.11 Odds and Ends

One of the reasons I look forward to the holiday season is that it provides the opportunity to get reacquainted with the inner workings of my FreeBSD system. During the rush of the rest of the year it seems that everything I learn is on a need-to-know basis. So with the excitement of a four year old on Christmas Eve, I break open

---

[10]`http://www.freshports.org/news.php`

the eggnog, pump up the volume on the PC speakers, and start reading through the notes I've made to myself over the past year.

It always reminds me of how I felt after my first successful FreeBSD install. After the initial "omg, I just installed Unix!", I sort of sat there in a stunned daze and wondered "now what?" There was just so much to learn, so many man pages to read, so many commands to try out. Not to mention the fact that I kept getting lost and couldn't remember where I was and where I had saved things.

Keeping Track

It was then that I acquired two habits which helped me scale the initial learning curve. The first was to subscribe to the freebsd-questions mailing list.[11] This is a fairly high volume list, but the information that can be learned from it is invaluable. In the beginning I'd set aside an hour a day to read through the responses. If something sounded interesting, I would try it out on my own system. If I couldn't get it to work, I appended that particular post to an ever-growing file of things to try again at a later date.

At first that file seemed huge; everything I read sounded interesting, and I wasn't very good yet at getting things to work. But after a few months of persistence, I noticed that I was making progress. It was like getting used to a new language. As I'd read through that file, the information in it seemed less strange and started to make more sense. Pieces were starting to fit together. One day as I was reading through the mailing list, someone asked a question and I actually knew the answer. That was a very good feeling.

The second habit I acquired was taking the time to document everything. I bought two notebooks. The first I labeled "stuff I tried"; the second I labeled "stuff that works". Since I have a knack for discovering all of the wrong ways to do something before I stumble upon a way that works, my first notebook filled up very quickly. I was, however, left with a record of all possible error messages and how I managed to get past them to a working solution. This became an invaluable troubleshooting tool. Knowing how to reproduce an error is as important as knowing how to accomplish something without errors.

The second notebook eventually turned into my little black book of accomplishments. Once I figured out how to do something, I didn't have to reinvent the wheel when I needed to do it again six months later. I could simply look it up and follow my own step-by-step instructions. It was also an excellent way to chart my progress as those empty pages slowly transformed into the stuff I knew how to do on a Unix system.

At some point, I retired those notebooks and started to maintain notes in my home directory. There are several ways to keep track of your own experimentations. The first is to record your input and resulting output using the **script** command. For example, I can keep track of the date I did some experiments with **snort**:

```
% script snort.dec.28.2002
```

This command tells the **script** utility to copy all input and output to a file called `snort.dec.28.2002`. When you use the **script** command, you'll receive a message stating the **script** has started and the name of the output file you specified. You will also be presented with a fortune, if you normally receive a fortune when you login. At this point, you can carry on as usual. Once you've finished recording what you set out to do, end the script by pressing **Ctrl-D**. You'll see a message like this:

```
Script done, output file is snort.dec.28.2002
```

---

[11]http://lists.freebsd.org/mailman/listinfo/freebsd-questions

The **script** utility is an excellent way to record how you accomplished something; it also creates a file that is handy to send to someone else so they can see what errors you are running across. It has its limitations, though, since it records everything, including escape characters. For example, here is the first line from one of my script files:

```
<-[1mdlavigne6@ <-[m:  cd /s o <-[K/ysr/ o <-[K o <-[K o <-[K o <-
[Kusr/ports/security/sn o o o rt
```

It's a bit hard to tell, but this is what script was recording:

```
% cd /usr/ports/security/snort
```

The resulting output is unreadable for several reasons. One, I use a customized prompt which contains control characters. Second, I had problems typing that day. Instead of /usr, I typed /s and had to backspace a character; than I typed /ysr and had to backspace three characters. Finally, I use tab completion; you can see that I tried to tab at sn but received a beep; I then tried to tab at sno and had my input completed to snort.

The **file** utility does warn that this happens:

```
% file snort.dec.28.2002
snort.dec.28.2002: ASCII English text, with CRLF, CR, LF line terminators, with escape
sequences
```

All is not lost, though. This command will get rid of most of the garbage characters:

```
% more snort.dec.28.2002 | col -b > snort.dec.28.2002.clean
```

The result is much more readable:

```
 1mdlavigne6@ m: cd /usr/ports/security/snort
```

```
% file snort.dec.28.2002.clean
snort.dec.28.2002.clean: ASCII English text
```

You'll find that if you use an editor during a **script** session, the results from the edit will be a bit messy when you re-read your **script** file. For this reason, I tend to use the **echo** command to send little comments to myself:[12]

```
% echo #once you open up /etc/rc.conf
% echo #change this line: linux_enable="NO"
% echo # to this: linux_enable="YES"
% echo # and add this line: sshd_enable="YES"
```

These comments help me to remember why I opened certain files and what I did when I was in there.

Another way of recording a session is to open an interactive shell:

---

[12]If you aren't using a C shell, the pound sign will start your comment, so put the echo arguments in single quotes.

```
% csh -i | & tee acid.dec.29.2002
```

Note: Technically the **-i** is not needed for this to work but I like to include it to remind me that the shell is interactive.

Again, you'll receive a fortune and everything you type will be recorded to the file name specified after the word **tee**. When you are finished, either press **Ctrl-C** or **Ctrl-D** or type the word **exit**. I find that this method produces less garbage than **script** so I don't need to clean up the file using the **col -b** command. However, if I try to use **vi** from an interactive shell, I'll receive this message:

```
ex/vi: Vi's standard input and output must be a terminal.
```

The **pico** editor will work, but the results will still be very messy when I read the resulting session file.

One of the cool things about recording to a file with either **script** or **csh -i** is that the results can be watched live from another terminal. For example, another user on the system can use the **tail** command to watch the file as it is created:

```
% tail -f acid.dec.29.2002
```

This can be very handy if you are troubleshooting a problem and need another user's input on the error messages you are receiving.

Finding Commands

So where do you go about finding all the commands on your FreeBSD system so you have something to try out? At least once a year I like to play with the **apropos** command to see which commands are on the FreeBSD system. For example, to see all of the built-in general commands, try:

```
% apropos '(1)'
```

If you happen to be half as curious as I am, give yourself a chunk of time before you try that command. If one of the descriptions piques your interest, read the associated man page. No matter how little or how much experience you have in Unix, you will always find commands you either haven't heard of or would like to learn more about. For example, I came across **systat**, one of those commands I can't believe I've lived without.

If you just type **systat** at a prompt, you probably won't be impressed. The full power of this command comes from having the man page open in one terminal and **systat** running from another. Any man page that includes a *pigs* switch has to be worth checking out. Since *pigs* is the default, type **:icmp** once you've started **systat**, then try a **ping** from another terminal. Once you've ended your **ping**, try **:ip** or **:tcp** or **:swap** or **:mbufs**. I'll leave it to you to try your own experiments so you can discover which switches are the most useful for your own needs.

Playing Around

I also remember to take the time to see which games come with the system:

```
% apropos '(6)'
```

Note: If you don't have any games installed you can choose to do so from the Distributions menu of **sysinstall**. Also, some games have been removed from the system but can be installed using **pkg_add -r freebsd-games**.

I discovered **grdc** just in time for my New Year's resolution of remembering to step away from the computer at least once a day in order to do some aerobic activity. The display is large enough for me to see what time it is from across the room, despite my myopia.

I also rediscovered **quiz**, a game I had forgotten about in the last few years. To see what quizzes are available, simply type **quiz** for a list. Each quiz type is on a line of its own and consists of at least two words. For example, if I type:

```
% quiz male female
lad?
```

I'll be given a male term and should type in the female equivalent. If I'm correct, I get a "Right!" and the next term. If I'm incorrect, I get a "What?" and another chance. If I give up and want to know the answer, I simply press **Enter**. Pressing **Ctrl-C** ends the game. The game can also be played the other way around by typing this instead:

```
% quiz female male
```

This utility includes quizzes for Latin, Greek, arithmetic, capitals, poetry, number sequences, and even Middle-Earth and Star Trek trivia.

Browsing Documentation

Some of the games on your system supplement the man page with additional documentation. This is a good time to mention that the documentation that comes in the /usr/share/doc directory is truly awesome when you are ready to delve deeper into the inner mysteries of Unix. You can also read and see the general layout of this documentation.

The documentation contains a who's who of Unix and many of the classic, "everybody should have a chance to read at least once" documents. It really is something to be able to read documentation from the very people who created Unix, the C programming language, the Fast File System, Sendmail, the Bourne shell, the C shell, **vi**, and so on. It's a good way to find out how things came to be and why they are the way they are.

Let's take a look at the contents of the documents directory:

```
% ls -F /usr/share/doc
IPv6/              faq@        psd/
atm/               handbook@   smm/
bind9/             ncurses     usd/
en@                ntp@
en_US.ISO8859-1/   papers/
```

You'll note that it is composed of several subdirectories. The psd is the Programmer's Supplementary Documents, the smm is the System Manager's Manual, and the usd is the User's Supplementary Documents. Those three subdirectories and the papers subdirectory each contain a file called contents.ascii.gz which gives a description of the documentation found in the associated subdirectory.

You may remember that a *.gz* extension indicates a gzipped file. You don't have to gunzip a file in order to read it. For example, to see the contents of the psd, simply use the **zmore** utility instead of **more**:

```
% zmore /usr/share/doc/psd/contents.ascii.gz
```

And if one of the documents looks interesting:

```
% zmore /usr/share/doc/psd/12.make/paper.ascii.gz
```

Over the holidays, I always find time to reread portions of the documentation. I also go through my extensive bookmark collection and revisit the homepages of some of the authors of that documentation. If you're unfamiliar with some of the who's who, you may enjoy the links in the Additional Resources.

Between those URLs and the documentation, you should have plenty of quality reading to keep you busy and learning about your FreeBSD system for quite a while.

Additional Resources

Original Article:

http://www.onlamp.com/pub/a/bsd/2003/01/23/FreeBSD_Basics.html

Dennis M. Ritchie

http://www.cs.bell-labs.com/who/dmr/

Ken Thompson

http://cm.bell-labs.com/cm/cs/who/ken/

Kirk McKusick

http://www.mckusick.com/

Brian Kernighan

http://cm.bell-labs.com/cm/cs/who/bwk/

Unixica

http://www.unixica.com/

1.12 FreeBSD for Linux Users

One of the minor irritations that comes with using another operating system is the change in the environment. Some of the first things many Linux users discover about a default FreeBSD installation are that it doesn't include **bash** and doesn't colorize the output of **ls**. Fortunately, if you've become accustomed to these features, it only takes a moment or so to integrate them into FreeBSD. First, as the superuser, add the **bash** package:

```
# pkg_add -r bash
```

That command will go out on the Internet, find the pre-compiled package, install it for you, and update /etc/shells. Note that the path for **bash** is different on FreeBSD, as it is a third-party application rather than part of the base operating system install:

```
$ which bash
/usr/local/bin/bash
```

Hint: in FreeBSD, user binaries that come with the operating system go in /bin and /usr/bin, system binaries in /sbin and /usr/sbin, and system configuration files in /etc. You'll find the equivalents for third-party applications in /usr/local/bin, /usr/local/sbin, and /usr/local/etc. This makes it easier to determine what did and didn't come with the operating system.

Then, from your regular user account, create an alias to **ls** to use the colorized switch:

```
% vi ~/.bashrc
alias ls='ls -G'
```

Once you've saved your file, type **bash** to start the shell and issue an **ls** command to test your change.

Modifying Existing User Accounts

Rather than typing **bash** every time you log in, you'll probably want to change the default shell of your regular user account to **bash**; this will require modifying the password database. Like most Linux distros, FreeBSD uses a shadow database. Unlike Linux, this isn't /etc/shadow. Instead, it's /etc/master.passwd, and — this is very important — you don't send this file directly to an editor.

Instead, use the **chpass** utility to update all of the password databases correctly. Here, I set the shell for the user *dru*:

```
# chpass -s /usr/local/bin/bash dru
chpass:  user information updated
```

Like the Linux command **usermod**, **chpass** has other switches; see **man chpass** for details. Alternately, if you're comfortable using the **vi** editor and prefer to see exactly what you're editing, use **vipw** instead. This will open up the password database in **vi** and update it correctly when you save your edits.

That reminds me. If you learned how to use **vi** in Linux, you probably instead learned how to use **vim**. FreeBSD, by default, uses **nvi**.

If you miss **vim**, simply type:

```
# pkg_add -r vim
```

Then, set **vim** as your default editor by adding this line to your ~/.bashrc file:

```
export EDITOR=/usr/local/bin/vim
```

Don't forget to type **. ~/.bashrc** to notify **bash** of the change to its configuration file.[13] Now **vipw** will use **vim** instead of **vi**. If you're editing files with tools that don't use the $EDITOR variable, and don't think you'll remember to type **vim** *filename* instead of **vi** *filename*, add an alias to **vim** in your ~/.bashrc file.

---

[13]That is a period and a space in the **. ~/.bashrc** to read and execute it within the current shell environment.

Creating User Accounts

Unix provides several utilities to create user accounts, and you'll probably find the utility you're used to using on a FreeBSD system. If you prefer to use an ncurses-type GUI, use the **sysinstall** menu. Its Configure option allows you to install software, create users, configure networking, and configure X.

Device Names

You'll find some minor differences in device names. For example, your first Ethernet NIC won't be /dev/eth0. Instead, the device name will indicate the chipset used in your NIC. Here's one way to find out your NIC name(s):

```
% dmesg | grep Ethernet
rl0:  Ethernet address:  00:05:5d:d2:19:b7
rl1:  Ethernet address:  00:05:5d:d1:ff:9d
ed0:  <NE2000 PCI Ethernet (RealTek 8029)> port 0x9800-0x981f irq 10 at device 11.0 on
pci0
```

This particular system has three Ethernet cards: two Realtek cards (rl0 and rl1) and one generic card (ed0). I found the names of the chipsets by sending those NIC names (minus their numbers) to **whatis**:

```
% whatis rl
rl(4) - RealTek 8129/8139 Fast Ethernet device driver
% whatis ed
ed(1), red(1) - text editor
ed(4) - NE2000 and WD-80x3 Ethernet driver
```

man 4 rl and **man 4 ed** describe which particular NIC models the specified chipset covers.

You'll also find that the names for your hard drives and partitions are different:

```
% df
Filesystem      1K-blocks      Used      Avail Capacity  Mounted on
/dev/ad0s1a       253678     65594     167790     28%   /
devfs                  1         1          0    100%   /dev
/dev/ad0s1e       253678     18482     214902      8%   /tmp
/dev/ad0s1f     13147670   6526230    5569628     54%   /usr
/dev/ad0s1d       253678     42232     191152     18%   /var
linprocfs              4         4          0    100%   /usr/compat/linux/proc
```

Compare that to the **df** output from a Red Hat system:

```
% df
Filesystem      1K-blocks      Used  Available  Use%  Mounted on
/dev/hda2        9506024   2080628    6942516    24%   /
/dev/hda1          99043      9275      84654    10%   /boot
none               63016         0      63016     0%   /dev/shm
/dev/cdrom        636408    636408          0   100%   /mnt/cdrom
```

Red Hat uses *hd* to represent an IDE hard drive; FreeBSD uses *ad*. Red Hat uses *a* to represent the primary master; FreeBSD uses *0*. Red Hat follows the *a* with a number representing the partition — in this case, *1* and *2* are the first two primary partitions. FreeBSD uses slices (hence the *s*) and this system has one FreeBSD slice divided into several partitions. By convention, partition *a* is / and *b* is /swap. This particular system also has *d* mounted on /var, *e* mounted on /tmp, and *f* mounted on /usr.

Note: Like Linux, FreeBSD uses the file /etc/fstab to determine how to mount filesystems; however, it does not use the file /etc/mtab. (If you've installed Linux compatibility, use **more /usr/compat/linux/proc/mtab** instead.) The commands **mount** and **df** list the currently mounted filesystems.

What Happened to /proc?

You're in for a surprise if you habitually poke about /proc for information on your hardware and the state of your running Linux system. Again, if you've installed Linux compatibility, you'll find most of what you're looking for in /usr/compat/linux/proc. However, also experiment with FreeBSD's powerful **sysctl** mechanism.

Typing **sysctl -a | more** is the equivalent of viewing every /proc entry at once, and then some. This is an excellent way not only to watch what happens on a running system but also to understand what the term "kernel state" means. I recommend you try this command at least once.

A judicious use of **grep** can help when you know what you're looking for. For example, to see current memory usage:

```
% sysctl -a | grep -i memory
Virtual Memory:  (Total:  614K, Active 185444K)
Real Memory:  (Total:  295928K Active 100972K)
Shared Virtual Memory:  (Total:  74960K Active:  68524K)
Shared Real Memory:  (Total:  43296K Active:  40048K)
Free Memory Pages:  36412K
p1003_1b.memory_protection:  0
p1003_1b.shared_memory_objects:  1
```

The superuser has the capability of changing many of the **sysctl** tunables on the fly. For example, to view then modify the system's TTL:

```
# sysctl -a | grep ttl
net.inet.ip.ttl:  64
# sysctl -w net.inet.ip.ttl=100
net.inet.ip.ttl:  64 -> 100
# sysctl net.inet.ip.ttl
net.inet.ip.ttl:  100
```

man sysctl and the Tuning with sysctl section of the Handbook have more information.[14]

Many Linux commands (e.g., **ps**, **top**, and **free**, to name a very few) query /proc for information on what is currently happening on the system. Similarly, many FreeBSD commands query **sysctl**. While you could manually send the information in /proc to a pager or grep through **sysctl -a**, it's often easier to have a command do the query and format the results for you. For example, on a FreeBSD 6.x system, **devinfo** will show your system resources, categorized by type of resource:

---

[14]http://www.freebsd.org/handbook/configtuning-sysctl.html

```
% devinfo -ru
Interrupt request lines:
0x0 (root0)
0x1 (atkbd0)
0x3 (sio1)
0x4 (sio0)
0x5 (rl0)
0x6 (fdc0)
0x7-0x8 (root0)
0x9 (acpi0)
0xa (pcm0)
0xb (uhci0)
0xc (psm0)
0xd (root0)
0xe (ata0)
0xf (ata1)
DMA request lines:
0-1 (root0)
2 (fdc0)
3-7 (root0)
I/O ports:
0x0-0xf (root0)
0x10-0x1f (acpi_sysresource0)
0x20-0x21 (root0)
<snip>
I/O memory addresses:
0x0-0x9ffff (root0)
0xa0000-0xbffff (vga0)
0xc0000-0xcbfff (orm0)
0xcc000-0xfbffffff (root0)
0xfc000000-0xfdffffff (agp0)
0xfe000000-0xffffffff (root0)
open if_tun units:
0-32767 (root0)
```

swapinfo will show your currently mounted swap devices:

```
% swapinfo
Device       1K-blocks    Used      Avail    Capacity
/dev/ad0s1b    637704      156     637548    0%
```

There are dozens of other useful utilities available. To find them, try these commands:

```
% apropos info | grep 8
% apropos stat | grep 1
% apropos stat | grep 8
```

Modules

Like Linux, the FreeBSD kernel supports the loading and unloading of modules. This allows an administrator to add or remove driver support without having to recompile the kernel or reboot the system. The possible modules are the files ending with the *.ko* extension in /boot/kernel.

To list the currently loaded modules:

```
% kldstat
Id  Refs      Address      Size     Name
1    10    0xc0400000    3348d8     kernel
2     1    0xc0735000     51ac8     acpi.ko
3     1    0xc3168000      6000     linprocfs.ko
4     1    0xc316e000     19000     linux.ko
```

If you're curious as to the meaning of each of the columns, see **man 2 kldstat**. Note that the usage and output is similar to Linux's **lsmod** command.

Linux also provides the **insmod** and **rmmod** commands to load and unload modules. The FreeBSD equivalents are **kldload** and **kldunload**. For example, to load USB scanner support:

```
# kldload uscanner.ko
```

To remove it when you're finished:

```
# kldunload uscanner.ko
```

Loading something that is already statically compiled into the kernel produces this error message:

```
# kldload snd_pcm.ko
kldload:  can't load snd_pcm.ko:  File exists
```

If you don't know what a module does, ask **whatis**. Suppose that I'm curious about the module if_pcn.ko. I won't include the *.ko* in my query. I also won't include the *if_*; it categorizes the module as an interface type. (Similarly, *snd_* represents the sound category.) That leaves *pcn*, making this command:

```
% whatis pcn
pcn(4) - AMD PCnet/PCI fast ethernet device driver
```

I think my NIC might fall into that category. **man 4 pcn** gives the actual NIC models covered by this particular kernel module.

FreeBSD Terminology

Here are the FreeBSD equivalents to some common Linux tasks, as well as some document references to start you in your own research.

You won't find **iptables**, **ipfwadm**, or **ipchains** on a FreeBSD system. However, FreeBSD does come with several built-in firewalls. **ipfw** provides a stateful firewall with an easily understandable rule syntax. **ipf** provides a different (often considered "more complex") rulebase that supports the chaining of rules. Newer FreeBSD versions also support OpenBSD's **pf**. The Firewall section of the Handbook is a good place to start.[15] It contains hyperlinks to several sites with more detailed documentation.

FreeBSD also supports NAT (IP masquerading) and bandwidth limiting (known as `dummynet`). Start with the Advanced Networking section of the Handbook.[16]

The author of `dummynet` has a useful `dummynet` tutorial[17] and Erudition has a comprehensive NAT tutorial[18].

FreeBSD also supports `netgraph` to augment the kernel's networking support and the See Also section of **man 4 netgraph** refers to the available netgraph modules. There are also several working examples found within the subdirectories of `/usr/share/examples/netgraph`.

Finally, FreeBSD supports the use of `gbde`[19] to encrypt disk partitions.

Once you're familiar with FreeBSD terminology and some of the design differences between Linux and FreeBSD, you'll find that most of your Linux skills easily transfer over to FreeBSD. As you read the FreeBSD Handbook and manpages, you're likely to discover new skills that you can practice on both operating systems.

Additional Resources

Original Article:

`http://www.onlamp.com/pub/a/bsd/2005/01/13/FreeBSD_Basics.html`

1.13 FreeBSD for Linux Admins

Over the past years, I've had the opportunity to teach introductory Linux and BSD classes. Since BSD users primarily attended the Linux classes and the Linux users primarily attended the BSD classes, both groups had an interest in finding out more about their open source counterparts.

Students expected to find differences, but they often found the particulars surprising. Some of the commands they customarily used had different switches or were missing entirely, and certain features had totally different implementations.

I'll cover some of the big-picture differences from the perspective of a Linux user being introduced to FreeBSD as well as the command equivalents between Linux and FreeBSD.

---

[15]`http://www.freebsd.org/handbook/firewalls.html`
[16]`http://www.freebsd.org/handbook/advanced-networking.html`
[17]`http://info.iet.unipi.it/~luigi/ip_dummynet/`
[18]`http://www.erudition.net/freebsd/NAT-HOWTO`
[19]`http://www.freebsd.org/handbook/disks-encrypting.html`

SysV vs. BSD: Runlevels

Most introductory Unix courses start with the differences between SysV and BSD. Students, unimpressed by this fascinating bit of theoretical trivia, tend to jot down a few notes dutifully, and then wait patiently for the hands-on portion of the class. Within the hour, though, someone will make a panicked discovery and shout out, "Where are my runlevels?" There's an inevitable and incredulous follow-up of "What do you mean there aren't any runlevels?" and "Where'd all my startup scripts go?"

Herein lies one of the tangible design differences between a SysV system such as Linux and a BSD system. Both systems manage to start and run just fine — they just do it differently. It's equally difficult convincing a Linux user that a Unix administrator can achieve all of the functionality of runlevels without using runlevels as it is to convince a BSD user that it takes an entire subdirectory structure of symlinks to manage services.

While there are some variations in number, most Linux distros will provide runlevels representing shutdown, reboot, single user, multiuser with command line, and multiuser with GUI modes. The /etc/inittab file describes these runlevels, and the **telinit** command allows administrators to tell the **init** process to change its current runlevel.

A BSD system is also capable of each of these **init** states, though it does so without using the inittab file or the **telinit** command. To reboot, use **reboot** or **shutdown -r**. To halt the system, use **halt** or **shutdown -h**. To enter single-user mode on a running system, type **shutdown now** and press **Return** when prompted to do so. To return to multiuser mode, type **exit**.

Whereas /etc/inittab sets the default runlevel on a Linux system, a BSD system uses /etc/ttys to determine whether the system will boot into multiuser command line or multiuser GUI. (Use the boot menu to select single-user mode at boot-up.) Like /etc/inittab, this file configures how many virtual terminals — those that accept keyboard input — to make available. The default configuration allows nine virtual terminals with the GUI residing on ttyv8 (accessible with **Alt-F9**). By default, the system boots into command-line mode and the user must type **startx** to start the GUI. However, if you miss having the system boot directly into a GUI login, edit /etc/ttys as the superuser and change the word off to on in the ttyv8 line.

Startup Scripts

On a Linux system, each runlevel has an associated subdirectory: rc0.d for runlevel 0, rc1.d for runlevel 1, and so on. Depending on the distribution, these subdirectories fall under either /etc or /etc/rc.d. Each subdirectory contains symlinks to startup scripts residing in /etc/init.d. The symlink names begin with either *S* (for start) or *K* (for kill) and tell **init** to act accordingly whenever the system enters that runlevel. After the letter comes a number that represents the order in which to run the scripts.

You won't find init.d or any of the runlevel subdirectories on a FreeBSD system. Instead, the system startup scripts live in /etc/rc.d, and the startup scripts for third-party applications stay in /usr/local/etc/rc.d. Instead of using symbolic links beginning with *S* or *K*, a handful of scripts in /etc whose names start with *rc* control which scripts run at startup and shutdown. **man rc** gives the names of these scripts and describes their operation. As an admin, you'll leave most of those *rc* scripts as is. To configure which services start at boot-up, instead edit the one file /etc/rc.conf.

Most of the scripts found in Linux's /etc/init.d and FreeBSD's /etc/rc.d share similar behavior. If you type only the script name, you'll receive a syntax message indicating which parameters you can send to that service. Here's an example from a FreeBSD system:

```
# /etc/rc.d/named
Usage: /etc/rc.d/named [fast|force] (start|stop|restart|rcvar|reload|status|poll)
```

You're probably unfamiliar with the **rcvar** parameter. It helps to determine the current /etc/rc.conf parameters of the service.

The Kernel

Instead of describing the design differences between a Linux and a FreeBSD kernel, I'll concentrate on the differences you'll encounter when recompiling a kernel.

To see which Linux kernel came with your distro, type **uname -r**.

In FreeBSD, the first number also refers to the major version number. As I write this, version 6.2 is the stable production release and version 5.5 is the legacy release. Both versions provide a development kernel known as CURRENT and various stable releases indicated by the second number. The FreeBSD Release Engineering webpage at http://www.freebsd.org/doc/en_US.ISO8859-1/articles/releng/ describes the release process in more detail.

The steps required to recompile a kernel also differ. Some Linux distros provide a mechanism to download Linux kernel source, or you can download it directly. After uncompressing the source, **cd** into your system's src directory and choose from one of three front ends available for modifying the Linux kernel configuration file:

- **make config** is a text-based series of many, many questions.

- **make menuconfig** provides an ncurses menu from the command line.

- **make xconfig** provides a menu from an X session.

Each front end provides an explanation for each Linux kernel configurable and allows you either to compile in that option statically or build it as a loadable module. Once you've saved your changes, use these commands to check for dependencies and to compile the kernel:[20]

```
# make dep
# make clean
# make bzImage
```

If you've chosen to create Linux modules, do these two commands next:

```
# make modules
# make modules_install
```

Finally, install the Linux kernel and update your boot loader:

```
# make install
```

---

[20]This is the process for a Linux 2.4 kernel; the 2.6 kernel is simpler.

Always double-check the changes to your boot loader configuration file; I've found that **make install** doesn't always make the modifications required to boot successfully into the new kernel.

On a FreeBSD system, use **sysinstall** to download the kernel sources. Better yet, use **csup** to keep your kernel sources up to date.

Once you have the sources, make a copy of /usr/src/sys/i386/conf/GENERIC and use your favorite editor to prepend # (the comment character) to the options you don't want to configure into your kernel. Refer to a file called NOTES in that same directory to see what each option means and to research other options you may wish to add. Once you've saved your changes, compile and install the new kernel. In this example I've saved the file as NEWFILE. The commands are:

```
# cd /usr/src
# make buildkernel KERNCONF=NEWFILE
# make installkernel KERNCONF=NEWFILE
```

By default, this compiles most kernel options as modules. If you prefer to compile everything statically, include this line in your kernel configuration file:

```
makeoptions MODULES_OVERRIDE=""
```

Installing Software

When it comes to installing software on an open source operating system, you usually have three choices available. The first is to install a precompiled binary. The advantage to this method is that it is very quick and usually painless, with the program and its dependencies recorded into a package management system. The disadvantage is that a precompiled binary may not be available for your particular operating system and architecture. If one is, keep in mind that it probably won't take advantage of your particular CPU's features and you will have no control over which features the distributor compiled into the binary. This usually isn't a big deal with desktop applications, but it can be for server applications.

Installing a precompiled binary in Linux depends upon which package management system came with your distro. Examples of popular package management system utilities are Red Hat's **rpm**, Debian's **apt-get**, and Gentoo's **emerge**. Some package management systems require you to find and download the binary and resolve dependency issues, while others fetch the binary and its dependencies for you.

Ease of use and syntax issues aside, having a package management system is always a good thing. It will maintain databases to keep track of which programs you have installed and which programs depend on which others. In theory, this should make it much easier to properly upgrade software without breaking dependencies and to monitor software for outstanding security patches. In reality, your mileage will vary with the package management system used, but it will still be much better than trying to remember what you installed and when.

FreeBSD provides a robust package management system. To install a precompiled binary in FreeBSD, use the **pkg_add** command with the remote fetch switch. For example, to install **curl**, a HTTP/FTP command-line download client, type:

```
# pkg_add -r curl
```

If there are any missing dependencies available as a precompiled binary, this command will also download and install them for you.

If you prefer to select packages from an ncurses menu, use **sysinstall** and choose Configure, then Packages.

The second method for installing software is to compile the binary yourself using your system's package management system. This will track the program itself and all of its dependencies; you also have a pretty good guarantee that the compile should succeed for your CPU and operating system type. Compiling your own binary allows you to take advantage of the program's **make** options. The assumption is that you've taken the time to research the available options for the particular application you wish to compile. The disadvantage is that it takes time to compile a binary, depending on the size of the binary and how much CPU and RAM is on the compiling system.

As an example, if your distro supports RPMs, you can download and compile a source RPM. These files end in src.rpm as opposed to something like i386.rpm. In FreeBSD, you instead use the ports collection. For example, to install Apache:

```
# cd /usr/ports/www/apache22
# make install clean
```

Of course, before issuing the **make** command, experienced admins read the Makefile in that directory to see which options to use for that compile.

The third method is to download and extract a source tarball. This method works on any Unix system but comes with a big disadvantage: the package management system in place cannot track the installed files. This means you have to remember what you installed, when you installed it, and what dependencies come with or rely on that program. It will also be very difficult to keep those programs up to date and to remember to check for security fixes on each program.

Sometimes this third method is a necessary evil. Perhaps you need to take advantage of a feature or security fix now and there currently isn't a precompiled binary or source RPM/port for that application for your operating system. Unless you really can't wait, however, you're better off waiting.

Documentation

One of the biggest improvements to open source operating systems over the past few years has been the proliferation of quality online documentation. Linux has The Linux Documentation Project. While everything here obviously comes from the Linux perspective, many of the articles concern third-party shells or software that apply well to non-Linux systems.

FreeBSD has the online FreeBSD Handbook and FreeBSD FAQ. These and other documentation resources also appear on FreeBSD systems in /usr/share/doc. The documentation describes pretty much anything you could ever want to do with a FreeBSD system.

One of the more noticeable differences between Linux distros and BSD systems is the quality of the man pages. An example that comes up in a Linux+ class is the man page for **ls**. For the exam, students need to know the **-F** switch. Here's the explanation from **man ls** on a Linux system:

```
-F, --classify
              append indicator (one of */=@|) to entries
```

Here's the explanation from a BSD system:

```
-F   Display a slash ('/') immediately after each pathname that is a
     directory, an asterisk ('*') after each that is executable, an at
     sign ('@') after each symbolic link, an equals sign ('=') after
     each socket, a percent sign ('%') after each whiteout, and a ver-
     tical bar ('|') after each that is a FIFO.
```

One of the lessons students learn is that if you don't find the information you want from a man page, see if there is a better man page! I've always had good luck with FreeBSD Hypertext Man Pages at `http://www.freebsd.org/cgi/man.cgi`.

The other man page that students find helpful is **man hier**, as it describes the file system hierarchy or directory structure layout. This is always a good command to run whenever you find yourself on an unfamiliar Unix operating system.

1.13.1 Additional Resources

Original Article:

`http://www.onlamp.com/pub/a/bsd/2004/11/11/FreeBSD_Basics.html`

2 Useful Unix Tricks

2.1 Useful Commands

FreeBSD comes with a lot of simple yet powerful commands designed to make your computing work easier. No matter how long you've used any type of Unix system, you'll still discover new shortcuts and new ways of doing things more efficiently. As my grandmother used to say, there's more than one way to skin a cat.

In this section, we'll discuss commands that help you remember who you are, where you are, how to find things, and how to start thinking like a Unix geek when it comes to accomplishing tasks.

Virtual Terminals

I love the concept of virtual terminals and usually run all eight along with an X session. At a typical moment, I'll have a PPP session running, another terminal with an email client open, a couple of terminals with different man pages open, another terminal where I'm trying out commands as *root*, another terminal where I'm trying out commands as a regular user — you get the idea. With this increased functionality comes increased confusion. I use several commands to help me navigate this mess.

If I forget which terminal I left a man page at, the PrintScrn key will scroll through all virtual terminals in increasing order. If I'm not running an X session, I can continue to rotate through terminals 1 to 8 forever. If I am running an X session, it will stop at terminal 9, the GUI.

If I enter a terminal and wish to know which one it is, I use the **tty** command:

```
% tty
/dev/ttyv4
```

Note that this is actually the fifth virtual terminal as they are numbered starting from zero (ttyv0). If I leave this terminal, **Alt-F5** will get me back there.

If I want to know who I am in this terminal, I can use **whoami**:

```
% whoami
root
```

If I want to know who is logged into any terminal, I can use **who**:

```
% who
genisis          ttyv0     Jun  3 15:45
genisis          ttyv1     Jun  3 15:46
genisis          ttyv2     Jun  3 21:09
genisis          ttyv3     Jun  3 21:10
```

```
genisis          ttyv4    Jun  3 21:27
genisis          ttyv5    Jun  4 09:40
genisis          ttyv6    Jun  4 09:43
genisis          ttyv7    Jun  4 10:46
```

Note the difference between **who** and **whoami**. On `ttyv4`, I originally logged in as *genisis*, then became superuser. The **who** command will tell you who has the login shell but does not return information on non-login shells. Also, because my X session is not a login shell, `ttyv8` does not display in this output.

If I forget where I am in the directory structure, I use **pwd** which will show my present working directory:

```
% pwd
/usr/home/genisis
```

Good rule of thumb: Never make or delete files or directories without first using **pwd** to double-check that you really are where you want to be.

Tracking Time and History

Now, if I've lost all track of time:

```
% date
Sun Jun  4 11:15:46 EDT 2000
```

or worse, can't remember what day it is:

```
% cal
      June 2000
Su Mo Tu We Th Fr Sa
             1  2  3
 4  5  6  7  8  9 10
11 12 13 14 15 16 17
18 19 20 21 22 23 24
25 26 27 28 29 30
```

or need to know what day Christmas falls on in the year 2020:

```
% cal 12 2020
    December 2020
Su Mo Tu We Th Fr Sa
       1  2  3  4  5
 6  7  8  9 10 11 12
13 14 15 16 17 18 19
20 21 22 23 24 25 26
27 28 29 30 31
```

or what day of the week the Declaration of Independence was signed:

```
% cal 07 1776
      July 1776
Su Mo Tu We Th Fr Sa
       1  2  3  4  5  6
 7  8  9 10 11 12 13
14 15 16 17 18 19 20
21 22 23 24 25 26 27
28 29 30 31
```

For two last geek trivia bits on **cal** to amaze your friends and confound your enemies, try:

```
% cal 9 1752
   September 1752
Su Mo Tu We Th Fr Sa
       1  2 14 15 16
17 18 19 20 21 22 23
24 25 26 27 28 29 30
```

The missing dates are due to the switch from the Julian to the Gregorian calendars. And:

```
% ncal -e
April 23 2000
```

will show which date Easter falls on; use **-o** if you want to know the date for Orthodox Easter.

By now, you're probably convinced that I'm a wonderful typist who has so carefully typed the calendars you are reading. Let's take a look at my history list:

```
% h
   110   date > /usr/home/genisis/cal
   111   cal > /usr/home/genisis/cal
   112   cal 12 2020 > /usr/home/genisis/cal
   113   cal 07 1776 > /usr/home/genisis/cal
   117   cal 9 1752 > /usr/home/genisis/cal
   122   ncal -e > /usr/home/genisis/cal
   134   h > /usr/home/genisis/cal
```

I hate to type, so I use the **>** (greater than) redirector a lot. This redirector is used if you want to save the results of a command to a file; the syntax is always the same:

```
% command > filename
```

I wanted you to see the output for each of the commands in the above history list, so I redirected them to a file, then pasted that file into my document. Note that I overwrote the same file seven times; this happened because I only used one **>** redirector.

Let's pretend you've posted a question to the FreeBSD questions list, and someone has asked you to supply the output of **uname -a**, **dmesg**, and `fstab`. You could use **>** to create three files and paste them into your email document. But you could also redirect all three outputs to one file by using the **>>** redirector to append instead:

```
% uname -a > /usr/home/genisis/help
% dmesg >> /usr/home/genisis/help
% cat /etc/fstab >> /usr/home/genisis/help
```

If I now enter:

```
% more /usr/home/genisis/help
```

I'll see the output of **uname -a**, **dmesg**, and my `fstab` file.

Let's look at these commands more carefully. I only used one **>** in the **uname -a** command because I was creating a new file and wasn't concerned with overwriting its contents. The command would have worked with **>>** but I saved myself a keystroke.

Because I used **>>** in the **dmesg** command, I didn't overwrite the **uname -a** portion of the file called `help`.

Note that I needed to use the **more** command with `/etc/fstab`. If I type:

```
% fstab >> /usr/home/genisis/help
fstab: Command not found:
```

will be the resultant error message. You can't redirect files; you can only redirect the output of commands. In this case, **more** is the command that read `/etc/fstab`; the result of that reading could then be redirected to `/usr/home/genisis/help`.

So you've successfully sent three commands to one file without overwriting each other's output. But why type in three sets of commands? Surely there must be a way to do this with one command. If I type:

```
% uname -a dmesg more /etc/fstab >> /usr/home/genisis/help2
usage: uname [-amnrsv]
```

will be the message I'll receive back. Take a look at that command again; it has everything you want to do, but how can you tell what is a command, what is a switch, and what is a file? If you're confused looking at your own command, imagine how your shell feels when it's trying to interpret what it is you want to do. We need some way of separating our commands; try:

```
% uname -a; dmesg; more /etc/fstab >> /usr/home/genisis/help3
```

This should yield the output of **uname -a** and **dmesg** to your terminal; if you

```
% more /usr/home/genisis/help3
```

you will only see the output of **more /etc/fstab**.

So, we're getting closer. We've separated the commands, now we want the shell to know that we want all three outputs in the file, not just the last command's output. One last try:

```
% (uname -a; dmesg; more /etc/fstab) >> /usr/home/genisis/help4
% more /usr/home/genisis/help4
```

and you should have the results you wanted to achieve. The parentheses tell your shell that you want to run the commands in the parentheses first, then redirect all of that output to your file.

Finding Stuff

FreeBSD comes with several handy utilities for finding information. Which utility you use depends on what it is you're trying to find. If you need to find an application, use **whereis**:

```
% whereis ls
ls: /bin/ls
```

If you need to find a file, use **locate**:

```
% locate fstab
/etc/fstab
```

If you find something but don't know what it is, use **whatis**:

```
% whatis ls
ls(1) - list directory contents
% whatis fstab
fstab(5) - static information about the filesystems
```

Note that **whatis** will include a manpage section number in parentheses. If you want additional information on the above, you can type:

```
% man 1 ls
% man 5 fstab
```

But what if you need to find a specific piece of text? You'll need to use the **grep** utility, which has a very simple syntax:

```
% grep whatyou'relookingfor filename
```

Let's suppose I can't remember if the bpf device is enabled or disabled in the default FreeBSD kernel configuration file. I could open up this file and start reading it, but it's quicker to ask:

```
% grep bpf /usr/src/sys/i386/conf/GENERIC
# The 'bpf' pseudo-device enables the Berkeley Packet Filter.
pseudo-device    bpf              #Berkeley packet filter
```

If I couldn't remember how far into this file the bpf option was, I could add the **-n** switch to **grep** which will list the line numbers of the entries:

```
% grep -n bpf /usr/src/sys/i386/conf/GENERIC
212:# The 'bpf' pseudo-device enables the Berkeley Packet Filter.
214:pseudo-device      bpf              #Berkeley packet filter
```

Of course, I can redirect this output to a file to email to the person who asked me in the first place:

```
% grep -n bpf /usr/src/sys/i386/conf/GENERIC \
      > /usr/home/genisis/reply
```

As another example, if you want the CPU information for your computer, you could run **dmesg**, turn on your scroll lock button, page up, and look for the line that describes your CPU. Or you could:

```
% dmesg | grep CPU
CPU: AMD-K6tm w/ multimedia extensions
     (199.96-MHz 586-class CPU)
```

to quickly receive the same information. Note, if you try the command this way:

```
% grep CPU dmesg
grep: dmesg: No such file or directory
```

will be the error message. **dmesg** is a command and you can only **grep** files. However, you can pipe the output of a command to **grep** so it can find a certain piece of text.

To summarize: when you use **grep**, ask yourself if what you're looking for will be found in a file or if it is the result of a command. If it's in a file, use:

```
% grep text filename
```

If it's the result of a command, use:

```
% command | grep text
```

Additional Resources

Original Article:

```
http://www.onlamp.com/pub/a/bsd/2000/08/09/FreeBSD_Basics.html
```

Introduction to Unix:

```
http://8help.osu.edu/wks/unix_course/intro-1.html
```

2.2 Finding Things in Unix

One of the most useful utilities to be found on any Unix system is the **find** command. This section will work you through the syntax of this command and provide you with some practical examples of its usage.

Table 2.1: Common find Primaries

-name	must be quoted when using wildcards
-type	e.g. **f**=file **d**=directory **l**=link
-user	name or UID
-group	name or GID
-perm	specify permissions
-size	rounded up to next 512 byte block or use *c* to specify bytes
-atime	last time file was read
-ctime	last time file's owner or permissions were changed
-mtime	last time file was modified
-newer	find files newer than given file
-delete	remove files found
-ls	gives same output as **ls -dgils**
-print	displays results of **find** command
-exec *command* {} \;	to execute a command; note the required syntax
-ok	use instead of exec to be prompted before command is executed
-depth	starts at lowest level in directory tree rather than root of given directory
-prune	used when you want to exclude certain subdirectories

Basic find Syntax

The command itself has a very simple syntax:

```
% find where_to_search expressions
```

The expressions are the part that can look confusing the first few times you use **find**. They are also the part that can vary from Unix system to Unix system, so you may want to take a quick peek at **find**'s manpage if you find yourself on a new system. The most common expressions that you can use on your FreeBSD system are listed in Table 2.1.

I'll be giving examples that show how to use and combine these expressions. Before doing that, what can **find** be used for? If you use the **whatis** command to see what it does, the answer may surprise you:

```
% whatis find
find(1) - walk a file hierarchy
```

In a nutshell, **find** is meant to recursively search directories to find any files that meet your specified expressions. This may not seem like such a big deal, but there aren't that many Unix utilities that can walk through a directory and all of its subdirectories. This ability proves quite useful, as not only can you find files, but you can do something with them as you find them.

Let's start with some simple examples and then work our way towards some more seemingly-complicated expressions. The simplest find you can do is to simply type this:

```
% find . -print
```

Since the dot represents your current directory, this **find** command will find all of the files in your current directory and all of its subdirectories, and then print the results to your screen.

On your FreeBSD system, **-print** is assumed if you forget to type it, so this command will also give the same result:

```
% find .
```

However, it's a good idea to get in the habit of using **-print**, in case you ever need to use **find** on a system that does not assume this action.

To find all of the files in your home directory, you should first make sure you are in your home directory, then repeat that **find** command, like so:

```
% cd
% find . -print
```

The **cd** command will always take you to your home directory. Since the **find** command can be used to do powerful things, it is always a good idea to first **cd** to the directory structure in which you wish to work. For the rest of this section, I will assume that you are in your home directory, so you won't inadvertently affect any files on your FreeBSD system that don't reside in your home directory.

Simple Expressions

The above examples demonstrated how easy it is to use **find**, but usually you are looking for something specific when you invoke the **find** command. This is where the other expressions come into play. Let's try to find a file with a specific name:

```
% touch file1
% find . -name file1 -print
./file1
```

Let's pick apart what I just did for a moment. I created an empty file named file1 using the **touch** command. I then told **find** to search my current directory (".") for a file named (**-name**) file1 and to print the results of the search to my screen. Also, I can tell that I only have one file named file1 in my home directory and all of its subdirectories, as only one result was displayed.

Often, when you need to use the **find** command, you are looking for more than one file. For example, you may want to find all of the files with a certain extension. I tend to download a lot of *.pdf* files and don't always remember to keep them in the same place. Occasionally, I like to collect them and put them in a directory I've created named pdfs. When this urge strikes, I can use the following **find** command to search my home directory and its subdirectories for all *.pdf* files:

```
% find . -name "*.pdf" -print
./pdfs/50130201a.pdf
./pdfs/50130201b.pdf
./pdfs/50130201c.pdf
./pdfs/IWARLab.pdf
./pdfs/DoS_trends.pdf
./pdfs/Firewall-Guide.pdf
./2000_ports.pdf
```

It looks like I've been pretty good lately, as I only have one *.pdf* file that is not in my pdfs directory. You'll note that in order to get this **find** command to work, I had to quote the "*" wildcard by typing *.pdf instead of just *.pdf. There are two other ways to quote, so the following two commands will yield the same results:

```
% find . -name \*.pdf -print
% find . -name '*.pdf' -print
```

More Complex Expressions

Let's add to that original command and see how the output changes. What if I was only interested in seeing which *.pdf* files were not in the pdfs directory? Let's repeat that **find** command, but pipe the results to **grep** so only that one file will be displayed:

```
% find .  -name "*.pdf" -print | grep -v "^\./pdfs/"
./2000_ports.pdf
```

Well, that command worked, but that syntax looks pretty scary; we better pick it apart. Whenever you use **grep -v**, you are creating a reverse filter, meaning that you want it to show the opposite of what follows. In my case, I'm not interested in the files that reside in the ./pdfs/ directory; I want to find the files that aren't, so I used the reverse filter. You'll note that I also quoted the whole expression. I also added a bit extra, that ^\ stuff. The ^ tells **grep** to only search the very beginning of a line for my expression. The \ is an extra quote so that **grep** does not interpret the dot as a special character. The whole thing put together told **grep** to just show me the files that don't live in the ./pdfs/ directory, so I received the desired output.

Brave enough to try something even more useful but complicated-looking? Let's get **find** to not only find this file, but move it to the correct directory using the following one-liner command:

```
% find .  -name "*.pdf" -print | grep -v "^\./pdfs/" | \
    xargs -J X mv X ./pdfs/
```

To see if it worked, let's repeat the original **find** command:

```
% find . -name "*.pdf" -print
./pdfs/50130201a.pdf
./pdfs/50130201b.pdf
./pdfs/50130201c.pdf
./pdfs/IWARLab.pdf
./pdfs/DoS_trends.pdf
./pdfs/Firewall-Guide.pdf
./pdfs/2000_ports.pdf
```

So it worked. Let's see why. Once **grep** finished filtering the **find** output, we piped that result to the **xargs** command to finish the job for us. The **-J** switch tells **xargs** to define a string to be replaced with arguments for the utility called by **xargs**. For example, before I ran the **find** command, I had no idea how many files needed to be moved. There may have been one, or there may have been several. I needed to let **xargs** know that regardless of how many files were found, I want them all moved and I want them all moved to the pdfs directory. That bit of magic was helped by the **-J** switch. To get the **-J** switch to work properly, I also defined a character (*X*) and put that character on either side of the **mv** command.

Searching by Time or Size

Remember that Unix filenames don't necessarily have extensions, so you may want to search for a more complicated pattern. Let's say I want to find any files that have bsd somewhere in their name. I would do this command:

```
% find . -name "*bsd*" -print
./.kde/share/icons/favicons/www.freebsd.org.png
./.kde/share/icons/favicons/www.freebsddiary.org.png
./.kde/share/wallpapers/bsdbg1280x1024.jpg
./mnwclient-1.11/contrib/freebsd
```

We can also find a file by more than just its name. For example, to find all the files that you have not read in more than (+) 30 days:

```
% find . -atime +30 -print
```

To see files you haven't modified, use **-mtime** instead, and to see files you haven't changed the owner or permissions of, use **-ctime**. The number after the + indicates how many days or 24-hour periods. To see which files were modified today, try:

```
% find . -mtime -1 -print
```

This will show what files were modified during the last 24 hours. Note that this time you should use the -, as you want to find the files from less than one day ago.

The other switch that deals with time is the **-newer** switch. The three time switches all use 24-hour periods. If you would like to be a bit more granular in your time than that, the **-newer** switch will compare a file's access, modification, and change times to within a minute. (The amin, cmin, and mmin switches can also be used to search by minute.) For example, to see if any of your dot files were changed since you last changed your .cshrc file, you could execute this command:

```
% find . -type f -name ".*" -newer .cshrc -print
```

You'll note that I've included some other new switches in this command. I specified a *type* of **f** for files, as I don't want to see any directories, just files. I told the **-name** switch that I was interested in seeing files that start with a dot. Finally, I used the **-newer** switch to indicate that I was interested in the files that were modified since I last modified my .cshrc file.

Since I've started to combine switches that indicate which files I'm interested in finding, I should mention that all switches are logically *anded* unless you use the **-o** or logical *or*. Since the switches are logically anded, I really told the **find** utility that I was only interested in files that were of a certain type *and* had a certain name *and* were newer than my .cshrc file.

Let's look at an example that shows the difference between a logical *and* and a logical *or*. If I wanted to see all of the files in my home directory that had not been accessed in the last seven days and are larger than 10 Mb, I would use this command:

```
% find . -atime +7 -size +20480 -print
```

However, if I wanted to see any files that either had not been accessed in the last seven days or that were over 10 MB in size, I would use this command instead:

```
% find . -atime +7 -o -size +20480 -print
```

You'll note that I had to do some math to come up with the number to give to the **-size** expression, since **-size** is looking for the number of 512-byte blocks. However, I could have used the **expr** command to do the math for me, like so:

```
% find .   -atime +7 -o -size +`expr 10 \* 1024 \* 2` -print
```

Note that in this example, everything between the backquotes (the ` on the far left of your keyboard) is what will do the required math. We still need the + in front of the first back quote, as we want to see files greater than 10 MB. You could also test what the results of the math will be by adding the **echo** command to the beginning of the command:

```
% echo find . -atime +7 -o -size +`expr 10 \* 1024 \* 2` -print
find . -atime +7 -size +20480 -print
```

Note: It is a good idea to **echo** complex commands first, to ensure that the stuff you've quoted will do what you expect before asking the **find** command to execute it.

Notice that I used the ` or backquote (the key on the far left of your PC keyboard). In Unix, whenever you want the output of one command passed to another command, put the command that will give the output between backquotes; this is known as command substitution. By putting the math that I wanted calculated between backquotes, the resulting calculation was passed to the **-size** switch and used by the **find** command.

The last thing I want you to notice is that I also had to quote the two asterisks (*) in the command using the backslash (\) character. When calculating math, * represents multiply; however, to the shell it represents a wildcard. By placing a \ before the *, the shell won't interpret it as a wildcard, so **expr** receives the * and will know that I want it to perform a multiplication.

Executing Commands

Next, let's say I have a large directory structure and I wish to search for a certain pattern and remove all of the files that match this pattern. There are several ways to do this with the find command, so let's compare some of these methods.

In my home directory, I have a directory called tmp that contains a subdirectory named tst. This tst directory has a lot of files and subdirectories, and some of these files end with a .old extension. Let's start by seeing just how many files live in my tst directory:

```
% cd /tmp/tst
% find . -print | wc -l
  269
```

Notice that when the **find** command ran, it printed each file found on a separate line. I could then pipe that result to the **wc** (word count) command using the switch that counted the lines (**-l**). This told me that I have 269 files (including directories, since to Unix, directories are really files) in my `tst` directory.

Let's see how many of these files have a *.old* extension:

```
% find . -name "*.old" -print | wc -l
  67
```

Now, how can I go about removing these `*.old` files? One way is to use the **-exec** switch and have it call the **rm** command like so:

```
% find . -name "*.old" -exec rm {} \;
```

Once that is finished, I can repeat this command to see if there are any remaining `*.old` files:

```
% find . -name "*.old" -print | wc -l
0
```

This command works, but it may not always be the best way to remove a large number of files. Whenever you use the **-exec** switch, a separate process is created for every file that **find** finds. This may not be an issue if you are only finding a small amount of files on your home computer. It may be an issue if you are finding hundreds or thousands of files on a production system. Regardless, this method does consume more resources and is slower than other methods.

Let's look at a second way to delete these files, this time using **xargs**:

```
% find . -name "*.old" -print | xargs rm
```

You'll note that I didn't have to include the \; string at the end of this command, as that string is used to terminate commands that are passed to **-exec**. By using **xargs** in this command, I will still remove all of the files that end in `.old`, but instead of creating a separate process for each file that is found, only one process is started through **xargs**. As **find** finds each file, it creates a list with each file on its own line. This list is passed to **xargs**, which takes all of the lines of the file and places them onto one line with a space to separate each file; it then passes this argument list of files to the **rm** command.

There is actually a third way to remove these files, using the **-delete** switch with **find**:

```
% find . -name "*.old" -delete
```

This command has the easiest syntax to use and is actually the most efficient way of removing files. The **-delete** switch doesn't even need to open a separate process: all of the files are removed by the **find** process. Also, this command should always work, whereas the **xargs** command may fail if **find** finds more files than can be passed to a command as an argument list. If you are searching a deep directory structure or have very long filenames, you may reach this limit. If you are curious as to the actual limit, there is a **sysctl** value that has been set for you:

```
% sysctl -a | grep kern.argmax
kern.argmax: 262144
```

The 262144 represents the maximum number of bytes (or characters) in an argument list.

Before moving on to some other switches, I should mention that you may want to verify which files **find** will find before removing them. In my examples, I was just removing old files in one of my test directories. If you are concerned that **find** may find some files you don't want deleted, run your command like this first:

```
% find . -name "*.old" -print
```

This will give you a list of all the matching files. If the list looks good, use the **-delete** switch to remove the files as in the example mentioned above.

Or, you can do the above in just one **find** command by using **-ok** like so:

```
% find . -name "*.old" -ok rm {} \;
```

The **-ok** will prompt for verification before executing the command that follows it. You'll note that I do have to use the **rm** command; I can't use the **-delete** switch. And, as with using **-exec**, I have to use the { } \; syntax in order for **-ok** to work.

Additional Switches

Let's take a look at some more switches. The **-ls** switch will give the inode number, number of blocks, permissions, number of hard links, owner, group, size in bytes, last modification time, and name for each file that is found. For example, the following command will show me the first ten directories in my home directory; you'll note that I specified that I only wanted to see directories by using the **-type d** switch.

```
% cd
% find . -type d -ls | head
976142    8 drwxr-xr-x  39 genisis  wheel 4096 Mar  3 17:52 .
1413099   2 drwxr-xr-x   2 genisis  wheel  512 Mar  3 13:38 ./pdfs
373539    2 drwxr-xr-x   2 genisis  wheel  512 Feb  6 12:38 ./tst
1087249   2 drwxr-xr-x   2 genisis  wheel  512 Oct  4 07:29 ./perlscripts
650764    2 drwx------   2 genisis  wheel  512 Mar  3 17:52 ./mail
706616    2 drwx------   4 genisis  wheel  512 Sep 22 14:29 ./.kde
706635    2 drwx------  11 genisis  wheel  512 Nov  7 12:36 ./.kde/share
706682    2 drwx------   3 genisis  wheel  512 Mar  2 18:36 ./.kde/share/fonts
```

Let's get a little fancier with the **-ls** switch. Earlier in the section, we piped some output to **wc -l** to see how many files contained a certain expression. Let's be a bit more particular and see how many subdirectories are in my home directory:

```
% find . -type d -print | wc -l
    256
```

71

Actually, there are only 255 subdirectories, as one of them is my current directory. Now, let's get a better idea of how this directory structure is laid out using this command:

```
% find . -type d -ls | awk '{print $4 - 2, $NF}' | \
    sort -rn | head
37 .
26 ./.kde/share/apps/kio_http/cache
18 ./.kde/share/apps
15 ./.gimp-1.2
9 ./tmp/tst
9 ./.kde/share
8 ./tmp/tst/h
8 ./tmp/tst/g
8 ./tmp/tst/f
8 ./tmp/tst/e
```

Wow, that's pretty cool. It looks like there are 37 subdirectories in my home directory, 26 subdirectories in the `.kde/share/apps/kio_http/cache` subdirectory, etc. Now, let's see how this **find** command worked. I started by using the **-ls** switch, which gave a fair bit of information regarding each directory as it was found. This information was piped to the **awk** utility, which is used to extract the data from certain fields. You'll note that in the original **-ls** output, the results were in certain fields: inode number, number of blocks, permissions, number of links, etc. I told **awk** to take the information from column 4 (which contains the number of links and is $4 to **awk**) and subtract 2 from that value (as I'm not interested in the directories . or ..). I also wanted to know the name of each directory; since this was the very last column, I used $NF to represent that field. By placing these instructions within the curly braces { }, I told **awk** to do this to every file that it received from the **find** command. I then piped the results from **awk** to the **sort** command; by using **-rn**, I told **sort** to sort the numerical output from largest to smallest so I could see which directories had the most subdirectories. I didn't want to bore you with all the output, so I also piped the final results to the **head** command so it would only display the first ten.

Another **find** switch is the **-perm** switch. An example is to search for any files that have their permissions set to 777, that is, set to read, write, and execute for everyone. This can be easily done with this command:

```
% find . -perm 777 -print
```

The above command searches for files with the exact permissions of 777. If you are concerned with only a certain bit, rather than all the permission bits, you can do something like this:

```
% find . -perm -4000 -print
```

This example will only yield files that have the SUID bit set. Another handy **find** command is this one:

```
% find . -perm -0002 -print
```

It will find all files that are writable by others. Note that you can use -0002, -002, -02, or -2 and receive the same result as leading 0s are assumed.

The last two switches I want to cover are useful when backing up or replicating directory structures. Let's start with **-depth**. Let's say I want to back up my entire home directory to a mounted directory named /backup. I can do this:

```
% find . -depth -print | cpio -dump /backup
```

This command may also work without the **-depth** switch, but not always. By default, **find** lists the files it finds by starting at the point mentioned in the **find** command, in my case . or my home directory. That is, it lists first the directory, and then the contents of that directory. If it encounters a directory that has read-only permissions, **find** will still provide a list of the contents of that directory to the **cpio** command, but **cpio** won't have permission to replicate the files in that subdirectory. It is interesting to note that **cpio** will still be able to create the directory, but as it does, it will set the permissions to read only, so it won't be able to create any files below that directory.

However, if you remember to use **-depth**, **find** will instead start its search at the lowest level, meaning it will list the contents of directories before it lists the directories themselves. This means that the files will already have been replicated by **cpio** before it sets the read-only permissions on the parent directory.

What if I don't want to replicate my entire home directory, just portions of it? This is where the **-prune** switch comes into play. Let's say I want to back up everything in my home directory except my tmp directory. I could do this:

```
% find . -type d -name tmp -prune -o -print | \
    cpio -dump /backup
```

You'll note that the syntax seems a little bit backwards. I used the **-name** switch to find any directories (**-type d**) named tmp and pass that list to **-prune**. I then used the logical or (**-o**) so that everything else will be printed and piped to **cpio**.

(The **cpio** utility is also covered in section 6.4.)

I hope the examples provided have helped you to become more comfortable with the **find** command and its syntax.

Additional Resources

Original Articles:

```
http://www.onlamp.com/pub/a/bsd/2002/02/21/FreeBSD_Basics.html
```

```
http://www.onlamp.com/pub/a/bsd/2002/03/14/FreeBSD_Basics.html
```

2.3 Read The Friendly Manpage! – A Tutorial

There are few things more frustrating to the FreeBSD novice than to be told to RTFM (Read The Friendly Manual), especially since the *F* does not always represent the word *Friendly*. Everyone quickly learns that they should always RTFM, but there are very few resources available to tell a novice how to find the information they need in the manual. Unless you've managed to befriend a very patient Unix guru, the fine art of manpage reading is learned through painful trial and error.

Introducing man

Most of the files that came with your FreeBSD system have explanations of their usage in the manual, which has been divided into sections to help categorize the different types of files. The **man** utility is used to format and display the section pertaining to the file in question. To find out what sections are available, type:

```
% whatis intro
intro(1)      - introduction to general commands (tools and utilities)
intro(2)      - introduction to system calls and error numbers
intro(3)      - introduction to the C libraries
intro(4)      - introduction to devices and device drivers
intro(5)      - introduction to file formats
intro(6)      - introduction to games
intro(7)      - miscellaneous information pages
intro(8)      - introduction to system maintenance and operation commands
intro(9)      - introduction to system kernel interfaces
```

Here you can see that the manual has been divided into 9 sections or categories. For example, section (1) deals with commands used by users, whereas section (8) deals with the commands or daemons used by your FreeBSD system. If you wish to read a bit more detail on the sections, type:

```
% man 1 intro
% man 2 intro
```

and so on for a quick explanation of what types of information are contained in each section of the manual.

Knowing the different sections of the manual is important, as some files have information in more than one section of the manual. Unfortunately, if you just type:

```
% man name_of_file
```

you will only be taken to the first section that exists for that file; if that file has entries in more than one section of the manual, they will not be displayed unless you specify the section for the **man** utility, like this:

```
% man number name_of_file
```

As an example, try these two commands. As each manpage opens, type "q" to quit and watch whether you receive your prompt back or a new manpage section:

```
% man passwd
% man -a passwd
```

The first command will open section 1 of the manual, describing how to use the **passwd** command to change your password.

The second command starts with section 1 of the manual, then goes to section 1 of the OpenSSL passwd command, and then goes to section 5 of the manual which describes the layout of the passwd database.

Try this:

```
% man who
WHO(1)   FreeBSD General Commands Manual   WHO(1)
% man utmp
UTMP(5)  FreeBSD File Formats Manual       UTMP(5)
% man init
INIT(8)  FreeBSD System Manager's Manual INIT(8)
```

Here we did not specify which section to open for the above three files, but the **man** utility automatically displayed the first section dealing with each file. It would appear that the first section dealing with utmp is section 5; to prove this to yourself, try:

```
% man 1 utmp
No entry for utmp in section 1 of the manual
% man 2 utmp
No entry for utmp in section 2 of the manual
% man 3 utmp
No entry for utmp in section 3 of the manual
% man 4 utmp
No entry for utmp in section 4 of the manual
% man 5 utmp
UTMP(5)   FreeBSD File Formats Manual   UTMP(5)
```

If you're really bored, you can try the same exercise with the **init** file and repeat from section 1 to section 9.

Headings

When the **man** utility displays a section of the manual for a specified file, it uses distinct headings that are formatted in boldface print. Let's open up a manpage and examine these headings in more detail:

```
% man who
WHO(1)   FreeBSD General Commands Manual   WHO(1)
```

Again, notice that the very first line in every manpage indicates which section of the manual you are reading.

NAME
```
     who -- display who is on the system
```

The first heading of every manpage is **NAME**. Whenever you use the **whatis** command, every **NAME** heading in the manual is scanned and those files whose **NAME** matches your query are displayed on your terminal like this:

```
% whatis who
biff(1)      - be notified if mail arrives and who it is from
from(1)      - print names of those who have sent mail
rusers(1)    - who is logged in to machines on local network
rwho(1)     - who is logged in on local machines
w(1)         - display who is logged in and what they are doing
who(1)       - display who is logged in
```

Note that our query for **who** matched both the name and description of every manpage containing the word who in the **NAME** heading.

The next heading in every manpage is **SYNOPSIS**:

```
SYNOPSIS
     who [-HmqsTu] [am I] [file]
```

Since we are in section 1 of the manpages, this is a very useful heading as it contains the syntax and switches used by the command. Here, the **who** command has two possible syntaxes which yield different results:

```
% who am i
genisis    ttyp0    Sep 24 10:52
% who
genisis    ttyv0    Sep 24 08:41
genisis    ttyv1    Sep 24 08:42
genisis    ttyv2    Sep 24 08:42
genisis    ttyv3    Sep 24 09:06
genisis    ttyv4    Sep 24 09:14
```

To understand the meaning of all the syntax options, scan the **DESCRIPTION** heading which immediately follows the **SYNOPSIS**.

```
DESCRIPTION
     The who utility displays information about currently logged on users.
     By default, this includes the login name, tty name, date and time of
     login, and remote hostname if not local.

The options are as follows:

  -H   Write column headings above the output.

  -m   Show information about the terminal attached to standard input only.

  -q   "Quick mode":  List the names and number of logged in users in columns.  All
other command line options are ignored.

  -s   Show the name, line and time fields only.  This is the default.

  -T   Indicate whether each user is accepting messages.  One of the following
characters is written:
       +  User is accepting messages.
       -  User is not accepting messages.
       ?  An error occurred.

  -u   Show idle time for each user in hours and minutes as hh:mm, '.'  if the user has
been idle less that a minute, and "old" if the user has been idle more than 24 hours.

  am I   Equivalent to -m.
```

The **DESCRIPTION** heading for who is fairly short and intuitive once you've tried running the command both ways. Let's look at a manpage with a longer **DESCRIPTION**:

```
% man ls
```

```
LS(1)    FreeBSD General Commands Manual    LS(1)
```

NAME
    ls - list directory contents

SYNOPSIS
    ls [**-ABCFGHILPRSTUWZabcdfghiklmnopqrstuwx1**] [file ...]

Unlike the **who** command, which has few switches, the **SYNOPSIS** for the **ls** command looks like the ingredients in alphabet soup. Note that the only part of the synopsis that is not enclosed by [] is **ls** itself; this means that all switches and files are optional. If you just type:

```
% ls
```

you will still get a listing of your current directory.

Remember that to Unix, everything is a file, including directories. So:

```
% ls /etc
```

will list the directory contents of /etc.

```
% ls /etc/rc.conf
/etc/rc.conf
```

won't yield much, but

```
% ls -l /etc/rc.conf
-rw-r--r-- 1 root wheel 187  Apr 3 09:11 /etc/rc.conf
```

will yield information on the rc.conf file.

The **SYNOPSIS** shows all legal switches, but the **DESCRIPTION** heading explains the usage of each switch, in the order they were listed in the **SYNOPSIS**. If I wish more information on what **-l** does, I can either use my page down key to look for it, or type slash and the text to search for:

```
/-l
```

to invoke the search function and receive the following explanation:

```
-1   (The lowercase letter ''ell.'')  List files in the long format,
     as described in The Long Format subsection below.
```

One can then page down and look for that subsection or keep pressing the **n** key (for next search match) until one finds it:

The Long Format
```
If the -l option is given, the following information is displayed
for each file:  file mode, number of links, owner name, group name, MAC
label, number of bytes in the file, abbreviated month, day-of-month file
was last modified, and the pathname.
```

The headings that follow the **DESCRIPTION** will vary depending on the manpage you are using. If the manpage you are reading has a **FILES** heading, it will list the full pathnames to the files (usually configuration files) associated with that command. For example, if we continue by typing **man who**, we'll see that it uses the following files:

FILES
```
/var/run/utmp
/var/log/wtmp
/var/log/wtmp.[0-6]
```

Each file listed will probably have an associated man page in section 5, since this is the section that deals with file formats. In this case, **man 5 utmp**, will yield useful information on the formats of these files.

Section 5 of the manpages is useful whenever you need more information on what a particular configuration file does and what type of information should be put into it. For example:

```
% man 5 resolv.conf
```

will bring you to section 5 of the manpage for resolver, so not only will you learn the syntax for the configuration file, you also learn what command reads this file.

Which brings us to the last heading seen in all manpages, the **SEE ALSO** heading. Here is the section for **man who**:

SEE ALSO
```
last(1),  users(1),  w(1),  utmp(5)
```

This heading is indispensable when you are learning a new command as it shows manpages that may shed additional light on the subject at hand.

In this example, **last, users,** and **w** are commands related to the **who** command and utmp is the configuration file read by the **who** command. We know all this thanks to the number placed in () next to each of these names.

If I was researching this topic further, I would try:

```
% man 5 utmp
```

and scan its **SEE ALSO** section. This would tell me that this file is also read by the user commands **last, w,** and **who,** and by the system commands **ac, init** and **pam_lastlog**. At that point I could do a **whatis** on any file that sounded intriguing, like this:

```
% whatis ac
ac(8) - connect time accounting
```

and if that description piqued my curiosity, I could learn more about this system command by doing this:

```
% man 8 ac
```

You'll find that once you know what to look for in a manpage, there isn't any shortage of useful information. If anything, you may find yourself being side-tracked as you navigate from one interesting manpage to another. I'm constantly amazed at how much other stuff I learn when I thought I was going to research something else.

Navigation

A couple of notes on navigation within manpages: Besides the handy / search key, you can also use **b** to go back one page, and once you've found what you are looking for, you can use **q** to quit. To find other navigation tricks, type **h** while in a manpage to receive the help screen on the summary of commands.

Where are the manpages for the built-in utilities and configuration files actually located on your FreeBSD system? To find out, try:

```
% whereis -m man
man:   /usr/share/man/man1/man.1
% ls -aF /usr/share/man
./            cat4/         en.ISO8859-1/      man3/         man9/
../           cat5/         en.ISO8859-15@     man4/         whatis
cat1/         cat6/         ja/                man5/
cat1aout/     cat7/         man1/              man6/
cat2/         cat8/         man1aout/          man7/
cat3/         cat9/         man2/              man8/
```

I used the **-a** and **-F** switches with the **ls** command to show all entries in /usr/share/man, and to include the / symbol after directory entries.

Note that the manpages themselves are stored in /usr/share/man. This directory contains subdirectories for all of the commands in each section of the manpages.

Many new FreeBSD users despair that they don't know what manpage to read because they don't know which command they need to accomplish a task. Next time you're bored and want to learn more about your FreeBSD system, try:

```
% ls /usr/share/man/man1
```

to receive a listing of the available manpages for the built-in utilities that came with your FreeBSD system. If you're half as curious as I am, you'll have several hours of interesting manpage reading ahead of you.

If you want to learn more about the built-in configuration files, try:

```
% ls /usr/share/man/man5
```

And to find out more about the system utilities that came with your FreeBSD system:

```
% ls /usr/share/man/man8
```

And my favorite time-killer:

```
% ls /usr/share/man/man6
```

You're probably better off not trying that last command at work; save it for a lazy Sunday afternoon.

And what about the cat subdirectories? The subdirectories that begin with man contain unformatted data; the subdirectories that begin with cat contain pre-formatted data. In just a moment, we'll do an exercise that will show the difference between formatted and unformatted data.

Compression and Formatting

But first, do an **ls** of the man1 and cat1 directories; here I've used **head** to just display the first ten lines for each.

```
% ls -C man1 | head
CC.1.gz            grep.1.gz          quota.1.gz
Mail.1.gz          grn.1.gz           ranlib.1.gz
[.1.gz             grodvi.1.gz        rcp.1.gz
addftinfo.1.gz     groff.1.gz         rcs.1.gz
addr2line.1.gz     grog.1.gz          rcsclean.1.gz
afmtodit.1.gz      grolbp.1.gz        rcsdiff.1.gz
alias.1.gz         grolj4.1.gz        rcsfreeze.1.gz
alloc.1.gz         grops.1.gz         rcsintro.1.gz
apply.1.gz         grotty.1.gz        rcsmerge.1.gz
apropos.1.gz       groups.1.gz        read.1.gz
% ls -C cat1 | head
CC.1.gz            grn.1.gz           rcp.1.gz
Mail.1.gz          grodvi.1.gz        rcs.1.gz
[.1.gz             groff.1.gz         rcsclean.1.gz
addftinfo.1.gz     grog.1.gz          rcsdiff.1.gz
addr2line.1.gz     grolbp.1.gz        rcsfreeze.1.gz
afmtodit.1.gz      grolj4.1.gz        rcsintro.1.gz
alias.1.gz         grops.1.gz         rcsmerge.1.gz
alloc.1.gz         grotty.1.gz        read.1.gz
apply.1.gz         groups.1.gz        readelf.1.gz
apropos.1.gz       gunzip.1.gz        readlink.1.gz
```

Notice that every file has a *.gz* extension. This means that all of the manpages have been compressed to conserve disk space. This is a good thing, as the online manual is huge. The utility used to compress the files is called **gzip**.

When I first discovered **gzip**, I thought, "What a great way to conserve disk space"; at the time I had a 602 MB drive and disk space was an issue. I merrily became the superuser (mistake number one), went to the root directory (mistake number two), and told **gzip** to compress every file on my FreeBSD system while giving me stats on how much space I had saved by issuing the command **gzip -rv** (trust me, you don't want to try that one). After I had finished rendering that installation of FreeBSD useless, I learned a valuable lesson: Keep the files that came compressed with FreeBSD compressed, and keep the files that came uncompressed with FreeBSD uncompressed.

However, feel free to compress any files you have created in your home directory; compression can also be very useful when you want to email a file to someone. Let's say I want to email a friend a PDF file; PDF files are notoriously large, and my poor friend is still using his old 14.4 kbps modem. I can save him some time downloading that email attachment if I do this first:

```
% ls -l ~/pdf_files/framerel.pdf
-rwxr-xr-x 1 genisis  wheel 31840 Sep 26 16:01 framerel.pdf
% gzip -v framerel.pdf
framerel.pdf:  32.9% -- replaced with framerel.pdf.gz
% ls -l framerel*
-rwxr-xr-x 1 genisis wheel 21392 Sep 26 16:01 framerel.pdf.gz
```

Notice that the **gzip** utility was able to compress this file by about a third of its original size; it also replaced the original file with its compressed counterpart and added a *.gz* extension to the original name.

When my friend receives this file, he won't be able to do anything with it until he uncompresses it like so:

```
% gunzip framerel.pdf
```

Note that my friend didn't have to specify the *.gz* extension as **gunzip** assumes the file it is unzipping will have a *.gz* extension and will complain if it doesn't.

This is also a good time to introduce the **file** utility; if anyone emails you an attachment or you happen to find a file on your FreeBSD system and don't know what type of data it contains, don't just send it to your screen using the **cat** or **more** commands. If it is not a text file, it may do nasty things to your screen. The **file** command will tell you what type of data is contained within the file like so:

```
% file framerel.pdf.gz
framerel.pdf.gz:  gzip compressed data, deflated, original filename, last modified:
Tue Sep 26 16:01:34 2000, os:  Unix
% gunzip frame*
% file framerel.pdf
framerel.pdf: PDF document, version 1.2
```

This is very useful information as I now know that the contents of this file will appear as random garbage characters unless I use a reader specifically designed to read pdf files. I was nice when I named this file with a pdf extension; I could have just as easily named it something less descriptive like open_me.

Let's compare these outputs to an executable file, say the **ls** command:

```
% whereis -b ls
ls: /bin/ls
% file /bin/ls
/bin/ls:  ELF 32-bit LSB executable, Intel 80386, version 1 (FreeBSD), statically
linked, stripped
```

And finally, let's compare it to a file I created using an editor and saved as myfile:

% **file myfile**
myfile: ASCII text

Out of the four file commands, the last command was the only one that revealed ASCII text; therefore, myfile is the only file that is safe to send to the **more** or **cat** commands or to a text editor.

Now, let's go back to the /usr/share/man directory to look at the difference between the unformatted man-pages contained in the man subdirectories and the formatted manpages contained in the cat subdirectories. Since all of the manpages have been **gzip**ped, they must first be uncompressed, then sent to a pager to view the data, then re-compressed to continue to conserve disk space. Fortunately, the **zcat** utility seamlessly does all three of these steps for you.

Let's **zcat** the motd manpage, as it is a nice short manpage that fits on one screen. We'll start with the unformatted version:

```
% cd /usr/share/man
% zcat man5/motd.5.gz
.\"     $NetBSD: motd.5,v 1.2 1994/12/28 18:58:53 glass Exp $
.\"
.\" This file is in the public domain.
.\" $FreeBSD: src/share/man/man5/motd.5,v 1.5 2001/07/14 19:41:09 schweikh Exp $
.\"
.Dd February 13, 1997
.Dt MOTD 5
.Os
.Sh NAME
.Nm motd
.Nd file containing message(s) of the day
.Sh DESCRIPTION
The file
.Pa /etc/motd
is normally displayed by
.Xr login 1
after a user has logged in but before the shell is run.
It is generally used for important system-wide announcements.
During system startup, a line containing the kernel version string is
prepended to this file.
.Pp
Individual users may suppress the display of this file by
creating a file named
.Dq Pa .hushlogin
in their home directories or through
.Xr login.conf 5 .
.Sh FILES
.Bl -tag -width $HOME/.hushlogin -compact
.It Pa /etc/motd
The message of the day.
.It Pa $HOME/.hushlogin
```

```
Suppresses output of
.Pa /etc/motd .
.El
.Sh EXAMPLES
.Bd -literal
FreeBSD 2.1.6.1-RELEASE (GENERIC) #0:  Sun Dec 29 03:08:31 PST 1996

/home is full.  Please cleanup your directories.
.Ed
.Sh SEE ALSO
.Xr login 1 ,
.Xr login.conf 5
```

Notice that this doesn't look anything like the output from **man motd**. Instead, this file contains remarks and formatting commands along with the actual data. Let's compare this to the pre-formatted version contained within the `cat` subdirectory:

% **zcat cat5/motd.5.gz**

```
MOTD(5)                   FreeBSD File Formats Manual                   MOTD(5)

NAME
     motd - file containing message(s) of the day

DESCRIPTION
     The file /etc/motd is normally displayed by login(1) after a user has
     logged in but before the shell is run.  It is generally used for impor-
     tant system-wide announcements.  During system startup, a line containing
     the kernel version string is prepended to this file.

     Individual users may suppress the display of this file by creating a file
     named ".hushlogin" in their home directories or through login.conf(5).

FILES
     /etc/motd          The message of the day.
     $HOME/.hushlogin  Suppresses output of /etc/motd.

EXAMPLES
     FreeBSD 2.1.6.1-RELEASE (GENERIC) #0:  Sun Dec 29 03:08:31 PST 1996

     /home is full.  Please cleanup your directories.

SEE ALSO
     login(1), login.conf(5)

FreeBSD 6.2                    February 13, 1997                    FreeBSD 6.2
```

Notice that the pre-formatted version looks like the manpage you are used to seeing, minus the highlighting. However, something very interesting happens if we try to save a formatted manpage into a file. Let's send the output of **zcat**ting the formatted `motd` manpage to a `test` file in our home directory:

```
% zcat man5/motd.5.gz > ~/test
```

If you view the `test` file using the **cat** utility it should look exactly like the **zcat**ted `motd.5.gz` file. If you send the `test` file to the **more** paging utility it should look exactly like a manpage, with highlighting included.

However, if you open up the `test` file using your favorite text editor, you'll see a mess. It's funny how a lot of ^H characters can make a file so unreadable. However, if you look very carefully, and mentally try to remove the ^H's, you should be able to recognize the text in your file. In case you're wondering, ^H is the control character for backspace which allows your terminal driver to doublestrike the previous character, which results in the highlighted text.

We've just discovered an interesting difference in functionality between the **cat** utility, the **more** utility, and an editor. By default, **cat** ignores control characters, **more** interprets control characters, and text editors display control characters. Thus we have an unhighlighted but readable file with **cat**, a highlighted file with **more**, and a mess with a text editor.

You can force **cat** to display control characters instead of ignoring them by using the **-v** switch. Try this:

```
% cat -v ~/test
```

Your output should display all of the ^H characters, just like the text editor did.

Understanding this behavior will come in handy if you ever want to send a manpage to a file: Perhaps you want to transfer some manpages to your non-Unix laptop or want to include some interesting snippets of a manpage when replying to an email. If you just redirect the output of the **man** command to a file like this:

```
% man motd > ~/test
```

your resulting file will contain all of those irritating ^H characters. However, if you pipe the output through the **col** command before sending it to your file, you will lose the ^H characters. Try it:

```
% man motd | col -b > ~/test
```

then send `~/test` to your favorite text editor to see the difference.

If you read the manpage for the col command, you'll discover why this works: it discards all of the control characters it doesn't recognize. And, fortunately for us, **col** doesn't recognize that many control characters.

This trick is also very handy if you ever transfer an ASCII file from an MS-DOS-based operating system to your FreeBSD system. If you've ever done this before, you've discovered that MS-DOS-based operating systems put a ^M at the end of every line to indicate the carriage return. You could use your arrow keys to navigate to each of these characters so you can press the delete key, but it is much easier to do this:

```
% col -b < dosfile > unixfile
```

This command tells **col** to strip the control characters from a file called `dosfile` and then send the results to a new file called `unixfile`.

Or, if it's too late and you've already opened up the file in **vi**, try this:

```
:%! col -bx
```

This will remove all of those pesky ^M or ^H characters without having to leave **vi**.

Putting it all Together

Now we can tie together all of this stuff to better understand how the **man** command works. When you type:

```
% man name_of_manpage
```

the **man** utility searches the `/usr/share/man` subdirectories, in order, for the first reference of the manpage you wish to view. You can alter this default behavior like so:

```
% man -a name_of_manpage
```

which will force **man** to read all of the subdirectories; this switch is useful if you think a manpage is in more than one section in the manual and you wish to view them all.

If **man** doesn't find the manpage here, it will then look in `/usr/local/man`. If you do a listing of this directory and its subdirectories, you will find the manpages for the programs you installed yourself: i.e., any ports or packages that you built.

Once **man** has found the manpage, the formatted copy is sent to a pager so it can be displayed on your screen one page at a time. The pager will correctly interpret the `^H` characters to expose the highlighted text. If you prefer to read your manpages without that glaring white text, you can start your manpage like so:

```
% man motd | col -b | more
```

You can substitute the word **more** with **less** if you prefer the **less** paging utility.

Additional Resources

Original Articles:

```
http://www.onlamp.com/pub/a/bsd/2000/10/04/FreeBSD_Basics.html

http://www.onlamp.com/pub/a/bsd/2000/10/11/FreeBSD_Basics.html
```

2.4 Working with Text

Once you have your FreeBSD system up and running, what do you spend most of your time doing? Why, working with and creating files, of course. In this section, I want to concentrate on manipulating text in files; we'll start with some useful commands that came with your FreeBSD system, then we'll examine some of the utilities in the ports collection.

The cat Utility

One of the most useful utilities for quick manipulation of text files is the **cat** utility. By default, **cat** will display the specified file to your screen. That is,

```
% cat filename
```

will display the contents of a file named `filename`.

You can also use **cat** to display multiple files like so:

```
% cat filename1 filename2 filename3
```

However, even the fastest speed-reader will miss most of the contents of the **cat** command if the contents of the file(s) are longer than one screen. To see the output displayed one screen at a time, pipe it to the **more** command like so:

```
% cat file1 file2 | more
```

Or, save yourself some typing (and be more efficient) and let the **more** utility directly display the files for you like so:

```
% more file1 file2
```

Both commands will get the job done, but if you use **cat**, it won't tell you when `file1` ends and `file2` begins, whereas **more** will. I usually use the **more** utility to display files, unless I'm absolutely certain that the file is only a few lines long. If the file you wish to view has been **gzip**ped and has a .gz extension, use the utilities **zcat** or **zmore** to view the file without having to **gunzip** it first.

You can also use **cat** as a quick and dirty editor to create a new file. By default, **cat** reads a file and sends its results to your terminal; to force it to instead read your input and send it to a file, you need to use the > redirector.

Note: One does have to be careful when redirecting — especially if you're quick with the **Enter** key — as it is easy to destroy existing files if you're not careful.

Try this in your home directory:

```
% cat > test
```

Notice that you've lost your prompt as the **cat** command is waiting for input to send to a file called `test`. Type what you want to appear in the file, and when you're finished, press **Enter**, then **Ctrl-D**. [1]

```
This is a test file
with a couple of lines of text

and a blank line.
^d
```

You should now have your cursor back. To view this new file, use **cat** without the redirector:

```
% cat test
```

---

[1]The carat îs also used as shorthand for pressing the **Control** key.

Simple, wasn't it? However, this is where redirection can be dangerous. If I already had a file named `test` in this directory, the redirection would happily overwrite that file without warning me first. I would be very unhappy if that file happened to be my thesis, or my resume, or any other file I may have been attached to — something to keep in mind when using **cat** with the **>** redirector.

You can also use **cat** to join multiple files into one file. This command:

```
% cat file1 file2 file3 > bigfile
```

will create a new file called `bigfile` out of the contents of `file1`, `file2`, and `file3` in that order. If there already is a file called `bigfile`, it will be destroyed (there's that **>** redirector, again), but you will still have your original three files.

The shell also understands the **>>** redirector, which appends (adds to the end) of a file. If the file does not already exist, shell will create the file for you. So if you type:

```
% cat file4 file5 >> bigfile
```

`bigfile` will contain the contents of files 4 and 5 after the earlier contents of files 1 to 3, while:

```
% cat file4 file5 >> newbigfile
```

will create a `newbigfile` that contains the contents of files 4 and 5. You'll notice that the **>>** redirector is much safer than the **>** redirector. However, if you're a fast typist, look before you press **Enter** and make sure you really did type **>>** instead of **>**.

Counting Text

Remember back in high school when you had to write those 1500 word essays? There may still be times when you need to know how many words or lines are in a file. You don't need a fancy editor to do this for you, and fortunately, your FreeBSD system is much quicker at counting than you are. If I were to type at the shell:

```
% wc wo*
     97     689    3717 working_with_text
```

the **wc** or word count command would tell me that this had 97 lines, 689 words, and 3717 bytes of information. If I wanted to see how this compared to the other articles in my directory, I could type this:

```
% wc /articles/*
    198    1326    8078 buildx.txt
    361    2411   13447 change_prompt
    431    2763   16147 cron_intro
    245    1556    9146 desktop.txt
    263    1768   10426 ethereal.txt
    351    2104   12855 howto_rtfm_part1
    374    2246   14018 howto_rtfm_part2
    363    2642   15523 intro_to
```

```
 334    1392    7987 loginshe.txt
 267    1528    8837 mountfs.txt
 321    2319   13712 networking_with_tcpip
 305    1524    9235 nfs.txt
 268    2101   11761 permissions_part1
 367    2235   12373 permissions_part2
 386    2063   12430 ppp.txt
 257    1478    8979 sharity.txt
 310    1738    9777 useful.txt
  97     689    3717 working_with_text
5498   33883  198448 total
```

If I just need to know the number of words, I would type:

```
% wc -w filename
```

and to just know the number of lines:

```
% wc -l filename
```

Using **wc** is a lot quicker than opening up an editor, hunting for my mouse under my piles of scrap paper, and trying to find the correct menu option.

To actually number the lines in a file, you can use a switch with the cat utility. Let's say I'm teaching a friend how to write a simple script; it will be easier on us both if I can refer to a line number when pointing out syntax. This command:

```
% cat -n /perlscripts/square
     1       #!/usr/bin/perl -w
     2
     3  print shift() **2, "\n";
     4
```

will show that this file has four lines: two lines with text and two blank lines. If I'm only interested in numbering the lines that contain text, I would use this command instead:

```
% cat -b square
     1       #!/usr/bin/perl -w
     2  print shift() **2, "\n";
```

I could now demonstrate to my friend the simply beauty of a Perl script; that one line of code (line 2 of the **cat -b** output) creates a script that will calculate the square of a number like so:

```
% ./square 43
1849
```

But you don't want to get me started on Perl; let's continue working with text files.

Spell Checkers

Let's say you're typing out that memo to your boss and you can't remember if the word "actually" has one or two "l"s. The quickest way to find out is to run the **look** utility like so:

```
% look actual
actual
actualism
actualist
actualistic
actuality
actualization
actualize
actually
actualness
```

Notice that I just supplied the root word "actual" and received all of the possibilities that could be added to that root, including the one I was looking for. I've yet to find a quicker way to get the correct spelling of a word, along with other possibilities that I may actually prefer.

However, if you are a terrible speller, you may prefer an interactive spell checker that will check an entire document for you. Both **aspell** and **ispell** in the ports collection will do this for you. Both utilities can be run from the command line, and **aspell** can be integrated into email readers and other editors. Let's take a quick look at both; I'll start with **ispell**. Become the superuser, make sure you're connected to the Internet, and type:

```
# pkg_add -r ispell
```

When it's finished installing, leave the superuser account and refresh your path by typing:

```
% rehash
```

Now let's create a quick text file with some spelling mistakes:

```
% cd
% cat > typos
This is a very quik file
to demunstrate my
terruble spelling.
^d
```

To spell check this file using **ispell**, type:

```
% ispell typos
```

which will highlight the first misspelled word and give you various options on dealing with the misspelling like so:

```
  quik         File: typos
This is a very quik
 file
00: quib
01: quick
02: quid
03: quin
etc.
[SP] <number> R)epl A)ccept I)nsert L)ookup U)ncap Q)uit e(X)it or ?  for help
```

Note the toolbar at the bottom of the screen. Since the correct spelling has been offered, if you press **r**, then **1**, and **Enter**, "quik" will be replaced with "quick," and **ispell** will move on to the next misspelled word. When you are finished, type **x** to save your changes; if you decide that you preferred your misspellings, use **q** to exit without saving the changes.

You can also add words to the **ispell** dictionary; this is most useful for acronyms or personal names. To do this, press **i** to insert into the dictionary. These inserts will be stored in a file in your home directory called .ispell_english. To find about the other useful features of **ispell**, use the **?** while in **ispell**, or read its manpage.

Although **ispell** is easy to use, it won't catch all of your misspellings. If I was a really terrible speller and had written this line in the typos file:

```
This is a veery kwik file
```

ispell would bypass the word "veery" completely and only offer the word "kaik" as a substitute for "kwik".

Let's try **aspell** on this file. Again, as *root* and while connected to the Internet, type:

```
# pkg_add -r aspell
```

Don't forget to leave the superuser account and **cd** back to your home directory when you are finished. Let's quickly overwrite that typos file with the **>** redirector:

```
% cd
% cat > typos
This is a veery kwik file.
^d
```

The syntax to use **aspell** is a little longer than **ispell**; don't forget the word **check**, or you'll receive a syntax error.

```
% aspell check typos
This is a *veery* kwik file.
1) very          6) veers
2) veer          7) weary
3) Vera          8) every
4) vary          9) verier
5) leery         0) were
```

```
i) ignore          I) Ignore all
r) Replace         R) Replace all
a) Add             x) Exit
?
```

Note that the misspelled word is in asterisks instead of highlighted; it did catch the word "veery" that **ispell** missed. Also, instead of a menubar at the bottom, the actions are mixed in with the possible spelling options. If we were to continue spell checking this file, **aspell** would also give a viable alternative to the word "kwik".

Usually I would tell you to read the manpage for **aspell** to see all of its features, but it does not have one. Instead, you'll have to:

```
% ls /usr/local/share/doc/aspell/man-html
```

to find its documentation. `manual.txt` is well worth browsing, especially if you would like to integrate **aspell** into your email reader.

Additional Resources

Original Article:

`http://www.onlamp.com/pub/a/bsd/2000/10/18/FreeBSD_Basics.html`

2.5 Using the vi Editor

OK, I admit it. I like using the **vi** editor. In fact, I have fond memories of using **vi** when I was teaching myself C++ while playing Peter Gabriel at full blast. I never became highly proficient at C++, but I can still type and get **vi**'s bell to go off in rhythm to any piece of music. I sort of miss that bell when I'm using another editor.

Everyone knows they should have a passing knowledge of **vi**, but most people groan at the thought of using it. I'd like to demonstrate some of the tricks that **vi** has up its sleeve. It really is a powerful little editor and I'm constantly amazed at its number of built-in shortcuts.

Getting Help

One of the more recent tips I learned is from UGU's tip of the day `http://www.ugu.com/sui/ugu/show?I=tip.today`. If you haven't heard of this great reference, you can read the archives or sign up to receive the daily tip.

Let's say that I've sent a file to a pager:

```
% more a_file
```

and I notice a typo as I'm reading through the file. If I type the letter **v**, the **vi** editor will be invoked and the bottom of my screen will show the name of the file and the line number my cursor is on. I can then correct the typo. To save the correction and go back to the pager, simply type **:wq** as usual.

What could possibly be more efficient than that?

The **vi** editor comes with a built-in help system which is useful for learning new shortcuts. If you type **:help** you'll see this at the bottom of your screen:

```
To see the list of vi commands, enter ":viusage<CR>"
To see the list of ex commands, enter ":exusage<CR>"
For an ex command usage statement
  enter ":exusage [cmd] <CR>"
For a vi key usage statement enter ":viusage [key]<CR>"
To exit, enter "q!"
Press any key to continue [: to enter more ex commands]:
```

For example, if I think I remember that **vi** uses the letter "o", but I can't remember for what, I can type:

```
:viusage o
  Key: o append after line
Usage: [count]o
Press any key to continue [: to enter more ex commands]:
```

Or, if I feel the need to kill an afternoon, I can enter **:viusage** and practice using the shortcuts I'm not familiar with. While this is handy, it can be quite overwhelming when you're first learning **vi**. One of the neatest tricks I learned was how to make a customized help screen. I picked up this tip from Steve Moritsugu's "Using Unix" (ISBN 0-7897-1632-1). I like to create a file with about ten commands I want to learn, and once I've mastered those, I'll edit the file with a new set of commands.

Let's create a help file for a beginner that shows the most basic commands:

```
% vi /tmp/help
echo"
:q!      abort without saving
:wq      write changes and quit
a        append text after cursor
i        insert text before cursor
o        open a new line below current line
O        open a new line above current line
x        delete character
dd       delete line
1p       restore most recently deleted text at cursor
u        undo last change (repeat to undo undo)
10G      go to line 10 (can use any line number)
G        go to last line
0        move to beginning of current line
$        move to end of current line"
```

Let's start with those commands; the trick is to make a help file that will fit on one screen. Don't forget the **echo** command and the quotation marks at the beginning and end of your file. Now, become the superuser, and type:

```
# ls -l /usr/bin/help
ls: /usr/bin/help: No such file or directory
```

Ignore the error message, it's a good thing. Now type:

```
# mv /tmp/help /usr/bin/help
# chmod 755 /usr/bin/help
# exit
```

To use the customized help screen while in a **vi** session, type:

```
:!help
```

Note that you have to remember to include the exclamation mark as you're really telling **vi** to execute a command you created called **help**.

set Commands

The **vi** editor also has quite a few **set** commands. It's useful to try them out first in a **vi** session and see which ones you like as you can invoke them permanently by creating a **vi** configuration file. Let's take a look at the **set** commands first, then create the file. From a **vi** session, type:

```
:set showmode
```

You'll note that a word appeared at the bottom right corner of your screen telling you what mode you are in. Some examples are Command, Insert, Replace, and Append modes.

Another handy **set** command allows you to turn on autowrap, meaning you never have to remember to press enter as **vi** will wrap your long lines for you. To set this option, type either:

```
:set wrapmargin=10
```

or

```
:set wm=10
```

If you would like to have each line numbered:

```
:set nu
```

If you decide that looks yucky, turn it off with:

```
:set nonu
```

In fact, any **set** command can be turned off by repeating it with no like so:

```
:set nowm=10
:set noshowmode
```

To see your current settings, type:

```
:set all
```

If you're unsure what each **set** command does, you'll find them in the **vi** man page if you do a search for "unset":

```
% man vi
/unset
```

Finally, if you set a **set** command during a **vi** session, it will be lost when you quit your **vi** session. To permanently keep a setting, create a file in your home directory called `.exrc` like so:

```
% vi ~/.exrc
set showmode
set wm=10
```

Include your favorite **set** commands, and when you're finished, save your changes with **:wq** to write and quit.

Executing Commands

One of the neatest things about the **vi** editor is that you can run commands without leaving **vi** and even save the command's output within your **vi** session. Let's say I'm typing along in my **vi** session and I need to see this month's calendar. I can type:

```
:! cal
```

Don't panic when you see this month's calendar appear at the bottom of your screen instead of your file. Once you're finished looking at the calendar, you can press any key to see your file again.

To insert this month's calendar into your file, place your cursor where you want it to appear, and type:

```
:!! cal
```

If you forget to have your cursor in the right place and end up inserting **cal**'s output in the wrong spot, don't forget that **u** will undo your change so you can try again.

The **!** command will run any command and **!!** will insert that command's output into your current file. To insert the contents of another file, try:

```
:!! cat /etc/fstab
```

Cut and Paste

The **vi** editor also has powerful cut-and-paste abilities. When you are in a **vi** session, you have the equivalent of 26 (for the 26 alphabet characters) clipboards available for your use. The **vi** editor also automagically stores your last nine deletions for you in separate buffers labeled from 1-9. You can save yourself a lot of typing if you remember to use these buffers.

There are only four letters one has to remember to do any cut-and-paste operation (Table 2.2).

Table 2.2: vi cut-and-paste

m	to mark the desired text
d or **dd**	to cut the text
y	to yank (copy) the text
p	to paste the text

When you're first learning to cut and paste, it is handy to **set showmode** as you have to be in Command mode to enter the cut-and-paste commands. You'll always be able to check you are in the right mode as the word "*Command" will appear in the bottom right corner of your screen. It's a good idea to practice on a file that is not important to you, but don't despair if you really muck up your file as you can always exit the **vi** editor without saving any of your changes with **:q!**.

Let's try some cut-and-paste operations. Open up or create a file that contains a couple of paragraphs worth of text. Move your cursor to the first line of a paragraph, and we'll manipulate the lines in that paragraph. My paragraph has six lines in it; to cut out those six lines, I'll type from command mode:

```
6dd
```

You'll note that this operation was silently effective, the lines just disappeared. If I type **u**, the lines reappear, if I type **u** again, they re-disappear as those lines are stored in **vi**'s buffer. Because they were my last deletion, they are in buffer number one.

To paste those lines, I'll put my cursor somewhere else in the file, and type:

```
"1p
```

The quotation mark tells **vi** to access its buffers; the **1** says I want the number one buffer (the last deletion); and the **p** says I want to paste those contents at the current cursor position. Again, this is silent, the lines magically appear. If my cursor was in the wrong spot, I can undo the changes with **u**, move the cursor and try again.

If you forget which buffer your deleted text is in, start with pasting the first buffer, undo that change with **u**, then repeat the command with the second buffer using dot like this:

```
"1pu.u.u.u.
```

until you find your text. You can cycle through all nine buffers this way.

Now let's try copying (yanking) text instead of deleting it. Because the numerical buffers only store deleted text, you instead want to save your copied text to one of the alphabetical clipboards. You can use any clipboard you want, you just have to tell **vi** which one you want to use.

I'll move to a different paragraph and yank (copy) three of its lines to clipboard letter a like so:

```
"a3y
```

You'll note that the lines didn't disappear this time. To see if it worked, I'll move my cursor to a different part of the file and paste in the contents of the a buffer:

```
"ap
```

Again, I told **vi** to access a buffer named *a* and to paste its contents at the current cursor position.

The contents of *a* will remain there until I end my **vi** session. If I want to copy more text, I'll probably send it to clipboard *b* and so on until I've cycled through all 26 clipboards.

Another way to copy and paste text is to mark the specific text. Move your cursor to any position in your file; I'll go to the middle of a paragraph and type:

```
ma
```

to start a mark named *a*. Now move your cursor to another position in your file; I'll go down to the end of a line a couple of paragraphs down and type:

```
y'a
```

This copies all of the marked text between the initial and ending cursor position to an unnamed buffer. Note that unnamed buffers are referred to by ' (single quote), whereas named buffers are referred to as " (double-quote). The bottom of my screen noted that I yanked 14 lines. I'll then move to another part of my file and paste it like so:

```
p
```

Now, let's get really fancy by copying the contents of our buffers into another file. Don't exit **vi** by using the **q** command or you will erase its buffers. In fact, you can tell **vi** to open up another file without leaving your current screen by using the **e** command like so:

```
:e newfile
```

If you've made any changes to your current file, **vi** will complain and tell you to save them first. If you don't want to save your changes, you can still enter the second file if you type:

```
:e! newfile
```

You'll note that **vi** will create an empty file called `newfile`. If I now type:

```
p
```

the contents of that unnamed buffer will be pasted into this new file. I can also copy in the contents of any named buffer by specifying its letter like so:

```
"ap
```

And I can even copy in a deletion from the previous file:

```
"1p
```

If you want to get back to the first file, repeat the **e** command and specify that file's name. No matter what file you are in, if you type **q**, you will exit **vi** and lose your buffers.

There are other ways to get text from one file to another using **vi**. Let's say I'm working in a large file and I want to copy (write) lines 100 to 125 to a new file. This command will do it:

```
:100,125w newfile
```

To see the results, I can open up `newfile` like so:

```
:e newfile
```

Or, if I want to send line 23 to the end of `existing_file`:

```
:23w >> existing_file
```

I've barely scratched the surface of what you can do in **vi**, but hopefully I've piqued your interest in this editor. Besides UGU and Steve Moritsugu's book, you'll also find more **vi** tips in "Unix Power Tools" (ISBN 0-596-00330-7)

Additional Resources

Original Article:

```
http://www.onlamp.com/pub/a/bsd/2001/10/25/FreeBSD_Basics.html
```

Garrett Hildebrand's **vi** Page:

```
http://hydra.nac.uci.edu/indiv/gdh/vi/
```

2.6 Customizing the Login Shell

For those users whose first operating system was not Unix, the concept of different login shells can be very confusing. It can take some time before you can consistently remember how to figure out which shell you are in, know which shells should be used for which purposes, and become comfortable with the features of each shell.

This section won't cover shell scripting or advanced shell tweaks; instead we'll concentrate on some differences between the C and Bourne shells. We'll also cover editing login and logout scripts, and learn something about login and non-login shells along the way.

Getting a Shell

By default, on a FreeBSD system, *root*'s login shell is **tcsh** (the extended C shell) and all other users are given a default login shell of **sh** (the Bourne shell). If you haven't customized your prompt, its appearance is a clue to which shell you are using. To test this, let's make two users. Log in as *root* and type **sysinstall**, then select Configure, User Management, and then User.

Note that the only section filled in is the Login shell field; it shows the default of a new user as /bin/sh.

Create a user called *test1*, add the user to the *wheel* group, assign a password you'll remember, and tab over to OK to add the user.

Create a second user called *test2*, add the user to the *wheel* group, assign a password, but this time change the Login shell field to read /bin/csh. Then tab over to OK to add the second user.

Exit **sysinstall** and type the word **logout** until your prompt looks like this:

```
login:
```

Login as *test1* and you'll receive the Bourne shell which looks like this for a normal user:

```
$
```

Now, **su** to *root* to see what the shell looks like to the superuser:

```
$ su
Password:
hostname#
```

Note that hostname will be replaced with the hostname of your computer.

Open up another virtual terminal that has the login: prompt. This time, log in as *test2* to see what the C shell prompt looks like to a regular user:

```
%
```

If you **su** to *root*, you'll see that the shell looks like the same to the superuser:

```
hostname#
```

Note that both superuser's prompts look the same. So how do you tell which user has which login shell? Try this:

```
# grep test* /etc/passwd
test1:test1:*:1005:0:User &:/home/test1:/bin/sh
test2:test2:*:1006:0:User &:/home/test2:/bin/csh
```

Login vs. Non-login Shells

If you type **logout** as either superuser, you should get this error message:

```
Not a login shell.
```

and you'll still have the same prompt. To leave superuser, you must type **exit**. Then *test1* should be back here:

```
$
```

(the Bourne shell) and *test2*, who has the C shell, should get this prompt back:

```
%
```

Let's try this one more time; have *test1* **su** to *root*, then type:

```
# whoami
root
# grep root /etc/passwd
root:*:0:0:Charlie &:/root:/bin/csh
```

If *test2* does the same thing, you should get the same results. The reason why both the superuser's prompts looked the same is that they both received *root*'s default C shell.

Now for the login shell error message. Open up another virtual terminal with a login: prompt and log in directly as *root*.

Since *root*'s login shell is the C shell, you should receive a prompt that looks like this:

```
hostname#
```

Now type **logout**. You should receive the login: prompt back without any error messages. This is an important concept. You can only **logout** of a terminal that you **login** to. If you only **su** to another user, you will receive that user's default shell, but it will be as a non-login shell. The only way to exit a non-login shell is with the **exit** command.

Open up yet another virtual terminal with a login: prompt and log in as *test1*. Your prompt should look like this:

```
$
```

Now, try this command and enter the password for *test2* when prompted:

```
$ su test2
Password:
%
```

Note that your shell has changed from the login Bourne shell to the non-login C shell. If you type:

```
% logout
Not a login shell.
```

However, if you type **exit**, your prompt changes back to

```
$
```

Now type **logout**:

```
$ logout
logout: not found
```

What happened now? You are in the Bourne login shell but it seems to have lost the logout command! We better try a:

```
$ man logout
```

If you go down a page, you'll see a list of commands and a comparison of those built into the C and the Bourne shells. Note that the C shell supports many more commands than the Bourne shell. Finally, note the Bourne shell's lack of built-in support for the **logout** command. The only way to leave the Bourne shell is with the **exit** command.

Shell History

Another difference between the two shells is their use of the **history** command. Log in as *test2* to enter the C shell, then type the letter **h** to view your command line history.[2] It will look something like this:

```
% h
     1      su
     2   exit
     3   whoami
     4   su root
     5   grep root /etc/passwd
     6   whoami
     7   su test1
     8   exit
     9   logout
    10   whoami
    11   exit
    12   h
```

Now try this, to repeat command number 10:

```
% !10
whoami
test2
```

---

[2]**h** is an alias for history. See section 2.7 for more details.

And this, to repeat the last command:

```
% !!
whoami
test2
```

If you want to repeat the last command that starts with "log":

```
% !log
logout
```

You can save yourself a lot of typing with the **history** command.

Now, log in as *test1*, and try the same **history** commands. You'll be disappointed to discover that your history starts from scratch and that the exclamation mark doesn't work in the Bourne shell. You need the C shell to get the added history functionality of **!** Fortunately, *root* gets the C shell by default.

test1 isn't out of luck, though. As *test1*, type **csh** — your prompt will change to:

```
%
```

Now, let's try **history** again:

```
% h     1  h
```

This is disappointing, though. By default, a user's history doesn't follow him when he changes shells. Let's make a bit of history and then try some commands:

```
% whoami
test1
% h     1  h
        2  whoami
        3  h
% !2
whoami
test1
```

If *test1* gets tired of the C shell, she can type **exit** and receive her Bourne shell back.

Login and Logout Scripts

Now let's do something useful with all of this knowledge. Let's have *test1* receive the current date and time when he logs into his login Bourne shell. While we're at it, we'll let *test2* receive a *fortune* when she exits her login C shell.

First, we need to know where **date** lives, so we can refer to its full pathname in the script:

```
$ which date
/bin/date
```

The Bourne shell supports login scripts, not logout scripts. The name of the Bourne shell's login script is
`.profile`. As *test1* open up `~test1/.profile` in your favorite editor and add the following line to the end of
this file:

```
/bin/date
```

and save your changes. Then type **exit** to log out and log back in as *test1*. If you see the current date and time,
you've just written your first login script on a Unix system.

The C shell supports both login and logout scripts. Not surprisingly, the files are named `.login` and `.logout`.
Log in as *test2* and try:

```
% pwd
/usr/home/test2
% ls -a | grep log
.login
.login.conf
```

You'll note that `.login` was created with the user; however, you must create your own `.logout` if you want
commands to execute when you log out of your login C shell. To view the file, type:

```
% more .login
```

And you should see that it ends with a command to execute **/usr/games/fortune**. Using your favorite editor
create a file named `.logout` which contains the line:

```
[ -x /usr/games/fortune ] && /usr/games/fortune freebsd-tips
```

and save your change. Now when you type **logout** or you **exit** your login shell, you should have a parting
fortune to read before receiving your new login prompt.

One last exercise to tie together all these concepts. As *root*:

```
# cp ~test2/.logout /root/
```

Log in and log out as *root* to see if you can get your fortunes both coming and going.

Now, log in as *test2* and **su** to *root*. Did you receive a fortune when you entered the non-login shell? How will
you leave this non-login shell? Will you receive a fortune when you leave the non-login shell?

Additional Resources

Original Article:

```
http://www.onlamp.com/pub/a/bsd/2000/08/02/FreeBSD_Basics.html
```

If you enjoyed learning this, I highly recommend that you check out the O'Reilly book, Unix Power Tools
(ISBN 0-596-00330-7). This is the type of book you can grow into. There are plenty of helpful tips for those
new to Unix, and the stuff you don't understand now you can go back to and use later as you progress from
newbie to pretty good user to Unix guru.

2.7 Understanding Shell Prompts

Occasionally, a user will write the FreeBSD questions mailing list asking how to customize his prompt. Inevitably, the responses will include:

- It depends on your shell

- Read the manpage for your shell

While this may seem a brush-off at first glance, it is actually useful advice as prompts are shell specific. Furthermore, if one was to answer with a secret recipe like this:

```
set prompt = "${e}[1m${USER}@`dirs`${e}[0m% "
```

the prompt might work, but the original user would have no understanding of why this cryptic string of seemingly random characters affected the look of his prompt.

Let's take a look at customizing the prompt for some of the more popular shells. By the end of this section, you should be able to decode the above recipe, and create your own custom-combo for your favorite shell.

Table 2.3 shows the default prompts for four different shells.

Table 2.3: Default Shell Prompts

Shell	Executable	Default Prompt
Bourne	sh	$
C	csh	%
tcsh	tcsh	%
Bash	bash	$

Unless you specify otherwise, any user you create will be placed in the Bourne shell. Since FreeBSD 4.1, the *root* account receives the tcsh shell by default. **bash** is not installed by default, but is available in the ports collection. Also note that the *root* user's prompt will be a #, regardless of the shell.

Shell Variables

Before we can customize the prompt, we need to know what a shell variable is. Every Unix shell is really a programming language; programming languages use variables to store information. Variables allow you to change or vary their value, hence their name. Your prompt is an example of a shell variable; if you could not change its value, you would be stuck with the defaults of $, %, or #.

Variables can be stored in a file that is read by the shell when you log in or change shells (as introduced on page 101). Table 2.4 shows which configuration file(s) can be read by each shell.

Table 2.4: Shell Configuration Files

Shell Name	Configuration File(s)
Bourne	.profile
C	.cshrc, .login, .logout
tcsh	.tcshrc, .cshrc, .login, .logout
Bash	.bash-profile, .bash_login, .profile, .bashrc, .bashlogout

Creating Aliases

Since we'll be mucking about with shell variables, let's create a test user account to try out our changes. Become the *root* user and type **sysinstall** and select Configure, User Management, and then User. Input a login ID for the test account and a password you'll remember, and change the Login shell to /bin/csh. When you're finished, leave **sysinstall**, **exit** out of the *root* account and log in as your test user.

Since you changed the user's shell to the C shell, your prompt should look like this:

```
%
```

The user will be in their home directory; to see the configuration files, type:

```
% ls -a
```

Note that the **-a** is required, as files that begin with a dot are hidden files. Now type:

```
% more .cshrc
```

to view the default settings for the C shell. Let's take a closer look at some of these entries:

```
alias h       history 25
alias j       jobs -l
alias la      ls -a
alias lf      ls -FA
alias ll      ls -lA
```

After the remarked-out comments section is a set of pre-defined aliases. Aliases are simply abbreviations for commands. Notice the alias called **la**: it is an abbreviation of **ls -a**. This means you could have typed **la** instead of **ls -a** to see your hidden files. Also note that you can type the letter **h** to receive your last 25 history entries; this sure beats typing the word **history**.

You can add your own aliases; they can be useful if you always want to use certain switches with a command. Some good aliases for beginners are:

```
alias ri rm -i #ask before deleting
alias mi mv -i #ask before moving over an existing file
```

Note that when you create an alias, you'll want to choose a name that is not already used by another command, like **ri** or **mi**. And be careful with aliases; if you get used to being prompted because of an alias, you may forget this is not the default behavior when you are at another computer or logged in as a different user.

Let's move down to the shell variables:

```
if ($?prompt) then
        # An interactive shell -- set some stuff up
        set filec
        set history = 100
        set savehist = 100
        set mail = (/var/mail/$USER)
        if ( $?tcsh ) then
                bindkey "^W" backward-delete-word
                bindkey -k up history-search-backward
                bindkey -k down history-search-forward
        endif
endif
```

Note the syntax is `set variable = [value]` where the value is in square brackets as it is optional. This syntax is specific to the C and **tcsh** shells.

A Custom Prompt

If you wish to change your prompt, the name of the C or tcsh shell variable is `prompt`. You can set as many values as you want for the `prompt` variable, as long as they are enclosed within quotation marks. The actual values differ slightly for the C shells and the **tcsh** shells. FreeBSD, PC-BSD and DesktopBSD users should follow the instructions for the **tcsh** shell; I've left in the instructions for the csh shell for those readers who are using other operating systems or who have changed their default shell to csh.

Let's try a very simple prompt that works in both the C and tcsh shells. Using your favorite text editor, open up the `.cshrc` file in your test user's home directory. Add the following line below your last **set** command line:

```
set prompt = "${USER}% "
```

Save the file and type **source .cshrc** to inform the shell about the change. Your prompt should now show your user name, followed by a % followed by a space, and then your cursor. Let's pick apart the string of characters we assigned to the prompt shell variable.

First off, we enclosed the entire value in quotation marks. It is good practice to always do this; it is mandatory if you have any spaces anywhere in your string of characters.

The `${USER}` is actually an environment variable. While shell variables are specific to a shell, environment variables are read by all programs (including shells). You can recognize variables as they always start with a $ and are usually enclosed in curly braces — {}. By convention, environment variables are named in upper case characters, while shell variables are in lower case. If you wish to see your other environment variables, type the following at your command prompt:

```
% env
```

If you wish to see your shell variables, type:

```
% set
```

The ${USER} environment variable contains your login name. We can tell the shell prompt variable to read this value when it sets your prompt.

Finally, we put a % after the login name to remind ourselves we are still in the C shell. I like a space between the % and the cursor, so I included one before the last quotation mark.

This prompt is useful as you will always be able to tell at a glance who you are logged in as at a virtual terminal.

I'm a very forgetful person and was forever using the **pwd** command to figure out where I was in the directory structure. Fortunately, this information can be included in the prompt. To do this in the C shell, replace your set prompt line with the following text:

```
alias cd 'chdir \!* && set prompt="'dirs'% "'
```

If you've typed the above without any typos, when you **source .cshrc**, you'll get the regular % prompt. However, after you type **cd**, your prompt will always tell you what directory you are in, with your home directory shortened to the ~ (tilde) symbol.

We actually had to do a bit of C shell programming to get this prompt to work. The C shell understands the ${cwd} or current working directory variable; unfortunately, this will only show what your current directory was when you logged in. We had to create an **alias** to the **cd** command if we wanted our prompt to continue to change as we changed directories.

We also had to use the backquote, the one on the same key as the ~ symbol. Don't confuse it with the single quote which is on the same key as the double quote. Back quotes are used for command substitution. We used it around the **dirs** command that tells the C shell to print out the name of the current directory. If you forget the backquotes, your prompt will literally display the word "dirs", instead of the result of the **dirs** command.

The other new characters we used were &&. This tells your shell that "I want you to do one thing, and when that successfully finishes, I want you to do this next". In summary, we told the shell that when we use the **cd** command, not only did we want it to change our directory, we also wanted it to set our prompt to show the name of the directory we changed to.

It is much easier to accomplish this same prompt in the **tcsh** shell, as it has a built-in variable for this purpose. The following string works for the **tcsh** shell:

```
set prompt = "%~ % "
```

The %~ is the built-in variable that shows the current working directory, with a ~ to represent the user's home directory. Again, I used the % to remind myself I was in the C shell (**tcsh** is really the C shell with extensions to its functionality), and I kept a space between my prompt and the cursor.

I usually like to remember both who I am and where I am, so I set my C shell prompt like this:

```
alias cd 'chdir \!* && set prompt="${USER}@'dirs'% "'
```

and my tcsh shell prompt like this:

```
set prompt = "${USER}@%~ % "
```

Notice that I've just joined all the desired commands together and enclosed them in quotation marks. I also put an @ as my separator between the username and the current working directory, so my prompt looks like this:

```
genisis@~ %
```

Bolding the Shell Prompt

We've input some useful information in our prompt, but it would be nice to have its text stand out so we don't confuse it with the other text on the screen. To bold your prompt in the C shell, replace your set prompt text with these lines:

```
set e="`echo x | tr x \\033`"
alias cd 'chdir \!* && set prompt="${e}[1m${USER}@`dirs`${e}[0m% "'
```

Since the C shell does not have a built-in variable for bolding text, we had to create our own variable which we called e. Because this is a shell variable, we gave it a name in lowercase; we then used our homemade variable when we set our prompt whenever we did this:

```
${e}
```

When we created e, we referred to the ASCII character *033*; this character represents the escape character. Every time we referenced ${e}, the shell did the equivalent of pressing the **Escape** key. Most terminals will interpret *ESC[1m* to mean "start bolding text." When you want to stop bolding text, *ESC[0m* tells the terminal to turn off that attribute.

If you prefer, you can underline text by replacing the *[1m* with *[4m*. Or you can cause your text to flash by using *[5m* instead. Don't forget to use *[0m* to turn off the attribute, or your whole screen will flash, which makes it very hard to work with text!

I usually change *root*'s prompt to be bold and flashing; this can be quite irritating, which reminds me to be *root* only when I absolutely have to be. To do this, become *root* and add the following lines to /root/.cshrc.

```
set e="`echo x | tr x \\033`"
alias cd 'chdir \!* && set prompt="${e}[1m${e}[5m${USER}@`dirs`${e}[0m% "'
```

Note that you can stack the *[1m* and *[5m* commands together; just remember to call ${e} before each one so it will include the Escape character.

Again, the **tcsh** shell has built-in variables to accomplish bolding and underlining, so you don't have to define your own variable first. To bold text in the **tcsh** shell, use this line to set your prompt:

```
set prompt = "%B%n@%~%b: "
```

In this command, %B starts bolding text and %b stops bolding. To underline text, use %U to start and %u to finish. The **tcsh** shell has many built-in variables that will let you put the date, time, your hostname, and colors into your prompt.

Finding Variables

We've only touched the surface of the possibilities of setting your prompt. You'll want to read the man page for your favorite shell to see what else you can set in that shell's prompt. For example, the C shell's executable is **csh**, so type **man csh** to read the man page for the C shell.

The first thing you'll notice about a shell's man page is that it is very long and contains a lot of advanced programming stuff you've probably never heard of. Fortunately, man pages have a search utility; the trick is to try to think of a word that is unique enough to zero in on what you're looking for. To do a search while in a man page, type a forward slash followed by the text you are looking for.

For example, you could try:

```
/shell variables
```

which will bring your cursor to the line that contains the words "shell variables". If you still aren't where you want to be, type **n** to go to the next occurrence of your search string.

A better search would be something more unique like:

```
/bold
```

This would bring you to the %B built-in variable if you were in the **tcsh** man page. Even if this wasn't the variable you were looking for, you would still be in the shell variable section of the man page.

Once you find an interesting shell variable or value, try it out in a test user account first to see if you like the results. You don't have to log out and back in to test every change. For example:

```
% source .cshrc
```

will force the C shell to re-read the .cshrc file and apply any changes you've made.

Additional Resources

Original Article:

```
http://www.onlamp.com/pub/a/bsd/2000/09/20/FreeBSD_Basics.html
```

2.8 Monitoring Unix Logins

This section will take a look at utmp, wtmp, and lastlog. These three files are read and updated whenever a user logs in to your FreeBSD system. However, you can't read these files directly, so we'll also look at the various utilities you can use to garner the information contained within these files. We'll then finish off the section with some utilities that deal with logins and terminals.

lastlog

Let's start with /var/log/lastlog. When a user logs in, the **login** utility reads this file to determine the last time that user logged in to your FreeBSD system; it will then make a new entry in this file to indicate the time of the new login. Let's see what happens when the user *genisis* logs into my FreeBSD system:

```
login: genisis
Password:
Last login:  Sat Feb 3 15:56:53 from biko
Copyright (c) 1992-2007 The FreeBSD Project.
Copyright (c) 1980, 1983, 1986, 1988, 1990, 1991, 1993, 1994
The Regents of the University of California.  All rights reserved.

Welcome to FreeBSD!
You have new mail.

You cannot kill time without injuring eternity.
```

Let's see what happened here. The **login** utility accepted the password for *genisis* and compared hash of it to the encrypted hash stored in /etc/master.passwd. It then read /var/log/lastlog to determine the last time this user had logged in (it looks like the last login occurred on Saturday from a computer named *biko*), and then displayed the copyright notice, my customized message of the day, an alert that mail was waiting, and a nice fortune cookie courtesy of Henry David Thoreau before presenting the user with a shell prompt.

It is possible to bypass these messages at login time. As the user *genisis*, I'll create an empty file called .hushlogin in my home directory:

```
% cd
% touch .hushlogin
```

I'll then logout and log back in again:

```
% exit
login: genisis
Password:
Alimony is a system by which, when two people make a mistake, one of them keeps paying
for it.
-- Peggy Joyce
```

Notice that the only thing the user *genisis* received this time was the fortune cookie. Remember, that fortune cookies are invoked by the shell's configuration file, so it came courtesy of the user's shell. However, this login may be a bit too quiet as the user won't receive any messages regarding pending password changes or any messages the administrator may have included in the message of the day.

utmp and wtmp

The second login record file is /var/run/utmp. This file contains information regarding users that are currently logged in and is read by the **w**, **who**, and **users** commands. Let's take a closer look at each of these utilities, starting with **users**:

```
% users
genisis test1 test2 test3
```

The **users** command is useful if you just need to know which users are logged in and don't want to sort through all the details of where they are logged in and what they are doing. However, if you need to know who is logged into which terminals, use the **w** command:[3]

```
% w
5:01PM up 3:30, 7 users, load averages:  0.04, 0.06, 0.02
USER    TTY  FROM LOGIN@ IDLE WHAT
genisis v0   -       1:31PM 1    more
genisis v1   -       1:32PM -    w
genisis v2   -       1:32PM 3:11 xinit /home/genisis/.x
genisis v3   -       1:46PM -    pico filename
test3   v4   -       4:51PM -    -tcsh (tcsh)
test1   p0   biko    4:50PM 10   -tcsh (tcsh)
test2   p1   biko    4:51PM 1    -tcsh (tcsh)
```

There are currently seven active logins on my FreeBSD system. The user *genisis* is physically sitting at my FreeBSD box and has logged into the first four virtual terminals (v0-v3). The user *test3* is also logged on locally using virtual terminal number 5 (v4). The user *test1* has logged into the first network terminal (p0) from a computer named *biko* and the user *test2* has logged into the second network terminal (p1) from the computer named *biko*.

The IDLE column shows how long it has been since a user typed anything at a terminal, and the WHAT column shows what process is currently running on each terminal. To find out all the processes running on each terminal, use the **-d** switch. Here I'll show the first ten lines of output:

```
% w -d | head
5:10PM up 3:39, 7 users, load averages:  0.00, 0.00, 0.00
USER      TTY    FROM LOGIN@  IDLE   WHAT
          219    -csh (csh)
          1085   _su (csh)
          1107   man w
          1108   sh -c /usr/bin/zcat /usr/share/man/cat1/w.1.gz | more
          1110   more
genisis   v0     -      1:31PM 10     more
          220    -csh (csh)
          1138   w -d
```

The **who** command gives output similar to the **w** command as it shows the user's login name, terminal name, time of login, and which computer the user logged in from:

```
% who
genisis    ttyv0   Feb  3 13:31
genisis    ttyv1   Feb  3 13:32
genisis    ttyv2   Feb  3 13:32
```

---

[3]More examples and details about **w** are in section 2.9.

```
genisis     ttyv3   Feb   3 13:46
test3       ttyv4   Feb   3 16:51
test1       ttyp0   Feb   3 16:50     (biko)
test2       ttyp1   Feb   3 16:51     (biko)
```

You'll receive different results if you run the **who** command with the **am i** option:

```
% who am i
genisis     ttyv1   Feb   13:32
```

It looks like *genisis* ran the above command at the second virtual terminal.

You can also tell the **who** command to read the /var/log/wtmp file instead of the default /var/run/utmp file:

```
% who /var/log/wtmp | head
genisis     ttyv0   Feb   3 13:25
shutdown            Feb   3 13:30
            ttyv0   Feb   3 13:30
reboot              Feb   3 13:31
genisis     ttyv0   Feb   3 13:31
genisis     ttyv1   Feb   3 13:32
genisis     ttyv2   Feb   3 13:32
genisis     ttyp0   Feb   3 13:34     (biko)
genisis     ttyv3   Feb   3 13:46
genisis     ttyp1   Feb   3 15:04     (biko)
```

Notice that this output also contains the times of reboots and shutdowns as the /var/log/wtmp file makes a record for every login, logout, date change, shutdown, and reboot. You can also access the information in the /var/log/wtmp file by using the **last** and **ac** commands. Let's compare the above output to the output from the **last** command:

```
% last | head
genisis ttyv4 Sun Feb 4 08:25 still logged in
genisis ttyv3 Sat Feb 3 20:43 still logged in
genisis ttyv2 Sat Feb 3 20:40 still logged in
genisis ttyv1 Sat Feb 3 20:40 still logged in
genisis ttyv0 Sat Feb 3 20:40 still logged in
reboot ~ Sat Feb 3 20:40
shutdown ~ Sat Feb 3 20:39
test3 ttyv4 Sat Feb 3 16:51 - 17:36 (00:44)
test2 ttyp1 biko Sat Feb 3 16:51 - shutdown (03:48)
test1 ttyp0 biko Sat Feb 3 16:50 - shutdown (03:48)
```

You'll notice that the entries are in reverse order, so you see the most recent events first. The last three columns are interesting as they show what time the user logged in, what time they logged out, and the duration of the login session. It also makes note if the user was forcibly logged out due to a shutdown or reboot.

The **last** command also supports several switches; a useful switch is the word **reboot**:

```
% last reboot
reboot                    Sat Feb  3 20:40
reboot                    Sat Feb  3 13:31
reboot                    Sat Feb  3 13:25
wtmp begins Sat Feb  3 13:25:04 2007
```

This will give a nice summary of the times and dates your FreeBSD system rebooted.

The ac Utility

The **ac** utility adds up the connection times that are recorded in /var/log/wtmp and can be used to get a rough idea of which users are using the most connection time. If you run **ac** without any switches, you'll be given a number that represents a total of all connection times contained within /var/log/wtmp:

```
% ac
        total   165.04
```

To see the total number of connection hours on a daily basis:

```
% ac -d
Feb  3  total       124.42
Feb  4  total        41.52
```

And to see the total hours for each user for the entire period of the /var/log/wtmp file:

```
% ac -p
        test1       4.12
        test2       4.11
        test3       0.75
        genisis   156.06
        total     165.04
```

To summarize: The utilities **w**, **who**, and **users** display information contained in the file /var/run/utmp; the utilities **last** and **ac** display the information contained in /var/log/wtmp.

Locking your Terminal

The last thing I'd like to mention in this section is locking unused terminals. Normally when a user finishes using a terminal, he or she will logout using either the **exit** or **logout** command. But sometimes a user needs to leave a terminal for a few minutes before finishing a session. It is good practice to lock your terminal if you need to be away from it, and your FreeBSD system comes with the **lock** utility for this purpose. If you just type **lock**, you'll be prompted for a Key (password) to unlock the terminal:

```
% lock
Key:
Again:
lock: /dev/ttyp0 biko timeout in 15 minutes
time now is Sun Feb  4 11:48:34 EST 2007
Key:
```

The terminal will now be locked for either 15 minutes or until the user returns and enters the key. If you don't want to be prompted to create a key when you invoke the lock utility, use **lock -p**; your key will be your login password. If you want to lock a terminal for more than 15 minutes, use **lock -n**. The only way to bypass a locked terminal is to know the key, wait for the timeout period, or to have the superuser send a kill signal to the PID of the **lock** process from a different terminal.

There is also a utility called **vlock** that you can install. As the superuser and while connected to the Internet:

```
# pkg_add -r vlock
```

Once installed, you can leave the superuser account. To use **vlock**:

```
% vlock
This TTY is now locked.
Use Alt-function keys to switch to other virtual consoles.
Please enter the password to unlock.
genisis's Password:
```

You'll note that this utility only uses the user's password as the key and that the terminal will be locked until a password is entered. However, the superuser can unlock this terminal directly by entering *root* and then the password for the *root* account:

```
genisis's Password: root
root's Password:
```

The **vlock** utility can also lock all the virtual terminals on a FreeBSD system without affecting network logins. If I type **vlock -a**, my screen will look like this:

```
The entire console display is now completely locked.
You will not be able to switch to another virtual console.
Please enter the password to unlock.
genisis's password:
```

At this point, my **Alt Function** keys no longer work and the machine is unavailable for users who physically walk up to my FreeBSD machine unless they happen to know the password for the user *genisis* or the *root* account. This feature is handy if your FreeBSD box is acting as a server as it will still accept network logins.

Additional Resources

Original Article:

```
http://www.onlamp.com/pub/a/bsd/2001/02/14/FreeBSD_Basics.html
```

2.9 Discovering System Processes

This section takes a look at processes. We'll see what a process is and how to view information regarding your processes. Then we'll look at doing useful things with this process information.

Like any other Unix system, FreeBSD is a multitasking, multiuser operating system. This means that a number of users can each be running a number of programs at the same time. It is the kernel's responsibility to ensure that each of these programs gets a fair turn at your computer's CPU and that each user receives the correct results from their program's execution.

The Process File System

When you start a program, it is loaded into RAM and is called a process, as its instructions need to be processed by the CPU. In order for the kernel to keep track of which programs are running and which user started which program, each process is assigned a process ID, or PID. Usually, the PID will be associated with, and have the same permissions as, the user who started the program and that user's primary group.

Not all programs are started by users; some are started by your FreeBSD system at boot time and are called daemons. Also, some programs will either start other programs or other instances of themselves. The original program is called the parent process, and the other processes are called its child processes.

When you installed FreeBSD, the process filesystem, or procfs, was created for you. However, depending upon your FreeBSD version, it may not be automatically mounted for you. If your /proc directory is empty, the superuser can mount procfs by adding the following line to /etc/fstab:

```
proc        /proc        procfs  rw        0  0
```

Once the superuser has saved these changes, **mount /proc** should mount procfs. If you get an error, check the line you added for typos.

You may have noticed that this filesystem is always 100% full when you display your free disk space like so:

```
% df | grep proc
Filesystem    Size   Used  Avail Capacity  Mounted on
procfs        4.0K   4.0K  0B    100%      /proc
```

This is normal, as the process filesystem is not supposed to contain files created by users; instead, it is read by commands such as **ps** and **w** so they can display which processes are currently running. Notice that the proc filesystem is mounted on /proc. Let's take a look at the contents of /proc using **ls** with the **-C** switch to sort the display into columns and the **-F** switch to mark directories with a trailing slash:

```
# ls -CF /proc
./       175/    2072/    301/     315/
../      176/    227/     307/     316/
0/       177/    261/     308/     317/
1/       178/    27/      309/     318/
110/     181/    273/     310/     319/
163/     197/    290/     311/     320/
166/     199/    292/     312/     4/
171/     2/      3/       313/     5/
173/     202/    30/      314/     curproc@
```

Note that every entry except one is a directory whose name is a number; that number refers to the PID of a running process. The last entry, curproc, is a symbolic link since it ends with the @ symbol. To find out what it is linked to, type:

```
# ls -l /proc/curproc
lr--r--r--  1 root       wheel 0 Apr  16 14:15 curproc@ -> 2072
```

It would appear that curproc is a symbolic link to another process. If you check out **man 5 procfs** you'll read that curproc refers to the current process making the lookup request; that is, my original **ls** command had a PID of 2072.

Now, let's see what type of information is recorded for each of the running processes by viewing the contents of one of these directories:

```
# ls -CF /proc/197
./        ctl        file@      mem       regs
../       dbregs     fpregs     note      rlimit
cmdline   etype      map        notepg    status
```

These all seem to be regular files except for the symbolic link named file; however, we have no idea what type of data they contain. Let's find out:

```
# file /proc/197/*
cmdline:  empty
ctl:      empty
dbregs:   MS Windows COFF Unknown CPU
etype:    empty
file:     symbolic link to /usr/sbin/inetd
fpregs:   data
map:      empty
mem:      empty
note:     empty
notepg:   empty
regs:     data
rlimit:   empty
status:   empty
```

Note: Even if your FreeBSD system does not mount the proc file system, it still keeps track of processes. You can use the **sysctl -a | more** command to view this information.

Process Utilities

It doesn't look like we'll be able to open up any of these files ourselves as they don't contain readable text. This makes sense for a filesystem that keeps track of data useful to the kernel. Even though you can't view the data directly, you can use the **w** and **ps** commands, which do know how to interpret and display the data contained within these files.

Let's start with the **w** command:[4]

---

[4]Also see section 2.8 for more **w** examples.

```
% whatis w
w(1) - display who is logged in and what they are doing
% w
10:43AM  up 17:50, 4 users, load averages: 0.00, 0.00, 0.00
USER     TTY     FROM    LOGIN@    IDLE    WHAT
genisis  v0      -       9:46AM    -       w
genisis  v1      -       Sat04PM   2:02    -csh (csh)
genisis  v2      -       Sat08PM   -       -csh (csh)
genisis  v3      -       Sat05PM   2:02    -csh (csh)
```

The first line displays the current time of day, how long your FreeBSD system has been up, the number of users currently logged in, and the number of jobs in the run queue averaged over 1, 5, and 15 minutes.

The remaining lines show the user's login name, the name of the terminal that user is logged in to, the host from which the user logged in, the time the user logged on, the time since the user last typed anything, and the name and arguments of the current process.

If we use the **-d** switch with the **w** command, we'll receive a slightly different output, as **w** will display all the processes that user has running on their terminal, like so:

```
% w -d
10:55AM  up 18:02, 4 users, load averages: 0.00, 0.00, 0.00
USER     TTY     FROM    LOGIN@    IDLE    WHAT
         2100                              -csh (csh)
         2104                              -su (csh)
         2235                              w -d
genisis  v0      -       9:46AM    -       w -d
         313                               -csh (csh)
genisis  v1      -       Sat04PM   2:14    -csh (csh)
         314                               -csh (csh)
genisis  v2      -       Sat08PM   -        -csh (csh)
         315                                -csh (csh)
genisis  v3      -       Sat05PM   2:14     -csh (csh)
```

The numbers under the TTY column are the PIDs of the processes. If you read the manpage for **w**, you'll find that it is a good utility to get a quick overview of who is currently logged in to which terminals and what they might be doing; however, it was not intended to provide detailed process usage information, as that is the job of the **ps** utility. If you simply type **ps** you'll receive basic information on the processes you have started, like so:

```
% ps
  PID      TT    STAT   TIME        COMMAND
  2100     v0    Ss     0:00.13     -csh (csh)
  2280     v0    R+     0:00.00     ps
  313      v1    Is+    0:00.13     -csh (csh)
  314      v2    Is+    0:00.21     -csh (csh)
  315      v3    Is     0:00.12     -csh (csh)
```

Reading the output from left to right, the default **ps** displays the PID, the name and type of the terminal, state, cpu time (including both user and system time), and the associated command for processes started by the user who ran the **ps** command.

State is a new term which can provide valuable information about your running processes. When reading the state (STAT) column, the first letter indicates the run state of the process. The valid values are:

- D - a process in disk (or other short term, uninterruptible) wait

- I - an idle process (sleeping for longer than about 20 seconds)

- L - a process which is waiting to acquire a lock

- R - a runnable process

- S - a process that is sleeping for less than about 20 seconds

- T - a stopped process

- W - an idle interrupt thread

- Z - a dead (zombie) process

In my output, I have one running process (the **ps** command), one C shell that hasn't done anything within the last 20 seconds, and three C shells that haven't done anything in more than 20 seconds. The + indicates that three of my processes are foreground processes, and the *s* indicates that four of my processes are session leaders. Don't worry if some of the state information doesn't hold profound meaning for you; some of it won't unless you are a programmer.

Note that the default **ps** will only show your processes; to view all the user processes running on your computer, use the **-a** switch:

```
% ps -a
  PID      TT    STAT    TIME        COMMAND
  2100     v0    Ss      0:00.18     -csh (csh)
  2403     v0    R+      0:00.00     ps -a
  313      v1    Is+     0:00.13     -csh (csh)
  314      v2    Is+     0:00.25     -csh (csh)
  315      v3    Is+     0:00.12     -csh (csh)
  316      v4    Is+     0:00.01     /usr/libexec/getty Pc ttyv4
  317      v5    Is+     0:00.01     /usr/libexec/getty Pc ttyv5
  318      v6    Is+     0:00.01     /usr/libexec/getty Pc ttyv6
  319      v7    Is+     0:00.01     /usr/libexec/getty Pc ttyv7
```

You may find it more useful to see which users started which commands; to do this, include the **-u** switch:

```
% ps -au
USER       PID    %CPU   %MEM   VSZ    RSS   TT     STAT   STARTED   TIME       COMMAND
genisis    2404   0.0    0.2    428    244   v0     R+     12:26PM   0:00.00    ps -au
root       273    0.0    0.4    620    448   con-   I+     4:53PM    0:00.02    /bin/sh /usr/loc
root       292    0.0    0.4    624    452   con-   I+     4:53PM    0:00.01    /bin/sh /usr/loc
<snip>
```

I find the output easier to read if I include the **-c** switch as it will only show the name of the command, instead of the path:

```
% ps -auc
USER      PID    %CPU   %MEM   VSZ   RSS  TT     STAT   STARTED   TIME     COMMAND
genisis   2414   0.0    0.2    428   244  v0     R+     12:31PM   0:00.00  ps
root      273    0.0    0.4    620   448  con-   I+     4:53PM    0:00.02  sh
root      292    0.0    0.4    624   452  con-   I+     4:53PM    0:00.01  sh
<snip>
```

We're still not seeing all of the processes on this system, though. To do this, include the **-x** switch to display the running daemons; this will be a longer output, so we'll pipe it to the **head** utility to see the first 10:

```
% ps -aucx | head
USER      PID    %CPU   %MEM   VSZ   RSS  TT     STAT   STARTED   TIME          COMMAND
root      10     98.2   0.0    0     8    ??     RL     Sat11AM   11463:00.06   idle
root      0      0.0    0.0    0     0    ??     WLs    Sat11AM   0:00.00       swapper
root      1      0.0    0.2    532   304  ??     ILs    Sat11AM   0:00.06       init
root      2      0.0    0.0    0     8    ??     DL     Sat11AM   0:00.11       g_event
root      3      0.0    0.0    0     8    ??     DL     Sat11AM   0:00.00       g_up
root      4      0.0    0.0    0     8    ??     DL     Sat11AM   0:00.20       g_down
root      5      0.0    0.0    0     8    ??     DL     Sat11AM   0:09.53       kqueue taskq
root      6      0.0    0.0    0     8    ??     DL     Sat11AM   0:09.53       acpi_task_0
root      7      0.0    0.0    0     8    ??     DL     Sat11AM   0:09.53       acpi_task_1
root      8      0.0    0.0    0     8    ??     DL     Sat11AM   0:09.53       acpi_task_2
```

Wow, no wonder the kernel needs to assign PIDs to keep track of what is happening on your FreeBSD system. If you instead pipe this output to **more** (to see it all) and find it hard to remember which column is which, add an **-h** to your switches to force **ps** to rewrite the column headings on every screen.

You may have noticed that our columns changed when we introduced the **-u** switch; the most notable new columns are %CPU and %MEM. Sometimes you may find it more useful for **ps** to display the processes by CPU or memory usage, rather than in numerical order. To sort by memory usage, include the **-m** switch; to sort by CPU usage, include the **-r** switch.

The switches I've mentioned are the most commonly used switches for the **ps** utility; you can read the manpage for **ps** to see what other switches are available so you can find out which combo of switches tweaks the output to your liking.

When using **ps**, you will most likely come across processes that you've never heard of before; use the **whatis** command to see if there are any manpages to shed light on the mystery. For example, being the very curious type, I tried the following:

```
% whatis init kqueue
init(8)                        - process control initialization
kqueue(2), kevent(2)           - kernel event notification mechanism
```

which kept me busy reading for a while.

Process Signals

When processes talk to each other, it is called interprocess communication. Processes aren't allowed to say just anything to each other; instead, your FreeBSD system comes with 32 possible predefined messages. These messages are called signals; you can view these signals with this command:

```
% kill -1
HUP INT QUIT ILL TRAP ABRT EMT FPE KILL BUS SEGV SYS PIPE ALRM TERM URG STOP TSTP CONT
CHLD TTIN TTOU IO XCPU XFSZ VTALRM PROF WINCH INFO USR1 USR2 LWP
```

Each signal has a numerical equivalent, and the signals are listed in numerical order; therefore, HUP=1, INT=2, etc. Processes are allowed to send these signals to each other; users are also allowed to send these signals to processes.

To find out what each of these signals does, read **man 2 sigaction** or **man 3 signal**. Table 2.5 summarizes each of the 32 signals, their resultant actions, and a brief description of each. Although users can send any of these signals, I've included an asterisk next to the signals most commonly used by users.

Table 2.5: Signals

Signal Name	#	Default Action	Description
*HUP	1	terminate process	terminal line hangup
*INT	2	terminate process	interrupt program
*QUIT	3	create core image	quit program
ILL	4	create core image	illegal instruction
TRAP	5	create core image	trace trap
ABRT	6	create core image	abort(3) call
EMT	7	create core image	emulate instruction executed
FPE	8	create core image	floating-point exception
*KILL	9	terminate process	kill program
BUS	10	create core image	bus error
SEGV	11	create core image	segmentation violation
SYS	12	create core image	non-existent system call
PIPE	13	terminate process	write on a pipe with no reader
ALRM	14	terminate process	real-time timer expired
*TERM	15	terminate process	software termination signal
URG	16	discard signal	urgent condition
*STOP	17	stop process	stop (cannot be ignored)
*TSTP	18	stop process	stop keyboard signal
CONT	19	discard signal	continue after stop
CHLD	20	discard signal	child status has changed
TTIN	21	stop process	background read attempted

TTOU	22	stop process	background write attempted
IO	23	discard signal	I/O is possible
XCPU	24	terminate process	CPU time limit exceeded
XFSZ	25	terminate process	file size limit exceeded
VTALRM	26	terminate process	virtual time alarm
PROF	27	terminate process	profiling timer alarm
WINCH	28	discard signal	Window size change
INFO	29	discard signal	status request from keyboard
USR1	30	terminate process	User defined signal 1
USR2	31	terminate process	User defined signal 2
THR	32	terminate process	thread interrupt

Some signals are used so often by users that they have been mapped to control characters. To view your control character mappings, look at the last four lines of the output of:

```
% stty -e
<snip>
discard dsusp   eof     eol     eol2    erase   erase2  intr    kill
^O      ^Y      ^D      <undef> <undef> ^H      ^H      ^C      ^U
lnext   min     quit    reprint start   status  stop    susp    time    werase
^V      1       ^\      ^R      ^Q      ^T      ^S      ^Z      0       ^W
```

The ^ (carat) symbol means to press your **Ctrl** key at the same time as the letter that follows it. Note that three signals have been mapped as control characters:

- ^C has been mapped to the INT signal, or signal 2

- ^\ has been mapped to the QUIT signal, or signal 3

- ^Z has been mapped to the TSTP signal, or signal 18 (even though it's called *susp* here)

Don't confuse the word *kill* in this output with the KILL signal (signal 9). ^U will erase an entire line, not send a signal 9. To prove this to yourself, type a long string of words at your prompt, then do a ^U.

Communicating with Processes

So, how do you send signals that haven't been mapped to control characters? Use the **kill** command.

```
% whatis kill
kill(1)    - terminate or signal a process
kill(2)    - send signal to a process
```

There's a couple of different ways to use **kill**; if you simply type:

```
% kill PID
```

the default TERM signal will be sent to the process with the PID that you indicated. If you wish to change the type of signal to send, you can specify the signal either by its name or by its number like so:

```
% kill -signal_name PID
% kill -signal_number PID
```

So:

```
% kill PID
% kill -TERM PID
% kill -15 PID
```

are all equivalent commands. Remember that Unix is case-sensitive; if you type this you'll receive an error:

```
% kill -term PID
term: Unknown signal; kill -l lists all signals.
```

So, now that we've seen the 32 possible messages and how to send them, let's look at examples of reasons you would want to send a signal to a process. Often when you're working your way through the FreeBSD Handbook or a tutorial, you'll learn how to make changes to a configuration file and will then be prompted to send a HUP signal. Most processes only read their configuration file when they first start up; the HUP signal tells a process to stop running; when that process restarts, it will reread its configuration file and your changes to that file will take effect. [5] Also, every time you log out of a terminal, a HUP signal is sent to all processes running on that terminal; this means that all processes that were running on that terminal will be stopped.

Note: If your FreeBSD system is 5.x or higher see if that process has an rc script before sending a HUP signal. Most operating system processes have a rc script in /etc/rc.d and many applications you've installed through ports or packages have a rc script in /usr/local/etc/rc.d. If there is a script, it is preferable to run it with the **reload** option than to use the **kill** command to send the HUP signal.

Sometimes you may start a process and wish to stop it before it is finished. For example, in a spurt of inspiration you might decide that you want to see the name of every file on your FreeBSD system, so you type this as superuser:

```
# find / -print | more
```

However, you soon grow tired of pressing the spacebar and decide that you really didn't want to see all of your files at this time. In other words, you want to send an interrupt signal. One way to do this is:

---

[5]Note that only some programs are written to listen to the HUP signal to mean reload configurations. Read the manpage or documentation for your desired program for information.

```
^C
```

You'll know that your INT signal worked as you'll get your prompt back.

Retry the same find command, but this time send a signal 3 like so:

```
^\
Quit  (core dumped)
```

If you use **Alt-F1** to return to the console, you'll see a message similar to this:

```
Nov 19 13:50:09 genisis /kernel:  pid 806 (find), uid 1001:  exited on signal 3
Nov 19 13:50:09 genisis /kernel:  pid 807 (more), uid 1001:  exited on signal 3 (core
dumped)
```

And if you do a directory listing at your original terminal, you should see a file called more.core. Normally, you won't be sending a signal 3 to a process unless you're a programmer and know how to use the debugger. I included the example to show the difference between a signal 2 and a signal 3; you can safely delete that *.core file.

Interprocess communication isn't much different than any other type of communication. You or another process can send a signal requesting a desired result, but it is up to the process receiving the signal to decide what it wants to do with that signal. Remember that processes are simply running programs; most programs use something called a signal handler to decide how and when to respond to signals. Usually if you send some type of termination signal, the signal handler will try to gracefully close all the files that process has opened to prevent data loss before the process itself closes. Sometimes, the signal handler will decide to just ignore your signal and will refuse to terminate the process.

However, some signals can't be ignored; for example, signal 9 and signal 17. Let's say that you wish to stop a process you've started, so you used **ps | grep** to find the PID of the process, used **kill** to send a TERM signal, then repeated your **ps | grep** to ensure it worked.

However, the second **grep** still shows that PID, meaning your TERM signal was ignored by that process. Either one of these commands should fix it:

```
% kill -9 PID
% kill -KILL PID
```

If you now repeat your **grep** command, you should just have your prompt echoed back at you, meaning that PID was indeed terminated.

You may ask, "Why not just always send a signal 9 if it can't be ignored?" Signal 9 does indeed kill a process, but it doesn't give it time to gracefully save all of its work first, meaning that you may lose some data. It's better to try sending another type of terminating signal first, and save signal 9 for those processes that stubbornly refuse to terminate. Also, remember that as a regular user you will only be able to send signals to processes that are owned by you. The superuser can send a signal to any process.

There may be times when you wish to terminate all the processes you own; this has different ramifications depending on whether you are a regular user or the superuser.

Let's demonstrate as a regular user. Log in to four different terminals and do a **ps** command to view your PIDs.

If I use a PID of *-1* when I invoke the **kill** command, I will broadcast the signal I specify to all of my processes. If I send a TERM signal like so:

```
% kill -1
```

then check my results with the **ps** command I may find that some of the original PIDs were terminated and that some of processes ignored that TERM signal. However, this is a bit more aggressive:

```
% kill -KILL -1
```

If you try this and scroll through your original four terminals, you'll see the login prompt at three of them. This last command killed all processes except the process you executed the **kill** command from, that is, all processes except the C shell you ran the **kill** command in.

You'll note that if you make a typo and forget the dash you'll receive this error as a regular user:

```
% kill 1
1: Operation not permitted
```

-1 is the special PID that represents all of your processes; *1* is the PID of the process named **init**. Only the superuser can kill the init process. Also, the superuser should only kill init if the superuser knows what he is doing!

Now let's see what happens if we repeat this exercise as the superuser. First, I'll run the **ps -acux** command on my test computer that is running all kinds of neat stuff so I'm guaranteed to see lots of processes.

Then I'll send the KILL signal to the special PID *-1* as the superuser:

```
% su
Password:
# kill -9 -1
```

That command was a little scarier as it even kicked me out of the C shell I executed the **kill** command from. Once I logged back in, I assessed the damage by repeating the **ps -acux** command.

When the superuser sends a signal to *-1*, it is sent to every process except the system processes. If that signal happened to be the KILL signal, you would be hearing complaints from users who happened to have a file open at the time and lost their data.

This is one of the reasons only the superuser is allowed to run the **reboot** and **halt** commands. When one of these commands is issued, a TERM signal is sent to PID *-1* to give all processes a chance to save their data; this is followed by a KILL signal to ensure that any remaining processes are terminated.

Note: Newer versions of FreeBSD include the NetBSD commands **pgrep** and **pkill** which allow you to search for and signal processes by their name instead of their PID.

Additional Resources

Original Articles:

http://www.onlamp.com/pub/a/bsd/2000/11/15/FreeBSD_Basics.html

http://www.onlamp.com/pub/a/bsd/2000/11/22/FreeBSD_Basics.html

2.10 The System Startup Daemon: init

A lot of neat stuff happens when you boot up your computer into FreeBSD. I won't cover all the details here, as the FreeBSD Handbook does an excellent job of explaining the bootup process. When you boot your computer, you have probably noticed that the kernel does a hardware probe and prints its results to your terminal. Once this probe is finished, the kernel starts two processes: process 0 (swapper) and process 1 (**init**).

Introducing init

The daemon responsible for process control initialization is **init**; without it, no other processes would be able to start. At boot time, **init** has two important jobs to do: first, it launches the startup scripts controlled by **rc**, then it initializes the terminals so they will be available for logins by users. Let's pick apart these functions, starting with **rc**:

```
% whatis rc
rc(8)     - command scripts for auto-reboot and daemon startup
```

The main script is /etc/rc and it calls the startup scripts located in /etc/rc.d. Let's take a closer look at this file:

```
% more /etc/rc
# System startup script run by init on autoboot
# or after single-user.
# Output and error are redirected to console by init,
# and the console is the controlling terminal.
# Note that almost all of the user-configurable behavior
# is no longer in this file, but rather in /etc/defaults/rc.conf.
# Please check that file first before contemplating any changes
# here.  If you do need to change this file for some reason, we
# would like to know about it.
```

OK, that's pretty clear; looks like we're not supposed to muck about with this file ourselves. There must be some pretty important stuff in here necessary for the proper bootup of our system. Let's skip through the file and look at some of its highlights to find out what actually is happening during this portion of startup. Note that **init** is recording all output and error messages to the terminal when the **rc** script is actually processed during bootup.

One of the first things **rc** does is set a path variable so it can find the executables on your FreeBSD system:

```
PATH=/sbin:/bin:/usr/sbin:/usr/bin
```

It then reads (sources) /etc/rc.subr to find the locations of any rc.conf files and load their contents:

```
. /etc/rc.subr
echo "Loading configuration files."
load_rc_config 'XXX'
```

The rest of the script calls **rcorder** to order the startup scripts in /etc/rc.d and then run the scripts to start the operating system followed by the third-party application processes.

Once we've reached the end of /etc/rc, **rc**'s job is finished. Let's recap what happened here: **init** called the **rc** script which read several global and local configuration files in order to properly create an environment where the system daemons and other processes could be started. Your operating system is now up and running, but at this point, there is no environment where a user can actually interact with that operating system. This is where **init**'s second important function kicks in.

Terminals

The configuration file /etc/ttys will be read to determine which terminals need to be initialized. Unlike /etc/rc, this file is often edited by the superuser to ensure that the desired terminals will be initialized by **init**.

In order to understand this file, we must realize that there are three types of terminals on your FreeBSD system. Virtual terminals start with ttyv followed by a number or letter; these are the terminals available for users physically seated at the FreeBSD computer. By default, the first of these virtual terminals, ttyv0, represents the console. Serial or dial-up terminals start with ttyd followed by a number; these terminals are available for users accessing your FreeBSD system remotely, using a modem. The last type of terminal is a pseudo or network terminal; these start with ttyp followed by a number or a letter and are used to access your FreeBSD computer over a network connection.

If we look at this file we'll see that it has been divided into three sections, with a section for each of the three types of terminals. Each section also has four columns, which I've summarized in Table 2.6.

Table 2.6: /etc/ttys Configuration

Column Name	What it Represents
name	The name of the terminal device.
getty	The program to start running on the terminal, which is typically **getty**. Other common entries include **xdm**, which starts the X Window System, or none, meaning no program.
type	For virtual consoles, the correct type is *cons25*. Other common values include *network* on pseudo-terminals, *dialup* for incoming modem ports, and *unknown* when the terminal type a user will try to connect with cannot be predetermined.
status	Must be *on* or *off*. If on, init will run the program specified in the getty column. If the word "secure" appears, this tty allows *root* login; to prevent *root* logins, use the word "insecure."

Let's start deciphering this file by looking at the virtual terminal section; note that it starts by setting up the console:

```
# If console is marked "insecure", then init will ask
# for the root password when going to single-user mode.
console none                            unknown off secure
```

If the **fsck** command runs into problems during bootup, **init** will put your FreeBSD system into single-user mode so the *root* user can fix the problem. If you set the console at *insecure* instead of the default *secure*, **init** will require the *root* password before you can continue.

```
ttyv0   "/usr/libexec/getty Pc"          cons25  on   secure
# Virtual terminals
ttyv1   "/usr/libexec/getty Pc"          cons25  on   secure
ttyv2   "/usr/libexec/getty Pc"          cons25  on   secure
ttyv3   "/usr/libexec/getty Pc"          cons25  on   secure
ttyv4   "/usr/libexec/getty Pc"          cons25  on   secure
ttyv5   "/usr/libexec/getty Pc"          cons25  on   secure
ttyv6   "/usr/libexec/getty Pc"          cons25  on   secure
ttyv7   "/usr/libexec/getty Pc"          cons25  on   secure
ttyv8   "/usr/X11R6/bin/xdm -nodaemon"   xterm   off  secure
```

You'll note that on my FreeBSD system I have eight virtual terminals in addition to the console; I can access each by pressing **Alt** and one of the **Function** keys. For example, **Alt-F1** accesses the console, **Alt-F2** accesses `ttyv1`, **Alt-F3** accesses `ttyv2`, etc. If I start an X session, it can be accessed by using **Alt-F8**. If I were to change the word *off* to *on* at `ttyv8`, I would receive an X terminal instead of the console at boot time. I could still use my **Alt Function** keys to access the other terminals. All of my virtual terminals are marked as *secure*, meaning they will accept *root* logins.

Now let's move on down to the dial-up terminals:

```
# Serial terminals
# The 'dialup' keyword identifies dialin lines to login, fingerd etc.
ttyd0   "/usr/libexec/getty std.9600"   dialup  off secure
ttyd1   "/usr/libexec/getty std.9600"   dialup  off secure
ttyd2   "/usr/libexec/getty std.9600"   dialup  off secure
ttyd3   "/usr/libexec/getty std.9600"   dialup  off secure
```

You'll notice that I have four available dial-up terminals, but they are all turned off. If I wanted users to access my FreeBSD computer using a modem, I'd have to turn at least one of these terminals on. I would also have to decide if I wanted these users to be able to log in as *root*; if not, I would change the word *secure* to *insecure*. You'll note that the getty column includes the number 9600, which represents a data transfer rate of 9600 bps. Since most modern modems are capable of higher rates, I would also probably change that number to 57600.

The last section in `/etc/ttys` is the network or pseudo terminal section. You'll note that there are a lot of these, 255 to be precise, that range from:

```
# Pseudo terminals
ttyp0   none          network
```

to

```
ttySv   none          network
```

and that none of them have been enabled by default.

If you ever become the superuser in order to make changes to `/etc/ttys`, you will have to remember to send a HUP signal to **init** so that it will use your changes. To do this, type:

```
# kill -1 1
```

as -1 is signal 1 (HUP) and 1 is process 1 (**init**).

The getty Program

Now, what is this **getty** program that keeps being mentioned in /etc/ttys? The description in **man 8 getty** states it well:

```
DESCRIPTION
The getty utility is called by init(8) to open and initialize the tty line, read a
login name, and invoke login(1).
```

So, **init** reads /etc/ttys and starts a **getty** process on every terminal you've told it to in that configuration file. Monitoring that terminal to see if anyone tries to log in is **getty**'s job. If someone does, **getty** will start the **login** program to verify that user's login name and password. If those check out, **login** will start up that user's login shell and place the user in their home directory. Once the user has a shell, or command interpreter, they now have a way of interacting with the operating system. It is now up to the shell to interpret a user's input and ensure that any necessary processes are started.

When a user logs out of their login shell, **init** is called in to start another **getty** process which will patiently monitor the terminal for another login attempt.

Let's tie together this whole process by looking at the output of the **ps** command on a freshly booted, default install of FreeBSD 6.2. If you include the **-ax** switches to include the system daemons you should see entries for: swapper, **init**, g_event, g_up, g_down, kqueue, acpi_task, yarrow, pagedaemon, vnlru, syncer, **adjkerntz**, **devd**, **syslogd**, **cron**, **sendmail**, **csh**, **ps**, and the terminals ttyv1 through ttyv7.

You should now be able to recognize most of these processes: swapper has a PID of 0 and **init** has a PID of 1. The **adjkerntz**, **syslogd**, **cron**, and **sendmail** processes were all successfully started by **rc**. I needed to run the **ps** command from a shell; in my case, it was from the C shell. **getty** processes are waiting for logins on virtual terminals 1-7. There is no **getty** process running on virtual terminal 8 as this terminal was marked *off* in /etc/ttys.

Additional Resources

Original Article:

http://www.onlamp.com/pub/a/bsd/2000/11/28/FreeBSD_Basics.html

FreeBSD Handbook: Booting Process

http://www.freebsd.org/doc/en_US.ISO8859-1/books/handbook/boot.html

FreeBSD FAQ: What is a virtual console and how do I make more?

http://www.freebsd.org/doc/en_US.ISO8859-1/books/faq/x.html#VIRTUAL-CONSOLE

FreeBSD Handbook: Dial-in Service

http://www.freebsd.org/doc/en_US.ISO8859-1/books/handbook/dialup.html

2.11 Where the Log Files Live

You know there are logs on your FreeBSD system somewhere; you've probably also heard that it is a good thing to read these logs on a regular basis. You may have even heard horror stories about logs filling up a user's hard drive. So how do we go about finding these mysterious logs?

Default Logs

Let's start by taking a look at the layout of our FreeBSD system using the trusty old command which explains our directory hierarchy:

```
% man hier
```

We'll then search for the word log and our first hit shows that the multi-purpose logs live in /var:

```
/log
   /var/    multi-purpose log, temporary, transient, and spool files
```

If you repeat the search by typing the **n** key, you'll see there is a subdirectory of /var called log/:

```
n
      log/     miscellaneous system log files
```

We're interested in the system log files, so let's take a look at the contents of /var/log:

```
% ls /var/log
Xorg.0.log       lpd-errs         sendmail.st
auth.log         maillog          setuid.today
cron             messages         setuid.yesterday
cups             mount.today      slip.log
debug.log        pf.today         userlog
dmesg.today      ppp.log          wtmp
dmesg.yesterday  scrollkeeper.log xferlog
lastlog          security
```

Your output may vary slightly depending upon your version of FreeBSD, which software you have installed on your FreeBSD system, and how long it's been since you've been in this directory. Being the curious type, you'll probably want to have a peek at each log to see what it contains. But before you start looking at files you didn't create, you'll want to first check that you have permission to view their contents. Here I'll take a look at the first few logs:

```
% ls -l /var/log/ | head
total 324
-rw-r--r--  1 root  wheel  39510 Nov  5 00:00 Xorg.0.log
-rw-------  1 root  wheel  28581 Sep 26 10:53 auth.log
-rw-------  1 root  wheel  81964 Nov  5 09:15 cron
```

```
drwxr-xr-x  2 root   wheel    512 Nov  5 09:15 cups
-rw-------  1 root   wheel    141 Nov  5 09:15 debug.log
-rw-------  1 root   wheel   3435 Nov  3 02:06 dmesg.today
-r--------  1 root   wheel   3382 Nov  2 02:06 dmesg.yesterday
-rw-r--r--  1 root   wheel  28168 Nov  5 09:15 lastlog
-rw-r--r--  1 root   wheel      0 Jul 28 09:10 lpd-errs
```

It looks like a regular user only has permission to view about half of the log files. If that user lives in the *wheel* group, they can view a few more, but only the superuser can view all of the system log files.

One last thing before looking at these files: you did not make these files, so you don't know what type of data they contain. Remember, you never open up an unknown file without first testing it with the **file** utility. Again, I'll check the first few logs:

```
% file /var/log/* | head
/var/log/Xorg.0.log:       ASCII English text
/var/log/auth.log:         writable, regular file, no read permission
/var/log/cron:             writable, regular file, no read permission
/var/log/cups:             directory
/var/log/debug.log:        writable, regular file, no read permission
/var/log/dmesg.today:      writable, regular file, no read permission
/var/log/dmesg.yesterday:  writable, regular file, no read permission
/var/log/lastlog:          data
/var/log/lpd-errs:         empty
/var/log/maillog:          ASCII text
```

Any file that has a type called data is usually non-printable. This means that you shouldn't try to send the lastlog file to your terminal using the **more** or **cat** commands or your favorite editor. It looks like the lpd-errs file is empty. The other files are writable or contain text, so they can be viewed by any user who has *r* permission to that file. Some of these files are quite large; if you are only concerned with the last bit, that is, the most recent part of the log, use the **tail** command like so:

```
% tail /var/log/maillog
```

This will display the last ten lines of the maillog; you'll note that maillog has very long lines that will wrap around your screen.

The Logging Daemon

Now you know which log files you can safely look at and satisfy your curiosity regarding their contents. But who put that information into those log files, and how can you specify what type of information you'd like to see in your log files? Sounds like we need to use the **apropos** command to see which manpages will shed some light on this subject. If you type:

```
% apropos system log
```

you'll receive a couple of screens full of possible manpages. Let's narrow our search a bit by adding some quotation marks:

```
% apropos "system log"
logger(1) - make entries in the system log
newsyslog(8) - maintain system log files to manageable sizes
syslog(3), vsyslog(3), openlog(3), closelog(3), setlogmask(3) - control system log
```

The double quotes tell **apropos** that you only want manpages that contain both words whereas the original search told **apropos** to return manpages that contained either word. This is why that last search yielded a lot fewer results.

We seem to be getting closer; it appears that FreeBSD uses the word syslog instead of system logs. Let's try:

```
% apropos syslog
newsyslog(8) - maintain system log files to manageable sizes
newsyslog(5) - newsyslog(8) configuration file
openpam_log(3) - log a message through syslog
syslog(3), vsyslog(3), openlog(3), closelog(3), setlogmask(3) - control system log
syslog.conf(5) - syslogd(8) configuration file
syslogd(8) - log systems messages
Sys::Syslog(3) - Perl interface to the UNIX syslog(3) calls
```

And we've hit paydirt; **syslogd** is the daemon responsible for logging system messages, and syslog.conf is its configuration file.

So, do you have permission to muck about with this syslog.conf file? To find out, do a long listing:

```
% ls -l /etc/syslog.conf
-rw-r--r--  1 root  wheel  903 Jul 28 09:10 /etc/syslog.conf
```

Looks like anyone can read it, but only the superuser will be able to modify it. Some parts of this file are self-explanatory, whereas others will require a read through **man 5 syslog.conf** before we start making any changes.

Each line in syslog.conf has two fields: the selector field (on the left), which specifies the type of message, and an action field (on the right), which specifies the action to be taken if a message matches the selection criteria. The selector field is separated from the action field by one or more tabs.

The selector field itself is divided into two parts separated by a period which represent *facility.level* where *facility* is what generated the message and *level* is the severity of the message. The possible values for facilities and levels are explained in **man 3 syslog**. Tables 2.7 and 2.8 provide a summary of the facilities and levels.

Let's use these tables to decipher what type of messages are sent to the console, that is, those irritating bold-white messages that show up on your first terminal. The corresponding line in /etc/syslog.conf reads as:

```
*.err;kern.warning;auth.notice;mail.crit      /dev/console
```

Note that the selector field is a bunch of facility.levels tied together with semicolons. Reading from left to right, this line tells **syslogd** to send the following types of messages to the console:

- error messages from all programs

Table 2.7: Syslog Facilities

Facility Name	What Program It Represents
AUTH	The authorization system: login(1), su(1), getty(8), etc.
AUTHPRIV	The same as AUTH, but logged to a file readable only by selected individuals.
CONSOLE	Messages written to /dev/console by the kernel console output driver.
CRON	The cron daemon: cron(8).
DAEMON	System daemons, such as routed(8), that are not provided for explicitly by other facilities.
FTP	The file transfer protocol daemons: ftpd(8), tftpd(8).
KERN	Messages generated by the kernel. These cannot be generated by any user processes.
LPR	The line printer spooling system: lpr(1), lpc(8), lpd(8), etc.
MAIL	The mail system.
NEWS	The network news system.
NTP	The network time protocol system.
SECURITY	Security subsystems.
SYSLOG	Messages generated internally by syslogd(8).
USER	Messages generated by random user processes. This is the default facility identifier if none is specified.
UUCP	The uucp system.
LOCAL0-7	Reserved for local use.
*	Specifies all facilities or programs except mark.

Table 2.8: Syslog Levels

Level Name	What It Represents
EMERG	A panic condition normally broadcasted to all users.
ALERT	A condition that should be corrected immediately.
CRIT	Critical conditions, e.g., hard device errors.
ERR	Errors.
WARNING	Warning messages.
NOTICE	Conditions that are not error conditions, but should possibly be handled.
INFO	Informational messages.
DEBUG	Messages that contain information normally used when debugging a program.
NONE	Special level to disable the facility.

- warning messages generated by the kernel

- notices regarding logins and **su**'s

- critical mail conditions

You should be able to use the same logic to see what types of messages are sent to which logs in the next seven lines:

```
*.notice;authpriv.none;kern.debug;lpr.info;mail.crit;news.err /var/log/messages
security.*                  /var/log/security
auth.info;authpriv.info     /var/log/auth.log
mail.info                   /var/log/maillog
lpr.info                    /var/log/lpd-errs
ftp.info                    /var/log/xferlog
cron.*                      /var/log/cron
```

However, to understand the rest of the file, we need to know the five possible actions listed in Table 2.9.

Also note that two of the lines in the file begin with an exclamation mark and don't have an action field after them like so:

```
!startslip
*.*              /var/log/slip.log
!ppp
*.*              /var/log/ppp.log
```

Occasionally you'll want to log the messages of a program that isn't covered by one of the built-in facilities. To add this program to /etc/syslog.conf, type the name of the program's executable on a line by itself with a ! in front of the name. On the next line, input the selector and action fields as you normally would.

Table 2.9: Syslog Actions

Syntax of Action	What It Does
/pathname	Messages are added to the end of the specified file.
@hostname	Messages are forwarded to the syslogd(8) program on the specified computer.
user1,user2,etc.	Messages are written to those users if they are logged in.
*	Messages are written to all logged-in users.
lcommand	Pipes the message to the specified command.

You'll find that **man 5 syslog.conf** has excellent examples covering just about every scenario you'll ever come across when configuring logging. If you do ever edit your `syslog.conf` file, don't forget to restart **syslogd**:

```
# /etc/rc.d/syslogd restart
Stopping syslogd.
Feb 18 16:22:49 dru syslogd:  exiting on signal 15
Starting syslogd.
# /etc/rc.d/syslogd status
syslogd is running as PID 64023.
```

Log Rotation

When you originally looked in your `/var/log` directory, you may have received a listing of a lot of files that ended in .0, .1, etc., and some of these files may have also been compressed (they had a *.bz2* extension). This is a result of the workings of **newsyslog**. Let's take a quick look in this utility's manpage:

```
% man newsyslog
NAME

newsyslog - maintain system log files to manageable sizes
DESCRIPTION
The newsyslog utility should be scheduled to run periodically by cron(8).  When it is
executed it archives log files if necessary.  If a log file is determined to require
archiving, newsyslog rearranges the files so that "logfile" is empty, "logfile.0" has
the last period's logs in it, "logfile.1" has the next to last period's logs in it,
and so on, up to a user-specified number of archived logs.  Optionally, the archived
logs can be compressed to save space.
```

In other words, if a logfile becomes too large, **newsyslog** will rename it with a .0 extension, possibly **bzip** it, and create a new file with the original log name. For example:

- `maillog.1.bz2` is the oldest maillog file; it has been compressed

- `maillog.0.bz2` is the second oldest maillog file; it is also compressed

- `maillog` is the current maillog that is being written to by **syslogd**

If you continue to read through the manpage for **newsyslog**, you'll learn how to tweak its configuration file `/etc/newsyslog.conf` so you can schedule when files will be renamed and compressed.

If you ever need to view the contents of a log that has already been compressed by **newsyslog**, you can use the **bzcat** utility like so:

```
% bzcat /var/log/maillog.0.bz2 | more
```

If you need to remove old log files to save space, it is safe to delete a log that ends with a either a number or a *.bz2* from the `/var/log` directory. If you need to do this often, there is no need to create a **cron** job; **newsyslog** will do this automatically. It will keep as many or as few backlogs as you desire and rotate through them when they reach a specified size. I would not recommend deleting uncompressed logs, though, as **syslogd** expects to be able to find the logfiles in the paths that you've specified in `/etc/syslog.conf`.

So, in the above example, it is safe to delete `maillog.0.bz2` and `maillog.1.bz2`, but don't delete `maillog`.

If you ever inadvertently delete an original logfile, you can create it using the **touch** utility:

```
# cd /var/log
# rm maillog        (oops)
# touch maillog
```

This will create an empty `maillog` file that **syslogd** can write to.

Other log and rotation examples are shown in section 10.8.

Additional Resources

Original Article:

`http://www.onlamp.com/pub/a/bsd/2000/11/08/FreeBSD_Basics.html`

2.12 Getting Cron to Do Our Bidding

Wouldn't it be great if you could get your FreeBSD system to automatically perform maintenance tasks on a regular basis and email you the results? Well, thanks to the built-in **cron** daemon and the **periodic** scripts, your FreeBSD system is already doing this for you. This section concentrates on FreeBSD's daemon to execute scheduled commands and learning how to configure the **cron** daemon to run your own commands and scripts.

Like most other daemons, **cron** is started for you when you boot into FreeBSD and continues to quietly run in the background. To prove to yourself that **cron** is indeed running, look for the word *cron* in the results of the process status command like so:

```
% ps -ax | grep cron
  97  ??  Is     0:07.71 /usr/sbin/cron -s
```

In this example, **cron** is running with a process ID of 97.

The **cron** daemon wakes up every minute and checks the *crontab*s (short for chron or time tables) to see if it needs to start the execution of a command or script. A *crontab* is simply a file containing a list of commands and the time each command should run. When you installed FreeBSD, a system crontab was created for you. You should not make any changes to this file; later on in the section, we'll use the **crontab** utility to make user crontabs that **cron** will read in addition to the system crontab.

The system crontab is stored in the /etc directory. We'll use the **more** command to safely view this file without risk of editing it. You'll want to be logged in to two virtual terminals as we'll be reading the file at one terminal, and trying other commands at the other terminal. At the first virtual terminal, type:

```
% more /etc/crontab
# /etc/crontab - root's crontab for FreeBSD
#
# $FreeBSD: src/etc/crontab,v 1.32 2002/11/22 16:13:39 tom Exp $
#
SHELL=/bin/sh
PATH=/etc:/bin:/sbin:/usr/bin:/usr/sbin
HOME=/var/log
#
#minute hour    mday    month   wday    who     command
#
*/5     *       *       *       *       root    /usr/libexec/atrun
```

As in many files, remarks begin with a #. The most useful remark is the labeling of the fields. Note that there are five time fields, a user field, and a command field. While the syntax may seem strange at first, each uncommented line in the crontab simply tells *cron* when you want it to run a specified command.

Table 2.10 shows the valid values for the five time fields.

Table 2.10: cron Time Fields

Field	Valid Values
minute	0-59
hour	0-23
dayofmonth	1-31
month	1-12 or first three letters of each month (not case-sensitive)
dayofweek	0-7 (where both 0 and 7 represent Sunday) or first three letters of each day (not case-sensitive)

Values can be a single number or three-letter word, or values can be a range. For example, 1-5 in the *dayofweek* field represents Monday to Friday. Values can also be separated by a comma: 1,15,30 in the *dayofmonth* field will run a command on the 1st, 15th, and 30th of each month.

All five time fields accept the * wildcard, which means "use every valid value" for that field. For example, to run a command every month, put a * in the *month* field.

135

You can also use the */number* value. For example a */2 in the *month* field means "run every second month." The system crontab has an example of this:

```
#minute hour    mday    month   wday    who     command
*/5      *       *       *       *       root    /usr/libexec/atrun
```

This line is read as: Every minute that is divisible by five (or every five minutes) of every hour of every day of every month, run the **atrun** command as *root*.

If you don't know what the **atrun** command does, type this at your other virtual terminal:

```
% whatis atrun
atrun(8) - run jobs queued for later execution
```

If that doesn't satisfy your curiosity, take a look through **man 8 atrun**.

One final table before continuing with /etc/crontab. You can replace all five time fields with one string value like in Table 2.11.

Table 2.11: cron String Values

String	What it Represents
@reboot	only runs the command when you reboot
@yearly	replaces 0 0 1 1 *
@annually	same as yearly
@monthly	replaces 0 0 1 * *
@weekly	replaces 0 0 * * 0
@daily	replaces 0 0 * * *
@midnight	same as daily
@hourly	replaces 0 * * * *

Return to the first virtual terminal to continue reading through /etc/crontab:

```
# Rotate log files every hour, if necessary
0       *       *       *       *       root    newsyslog
```

Again, the comment is useful: Every minute that is 0 of every hour of every day of every month, run the **newsyslog** command. And what does the **newsyslog** command do?

```
% whatis newsyslog
newsyslog(8) - maintain system log files to manageable sizes
```

It is introduced in section 2.11.

Continuing in the crontab:

```
# Perform daily/weekly/monthly maintenance
1    3    *    *    *    root    periodic daily
15   4    *    *    6    root    periodic weekly
30   5    1    *    *    root    periodic monthly
```

Notice that the daily/weekly/monthly maintenance scripts use scattered times. The daily script runs every morning at 3:01 A.M.; if you sleep anywhere near your FreeBSD box, you may have heard your hard drive churning at this strange hour. The weekly script runs every Saturday morning at 4:15 A.M., and the monthly script runs on the first day of every month at 5:30 A.M. It is a good thing to run maintenance scripts during times when your computer's processor should be free (e.g., the middle of the night), and to not run the scripts all at the same time to prevent your processor from getting bogged down.

Where does **periodic** find the periodic scripts? At your second virtual terminal, try this:

```
% ls /etc/periodic
daily      monthly      security      weekly
% ls -F /etc/periodic/weekly
310.locate*    330.catman*    400.status-pkg*
320.whatis*    340.noid*      999.local*
```

The **-F** to the **ls** command puts a * after all executables; therefore, /etc/periodic contains subdirectories that contain the scripts that **cron** runs daily, weekly, and monthly. If you're truly curious, you can view any of these scripts with the **more** command.[6] As a side note, if you are learning shell scripting, viewing these built-in scripts provides practice in recognizing proper syntax.

Since the results of these scripts are mailed to *root*, *root* can use a mail reader to check for any problems. Become the superuser and open up your favorite email reader to see the messages sent from **cron**.

If you've never done this before, you may have hundreds of messages, depending on how long your computer has been turned on. If you always shut off your computer at night, you won't have any, as the scripts all run after midnight.

If you have any messages, you should have at least one called daily run output. If you read this message, you'll see that **cron** has a lot of work to do every morning at 3:01. You'll also note that the security check was sent in a separate email message called security check output. This message is well worth reading as it contains the results of checking setuid files, uids of 0, passwordless accounts, kernel log messages, failed logins, and refused connections.

Once you've finished reading the messages, you can safely delete them. Don't forget to leave the superuser account when you exit the email reader.

So far, we've looked at the system crontab, which should be left as is. Now we want to look at making your own crontab file to put in the commands that you want **cron** to execute. By default on a FreeBSD system, any user can create his own crontab file. These crontabs will be stored in /var/cron/tabs. As superuser, if you:

```
# ls /var/cron/tabs
#
```

---

[6]These periodic scripts are covered in section 2.13.

you'll note that this directory is empty by default. Once you create a crontab, it will create a file with the same name as the user. Never edit this file directly using a text editor; instead, use the **crontab** utility to create or modify your crontab file.

You may be wondering what types of commands or scripts you would want **cron** to run for you. Ask yourself what types of commands you run regularly, or should run regularly but sometimes forget to run. For example, you may wish to remove old *.core files or dead.letter files. [7] Perhaps you would like to flush your browser cache on a regular basis.

Once you know what you'd like **cron** to do for you, decide which command or group of commands will accomplish this task. Every entry in a crontab must be one line; It is OK if the line wraps around your screen as long as you don't press enter. If the command is very long, it may be easier to enter the command into a script and reference the script in **crontab**. Let's do an example of each.

If I want to find files with certain extensions and remove them, I can enter a command like this (you would enter this all on one line):

```
find / \( -name "*.core" -or -name "dead.*" \) -print -exec rm -rf {} \;
```

Let's see if we can interpret this gobblygook. This is all one **find** statement and **find** statements always look like this:

```
find starting_here look_for_this then_do_this
```

So, when I typed **find /**, I told **find** to start looking at the root of the filesystem.

I then told **find** to look for files whose names (**-name**) end with either *.core* or begin with *dead*. Because I wanted **find** to eventually remove both types of these files, I put both names within parentheses. I also had to quote both parentheses with the backslash character so the shell wouldn't try to interpret the parentheses.

Once **find** has found these files, I told it to execute (**-exec**) the **rm -rf** command to remove these files. Whenever you use **-exec**, you must end the find statement with **\;** (backslash and semicolon) or it won't work. The **{}** (braces) tell **-exec** to use whatever **find** found as the variable to work on.

Now, that wasn't so bad, was it? Let's get even fancier and create a simple shell script to clear the Netscape cache. If you're not using Netscape, you can practice modifying the script to clear the cache used by your browser.

```
#!/bin/sh
#First, double-check that the user is not
#currently using Netscape
#Then remove the contents of all the subdirectories
#in the Netscape cache
if ! (`ps wxu $USER | grep -q [n]etscape`)
        then
        echo "Clearing Netscape cache..."
        rm -rf ~/.netscape/cache/*
fi
echo "Exiting...."
```

---

[7] Removing core files and other old files can be done by the daily scripts also, see section 2.13 for another example.

Let's pick apart what we just typed in here. All scripts begin with a shebang or that **#!** character followed by the full pathname to the program that will interpret the script. We've created a Bourne shell script as we've indicated that the **sh** command will be responsible for interpreting this script.

We then included four comment lines (they begin with the **#** character) to remind ourselves of the purpose of this script.

Then we get to the actual meat of the script. It is composed of an if statement which begins with **if** and ends with **fi**. The first line of the if statement sets a condition that will either be true or false:

```
if ! (`ps wxu $USER | grep -q [n]etscape`)
```

The **!** is the *not* operator, which tells if to only activate the then clause if what is in the parentheses is not true. Basically, use the **ps** with **grep** commands to search for the first instance of Netscape for this user.[8] If there is no process ID dealing with Netscape, continue the script by **echo**ing the text enclosed in quotes:

```
echo "Clearing Netscape cache..."
```

and by clearing the Netscape cache in that user's home directory:

```
rm -rf ~/.netscape/cache/*
```

However, if there is a process ID dealing with Netscape, leave the if statement instead of executing the then clause.

Save your file; I saved mine as `clean`. You can call your script whatever you want, just don't give it a name that is already being used by another command. To double-check, try this in another virtual terminal:

```
% whereis -b potential_scriptname
```

If your answer is a pathname, there already is a command with that name, so try another name. If all you get is an echo like this:

```
% whereis -b clean
clean:
```

it is probably safe to use that name for your script.

Once you've saved your script, you still need to use the **chmod** command to make it executable:

```
% chmod +x clean
```

It is also a good idea to create a `bin` directory in your home directory to store your scripts:

```
% mkdir ~/bin
% mv clean ~/bin
```

---

[8]The brackets [n] around the "n" in the regular expression are used to help fine-tune the match so the **grep** process is not matched too. Also see **man pgrep** for another idea.

Finally, always test that your script actually works before telling **cron** to use it. If you are in the `bin` directory, type:

```
% ./clean
```

If you're in any other directory, type:

```
% clean
```

If you are in the C shell and receive a "Command not found" message, type:

```
% rehash
```

to reread your path statement and try again.

If you receive an error message when your script executes, you most likely have a typo somewhere in your file. Look for the typo and try running your script again until it runs without any error messages.

Now we're ready to create a crontab file to tell **cron** to run our script and our **find** command. Log in as a regular user; I'm logged in as the user *genisis*. Now type:

```
% crontab -e
```

to invoke the **crontab** utility in editor mode. If you're real quick, you'll see this message before entering **vi**:

```
crontab: no crontab for genisis - using an empty one
```

Since we're in **vi**, press **Escape** then **i** to enter insert mode; then enter the following text. Make sure you do not press the **Return** key when you type in the **find** command; **vi** will wrap the text for you to fit your screen.

```
# every morning at 4:32 search and
# destroy all core or dead files
32 4 * * * find /home/genisis/ \( -name "*.core" -or -name "dead.*" \) -print ⇓
     -exec rm -rf {} \;
# run the script that clears the Netscape
# cache every morning at 2:48
48 2 *  *  *  /home/genisis/bin/clean
```

Note that the syntax is slightly different than in the system crontab file as there is no who field. Since this crontab will have the same name as the user, the who will be the user who made the crontab. When you are finished, double-check for typos, then press **Escape** and then **:wq** to save your changes and quit. If you input an invalid value in the time fields, **crontab** will complain and ask if you want to re-enter the editor. Say yes, and look for your typo. Otherwise, you should see this message:

```
crontab: installing new crontab
```

Tomorrow when you check your email, you will see two emails from **cron** with the results of your crontab entries. If your commands were successful, they should look like this:

```
From genisis@.istar.ca.   Thu Sep 14 04:38:31 2000
Date:  Thu, 14 Sep 2000 04:38:50 -0400 (EDT)
From:  genisis (Cron Daemon)
To:  genisis
Subject:  cron <genisis@istar.ca> find /home/genisis/ \( -name "*.core" -or -name
"dead.*" \) -print -exec rm -rf {} \;

/usr/home/genisis/dead.letter
/usr/home/genisis/netscape.bin.core
```

```
From genisis@.istar.ca.   Thu Sep 14 02:51:36 2000
Date:  Thu, 14 Sep 2000 02:52:01 -0400 (EDT)
From:  genisis (Cron Daemon)
To:  genisis
Subject:  cron <genisis@istar.ca> /home/genisis/bin/clean
```

```
Clearing Netscape cache...
Exiting....
```

A few final notes on crontabs … if you ever want to view your crontab, you can type:

% crontab -l

If you want to make changes to your crontab, use **crontab -e** again.

Only *root* can see which users have installed crontabs. Become the superuser and try this:

 # ls /var/cron/tabs
```
genisis
```

You should see a new entry with the same name as the user who just created the crontab.

Additional Resources

Original Article:

```
http://www.onlamp.com/pub/a/bsd/2000/09/27/FreeBSD_Basics.html
```

2.13 Understanding the Automatons

Now that you are comfortable with **cron**, let's take a closer look at the actual **periodic** scripts that **cron** calls to be executed on a daily, weekly, and monthly basis.

It's always a good idea to be aware of what scripts are running on your computer. Scripts, after all, do stuff that make them a double-edged sword. On the plus side, they can keep you posted on the overall health of your computer and take care of routine housekeeping tasks for you. With the built-in scripts, you don't have to know how to write a shell script in order to perform routine tasks as your FreeBSD system comes with many pre-made scripts that are automatically run for you. On the negative side, any script can be vulnerable to exploits by malicious users. Just as you shouldn't run services on your computer that you don't need, you should only run the scripts that are useful to you and disable the ones you don't need.

The periodic Directories

The scripts themselves are found in /etc/periodic/ and are placed in the appropriate subdirectory depending on whether they will be run daily, weekly, or monthly or if they deal specifically with security:

```
% ls -F /etc/periodic
daily/     monthly/     security/     weekly/
```

Each script in these subdirectories begins with a number to indicate the order in which the scripts in that directory will be run. That is, a script beginning with the number 120 will run before the script beginning with the number 300. Also, these scripts are executable files as indicated by the * in the output of **ls -F**:

```
% ls -F /etc/periodic/weekly
310.locate*    330.catman*    400.status-pkg*
320.whatis*    340.noid*      999.local*
```

Finally, these are Bourne shell scripts (that is, they all begin with the line #!/bin/sh) meaning you can test the output of any of these scripts like:

```
% /etc/periodic/daily/430.status-rwho
Local system status:
8:25AM up 19 days, 21:34, 7 users, load averages:  0.41, 0.38, 0.29
```

You may remember that **cron** uses the system crontab file to determine when the scripts in each directory are to be run. The **periodic** program has its own separate configuration file called periodic.conf which is used to specify which of the daily, weekly, and monthly scripts you want to be included in the run, and which you wish to disable.

The periodic Configuration File

Your FreeBSD system comes with a default periodic.conf file; let's take a look at the first 20 lines of that file:

```
% head -20 /etc/defaults/periodic.conf
#!/bin/sh
# # This is defaults/periodic.conf - a file full  of useful variables that
# you can set to change the default behaviour of periodic jobs on your
# system.  You should not edit this file!  Put any overrides into one of the
# $periodic_conf_files instead and you will be able to update these defaults
# later without spamming your local configuration information.
# The $periodic_conf_files files should only contain values which override
# values set in this file.  This eases the upgrade path when defaults
# are changed and new features are added.
# For a more detailed explanation of all the periodic.conf variables, please
# refer to the periodic.conf(5) manual page.
# $FreeBSD: src/etc/defaults/periodic.conf,v 1.33.2.2 $
# What files override these defaults ?
periodic_conf_files="/etc/periodic.conf /etc/periodic.conf.local"
```

This file makes it pretty clear that you should not make any changes to it and offers two locations to store your own customized version of `periodic.conf`. If you try to find the files that override the defaults, you'll see that they don't exist as it is up to you to create them:

```
% more /etc/periodic.conf
/etc/periodic.conf: No such file or directory
% more /etc/periodic.conf.local
/etc/periodic.conf.local: No such file or directory
```

Before you start making your customized file, it is a good idea to know what each script does so you can decide whether or not you want it to be executed by the **periodic** program.

Let's take a quick look at each script, what it does, and whether or not it runs by default. These details are described in **man periodic.conf** which I've summarized in Tables 2.12, 2.14, and 2.15.

Table 2.12: Daily Periodic Scripts

Name of script	Action	Default
100.clean-disks	removes all matching files	NO
110.clean-tmps	clears temporary directories	NO
120.clean-preserve	removes old files from `/var/preserve`	YES
130.clean-msgs	old system messages purged	YES
140.clean-rwho	old files in `/var/rwho` purged	YES
150.clean-hoststat	old files in `/var/spool/.hoststat` purged.	YES
200.backup-passwd	backup master.passwd and group files and modifications reported	YES
210.backup-aliases	aliases file backed up and modifications displayed	YES
300.calendar	runs calendar -a daily	NO
310.accounting	rotates daily accounting files	YES
330.news	runs `/etc/news.expire`	YES
400.status-disks	runs df(1) and dump -W	YES
405.status-ata-raid	runs atacontrol status on ataraid arrays	NO
406.status-gmirror	runs gmirror status	NO
407.status-graid3	runs graid3 status	NO
408.status-gstripe	runs gstripe status	NO
409.status-gconcat	runs gconcat status	NO
420.status-network	runs netstat -i	YES
430.status-rwho	runs uptime(1)	YES

440.status-mailq	runs mailq(1)	YES
450.status-security	runs `/etc/security`	YES
460.status-mail-rejects	summarizes mail rejections logged to `/var/log/maillog`	YES
470.status-named	summarizes denied zone transfers	YES
500.queuerun	manually runs the mail queue	YES
999.local	list of extra scripts in `/etc/daily.local`	

The Daily Scripts

You'll notice that there are quite a few scripts and most of them are enabled by default. Let's become the superuser and copy the default file to the file that we'll customize:

cp /etc/defaults/periodic.conf /etc/periodic.conf

I'll then open up /etc/periodic.conf in my favorite text editor and pick through the interesting lines. Let's start with this bit:

```
# Daily options
# These options are used by periodic(8) itself to determine what to do
# with the output of the sub-programs that are run, and where to send
# that output.  $daily_output might be set to /var/log/daily.log if you
# wish to log the daily output and have the files rotated by newsyslog(8)
daily_output="root"        # user or /file
daily_show_success="YES"   # scripts returning 0
daily_show_info="YES"      # scripts returning 1
daily_show_badconfig="NO"  # scripts returning 2
```

You'll note that by default, the results of running the daily scripts are emailed to *root*. If you check *root*'s email, you'll see messages with the subject "hostname daily run output" and if you read one of those messages, the output should match up to the daily scripts that are marked as YES. You can have the output sent to another user by replacing *root* with a user name or email address on the `daily_output` line.

Alternatively, you can specify that the output be sent to a file, usually `/var/log/daily.log`. This file doesn't exist by default, so you'll want to create it by using **touch /var/log/daily.log**.

Let's continue by taking a look at the daily scripts. You'll note there is a logic to the layout of the scripts: The first scripts clean out old files, these are followed by backup scripts, which are followed by scripts which run some useful utilities.

```
# 100.clean-disks
daily_clean_disks_enable="NO"        # Delete files daily
```

```
daily_clean_disks_files="[#,]* .#* a.out *.core *.CKP .emacs_[0-9]*"
daily_clean_disks_days=3          # If older than this
daily_clean_disks_verbose="YES"   # Mention files deleted
```

This script is disabled by default but you may want to consider enabling it if disk space is an issue on your system. If you do enable this option, backup your important files first and check the output to ensure this script didn't delete any files you were attached to. This is especially important if you decide to add your own extensions to the files list.

The next script is also disabled by default and may be worth enabling if disk space is an issue:

```
# 110.clean-tmps
daily_clean_tmps_enable="NO"      # Delete stuff daily
daily_clean_tmps_dirs="/tmp"      # Delete under here
daily_clean_tmps_days="3"         # If not accessed for
daily_clean_tmps_ignore=".X*-lock quota.user quota.group"  # Don't delete these
daily_clean_tmps_verbose="YES"    # Mention files deleted
```

The next script cleans out /var/preserve. If you don't know what a directory does on your FreeBSD system, **man hier** is the best place to look. Here I'll search that man page for the word preserve:

```
% man hier
/preserve
preserve/  temporary home of files preserved after
           an accidental death of an editor; see (ex)1
```

Now that you know what preserve is for, you can decide whether or not to keep this script enabled.

```
# 120.clean-preserve
daily_clean_preserve_enable="YES"   # Delete files daily
daily_clean_preserve_days=7         # If not modified for
daily_clean_preserve_verbose="YES"  # Mention files deleted
```

The next script cleans out messages sent by the **msgs** utility. If you don't use this utility, you can disable this script as there won't be any messages to delete. If you're not sure if you're using this utility, you probably aren't, but you can doublecheck by reading **man msgs**.

```
# 130.clean-msgs
daily_clean_msgs_enable="YES"     # Delete msgs daily
daily_clean_msgs_days=            # If not modified for
```

For the next script, it is again helpful to read the man page for the utility, in this case **rwho**. If your FreeBSD computer is not hooked up to a Unix LAN, you can disable this script as /var/rwho will always be empty.

```
# 140.clean-rwho
daily_clean_rwho_enable="YES"     # Delete rwho daily
daily_clean_rwho_days=7           # If not modified for
daily_clean_rwho_verbose="YES"    # Mention files deleted
```

The next script purges the hoststat table maintained by **sendmail** if it was started with the **-bh** flags. Your system isn't using this table if you just get your prompt back after running **hoststat** as the superuser.

```
# 150.clean-hoststat              # Purge sendmail host
daily_clean_hoststat_enable="YES"   # status cache daily
```

Now we get to the two backup scripts. You definitely want your password and group files backed up daily. This script not only backs them up, it will also report if either of those two files had any changes made to them that day. The output of this script should be checked on a daily basis.

```
# 200.backup-passwd
daily_backup_passwd_enable="YES"   # Backup passwd & group
```

It is a good idea to have a backup of your mail aliases file; whether or not you want to have it backed up daily is up to you.

```
# 210.backup-aliases
daily_backup_aliases_enable="YES"   # Backup mail aliases
```

The **calendar** utility is interesting, but not enabled by default. If you like the **fortune** program and enjoy reading trivia, you might consider enabling this script. There are a few steps involved in setting up **calendar**.

First, decide which calendar file you think you or your users would enjoy reading. The possible files are found in /usr/share/calendar:

```
% ls -F /usr/share/calendar
calendar.all          calendar.holiday      calendar.world
calendar.australia    calendar.hungarian    de_AT.ISO_8859-15/
calendar.birthday     calendar.judaic       de_DE.ISO8859-1/
calendar.christian    calendar.lotr         de_DE.ISO8859-15@
calendar.computer     calendar.music        fr_FR.ISO8859-1/
calendar.croatian     calendar.newzealand   fr_FR.ISO8859-15@
calendar.freebsd      calendar.russian      hr_HR.ISO8859-2/
calendar.french       calendar.southafrica  hu_HU.ISO8859-2/
calendar.german       calendar.ukranian     ru_RU.KOI8-R/
calendar.history      calendar.usholiday    uk_UA.KOI8-U/
```

Each of the files are in plain text so you can safely send them to a pager to see their contents or edit the contents as you wish. Some calendar files contain the actual trivia:

```
% more /usr/share/calendar/calendar.computer
01/01   AT&T officially divests its local Bell companies, 1984
01/01   The Epoch (Time 0 for UNIX systems, Midnight GMT, 1970)
01/03   Apple Computer founded, 1977
01/08   American Telephone and Telegraph loses antitrust case, 1982
01/08   Herman Hollerith patents first data processing computer, 1889
01/08   Justice Dept. drops IBM suit, 1982
01/10   First CDC 1604 delivered to Navy, 1960
01/16   Set uid bit patent issued, to Dennis Ritchie, 1979
01/17   Justice Dept. begins IBM anti-trust suit, 1969 (drops it, 01/08/82)
01/24   DG Nova introduced, 1969
```

While other calendar files are used to specify which trivia files to include:

```
% more /usr/share/calendar/calendar.all
#include <calendar.world>
#include <calendar.croatian>
#include <calendar.french>
#include <calendar.german>
#include <calendar.hungarian>
#include <calendar.southafrica>
#include <calendar.russian>
#include <calendar.usholiday>
```

Any user aware of this directory can see what trivia is suited to today's and tomorrow's date by invoking the desired calendar file with the **-f** switch like so:

```
% calendar -f /usr/share/calendar/calendar.birthday
Nov  4  King William III of Orange born, 1650
Nov  5  Roy Rogers born, 1912
```

Note that this command will fail if a user isn't in this directory or doesn't specify the full path name to the desired calendar file. To fix this, tell the user to create a directory in their home directory and to copy the desired calendar file(s) to it:

```
% cd
% mkdir .calendar
% cp /usr/share/calendar/calendar.world .calendar/calendar
```

I like calendar.world as it includes birthdays, computer, music, history, and holidays. Since I've saved the file as calendar, I can now simply type **calendar** with no arguments, regardless of what directory I'm in:

```
% calendar
Nov  4  King William III of Orange born, 1650
Nov  5  Roy Rogers born, 1912
Nov  4  UNIVAC I program predicts Eisenhower victory based on 7% of votes, 1952
Nov  4  Iranian militants seize US embassy personnel in Teheran, 1979
Nov  4  Soviet forces crush the anti-communist revolt in Hungary, 1956
Nov  5  Guy Fawkes' Plot, 1605
Nov  4  Flag Day in Panama
Nov  4  Will Rogers Day
```

Which brings us back to the **periodic** script that deals with **calendar**. If you enable this script, it will email the customized **calendar** output to every user who has created a .calendar in their home directory. As a side note, the superuser can do this at any time. Once you've set up your .calendar directory, become the superuser and type:

```
# calendar -a
```

If you check your email, you'll have a new message with a subject of "Day_of_the_Week Calendar". If your users think this is a cool feature, enable the **periodic** script and show them how to set up their .calendar directory.

```
# 300.calendar
daily_calendar_enable="NO"    # Run calendar -a
```

System accounting is off by default, so disable this script if you don't plan on enabling system accounting. If you're not sure what system accounting does, **man sa** gives a list of what statistics will be gathered. If you decide to enable system accounting, consider changing daily_accounting_compress to **YES** and keep an eye on your disk-space usage.

```
# 310.accounting
daily_accounting_enable="YES"    # Rotate acct files
daily_accounting_compress="NO"   # Gzip rotated files
daily_accounting_flags=-q        # Flags to /usr/sbin/sa
daily_accounting_save=3          # How many files to save
```

You should disable the news script; even if you are running a news server as it should have a built-in mechanism to handle expired news articles.

```
# 330.news
daily_news_expire_enable="YES" # Run news.expire
```

You'll probably want to keep the disk status script enabled, and you should check its output on a daily basis to ensure you are not running out of disk space.

```
# 400.status-disks
daily_status_disks_enable="YES"              # Check disk status
daily_status_disks_df_flags="-k -t nonfs" # df(1) flags for check
```

Note that you can change the flag line to include the switches you prefer to pass to the **df** utility. Since I don't use NFS and I like to keep track of my free inodes and see the output in human readable format, my line looks like this:

```
daily_status_disks_df_flags="-h -i"      # df(1) flags for check
```

Which gives me this output:

```
Filesystem     Size  Used  Avail Capacity iused      ifree %iused  Mounted on
/dev/ad0s1a    496M   75M   381M    16%     2330      63460    4%   /
devfs          1.0K  1.0K    0B    100%        0          0  100%   /dev
/dev/ad0s1e    496M   38K   456M     0%       28      65762    0%   /tmp
/dev/ad0s1f    140G   37G    91G    29%   495229   18417025    3%   /usr
/dev/ad0s1d    1.9G  117M   1.7G     6%     5704     276918    2%   /var
linprocfs      4.0K  4.0K    0B    100%        1          0  100%   /usr/compat/
```

instead of the default output, which would look like this:

```
Filesystem   1K-blocks     Used    Avail Capacity  Mounted on
/dev/ad0s1a    507630     76792   390228    16%     /
devfs               1         1        0   100%     /dev
/dev/ad0s1e    507630        38   466982     0%     /tmp
/dev/ad0s1f 146331194 39255190 95369510    29%     /usr
/dev/ad0s1d   2012718    119590  1732112     6%     /var
linprocfs           4         4        0   100%     /usr/compat/linux/proc
```

Scripts 405.* through 409.* may or may not be on your system, depending upon your version of FreeBSD. ataraid was introduced in FreeBSD 5.2. GEOM was introduced in FreeBSD 5.3 and **gmirror**, **graid**, **gstripe**, and **gconcat** are all GEOM-based RAID utilities.

The first line in the network status script runs the **netstat** utility; if you don't want the script to resolve IP addresses to network names, change the second line to NO. It's up to you to decide if the output of this script is useful enough to you to warrant keeping it enabled.

```
# 420.status-network
daily_status_network_enable="YES"  # Check network status
daily_status_network_usedns="YES"  # DNS lookups are ok
```

The output of the next script depends on whether or not the **rwho** daemon is running. If it is not, it will show the uptime of your local system; if it is, it will show the uptime for each machine in your LAN.

```
# 430.status-rwho
daily_status_rwho_enable="YES"  # Check system status
```

The next script runs **mailq**, the output of which will let you know if there is any mail stuck in the queues.

```
# 440.status-mailq
daily_status_mailq_enable="YES"             # Check mail status
daily_status_mailq_shorten="NO"             # Shorten output
daily_status_include_submit_mailq="YES"     # Also submit queue
```

The security script is probably the most important script run by **periodic**, and its output should be checked on a daily basis. You'll note that the output is mailed separately from the rest of the daily output scripts, and can be mailed to a different user (the default user is *root*). Also, keep the inline line set at NO; if you set it to YES, it will be sent to the terminal instead of to a user. You do want a trusted user to read this output on a daily basis, in case further investigation is required.

```
# 450.status-security
daily_status_security_enable="YES"    # Security check
# See ''Security options'' below for more options
# Security options
daily_status_security_inline="NO"       # Run inline ?
daily_status_security_output="root"   # user or /file
daily_status_security_noamd="NO"        # Don't check amd mounts
daily_status_security_logdir="/var/log"  # Directory for logs
daily_status_security_diff_flags="-b -u"  # flags for diff output
```

The security check runs the scripts found in `/etc/periodic/security`. These have been summarized in Table 2.13.

Table 2.13: Security Scripts

Name of script	Action	Default
100.chksetuid	checks for new SUID files	YES
200.chkmounts	reports on newly mounted filesystems	YES
300.chkuid0	checks for users with UID of 0	YES
400.passwdless	checks for users with empty passwords	YES
500.ipfwdenied	log entries for packets denied by IPFW firewall	YES
510.ipfdenied	log entries for packets denied by ipf firewall	YES
520.pfdenied	log entries for packets denied by pf firewall	YES
550.ipfwlimit	display IPFW rules which reached verbosity limit	YES
600.ip6fwdenied	log entries for packets denied by IPFW firewall	YES
650.ip6fwlimit	display IPFW rules which reached verbosity limit	YES
700.kernelmsg	display dmesg entries	YES
800.loginfail	display failed logins	YES
900.tcpwrap	connections denied by TCP Wrappers	YES

The security check looks for well-known vulnerabilities, meaning that anything in its output should be looked at to ensure your system hasn't been compromised. Let's take a quick look at some of these checks:

100.chksetuid

Setuid files are one of the oldest known vulnerabilities in Unix systems. Fortunately, your FreeBSD system keeps a list of which files are setuid in `/var/log/setuid.today` and `/var/log/setuid.yesterday`. This script checks to see if there are any differences between these two files; that is, it can notify you if a new setuid file shows up on your system. If it does, you want to be aware of it.

300.chkuid0

By default, the only users on your system that have a UID of 0 are *root* and *toor*. An UID of 0 means that that user has *root* access to your FreeBSD system, so you should be very suspicious if a new user shows up under this section of the output.

400.passwdless

We all know that user accounts without passwords are a bad thing. The daily security output will notify you if any passwordless accounts show up so you can rectify the situation.

500.ipfwdenied

This script will check `/var/log/ipfw.today` for you and give you the stats on how many packets were rejected for each of your logged deny rules.

550.ipfwlimit

This script will tell you which IPFW rules reached their logging limits.

700.kernelmsg

This script will show the contents of `/var/log/dmesg.today`, meaning it will show the system messages.

900.tcpwrap

If you've configured TCP Wrappers, any warning messages will be recorded for you.

The Rest of the Daily Scripts

Leaving the security script, let's move on to the next script, which will show you if any mail was rejected.

```
# 460.status-mail-rejects
daily_status_mail_rejects_enable="YES"   # Check mail rejects
daily_status_mail_rejects_logs=3         # How many logs to check
```

The **status-named** script can be disabled if you are not running a DNS server. If you are running a DNS server, check the output of this script, as it will let you know if your DNS server denied any zone transfers. A zone transfer request from a machine that is not one of your secondary DNS servers may indicate that someone is trying to gather information about your network.

```
# 470.status-named
daily_status_named_enable="YES"
daily_status_named_usedns="YES"   # DNS lookups are ok
```

The next script ensures that **sendmail**'s queue is processed at least once per day. You don't have to run this script, as by default **sendmail** will check its queue every 30 minutes for undeliverable mail and will try to resend any messages at that point.

```
# 500.queuerun
daily_queuerun_enable="YES"    # Run mail queue
daily_submit_queuerun="YES"    # Also submit queue
```

Finally, there is a script which can run `/etc/daily.local`; this file doesn't exist but you can create one containing your custom commands:

```
# 999.local
daily_local="/etc/daily.local"     # Local scripts
```

Weekly and Monthly Scripts

That's it for the built-in daily scripts; let's move on to the weekly scripts.

Table 2.14: Weekly Scripts

Name of script	Action	Default
310.locate	runs `/usr/libexec/locate.updatedb`	YES
320.whatis	runs `/usr/libexec/makewhatis.local`	YES
330.catman	runs `/usr/libexec/catman.local`	NO
340.noid	locate files with an invalid owner or group (orphans)	NO
400.status-pkg	uses pkg_version(1) to list out of date installed packages	NO
999.local	list of extra scripts in `/etc/weekly.local`	

You'll note that you're once again given the option to specify where to send the weekly output, and again, the default is to email it to *root*.

```
# Weekly options
# These options are used by periodic(8) itself to determine what to do
# with the output of the sub-programs that are run, and where to send
# that output.  $weekly_output might be set to /var/log/weekly.log if you
# wish to log the weekly output and have the files rotated by newsyslog(8)
weekly_output="root"        # user or /file
weekly_show_success="YES"   # scripts returning 0
weekly_show_info="YES"      # scripts returning 1
weekly_show_badconfig="NO"  # scripts returning 2
```

The first two scripts update the **locate** and **whatis** databases; if you've ever heard your hard drive churning around 4:00 on a Saturday morning, this is the reason why. Since **locate** and **apropos** are two of my favorite commands, I keep these scripts enabled.

```
# 310.locate
weekly_locate_enable="YES"   # Update locate weekly
# 320.whatis
weekly_whatis_enable="YES"   # Update whatis weekly
```

The next script is disabled by default; if you have lots of disk space and read a lot of man pages, you may find that enabling this script speeds up using the **man** utility.

```
# 330.catman
weekly_catman_enable="NO"        # Preformat man pages
```

The next script is also disabled. Enable it if you want to be aware of any files on your system that don't have a valid owner or group.

```
# 340.noid
weekly_noid_enable="NO"        # Find unowned files
weekly_noid_dirs="/"           # Look here
```

The last built-in weekly script is interesting, and may be worth enabling if you like to keep up-to-date with the ports tree. It will compare your already installed ports with /usr/ports/INDEX and make a list of which ports have a newer version number and should be updated.

```
# 400.status-pkg
weekly_status_pkg_enable="NO"           # Find out-of-date pkgs
pkg_version=pkg_version                  # Use this program
pkg_version_index=/usr/ports/INDEX-t  # Use this index file
```

You also have the option to create and use your own custom script called /etc/weekly.local:

```
# 999.local
weekly_local="/etc/weekly.local"     # Local scripts
```

Table 2.15: Monthly Scripts

Name of script	Action	Default
200.accounting	does login accounting using the ac(8) command	YES
999.local	list of extra scripts in /etc/monthly.local	

There is only one built-in monthly script and you are again given the option of where to send its output:

```
# Monthly options
# These options are used by periodic(8) itself to determine what to do
# with the output of the sub-programs that are run, and where to send
# that output.  $monthly_output might be set to /var/log/monthly.log if you
# wish to log the monthly output and have the files rotated by newsyslog(8)
monthly_output="root"                # user or /file
monthly_show_success="YES"           # scripts returning 0
monthly_show_info="YES"              # scripts returning 1
monthly_show_badconfig="NO"          # scripts returning 2
# 200.accounting
monthly_accounting_enable="YES"   # Login accounting
# 999.local
monthly_local="/etc/monthly.local"     # Local scripts
```

The accounting script will show the accounting statistics gathered by the **ac** command. If these statistics aren't useful to you, disable this script.[9]

---

[9]Login accounting is introduced in section 2.8.

Additional Resources

Original Articles:

http://www.onlamp.com/pub/a/bsd/2001/11/08/FreeBSD_Basics.html

http://www.onlamp.com/pub/a/bsd/2001/11/21/FreeBSD_Basics.html

Unix Security Checklist:

http://www.cert.org/tech_tips/usc20_full.html

DNS & BIND: Security Chapter

http://www.oreilly.com/catalog/dns4/chapter/ch11.html

2.14 Adding Users to FreeBSD

FreeBSD is a multiuser environment; one of the main tasks of a system administrator is to create user accounts and provide a secure environment for users to do their work in. To accomplish this effectively requires some pre-planning before any users are created.

Even if you are the only user on your home-based FreeBSD system, you will still need to create at least one user account to do your regular work in. Remember, you only use the superuser account for tasks that require superuser permissions.

It is a good idea to practice planning like an administrator on your own FreeBSD system, as you will gain the skills that will be essential when you begin to administer in a real production environment.

Naming Policies

A lot of stuff happens in the background when you create a user: several databases are updated, a mail folder is created, and a home directory for the user is created. When you create the user, you will have to supply a fair amount of information, including the username and password. Let's concentrate on user policies and creating user accounts.

Every user account you create must have a unique name across your FreeBSD system. This is easy to accomplish in a small environment, but a little harder to manage if you have to create dozens, hundreds, or even thousands of users. To help ensure uniqueness, you should have a user naming policy. If there is no existing policy in place and you need to create a naming scheme, keep in mind that there are a few restrictions on user names. First, they are limited to 16 characters, and some protocols, such as NIS, require a user name limit of eight characters. Second, they cannot begin with the hyphen character. And third, you should avoid the use of capital letters and periods as these may confuse some mail programs.

An example policy in a small environment would be to create user names using the first name and last initial of the user. You might have to modify this slightly to avoid conflicts. For example, if you needed to create accounts for Mike Smith and Mike Spencer, you could create *mikes* and *michaels* or *mikesm* and *mikesp*.

Another policy would be to create user names using the last name and first initial of the user, with possible modifications to avoid conflicts. If you need to create accounts for Mark Smith and Michelle Smith, you could create *smithma* and *smithmi*.

In a larger environment, you might want to use a certain number of characters for the first name and a certain number of characters for the last name. For example, if the policy is the first four characters of the user's first name followed by the first four characters of their last name, Mark Smith would become *marksmit* and Michelle Smith would become *michsmit*. You'll still need a backup plan for users whose first or last names are shorter than the specified amount of characters. For example, if I needed to create an account for My Lee using the above policy, I could create *my_lee*.

Unless you are in an extremely small environment, it's wise to avoid non-descriptive nicknames such as the *biko* and *genisis* that I use on my home system.

To summarize, a good user naming policy is aware of the restrictions placed on usernames and has a contingency method to avoid naming conflicts.

Creating User Accounts

Once you've decided on a naming scheme, you can create the user accounts using the **adduser** utility:

```
% adduser
adduser: ERROR: you must be the super-user (uid 0) to use this utility.
```

Oops. Looks like this is an administrative task that requires *root* permissions. Let's try this again.

```
% su
Password:
# adduser
Username: dlavigne
Full name: Test Account
Uid (Leave empty for default):
Login group [dlavigne]:
Login group is dlavigne. Invite dlavigne into other groups? []
Login class [default]:
Shell (sh csh tcsh nologin) [sh]: tcsh
```

Here the **adduser** script read a file called /etc/shells which contains the paths to all of the shells installed on the system; it then displayed the possible shells available for the user. Note that the default shell offered to users was the Bourne shell (sh), but I changed it to tcsh.

```
Home directory: [/home/dlavigne]:
Use password-based authentication? [yes]:
Use an empty password? (yes/no) [no]:
Use a random password? (yes/no) [no]:
Enter password []: mypassword
Enter password again []: mypassword
Lock out the account after creation? [no]:
Username    : dlavigne
Password    : *****
Full Name   : Test Account
Uid         : 1001
Class       :
Groups      : dlavigne
```

```
Home          : /home/dlavigne
Shell         : /bin/tcsh
Locked        : no
OK? (yes/no): yes
adduser: INFO: Successfully added (dlavigne) to the user database.
Add another user? (yes/no): no
Goodbye!
```

Behind the Scenes

Now that I've successfully created a user, I'll leave the superuser account. Let's log in as the new user, see what they have, and summarize what happened here:

```
login: dlavigne
Password:
% pwd
/usr/home/dlavigne
% ls -la
total 20
drwxr-xr-x 2 dlavigne dlavigne 512 Dec 30 11:21 ./
drwxr-xr-x 6 root     wheel    512 Dec 30 10:44 ../
-rw-r--r-- 1 dlavigne dlavigne 628 Dec 30 10:44 .cshrc
-rw-r--r-- 1 dlavigne dlavigne 299 Dec 30 10:44 .login
-rw-r--r-- 1 dlavigne dlavigne 160 Dec 30 10:44 .login_conf
-rw------- 1 dlavigne dlavigne 371 Dec 30 10:44 .mail_aliases
-rw-r--r-- 1 dlavigne dlavigne 331 Dec 30 10:44 .mailrc
-rw-r--r-- 1 dlavigne dlavigne 722 Dec 30 10:44 .profile
-rw------- 1 dlavigne dlavigne 276 Dec 30 10:44 .rhosts
-rw-r--r-- 1 dlavigne dlavigne 852 Dec 30 10:44 .shrc
```

You'll note that a home directory was created for the user and that it contains a lot of files that begin with a period or dot. These files were copied from the skeleton directory:

```
% ls -l /usr/share/skel
total 16
-rw-r--r-- 1 root wheel 628 Nov 20 07:01 dot.cshrc
-rw-r--r-- 1 root wheel 299 Nov 20 07:01 dot.login
-rw-r--r-- 1 root wheel 160 Nov 20 07:01 dot.login_conf
-rw------- 1 root wheel 371 Nov 20 07:01 dot.mail_aliases
-rw-r--r-- 1 root wheel 331 Nov 20 07:01 dot.mailrc
-rw-r--r-- 1 root wheel 722 Nov 20 07:01 dot.profile
-rw------- 1 root wheel 276 Nov 20 07:01 dot.rhosts
-rw-r--r-- 1 root wheel 852 Nov 20 07:01 dot.shrc
```

Note that the eight files created in our new user's home directory were copied from the template files contained in this directory. Also note that only the superuser can edit the files contained in the skel directory. For example, if you wished all users to receive a customized shell prompt, the superuser could modify the /usr/share/skel/dot.cshrc file which would then be copied to users' home directories as you created the users. Also, the superuser can also place any other dot files he wishes users to receive in the skel directory; for example, you can create a customized .xinitrc file for users.

Password Databases

When the superuser creates a user account, an entry for that user is added to the password database. Your FreeBSD system actually has four password database files that need to be updated. Let's summarize these files before taking a detailed look at their format. The first file is called /etc/passwd, and it is an ASCII text file readable by anyone:

```
% file /etc/passwd
/etc/passwd: ASCII text
% ls -l /etc/passwd
-rw-r--r--  1 root  wheel  1054 Dec 30 13:00 /etc/passwd
```

The permissions on this file need to stay the way they are or most of your FreeBSD utilities would stop working. However, it would be a security risk to store passwords in a file readable by anyone; for this reason, an * (asterisk) is used in the portion of this file where the password would normally be stored.

The second file is the shadow password file, or /etc/master.passwd. This file contains the encrypted hashes of users. We'll be taking a deeper look at encryption and hashes in sections 9.1 and 9.9 and other sections; for now, think of a hash as the value that FreeBSD uses to determine if a user's password is valid.

Let's see what type of file this is and who can read it:

```
% file /etc/master.passwd
/etc/master.passwd: writable, regular file, no read permission
% ls -l /etc/master.passwd
-rw-------  1 root  wheel  1226 Dec 30 13:00 /etc/master.passwd
```

The shadow password file is still in plain, ASCII text, but it is only readable and writable by *root*.

The third and fourth password files are called /etc/pwd.db and /etc/spwd.db. Let's take a look at their file types:

```
% file /etc/*pwd.db
/etc/pwd.db: Berkeley DB 1.85 (Hash, version 2, native byte-order)
/etc/spwd.db: Berkeley DB 1.85 (Hash, version 2, native byte-order)
```

These definitely aren't ASCII text files, so don't try to open them up with **cat**, **more**, or a text editor. These two files contain the same information as the ASCII text files, but in a database form that improves performance. Since /etc/pwd.db is the database equivalent of /etc/passwd, it doesn't contain any hashes. The *s* in /etc/spwd.db represents the shadow, so it is the database equivalent of /etc/master.passwd and does contain the hashes.

Now that we're familiar with the names of the four password files, let's take a look at the type of information they contain. As the superuser, send /etc/master.passwd to your screen; it should look something like this:

```
% su
Password:
# head /etc/master.passwd
# $FreeBSD: src/etc/master.passwd,v 1.40 2005/06/06 20:19:56 brooks Exp $
root:$1$hnH/w50a$tPdv5HZRsDP46FtsW8eXH/:0:0::0:0:Charlie &:/root:/bin/csh
```

```
toor:*:0:0::0:0:Bourne-again Superuser:/root:
daemon:*:1:1::0:0:Owner of many system processes:/root:/sbin/nologin
operator:*:2:5::0:0:System &:/:/sbin/nologin
bin:*:3:7::0:0:Binaries Commands and Source,,:/:/sbin/nologin
tty:*:4:65533::0:0:Tty Sandbox:/:/sbin/nologin
kmem:*:5:65533::0:0:KMem Sandbox:/:/sbin/nologin
games:*:7:13::0:0:Games pseudo-user:/usr/games:/sbin/nologin
```

Not the most friendly looking file, is it? It'll be a lot easier to read once we understand its format. Each line in the file contains one user's record, and each record consists of ten fields separated by colons. The fields are always in the following order:

```
name:hash:uid:gid:class:change:expire:gecos:home_dir:shell
```

Let's pick apart the record for the user *dlavigne* that was created using the **adduser** utility. Its record looks like this:

grep dlavigne /etc/master.passwd
```
dlavigne:$1pZV8Ju.2sEqsY:1001:1001::0:0:Test Account:/home/dlavigne:/bin/tcsh
```

The first field (dlavigne) is the username this user uses to log in to the system.

The second field ($1pZV8Ju.2sEqsY) is the encrypted hash; fortunately for dlavigne, this is not the password that she types in at login time. There is no way to tell what her actual password is from just reading this file. If you have a blank entry in this field, that user is not using a password, and you can tell by just reading this file. Also note that most of the system accounts have an asterisk in the second field; this means that a regular user won't be able to try to log in using one of these accounts.

The third field (1001) is the UID (user ID) of the user; this is how FreeBSD differentiates between users, so it must be unique. By default, FreeBSD starts creating UIDs at 1000, so all users I've created have a UID of 1000 or greater. Note that the users *root* and toor have a UID of 0; this means they have full superuser access to the system.

The fourth field (1001) is the primary GID (group ID) of the user. By default, when you create a user in FreeBSD, a group of the same name is also created.

The fifth field (blank) is the class of the user. Classes can be used to determine environment settings, session accounting, and resource limits. By default, this field is blank.

The sixth field (0) represents the time until the password needs to be changed. By default this field is set to zero, meaning the user never has to change his password.

The seventh field (0) represents the time until the user account expires; if a user account expires, that user will no longer be able to log in. By default, this field is set to zero, meaning that the account will never expire.

The eighth field (Test Account) contains the user's gecos information. This can include the user's full name, office location, work phone number, and home phone number, each separated by commas. The origin of the term gecos is interesting; when Unix was first being developed at Bell Labs, the main computer ran the General Electric Computer Operating System (gecos), and the information regarding the location of the users using this computer was placed in the gecos field of the password file.

The ninth field (/home/dlavigne) is the user's home directory. This is where they will be placed when they log in.

The tenth field (/bin/tcsh) is the path to the user's shell. Remember that the default shell is the Bourne shell, but we changed it to the **tcsh** shell when we ran the **adduser** utility.

Let's quickly compare the /etc/master.passwd file to the /etc/passwd file. I don't need to be the superuser to read this file, so I'll exit out of the superuser account first:

```
# exit
% head /etc/passwd
# $FreeBSD: src/etc/master.passwd,v 1.40 2005/06/06 20:19:56 brooks Exp $
root:*:0:0:Charlie &:/root:/bin/csh
toor:*:0:0:Bourne-again Superuser:/root:
daemon:*:1:1:Owner of many system processes:/root:/sbin/nologin
operator:*:2:5:System &:/:/sbin/nologin
bin:*:3:7:Binaries Commands and Source,,,:/:/sbin/nologin
tty:*:4:65533:Tty Sandbox:/:/sbin/nologin
kmem:*:5:65533:KMem Sandbox:/:/sbin/nologin
games:*:7:13:Games pseudo-user:/usr/games:/sbin/nologin
```

Note that it is similar to the shadow password file except that all of the password fields contain an * instead of the user's hash. Also, the fields that were blank or had a value of 0 have been omitted in this file.

Making Changes

You may have noticed that when we did the long listing for the password files using the **ls -l** command, only *root* had permission to write to the password files. It is important to note that *root* does not edit these files by opening them directly into a text editor. It is critical that a change made to one password file is sent to the other password files when that change is made; this is the job of the system utility called **pwd_mkdb**. If *root* needs to change a password file, he needs to use a utility which will send its changes to **pwd_mkdb**.

An example of a utility used for this purpose is **vipw**. The command **vipw** opens up the entire password file in the editor defined by the environment variable EDITOR, which is usually **vi**, hence the name **vipw**. If for some reason your default editor is not **vi**, you should probably avoid using the **vipw** utility or change EDITOR back to **vi**. Other editors use word-wrap, which can wreak havoc with system files such as your password file; this is not a good thing. To use this utility, you need to be comfortable using the **vi** editor and know what each of the ten fields represents and what values are acceptable in each field. For these reasons, only the superuser is allowed to use this utility.

Another utility that can be used to edit the password files is **chpass**, which is also called **chfn** or **chsh**. These utilities can be used by any user to change some of their own values in the password file. I'll log in as the user *dlavigne* and run the **chpass** utility:

```
login: dlavigne
Password:
% chpass
#Changing user  information for dlavigne.
Shell: /bin/tcsh
Full Name: Test Account
Office Location:
Office Phone:
```

```
Home Phone:
Other information:
/etc/pw.m32496: unmodified: line 1
```

Notice that a regular user is limited to changing only their own default shell and gecos information fields. I'll add an office phone number and see what happens. Since I'm in the **vi** editor, I'll arrow over to the correct spot in the file, press the **Escape** key followed by an **a** to enter append mode, and type in the phone number **123-4567**. I'll then press **Escape** again, followed by **:wq** to save my changes and quit the **vi** editor. The following will be displayed on my screen:

```
Password:  mypassword
chpass: user information updated
```

If I then look for the relevant entry in /etc/passwd, I should be able to see the change:

```
% grep dlavigne /etc/passwd
dlavigne:*:1001:1001:Test Account„123-4567:/home/dlavigne:/bin/tcsh
```

Notice the addition of the two commas in the gecos field to indicate what values you are reading. They will always be in this order:

```
full_name,office_location,work_phone,home_phone
```

so I know that 123-4567 is the work phone number of the user *dlavigne.*

Now, I'll run the **chpass** utility as the superuser. If I give a username as an argument to this command, I can edit the entries that pertain to that user. Let's see what the superuser can do to the entries for the user *dlavigne*:

```
% su
Password:
# chpass dlavigne
#Changing user  information for dlavigne.
Login: dlavigne
Password: $1pZV8Ju.2sEqsY
Uid [#]: 1001
Gid [# or name]: 1001
Change [month day year]:
Expire [month day year]:
Class:
Home directory: /home/dlavigne
Shell: /bin/tcsh
Full Name: Test Account
Office Location:
Office Phone: 123-4567
Home Phone:
Other information:
/etc/pw.B32584: unmodified: line 1
```

You should be able to recognize all of the ten fields for this user. The superuser account can modify the record for any user using the **chpass** command followed by the username. If the superuser just types **chpass**, he will be able to modify the record for the *root* user account. The **chpass** utility does have a few switches the superuser can use to modify a particular field in a user's record; see **man 1 chpass** for details.

The utility that is used to safely change a user's password in all of the password database files is the **passwd** utility. As the user *dlavigne* I'll change my password using the **passwd** command:

```
% passwd
Changing local password for dlavigne
Old Password:
New password: newpassword
Retype new password: newpassword
%
```

When a user changes their password, they are prompted for the old password; this prevents other users from changing a user's password for them.

What if a user forgets their password? All is not lost, as the superuser can change a user's password for them; when the superuser changes a user's password, she will not be prompted for the user's old password:

```
% su
Password:
# passwd dlavigne
Changing local password for dlavigne.
New password: anotherpassword
Retype new password: anotherpassword
```

Note that the superuser uses the username as an argument to the **passwd** utility; if there is no username, the password for the *root* account will be changed.

The last utility I want to look at that changes the password files is the **rmuser** utility. This utility is used to remove user accounts and anything associated with that user; therefore, it can only be run as the superuser. Let's remove that *dlavigne* account:

```
# rmuser
Please enter one or more usernames: dlavigne
Matching password entry:
dlavigne:$1$P6kMmPWG$rZiu/HfaIPVwJC6hdOImc/:1002:1002::0:0:dlavigne:/home/dlavigne ⇓
   :/bin/tcsh
Is this the entry you wish to remove? y
Remove user's home directory (/home/dlavigne)? y
Removing user (dlavigne): mailspool home passwd
```

This is a pretty effective utility; not only did it remove the user from the password files, it also removed the user's home directory, mail file, and any files belonging to the user in the temporary directories. You should also note that before I deleted the *dlavigne* user, its password field was no longer empty; it looked like the **passwd** utility had been successful in updating the password database.

Additional Resources

Original Articles:

```
http://www.onlamp.com/pub/a/bsd/2001/01/03/FreeBSD_Basics.html
http://www.onlamp.com/pub/a/bsd/2001/01/10/FreeBSD_Basics.html
```

3 Ports, Packages, and PBIs

3.1 Ports Tricks

One of the many reasons to love FreeBSD is its ports collection where nearly 17,000 applications are available and easy to install. In this section, I'd like to share some of my favorite ports tricks.

Even if you've been using the ports collection for a while, a read through **man ports** may reveal some tricks you were unaware of. If you have lots of disk space but a slow or intermittent Internet connection, this tip from the manpage is a real gem:

```
# cd /usr/ports
# make readmes
```

You may want to go grab some lunch while the command does its thing. When it's finished, you'll have a new file called /usr/ports/README.html. Open that file in your favorite web browser and you'll find some very handy hyperlinks. First, there is a link to the FreeBSD Handbook, which can be accessed either offline from your hard disk, or online from the FreeBSD web site. Next, there is a link to the Porter's Handbook. If you've ever wondered at the magic behind a port's Makefile or had the urge to make your own port, this is the file to read.

Next, there is a list of hyperlinks to each of the subdirectories in /usr/ports. Don't let the simplicity fool you. Select a subdirectory and one of its applications. I'll click on Editors –> AbiWord2. The resulting page contains hyperlinks to the port's description, web site, and maintainer's email address, as well as the email address of the ports mailing list. It also contains a list of all of the port's dependencies. Granted, all of this information was already on your hard drive, but you can't beat accessing it via one bookmarkable web page that is available offline.

Making a Package Repository

Another handy trick is making a package repository. This can be both a time- and bandwidth-saver if you need to install software on multiple machines in a network. It is also ideal for installing software on server machines, as you don't have to install the entire ports collection just to install your required applications.

Pick a machine in your network to contain the package repository. Only this machine will need the ports collection; it won't be required on the rest of the machines in the network. Start by creating a directory to hold the packages:

```
# mkdir /usr/ports/packages
```

Then create the packages you need. Here, I'll create two packages:

```
# cd /usr/ports/www/lynx
# make package-recursive
# cd /usr/ports/mail/getmail
# make package-recursive
<snip output except for last few lines>
Creating package /usr/ports/packages/All/getmail-4.7.3.tbz
Registering depends: python24-2.4.4.
Creating package /usr/ports/packages/All/python24-2.4.4.tbz
```

Note: You will receive an error if the requested software is already installed on this system. You can bypass that error and create the package by including this option:

```
# make FORCE_PACKAGE_RECURSIVE=yes package-recursive
```

When you use **make package-recursive**, the requested package and any of its dependencies are created and stored in a subdirectory of /usr/ports/packages.

Once you've populated /usr/ports/packages with the packages required by your network, set up an NFS mount to share the package repository. The easiest way to do this is with **sysinstall**. On the machine holding the packages, type **sysinstall**, then choose Configure, then Networking, and then NFS server. You should see the following message:

> Operating as an NFS server means that you must first configure an /etc/exports file to indicate which hosts are allowed certain kinds of access to your local file systems. Press [ENTER] now to invoke an editor on /etc/exports

Unless you've changed your default editor, /etc/exports[1] will be opened in **vi**. The default file contains some example syntax. The following line limits access to /usr/ports/packages to the computers on network 192.168.2.0 using the default subnet mask for that network:

```
/usr/ports/packages -network 192.168.2.0 -mask 255.255.255.0
```

Once you've saved your changes, exit **sysinstall** and initialize the NFS server:

```
# /etc/rc.d/nfsd start
Starting nfsd.
# /etc/rc.d/nfsd status
nfsd is running as pid 103 104 105 106 107.
```

Next, you'll need to create NFS clients on each machine that is to use the package repository. This time, in **sysinstall**, choose NFS client. You won't be prompted for anything; you'll just check off the box. Once you've exited the utility, type:

```
# /etc/rc.d/nfsclient start
NFS access cache time=60
```

---

[1]More details about /etc/exports and setting up an NFS server are covered in section 8.15.

Then, check to see if you can access the package repository. In my example, 192.168.2.12 is the machine containing the packages:

```
# mount 192.168.2.12:/usr/ports/packages /mnt
# ls /mnt
All     Latest  ipv6    mail    python  www
```

You'll note that subdirectories were created for mail/getmail and www/lynx. The ipv6 and python subdirectories were for dependencies of those packages. The All subdirectory is quite handy:

```
# ls /mnt/All
getmail-4.7.3.tbz       lynx-2.8.6.4.tbz    python24-2.4.4.tbz
```

I'll now try to add a package:

```
# pkg_add /mnt/All/lynx-2.8.6.4.tbz
```

Once I receive my prompt back, I'll check that the application did indeed install:

```
# pkg_info | grep lynx
lynx-2.8.6.4    A non-graphical, text-based World-Wide Web client
```

Note: Either NFS export the All subdirectory or train your users to refer to it when adding packages as this directory contains the dependency packages as well. Otherwise the package install will fail if it can't find a dependency:

```
# pkg_add /mnt/mail/getmail-3.1.7.tbz
pkg_add: could not find package python-2.2.3_2 !
# pkg_add /mnt/All/getmail-3.1.7.tbz
#
```

Also, when a user is finished, remind them to **cd** out of the NFS share and unmount it:

```
# cd
# umount /mnt
```

Showing Dependencies

OK, what else can one do with ports? I've already shown you one way to view a port's dependencies using **make readmes**. Another way is to do this:

```
# cd /usr/ports/graphics/xpdf
# make pretty-print-build-depends-list
This port requires package(s) "autoconf-2.59_2 expat-2.0.0_1 fontconfig-2.4.2_1, 1
freetype2-2.2.1_1 gettext-0.16.1_1 gmake-3.81_1 imake-6.9.0_1 libdrm-2.0.2
libiconv-1.9.2_2 m4-1.4.8_1 open-motif-2.2.3_2 perl-5.8.8 pkg-config-0.21
t1lib-5.1.1,1 xorg-libraries-6.9.0_1" to build.
```

Searching Ports

The ports collection also includes a search feature. This is extremely useful, especially if you already know what type of application you want and wish to know which ports are available to fulfill that need. For example:

```
# cd /usr/ports
# make search key=dvd | more
```

The result will be a list of all ports dealing with DVDs. Here is the first result in the search, to give you an idea of the information that can be gathered:

```
Port:   amarok-1.4.5_5
Path:   /usr/ports/audio/amarok
Info:   Media player for KDE
Maint:  mich@FreeBSD.org
B-deps: OpenEXR-1.4.0 aalib-1.4.r5_2 arts-1.5.6_1,1 artswrapper-1.5.3 aspell-0.60.5
atk-1.18.0 bitstream-vera-1.10_3 cairo-1.4.4 cdrtools-2.01_6 cups-base-1.2.1
<snip>
R-deps: OpenEXR-1.4.0 aalib-1.4.r5_2 arts-1.5.6_1,1 artswrapper-1.5.3 aspell-0.60.5
atk-1.18.0 bitstream-vera-1.10_3 cairo-1.4.4 cdrtools-2.01_6 cups-base-1.2.1
<snip>
WWW: http://amarok.kde.org/
```

The B-deps are the build dependencies (software required to successfully compile the application), while the R-deps are the run dependencies (software required to successfully run the application).

If instead you just want to search for a port's name, use **search name=** instead. For example, if I know I want to build firefox and want to see which versions are available but don't care about dependencies, this will do the trick:

```
# make search name=firefox | grep Port
Port:   de-bsdforen-firefox-searchplugin-0.2_1
Port:   de-bsdgroup-firefox-searchplugin-0.2_1
Port:   firefox-2.0.0.3,1
Port:   firefox-3.0.a2,1
Port:   firefox-i18n-2.0.0.3
Port:   firefox-remote-20040803_1
Port:   firefox-1.5.0.11,3
Port:   linux-firefox-2.0.0.3
Port:   linux-firefox-devel-3.0.a2007.03.21
Port:   xpi-firefox-showcase-0.9.2.3
```

If you find the search facility useful, it is a good idea to first run **make index** from /usr/ports to ensure your ports index is completely up to date. This is another command that takes a while, so don't execute it if you're in a hurry.

Displaying the Currently Installed Packages and Ports

Let's move on to **pkg_info**. This utility is used to display the currently installed packages and ports on a system. Unless you've read this manpage before, you're missing out on a lot of useful switches.

When using **pkg_info**, you can use **-a** in combination with other switches to gather information on all installed software. Alternately, specify the name of the particular application you wish to gather information about. For example:

```
% pkg_info -ac
```

shows the one-line comment of every installed application, whereas:

```
% pkg_info -c lynx-2.8.6.4
```

will show the one-line comment for lynx-2.8.6.4. If you'd rather read the long description, use **-d** instead of **-c**.

If you're like me and hate typing, or, for that matter, remembering the version number of an application, include **-x**:

```
% pkg_info -xc lynx
```

The above command will show the one-line comment of every application that starts with **lynx**. Besides saving your memory cells for other purposes, it's an excellent way to find out if more than one version of **lynx** happens to be installed on your system.

Reading Post-Installation Messages

After installing a port, it's useful to see if there were any messages, as these often contain configuration instructions. For example, here is the message for /usr/ports/mail/messagewall:

```
% pkg_info -xD messagewall
Messagewall has been installed, now create the chroot environment:
        mkdir /home/mwall
        groupadd mwall
        useradd -g mwall mwall
        mkdir /home/mwall/pids
        chown mwall:mwall /home/mwall/pids
        mkdir /home/mwalla
        groupadd mwalla
        useradd -g mwalla mwalla
        mkdir /home/mwalla/pids
        chown mwalla:mwalla /home/mwalla/pids
copy the virus patterns into your environment
        cp /usr/local/etc/messagewall/virus.patterns /home/mwall
and don't forget to edit your configfile!
```

A very useful switch is **-L**, as it gives the full pathname to every file that was installed with the application:

```
% pkg_info -xL lynx | head
Information for lynx-2.8.6.4:
Files:
/usr/local/man/man1/lynx.1.gz
/usr/local/bin/lynx
/usr/local/etc/lynx.cfg.default
/usr/local/share/doc/lynx/CHANGES
/usr/local/share/doc/lynx/COPYHEADER
/usr/local/share/doc/lynx/COPYHEADER.asc
/usr/local/share/doc/lynx/COPYING
```

From the output, I now know that **lynx** installed with a manpage, that the location of the application itself is **/usr/local/bin/lynx**, that there is a default configuration file, and that there is a directory containing documents regarding **lynx**. Usually, I'm not interested in every file that was installed.

Checking Dependencies Before Uninstalling

Before uninstalling an application, it is always a good idea to see if any other packages require that application as a dependency. For example, you've typed **pkg_info | more** and see this application:

```
ORBit2-2.14.7
```

You think to yourself, "I don't remember installing, or even ever using, this application. Maybe I should just get rid of it." This command will tell you if it was instead installed by another application that you do need:

```
% pkg_info -Rx ORBit | head -5
Information for ORBit2-2.14.7:
Required by:
en-openoffice.org-US-2.1.0
gimp-2.2,2
```

Ahh, looks like this application is useful, after all. But, don't worry. If you did try to uninstall this application, **pkg_delete** would complain because it is required by those other applications. However, it is always nice to be aware of these things ahead of time.

Checking the Disk Space Your Ports Use

What happens if you go a little install-crazy and end up with more applications than disk space? Use the size switch to determine how much space an application's files are using. Send the output to either a pager:

```
% pkg_info -as | more
```

or to a file that you can read at your leisure:

```
% pkg_info -as > sizes
```

You'll then have an idea of which applications are using the most space so that you can decide which ones are worth uninstalling. Remember, you also have the comment switch and the dependencies switch to help you in your decision.

Checking the Status of Installed Ports

Yet another way to find out what software is installed on your system is to use **pkg_version**.

```
% pkg_version | more
```

will list each installed application, in alphabetical order. You'll note that each application is followed by one of these three symbols:

= the application is up to date.

< there is a newer version of the application available.

> your index may be out of date.

So, to determine which applications require upgrading:

```
% pkg_version -l "<"
```

Note that you need to place quotes around the **<**, or your shell will complain about a missing name for your redirect. If you don't receive any output, congratulations! All of your applications are up to date. If you do receive some output, you know which applications require an upgrade.

Alternately, this command will show all applications that are out of date:

```
% pkg_version -L "="
```

See **man pkg_version** if you didn't catch the difference between **-l** and **-L**.

If you prefer a more verbose output than =, <, or >, try this command:

```
% pkg_version -v | more
```

Usually, you run **pkg_version** after using **csup** to retrieve the latest ports updates. If for some reason you're not using **csup**, you can still check your installed ports against the latest ports tree:

```
% pkg_version -v \
  ftp://ftp.freebsd.org/pub/FreeBSD/branches/-current/ports/INDEX \
  | more
```

Note that that command is one long line. Alternately, use **-l** or **-L** with that URL to find your out of date applications.

All of the utilities mentioned in this section came with your FreeBSD system.

Additional Resources

Original Article:

```
http://www.onlamp.com/pub/a/bsd/2003/08/07/FreeBSD_Basics.html
```

3.2 portupgrade

In the previous section, we took a look at the built-in utilities that can be used to manage the FreeBSD ports collection. In this section, I'd like to continue in that vein.

Ports Structure

First, let's review the ports structure, where it's installed on your system, and how you can keep it up to date.

When you installed FreeBSD and chose to install the ports collection, /usr/ports and its files and subdirectories were created for you. If you **ls /usr/ports**, you'll see that it contains subdirectories that logically divide the ports collection. For example, there are subdirectories for mail, www, and databases. Each subdirectory contains subdirectories for applicable applications, so www has subdirectories for **mozilla** and **lynx**. Each of those subdirectories contains the information needed in order to install that particular application. For example:

```
$ ls -F /usr/ports/www/firefox
CVS/            distinfo     pkg-descr
Makefile        files/       pkg-message
```

We were actually gathering information from the Makefile, pkg-descr, and pkg-message files with some of the utilities and switches we covered in the previous section.

The ports collection is constantly being updated and new ports are added on a daily basis. If you're the curious type and like to see a layout of which ports were added when, you'll find http://www.freshports.org an invaluable resource.

It's great to have such a dynamic ports collection, but it does mean that your ports tree, the /usr/ports directory structure, can quickly become out of date. To keep in sync with the changes and ensure that you always have the ability to build any available port, use **csup**.

Syncing Your Ports Tree

Starting with FreeBSD 6.2, **csup** is part of the base system meaning you don't have to install the third-party **cvsup-without-gui** application. You can either create your configuration file by hand or edit the sample one provided in /usr/share/examples/cvsup/cvs-supfile.

csup can be used to keep both your operating system and your ports collection up to date. If you're only interested in keeping your ports tree in sync, a configuration file similar to this will do it:

```
# more /root/cvs-supfile
*default host=cvsup.ca.freebsd.org
*default base=/usr/local/etc/cvsup
*default prefix=/usr
*default release=cvs delete use-rel-suffix compress
ports-all tag=.
```

The file can be invoked with this command as the superuser:

```
# csup /root/cvs-supfile
```

The first time you use this file **csup** may complain about a missing subdirectory; simply **mkdir** it and try again. Also note that the =. in the ports-all line is important, so double-check that your file has it.

That **csup** command will download all of the latest bits of the ports collection and add them to your ports tree. This is the type of command that benefits from being run on a daily basis, so you might wish to add it as a **cron** job.

The **csup** process also updates a file called /usr/ports/INDEX. This file contains a list of all of the ports in your ports tree. To see how up to date your ports tree is, use this command:

```
% ls -l /usr/ports/INDEX
-rw-r--r--  1 root   wheel   3678738 May 17 17:04 INDEX
```

That particular machine was installed on May 17 and I haven't kept its ports tree up to date. If I compare that system to my main machine, which is **csup**ed daily:

```
# ls -l /usr/ports/INDEX
-rw-r--r--  1 root   wheel   3912366 Aug 17 08:50 INDEX
```

you'll see that the size of the file, and thus the number of port entries, has grown considerably in that three-month period.

Installing portupgrade

Let's take a look at **portupgrade**, a feature-rich port designed to help you get the most out of the ports collection.

Start by installing portupgrade:

```
# pkg_add -r portupgrade
```

This will install over a dozen useful utilities. Let's take a trick from the last section and see which manpages, and hence, which utilities (in man1) and which configuration files (in man5) were installed:

```
% pkg_info -xL portupgrade | grep man
/usr/local/man/man1/pkg_deinstall.1.gz
/usr/local/man/man1/pkg_fetch.1.gz
/usr/local/man/man1/pkg_glob.1.gz
/usr/local/man/man1/pkg_sort.1.gz
/usr/local/man/man1/pkgdb.1.gz
/usr/local/man/man1/portcvsweb.1.gz
/usr/local/man/man1/portsclean.1.gz
/usr/local/man/man1/portsdb.1.gz
/usr/local/man/man1/portupgrade.1.gz
/usr/local/man/man1/portversion.1.gz
/usr/local/man/man5/pkgtools.conf.5.gz
/usr/local/man//man1/pkg_which.1.gz
/usr/local/man//man1/portinstall.1.gz
/usr/local/man//man1/ports_glob.1.gz
```

It is time well spent to skim through those manpages. You'll get an idea of the power and the flexibility of the ports collection and will uncover tips and tricks you've never thought of. However, don't be dismayed if you feel a bit overwhelmed by the amount of available information. In the next few sections, I'll walk you through some concrete examples to get you started in using these utilities effectively.

Updating the Ports Database

OK, we're finally ready for **portupgrade** and its suite of utilities. After each **csup**, run this command:

```
# portsdb -Uu
```

The first time you use this command, a database called INDEX-6.db will be created in /usr/ports. This database will be updated every time you repeat that **portsdb** command after a fresh **csup**. If you use the **file** utility, you'll see that you won't be able to access the contents of INDEX-6.db, since it is not an ASCII text file:

```
% file /usr/ports/INDEX-6.db
/usr/ports/INDEX-6.db: Berkeley DB 1.85/1.86 (Btree, version 3, native byte-order)
```

However, several of the **portupgrade** utilities will use this database. The Btree refers to a type of database algorithm that is designed to quickly search through a large amount of data. This is ideal for the ports collection — we'll find that some of the **portupgrade** utilities are faster and more efficient than the built-in utilities we saw in the last section, because of that Btree.

You'll have to be patient, as **portsdb** takes a while to run.

Note: This command is equivalent in functionality and reduces the amount of waiting time:

```
# cd /usr/ports
# make fetchindex
# portsdb -u
```

Once your INDEX is up to date, you're ready to use **portversion** to see if any of your installed ports need upgrading. Remember this command?

```
# portversion -l "<"
```

If you receive any output, your next step is to upgrade those out-of-date ports. Not surprisingly, we'll use **portupgrade**, which is also called **portinstall**.

Upgrading the Ports

In its simplest form, **portupgrade -a** will upgrade all (**-a**) of your out-of-date ports. However, over time you may end up with ports that refuse to upgrade. This seeming anomaly is not a limitation of **portupgrade**, but rather points to the reality of dependencies.

A port has two types of dependencies. The first is called a build dependency and refers to any other ports that need to be installed before this port will successfully install. The second type of dependency refers to other ports that depend upon the particular port you wish to upgrade. You may remember from the previous section that **pkg_delete** won't let you uninstall an application if other applications depend upon it.

If you just upgrade an application but don't check to see if its dependencies also need upgrading, you'll eventually end up with applications that refuse to upgrade. To prevent this from happening, use the two recursive switches with **portupgrade**, like so:

```
# portupgrade -arR
```

The **-R** will check the build dependencies and the **-r** will check the applications that depend upon the port being upgraded. This will prevent your system from having outdated dependencies and software incompatibilities.

Occasionally, when you use **portupgrade** or one of its utilities, you'll see a message asking you to run **pkgdb -F**. As you may have guessed from the name, this utility updates a package database. That database is found at /var/db/pkg/pkgdb.db. Again, this database uses a Btree to optimize search time.

If you're ever asked to run **pkgdb -F**, do it. However, don't interrupt this command, or you'll end up with an inconsistent database. If you're ever in that unfortunate situation, this command will fix the inconsistencies:

```
# pkgdb -fu
```

That's a pretty easy switch combo to remember, as similar thoughts will probably be running through your head at the time.

Running **pkgdb** with **-F** will interactively fix the database. This means that **pkgdb** will pause to ask you what you would like it to do before doing it. If you find it intimidating coming up with the correct responses to **pkgdb**'s enquiries, use **-fu** instead, and it will quietly do what it thinks is best. If you're really paranoid, an alternative is **-Fa**, which tells **pkgdb** to only fix the discrepancies that can be fixed securely.

This all sounds scarier than it really is. It's very rare that you'll ever be asked to run **pkgdb -F**. **pkgdb** is usually used for other purposes, which is why it's also called **pkg_which**.

Using pkg_which

pkg_which (or **pkgdb**) can be used to find out to which application a file belongs. Here's a simple example showing the difference between the built-in **which** command and **pkg_which**:

```
% which pkgdb
/usr/local/sbin/pkgdb
```

which is used to find the path to an application. **pkg_which** will tell me to which port the specified application belongs:

```
% pkg_which pkgdb
portupgrade-2.2.6_3,2
```

This command is equivalent:

```
% pkgdb pkgdb
portupgrade-2.2.6_3,2
```

Here's another example. Let's say you're poking about /usr/local, the directory structure containing the files used by installed applications. You find a whole bunch of files and don't have a clue where they came from or to which application they belong. Here's a job for **pkg_which**. Take a look at this example snippet from my system:

```
% ls /usr/local/bin/yaf*
/usr/local/bin/yaf-cdda*      /usr/local/bin/yaf-tplay*
/usr/local/bin/yaf-mpgplay*   /usr/local/bin/yaf-vorbis*
/usr/local/bin/yaf-splay*     /usr/local/bin/yaf-yuv*
```

If you're like me, those files hold absolutely no meaning to you. Let's see to which applications they belong:

```
% pkg_which /usr/local/bin/yaf*
kdemultimedia-mpeglib_artsplug-3.5.6
kdemultimedia-mpeglib_artsplug-3.5.6
kdemultimedia-mpeglib_artsplug-3.5.6
kdemultimedia-mpeglib_artsplug-3.5.6
kdemultimedia-mpeglib_artsplug-3.5.6
kdemultimedia-mpeglib_artsplug-3.5.6
```

pkg_which contains a few useful switches. One is the **-o**, or origin, switch. Say you can't remember where in the ports tree **kdemultimedia-mpeglib_artsplug-3.5.6** came from. Try this:

```
% pkg_which -o kdemultimedia-mpeglib_artsplug-3.5.6
audio/mpeglib_artsplug
```

The output indicates that the name of the subdirectory from which that application was built is /usr/ports/audio/mpeglib_artsplug.

Before going further, let's summarize the steps you can take to keep your installed software up to date:

1. Run **csup** to sync the ports tree.

2. Run **portsdb** to update INDEX-6.db.

3. Use **portversion** to determine which applications need upgrading.

4. Use **portupgrade** to upgrade those applications.

Additional portupgrade Switches

We've already seen that **portupgrade -arR** will properly upgrade all out-of-date applications. However, **portupgrade** comes with several switches to let you pick and choose which applications to upgrade and how to do it.

One option that is useful if you don't have a constant Internet connection is **-F**. Typically, when you upgrade, **portupgrade** will go out on the Internet as it needs a file, then spend the time building that file. If you're doing a large upgrade such as KDE, it may need to go on the Internet every so often over a period of hours.

This command will go out on the Internet and retrieve all of the files needed to upgrade your ports, but won't install anything:

```
% portupgrade -aFrR
```

Once you've downloaded the necessary files, you can disconnect from the Internet and use carry on as usual.

Another available switch is **-n**. This switch simply tells you what **portupgrade** would do without actually doing it. This is very useful if you are the nervous or the paranoid type and want to know ahead of time what is going to happen to your installed software.

Here's an example output:

```
# portupgrade -anrR
---> Session started at: Sun, 17 Aug 2003 22:06:00 -0400
<a page of output snipped>
---> Reporting the results (+:done / -:ignored / *:skipped / !:failed)
- lang/ruby16 (ruby-1.6.8.2003.04.19)
- net/cvsup-without-gui (cvsup-without-gui-16.1h)
+ lang/ruby16-shim-ruby18 (ruby-shim-ruby18-1.8.0.p2.2003.04.19)
+ databases/ruby-bdb1 (ruby-bdb1-0.1.9)
- sysutils/portupgrade (portupgrade-20030723)
- www/lynx (lynx-2.8.4.1d)
---> Session ended at: Sun, 17 Aug 2003 22:06:02 -0400 (consumed 00:00:02)
```

Let's take a look at that output. **portupgrade** systematically went through every installed port on the system, then put its results into a report. Each line in the report shows the port's origin, the currently installed version, and a symbol indicating whether or not it needs to be upgraded. This particular report shows that two ports need upgrading. They are the ones on lines that begin with a + (plus). If I compare this report to **portversion**, I'll see similar results, written in a different fashion:

```
# portversion -l "<"
ruby-bdb1
ruby-shim-ruby18
```

If you're cautious about what gets upgraded on your system, you might also enjoy the **-i**, or interactive, switch. Add it to your **portupgrade** switches and **portupgrade** will pause for your input before upgrading an application or any of its dependencies. A pause will look like this:

```
---> Upgrading 'ruby-bdb1-0.1.9' to 'ruby-bdb1-0.2.1'
     (databases/ruby/bdb1)
OK? [yes]
```

Notice the default response of *yes* in the square brackets. That means if you press **Return**, you are saying yes. If you decide you'd rather not upgrade this port, type in the word **no** instead.

The last switch I'd like to cover is the **-l**, or log, switch. This switch is invaluable if you're ever in the situation where a port refuses to install and you need to send the output of the failed install to someone else. Here, I'll upgrade one specified port and send the output to a file called logfile:

```
# portupgrade -rR ruby-shim-ruby18 -l logfile
```

You probably don't want to use the **-l** switch with the **-a** switch, especially if you have a lot of ports that need upgrading. No one is going to want to wade through a log file that large!

Additional Resources

Original Article:

`http://www.onlamp.com/pub/a/bsd/2003/08/28/FreeBSD_Basics.html`

FreeBSD Handbook: Using CVSup

`http://www.freebsd.org/doc/en_US.ISO8859-1/books/handbook/cvsup.html`

Cleaning Up Ports:

`http://www.onlamp.com/pub/a/bsd/2001/11/29/Big_Scary_Daemons.html`

3.3 Cleaning and Customizing Your Ports

Anyone who installs or uninstalls software soon realizes what a messy business this can be. Installations can clutter the hard drive with temporary files, unread READMEs, and unnoticed directories. Sometimes a program uninstall will leave behind souvenirs: files that are no longer required but still take up disk space. Worse, an install might overwrite, or an uninstall might remove, libraries that were being used by other applications. These frustrations seemingly transcend operating-system boundaries and often result in a user reinstalling the operating system from scratch just to start over with a clean slate.

Keeping Your Ports Clean

Fortunately, there are tools available to help you intelligently manage software installation and keep your FreeBSD system happily humming along for years. For example, when you install a port, remember to include the **clean** target:

```
# make install clean
```

This will tell **make** to clean out its working directory once the port has successfully installed. If you forget to **clean**, you'll soon find that working directories can consume a lot of disk space.

Depending upon your needs and the amount of disk space you have to work with, you might consider using this command instead:

```
# make install distclean
```

When you install a port, the required source files are downloaded from the Internet and copied into /usr/ports/distfiles. If you ever want to reinstall that port, the necessary source files are already on disk. **distclean** tells **make** to erase those files once the port is successfully installed. When deciding whether or not to use **distclean**, balance your available disk space with the speed and reliability of your Internet connection. Also, for license reasons, some ports require you to fetch the source manually and save it to /usr/ports/distfiles. I find it more convenient to save those files on disk, so I don't use **distclean** when building those ports.

Those two switches can go a long way in conserving disk space. However, if you've installed **portupgrade**, check out the **portsclean** utility that came with it. As the name suggests, this utility is designed to clean out what may have been left behind from using the ports collection.

I have a system that I use to test applications, meaning I've used it to install and uninstall hundreds of ports. I usually remember to use **clean** and sometimes remember to use **distclean**. Let's take a look at its current condition and see if **portsclean** will make a difference. First, I'll check how much disk space is free on /usr:

```
% df /usr
Filesystem    1K-blocks    Used    Avail Capacity  Mounted on
/dev/ad0s1f   13360662  6189648  6102162    50%     /usr
```

Next, I'll look for disk hogs in /usr/ports. This command will show the disk usage, sorted by largest usages first and piped to **head** so I can see the top ten disk wasters:

```
# du /usr/ports | sort -rn | head
3110862 /usr/ports
1848846 /usr/ports/distfiles
822278  /usr/ports/editors
816710  /usr/ports/editors/openoffice-devel
816592  /usr/ports/editors/openoffice-devel/work
604784  /usr/ports/editors/openoffice-devel/work/oo_644_src
362536  /usr/ports/distfiles/KDE
295404  /usr/ports/distfiles/openoffice
211718  /usr/ports/editors/openoffice-devel/work/mozilla
211654  /usr/ports/editors/openoffice-devel/work/mozilla/work
```

Hmmm. Looks like I haven't used **distclean** as much as I thought, and I still have working files left behind from the OpenOffice build.

I'll start by cleaning out all of those missed working directories:

```
# portsclean -C
```

Did it make a difference in disk space?

```
# df /usr
Filesystem  1K-blocks    Used    Avail Capacity  Mounted on
/dev/ad0s1f  13360662  5160664  7131146    42%     /usr
```

Oh yeah. I just increased my disk capacity by 8%. Remember, cleaning out working directories is a good thing, as they are only used during the build process. They aren't needed once the port successfully installs.

The next **portsclean** switch is pretty cool. Let's say you've decided to keep /usr/ports/distfiles intact. For the past few years. And you've uninstalled a few applications along the way, and upgraded others to the latest versions. There's a very good chance that some outdated and unneeded source files are collecting dust in /usr/ports/distfiles. To find and remove those relics:

```
# portsclean -DD
Detecting unreferenced distfiles...
```

and to check out the impact:

```
# df /usr
Filesystem  1K-blocks    Used    Avail Capacity  Mounted on
/dev/ad0s1f  13360662  4092490  8199320    33%     /usr
```

Whoa. Another 9% in disk savings. I should also see a major difference in the **du** command:

```
# du /usr/ports | sort -rn | head
1011998 /usr/ports
780760  /usr/ports/distfiles
161724  /usr/ports/distfiles/openoffice
137010  /usr/ports/distfiles/staroffice52
122648  /usr/ports/distfiles/KDE
55478   /usr/ports/distfiles/xc
24936   /usr/ports/distfiles/rpm
20536   /usr/ports/devel
18194   /usr/ports/distfiles/AbiWord
17704   /usr/ports/distfiles/ghostscript
```

Notice that while disk usage has decreased considerably, my system still holds the distfiles referenced by my currently installed applications.

Customizing Available Ports

Let's move on to customizing how you interact with the ports collection. When you installed **portupgrade**, the files /usr/local/etc/pkgtools.conf and /usr/local/etc/pkgtools.conf.sample were installed for you. By default, both files are the same. Make any changes to /usr/local/etc/pkgtools.conf and keep /usr/local/etc/pkgtools.conf.sample as is, to remind you of the original settings.

If you take the time to read this file, you'll find that it is well commented and chock full of neat and useful advice designed to help you get the most out of your ports. I'll highlight some of the more useful options, but do take the time to check out the full file yourself.

For starters, this file allows you to set the environment variables used by the **portupgrade** suite of utilities. For example, the default temporary directory is /var/tmp. This default can cause problems on small hard drives where disk space is limited on /var. To change this default, search for this line in /usr/local/etc/pkgtools.conf:

```
#    ENV['PKG_TMPDIR'] ||= '/var/tmp'
```

and change it to something like this:

```
ENV['PKG_TMPDIR'] ||= '/usr/tmp'
```

Remember to remove the comment (#) and to ensure the new temporary directory exists.

Another useful setting is the ignore categories section:

```
# IGNORE_CATEGORIES: array
#
# This is a list of port categories you want the pkgtools to ignore.
# Typically you want to list language specific categories of the
# languages you don't use.
```

```
#
# After configuring this list, you need to rebuild the ports
# database to reflect the changes. (run 'portsdb -Ufu')
#
# e.g.:
#    IGNORE_CATEGORIES = [
#       'chinese',
#       'french',
#       'german',
#       'hebrew',
#       'japanese',
#       'korean',
#       'russian',
#       'ukrainian',
#       'vietnamese',
#    ]
IGNORE_CATEGORIES = [
]
```

Here, the comments are quite clear. If you decide to take advantage of this option, remove the # from categories you wish to ignore. While the language categories are suggested, you can ignore any category. For example, if you never plan on installing applications from the astro or irc categories, you can include those. Here is a sample edit:

```
IGNORE_CATEGORIES = [
    'chinese',
    'german',
    'hebrew',
    'japanese',
    'korean',
    'russian',
    'ukrainian',
    'vietnamese',
    'astro',
]
#         IGNORE_CATEGORIES = [
#       ]
```

Notice that I remarked the default empty IGNORE_CATEGORIES section. I then removed the remarks from the section listing the categories I'd like to be ignored. I also used the same format to add the astro category. Don't forget to follow the directions in the comments and:

portsdb -Ufu

once you've saved your edits to this section.

Customizing Individual Port Build Options

One of the handiest settings in this file is the MAKE_ARGS section. Some ports allow you to customize how they build by specifying certain arguments. These arguments are found in the port's Makefile and are usually invoked like this:

```
# cd /usr/ports/www/bluefish
# make WITH_TIDY=yes install clean
```

The above make command is equivalent to this invocation:

```
# make -DWITH_TIDY install clean
```

If you ever plan on using **portupgrade** to upgrade **bluefish** and wish to use the same arguments, you have a choice. Either count on your ability to remember to use the **-m** switch to specify your **make** arguments with **portupgrade**:

```
# portupgrade -rRm '-DWITH_TIDY' bluefish
```

or spend a moment and add those switches to /usr/local/etc/pkgtools.conf:

```
MAKE_ARGS = {
    'www/bluefish-*' => 'WITH_TIDY=1',
}
```

Let's pick that apart, as it looks a bit complicated and the syntax is rather picky. Notice that the entire MAKE_ARGS section is enclosed within curly brackets. Within those brackets are the particular ports and their **make** arguments. This means you can keep adding ports to this section, each on their own line, ensuring that all of the ports are between those brackets.

The name of the port itself must be quoted in single quotes and includes the name of its subdirectory in the ports collection. The name is followed by the wildcard -*.

The **make** arguments themselves are also enclosed between single quotes located after the =>. Note that the number *1* is used instead of the word yes and that the arguments are separated by a space.

It's worth your while to spend the few minutes it takes to add your arguments to this section whenever you first build a port that uses arguments. You'll eventually upgrade that port, and it is highly unlikely that you'll even remember that it used arguments, let alone what those actual arguments were.

Ports Tools

Let's finish this series by peeking at the tools section of the ports tree. If you haven't discovered it on your own yet, take a look at:

```
% more /usr/ports/Tools/scripts/README
```

Gee, just when you thought you knew everything there was to know about ports, you find there's a whole new stash of useful utilities. Since these are all scripts, don't forget to put a ./ in front of the name as you try out each of the scripts:

```
# cd /usr/ports/Tools/scripts
# ./consistency-check
```

I'd suggest trying out each script that piques your interest as you read its description in the README file. If you find some new favorites, consider either copying them or symlinking them to ~/bin so they will be in your path.

Additional Resources

Original Article:

```
http://www.onlamp.com/pub/a/bsd/2003/09/18/FreeBSD_Basics.html
```

3.4 make for Nonprogrammers

If you're a typical FreeBSD user, you don't have a background in C programming. Yet, if you've ever used **make world** to upgrade your operating system or issued **make install** somewhere within your ports tree, you've compiled C code.

This section covers some **make** basics so you have an idea what is happening behind the scenes. It also examines some of the options you have available when issuing **make** commands.

Why C?

You may be wondering why you should care about C if you have no intention of becoming a C programmer. The reason is simple: most operating systems (including FreeBSD) are written in C, as are many executable programs. As an example, use the **file** command to see the type of third-party programs installed on your system:

```
% file /usr/local/bin/* | more
```

You'll find some Bourne shell scripts and perl scripts, but much of the rest will be executables and say something like "ELF 32-bit LSB executable, Intel 80386, version 1 (FreeBSD), dynamically linked (uses shared libs), stripped."

Keep in mind that you can run FreeBSD for years without ever typing **make**. Simply install the operating system from scratch whenever you want to upgrade to a new version. Leave the kernel as is. That's right, the kernel is also written in C, which is why you type **make buildkernel** and **make installkernel**. Don't install the ports collection, and always install software using **pkg_add -r**. Think of all the disk space you'll save, as you'll have no need to install src or ports.

However, you won't be taking full advantage of the many benefits of an open source operating system — other than the free price tag.

make Basics

OK, so what is **make**, anyway? According to **man make**, it maintains program dependencies. As any C programmer who has ever worked on a software project can tell you, there can be literally hundreds of source files, header files, and object files to compile and link in order to generate an executable program. **make**'s job is to ensure that everything happens in the correct order.

In order for **make** to do its thing, it reads a Makefile in the same directory from which you run the **make** command. For example, say I try this in my home directory:

```
% cd
% make
make: no target to make.
```

That message means that there isn't a file called Makefile in the directory. However, suppose I issue the same command (as superuser) from somewhere in the ports tree:

```
# cd /usr/ports/shells/bash
# make
```

Then it will go out on the Internet looking for some source code to compile. This makes sense, as you need C source code in order to make this program.

How did **make** know to go to the Internet looking for that source code, and more importantly, how did it know which specific FTP site contained the source code it needed? If you guessed that the instructions were in a Makefile in that directory, you are correct:

```
# ls /usr/ports/shells/bash
CVS        distinfo   pkg-deinstall   pkg-install
Makefile   files      pkg-descr       pkg-plist
```

If you read through that Makefile, you'll find a MASTER_SITES variable that lists the URLs to sites containing the required source code.

Note: In case you're wondering where that downloaded source ends up, it is copied to /usr/ports/ distfiles/ as a tarball. **make** then extracts this tarball into a subdirectory of your current directory called work. Typing **make install clean** will delete work — don't type **clean** if you want to keep the work directory.

Deciphering the *Makefile* for a Port

You don't have to be that brave to wade through a port's Makefile, as most of the uppercase variables have explanatory names. If you come across one that isn't self-explanatory or want a bird's-eye view of what each variable does, check out the **make** file that explains the format of port Makefiles:

```
% more /usr/ports/Mk/bsd.port.mk
```

Knowing the names of some of these variables can be useful to you, not just **make**. For example, I can search for the MAN variable to determine which man pages a port will install:

```
% grep MAN /usr/ports/mail/postfix/Makefile
MAN1=   postalias.1 postcat.1 postconf.1 postdrop.1 postfix.1 postkick.1
MAN5=   access.5 aliases.5 bounce.5 canonical.5 cidr_table.5 generic.5
MAN8=   anvil.8 bounce.8 cleanup.8 discard.8 error.8 flush.8 local.8 master.8
```

The MAN variable uses a number to represent the section of the manual. By using **grep** to search for this variable, I know that this port will install six man pages into section 1, six into section 5, and eight into section 8. Looks like I'll be doing a lot of reading if I install this port!

make Targets

Besides using **grep** to glean information out of a Makefile, you can also take advantage of **make** targets. Target is the proper term for the action word(s) you type after **make**. For example, you've probably used the **install** and **clean** targets when building a port. Not surprisingly, /usr/ports/Mk/bsd.port.mk contains a list of all the targets supported when compiling a port. You can find this list by using **/** (slash) to search for the "Default targets" section once you've opened this file in a pager.

However, you may find it easier to read **man ports**, as it further explains the common targets.

If you've never done anything fancier than **make install**, you should practice using each of the targets on a test system, as they may not necessarily work the way you think they would after reading the descriptions.

For example, try running **make configure** instead of **make install** from /usr/ports/shells/bash. At first glance, this looks like a normal compile, as **make** goes out looking for source code, extracts it, and configures it for your system. Note that it doesn't actually build the code or install the program, though.

If you read **man ports** carefully, you'll see that the usual **make install** is really a whole bunch of targets run in this order: **config, fetch, checksum, depends, extract, patch, configure, build,** and finally **install**. If you specify any other target, **make** will start at **config** and run every target up to and including the specified target. So, **make configure** does everything from **make config** to **make configure**.

Next, run **make configure** from /usr/ports/mail/postfix. The **make** process will begin, and depending upon the speed of your Internet connection, some moments later you'll see a dialog menu box where you can pick and choose which options to pass to the configuration script.

This may have bitten you before: you type **make install**, leave your computer to attend to something else, and come back an hour later only to find not a newly compiled program but instead a dialog menu waiting for your input. Wanna know a secret? The ports that pop up such menus often have a scripts directory containing a **dialog** script called configure. If you see such a directory when you **cd** into a ports skeleton, stick around, as it will ask you for some interaction before the build begins.

Understanding make config

You may be wondering what the difference is between **make configure** and **make config**. I've shown so far that **make configure** runs after several targets and may or may not require the user to interact with a **dialog** script.

In contrast, the **config** target is the first to run and always uses a **dialog** script to allow you to configure OPTIONS. Note that OPTIONS is uppercase on purpose; it refers to a **make** variable.

For example:

```
# cd /usr/ports/multimedia/xmms
# make config
===> No options to configure
```

That shouldn't be surprising, as the Makefile doesn't use any OPTIONS:

```
# grep -w OPTIONS /usr/ports/multimedia/xmms/Makefile
#
```

However, this Makefile does use this variable:

```
# grep OPTIONS /usr/ports/graphics/kdegraphics3/Makefile
OPTIONS=  IMLIB "Build Kuickshow, a fast and versatile image viewer" off \
```

Note that the trailing backslash (\) indicates that there are more options; to see more, change **grep** to **grep -A 5** to see the five lines starting at (After) OPTIONS.

Now try:

```
# cd /usr/ports/graphics/kdegraphics3
# make config
```

A **dialog** script immediately opens, displaying all of the possible options. Those enabled in the Makefile will be on by default, whereas those tagged as off will not. Once you make your own selections and tab over to OK, you'll receive your prompt back, as **make config** is the first and only target to run.

Did you know that /var/db/ports/ often saves your selected OPTIONS for you?

```
# more /var/db/ports/kdegraphics/options
# This file is auto-generated by 'make config'.
# No user-servicable parts inside!
# Options for kdegraphics-3.5.6
_OPTIONS_READ=kdegraphics-3.5.6
WITHOUT_IMLIB=true
WITH_GPHOTO2=true
WITHOUT_SANE=true
```

You can also view your selections from within the port's directory using the **showconfig** target:

```
# pwd
/usr/ports/graphics/kdegraphics3
# make showconfig
===> The following configuration options are available for kdegraphics-3.5.6:
     IMLIB=on "Build Kuickshow, a fast and versatile image viewer"
     GPHOTO2=on "Enable support for digital cameras"
     SANE=off "Build Kooka, a SANE scanner frontend for KDE"
===> Use 'make config' to modify these settings
```

Should you change your mind, you can always rerun **make config**. Alternatively, remove the *config* options using:

```
# make rmconfig
===> Removing user-configured options for kdegraphics-3.5.6
# more /var/db/ports/kdegraphics/options
/var/db/ports/kdegraphics/options: No such file or directory
```

Your World's Makefile

Quick, what directory are you in when you issue a **make** command to upgrade the operating system or build a new kernel? There has to be a Makefile[2] in that directory, or else your **make** command would fail. Take a look at it:

```
% more /usr/src/Makefile
```

This is an interesting Makefile that starts off mentioning targets you've probably used before, such as **build-world**, **buildkernel**, **installkernel**, and **installworld**. However, search for Targets and you'll see this section:

```
# Targets that begin with underscore are internal targets intended for
# developer convenience only.  They are intentionally not documented and
# completely subject to change without notice.
TGTS=   all all-man buildenv buildkernel buildworld check-old checkdpadd \
        clean cleandepend cleandir delete-old delete-old-libs depend \
        distribute distributeworld distrib-dirs distribution everything\
        hierarchy install installcheck installkernel installkernel.debug \
        reinstallkernel reinstallkernel.debug installworld \
         kernel-toolchain libraries lint maninstall \
         obj objlink regress rerelease tags toolchain update \
        _worldtmp _legacy _bootstrap-tools _cleanobj _obj \
        _build-tools _cross-tools _includes _libraries _depend
        build22 distribute32 install32
```

Note: It's one thing to try new **make** targets in the ports tree — the worst that can happen is you'll end up installing an application. However, if you have the urge to deviate from the targets described in the Handbook for safely upgrading the operating system or a kernel, practice on a test system that doesn't contain any data you'd miss should something go terribly wrong.

The rest of the Makefile describes the documented targets. There are a few interesting things to note. The Handbook cautions against using **make world**. This Makefile explains further:

```
# world
# Attempt to rebuild and reinstall everything. This target is not to be
# used for upgrading an existing FreeBSD system, because the kernel is
# not included. One can argue that this target doesn't build everything
# then.
```

---

[2]Or BSDmakefile or lowercase makefile, but those filenames are rarely used.

```
world:
        @echo "WARNING: make world will overwrite your existing FreeBSD"
        @echo "installation without also building and installing a new"
        @echo "kernel.  This can be dangerous.  Please read the handbook,"
        @echo "'Rebuilding world', for how to upgrade your system."
        @echo "Define DESTDIR to where you want to install FreeBSD,"
        @echo "including /, to override this warning and proceed as usual."
        @echo "You may get the historical 'make world' behavior by defining"
        @echo "HISTORICAL_MAKE_WORLD.  You should understand the implications"
        @echo "before doing this."
```

This file also indicates that make kernel is really **make buildkernel** followed by **make installkernel**. That means that you could replace:

make buildkernel KERNCONF=*NEW* **&& make installkernel KERNCONF=***NEW*

with:

make kernel KERNCONF=*NEW*

Note that the Makefile assumes GENERIC unless you specify another kernel with KERNCONF.

The last target I want to mention is **make update**. If you try typing that as is, you'll just receive your prompt back, meaning nothing happened. This is because this target reads the file /etc/make.conf to see exactly what you'd like to update.

On my test system, I already had **csup** up and running and had created a sup file in /root/cvs-supfile. So, I added these lines to /etc/make.conf:

```
SUP_UPDATE=         yes
SUP=                /usr/bin/csup
SUPFLAGS=           -g -L 2
SUPFILE=            /root/cvs-supfile
```

If you haven't yet created a configuration file yet for **csup**, replace that SUPFILE line with these:

```
SUPHOST=            cvsup.ca.freebsd.org
SUPFILE=            /usr/share/examples/cvsup/standard-supfile
PORTSSUPFILE=       /usr/share/examples/cvsup/ports-supfile
DOCSUPFILE=         /usr/share/examples/cvsup/doc-supfile
```

When filling in SUPHOST=, please choose a mirror geographically close to you. You'll find a list of mirrors at http://www.freebsd.org/doc/en_US.ISO8859-1/books/handbook/cvsup.html#CVSUP-MIRRORS. Also, review the three files in /usr/share/examples/cvsup to pick and choose which parts of the operating system, ports, and docs you wish to update.

When you've finished, run **make update** from /usr/src to update the specified sources.

Conclusion

Perhaps you've wondered how some people on the mailing lists knew about commands that went beyond **make install**. You found out what files they read to learn that information. Just remember, if you want to try out some new **make** targets for yourself, use a testing system and back up any data that is important to you first.

Additional Resources

Original Article:

`http://www.onlamp.com/pub/a/bsd/2005/03/24/FreeBSD_Basics.html`

FreeBSD Handbook: Rebuilding World

`http://www.freebsd.org/doc/en_US.ISO8859-1/books/handbook/makeworld.html`

3.5 Building Binary PC-BSD Packages

FreeBSD is starting to make waves in the desktop arena, and not just as the Darwin core of the popular Mac OS X operating system. Several FreeBSD-based desktop projects have emerged in the past few years and have matured to the point where a nontechnical user can easily install a system fully configured for sound, a network, and applications. In addition to ease of use, benefits include no cost, the BSD license, and the stability and security inherent in FreeBSD.

One of these projects is PC-BSD, which provides two additional features that make it a strong contender in the desktop market. The first is the Online Update Manager, which with a click of the mouse allows a user either to schedule or to manually check for updates to the operating system and installed applications. If necessary updates exist, the system automatically downloads and applies them, making it a trivial task to keep the system patched.

The second feature is a GUI application installer and uninstaller. While advanced users can still use the FreeBSD ports and packages collection, casual users can simply download a PBI (PC-BSD package), double-click on it, and watch as the GUI installer performs its magic.

PBIs have the advantage of being entirely self-contained. That means casual users won't inadvertently overwrite existing libraries or files by installing and uninstalling applications.

This section shows how to create your own PBI, using Digikam as an example of a rather complex package with many library dependencies. While most PBIs will be easier to generate, I want to demonstrate most of the gotchas you may run across when generating your own PBIs.

While casual users won't be making their own PBIs, you don't have to be a programmer to do so. If you have basic Unix skills, are comfortable with the FreeBSD packages collection, and have a meticulous nature, you can easily create your first PBI in the space of an afternoon. This section assumes that you are working on a freshly installed PC-BSD system.

Step 1: Create Your Staging Area

Start by double-checking that there is an existing FreeBSD package in the `packages/All/` subdirectory at the FreeBSD ftp site for your FreeBSD release.

Next, become the superuser and create a directory for the application in your regular user account's home directory:

```
% pwd
/home/dru
% su
Password:
# mkdir -p pbi/digikam
# cd pbi/digikam
```

Step 2: Download the FreeBSD Package and Any Required Libraries

Using the exact name of the package, you can fetch it directly:

```
# fetch ftp://ftp.freebsd.org/pub/FreeBSD/releases/i386/ ⇓
6.2-RELEASE/packages/All/digikam-0.8.1_4.tbz
```

Next, install the package to make sure you don't have any missing dependencies. If you're lucky, it will just install and you'll get your prompt back. If you instead get error messages, you will have to fetch the missing dependencies:

```
# pkg_add digikam-0.8.1_4.tbz
pkg_add: could not find package sqlite-3.3.7 !
pkg_add: could not find package libexif-0.6.13 !
<snip 7 other missing packages>
# fetch ftp.freebsd.org/pub/FreeBSD/releases/i386/ ⇓
6.2-RELEASE/packages/All/sqlite-3.3.7.tbz
# fetch ftp.freebsd.org/pub/FreeBSD/releases/i386/ ⇓
6.2-RELEASE/packages/All/libexif-0.6.13.tbz
<snip 7 other fetches>
```

Then try to install the package again:

```
# pkg_add digikam-0.8.1_4.tbz
```

Don't worry if you receive warnings indicating that some software has a greater revision number than is required. You can double-check the install was successful with:

```
# pkg_info | grep digikam
digikam-0.8.1_4    Photo album manager for KDE with gphoto2 backend
```

Step 3: Prepare the Tarball and Install/Uninstall Scripts

Packages are really compressed tarballs, so start by uncompressing them:

```
# bunzip2 *.tbz
```

As you untar each package, you can remove the original tarball:

```
# tar xvf digikam-0.8.1_4.tbz && rm digikam-0.8.1_4.tar
# tar xvf sqlite-3.3.7.tbz && rm sqlite-3.3.7.tar
<snip 8 other untars>
```

Notice that this created several subdirectories, one of which is bin/. The PBI you create will be a compressed snapshot of this bin/ directory. The rest of this section will show you how to put all the required pieces into it.

The first piece will be a new tarball named base_changes.tar, which contains everything except the contents of bin:

```
# tar cv --exclude bin -f bin/base_changes.tar .
```

Next, create an install script and set it as executable:

```
# more bin/PBI.SetupScript.sh
#!/bin/sh
cd /usr/local/MyPrograms/$1
tar xvjpf base_changes.tar
rm base_changes.tar
# chmod +x bin/PBI.SetupScript.sh
```

Then create an uninstall script:

```
# more bin/PBI.RemoveScript.sh
#!/bin/sh
cd /usr/local/MyPrograms
rm -Rf $1
# chmod +x bin/PBI.RemoveScript.sh
```

Notice that when the PBI installs, everything it needs (base_changes.tar) untars into /usr/local/ MyPrograms/$1, where *$1* represents the name of the PBI. Uninstalling the PBI removes that entire directory.

Because you can use these scripts with any PBI, I keep a copy in my pbi/ directory so I don't have to re-create them:

```
# cp bin/PBI.* ~dru/pbi
```

Step 4: Copy Libraries

Now it's time to create a lib/ directory in your staging area's bin/ directory:

```
# pwd
/home/dru/pbi/digikam/bin
# mkdir lib
```

Unless you have a very simple application, there can be many dozens of libraries that you need to locate and copy into that custom lib/ directory. **ldd** will give you the names, but you don't want to spend hours copying pathnames when a script will do it in under a second. This script will work every time, so ~user_account/pbi/ is a good place to keep it.

```
# more ~dru/pbi/lib.sh
#!/bin/sh
# this script requires you to input the name of an executable
# which is referred to as $1 in the script
# copy the output of ldd into a file
# ldd gives the paths to required libraries
ldd $1 > $1_lib.sh
# these statements clean up the output of ldd
# and transforms it into a series of "cp path lib" statements
cat $1_lib.sh | cut -d = -f 2 | cut -d '(' -f 1 > $1_tmp1
sed 's/\>/cp/g' $1_tmp1 > $1_tmp2 ; mv $1_tmp2 $1_tmp1
sed 's/$/ lib/g' $1_tmp1 > $1_tmp2 ; mv $1_tmp2 $1_lib.sh
# this transforms the first non-path line
# into a shebang
sed 's/.*\:.*/\#\!\/bin\/sh/'g $1_lib.sh > $1_tmp1 ; mv $1_tmp1 $1_lib.sh
# this makes the resulting file executable
chmod +x $1_lib.sh
echo "Run the script $1_lib.sh to copy the required libraries"
```

When finished, make the script executable:

```
# chmod +x ~dru/pbi/lib.sh
```

As this script takes an executable as an argument, find out the names of your package's executables:

```
# pwd
/home/dru/pbi/digikam/bin
# file * | grep LSB
dcraw:  ELF 32-bit LSB executable, Intel 80386, version 1 (FreeBSD), dynamically ⇓
 linked (uses shared libs), stripped
digikam: ELF 32-bit LSB executable, Intel 80386, version 1 (FreeBSD), dynamically ⇓
 linked (uses shared libs), stripped
<snip>
```

This particular package has dozens of executables, and you need to run **lib.sh** for each one. Note that **lib.sh** makes a script that copies the libraries needed by that executable. As you create each script, run it and then remove it:

```
# ~dru/pbi/lib.sh dcraw
Run the script dcraw_lib.sh to copy the required libraries
# ./dcraw_lib.sh && rm dcraw_lib.sh
# ~dru/pbi/lib.sh digikam
Run the script digikam_lib.sh to copy the required libraries
# ./digikam_lib.sh && rm digikam_lib.sh
<snip>
```

When you finish, you'll have a populated `lib/` directory:

```
# ls lib | wc
79   79   1055
```

Next, double-check whether your package has any `lib/` subdirectories:

```
# ls -F ~dru/pbi/digikam/lib | grep "/"
gphoto2/
gphoto2_port/
imlib2/
kde3/
```

If there are any, create those subdirectories in your `bin/lib/` and copy the appropriate library files over:

```
# pwd
/home/dru/pbi/digikam/bin/lib
# mkdir gphoto2 gphoto2_port imlib2 kde3
# cp -R ~dru/pbi/digikam/lib/gphoto2/* gphoto2
# cp -R ~dru/pbi/digikam/lib/gphoto2_port/* gphoto2_port
# cp -R ~dru/pbi/digikam/lib/imlib2/* imlib2
# cp -R ~dru/pbi/digikam/lib/kde3/* kde3
```

Step 5: Look for an Icon and Cleanup `bin/`

Adding an icon to your PBI is nice. Check whether one came with your package:

```
# grep -w icons ../+CONTENTS
share/apps/digikam/icons/hicolor/32x32/actions/addimagefolder.png
<snip large output>
```

This package definitely came with many icons, and this is the one I'm looking for:

```
# cp ../share/icons/crystalsvg/128x128/apps/digikam.png .
```

If your package doesn't have any icons, choose your favorite from a subdirectory of `/usr/local/share/icons/crystalsvg/128x128/` and copy it to `bin/`.

When you finish, uninstall the package and its dependencies so they won't interfere when you test the PBI:

```
# pkg_delete -rx digikam
```

Finally, double-check `bin/` to ensure that it contains only the tarball, the install and uninstall scripts, the binaries, and the `lib/` directory.

Step 6: Create the PBI

PC-BSD provides a GUI tool which turns the contents of your staging area's `bin/` directory into a PBI. Simply double-click on the downloaded file to install the Package Creator. By default, it will place an icon on the desktop and an entry into the Programs menu.

Open up the Package Creator and fill in the first screen with your details:

Package Name: Digikam

Package Version: -0.8.1_4

Author: Gilles Caulier

Website: `http://www.digikam.org/`

Note: The `http://www.freshports.org` description for your application should include the URL to the application's website. The name of the primary author of the application is usually somewhere at the website for the application.

In the next screen, you can keep the default No for Display License unless the application requires the user to read and agree to a license.

In the next screen, browse the Package Directory and select your bin directory:

`/home/dru/pbi/digikam/bin/`

Under Library Support, select Specify Library Directory, click on the Browse button, and double-click on lib/.

In the next screen, click on Default Program Icon and select your PNG.

Click on Add under Package Executables and type in the program name. Click on the Browse button for Program Executable and select the executable. (In my case it was **digikam**).

Some programs (for example, Wireshark) need superuser access in order to run. Digikam does not, so I didn't select that option. Click on Save, and then on Next when finished.

Some programs require Mime Types, which you can add in the next screen. (Digikam does not.) The program will then create your PBI–it may take a few minutes, depending on the size of the tarball and the number of libraries. It will tell you when it finishes, and it will place the PBI in that user account's home directory. If you like, click on the Save preset button, which will save all the details to a `.pbc` file. That can save you some typing the next time you create a PBI.

Step 7: Test the PBI

It's important to test that your PBI successfully installs and uninstalls and that the program works with all its features.

I like to move the PBI to the Desktop so I can double-click on it:

```
# mv ~dru/Digikam-0.8.1_4-PV.pbi ~dru/Desktop/
```

Now leave the superuser account so you're acting as a regular user, and double-check that the application is not currently installed:

```
# exit
% pkg_info | grep digikam
%
```

Double-click on the PBI and see what happens. It should prompt you for the superuser password; click on Next twice and then on Finish. You should now have an icon for your application on the desktop. Double-click on it to launch the application, and try all its features to make sure they work.

Once you've confirmed that the application works, double-check that your uninstall script works. Go to Computer -> PC-BSD Settings -> Remove Programs and remove your program. When that finishes, make sure there is no longer a directory for your application in /usr/local/MyPrograms/.

When Things Don't Work

If you get an error when you launch your program, double-check the contents of the subdirectory for your application under /usr/local/MyPrograms/. If you're missing subdirectories or files, check for a typo in your install script that prevented the tarball from untarring. Likewise, if your application directory remains after uninstalling the program, you have a typo in your uninstall script.

If all the files seem to be there, you may have inadvertently missed running **lib.sh** on one of the executables and therefore have some missing libraries. Review your history, and if you find your error, add the missing libraries, regenerate a PBI, and test again.

Sometimes the application will launch but features will be missing. In the example of Digikam, the initial splash screen was missing, as were most of the menus. That happens when an application shares files with existing applications such as KDE. To find those files, I checked out the package list for Digikam at http://www.freshports.org.

It was the share files I missed. Because I don't want to interfere with existing applications or copy files outside the self-contained application directory, I used symbolic links. I like to add links one at a time at the command line and relaunch the application to see what happens. Once I knew which symbolic links added the missing features, I added them to **PBI.SetupScript.sh** and regenerated the PBI. In the case of Digikam, the following links added the missing features. (On the command line, replace *$1* with the name of the directory, as *$1* will work only in the script.)

```
% ln -s \
   /usr/local/MyPrograms/$1/applications/kde/showfoto.desktop \
   /usr/local/share/applications/kde
% ln -s \
   /usr/local/MyPrograms/$1/share/applnk/Graphics/digikam.desktop \
   /usr/local/share/applnk/Graphics
% ln -s /usr/local/MyPrograms/$1/share/apps/digikam/ \
   /usr/local/share/apps/digikam
% ln -s /usr/local/MyPrograms/$1/share/icons/hicolor/ \
   /usr/local/share/icons/hicolor
```

Note: Don't forget the trailing / when creating directory symbolic links.

Finally, if your application relies on GTK+ or Pango, follow the directions at http://faqs.pcbsd.org/19_320_en.html.

Step 8: Upload the PBI

Once you've tested your PBI, you can submit it for inclusion on the PC-BSD site so other PC-BSD users can use it.

This is a two-step process. Start by posting a message to `http://forums.pcbsd.org/viewforum.php?f=32`.

Make sure your posting includes the required PBI information listed at `http://forums.pcbsd.org/viewtopic.php?t=5142`. If the PBI testers run across any problems with your PBI, they will reply to your posting. Otherwise, they'll let you know when the PBI is approved and added to the pbiDIR website.

Next, upload your PBI to a FTP server. If this is your first PBI, click on the private message button on the PBI team profile at `http://forums.pcbsd.org/profile.php?mode=viewprofile&u=37`. The PBI team will send you the login information you will need to access the ftp server.

If you haven't had a chance to check out PC-BSD for yourself, I highly recommend it as a desktop for both advanced and casual BSD users. If there currently isn't a PBI for your favorite application, set aside an afternoon and see if you can generate one yourself. You'll find it to be a very satisfying, and possibly addictive, experience.

Additional Resources

Original Article:

`http://www.onlamp.com/pub/a/bsd/2006/01/05/FreeBSD_Basics.html`

PC-BSD website:

`http://www.pcbsd.org`

PBI website:

`http://www.pbidir.com`

3.6 Interesting Ports

Whenever I get a chance to roam through the ports collection, I always end up feeling like a kid in a candy store.

At the moment, there are nearly 17,000 ports to choose from and they're nearly all just a **pkg_add -r** away. In this section, I'd like to concentrate on some of the more useful ports I've come across, but I'm sure I'll also wander a bit into the less-than-useful-but-worth-trying-out-anyways ports as well.

As a reminder, if you install software and use either **csh** or **tcsh** as your shell, type **rehash** so the new executable will be in your path. If you're curious as to where the executable was installed, **which *name_of_application*** should reveal the path.

Subnetting Utilities

As any of my students can attest, I'm a stickler for ensuring they know how to quickly calculate anything possible in IPv4 addressing land. From subnet masks to CIDR notation to broadcast IDs to Cisco wildcard bit masks, they end up learning far more about TCP/IP than they could have anticipated. If you're a bit rusty on your calculations, there are several utilities in the ports collection that deal with subnet masks and IPv4 addressing.

Note: You can learn more about subnetting with 3com's "Understanding IP Addressing: Everything You Ever Wanted to Know" from `http://www.3com.com/other/pdfs/infra/corpinfo/en_US/501302.pdf`.

The **whatmask** utility is a very quick way to see a subnet mask in CIDR notation, regular notation, or its wildcard bit mask equivalent. (Wildcard bit masks are used in Cisco access lists.) If you just type **whatmask**, you'll see that it uses a very basic syntax:

```
% whatmask
whatmask version 1.2, Copyright (C) 2001-2003Joe Laffey <joe@laffeycomputer.com>
This binary compiled on Feb 15 2007 at 02:41:56
Visit:  http://www.laffeycomputer.com/software.html for updates.
whatmask comes with ABSOLUTELY NO WARRANTY; for details see the COPYING file
that accompanied this distribution.  This is free software, and you are welcome
to redistribute it under the terms of GNU PUBLIC LICENSE.
Given a mask:    whatmask <CIDR bits>
               - or - whatmask <subnet mask>
               - or - whatmask <hex subnet mask>
               - or - whatmask <wildcard bit mask>
 Note:  whatmask will autodetect the input and show you all four.
```

I'll try the following:

```
% whatmask 255.255.255.224
---------------------------------------------
        TCP/IP SUBNET MASK EQUIVALENTS
---------------------------------------------
CIDR = ....................: /27
Netmask = .................: 255.255.255.224
Netmask (hex) = ...........: 0xffffffe0
Wildcard Bits = ...........: 0.0.0.31
Usable IP Addresses = .....: 30
```

Very short and sweet, and this can save a few brain cells when you're in a hurry and don't feel like doing math. If you also need to determine the subnet IDs, broadcast addresses, and host IDs provided by a subnet mask, you can save yourself some calculations using the **ipcalc** utility. Once installed, type **ipcalc** for its syntax:

```
% ipcalc
Usage: ipcalc [options] <ADDRESS>[/]<NETMASK> [NETMASK]
ipcalc takes an IP address and netmask and calculates the resulting broadcast,
network, Cisco wildcard mask, and host range. By giving a second netmask, you
can design sub- and supernetworks. It is also intended to be a teaching tool
and presents the results as easy-to-understand binary values.
-n --nocolor   Don't display ANSI color codes.
-b --nobinary  Suppress the bitwise output.
-c --class     Just print bit-count-mask of given address.
-h --html      Display results as HTML (not finished in this version).
```

```
-v --version    Print Version.
-s --split n1 n2 n3
                  Split into networks of size n1, n2, n3.
-r --range      Deaggregate address range.
   --help       Longer help text.
```

I personally found the ANSI color codes to be ugly, so I used **-n** when I tried the following example:

```
% ipcalc -n 192.168.10.40/27
Address:    192.168.10.40           11000000.10101000.00001010.001 01000
Netmask:    255.255.255.224 == 27 11111111.11111111.11111111.111 00000
Wildcard:   0.0.0.31                 00000000.00000000.00000000.000 11111
=>
Network:    192.168.10.32/27        11000000.10101000.00001010.001 00000 (Class C)
HostMin:    192.168.10.33           11000000.10101000.00001010.001 00001
HostMax:    192.168.10.62           11000000.10101000.00001010.001 11110
Broadcast:  192.168.10.63           11000000.10101000.00001010.001 11111
Hosts/Net:  30                      Class C, Private Internet
```

A utility with a similar function but slightly different output is **cidr**. It has a fairly long syntax, so I'll snip a bit of its output:

```
% cidr
<snip>
Short form:
cidr <ipaddress/prefix> [-H]
Note: Short form only supports dotted-quad IP address and
      decimal(integer) prefix.  Host list ("-H") is optional.
<snip the Long form section>
```

And I'll try out the same example:

```
% cidr 192.168.10.40/27
ip address..........: 192.168.10.40
netmask.............: 255.255.255.224
network address.....: 192.168.10.32
broadcast address...: 192.168.10.63
please wait while host addresses are validated...
total host addresses: 30
```

If I had included the **-H**, it would have also printed out each host IP address on a separate line. That output might be handy to send to a printer if I was making an inventory of a network.

The last related utility I'll demonstrate is **ipsc**:

```
% ipsc
usage: ipsc [options] <addr/mask | addr/offset | addr>
        -C <class> Network class (a, b, or c).  Must be used with -B
```

```
      -B <bits>    Subnet bits (must be used with -C)
      -i <if>      Reverse engineer an interface (e.g. eth0)
      -a           Print all information available
      -g           Print general information
      -s           Print all possible subnets
      -h           Print host information
      -c           Print CIDR information
      -v           Print the program version
      -?           Print this help message
Report bugs to dan@vertekcorp.com
```

The most interesting feature of this utility is the **-i** option. Let's see what happens when I use it and specify my outbound NIC:

```
% ipsc -i ed1
Network class:          A
Network mask:           255.0.0.0
Network mask (hex):     FF000000
Network address:        24.141.116.0
Subnet bits:            14
Max subnets:            16384
Full subnet mask:       255.255.252.0
Full subnet mask (hex): FFFFFC00
Host bits:              10
Hosts per subnet:       1024
Bit map:                nnnnnnnn.ssssssss.sssssshh.hhhhhhhh
```

This utility also gives a rather exhaustive output when you use the **-a** switch. I'll do that with the same example I used for the other utilities:

```
% ipsc -a 192.168.10.40/27
Network class:          C
Network mask:           255.255.255.0
Network mask (hex):     FFFFFF00
Network address:        192.168.10.32
Subnet bits:            3
Max subnets:            8
Full subnet mask:       255.255.255.224
Full subnet mask (hex): FFFFFFE0
Host bits:              5
Hosts per subnet:       32
Bit map:                nnnnnnnn.nnnnnnnn.nnnnnnnn.ssshhhhh
Subnet 1:               192.168.10.0      192.168.10.31
Subnet 2:               192.168.10.32     192.168.10.63    *
Subnet 3:               192.168.10.64     192.168.10.95
Subnet 4:               192.168.10.96     192.168.10.127
Subnet 5:               192.168.10.128    192.168.10.159
Subnet 6:               192.168.10.160    192.168.10.191
Subnet 7:               192.168.10.192    192.168.10.223
```

```
Subnet 8:                    192.168.10.224   192.168.10.255
IP address:                  192.168.10.40
Hexadecimal IP address:      C0A80A28
Address allocation range:    192.168.10.32 - 192.168.10.63
Full subnet mask:            255.255.255.224
Subnet mask:                 0.0.0.224
Subnet ID:                   0.0.0.32
Network ID:                  192.168.10.0
Host ID:                     0.0.0.40
Cisco Wildcard:              0.0.0.31
CIDR notation:               192.168.10.0/27
Route/Mask:                  192.168.10.0 / 255.255.255.224
Hexadecimal route/mask:      C0A80A00   / FFFFFFE0
Supernet max:                0
```

Logging Utilities

Let's leave TCP/IP land and take a look at some utilities that deal with logs. If you're using Sendmail, you might want to take a look at **mreport**. If you just type **mreport**, you'll receive a summary of your Sendmail log:

```
% mreport
       [hostname] [/var/log/maillog]
[ 24] 101080 owner-freebsd-questions@FreeBSD.ORG    genisis@localhost
[  3]  11067 owner-freebsd-security@FreeBSD.ORG     genisis@localhost
[  2]   7858 firewall-wizards-admin@nfr.com         genisis@localhost
[  2]   6407 owner-freebsd-newbies@FreeBSD.ORG      genisis@localhost
[  1]   6158 owner-freebsd-advocacy@FreeBSD.ORG     genisis@localhost
[  2]   3913 root                                   root
[  1]   3415 tsmith@example.com                     genisis@localhost
[  1]   3176 shrdlu@example.org                     genisis@localhost
[  1]   2378 listserv@example.net                   genisis@localhost
[  1]   2183 maria@example.org                      genisis@localhost


=====================
Total Bytes        : 147635
Number of Records  : 10
---------------------
Host Name          : hostname
Input File         : /var/log/maillog
Output File        : stdout
First Record       : Jul 15 01:30:51
Last Record        : Jul 15 09:35:51

---------------------
Time Taken         : 10729 µs
=====================
mreport-0.9 by Jason Armstrong
```

If you read the man page for this utility, you'll see that the number in the brackets [ ] represents the number of emails, followed by the size in bytes; who the email is from; and who the email is destined for. There are also switches to customize how the output is sorted. Several examples are cited in the man page to get you started.

Another utility that deals with logs is **colorize**. A configuration file describing which colors are associated with which key terms will be installed to `/usr/local/etc/colorizerc` and can be edited to your preference. You can also apply various attributes such as *bold* or *blink* to key terms in this file.

To actually use the utility, use the < redirector to receive input from the desired log file. You may have to remain as the superuser depending upon the permissions set on the log file. For example, to view the security log:

```
# colorize < /var/log/security
```

Unfortunately, you can't send output to a pager utility and there isn't a switch to page the results. You can see the beginning or end of a large log if you pipe the results to either **head** or **tail** like so:

```
# colorize < /var/log/maillog | head
# colorize < /var/log/maillog | tail
```

One of the more interesting available switches allows you to create a colorized HTML version of a log. Here I'll create a page called `security.html` and send it to my home directory:

```
# colorize -h < /var/log/security > ~genisis/security.html
```

If you don't see color in your html file, include the **–nocss** in the above command.

Formatting Utilities

There are several nifty utilities that deal with handling documents in various formats. I'll take a look at **ascii2pdf** and **catdoc**.

The utility **ascii2pdf** can quickly convert an ACSII file to PDF format. To use, simply specify the name of the file you wish to convert; it will create a second file with the same name but with a *.pdf* extension. To view the new PDF file, you can use the **acroread** port.

If you just want to read a Word document at the command line without converting it to another format first, try **catdoc**. You should be able to use it to read any Word document like so:

```
% catdoc filename.doc | more
```

Or, to convert it to ASCII, I could redirect the output to another file:

```
% catdoc filename.doc > filename.txt
% more filename.txt
```

Note: Since this was originally written, OpenOffice provides an excellent way to read, modify, and export Word documents to other formats. **catdoc** is still useful if you need to work with a Word document at the command line.

Humorous Utilities

A utility that falls into the easily amused category is **oneko**. You may want to start it from **xterm** by typing **/usr/local/bin/oneko**; this way, if you get tired of watching the antics of the kitten as it follows your mouse, you can quickly kill it from the **xterm**. A similar utility is **xneko**, but I found it rather cruel to watch the kitten try to scratch its way out of its box in order to chase the mouse. Your mileage may vary.

Finally, try out the **cowsay** utility. Read the well-written man page and see the care that was taken when this utility was created. Try each of the numerous switches. As you do so, you'll probably shake your head in wonder like I did and ask yourself, "Why?" The only answer I could come up with is "Why not?"

Pruning Installed Ports

I first learned about **pkg_cutleaves** from Richard Bejtlich's weblog at http://taosecurity.blogspot.com/. Richard has the uncanny ability of keeping abreast of my three favorite subjects: FreeBSD, the ports collection, and security.

If you use **portupgrade** to keep your ports up-to-date, consider adding **pkg_cutleaves** to your repertoire. This interactive Perl script searches your ports database for leaves, or software that isn't a dependency of any other installed program. This gives you the opportunity to clean your drive of those orphaned programs you no longer use or were dependencies of software you've since uninstalled.

Once you've installed **pkg_cutleaves**, take a minute to read **man pkg_cutleaves**. Then, as the superuser:

```
# pkg_cutleaves
Package 1 of 73:
abiword-2.4.6 - An open-source, cross-platform WYSIWYG word processor
abiword-2.4.6 - [keep]/(d)elete/(f)lush marked pkgs/(a)bort? k
** Keeping abiword-2.4.6.
```

On this particular system, I have 250 installed ports, of which 73 are entirely independent. **pkg_cutleaves** will show each of these and will pause while I decide to keep or remove the port. I've chosen to keep **abiword** but to delete **apache-ant** since I have a vague memory of it being a dependency of some application I've long ago uninstalled:

```
Package 2 of 73:
apache-ant-1.7.0 - Java- and XML-based build tool, conceptually similar to make
apache-ant-1.7.0 - [keep]/(d)elete/(f)lush marked pkgs/(a)bort? d
** Marking apache-ant-1.7.0 for removal.
```

I'll carry on until I've made a decision on each of the 73 ports. Once I'm finished, **pkg_delete** will carry out the requested deletions. In this example, I've chosen to delete 25 ports:

```
Package 73 of 73:
zip-2.32 - Create/update ZIP files compatible with pkzip
zip-2.32 - [keep]/(d)elete/(f)lush marked pkgs/(a)bort? k
** Keeping zip-2.32.
Deleting apache-ant-1.7.0 (package 1 of 25).
---> Deinstalling 'apache-ant-1.7.0'
```

When these deletions complete, **pkg_cutleaves** reprocesses the ports database to see if any of those deletions resulted in new leaf packages:

```
Go on with new leaf packages ((y)es/[no])? y
```

This process will continue until I've dealt with all leaves. At that point it will provide a summary of the uninstalled packages:

```
Didn't find any new leaves, exiting.
** Deinstalled packages:
apache-ant-1.7.0
<snip>
** Number of deinstalled packages: 53
```

The next time you run **pkg_cutleaves**, it will ask you again about the ports you chose to keep. If you know you want to keep these and find it irritating to confirm this every time, create a file called /usr/local/etc/pkg_leaves.exclude containing the names of those ports you wish to keep:

```
abiword
```

Remember to include the **-x** (exclude) switch:

```
# pkg_cutleaves -x
```

This tells **pkg_cutleaves** to read your exclude file. For those occasions when you don't want it to read your exclude file, don't include that switch.

Improving Your Fortunes

The next utility is for those of you who enjoy BOFH (Bastard Operator From Hell) humor. If that strikes your funny bone, you can add BOFH-style fortunes to your system by installing **fortune-mod-bofh**. Once installed, try a random fortune:

```
% fortune /usr/local/share/games/fortune/bofh
BOFH excuse #419:
overflow error in /dev/null
```

If you'd like these fortunes to appear randomly with the rest of your fortunes, copy them into the system fortune directory as the superuser:

```
# cp /usr/local/share/games/fortune/bofh* /usr/share/games/fortune/
```

Once you've copied over the BOFH files, you can specify you'd like a BOFH fortune by typing:

```
% fortune bofh
```

This is many keystrokes shorter than the previous incantation. If you're a Futurama fan, repeat the steps above for the **fortune-mod-futurama** utility:

```
# pkg_add -r fortune-mod-futurama
# cp /usr/local/share/games/fortune/futurama* \
   /usr/share/games/fortune/
# exit
% fortune futurama
Fry: I want to see the edge of the universe.
Amy: Ooh, that sounds cool.
Zoidberg: It's funny.  You live in the universe but you never do these things 'til
someone comes to visit.
```

Star Trek fans may enjoy **fortune-mod-ferengi_rules_of_acquisition**. There is also a **fortune-mod-bible** and Romanian jokes in **fortune-mod-culmea-culmilor**.

It's funny that this fortune made me wistful for a Douglas Adams fortune. A quick Google search located that there is indeed a fortune-hitchhiker project at `http://www.splitbrain.org/projects/fortunes/hg2g`. Download `fortune-hitchhiker.tgz`, then:

```
# tar xzvf fortune-hitchhiker.tgz
# cp fortune-hitchhiker/hitchhiker* /usr/share/games/fortune
# exit
% fortune hitchhiker
"'You know,' said Arthur, 'it's at times like this, when
I'm trapped in a Vogon airlock with a man from Betelgeuse,
and about to die from asphyxiation in deep space that I
really wish I'd listened to what my mother told me when I
was young.'
'Why, what did she tell you?'
'I don't know, I didn't listen.'"
  -- Arthur coping with certain death as best as he could.
```

Perhaps another Hitchhiker fan will add this to the ports collection.

Making Subjects and Verbs Agree

The next port intrigued me as it's named after one of my favorite childhood literary characters:

```
# pkg_add -r queequeg
```

This will install the **qq** Python script, which can run against any text, LaTeX, or HTML file, like so:

```
% qq filename
```

The Queequeg (`http://queequeg.sourceforge.net/index-e.html`) project's goal is to help the non-native English writer match a singular or plural noun to the correct verb conjugation. At this point, the project developers are still working on filtering out false positives so the resulting output may still be too frustrating for those who lack a solid command of English grammar. However, if English grammar is your forté and you have some time to donate, this project is looking for beta testers. If it matures, it will be an excellent tool for non-English developers to easily create manpages in natural English.

Additional Resources

Original Articles:

`http://www.onlamp.com/pub/a/bsd/2001/07/19/FreeBSD_Basics.html`

`http://www.onlamp.com/pub/a/bsd/2004/03/25/FreeBSD_Basics.html`

3com's Understanding IP Addressing: Everything You Ever Wanted to Know

`http://www.3com.com/other/pdfs/infra/corpinfo/en_US/501302.pdf.`

3.7 Browsing through the Ports Collection

Whenever I have too much time on my hands, I can be found perusing the FreeBSD ports collection. I provide endless amusement for my daughter as I show off my latest geek discoveries; to paraphrase her favorite Dogbert quote, I've entered the state of "nerdvana."

As a reminder, you should be able to install the package of almost any port using **pkg_add -r *portname*** as the superuser. You can browse port descriptions at `http://www.freshports.org` and use its search feature to find interesting applications. Once you've installed a new application, leave the superuser account to try it out. If you are using the C shell, you may have to type **rehash** so the newly-installed application will be in your path.

3.7.1 System Utilities

One of my first stops in the ports collection is usually the `sysutils` category, as it contains many small but useful utilities. One such useful utility is **symlinks**, which will find and identify all symlinks on your system. This utility comes with a short little manpage showing all of its switches. I decided to see all the symlinks on my system, so I became the superuser (so I would have permission to scan all directories) and ran the utility like so:

```
% su
Password:
# symlinks -vr /
other_fs: /home -> usr/home
other_fs: /etc/rmt -> /usr/sbin/rmt
other_fs: /etc/termcap -> /usr/share/misc/termcap
other_fs: /etc/namedb -> /var/named/etc/namedb
relative: /etc/aliases -> mail/aliases
other_fs: /sbin/nologin -> /usr/sbin/nologin
other_fs: /sys -> usr/src/sys
other_fs: /compat -> usr/compat
```

In less than a second, every symlink on my system had been listed. Very handy utility for this purpose.

Another handy utility **pkg_tree**, will list all of the ports and packages installed on your system in a tree-like structure, so you can see their dependencies.

If you've built more than a couple of packages or have built a mega-port such as Gnome or KDE, you'll definitely want to page the output; here I'll instead show the first ten lines with **head**:

```
% pkg_tree | head
ORBit2-2.14.7
|\__ pkgconfig-0.21
|\__ perl-5.8.8
|       \__ libiconv-1.9.2_2
|       \__ gettext-0.16.1_1
|       \__ glib-2.12.11
|       \__ libIDL-0.8.8
OpenEXR-1.4.0
|       \__ pkg-config-0.21
aalib-1.4.r5_2
```

The last utility I'll mention in this category is **fortunelock**. This is a short and sweet program with a short little manpage. If you need to leave a terminal and don't want to log out first, type:

```
% fortunelock
```

It will prompt you for a password and ask you to repeat it. Once you've done so, it will repeat random fortunes until you return and re-enter the password. Passersby will at least be entertained by your terminal, even if they don't know the password to access it.

One of my favorite ports is in the textproc category and is called **glimpse**. I have a lot of articles and whitepapers stashed away in my home directory, and this utility is indispensable for finding a certain line of text. It is similar to the **locate** utility in that it builds a database; because of this database, searches are blazingly fast, almost instantaneous.

The first time you want to use **glimpse**, go to your home directory (I'm assuming the information you want to find is somewhere in your home directory and its subdirectories) and build the database like so:

```
% cd
% glimpseindex -o .
This is glimpseindex version 4.12, 1999.
Indexing "/usr/home/genisis" ...
Size of files being indexed = 6437564 B, Total #of files = 850
Index-directory: "/usr/home/genisis"
Glimpse-files created here:
-rw-------  1 genisis  wheel   35658 Jan 13 19:52 .glimpse_filenames
-rw-------  1 genisis  wheel    3400 Jan 13 19:52 .glimpse_filenames_index
-rw-------  1 genisis  wheel       0 Jan 13 19:51 .glimpse_filetimes
-rw-------  1 genisis  wheel  510659 Jan 13 19:52 .glimpse_index
-rw-------  1 genisis  wheel     863 Jan 13 19:52 .glimpse_messages
-rw-------  1 genisis  wheel  342572 Jan 13 19:52 .glimpse_partitions
-rw-------  1 genisis  wheel     130 Jan 13 19:52 .glimpse_statistics
-rw-------  1 genisis  wheel  262144 Jan 13 19:52 .glimpse_turbo
```

The indexing will churn along for a few minutes, depending on how large your home directory is. You'll note that it will make several hidden files in your home directory that all begin with *.glimpse*. Once you've made the database, try to find something. As an example, I know that somewhere I have a file that tells me the modem code for "auto answer," but I can't remember which file, so I'll try:

```
% glimpse "auto answer"
/usr/home/genisis/unix:    no result codes (Q1), and auto answer (&S0=1). ⇓
     Then write the
/usr/home/genisis/unix:    at&s0=1    turn on auto answer
```

Not only is the modem code located in /usr/home/genisis/unix, I don't even have to read the file as, it also returned the modem code I was looking for. See why this is one of my favorite utilities?

The manpage for **glimpse** has several examples on how to fine-tune your search. If you use this utility often and are constantly creating and removing files from your home directory, you may want to consider running **glimpseindex** as a **cron** job. I usually just rerun **glimpseindex** whenever I can't find what I'm looking for.

Miscellaneous Utilities

While I was in the textproc section, I also came across an interesting utility known as **dadadodo**. Even if you decide not to install this utility, I highly recommend checking out http://www.jwz.org/dadadodo/; it's well worth a visit.

To run the utility, simply type:

```
% dadadodo name_of_a_file
```

I've found that saved emails, especially boring, overly technical ones, make great input files. With a utility like this, one could quit their day job to become either a poet or a fortuneteller.

Keyboard Practicer or **kp** is a very user-friendly GUI interface to practice your typing skills. Run it from an X Window session. The default mode is to show a Dvorak layout; if you're using a regular keyboard, go to Options –> Keyboard and choose Qwerty.

Then, just start typing what you see in the top section without looking at your fingers. If you're not sure where the key is located, don't look at your fingers; instead, notice which key is highlighted on your monitor. This program will keep track of your mistakes and your speed in wpm (words per minute). If you want to practice typing another file, go to File –> Load file which will show you all of the files in your home directory. Highlight one to practice typing and to see if you can improve your speed.

pib provides an intuitive graphical interface to using the ports collection. You will have to remain the superuser to actually install ports using the **pib** utility. You can start **pib** by either adding an icon to your windows manager or by opening up an **xterm** and typing **/usr/local/bin/pib**.

Once **pib** starts, you'll be presented with a window that displays all the subdirectories of /usr/ports. If you double-click on a category, you'll get a listing of the available ports in that category. If you double-click on a port, a summary of its description, the name and email address of its maintainer, and a list of its dependencies will be displayed. If you want to read its full description, click on the question mark "?" next to its description.

Let's click on the Function menu, then click on the word Search. Here is an interface to search the ports Index. For example, if you know what you'd like a utility to do, but don't know the name of the port that will do it, try a keyword search with the comment button depressed. You can double-click on any search result to be taken to the information available for that port.

Let's actually build something using **pib**. Click on the misc directory, then on **figlet**. Click on the Function menu, then on Maker. You should notice the word figlet-2.2.1 in the upper right-hand corner, followed by eight buttons; the first seven buttons will be used to make this utility. Start by clicking on the Clean button and watch as the **make** utility does its stuff on your screen; when you receive your cursor back, click on the Accept button in the lower left-hand corner, and then click on the Fetch button. Continue this process until you've cycled your way through the first seven buttons. The one dubious benefit of **pib** is that you do get to see all the functions **make** goes through to install a port, as there is no mega-button that you can click on to do everything for you.

Before we use **figlet**, let's take a look at your MOTD. Every time you log in, you receive a message telling you which version of FreeBSD you are using and how to get help using FreeBSD. While this is a useful message, it's not very exciting after you've read it a few hundred times. Fortunately, the file that provides this message is editable by the superuser and can contain whatever the superuser deems appropriate for his users to read at login time.

Let's customize this file (/etc/motd) using our new **figlet** utility. Try the following as the superuser:

```
# figlet "Welcome to FreeBSD 6.2\!\!" > /etc/motd
```

then log out and back in to see your results. You'll note that **figlet** took the text contained within the quotes and wrote it in a more interesting manner. We had to use the backslash \ to prevent the shell from interpreting the double exclamation marks as a **history** command. If you don't believe me, try the above command again without the \'s and see what happens when you log out and back in. Finally, we used the single > redirector, which overwrote our original /etc/motd file.

Let's try a more seasonal message:

```
# figlet -f bubble "SEASONS GREETINGS \!\!" > /etc/motd
```

When you log out and back in, you should receive this:

figlet comes with several dozen different fonts; see **man figlet** for details.

In my search for interesting ports, I usually go to http://www.freshports.org at least once a week to keep abreast of which ports have been recently added. One that caught my eye was **nonsense**; any port with a name like that and a link to its homepage is just asking to be tried out:

```
% nonsense -F
It's a crime for a teenager to have fun without a license in Houde, Oklahoma.
% nonsense -f /usr/local/share/nonsense/data/insults.data
Thou pribbling tardy-gaited strumpet!
```

Save this utility for a rainy day, as it is a good time-waster; I spent far too much time in the random insults and fortune sections.

If you don't receive a humorous fortune when you log in, you probably didn't install the fortune utility when you installed FreeBSD. To rectify this situation, become the superuser and type **sysinstall** then choose Configure, then Distributions, then arrow down to Games and use your spacebar to select it; press **Enter** and choose your

Installation Media. Once it is finished, exit out of **sysinstall**. Now when users log in, they should receive a fortune.

Now that you have the **fortune** program, you can install additional fortunes as you come across them. This is how I added the Humorix fortunes from `http://humorix.org/downloads/#Fortunes`: I saved the file `humorixfortunes-1.4.tar.gz` to my home directory. I then typed:

```
% tar xzvf humo*
% ls humorixfortunes-1.4
humorix-misc         humorix-stories
humorix.misc.dat     humorix-stories.dat
```

These files need to be copied to `/usr/share/games/fortune/`, as this is the directory where the **fortune** databases are stored. Since only the superuser has write permission to the `fortune` directory, I copied the files like so:

```
% su
Password:
# mv humorixfortunes-1.4/* /usr/share/games/fortune/
```

The *humorix* files are now available for use by the **fortune** program. Type **fortune** to receive a fortune.

Well, we've lingered a bit in the amusing, let's move over to the obscurely useful. As any of my students can attest to, I spend far too much time reading RFCs and forcing my students to do so as well. Of course, I was intrigued by a port called **rfc**. Once installed, I typing **rfc** will diplay the switches available for the utility. Before you can use the utility, you must first build the index by typing:

```
% rfc -i
Modem users one moment, it's about 400k (doesn't need to be updated often)
original lines = 0       /usr/local/etc/rfc-index
new lines      = 18304 /usr/local/etc/rfc-index
```

You're now ready to use the **rfc** utility like so:

```
% rfc -l 1
```

and I was able to read RFC number 1 without the hassle of going out and looking for it. But that's not the end of this utility's usefulness. RFC 1700 (the RFC for assigned numbers) has its own switches to allow for quick searches. For example:

```
% rfc -p ip 6
Making connection to server....
http://www.iana.org/assignments/protocol-numbers
    6    TCP    Transmission Control    [RFC793]
[RFC793] Postel, J., "Transmission Control Protocol - DARPA
    Internet Program Protocol Specification", STD 7, RFC 793
    USC/Information Sciences Institute, September 1981.
% rfc -p port doom
```

```
Making connection to server....
http://www.iana.org/assignments/port-numbers
doom      666/tcp     doom Id Software
doom      666/udp     doom Id Software
#                     <ddt&idcube.idsoftware.com>
```
% rfc -p port 1433
```
Making connection to server....
http://www.iana.org/assignments/port-numbers
ms-sql-s   1433/tcp    Microsoft-SQL-Server
ms-sql-s   1433/udp    Microsoft-SQL-Server
```

But wait, it gets better. If I type:

% rfc -n -i
```
One moment, it's fairly small (doesn't need to be updated often)
original lines  = 0    /usr/local/share/misc/nmap-services
new lines       = 0    /usr/local/share/misc/nmap-services
```

I'll build the index for all known unregistered and trojan port numbers. Once I've created this index, if I want to check a suspicious port:

% rfc -n 12345
```
Looking up service...
NetBus    12345/tcp  # NetBus backdoor trojan or Trend Micro Office Scan
```

I can tell this is a utility I'll miss when I'm not sitting at my FreeBSD box.

The last utility I want to mention is **powershell**. Once you've built it, open up an X session and either create an icon for PowerShell within your windows manager, or start it from an **xterm** by typing **powershell**. You can view a screenshot at http://powershell.sourceforge.net/pshell1.jpg.

The first time you start **powershell**, it doesn't look much more exciting than an **xterm**. In order to fully appreciate PowerShell, tweak it a bit. With your mouse, click on the Edit menu, then Preferences, then the Menus button. If you have installed **pine**, **emacs** or **lynx**, their paths are incorrect for FreeBSD; change /usr/ bin to the correct path of /usr/local/bin, press the Update button and then Apply your changes.

Now you're ready to use PowerShell. If you either click on the File menu or right-click on the taskpad, you can start another **tcsh** shell, **bash** shell, or **pico**, **pine**, **lynx**, or **emacs**. Everything you start will be given its own labeled tab, and you can run as many of these as you have the inclination to. It's a simple matter of clicking on the appropriate tab to quickly switch from shell to editor to surfboard.

You'll find that PowerShell's help file is actually helpful, and the utility is quite configurable. It is the ideal utility for the power user who insists on doing several dozen things at once; this utility just may save me from wearing out my **Ctrl-Alt Function** keys.

Additional Resources

Original Articles:

http://www.onlamp.com/pub/a/bsd/2002/01/24/FreeBSD_Basics.html

http://www.onlamp.com/pub/a/bsd/2000/12/20/FreeBSD_Basics.html

4 Bag of Tricks

4.1 SETI@home

If you've ever watched the movie Contact and felt the excitement that comes from the possibility of finding intelligent signals from outer space, you may find the SETI@home project interesting. Even if you're not interested in extraterrestrial life, this project does provide an interesting example of collaborative computing.

In this section, I'd like to demonstrate the usage of the **setiathome** client.

Before I begin, what is collaborative computing? In a nutshell, it is a way to harness the processing power of CPUs running on many different computers so they can all work on a common project. Those who participate in a collaborative project donate idle CPU cycles to help process vast amounts of research data.

There are several such projects on the Internet, all of which give you the possibility of fame and fortune. The first is http://distributed.net which has been hosting various projects since 1997, usually dealing with the strength of encryption algorithms.

Another collaborative project deals with a mathematical concept known as Mersenne primes and can be found at http://www.mersenne.org/.

Installing and Connecting to the Client

It is the SETI@home project we will be concentrating on. OK, without any further ado, let's become the superuser and install the **setiathome** client:

```
% su
Password:
# pkg_add -r boinc-setiathome-enhanced
```

Unless you already have a SETI account, take a moment to register at http://setiathome.berkeley.edu/ create_account_form.php. You'll receive a confirmation email containing your key which is a long string of hex characters. Once you have your key, start the client as the super user:

```
# boinc_client
2007-04-27 12:53:50 [--] Starting BOINC client version 5.8.15 for i386-portbld-freebsd
2007-04-27 12:53:50 [--] log flags:  task, file_xfer, sched_ops
2007-04-27 12:53:50 [--] Libraries: libcurl/7.16.1 OpenSSL/0.9.7e zlib/1.2.3
2007-04-27 12:53:50 [--] Data directory:/usr/home/dru
2007-04-27 12:53:50 [--] Processor:  1 i386 Intel(R) Pentium(R) processor 1500
Mhz [] [sse sse2 mmx]
2007-04-27 12:53:50 [--] Memory:  502.85 MB physical, 0 bytes virtual
2007-04-27 12:53:50 [--] Disk:  27.11 GB total, 17.47 GB free
```

```
2007-04-27 12:53:50 [--] No general preferences found - using BOINC defaults
2007-04-27 12:53:50 [--] This computer is not attached to any projects
2007-04-27 12:53:50 [--] Visit http://boinc.berkeley.edu for instructions
```

You'll lose your prompt, so from another terminal or **xterm**, attach to the project. You may find it easiest to cut/paste your key:

```
# boinc_cmd -project_attach http://setiathome.berkeley.edu yourkeyhere
```

You should just get your prompt back in the terminal from which you ran **boinc_cmd**. You should also see a whole bunch of status messages from where you ran the **boinc_client** command as your client downloads project files and starts to compute them.

SETI@home is now working quietly in the background, processing your job order. The files it uses will be stored in `/var/db/boinc/projects/setiathome.berkeley.edu`.

Using the GUI

Once you've attached to the project you can now start and use the gui Boinc Manager (shown in Figure 4.1):

```
# boinc_gui
```

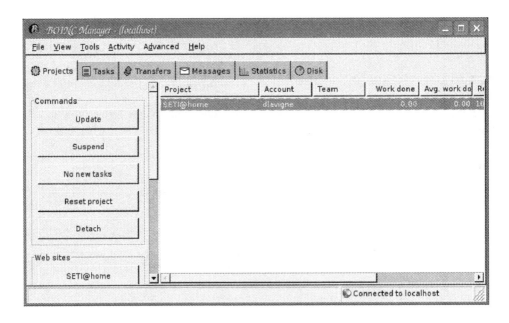

Figure 4.1: BOINC Manager

The manager can be used to Suspend the client or Detach from the client.

Click on Your preferences to review your current settings such as amount of disk space to use, how often to connect to the project, and whether or not to be active when laptop is running on batteries or while the computer is in use.

Click on the Help button to access the BOINC wiki which has lots of useful tips for usage and troubleshooting. The Help menu provides an overview of the features available in the BOINC Manager.

Click on the Messages tab to see a history of the client's actions.

A few final notes about the SETI@home application. If your firewall allows you to make outbound connections on port 80, meaning you are able to surf the Internet, you shouldn't have any problems using the **setiathome** client. The default preferences for the client shouldn't have any impact on your system's performance as they take advantage of idle CPU cycles.

I hope you enjoyed this and will check out the world of collaborative computing. Who knows, maybe some day I'll see your name in the papers as the person whose CPU discovered something interesting.

Additional Resources

Original Article:

```
http://www.onlamp.com/pub/a/bsd/2002/02/07/FreeBSD_Basics.html
```

Seti@Home Project:

```
http://setiathome.berkeley.edu/
```

4.2 Running Windows Applications on FreeBSD

One of the neatest things about FreeBSD is that if it is running on a dual-boot computer, you don't have to exit FreeBSD to access data contained on the other operating system's partition. It is a simple matter to mount the other partition and to then read, write, or even delete the files contained on that partition. Ah, but what about running executable files, you may ask? If that other operating system is made by Microsoft and you're running the Windows emulator (Wine) on your FreeBSD system, it is possible to run many Windows applications from your FreeBSD system.

In this section, I want to demonstrate building and using Wine. If things go well, I'll push my luck by also attempting to run some Windows applications on a computer totally dedicated to FreeBSD — it does not contain a Microsoft partition anywhere on its hard drive.

Installation

I'll start by installing Wine on two of the machines in my network. The first machine dual-boots Windows 98 and FreeBSD 4.3-Release. The second machine has been totally and dangerously dedicated to FreeBSD 6.2. I'll become the superuser and install on each machine:

```
% su
Password:
# pkg_add -r wine
```

I also need to check each machine's kernel configuration file to ensure it contains all of the options needed to run Wine. GENERIC does; if you've changed your kernel configuration file, check for these options:

```
# grep SYSV /usr/src/sys/i386/conf/MYKERNEL
options SYSVSHM #SYSV-style shared memory
options SYSVMSG #SYSV-style message queues
options SYSVSEM #SYSV-style semaphores
```

where you replace *MYKERNEL* with the name you used for your custom kernel configuration file. If these lines are missing, you will have to add them and recompile your kernel, using the instructions in the FreeBSD Handbook.

If you type **pkg_info -Lx wine | more** after the install you'll see that nearly a dozen man pages were installed as well as several READMEs in `/usr/local/share/doc/wine`. I also found the Wine HOWTO at `http://www.la-sorciere.de/Wine-HOWTO/book1.html` to be very helpful in setting up Wine for the first time.

Mounting the Windows 98 Partition

Let's start by trying to run Wine on the system that dual-boots FreeBSD 4.3-Release and Windows 98. To run Wine on this machine, I'll have to:

1. Find and mount the Windows partition.

2. Double-check Wine's configuration file.

3. Test the configuration by seeing if I can run a Windows application.

It's been a while since I set up this computer, so I'll use **sysinstall** to double check my partitioning scheme. As the superuser I'll type **sysinstall**, then Configure, then Fdisk. My output looks like this:

```
Offset           Size(ST)        End      Name     PType   Desc
       0               63         62        -         6    unused
      63          4176837    4176899      ad0s1       2       fat
 4176900          4016250    8193149      ad0s2       3    freebsd
```

When I'm finished, I use **q** to quit this screen, and cancel my way out of **sysinstall**. It looks like Windows is on the fat partition known to FreeBSD as `ad0s1`. In order to mount this partition, I first have to create a mount point which I'll call `dos`:

```
# mkdir /dos
```

I should also check the permissions of the mount point:

```
# ls -l / | grep dos
drwxr-xr-x  2 root  wheel   512 Aug 31 13:07 dos
```

This looks good as all users have read and execute permissions, but only the *root* user has write permission.

Before adding a permanent mount entry to `/etc/fstab`, I'll ensure that I can first manually mount that partition without any errors:

```
# mount -t msdos /dev/ad0s1 /dos
```

Note that I specified the filesystem type with **-t msdos**, the partition's name with /dev/ad0s1 and the mount point with /dos. Because I just received my prompt back, the mount was successful — I can verify this with the **df** command:

```
# df -h
Filesystem    Size    Used    Avail   Capacity   Mounted on
/dev/ad0s2a    97M     36M     53M      40%       /
/dev/ad0s2f   1.7G    567M    1.0G      35%       /usr
/dev/ad0s2e    19M    2.0M     16M      11%       /var
procfs        4.0K    4.0K      0B     100%       /proc
/dev/ad0s1    2.0G    783M    1.2G      38%       /dos
```

I can also verify the contents of the mounted partition using **ls**; I'll include the **-F** switch so I can tell the directories from the files as the directories will be followed by a /.

```
# ls -F /dos
AUTOEXEC.BAT*    COMMAND.COM*    MSDOS.SYS*       SCANDISK.LOG*
BOOT.INI*        CONFIG.SYS*     My Documents/    SETUPLOG.TXT*
BOOTLOG.PRV*     DETLOG.TXT*     NETLOG.TXT*      WINDOWS/
bootsect.bsd*    IO.SYS*         Program Files/   RECYCLED/
ntdetect.com*    ntldr*
```

If you've never mounted another operating system's partition before, you may want to take a few minutes to get used to **cd**'ing and **ls**'ing the contents of that partition from your FreeBSD prompt. Take note that many of the files are in uppercase — when you wish to access a file, type it in exactly as it appears as FreeBSD is case sensitive. Also, some files have spaces in them. To access these files, you can either start to type in the name and then use your **Tab** key to auto-complete the name, or else use a backslash to escape the space like so:

```
# ls Program\ Files
```

If you want to have your Windows partition mounted for you at boot time, carefully add the following line to your /etc/fstab file:

```
/dev/ad0s1    /dos    msdos    rw    0    0
```

Make sure that you use the right partition name as yours may not be ad0s1 like mine is. Double-check that you don't have any typos before saving your changes. I always like to ensure that my changes to /etc/fstab worked, so I'll test it by using the shorter version of the **mount** command, which forces **mount** to look for the rest of the information it needs in this file. Note that I had to unmount the partition first before I could try remounting it:

```
# umount /dos
# mount /dos
```

You can ensure that the partition is mounted by repeating the **df -h** command.

Configuring Wine on Dual-Boot System

Newer versions of Wine no longer use the `wine.conf` file for Wine configuration. In theory, you should be able to run a Windows executable by giving the full path to the executable. For example, as a regular user from an X Window session, I'll open up an **xterm** window and look for a Windows application to execute:

```
% ls /dos/WINDOWS | more
```

I notice PROGMAN.EXE and am intrigued as that is the Windows Program Manager. I'll see if I can get it to work from FreeBSD:

```
% wine /dos/WINDOWS/PROGMAN.EXE
```

Remember to give the full path exactly as you see it from FreeBSD's perspective. Also, use the command **wineconsole** instead for any command line Windows programs such as **ping** or **ipconfig**.

After a few seconds, I'm greeted by Program Manager. Clicking on the File menu, I select the Run option and then click on the Browse button. I'm greeted by a list of all of the programs running on my Windows partition.

Now the fun begins as I use trial and error to see which applications I can get to run. I'll start with Windows Calculator, so I'll click on CALC.EXE and press the Open button, then the OK button. And, voila, I'm using Windows Calculator. You could easily wile away an afternoon testing each application to prove to yourself which ones work. Or, you could search the application database at `http://appdb.winehq.org/` to view the over 6000 applications which are known to work. While there you can also click the Submit Application hyperlink if you successfully test an application not currently in the database.

Note: You will probably still experience trial and error when using the database; some applications which were supposed to run perfectly did not on my totally dedicated FreeBSD system.

Running External Applications

Now, let's try something a little more interesting. I'll become the superuser and see if I can install and then run a Windows application using Wine. The instructions are the same regardless of whether you have a currently mounted Windows partition or a system totally dedicated to FreeBSD.

Once you've located a program which looks interesting and have downloaded it's installation program, use **wine** to run it. Wine will automagically create a `~/.wine/drive_c/Program\ Files/` for you as well as a subdirectory for the application you are installing. Here I'll demonstrate the installation of:

```
% wine -winver win98 -managed solsuite.exe
```

Now when I repeat the wine command, the installation wizard for the program begins. I follow through the prompts and watch as the files are copied over to their correct destinations. At the very end, the install appeared to hang, but it said that there was 0 minutes, 0 seconds remaining. I took my chances and used a **Ctrl-C** to end the install. Then I typed:

```
% cd Program\ Files/SolSuite
% wine -winver win98 -managed Solsuite.exe
```

And it's time to phone up the neighbors and show off. I've successfully installed and run a Windows application from FreeBSD and renewed my interest in card games in the process.

As a final test, I'll reboot this computer into Windows 98. I'll click on the Start menu –> Programs, and I see a new entry for Solsuite-Solitaire Card Games, but it's empty. Not to be deterred, I go into Explorer and double-click on Program Files then SolSuite and I see all the executables which is a good sign. I then double-click on the Windows folder, Start Menu, Programs, and Solsuite, and use my right mouse button to drag SolSuite.exe into this folder. Doing this will give me a menu where I'll choose to Create Shortcut Here.

I'll now return to my Start button, Programs, Solsuite, and Shortcut to SolSuite, and I'm again prompted to choose my favorite card game. I'm impressed.

Now for the ultimate challenge. I'll move over to the computer that is totally dedicated to FreeBSD. Its hard drive is completely formatted with UFS and there are no Windows files on this computer. I'll start by becoming the superuser and creating some directories and empty files which Microsoft applications expect to see:

```
# su
Password:
# mkdir -p /usr/local/lib/win/windows
# cd /usr/local/lib/win/windows
# mkdir system
# touch win.ini
# cd system
# touch shell.dll shell32.dll winsock.dll wsock32.dll
```

Still as the superuser, I'll go back to http://download.com and download the executable for **Solsuite 2001**, this time saving it to /usr/local/lib/win. I'll then startup an X Window session, open up an xterm window and type:

```
# cd /usr/local/lib/win
# wine -winver win95 -managed solsuite.exe
```

Again, the installation program does its thing. I receive an error message about not being able to find Explorer.exe, but I ignore it. When it's finished, I then type:

```
# cd Program\ Files/SolSuite
# wine -winver win95 -managed SolSuite.exe
```

It's a bit slow (but this is an older computer) and I have to tweak my display settings, but I'm playing a Windows card game on a box totally dedicated to FreeBSD. A person could get a bit giddy indulging in the Wine.

It looks like Wine is one of the FreeBSD ports that you could have a lot of fun with. If you experiment with it and find an application that works but isn't listed yet in the database, submit your entry to one of the sites I mentioned in this section.

TheOpenCD

The other piece of software I found made me glad I had a Windows 2000 Professional install kicking around in my home network. How many times have you seen your Windows friends struggling with expensive yet virus-ridden software? Yes, they'd love a more affordable solution, but they don't have the time, energy, or courage to take the Unix plunge. Perhaps they do, but they don't completely believe that they'll be as productive on a Unix system. Maybe they still think there's a catch to free software. Don't you wish they could just install some decent open source software on the operating system they most prefer?

Well, now there's an easy way to introduce open source software to a Microsoft operating system using TheOpenCD. I burnt the .iso so I could check it out.

The CD itself autoruns on a Windows system. However, TheOpenCD's web site breaks down the contents and layout of the CD so you can see for yourself what is available in the following categories:

- Productivity

- Design

- Internet

- Games

- Multimedia

Once the user clicks on a category, a slide appears for each program. Each slide contains a description of the program, screenshots, and a hyperlink to the program's web site. More importantly, the Install button invokes a Windows installer for the specified program.

I must admit that I took great joy in installing GIMP, OpenOffice, PDFCreator, Blender, and FileZilla on a 2000 system. I also thoroughly enjoyed the Movies & Demos that came with the Blender 3D slide. I even discovered some new software that I hadn't previously known of.

I found the CD easy to use with an attractive layout. The creators of the CD also accept program nominations where you can present the case for including additional software on the CD. I think this CD will make its way into quite a few conventions and installathons over the next year. Check it out for yourself, and maybe burn a few for your friends and family.

Additional Resources

Original Articles:

http://www.onlamp.com/pub/a/bsd/2001/09/21/FreeBSD_Basics.html

http://www.onlamp.com/pub/a/bsd/2004/09/24/FreeBSD_Basics.html

FreeBSD Handbook: Configuring the FreeBSD Kernel

http://www.freebsd.org/doc/en_US.ISO8859-1/books/handbook/kernelconfig.html

TheOpenCD:

http://theopencd.org

4.3 Multi-Platform Remote Control

In this section, I'd like to take a look at TightVNC, the Virtual Network Computing project originally from ATT Laboratories. With TightVNC, you can access the desktop of any PC in your network, regardless of the operating system it is using. For example, from your FreeBSD computer you can access the desktop of a Windows XP/2000/Vista desktop or server, another *BSD computer, or a Linux, SCO or Solaris system. You will be able to do anything from that desktop as if you were physically at the other machine. The reverse is also true, meaning you can access your FreeBSD computer from any of the above listed operating systems.

This functionality is extremely handy if you are an administrator of a network, as you can check the status and change the configurations of any PC in your network without leaving your desk. In my home network, I've found it to be an economic alternative to a KVM switch when I had more PCs than monitors and mice. As an instructor, it's an invaluable teaching tool as I can have the desktops of several operating systems minimized in my menubar.

Because of its functionality and ease of use, you may want to consider running TightVNC only on your local LAN. It's one thing for you to be able to access any of your PCs, but you probably wouldn't want to give that functionality to a stranger. TightVNC does have some built-in security measures, and I'll point them out as we come across them.

Installation and Starting the Server

In my home LAN, I have the following computers:

10.0.0.1 running FreeBSD 6.2

10.0.0.2 running WinXP

10.0.0.3 running 2000 Professional

In this demonstration, I won't be going through the firewall on my other FreeBSD computer, so I won't have to change my ruleset. Also, all PCs on my LAN have already been set up for Internet connectivity, so I can build TightVNC on each of them.

Let's start by installing TightVNC. On the FreeBSD computer:

```
# su
Password:
# pkg_add -r tightvnc
```

On the XP and 2000 PCs, I used my Web browser to navigate to www.tightvnc.com/download.html. I downloaded and ran the self-installing package (.exe) for the latest stable version for Windows. Detailed installation instructions for Windows, including how and why you would want to install it at a service are available at http://www.tightvnc.com/winst.html

Like any other TCP/IP application, TightVNC contains two components: a server and a client (also known as the viewer). You use the viewer to access another PC; however, that PC must be running the server so it can listen for and authorize the connection.

If I now go to Start -> Programs on the Windows systems, I have a new heading for TightVNC that contains all of the server tools. I'll click on Launch TightVNC Server which will bring up the Properties dialog. This box contains a section to type in a password, which is VNC's first security feature. This password is used to authorize connections to the computer running the TightVNC server. If a user knows the password, he will have access to that computer; his permissions will be the same as the user who started the TightVNC server. For example, on my XP box, I'm currently logged in as administrator, which is the equivalent of the *root* account in FreeBSD. Accordingly, I'll probably want to set a unique and difficult password to prevent users other than myself from gaining administrative access through TightVNC.

I'll type in the password and press OK. I now have a new icon in my system tray next to the clock. If I right-click this icon, I can view the properties, kill any clients or stop the TightVNC server.

Using the Client

Let's see if I can access the 2000 system from the FreeBSD computer. On FreeBSD, the server component is called **vncserver** and the client component is called **vncviewer**, both of which installed with man pages.

I'll start my favorite windows manager, open an **xterm** and type **vncviewer**. A small box appears that prompts for the VNC Server. I can type in either the hostname or the IP address of the Windows server; I decide to type in 10.0.0.3. Another box appears prompting for the password, so I type in the password I created when I set up the VNC server on the Windows computer. At that point, the Windows Server's desktop appears on my screen.

These two computers happen to be side by side on my network, so I'm now seeing the Windows desktop in stereo. As I move the cursor on my FreeBSD box, I can watch it move simultaneously on both monitors. As my cursor goes to the Start menu and I see the ShutDown option, my mind wanders to all sorts of evil April Fools pranks I could play on unsuspecting users in my network. I envision the horror on another user's face as I slowly open a command prompt and type fdisk, or perhaps format C:. But seriously, VNC is an effective administrative tool. If you don't want users to access another computer, don't run the VNC server on it. If you don't want all users accessing a VNC server, set a tough password and only give it to authorized users.

Now, let's try running the VNC server on the FreeBSD computer and accessing it from the WinXP computer. Remember, whenever users connect to a VNC server, they will inherit the permissions of the user who started that VNC server. For this reason, don't start the VNC server as *root*. Also, keep in mind that if the user who starts the VNC server has permission to become the superuser, then so will the person who accesses the VNC server.

On the FreeBSD computer, I'll start the VNC server as the user *genisis*:

```
% vncserver
You will require a password to access your desktops.
Password:
Verify:
xauth: creating new authority file /home/genisis/.Xauthority
New 'X' desktop is genisis:1
Starting applications specified in /home/genisis/.vnc/xstartup
Log file is /home/genisis/.vnc/genisis:1.log
```

Note that I was again prompted for a password, just like I was when I started the VNC server on the Windows computer. Several files were also created in *genisis'* home directory, including a log file for troubleshooting purposes. Take note of the number 1 as this is the number of the display that the client will make a connection to. If I was to repeat the **vncserver** command, then I would receive the same output, but with a display number of 2 and could repeat for as many connections as I was willing to listen for.

To ensure that the server is running, I can do a search through the running processes by **grep**ing the **ps** command like so:

```
% ps -acux | grep vnc
genisis 20310  0.0  2.4  3556 3068  p0- I  8:36AM  0:00.20 Xvnc
```

You'll note that the actual name of the server is **Xvnc**. Again, the owner of this process is *genisis* so any connections to this server will have all of the permissions of the user *genisis*.

I'll also double check what port this server is listening on by searching through the socket table:

```
% sockstat -4 | grep vnc
USER      COMMAND   PID  FD PROTO  LOCAL ADDRESS   FOREIGN ADDRESS
genisis   Xvnc    20310   0 tcp4   *:6001          *:*
genisis   Xvnc    20310   3 tcp4   *:5901          *:*
genisis   Xvnc    20310   4 tcp4   *:5801          *:*
```

Note that the one process (PID 20310) is actually listening on three ports: 6001, 5901 and 5801. VNC uses the following numbering scheme for its ports:

580x allows you to access the VNC server from a Web browser

590x allows you to access the VNC server from a network connection

600x means it is listening for X11 connections

In each case, the x represents the display number you were given when you started the VNC server; in our case it is 1.

Now that my FreeBSD box is listening for VNC connections, I'll go to the WinXP computer. When I unzipped the VNC program that I downloaded, a VNC folder was created. When I double-click on this folder, I see that it contains another folder called vncviewer that contains an executable called vncviewer. I'll double-click this executable, which will bring up the Connection details box that prompts me for the name of the VNC viewer in the format host:display. When I type in 10.0.0.1:1, I'll receive the VNC Authentication box, which prompts for the Session password. Once I type this in, I'll receive a **twm** desktop with the following written in the blue title bar: genisis's X desktop (genisis:1)

At this point, I can type in whatever I want into the **xterm** and I can do anything to my FreeBSD computer from the WinXP computer that the user *genisis* has permission to do.

If you don't like the default window manager of **twm**, you can experiment running other windows managers. Since the pixel information required to redraw the screen is being sent over the network, you'll probably want to consider one of the more light-weight windows managers. Since Windowmaker is already installed on my FreeBSD computer, I typed **wmaker** into the **xterm** and was greeted by the familiar Windowmaker desktop. For some reason, I was also able to load Xfce, but it refused to load the menubar, leaving it functionally useless. If you experiment on your own and find a windows manager that works for you, you can tell your VNC server to permanently change the default windows manager.

To do so, you'll have to kill the running VNC server and edit VNC's xstartup file. I'll do this as the user *genisis*:

```
% killall Xvnc
% cd ~genisis/.vnc
% more xstartup
```

```
#!/bin/sh
xrdb $HOME/.Xresources
xsetroot -solid grey
xterm -geometry 80x24+10+10 -ls -title "$VNCDESKTOP Desktop" &
twm &
```

That last line that says twm &, I'll edit to read wmaker &. I'll then restart the VNC server using the **vncserver** command. When I reconnect from the WinXP computer, I now have the Windowmaker windows manager instead of **twm**.

Another handy way to attach to a VNC server is from a Java enabled Web browser. I'll open Internet Explorer from the WinXP computer and type in the following URL: http://10.0.0.1:5801.

Remember that the VNC server listens for Web requests from port 580x; since my server is listening on display number 1, I replaced the x with the number 1. In the Web browser, a VNC Authentication page is displayed that prompts for the password. Once I type in the password, I'm once again greeted with the Windowmaker display running on my FreeBSD computer.

A quick note on the difference in the displays depending on whether the VNC server is running on a Microsoft machine or a FreeBSD computer. Unlike Unix, Microsoft does not use the concept of an X Server that can listen for multiple connections. Instead, it uses profiles to distinguish one user's desktop from another. Since Microsoft operating systems are single user, only one profile can be run at a time; which profile is used depends upon who has logged in. For this reason, when you access a Microsoft machine using VNC, you will get the actual desktop that is currently running on that computer, including that user's wallpaper, shortcuts, etc.

In contrast, FreeBSD is a multi-user operating system and the X Server is capable of listening for multiple connections, each of which is assigned a sequential number. When you access a FreeBSD computer running VNC, you must specify the number of the display you would like to connect to. You'll then receive a default desktop, not the desktop of the user who started the VNC server.

On the Microsoft computers in your network, you don't have to install VNC on each machine you want to connect from, just those that will be running the server. The **vncviewer** easily fits on a floppy; simply copy the executable onto a floppy and take it with you when you want to initiate a VNC connection to another computer in your network.

This section should get you started on the possibilities available to you by using VNC on your LAN. To discover the other built-in features on VNC, check out the documentation that was installed on your FreeBSD computer or from the VNC Web site. They contain instructions on how to run VNC as a service in Windows, how to run VNC through an SSH tunnel and how to run VNC through a firewall.

Additional Resources

Original Article:

http://www.onlamp.com/pub/a/bsd/2001/08/23/FreeBSD_Basics.html

4.4 An Introduction to Webmin

I want to spend some time in the Webmin utility, which can be installed from the ports collection. We'll do a bit of background to see why you would want this utility, and what issues to be aware of before using it. We'll then look at configuring Webmin for secure access and at the powerful options that come with the Webmin utility.

Introduction

Admit it: When you think of using pretty GUI administrative utilities, Unix is usually not the first operating system that springs to mind. However, the operating systems that do provide nice-looking utilities usually don't let you configure the system any deeper than the vendor wants you to. Fortunately, with FreeBSD and the ports collection, you can have the best of both worlds.

One of the reasons I love FreeBSD is that the only limitation to what I'm allowed to configure on my systems is my own willingness to learn how to do what I'd like to do. FreeBSD's built-in commands are efficient and powerful; Webmin provides a graphical interface to many of these built-in commands.

When you install Webmin you are actually installing the Webmin server, which can only be installed on Unix machines. The Webmin server contains Perl modules that let you view and manipulate processes, users, groups, networking configurations, disk quotas, cron jobs, logs, system daemons, and much more.

Once the Webmin server is installed, you can use any web browser from any operating system to access these modules in order to actually configure your FreeBSD computer. In other words, you install the Webmin port on the FreeBSD computer you wish to administer; you then use a web browser to connect to the computer running the Webmin server.

This is actually a powerful concept as it allows both local and remote administration of your FreeBSD computer using a familiar graphical interface. Configurable aspects of your computer will appear as icons and hyperlinks from within your web browser.

Since we will be using a utility with such great functionality, there are a few things we need to consider when installing this package. Keep in mind that these considerations are actually good practice for any type of system administration.

When you configure Webmin, you will be prompted for the following information:

- a port number the Webmin server will accept requests on

- your computer's host name

- a user name for accessing the Webmin server

- a password

- confirmation that you already have Perl 5 installed

- confirmation that you wish to use SSL

Let's go through this checklist one point at a time.

Any port in a storm

Since the Webmin server will be waiting for requests from Webmin clients, it must be given a TCP/IP port number to listen on. Normally when you type a URL into a web browser, you type something like this:

```
http://www.freebsd.org
```

However, your web browser is actually assuming this:

```
http://www.freebsd.org:80
```

That is, your browser assumes that the Web server software on a host named www.freebsd.org is listening for web requests on port 80, which is the default listening port for web servers.

However, when you use your web browser to access your Webmin server, you want to configure your FreeBSD computer, not access a web page; therefore, you must tell your web browser what port the Webmin server listens on by typing this instead:

```
http://yourhostname:port_number
```

The default Webmin port number is 10000, but I strongly recommend that you change this to prevent unauthorized users from trying to access your Webmin server. When deciding on a port number, pick a number between 1024 and 65,535. You'll want to choose a number that is not potentially being used by another service; to doublecheck, do this:

```
% grep -w your_number /etc/services
```

For example, If I try:

```
% grep -w 10101 /etc/services
```

I will just receive my prompt back, meaning this port number is probably not being used by another service. However:

```
% grep -w 8668 /etc/services
```

will show that 8668 is the listening port that is used by **natd**, so I should probably try another port number.

Once you've settled on a port number, either commit it to memory or record it in a safe place, as you'll need it to access your Webmin server.

Host name

Next on the checklist is your computer's host name. If you will only be using Webmin locally, meaning your web browser and the Webmin server are on the same computer, type in either your computer's private IP address or the host name you created when you installed your FreeBSD computer. If you wish to access your computer remotely over the Internet, you will need to use the FQDN (fully qualified domain name) that you've purchased or the static IP address issued to you by your ISP.

User name and password

Next is the user name. Webmin will offer to use the default user name of *admin*. Please change this to a more non-intuitive name. Whenever someone tries to contact your Webmin server, they will be prompted for a user name and password. If these check out, that user will have unlimited access to your FreeBSD computer, so it is worth choosing a user name that no one else would think of using.

The same goes for the password. Webmin's default password is blank, meaning there is no password. You definitely want to change that default. You'll be glad you did when we start going through the powerful features built into the Webmin server.

The last thing the install utility will ask is if you wish to use SSL. If you will be accessing your computer remotely, you should. SSL will encrypt all the data passing between the computer hosting Webmin and the computer you are sitting at with your browser. This is a very good thing, as this data is passing over the Internet, which is a very insecure network. (SSL is part of the base system.) If you build Webmin without SSL support and change your mind later, you can easily configure SSL support without reinstalling Webmin.

Installation & Configuration

Become the superuser, make sure you're connected to the Internet, and type:

```
# pkg_add -r webmin
```

At the end of the install you will see this message:

```
===================================
To reconfigure webmin you should
run the following command as root:

  ${LOCALBASE}/lib/webmin/setup.sh

You won't have to perform this step
after every webmin upgrade.
Since 1.150_2, to run webmin from
startup, add webmin_enable="YES"
in your /etc/rc.conf.
===================================
```

Note that if the Webmin server is not running, users will see the following error message when they attempt to connect to the Webmin server from their web browsers:

The server may not be accepting connections or may be busy. Try connecting again later.

Before running that setup script and starting the server for the first time, add that line to /etc/rc.conf first. After saving your changes run the script:

```
# /usr/local/lib/webmin/setup.sh
***********************************************************************
          Welcome to the Webmin setup script, version 1.330         *
***********************************************************************
Webmin is a web-based interface that allows Unix-like operating
systems and common Unix services to be easily administered.

Installing Webmin in /usr/local/lib/webmin ...

***********************************************************************
Webmin uses separate directories for configuration files and log files.
Unless you want to run multiple versions of Webmin at the same time
you can just accept the defaults.

Log file directory [/var/log/webmin]:
***********************************************************************
Webmin is written entirely in Perl.  Please enter the full path to the
Perl 5 interpreter on your system.
```

```
Full path to perl (default /usr/bin/perl):
Testing Perl ...
Perl seems to be installed ok
*********************************************************************
Operating system name:    FreeBSD
Operating system version:  6.2
*********************************************************************
Webmin uses its own password protected web server to provide access
to the administration programs.  The setup script needs to know :
 - What port to run the web server on.  There must not be another
   web server already using this port.
 - The login name required to access the web server.
 - The password required to access the web server.
 - If the webserver should use SSL (if your system supports it).
 - Whether to start webmin at boot time.

Web server port (default 10000): 10101
Login name (default admin): drulav
Login password: mypassword
Password again: mypassword
Use SSL (y/n): y
*********************************************************************
```

You should receive a bunch of messages as the script finishes its configurations. When finished, start the server and double-check its status:

```
# /usr/local/etc/rc.d/webmin start
Starting webmin.
# /usr/local/etc/rc.d/webmin status
webmin is running as pid 5992.
```

Note that if you chose to use SSL, your connection URL will start with *https* instead of *http*. If a user types **http** instead they will receive this error message in their browser:

> Error - Bad Request
>
> This web server is running in SSL mode. Try the URL https://localhost:10101 instead.

If you are using SSL, your browser will prompt you to accept the certificate which was created for you. You'll also notice that your browser will show an icon for either a key or a closed lock, depending upon which web browser you are using; this indicates that the data is secure as it is being encrypted. Once you've been authenticated, your screen should look similar to Figure 4.2.

Configurations from within Webmin

Let's start with the Webmin Configuration hyperlink. This is where you'll be able to configure most of the additional security measures, which will be especially useful if you are accessing your Webmin server over the Internet. You'll want to poke about yourself, but here's a quick summary of some the security related options:

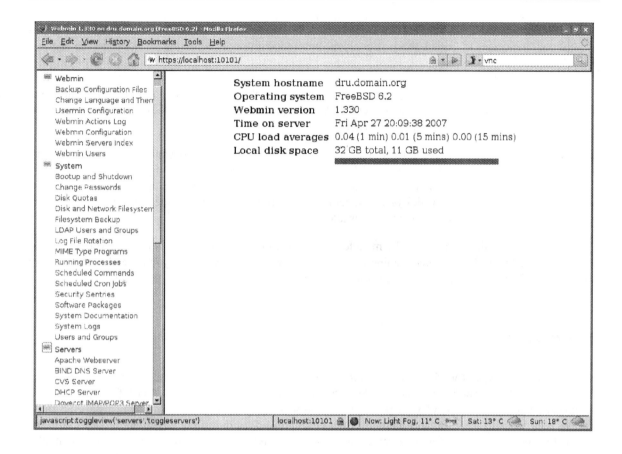

Figure 4.2: Webmin Main Menu

- **IP Access Control:** If you always access your Webmin server from the same computer or group of computers, you can tell Webmin to only accept connections from that/those computer/s. The default is to accept connections from any computer in the world that happens to know your IP address or FQDN and Webmin port number.

- **Ports and Addresses:** If your computer has more than one IP address, Webmin will bind its port to all IP addresses, meaning it will be listening for requests on all the NICs on the computer hosting the Webmin server. If you don't want it to do that, you can tell Webmin which IP address to listen on. For example, if your Webmin server has an interface connected to your LAN and another interface connected to the Internet, you can use this screen to only bind the Webmin port to the NIC attached to your LAN. This will restrict Webmin access to computers from within your LAN. Also, if you ever want to change the listening port number, this is where you do it.

- **Logging:** It is always good practice to log connections, and then take the time to actually read the logs. By doing this, you will know if anyone other than yourself is trying to access your Webmin server. By default, logging is enabled; use this screen to fine-tune what gets logged.

- **Proxy Servers and Downloads:** If your Webmin server is located behind a firewall, you may need to configure the IP address of the firewall in order for users to access certain modules on your Webmin server.

- SSL Encryption: If you didn't install Webmin with SSL support, this is where you can enable this support if you later decide to. Again, this is strongly recommended if you are accessing Webmin over the Internet.

Note: If you ever screw up your configuration and are no longer able to access your Webmin server, all is not lost. Become the superuser on the computer running Webmin, look for and then edit the offending configuration in the `/usr/local/etc/webmin/miniserv.conf` file.

Now, click on the Webmin Users link. You should see the user you created. If you click on that username, you'll receive a listing of all the Webmin modules that user is allowed to access. If you ever decide to give another user access to your Webmin server, you have very fine control over what that user will be able to view and modify. For example, if you click on the Sendmail Configuration link, you can specify which configuration files that user can modify, and whose email he is allowed to read.

If you spend some time clicking on the modules in this section, you'll get an idea of what you're capable of doing to the FreeBSD computer running the Webmin server. Aren't you glad you created a non-intuitive username and hard to guess password, and you're reading the logs of all connection attempts?

System Section

Now let's see what type of work we can do from the Webmin interface. Expand System and click on Software Packages, then the Package Tree button. You should receive the graphical equivalent of the **pkg_info -a** command. Now click on one of your packages to read its description and the date it was installed. Those who've been around FreeBSD for a while may not be impressed, as this is the equivalent of **pkg_info -Dx**. Try clicking on the List Files button. Ever install a port and wondered where it put everything and what all it created on your FreeBSD system? Wonder no more, as you now have a hyperlinked list of all the files that were installed with that port, as well as their locations, size, and ownership.

Next try Running Processes. This is just a graphical output of the **ps** command, but I love its layout. All running processes can be sorted by PID, user, memory, and CPU. If you sort by PID, you'll receive a tree-like structure, with every child process slightly to the right of its parent process. Each process has a hyperlink to further details about that process. If you need to send a signal to a process, you can choose the type of signal from a drop-down menu. (Do a **man 1 kill** to learn more about signals — and never **kill** a process if you don't know what that process does).

The Scheduled Cron Jobs hyperlink displays a listing of all users' **cron** jobs. You can edit and create new **cron** jobs using this interface. If you are a visual person, you may find it easier to click on the desired time slots rather than remembering where to place the right number in **vi** using the **crontab** utility.

Next try Users and Groups. If you haven't yet figured out what users and groups get installed with FreeBSD, here's your chance to see them all. Click on an existing user to see their details. Note that you can change a user's login shell or home directory and set password restrictions and account expiry from this screen. Go back a screen and click on Create a new user. You have more options in this screen than in the equivalent **sysinstall** screen.

The last link I want to look at in the System section is System Logs. If you click on this link, you'll get a listing of all your system logs and their locations. If you click on one of the logs, you can set its logging facilities and priorities. Even handier, you can click the View logfile button. It will display the last 20 lines by default, but you can change this by typing in another number and pressing the Refresh button.

Servers & Networking Sections

The Servers section is where you'll see that Webmin is a utility you can grow into as you learn more about your FreeBSD system. As you learn how to build and administer Apache Web servers, BIND DNS servers, MySQL database servers, Samba servers, and Squid proxy servers, you'll have a nice GUI interface to access their configuration files either locally or remotely. None of the servers I just mentioned are built by default, but they can all be added using FreeBSD's ports collection.

I would like you to click on the hyperlink for Sendmail Configuration, as a working Sendmail server is installed with your FreeBSD system. You should get a screenful of configuration icons; however, you won't want to muck about with these unless you know what you're doing. For now, you might just want to take note that each icon is much more user-friendly than the Sendmail configuration file.

The icon I'd like to look at is the one labeled User Mailboxes. When you click on this link, you'll receive a table showing all users and how much mail (in bytes) is in their mailbox. Very handy to see which users on your system aren't deleting their mail. If you click on a user, you will see all of their email messages. You can click on a message to read, reply, forward, or delete it. This could provide a very handy way for users to access their email from a browser on any computer with an Internet connection. It would just be a matter of creating another username and password to the Webmin server, and removing that user from all modules except Sendmail Configuration in the Webmin Users link under the Webmin section. Don't forget to change all the default *yes*es to *no*s and only give them permission to read their own email.

In the Networking section click on Network Configuration, then Network Interfaces. This screen shows your current configurations and which interfaces are configured to run at boot time. If you click on an interface, you can change its IP address, subnet mask, and toggle its status as being up or down. If you return to the Network Configuration screen, you'll also see hyperlinks to change your default gateway, edit /etc/resolv.conf, and edit /etc/hosts via a GUI screen.

Working with Modules

In the Webmin section, click on Webmin Configuration, then the Webmin Modules link. If you scroll down to the bottom half of the screen, you'll see all of the currently installed Webmin modules. If you see any modules that you don't plan on using, you can mark and delete them; they will no longer show up in your browser when you access the Webmin server.

You can also install new modules from this screen. If you surf over to http://www.webmin.com/third.html, you'll get a description of modules you can install. The modules themselves are very small files that end with a *.wbm* extension. One of my favorite add-on modules is the Network Utilities module that installs into the Networking section. This is how I installed it:

```
# mkdir /usr/local/webmodules
```

In my browser I right-clicked the module to save it into this directory. I then clicked the ellipse (the button with ... in it) next to the From uploaded file box. Once I had located the downloaded module, I clicked the Install Module button, and I was finished.

To see if it worked, I expanded the Networking section, and I had a new hyperlink called Network Utilities. When I enter this screen, I get icons to Ping, Traceroute, Lookup, Nmap, Whois, and Dig utilities, as well as a handy IP Subnet Calculator[1]. I have the option of typing in an IP address or hostname; I can then Ping It!, Trace It!,

---

[1]Have a look at section 3.6 for some other subnetting utilities.

Look Up!, Scan It!, or Dig It!. Note that the **nmap** utility is the only one that is not installed by default with your FreeBSD system. If you wish, you can install it from the ports collection; please keep in mind that you can get yourself into legal trouble if you **nmap** hosts other than those in your own network.[2]

Not only can you easily add modules to your Webmin server, you can also upgrade your entire Webmin server without losing your customized configurations. Go back to Webmin Configuration and click on the Upgrade Webmin hyperlink to find the screen that allows you to do this.

Hopefully this section has piqued your interest in Webmin and you will spend some time discovering for yourself what you can do with this powerful utility.

Additional Resources

Original Articles:

`http://www.onlamp.com/pub/a/bsd/2000/10/25/FreeBSD_Basics.html`

`http://www.onlamp.com/pub/a/bsd/2000/11/01/FreeBSD_Basics.html`

4.5 Webmail with Usermin

As a software junkie, I'm always coming across new programs to experiment with. As I find programs I like, I add them to my mental bag of tricks so they're ready whenever a client asks, "What's the best program to do *x*?" In this section, I'll demonstrate how I used an old favorite as a lightweight webmail program as well as a new favorite I just ran across.

On one of my routine visits to a network I administer, the owner mentioned he was thinking of adding webmail functionality. Since he had only a dozen or so users, he didn't want anything too complicated, just a small program with which people could check their mail while away from the office. If he had to, he could take the time to write and test a few scripts himself, but he preferred not to spend his time reinventing the wheel.

We went to the Mail category of `http://www.freshports.org` to see the available FreeBSD options. Things looked hopeful, as more than half a dozen webmail programs were there. We took a closer look at each program to see which best suited his particular network. A few required Apache 1.*x* and wouldn't work with his server running Apache 2.*x*. Still others needed an IMAP server. His server has happily run **popa3d** for the past few years, and he was hesitant to learn, install, and test an IMAP server on a production system. (I know IMAP4 is more secure than POP3; I also know better than to tempt the network gods by replacing working software with something better.) This narrowed our choices down to two applications.

We looked at the smaller application, but the owner didn't like the interface. The larger one's interface looked quite nice, judging from the web site's screenshots, so we agreed to install the application on a test system to see how easy it was to configure. That was when the fun began.

The install itself resulted in hundreds of SUID scripts, which started my heart going. Even the owner couldn't believe how big the program was. We then started wading through reams of documentation, soon followed by scouring the Internet for error messages when the scripts refused to run. After a couple of hours of this, the owner teetered between "Why did I even want a webmail program?" and "Forget this, let's try that IMAP thing."

That's when I began to mentally scan through my toolkit. I've used Webmin on many an occasion to check email as an administrator. Obviously Webmin wouldn't help here, as it's a remote administration tool. However, Webmin does have a user equivalent — called, not surprisingly, Usermin.

---

[2]**nmap** is introduced in section 10.5.

Installing Usermin

While the owner took a break, I did this:

pkg_add -r usermin

When the install finished, I followed the instructions left by the pkg-message:

```
# /usr/local/lib/usermin/setup.sh
**********************************************************************
*            Welcome to the Usermin setup script, version 1.260     *
**********************************************************************
Usermin is a web-based interface that allows Unix-like operating
systems and common Unix services to be easily administered.
Installing Usermin in /usr/local/lib/usermin ...
**********************************************************************
Usermin uses separate directories for configuration files and log files.
Unless you want to run multiple versions of Usermin at the same time
you can just accept the defaults.

Config file directory [/usr/local/etc/usermin]:
Log file directory [/var/log/usermin]:

**********************************************************************
Usermin is written entirely in Perl. Please enter the full path to the
Perl 5 interpreter on your system.
Full path to perl (default /usr/bin/perl):
Testing Perl ...
Perl seems to be installed ok
**********************************************************************
Operating system name:    FreeBSD
Operating system version: 6.2
**********************************************************************
Usermin uses its own password protected web server to provide access
to the administration programs. The setup script needs to know :
- What port to run the web server on. There must not be another
  web server already using this port.
- If the webserver should use SSL (if your system supports it).
Web server port (default 20000): 8080
Use SSL (y/n): y
**********************************************************************
Creating web server config files..
..done
Attempting to start Usermin mini web server..
..done
**********************************************************************
Usermin has been installed and started successfully. Use your web
browser to go to
```

```
https://dru.domain.org:8080/
```

```
and login as any Unix user on your system.
```

```
Because Usermin uses SSL for encryption only, the certificate
it uses is not signed by one of the recognized CAs such as
Verisign. When you first connect to the Usermin server, your
browser will ask you if you want to accept the certificate
presented, as it does not recognize the CA. Say yes.
```

Note that I chose a random port of 8080, which users must specify in their browser in order to connect. Since I also chose SSL, users must use https in their URL. They will have the added bonus of encrypted connections, so accessing their mail with Usermin will be more secure than doing so with a POP3 client.

Note that while this particular client had an Apache web server, that's not a requirement in order to use Webmin or Usermin.

Before configuring Usermin, I added this line to /etc/rc.conf:

```
usermin_enable="YES"
```

to ensure that Usermin will restart should the system ever reboot.

Pruning Usermin

When the owner returned from his break, I had him type in the URL and log in with his username in order to check out the Usermin interface. You can do the same at the Usermin screenshots page at http://www.webmin. com/uscreens.html or examine Usermin's standard modules list at http://www.webmin.com/ustandard. html.

We went through the modules together and agreed to keep our installation very simple and lightweight. The only modules we retained were named Read Mail and Change Password. Since Usermin is a user program and you don't want users mucking about with each other's settings, you actually need Webmin to configure Usermin. If you don't already have Webmin and wish to configure Usermin, install Webmin with:[3]

pkg_add -r webmin

At the end of the install, run the **/usr/local/lib/webmin/setup.sh** script. Be sure to choose a different port number and choose a unique username and password for the administrative account. Open a second tab in your browser and open your URL using the Webmin port number. This will allow you to test your changes from the user's perspective as you make them in the other tab of your browser.

Click on Webmin in the left pane to expand this section and locate Usermin Configuration. You can then click on Usermin Modules to delete the modules you don't want to use. Use the **Ctrl** key to select multiple modules to delete. Note that once a module is deleted, you have to reinstall it before you can use it again.

After I configured the site, I still had an extra module I didn't want: Running Processes wouldn't delete, as Change Password depended upon it. However, I went into Available Modules and unchecked Running Processes. Note that this screen won't actually delete the module but it will hide its existence from users.

---

[3]Installing Webmin is covered more in section 4.4.

Depending upon your needs, you can further tighten up Usermin's security. If, for example, you use Usermin to check your own mail from work and have a static IP, you can restrict connections to that IP in IP Access Control. If you or your users don't have static IPs, instead use Allowed Users and Groups to restrict who can connect. Users who don't match the list will receive the message "Login failed. Please try again".

Also consider reviewing the defaults in Authentication. For example, by default there are password timeouts but authentication failures go unlogged.

All in all, my client was pleased with how easy it was to configure Usermin and get a decent-looking and functional webmail program. Now I have a new trick to pull out of my sleeve the next time someone is shopping around for a similar solution.

Additional Resources

Original Article:

`http://www.onlamp.com/pub/a/bsd/2004/09/24/FreeBSD_Basics.html`

5 Filesystems

5.1 An Introduction to Unix Permissions

When I was first learning Unix, it seemed that everything I tried to do resulted in the very irritating "Permission denied" message. I also quickly learned that if *root* starts messing with permissions before *root* knows what he is doing, many of the neat utilities that come with Unix stop working.

Viewing Permissions

Unix uses three base permissions: read (r), write (w), and execute (x). To view the permissions on your FreeBSD system, use the **ls** command with the **-l** (show long listing) and **-a** (show all files) switches. Here I'll show the first ten entries on the root filesystem:

```
% ls -la / | head
total 69
drwxr-xr-x 16 root wheel       512 Aug  9 11:36 .
drwxr-xr-x 16 root wheel       512 Aug  9 11:36 ..
-rw-r--r--  1 root wheel       658 Jul 26 23:14 .cshrc
-rw-r--r--  2 root wheel       251 Jul 26 23:14 .profile
drwxrwxr-x  2 root operator    251 Jul 26 23:14 .snap
-r--r--r--  1 root wheel      4735 Jul 26 23:14 COPYRIGHT
drwxr-xr-x  2 root wheel      1024 Aug  9 07:45 bin
drwxr-xr-x  3 root wheel       512 Aug  8 17:14 boot
drwxr-xr-x  2 root wheel       512 Aug  8 13:03 cdrom
```

Let's pick apart this output. This long listing starts with:

```
total 69
```

is the number of 512-byte blocks used by the files within this directory. You only get this information if you do a long listing on a directory; to see the difference, do a long listing on a file, like so:

```
% ls -l /.cshrc
-rw-r--r--  1 root  wheel  658 Jul 26 23:14 /.cshrc
```

After the total block information is a listing of the files in the specified directory. To Unix, everything is a file; this means that data files, directories, device entries, and links are all considered to be files. The very first letter in a file's **ls -la** listing states what type of file it is. For example:

```
drwxr-xr-x  2 root wheel    1024 Aug  9 07:45 bin
-rw-r--r--  1 root wheel     658 Jul 26 23:14 .cshrc
lrwxrwxrwx  1 root wheel       9 Aug  8 17:15 home -> /usr/home
```

bin is a directory as its listing begins with the letter *d*.

.cshrc is a regular file as its listing begins with the dash "-" character.

home is a symbolic link as its listing begins with the letter *l*. You'll also note that symbolic links use a -> to indicate the files that are linked.

The next nine characters represent the file's permissions. Permissions are always listed in the order of read, write, and execute. If the letter is listed, the permission is granted; if there is a - (dash) instead of the letter, that permission is denied. The permissions are repeated three times to represent owner, primary group, and everyone else. Consider the following listing:

```
-rw-r--r--  1 root wheel     658 Jul 26 23:14 .cshrc
```

As before, .cshrc is a regular file as its listing begins with a -. The owner of the file (*root*) has read and write permissions, but not the execute permission. Anyone in the primary group (*wheel*) has read permission to this file, but not write or execute permission. Everyone else has read permission, but not write or execute permission.

Note that the owner of the file is listed after the permissions; the primary group of the file is listed after the owner. This is followed by the size of the file in bytes, the date and time the file was last modified, and finally the name of the file.

Understanding rwx

What a person can actually do with a file depends on both the file's permissions and the permissions of the directory the file lives in. Let's look at the meanings of *r*, *w*, and *x* for regular files and directories, and then see if we can predict what a regular user can do with a file. Note that I said regular user; the *root* user is not subject to permissions — one of the many reasons not to be *root* any longer than absolutely necessary.

If read (r) is set on a file, permission is given to view (not change) the contents of the file using an editor or a utility such as **cat** or **more**. If read is set on a directory, permission is given to list the contents (or files and subdirectories) within the directory using the **ls** command.

If write (w) is set on a file, permission is given to change the contents of the file using an editor or a redirector. If write is set on a directory, permission is given to change the contents of the directory; meaning you can create, move, or delete files within the directory.

If execute (x) is set on a file, it can be run as a program or a shell script. If execute is set on a directory, permission is given to **cd** into that directory.

In order to determine what a regular user can do to the /.chsrc file, we'll need to look at the permissions for both the .cshrc file and the / directory. I've snipped the output of **ls -la** to just give the two entries we're interested in:

```
% ls -la /
drwxr-xr-x 16 root wheel     512 Aug  9 11:36 .
-rw-r--r--  1 root wheel     658 Jul 26 23:14 .cshrc
```

Note that the . (period or dot) represents the current directory. Root is a strange directory as it is the root of your system. Normally the double .. represents the parent directory, or previous directory; since root is the beginning, both . and .. represent root, so their listings are identical.

So, what should a regular user be able to do with this file? They have *rx* permissions to the directory and *r* to the file. Looks like they'll be able to open up the file in an editor, but not make any changes to it. Will they be able to copy, move, or delete the file? Let's try and see.

If I open up the file in my favorite editor, I can read it fine, but I can't save any changes I make to it. So far, so good. Now I'll try:

```
% cp /.cshrc /mycopy
cp: mycopy: Permission denied
% mv /.cshrc /mycopy
mv: rename .cshrc to mycopy: Permission denied
% rm .cshrc
override rw-r--r--  root/wheel for .cshrc? y
rm: .cshrc: Permission denied
```

As we expected, we could **cd** into the directory, but we couldn't copy, move, or remove the file within that directory, even though we were teased a bit during the remove operation.

What will happen if we try to copy or move this file to another directory, say our home directory? Let's first look at the permissions on our home directory:

```
% ls -la ~
drwxr-xr-x  12 genisis  wheel  1024 Aug 15 11:34 .
```

Note that ~ (tilde) is an abbreviation for your home directory; this saves a lot of typing. Now let's retry our commands:

```
% cp .cshrc ~/myfile
% mv .cshrc ~/myfile
mv: rename .cshrc to /home/genisis/myfile: Permission denied
```

Note that I didn't get an error message when I copied the file to my home directory; this means the command was successful. However, I wasn't able to move that same file into my home directory. This strange behavior makes sense if you understand what actually happens when you move and copy files.

Remember that everything is a file to Unix. Regular files contain data, such as text. A directory is really just a file which contains a list of the other files that live within the directory. In order to move a file, you have to remove the file from this list. If you don't have write permission to the directory, you can't change the list, so you won't be able to move the file.

In order to copy a file, you have to add the name of the new file to the list of the directory you want to copy the file to. When we tried to copy the .cshrc file within the / directory, we didn't have write permission to the / directory, so we couldn't copy the file. However, when we tried to copy .cshrc to our home directory, we had write permission to our home directory, so the copy was successful.

Specialty Permissions

Unix also understands three specialty permissions that allow us to fine-tune the default permissions. The first specialty permission is called the SUID, or set user id bit. If you do a long listing, and see either an *s* or an *S* instead of an *x* in the owner section of the permissions, this bit has been set.

The SUID bit can allow a user to temporarily gain *root* access, usually in order to run a program. For example, only the *root* account is allowed to change the password information contained in the password database; however, any user can use the **passwd** utility to change their password. Let's do a long listing on the **passwd** command to see why. Here I'll use backticks to send the full pathname to **passwd** as found by the **which** command to a long listing:

```
% ls -l `which passwd`
-r-sr-xr-x  2 root  wheel  26260 Jul 26 23:12 /usr/bin/passwd
```

Because the SUID bit has been set on the **passwd** utility and it is owned by *root*, it will become *root* in order to modify the password database, allowing the user to change their password.

If the SUID bit appears as a lowercase *s*, the file's owner also has execute permission to the file; if it appears as an uppercase *S*, the file's owner does not have execute permission.

The second specialty permission is the SGID, or set group id bit. It is similar to the SUID bit, except it can temporarily change group membership, usually to execute a program. The SGID bit is set if an *s* or an *S* appears in the group section of permissions. An example of a file with the SGID bit set is **netstat**:

```
% ls -l `which netstat`
-r-xr-s---  1 root  kmem  114872 Jul 26 23:12 /usr/bin/netstat
```

Since **netstat**'s SGID bit is set with an *s* instead of an *S*, execute permission has also been set.

The third specialty permission is the directory sticky bit. This bit is essential if you have a directory that is used by more than one user. Remember the permissions for your home directory?

```
% ls -la ~
drwxr-xr-x  12 genisis  wheel  1024 Aug 15 11:34 .
```

The owner has full access to the directory, but all other users, including members of the owner's primary group, only have *rx*. Only the owner will be able to create and delete files from his home directory, which is a good thing.

However, these permissions aren't suitable for a shared directory where many users have to be able to create, modify, and possibly remove files from the directory. If you create a directory and give either a group or everyone write access to the directory, users will be able to create and modify files within the directory.

Unfortunately, write access to a directory also means that users can delete any file within the directory, even if they don't own the file. This is not nice, especially considering that once a file is deleted in Unix, it is gone forever.

This is where the directory sticky bit comes in. This bit is set if a *t* or a *T* appears instead of an *x* in the everyone section of permissions like so:

```
% ls -l / | grep tmp
drwxrwxrwt   9 root   wheel   512 Aug 31 10:48 tmp/
```

When the directory sticky bit is set, users will still be able to create and modify files within the directory, but they will only be able to delete files which they themselves created.

All permissions on your FreeBSD system will be a combination of these base and specialty permissions.

Octal Mode

Next, we'll be using **chmod** to change permissions. But first, never, ever, ever change the default permissions on the files and directories that came with your FreeBSD system. The creators of FreeBSD understand permissions; unless you are a systems administrator or a security engineer with a good reason to change these defaults, please leave well enough alone.

Instead, we'll be creating test directories and test files to practice with. Once you're comfortable with setting permissions, you'll be able to create your own directories and set their permissions according to your needs.

Let's start by taking a look at the **chmod** command. There are two modes of operation for **chmod**: absolute mode (which uses numbers) and symbolic mode (which uses letters).

In absolute mode, **chmod** uses four numbers to represent the following four sets of permissions:

- Specialty permissions (SUID, SGID, directory sticky bit)
- Base permissions for the owner of the file (*rwx*)
- Base permissions for the primary group of the file (*rwx*)
- Base permissions for everybody else (*rwx*)

Instead of using the letters *r*, *w*, *x*, *s*, or *t*, it uses the numbers 4, 2, and 1 in this order:

```
421 421 421 421
```

In the first set of numbers, 4 = SUID, 2 = SGID, and 1 = directory sticky bit. In the next three sets of numbers, 4 = read, 2 = write, and 1 = execute; again the order is owner, group, and everyone else. If a permission is to be denied, a 0 is used, not the - symbol.

So, if I wanted to set the SUID bit on a file, give its owner full access, and give the primary group and everyone else read and execute access, I would want permissions like this:

```
400 421 401 401
```

To set this using **chmod**, I must first total each set of permissions like so:

```
400 = 4+0+0 = 4
421 = 4+2+1 = 7
401 = 4+0+1 = 5
401 = 4+0+1 = 5
```

so I can tell **chmod** this:

```
% chmod 4755 name_of_file
```

Let's try this and see if it works. As a regular user, **cd** into your home directory and create a test file. In this example, I am logged in as the user *genisis*; if I type **cd** without any arguments, I will be taken to *genisis*' home directory.

```
% cd
% touch test
% ls -la test
-rw-r--r--  1 genisis  wheel  0 Aug 19 11:27 test
% chmod 4755 test
% ls -la test
-rwsr-xr-x  1 genisis  wheel  0 Aug 19 11:27 test
```

Note that whoever creates a file becomes the owner of the file. And the group of the new file will be inherited from the group of the directory it is in. Only the owner of the file (and *root*) can change the permissions of a file.

Now, how would you use **chmod** to change the file back to its original permissions? Let's see if we can do the math and get it to work. Our original permissions looked like this:

```
-rw-r--r--  1 genisis  wheel  0 Aug 19 11:27 test
```

There isn't an *s*, *S*, *t*, or *T* in the original permissions, so the first set will be $0 + 0 + 0 = 0$.

The owner has *rw* which is $4 + 2 + 0 = 6$.

The group has *r* which is $4 + 0 + 0 = 4$.

Everyone else has *r* which is $4 + 0 + 0 = 4$.

So let's see if the following works:

```
% chmod 644 test
% ls -la test
-rw-r--r--  1 genisis  wheel  0 Aug 19 11:27 test
```

Note that the following command would yield the same result:

```
% chmod 0644 test
```

However, you can omit the 0 if it represents the specialty permissions.

Symbolic Mode

Now let's try **chmod** in symbolic mode. The syntax for symbolic mode is a bit longer:

```
% chmod who operator permission filename
```

where who can be:

u = user (owner)

g = group

o = others

a = all, or ugo

and operator can be:

+ add this permission

- take away this permission

= make this permission equal to

and the permissions can be *r*, *w*, *x*, *s*, *t*, and *X*. Note that there is no capital *S*; if you want to keep the execute bit when you set the SUID or SGID bits, use both *s* and *x*. If you want to set the SUID bit, use *s* with a who of *u*; to set the SGID bit, use *s* with a who of *g*. To set the sticky bit, use *t* with a who of *o*.

Let's try our original example in symbolic mode. We started with:

```
-rw-r--r--  1 genisis  wheel  0 Aug 19 11:27 test
```

and want to end up with:

```
-rwsr-xr-x  1 genisis  wheel  0 Aug 19 11:27 test
```

so let's try this:

```
% chmod a+sx test
% ls -la test
-rwsr-sr-x  1 genisis  wheel  0 Aug 19 13:05 test
```

Close, but no cigar. Since we specified a who of *a* (or everyone), we set both the SUID and SGID bits. Let's try again:

```
% rm test
% touch test
% chmod u+s go+x test
chmod: go+x: No such file or directory
```

We got a syntax error on that command because **chmod** expects the who, operator, and permissions to be a string of characters without any spaces. Whatever follows the space is interpreted as the name of the file whose permissions are being set. Let's try again:

```
% chmod u+s,go+x test
% ls -la test
-rwSr-xr-x  1 genisis  wheel  0 Aug 19 13:16 test
```

Almost there; we seem to have set the SUID bit and given everyone except the owner execute permission. One more try:

```
% rm test
% touch test
% chmod u+sx,go+x test
% ls -la test
-rwsr-xr-x  1 genisis  wheel  0 Aug 19 13:22 test
```

Success. You can see that it is a good idea to always doublecheck your permissions using **ls -la** after using the **chmod** command to make sure you actually set the permissions you intended.

Remember that what a user can do with a file depends on both the file's permissions and the directory's permissions. Let's make a test directory in our home directory to store some test files:

```
% cd
% mkdir testdir
% cd testdir
% touch testfile
% ls -la
total 2
drwxr-xr-x   2 genisis  wheel    512 Aug 20 10:24 .
drwxr-xr-x  14 genisis  wheel   1024 Aug 20 10:23 ..
-rw-r--r--   1 genisis  wheel      0 Aug 20 10:24 testfile
```

Note the interesting behavior with the times. The parent directory was last modified when testdir was created, as its name had to be added to the parent directory's list. Remember that a directory is simply a file containing a list of the directory's contents. Similarly, the testdir directory was modified the same time that the testfile was created, as it also had to be added to its directory list.

Now, I want you to logout and login as a different user (other than *root*). Looking at the permissions for the testdir directory, will that user be able to **cd** into that directory, use the **ls** command, read a file, change a file, create a file, or remove a file? As you try this exercise, remind yourself which permission is allowing or preventing that user from doing something in the testdir directory. I'll login as the user *biko*:

```
% exit
login: biko
Password:
% cd ~genisis/testdir
```

Note the shortcut to return to *genisis*' home directory. Looks like the execute permission for everyone on testdir allowed *biko* to **cd** into it.

```
% ls -la
total 2
drwxr-xr-x   2 genisis   wheel    512 Aug 20 10:24 .
drwxr-xr-x  14 genisis   wheel   1024 Aug 20 10:23 ..
-rw-r--r--   1 genisis   wheel      0 Aug 20 10:24 testfile
```

Looks like the read permission for everyone on the `testdir` directory allowed *biko* to list its contents.

```
% more testfile
```

Looks like the read for everyone on the `testfile` allowed its contents to be read. Even though the file was empty, *biko* did not receive an error message.

```
% touch myfile
touch: myfile: Permission denied
```

Looks like *biko* doesn't have write permission to this directory, so he won't be creating any files in it.

```
% rm testfile
override rw-r--r--  genisis/wheel for testfile? y
rm: testfile: Permission denied
```

Again, lack of write permission will prevent *biko* from removing files from this directory.

```
% mv testfile ~
mv: rename testfile to /home/biko/testfile: Permission denied
```

This is a move operation; *biko* would need write permission on the `testdir` directory for this to work.

```
% cp testfile ~
```

This copy operation was successful as *biko* does have write permission on his home directory.

```
% ls -la >> testfile
testfile: Permission denied.
```

Here I was trying to append the results of **ls -la** to the end of the `testfile`. If *biko* had write permission, he would be able to do this.

Now, how would we give *biko* permission to create files in this directory but not delete any files which were created by *genisis*? See if you can come up with a solution in both absolute and symbolic mode before testing your theory. Note, you have a choice of giving permission to the primary group, to everyone else, or to both. You'll have to log in as the original user who made the `testdir` directory in order to change its permissions. And don't forget to change your directory's sticky bit.

Using Groups

Now is a good time to mention *groups*, as group membership is an important consideration when setting permissions. To see what groups you belong to, simply type:

```
% groups
```

To see what groups anyone else belongs to, add their login name to the end of the **groups** command like so:

```
% groups genisis
wheel
% groups biko
biko
```

Here I have two users who don't live in the same group. If I wanted them to share a directory, I could set permissions on everyone, but this would also give permissions to everyone else. Alternately, I could make them members of the same group and set permissions for the group. With this method, I may also have to change the primary group of the file using the **chown** command. Let's create a group called *projects* and add these two users to it. Become *root*, as only *root* can make new users or groups. We'll use the **pw** command to create the group; first, we'll type **pw** to get the syntax:

```
# pw
usage:
  pw [user|group|lock|unlock] [add|del|mod|show|next] [help|switches/values]
```

Then we'll add a group with the fairly straightforward syntax:

```
# pw group add projects
```

Then we'll verify that it worked like so:

```
# grep projects /etc/group
projects:*:1006:
```

Our new group is showing up in the /etc/group database with a group ID of 1006. Now, I'll want to add the users *genisis* and *biko* to the group like so:

```
# pw groupmod projects -M genisis,biko
# grep projects /etc/group
projects:*:1006:genisis,biko
```

Everything looks good; one last test to verify:

```
# groups genisis
wheel projects
# groups biko
biko projects
```

Note that you can belong to more than one group at a time in FreeBSD. Now all we have to do is change the primary group of the `testdir` directory so we can give permissions to just *genisis* and *biko*. The user *genisis* can do this, as she owns the directory, so we'll exit out of the *root* account and log back in as *genisis*. Then:

```
% cd
% chown :projects testdir
```

Note that the **chown** command requires a full colon (:) to indicate you want to change the primary group, not the owner of the file or directory.[1]

Now, let's see if the change was successful:

```
% ls -la testdir
total 2
drwxr-xr-x   2 genisis  projects   512 Aug 20 10:24 .
drwxr-xr-x  14 genisis  wheel     1024 Aug 20 11:45 ..
-rw-r--r--   1 genisis  wheel        0 Aug 20 10:24 testfile
```

We can now set permissions for the *projects* group, and it will only affect the users *genisis* and *biko*.

I'd like to end this section with some common permissions to set on directories that you create.

If you create a directory that will contain private data that you only want yourself to access, set its permissions to 700. Users will be able to see the directory, but they won't be able to **cd** into it, list its contents, or modify any of the files in it. Keep in mind that *root* is not subject to permissions, so nothing is really hidden from the *root* account.

If you wish to have a directory inaccessible to a group of users, set its permissions to 707 or 705. This works, as FreeBSD stops reading permissions when it finds a match. This means that FreeBSD first checks to see if you are the owner of the file; if you are, you are subject to the owner's permissions. If you are not the owner, it then checks to see if you belong to the primary group of the file; if you do, you are subject to that group's permissions. If you don't, you are subject to the permissions of everyone else.

If you want a group to be able to write files, but only delete their own files, set the directory's permissions to 1775.

Practice reading directory listings to determine what you can and can't do with a file. When you see a listing, think which **chmod** command would have set that permission. Before you know it, you'll be able to look at a listing and know how to change its permissions so your users can do what you want them to do.

Additional Resources

Original Articles:

http://www.onlamp.com/pub/a/bsd/2000/09/06/FreeBSD_Basics.html

http://www.onlamp.com/pub/a/bsd/2000/09/13/FreeBSD_Basics.html

---

[1]The **chgrp** command can also be used to change the group id of a file.

5.2 Dividing Your Data

In the next few sections, I'll look at how FreeBSD stores data on your hard disk. To store data on a hard drive, the drive must first be divided into logical storage units, and each unit must be assigned an address. The file system will save data to these storage units and keep track of which storage units contain which files.

Like any other version of Unix, FreeBSD uses inode (index number) tables to record where files are physically located on disk.[2] Before any inode tables can be created, the disk storage units must be created and given addresses. Let's summarize the steps involved in this process:

- The **fdisk** utility is used to view and create the BIOS partition table which defines up to four disk "slices."

- The **bsdlabel** utility is used to view and create the Unix partition table which defines up to eight Unix "partitions."

- The **newfs** utility is used to actually create a filesystem on each Unix partition.

- Every filesystem will then maintain its own inode table.

The BIOS Parition Table

Notice that your FreeBSD system contains both a BIOS partition table and a Unix partition table. This is necessary as FreeBSD is a Unix operating system, meaning it understands the Unix partition table; however, FreeBSD is also an operating system which runs on a PC (personal computer). PCs require software known as the BIOS in order to initialize the computer, discover the physical geometry of the drives, and locate the software that will boot the desired operating system.

One of the instructions in the BIOS is to look at the contents of the first sector of the first hard disk. This sector is 512 bytes in size; out of those 512 bytes, 64 bytes have been set aside for the BIOS partition table. Every entry in the BIOS partition table consists of 16 bytes, therefore there is only enough room to describe four BIOS partitions.

The BIOS partition table can be viewed or changed using a **fdisk** utility. If you change the BIOS partition table, you are actually slicing your physical disk into as many as four logical disks. FreeBSD users prefer to call these logical disks "slices" so they won't be confused with the partitions described by the Unix partition table.

You may be familiar with the DOS **fdisk** utility; I'd like to compare it to the FreeBSD **fdisk** utility so you can see the similarities between the two programs. I'll start by showing the output from one of my PCs; I booted this PC with a DOS boot disk, then ran **fdisk** from the floppy prompt:

```
        Microsoft Windows 95
        Fixed Disk Setup Program
(C)Copyright Microsoft Corp/ 1983 - 1995
FDISK Options
Current fixed disk drive: 1
Choose one of the following:
1. Create DOS partition or Logical DOS Drive
2. Set active partition
3. Delete partition or Logical DOS Drive
4. Display partition information
Enter choice: [4]
```

---

[2]Inodes are covered in more detail in section 5.3.

Here we've entered the main menu of the DOS **fdisk** utility. I don't want to change the BIOS partition table, so I'll choose option 4 to display the partition information.

```
Display Partition Information

Current fixed disk drive:  1

Partition  Status  Type  Volume Label  Mbytes  System  Usage
C: 1         A     PRI DOS              204    FAT16    3%
   2               Non-DOS             3193             52%
   3               EXT DOS             2753             45%

Total disk space is   6150 Mbytes (1 Mbyte = 1048576 bytes)

The Extended DOS Partition contains Logical DOS Drives.
Do you want to display the logical drive information (Y?N)......?[Y]
```

Notice that I have sliced up my hard drive into three slices, which DOS calls partitions. The first slice has a status of A for active, meaning that it contains boot code in order to boot an operating system. It is 204 Mbytes in size and has been formatted with the FAT16 file system.

The second slice is 3,193 Mbytes and contains my FreeBSD partitions. This file type is not recognized by the DOS fdisk utility and has been simply labeled as non-DOS.

The third slice is a 2,753-Mbyte extended partition. Notice that you must enter another screen to see the layout of the extended partition. Extended partitions were designed to allow you to slice your hard drive into more than four slices; the extended partition is simply a pointer to another area on disk which contains yet another table to describe the layout of the logical partitions contained within the extended partition. Unfortunately, these logical partitions are truly logical as they cannot contain boot code, and many operating systems will not install on an extended partition. I'll press **Y** to enter into the screen that will show these logical partitions:

```
Display Logical DOS Drive Information

Drv Volume Label Mbytes System Usage
D: 1396 FAT16 51%
E: 361 FAT16 13%

Total Extended DOS Partition size is 2753 Mbytes (1 Mbyte = 1048576 bytes)
```

Let's summarize the information we've gleaned out of the DOS **fdisk** utility. This PC has one hard drive of 6,150 Mbytes. It has been sliced up and labeled as shown in Table 5.1.

DOS uses the following naming scheme for its slices:

- Primary slices are labeled first, starting with the letter C as the letters A and B are reserved for floppy drives.

- Once the primary slices have been labeled, the logical slices are then labeled.

- Extended slices and unknown slices are not labeled.

Table 5.1: DOS fdisk Slices

DOS slice name	DOS slice type	Slice size	Filesystem
C:	primary	204 Mbytes	FAT16
D:	logical	1,396 Mbytes	FAT16
E:	logical	361 Mbytes	FAT16
none	unknown	3,193 Mbytes	unknown

Let's compare this to the output from FreeBSD's **fdisk** utility. If you just type **fdisk** at a prompt, it will display the contents of the BIOS partition table. However, if you try to run **fdisk** as a regular user, you'll receive this message:

```
% fdisk
fdisk: can't open device /dev/ad0
fdisk: cannot open disk /dev/ad0: Permission denied
```

Only the superuser has permission to access the device that represents my first IDE disk; this is a good thing, as all **fdisk** utilities give you the option to modify the slices that have been defined on a hard disk. If you modify a slice, you lose all the data on that slice. Don't worry, the superuser won't be able to modify a slice if he just types **fdisk** to view the BIOS partition table; the superuser has to actually specify a drive and a switch in order to change a slice. I'll become the superuser and try that view command again:

```
# fdisk
****** Working on device /dev/ad0 ******
parameters extracted from in-core disklabel are:
cylinders=784 heads=255 sectors/track=63 (16065 blks/cyl)

parameters to be used for BIOS calculations are:
cylinders=784 heads=255 sectors/track=63 (16065 blks/cyl)

Media sector size is 512
Warning:  BIOS sector numbering starts with sector 1
Information from DOS bootblock is:
The data for partition 1 is:
sysid 6,(Primary "big" DOS (> 32MB))
start 63, size 417627 (203 Meg), flag 80 (active)
beg:  cyl 0/ sector 1/ head 1;
end:  cyl 25/ sector 63/ head 254
The data for partition 2 is:
sysid 165,(FreeBSD/NetBSD/386BSD)
start 417690, size 6538455 (3192 Meg), flag 0
beg:  cyl 26/ sector 1/ head 0;
end:  cyl 432/ sector 63/ head 254
The data for partition 3 is:
```

```
sysid 5,(Extended DOS)
start 6956145, size 5638815 (2753 Meg), flag 0
beg:  cyl 433/ sector 1/ head 0;
end:  cyl 783/ sector 63/ head 254
The data for partition 4 is:
<UNUSED>
```

If you take a close look at this output, you'll notice that FreeBSD's **fdisk** utility yields the same information as the DOS **fdisk** utility plus more detailed information regarding the physical layout of the disk. This information is always contained in the BIOS partition table, but not all of the information is displayed with the DOS **fdisk** utility.

Hard drives are divided into logical units known as cylinders and sectors. My FreeBSD slice (partition 2) starts at cylinder 26/sector 1 and ends at cylinder 432/sector 63. Since cylinders are comprised of 63 sectors, we've started at the beginning of cylinder 26 and ended at the end of cylinder 432, for a total of 407 cylinders. We'll see that cylinder information again when we look at the Unix partition table.

You can also use the **fdisk** utility to view a summary of the BIOS partition table if you include the **-s** switch:

```
# fdisk -s
/dev/ad0: 784 cyl 255 hd 63 sec
Part        Start        Size Type Flags
  1:           63      417627 0x06 0x80
  2:       417690     6538455 0xa5 0x00
  3:      6956145     5638815 0x05 0x00
```

This output again shows three defined slices. It also shows the starting address of each slice, and the size of each slice in sectors. The type of each slice is written in hex as hex values always begin with 0x. The hex value a5 is equivalent to the decimal number 165 which is the magic number used by FreeBSD; the hex value 06 is equivalent to the decimal number 6 which is the magic number for FAT16; the hex value 05 is equivalent to the decimal number 5 which is the magic number for a DOS extended partition. Only one flag can be set to 0x80 as this represents the active partition and a BIOS partition table can only have one active partition.

Let's summarize the BIOS partition table: It is used by a PC's BIOS to determine the physical layout of a hard disk which may have been logically divided into as many as four slices. Normally, users create multiple slices when they wish to run multiple operating systems. If a slice is to contain a Microsoft operating system, it must first be formatted with a file system that the operating system understands. The formatting process will create a table on that slice which will be used by the file system to keep track of where data is stored on that slice.

Unix Partition Table

The nice thing about slicing up a hard drive is that you can reformat a slice (which destroys the table for that slice, meaning you'll no longer be able to find the data on that slice) without affecting the data on the other slices of the disk. However, a slice formatted for a Microsoft operating system can only contain one file system; that is, you can't have two or more file systems on a slice that contains a Microsoft operating system.

If a slice is to contain the FreeBSD operating system, the Unix partition table will be written to that slice. A FreeBSD slice can contain up to eight partitions, and each partition can be either a separate file system or a swap partition.

If you run the **bsdlabel** utility without any switches, you will be able to safely view the Unix partition table of the specified slice without modifying it; again, only the superuser can use this utility as only the superuser has permission to access the disk's device name. My PC is running FreeBSD 6.2, so its IDE drive is called ad0. Drives are numbered starting with the number 0 and slices with the number 1; since my first FreeBSD slice is on my first drive, I'll specify the device like so:

```
# bsdlabel ad0s1
# /dev/ad0s1:
8 partitions:
#    size    offset      fstype    [fsize bsize bps/cpg]
a:  102400        0      4.2BSD        0     0     0
b:  270976   102400        swap
c: 6538455        0      unused        0     0 # "raw" part, don't edit
e:   40960   373376      4.2BSD        0     0     0
f: 6124119   414336      4.2BSD        0     0     0
```

The Unix partition table looks quite different from the BIOS partition table. All of these entries live in that one FreeBSD slice which the BIOS sees as partition 2. Notice that this one slice has been assigned five letters, but the letter *c* shows a filesystem type of unused. By convention, the letter *c* represents the entire slice, so the actual filesystems will be assigned the letters *a-b* and *d-h*. On this FreeBSD slice, there are three separate filesystems lettered *a*, *e*, and *f*. The swap partition has been assigned the letter *b*.

Each filesystem is defined by its cylinder groups, which are simply a bunch of cylinders grouped together. Each filesystem is only responsible for the data stored on its cylinder group. With a bit of math we can figure out how big this slice is in megabytes. There are 6,538,455 sectors and each sector is 512 bytes. If we multiply the number of sectors by the number of bytes, we'll get the total number of bytes. If we divide this result by 1,024, we'll get the number of kilobytes; if we divide that result by another 1,024, we'll get the number of megabytes:

6,538,455 * 512 = 3,347,688,960 bytes
3,347,688,960 / 1,024 = 3,269,227 kilobytes
3,269,227 / 1,024 = 3,192 megabytes

which just happens to be the size reported by the **fdisk** utility.

How Filesystems Work

The **bsdlabel** utility can be used to create the Unix partition table, but it does not actually create the filesystems. Instead, it creates a disk pack label which is read by the **newfs** utility. It is the **newfs** or new filesystem utility which creates the actual filesystems and their associated inode tables. Let's start by taking a closer look at formatting and filesystems in general so we can gain a better appreciation of **newfs**.

There are two types of hard drive formatting. When you purchased your hard drive, it most likely was already low level formatted for you by the manufacturer. Low-level formatting creates the tracks and sectors on the drive; the intersection of these tracks and sectors creates the units of storage known as physical blocks, which are 512 bytes in size.

The second type of formatting is called high-level formatting. This type of formatting installs a particular file system onto a slice of your physical drive using a utility such as DOS's **format** or FreeBSD's **newfs**. Some examples of file systems are FAT16, FAT32, NTFS, and UFS. Different file systems may vary in performance, but they usually have two features in common:

- They require some type of table to map block addresses to the files contained within the blocks.

- They may also use a logical block addressing scheme to try to optimize read/write performance.

Let's pretend you're a file system for a moment. Your goal is to quickly store (write) and find (read) data given the following physical limitations:

- You've been assigned an area called a cylinder.

- Your cylinder has 255 horizontal lines running through it (tracks) and also 63 vertical lines running through it (sectors).

- Where these lines intersect, a storage unit (block) has been created for you to place files into; every block is the same size (512 bytes).

So, how many storage blocks do you have on your cylinder?

255 * 63 = 16,065

If you put one file in each storage block, you can save up to 16,065 files. If you create a table for yourself and number it from 1 to 16,065, you can simply record the name of each file next to a free number as you save the file to the block represented by that number. If you delete a file, you have to remember to remove its name from your table. If you want to move a file, you can look it up in your table, erase it from the old location, and write its name next to its new block number. You would also quickly learn that you didn't have to go to all the trouble of physically moving a file from one storage block to another storage block; it is much easier to simply change the entry for that file in your table.

In its simplest form, this is how all file systems keep track of your files. If this was a Unix file system, that table would be called the inode table.

Unfortunately, simplicity results in lousy hard disk usage. The ability to save files in 512-byte storage units would be great if every file created by users was 512 bytes in size. But, as you know, files vary greatly in size, from just a few bytes to several kilobytes.

Still thinking as a file system, how would you save a file that was 100 bytes in size? If you simply place this file by itself into a storage block, you've wasted 412 bytes of hard disk space. Save enough small files, and you end up wasting a lot of your disk space. What would happen if you saved 16,065 one-byte files? You would use up all your blocks with 16,065 bytes worth of data. Even though there may be several MB of free disk space on your cylinder, you have run out of the blocks to place files into. In Unix, this is called running out of inodes (or inode table entries), and it is not a good thing.

Continuing to think like a filesystem, it would make sense not to devote an entire physical block to one small file. However, you now have to re-think how you're going to organize your table to deal with the fact that there may be more than one file in a block. If you simply start stuffing in as many files as will fit into a 512-byte block, how are you going to keep track of where one file ends and another file begins? What if you remove a 10-byte file and replace it with an 8-byte file — how will you keep track of that extra two bytes in case you want to stuff in two more 1-byte files? You should be able to see that such a scheme would quickly become unworkable.

Most filesystems use the concept of fragments. A fragment is a logical division of a block. Each fragment will be assigned an address so it can have an entry in the filesystem table. As a simple example, a filesystem may choose to divide each physical block into four fragments. This effectively multiplies your number of blocks by four while reducing the block size by four. For example, if you started with 16,065 physical blocks that were each 512 bytes in size, a fragment size of 4 would give you 64,260 logical blocks that were each 128 bytes in size. Each fragment can be treated as a storage block and only store one file, meaning the table now has 64,260 entries, but you still don't have to worry about about keeping track of multiple files per logical storage unit.

Now let's look at the other end of the scale. What happens if you need to store files larger than your physical or logical block size? You're obviously going to need to use more than one block to store that file. Pretend you need to save a 1,000-byte file. This will require two physical blocks (512 * 2), so you will need to make two entries in your table for this one file. You'll also have to re-think how you are going to make those entries, as order is now important. It's not enough to know that this file lives in, say, blocks 3 and 4; you also need to know that the first 512 bytes of that file lives in block 3, and the remainder of that file lives in block 4.

If you are a filesystem that chose to use fragments, your job is actually harder when you need to save a large file. If you save that same 1,000-byte file with a fragment size of 4, you'll have to make eight entries in your table and ensure that you remember which order to keep those eight entries in.

Up to this point, we've only looked at the considerations for saving or writing files. Another important consideration for a filesystem is its read performance. The whole point of saving files to disk in the first place is so that users can access files when they need to. In order for a user to access a file, the filesystem must find out which block or blocks that file has been stored in, and then copy the contents of those disk blocks to RAM so the user can actually manipulate the data within the file.

There are several things a filesystem can do to increase read performance. One is to actually increase the logical block size, meaning that several physical blocks are grouped together into one large virtual block. When a user wishes to access a file that is contained on a physical block, the entire virtual block is loaded into RAM. This saves a lot of transferring of individual blocks from disk to RAM and then back to disk. If several blocks have already been pre-loaded into RAM, it is quite likely that all the data that user required was transferred to RAM in one transfer.

Let's see if we can summarize the considerations of a file system:

- There is a finite number of storage blocks, and every storage block has a numbered entry in a table, which in Unix is called the inode table.

- If you run out of inode numbers, you have run out of storage blocks; this means that you can no longer create and store files, regardless of how much disk space is left on your drive.

- If you need to store a lot of small files, you should fragment your block size to create more inode numbers.

- If you wish to increase read performance, you should create a large virtual block size so more blocks are loaded into RAM per disk transfer.

newfs Defaults

Now, let's see how this applies to FreeBSD. When you use **newfs**, you are formatting your partition with UFS2, or the Berkeley Unix File System. Let's take a peek at **man 8 newfs** to see what the defaults are for this file system:

We're interested in some of the switches; let's start with the **-b** switch:

```
-b block-size
The block size of the file system, in bytes.  It must be a power of 2.  The default
size is 16384 bytes, and the smallest allowable size is 4096 bytes.  The optimal
```

block:fragment ratio is 8:1. Other ratios are possible, but are not recommended, and may produce poor results.

Notice that this is the block size for the file system; the physical block size is always 512 bytes. 16384 bytes is actually 32 physical blocks, so this switch deals with the virtual block size or how many blocks are loaded into RAM at once. Remember that this is done to increase read performance and is one of the reasons why UFS2 is fast.

Now let's look at the **-f** switch:

```
-f frag-size
The fragment size of the file system in bytes.  It must be a power of two ranging in
value between blocksize/8 and blocksize.  The default is 2048 bytes.
```

UFS2 uses fragments, but it fragments the virtual block size, not the physical block size. The default fragment size is actually four physical blocks or 2048 bytes. Now the **-i** switch:

```
-i bytes
Specify the density of inodes in the file system.  The default is to create an inode
for every (4 * frag-size) bytes of data space.  If fewer inodes are desired, a larger
number should be used; to create more inodes a smaller number should be given.  One
inode is required for each distinct file, so this value effectively specifies the
average file size on the file system.
```

By default, there is one inode for every 8192 bytes worth of disk space and every file requires its own inode number. Since an inode represents the storage unit for one file, this default assumes an average file size of 8192 bytes.

There are two other switches worth mentioning at this point, as they affect the read/write performance of the FFS filesystem. The first one is the **-m** switch:

```
-m free space
The percentage of space reserved from normal users; the minimum free space threshold.
The default value used is defined by MINFREE from <ufs/ffs/fs.h>³, currently 8%.  See
tunefs(8) for more details on how to set this option.
```

All filesystems suffer when you start to get low on available storage blocks. Filesystems like to store files from the same directory in contiguous (next to each other) blocks; this gets harder to do as the number of available blocks decreases and the filesystem has to start searching for empty blocks. The designers of UFS noticed that performance drastically decreases when a filesystem gets around 90% full. When a filesystem reaches the default free space threshold (8%), meaning the filesystem is 92% full, it won't let regular users save any more files. Instead the users will receive an error message and will probably start complaining to the administrator to rectify the situation. The superuser will still be able to save files and use up the remaining blocks, but his time would be better spent in coming up with a plan to save the filesystem before it runs out of storage blocks.

The second switch that deals with free space is the **-o** switch:

---

[3]That's the header file at /usr/include/ufs/ffs/fs.h.

```
-o optimization
```
(space or time). The file system can either be instructed to try to minimize the time
spent allocating blocks, or to try to minimize the space fragmentation on the disk.
If the value of minfree (see above) is less than 8%, the default is to optimize for
space; if the value of minfree is greater than or equal to 8%, the default is to
optimize for time. See tunefs(8) for more details on how to set this option.

Most filesystems use an algorithm to determine which blocks should be used to store which files. This switch tells the UFS algorithm to optimize itself for speed or time. However, when the filesystem meets the minfree threshold, finding free blocks or space becomes much more important than speed.

From the default parameters, you can see that UFS has been optimized for speed, while still creating a fair number of inodes to record where files have been stored. For most installations, the default values will be fine; in later sections, we'll look more in-depth on how to determine if the default values are not sufficient for your system and what to do about it.

At this point, you've probably learned more about filesystems than you care to admit. The next section takes a look at cylinder groups, superblocks, and what type of information is actually recorded in an inode entry.

Additional Resources

Original Articles:

```
http://www.onlamp.com/pub/a/bsd/2001/02/21/FreeBSD_Basics.html
```

```
http://www.onlamp.com/pub/a/bsd/2001/02/28/FreeBSD_Basics.html
```

5.3 Understanding Filesystem Inodes

While looking at partition tables and file systems we've discovered that your PC finds your FreeBSD slice by reading the BIOS partition table. That FreeBSD slice has a Unix partition table that contains the disk packing label, which describes the layout of the filesystems on that slice. We can finally take a look at inodes: what they are and what information about them is available to you on your FreeBSD system.

The superblock

Let's start by taking another look at the output of the **bsdlabel** command from one of my FreeBSD systems; I've snipped the output to just show the layout of the partitions:

```
# bsdlabel ad0s1
<snip>
8 partitions:
#     size offset fstype [fsize bsize bps/cpg]
a:  102400      0 4.2BSD    0    0     0
b:  270976 102400   swap
c: 6538455      0 unused    0    0        # "raw" part, don't edit
e:   40960 373376 4.2BSD    0    0     0
f: 6124119 414336 4.2BSD    0    0     0
```

Notice that partitions *a*, *e*, and *f* are to be formatted with the filesystem type 4.2BSD, meaning the Berkeley Unix File System (UFS).

Basically, a hard drive is composed of a number of circular disks called platters. Each platter has been divided into circular tracks; a cylinder is the same track on all the platters. If you could separate all the cylinders on your hard drive, you would end up with a series of increasingly smaller sized rings with each ring being the thickness of your hard drive.

A partition is simply a cylinder group, or a group of adjacent cylinders logically joined into a wider, doughnut-shaped ring. If a partition is formatted with a filesystem, that filesystem will maintain one inode table to keep track of any data placed on that cylinder group. To summarize:

- A filesystem is responsible for one cylinder group.

- A cylinder group has one inode table.

Each partition that has been formatted with a filesystem has three distinct areas:

- an area known as the superblock

- an area that contains the inode entries

- the remaining area, which is used to store files

The superblock describes the parameters of the filesystem, such as the number of blocks, the size of the blocks, the size of the fragments, and the number of inodes. (If you're curious as to what else is defined in the superblock, you'll find all the parameters in **man 5 fs**.) These parameters were determined by the **newfs** command and any switches you may have passed to that command when you created the filesystem. This means that if at a later date you discover that you will run out of inodes before you run out of disk blocks, you will have to recreate the filesystem in order to change these parameters. You'll need to back up your data and test your backup first, as recreating the filesystem with the **newfs** utility will destroy all of the existing data on that cylinder group.

Inodes

After the superblock area is the area that contains all of the inode entries. Each inode entry is 128 bytes in size and contains information about the file that it represents; this information is known as the file's metadata. You can find out for yourself what this metadata is by reading the file `/usr/include/ufs/ufs/dinode.h`; even though this is a C file, it is well commented and not too hard to figure out. I've summarized its contents by listing the metadata that an inode keeps track of:

- the permissions of the file

- the file link count

- old user and group ids

- the inode number

- the size of the file in bytes

- the last time the file was accessed (atime)

- the last time the file was modified (mtime)

- the last inode change time for the file (ctime)

- direct disk blocks

- indirect disk blocks

- status flags (chflags)

- blocks actually held

- file generation number

- the owner of the file

- the primary group of the owner of the file

Notice that the name of the file is not part of the inode's metadata. The filesystem doesn't care what the name of the file is; it only needs to know what inode number is associated with that file.

Much of a file's metadata can be viewed by doing a long directory listing. Let's take a look at the long listing for the root directory by using the **ls** command with the **-l** switch.[4]

You should see seven columns of output that represent each file's:

- permissions

- link count

- owner

- group

- size in bytes

- mtime

- pathname

You should be able to recognize the first six as part of the metadata contained in each file's inode.

You can also find out the inode number of each file by adding the **-i** switch to the **ls** command. If you try this you will notice an extra column to the long listing; the number in the first column is the inode number for that file. Inode number 2 will be mentioned several times: dev, tmp, usr, and var. Inode 2 is always the first inode of a filesystem and represents the root or starting point of that filesystem. We can use the **df** command to see which filesystems have been mounted on this system:

```
% df
Filesystem   1K-blocks    Used    Avail Capacity  Mounted on
/dev/ad0s2a      49583   27729    17888    61%    /
/dev/ad0s2f    2967289  737169  1992737    27%    /usr
/dev/ad0s2e      19815    3647    14583    20%    /var
/dev/ad0s2d     131231       1   120732     0%    /tmp
```

---

[4]This is covered in more detail in section 5.1.

Not surprisingly, usr, var, and tmp show up as mounted filesystems. Don't forget that each filesystem maintains its own inode table; that is, inode 2 for usr is a different inode entry in a completely different inode table than the inode 2 entry for var. The only thing these inode entries share in common is the number 2, as they are both the root entry for their respective filesystems.

The **df** or disk free utility has a switch that will tell you how many inodes are on each filesystem. Let's run that utility again with the **-i** switch:

```
% df -i
Filesystem  1K-blocks    Used    Avail Capacity iused   ifree
/dev/ad0s2a     49583   27729    17888     61%    1074   11468     9%  /
/dev/ad0s2f   2967289  739993  1989913     27%   90852  655130    12%  /usr
/dev/ad0s2e     19815    3645    14585     20%     391    4663     8%  /var
/dev/ad0s2d    131231       1   120732      0%       1   33277     0%  /tmp
```

It's a good idea to run this command on a regular basis to ensure that your filesystems are not running out of either disk storage blocks or inode entries.[5] Unless you are creating a large number of very small files, you will probably run out of disk blocks long before you run out of inodes. Knowing whether or not you've created enough inodes while leaving enough storage blocks is a matter of experience, as it depends upon what your FreeBSD system is used for and what types of files are created by your users. If you run this command often, you'll get an idea of what is normal for your system; you'll also learn if the defaults are not appropriate for your system.

The last thing I'd like you to notice about an inode is that it keeps track of three different times: the file's mtime, atime, and ctime.

A file's mtime is its last modification time; that is, when the actual contents of the file were last changed. For example, if you open a file with your favorite text editor and add or delete some text, you have modified the contents of that file. When you save your changes, the inode will update the mtime of that file. Remember that **ls -l** will show the mtime of the file.

A file's atime is the last time that file was accessed. For example, if you read a file using a pager, you will access the file and the inode will update the atime for that file. You can view a directory listing by atime instead of the default mtime by using the switches **ls -lut**.

The ctime is updated whenever the inode itself is changed. For example, if you change the permissions, owner, or group of a file you are actually making changes to that file's inode, so the ctime will also be updated. To see a listing by ctime, use the switches **ls -lc**.

If you take a close look at those last three **ls** listings, you'll note that the times are indeed different and reflect the three types of times recorded by each file's inode.

The **stat** utility can also be used to print out inode contents. Here is an example output:

```
% stat myfile
87 1719610 -rw-r--r-- 1 dru wheel 6889624 26726 "May 28 14:32:17 2007" "May 28
14:07:27 2007" "May 28 14:07:27 2007" "May 21 18:54:28 2007" 4096 56 0 myfile
```

The output is similar to **ls -li** with a few extra fields. The first number (in this case, 87) refers to the ID of the device containing the file; the second number is the inode number. The four date fields represent: atime, mtime, ctime, and birthtime (when the inode itself was created)[6]. All of the fields are detailed in **man 2 stat**.

---

[5]See section 2.13 and read about the daily_status_disks_enable daily job.

[6]By the way, some filesystems do not record any creation time, so may show "Jan 1 00:00:00 1970" as the birthtime.

Additional Resources

Original Article:

`http://www.onlamp.com/pub/a/bsd/2001/03/07/FreeBSD_Basics.html`

5.4 Mounting Other Filesystems

Anyone who has ever worked in a networked environment running different operating systems using different filesystems knows the frustration of trying to get every computer to see the data on every other computer. Even on my multi-boot test computer, Windows NT can't see the data on my FAT32 partition, Windows 98 can't see the data on my NTFS partition, DOS can't see data on either partition — and these operating systems are all installed on the same hard drive.

Fortunately, I also have FreeBSD installed on this computer, and it has no problem accessing the data anywhere on that hard drive, thanks to the **mount** command.

mount Basics

The **mount** command is one of the most powerful commands available to *root*. It allows *root* to mount filesystems so users can access either data physically located on a device cabled to that computer or data physically located on other computers that understand the **mount** command.

The syntax for the **mount** command itself is simple:

`mount [-t filesystem] devicename mountpoint`

Let's start with some common device names in Table 5.2.

Table 5.2: Common Device Names

Device	Name
Floppy	`/dev/fd0`
CD-ROM	`/dev/cd0`
SCSI drives	`/dev/sd0s#`
IDE drive	`/dev/ad0s#`
Flash drive	`/dev/da#s#`

Each device is numbered starting with 0 (zero). Storage devices will also have the sub partition unit, or slice number appended to them. The slice number (represented above as *s#*) consists of the letter *s* and a number.

For example, my test computer has one IDE drive that has been partitioned as follows:

- 200 MB FAT partition containing DOS.

- 1.8 GB partition containing FreeBSD 4.0.

- 500 MB NTFS partition containing Windows NT Server 4.0.

- 1.5 GB FAT32 partition containing Windows 98.

If I boot to DOS, it only recognizes a partition named C:.

If I boot to NT, it sees a FAT partition called C: and an NTFS partition called D:.

If I boot to Windows 98, it sees a FAT partition called C: and a FAT32 partition called D:.

Because they don't recognize each other's filesystems, both Windows 98 and NT think they reside on a partition called D, even though they reside on different partitions of my hard drive.

FreeBSD's logic makes a bit more sense, as it sees my drive like this:

- `/dev/ad0s1` as FAT

- `/dev/ad0s2` as FreeBSD

- `/dev/ad0s3` as NTFS

- `/dev/ad0s4` as FAT32

since I've sliced my first IDE drive into four sections.

If you are multi-booting your FreeBSD computer, you can check out the device names for your partitions with **sysinstall**. As *root*, type **sysinstall** and choose Configure, then Fdisk, and then use your spacebar to select the drive.

The Name column will list the device name; the Desc column will list the type of filesystem. If you used DOS **fdisk** to partition your hard drive, it will only show two entries: one for the primary partition and the other for the extended partition. An Intel BIOS may support up to four primary partitions, but DOS-based **fdisk** utilities will only let you create one primary partition, and FreeBSD's **fdisk** utility does not show logical partitions.

The **mount** command also requires you to specify a mountpoint. A mountpoint is simply an empty directory you've created as a reference point to access mounted data. The mounted data is not actually placed in this directory; instead, think of the mountpoint as a virtual shell where you can use your Unix commands to manipulate the mounted data. It is important that you keep your mountpoint directories empty; use other directories for storing files.

Mountpoints are usually created as subdirectories of `/`; FreeBSD has already created two mountpoints for you: `/cdrom` and `/mnt`.

When you create your mountpoints, give them useful names such as `/floppy`, `/ntfs`, `/fat32`, or `/fat`.

Now for the filesystem: notice that I put **-t filesystem** in brackets when I gave the syntax for the **mount** command. The filesystem switch is optional as FreeBSD assumes you want to mount the UFS (Unix File System) unless you specify otherwise. The most common filesystem types you'll probably specify are listed in Table 5.3.

Table 5.3: Common Filesystem Types

Filesystem Type	Description
-t msdos	for floppies and flash drives or FAT16 and FAT32 partitions
-t cd9660	for data CDROMs
-t ntfs	for primary NTFS partitions

Mounting Floppies

A few notes on floppies and Unix: If you are used to sticking a floppy into the floppy drive of a Windows computer and then ejecting it at will, it'll take some getting used to how Unix computers treat floppies.

Both hard drives and floppies contain filesystems that must be mounted for their data to be accessed. Only *root* can mount filesystems, so you must be *root* to mount a floppy.[7] Also, you can't just eject a mounted floppy; you must tell Unix to unmount it first.

Keep in mind that hard drives are considered to be permanent storage devices, while floppies are temporary storage devices, but Unix treats them the same as hard drives. You wouldn't dream of physically removing your hard drive and adding another one while your computer was booted into an operating system on that first hard drive. For the same reason, don't mount a floppy and then eject it without telling Unix to unmount it first.

It is possible to format a floppy with DOS from FreeBSD. To format a floppy, do not mount it first. Remember, you mount filesystems, and you don't have a filesystem until you format. As *root*, put a floppy in your floppy drive, then type:

```
# fdformat /dev/fd0
Format 1440 floppy '/dev/fd0'? (y/n): y
```

When it is finished processing:

```
# bsdlabel -w -r /dev/fd0 fd1440
# newfs_msdos -f 1440 fd0
```

You can now mount that floppy like this:

```
# mount -t msdos /dev/fd0 /floppy
# ls /floppy
```

The **ls** command should confirm that there is nothing on the floppy. Let's copy something onto the floppy:

```
# cp /etc/fstab /floppy
# ls /floppy
fstab
# more /floppy/fstab
```

---

[7]Or the superuser can set up the system to allow others to mount filesystems — see section 1.2 for one example.

You should be able to hear your floppy drive churn as you view the contents of `fstab`. If you **cd /floppy** and then try to unmount it:

```
# umount /floppy
umount: unmount of /floppy failed: Device busy
```

You can't unmount a filesystem if it is your present working directory. Let's try again:

```
# cd ~
# umount /floppy
```

It is now safe to eject the floppy from the floppy drive.

Now let's try a CD-ROM. Put a data CD-ROM, not a music CD-ROM, into your CD-ROM bay and type:

```
# mount /cdrom
# ls /cdrom
```

You should be able to see the contents of the CD. Why did the shortened **mount** command work? Remember that FreeBSD already created a mountpoint called /cdrom for you? Well, it also added an entry to a file that is read by the **mount** command if you don't specify a device name. Try this:

```
# grep cdrom /etc/fstab
/dev/cd0    /cdrom      cd9660   ro,noauto 0    0
```

Notice that there is an entry for /cdrom with its options set at noauto. This tells FreeBSD not to mount your CD-ROM automatically when you boot; however, this entry now shortens the **mount** command for when you do want to mount a CD-ROM. Let's unmount the CD-ROM and add an entry to at the end of the /etc/fstab file to shorten the **mount** command for floppies:

```
# umount /cdrom
# vi /etc/fstab
```

And go to the end and add the new line:

```
/dev/fd0    /floppy    msdos    rw,noauto    0    0
```

Make sure you tab over to keep your columns neat; also, make sure it all fits on one line. Doublecheck for typos before saving this file.

Now, insert a floppy into your floppy drive and try:

```
# mount /floppy
# ls /floppy
# umount /floppy
```

Mounting other Partitions

I can also mount my C:\ drive while in FreeBSD; since its device name is /dev/ad0s1, I issue this command:

```
# mount -t msdos /dev/ad0s1 /fat
```

I can then freely edit and delete files within /fat — which is really the C:\ drive — using my favorite Unix commands. I can also copy files back and forth between C:\ and FreeBSD.

If I want to get real fancy, I'll also mount my FAT32 partition:

```
# mount -t msdos /dev/ad0s4 /fat32
```

and I can copy a file from C:\ to what Windows 98 calls the D:\ partition:

```
# cp /fat/test.txt /fat32/test.txt
```

Saves a lot of rebooting if I just want to move some files around. If I want to save myself some typing when I wish to access these filesystems, I'll add the following lines to the end of /etc/fstab:

```
/dev/ad0s1   /fat          msdos   rw      0     0
/dev/ad0s4   /fat32        msdos   rw      0     0
```

Because these file systems are located on my permanent storage device, I can have FreeBSD mount them at every boot; therefore, I haven't set the Options to noauto.

If I've rebooted since adding these lines to /etc/fstab, these partitions will be mounted for me. I can simply use the commands **cd /fat** or **cd /fat32** to access the data on these partitions.

This section focused on accessing the file systems of devices physically attached to your FreeBSD computer. The next will discuss how to access data located on Microsoft computers within your network.

Additional Resources

Original Article:

http://www.onlamp.com/pub/a/bsd/2000/07/05/FreeBSD_Basics.html

5.5 Accessing MS-DOS Filesystems

In this section, I'd like to take a look at two utilities from the ports collection that can be used to manipulate data contained on MS-DOS file systems. The suite of DOS-like command line utilities found in **mtools** can manipulate MS-DOS data contained on floppies, another partition on your hard drive, Jaz drives, and Zip drives. The program **mtoolsfm** provides a nice GUI interface to access MS-DOS data on a floppy and to quickly transfer data between your home directory and an MS-DOS formatted floppy.

The nice thing about both utilities is that they allow a user to transparently access this data without having to first mount the filesystem. Remember that normally only the superuser can mount filesystems. If you are an administrator or have family members using your FreeBSD system, you don't want the hassle of mounting a filesystem every time someone wants to access data on a floppy. Also, as a new user you may still forget to unmount the filesystem before removing your floppy; if you've ever tried this, you have discovered that FreeBSD may panic, reboot, or give you nasty error messages for doing so.

Using mtools

So let's install both utilities and take a look at using them. Become the superuser, ensure that you are connected to the Internet, and:

```
# pkg_add -r mtools
# pkg_add -r mtoolsfm
```

Once the installs finish, leave the superuser account by typing **exit**. If you are using the C shell, type **rehash** to make your shell aware of your new programs.

Let's take a look at **mtools**. If you just type its name, it will give you a list of the tools that are available for your use:

```
% mtools
Supported commands:
mattrib, mbadblocks, mcat, mcd, mclasserase, mcopy, mdel, mdeltree
mdir, mdoctorfat, mdu, mformat, minfo, mlabel, mmd, mmount
mpartition, mrd, mread, mmove, mren, mshowfat, mtoolstest, mtype
mwrite, mzip
```

If you have ever used DOS before, most of these program names should be familiar to you; the only difference is that they all begin with the letter m. Each of these utilities has an associated manpage so you can view its syntax. Sections 1 and 5 of the manual have entries for **mtools** itself.

Let's see what happens if we type **mcd**:

```
% mcd
A:/
```

That doesn't look too bad, as that's the prompt used by MS-DOS to represent your floppy drive. Experienced DOS users will note that the slash is Unix style instead of DOS style. Let's see if we can see the contents of a floppy using the **mdir** command:

```
% mdir
Can't open /dev/fd0:  No such file or directory
Cannot initialize 'A:'
```

Oops, I'm so embarrassed; I forgot to put a floppy in the drive. Let's try again with a floppy in the drive:

```
% mdir
Can't open /dev/rfd0: Permission denied
Cannot initialize 'A:'
```

Before we start messing about with permissions, we should first check the **mtools** configuration file to see what it is looking for. If you **man 5 mtools** you'll discover that the name of the configuration file is mtools.conf, and it is located in /usr/local/etc. Let's see who has the right to access this file and make changes to it:

```
% ls -l /usr/local/etc/mtools.conf
-r--r--r--  1 root    wheel  3969 Dec  2 11:50 /usr/local/etc/mtools.conf
```

Looks like anyone will be able to read this file, but only the superuser will be able to make changes to it. Let's take a look at this file first:

```
% more /usr/local/etc/mtools.conf
# Example mtools.conf files.  Uncomment the lines which correspond to
# your architecture and comment out the "SAMPLE FILE" line below
# A note on permissions:  a user must have read and write permissions for the
# devices named here in order to access the DOS file systems.  You might give
# ALL USERS access to ALL FLOPPY DISKS via the command
#     chmod a+rw /dev/*fd* /dev/fd[0-9]*
# # FreeBSD floppy drives
drive a: file="/dev/fd0"
drive b: file="/dev/fd1"
```

Looks like we need to give our users permissions to access the floppy device; fortunately, the lines specific to FreeBSD floppy drive device names have already been uncommented for us so we don't need to make any changes to this configuration file.

Let's look at the existing permissions for /dev/fd0, which will be seen as A: by **mtools**:

```
% ls -l /dev/fd0
crw-r-----  1 root    operator  0, 76 Oct  3 08:51 /dev/fd0
```

There's our problem. As mtools.conf stated, users need *rw* to access the device, but users only have *r*. Since this file is owned by *root*, we'll have to become the superuser to change its permissions; since I only have one floppy drive, I'll just add *rw* to the one device:

```
% su
Password:
# chmod a+rw /dev/fd0
```

I'll also add this line to /etc/devfs.conf to ensure the new permissions are retained should the system reboot:

```
perm fd0 0666
```

When finished, leave the superuser account and try your **mdir** command again as a regular user; you should be able to see the contents of your floppy drive.

Let's get a little fancier than this. I have a FAT partition at the beginning of my hard drive; let's see if **mtools** can access it. There were some lines in mtools.conf that dealt with hard drives:

```
# IDE hard disks
#   first disk on the first IDE interface (wd0) slice 1 (s1)
drive c: file="/dev/ad0s1"
```

As superuser, I'll check the permissions on this device and change them so users can access the C: drive:

```
# ls -l /dev/ad0s1
crw-r-----  1 root  operator 0, 89 Oct 4 15:58 ad0s1
# chmod a+rw /dev/ad0s1
```

Then, as a regular user, I'll see if I can access data on both the A: and C: drives:

```
% mcd a:
% mdir
 Volume in drive A has no label
 Volume Serial Number is 3505-18E3
Directory for A:/
dru3     txt   2846 11-28-2000  21:46
inetdc 1 txt  13669 10-05-2000  21:22  inetd.conf.txt
cisco    doc  10752 11-13-2000  18:07
       3 files        27 267 bytes
                    1 428 698 bytes free
% mcd c:
% mdir
 Volume in drive C has no label
 Volume Serial Number is 39D0-A67B
Directory for C:/
bootsect bsd    512 10-04-2000 15:22
confer 1    <DIR>    11-01-2000 20:39 conferencing server
sybex       <DIR>    11-10-2000 20:18 Sybex
       3 files           512 bytes
                  492 470 272 bytes free
```

Now, I know that there are some hidden files on my C: drive; if I take a look at **man mdir**, I'll see that **-a** will show hidden files. Let's try that command again:

```
% mdir -a
 Volume in drive C has no label
 Volume Serial Number is 39D0-A67B
Directory for C:/
bootsect dos     512    10-04-2000 15:33
config   sys       0    10-04-2000 15:40
autoexec bat       0    10-04-2000 15:40
io       sys       0    10-04-2000 15:40
msdos    sys       0    10-04-2000 15:40
bootsect bsd     512    10-04-2000 15:22
msdownld tmp <DIR>      10-04-2000 16:10
confer 1     <DIR>      11-01-2000 20:39 conferencing server
recycled     <DIR>      11-01-2000 21:01 Recycled
sybex        <DIR>      11-10-2000 20:18 Sybex
arcldr   exe 148992     12-07-1999 12:00
arcsetup exe 162816     12-07-1999 12:00
```

```
ntldr          214416    12-07-1999 12:00
ntdetect com    34468    11-25-2000 21:45
boot     ini      214    11-25-2000 20:00
pagefile sys 104857600 11-25-2000 19:51
        16 files      105 419 530 bytes
                      492 470 272 bytes free
```

Let's see if I can read one of these files:

```
% mtype boot.ini
[boot loader]
timeout=30
default=multi(0)disk(0)rdisk(0)partition(3)\WINNT
[operating systems]
multi(0)disk(0)rdisk(0)partition(3)\WINNT="Microsoft
  Windows 2000 Server" /fastdetect
C:\bootsect.bsd="FreeBSD"
```

Let's see if I can copy this file onto my floppy:

```
% mcopy boot.ini a:
```

My floppy drive is churning, which is a good sign. Let's double-check that it worked:

```
% mdir a:
 Volume in drive A has no label
 Volume Serial Number is 3505-18E3
Directory for A:/
dru3     txt    2846 11-28-2000   21:46
inetdc 1 txt   13669 10-05-2000   21:22   inetd.conf.txt
boot     ini     214 12-03-2000   11:25   boot.ini
cisco    doc   10752 11-13-2000   18:07
        4 files        27 481 bytes
                    1 428 484 bytes free
```

It is nice to be able to easily transfer files from my NT boot partition to a floppy while I'm in my FreeBSD system. I can just as easily send files back and forth between FreeBSD and my C: drive or A: drive.

A few things to note about **mtools**. It supplies DOS-like utilities, and DOS is quite limited. For example, I won't be able to read the file on my floppy drive called `cisco.doc` as DOS does not recognize the doc extension. If you are working in both your A: and C: drives, you'll have to **mcd** between them like so:

```
% mcd a:   (to view and manipulate data on A:)
% mcd c:   (to view and manipulate data on C:)
```

Also, make sure you are only trying to access MS-DOS filesystems; that is, don't try to view the contents of a floppy formatted with a Unix filesystem.

Using mtoolsfm

Now let's take a look at **mtoolsfm**. This utility is easier to work with as it has a very intuitive interface. Since it is a GUI, you will have to run it from an X Window session. I've placed a shortcut to it in my Xfce toolbar. If you don't know how to create shortcuts in your windows manager yet, open up an **xterm** and type **mfmtools**.

When the utility opens up, you'll see a window with two panes; by default, both panes will show the contents of your home directory. Directories have a folder icon, and their names and attributes show up in blue type. Files have an icon that looks like a sheet of paper, and their attributes show up in black type. If you click on the Options menu with your mouse, you can select Show dot files to also view your hidden files.

Insert your floppy; at the menu bar on top of one of the panes, click on the arrow and select a: instead of the default Harddisk. You should now see the contents of your floppy. By highlighting a file on the floppy and clicking on the Copy button with the appropriate arrow, you can copy the file over to your home directory. Or by clicking a file on your home directory, you can quickly copy it over to the floppy.

Click on the File menu just above a pane; here you'll see options to delete, rename, or print the highlighted file. You can also create a new directory using this menu. If you remove a floppy and insert a new one, use the View menu, Refresh option to see the contents of the new floppy.

Though somewhat limited, **mtoolsfm** is a very quick way to manipulate the contents of your home directory in a visual way. I also find it to be a painless method of sending files back and forth between a floppy and my home directory.

Additional Resources

Original Article:

http://www.onlamp.com/pub/a/bsd/2000/12/13/FreeBSD_Basics.html

5.6 Using FreeBSD's ACLs

Since version 5.0, FreeBSD has implemented something known as ACLs (Access Control Lists). ACLs came to FreeBSD as part of the TrustedBSD project. As the name suggests, they give a user finer access control over permissions.

Why Would I Want to Use ACLs?

While ACLs don't change the standard Unix permissions of (r)ead, (w)rite, and e(x)ecute, they do give you better control over whom those permissions affect. Here's a simple example — as a regular user, create a test file in the system's temporary directory:

```
% touch /tmp/test
% ls -l /tmp/test
-rw-r--r--  1 dru  dru  0 Jul 26 15:43 /tmp/test
```

I've chosen this directory as all users have write access here and it is a good place to test out permissions. However, don't keep important files here, because they are likely to disappear, depending on how the system administrator has configured the cleaning of this directory!

In this example, the creator of the file, *dru*, has *rw* access; anyone in the group *dru* has *r* access; and everyone else has *r* access. Note that when you create a user in FreeBSD, you also get a group of the same name with that user as the only member.

Now suppose that I need to give the users *rob* and *toby* write access to this file. As the permissions stand now, they might be able to open the file in an editor, but they won't be able to save any changes, as they are neither the user *dru* nor a member of the *dru* group. They fall into other, which has read permission only.

Before ACLs, the typical solution to this dilemma was to modify group memberships. I could, for example, ask the system administrator to add *rob* and *toby* to the *dru* group. I could then use **chmod** to add write permission to the *dru* group for this file. This is slightly better than giving write permission to other, as that would allow anyone on the system to write to that file.

Alternatively, the system administrator could carefully plan out which users need access to which files and then create groups and assign users to those groups. Then, assuming a user belonged to the required group, she could use the **chgrp** command on the files she created in order to change group ownership.

Neither system is perfect, however. For one, it requires bugging the system administrator, which is inconvenient when all you want to do is share your own files. Further, consider another scenario. Suppose that *dru*, *rob*, and *toby* have all been made members of the newly created workgroup group. All three group members can write to any files with write permission for workgroup, regardless of which one originally created the file. But what if *dru* wants *rob* to write to one of these files but not *toby*?

This is starting to sound pretty complicated, isn't it? Fortunately, this is the reason behind ACLs. Without having to ask the administrator to make a bunch of groups or having to use **chgrp**, *dru* can easily pick and choose through her files and decide which files *rob* gets write access to; she can also give *toby* write access to a different set of files.

This section shows how you, as the system administrator, can prepare a FreeBSD system for ACLs. I'll then demonstrate a GUI utility, which will allow your users to easily control the ACLs on their own files. Finally, I'll show you how to back up files containing ACLs.

Preparing the System

If you're using FreeBSD 5.1 or later, ACL support is already built into your kernel and UFS2 filesystem. With earlier versions of FreeBSD, see Daniel Harris's article on ACLs at http://www.onlamp.com/pub/a/bsd/2003/08/14/freebsd_acls.html for instructions for compiling ACL support into FreeBSD.

You simply need to decide on which filesystem(s) you wish to use ACLs:

```
# df
Filesystem  1K-blocks     Used   Avail Capacity  Mounted on
/dev/ad0s1a    253678    35764  197620    15%    /
devfs               1        1       0   100%    /dev
/dev/ad0s1e    253678       22  233362     0%    /tmp
/dev/ad0s1f   8077406  3045460 4385754    41%    /usr
/dev/ad0s1d    253678    21048  212336     9%    /var
```

On my system, I wanted to enable ACLs only for users, so I configured only the /usr filesystem.

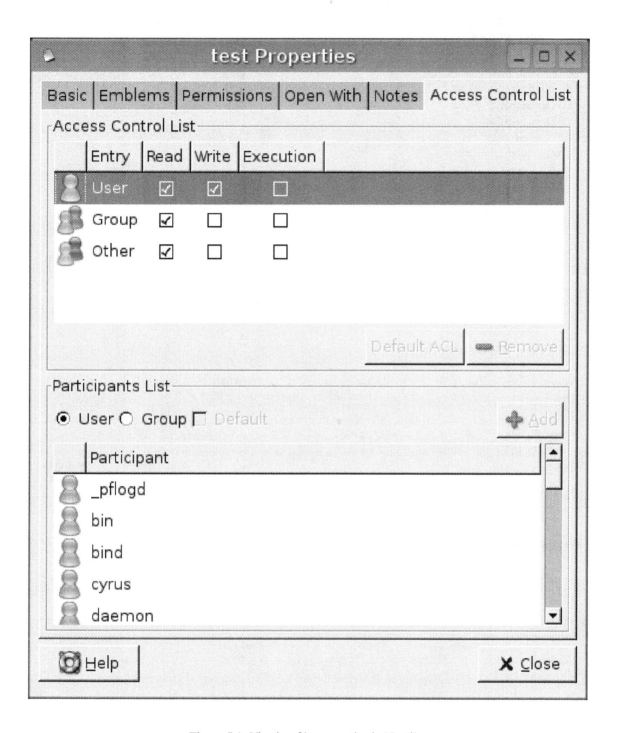

Figure 5.1: Viewing file properties in Nautilus

The FreeBSD Handbook explains the advantages of using the **tunefs** command to enable ACLs. The disadvantage is that it requires bringing the system down to single-user mode and unmounting the filesystem. Choose a time that will least impact users; once you're sure no one is connected to the system, use the following:

```
# shutdown now
Enter full pathname of shell or RETURN for /bin/sh:
# /sbin/umount /usr
# /sbin/tunefs -a enable /dev/ad0s1f
tunefs: ACLs set
# /sbin/mount /usr
```

Use your output from **df** to know the name of the device on which you wish to enable ACLs.

Then, to see if it worked:

```
# /sbin/mount | grep acl
/dev/ad0s1f on /usr (ufs, local, soft-updates, acls)
```

When finished, type **exit** to bring the system back to multiuser mode. That's it. ACLs are now enabled on /usr.

Installing and Using the GUI

If you do a Google search for "FreeBSD acl", you'll find several articles and how-tos. Each of these gives examples on using the main ACL command line utilities, **getfacl** and **setfacl**.

While **getfacl** is straightforward, the syntax for **setfacl** can get a bit hairy — more than enough to scare off most of your users. Here, a GUI is beneficial, as it allows users to easily determine and control who has what permissions. **eiciel** provides an intuitive GUI and is available as a FreeBSD package or port. It also works on Linux systems and is a part of the Nautilus file manager, which among other things adds a properties sheet to files, allowing a user to easily view and manage file permissions, icons, and the Open With utility.

You can quickly add the binary package using:

```
# pkg_add -r eiciel
```

Once you have installed the package, leave the superuser account and enter an X session as a regular user.

There are two ways to access the newly installed ACL GUI. One is to start Nautilus. The user *dru* has three files in her home directory called test, file1, and myfile. Figure 5.1 shows what happens when the user right-clicks on test and selects Properties from the menu.

The **eiciel** installation has added an Access Control List tab to Nautilus. You can see from the figure that this tab provides a GUI representation of the following permission set:

```
% ls -l test
-rw-r--r-- 1 dru  dru  0 Jul 27 09:09 test
```

The other method is to start **eiciel** directly. Click on the Open button to select the test file, which will show the ACLs window (Figure 5.2).

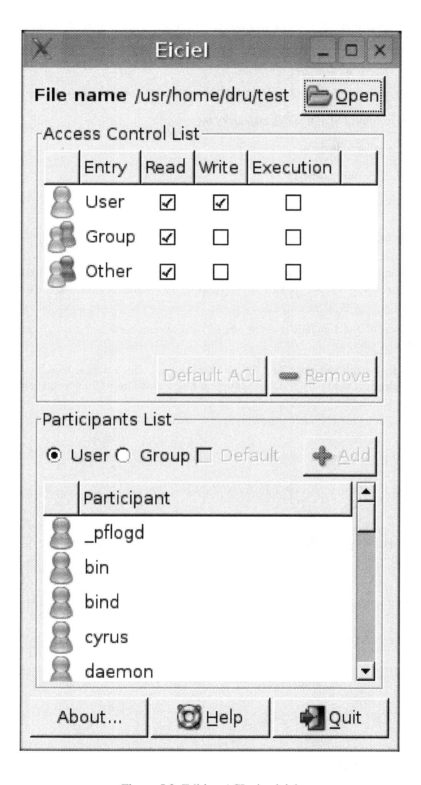

Figure 5.2: Editing ACLs in eiciel

I prefer to use the nautilus method, as it also includes the Permissions tab, which allows me to view and change:

- the file owner

- the file group, including a tab to scroll through groups *dru* is a member of; similar to **chgrp**

- special flags, to control SUID, SGID, and sticky bit

- the text view, similar to **ls -l**

- the number view; in this case, 644

Understanding ACL Masks

Look again at the bottom portion of Figure 5.1. Here, you can view the users and groups on the system. Double-clicking on the user *rob* will add two items to the top portion, or Access Control List, of the screen as shown in Figure 5.3.

Note: Newer versions of **eiciel** include a check box to show system participants (accounts) which aren't displayed by default.

Notice that the entries for *rob* and mask have full *rwx* permissions, which is more than *dru* has as the owner of the file. What is happening here? By double-clicking on *rob*, I added an ACL, which I can verify with a long listing on my home directory:

```
% ls -l
drwx------  2 dru  dru    512 Jul 26 10:35 Desktop
-rw-r--r--  1 dru  dru      0 Jul 27  9:22 file1
-rw-r--r--  1 dru  dru      0 Jul 27  9:22 myfile
-rw-r--r--+ 1 dru  dru      0 Jul 27 10:03 test
```

See that + at the end of the permission set for test? That indicates that an ACL has been set on that file. I can view it with **getfacl**:

```
% getfacl test
#file:test
#owner:1001
#group:1001
user::rw-
user:rob:rwx
group::r--
mask::rwx
other::r--
```

That output is basically the text representation of Figure 5.3.

Why did *rob* get *rwx*, and what is this mask entry? By definition, an ACL mask determines the maximum allowable permissions. It's worth doing two things to make sure you understand that fully.

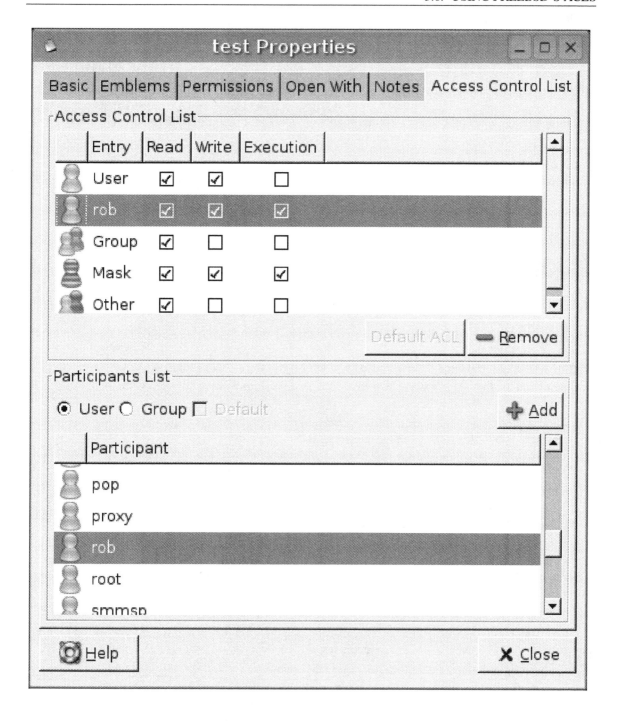

Figure 5.3: Adding to a user's ACL

First, uncheck the execute permission from the *rob* entry. Note that I can give *rob* any combination of read, write, or execute that I desire. From the perspective of the person using this GUI, she can simply double-click on the user to add them, and uncheck the permissions she doesn't want the user to have.

What happens if you change that mask entry? Put *rob* back as *rwx*, but remove execute from mask. As soon as you do that, the execute permission next to *rob*, or any other user with execute, will display a red exclamation mark. The GUI also displays a message that a red exclamation mark means "an ineffective permission."

This makes sense if you go back to the definition of an ACL mask. Now the maximum allowable permission set is *rw*, meaning that anyone who appears to have execute really doesn't. While the GUI gives a nice visual, **getfacl** will also indicate the effective permissions:

```
% getfacl test
#file:test
#owner:1001
#group:1001
user::rw-
user:rob:rwx     # effective: rw-
group::r--
mask::rw-
other::r--
```

Understanding Directory ACLs

A file can have only one ACL, its "access ACL." Most users will be happy with the ability to fine-tune the permissions on the files they create, as demonstrated in the previous section. Directories are more complex, as they can have up to three types of ACLs:

- An *access ACL* affects access to the directory itself.

- The *default directory ACL* sets the default permissions on any subdirectories created within the directory.

- The *default access ACL* sets the default permissions on any files created within the directory. Note that if the default directory ACL is not set, subdirectories will also inherit this ACL. However, if the default directory ACL is set, that value will override the value of this ACL.

The current FreeBSD implementation supports only the first two types of directory ACLs, so double-check the effective permissions on any files you create in directories containing ACLs. To see how this works, create a directory called `folder`.

Note: If you're planning on setting an ACL on a directory, do so before you add any files or subdirectories to that directory. This is because only objects created after the ACL can inherit the ACL. If you add an ACL to a directory that already contains files or subdirectories, always double-check that they contain the desired ACLs.

Look at the ACL properties for `folder` (Figure 5.4). It looks similar to a file, except the Default ACL button is no longer grayed out and there is a new Default check box under the Participants list. The User, Group, and Other permissions affect access to the directory itself and therefore represent the first type of ACL or the access ACL.

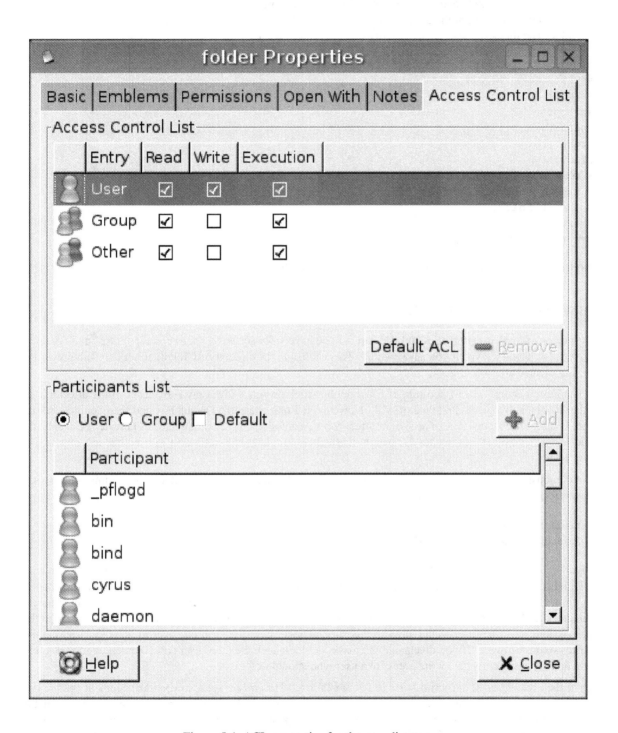

Figure 5.4: ACL properties for the new directory

Click on that Default ACL button. As Figure 5.5 shows, there are now four additional entries. These represent the second type of ACL, or the default directory ACL, and affect only subdirectories. Verify this by creating a subfolder and file:

```
% getfacl folder
#file:folder
#owner:1001
#group:1001
user::rwx
group::r-x
other::r-x
% mkdir folder/subfolder
% touch folder/testfile
% ls -l folder
drwxr-xr-x+ 2 dru   dru   512 Jul 27 12:23 subfolder
-rw-r--r--+ 1 dru   dru     0 Jul 27 12:23 testfile
```

Notice that `subfolder` inherited the directory permissions but `testfile` did not.

Adding a User to a Directory ACL

If I go back to `folder` properties and add *rob*, will he have write access to `folder/subfolder/` and `folder/testfile`? Good for you if you answered no. This change to the directory ACL will affect only subdirectories or files created after the change.

I also have a choice when I add *rob*. If I just double-click on *rob*, I give only *rob* access to the directory. In other words, I change the first type of ACL. However, if I first check the Default box and then double-click on *rob*, I change the second type of access, or affect *rob*'s permissions on the subdirectories I create. I can actually add *rob* both ways. If the icon has a D over it, it affects subdirectories; if it doesn't, it affects access only to this directory.

For demonstration purposes, add both versions of *rob* and leave them with the default *rwx* permissions. To see the effect, create another test subdirectory and file:

```
% mkdir folder/subfolder2
% touch folder/testfile2
```

Figure 5.6 shows the effective ACLs. As expected, the default directory ACL, represented by the *rob* icon with a D, inherited *rwx* from the parent directory. Note that the access ACL, represented by the *rob* icon without a D, shows that *w* is an ineffective permission. In other words, because it represented access only to the parent directory, it doesn't give *rob* any inherited permissions on this subdirectory; therefore, *rob* is subject to the permissions any other user would have on this subdirectory. However, you can override this by checking the write box in the mask. If you do change the mask, double-check the other users on your screen to make sure you don't inadvertently give write access to a user who shouldn't have it.

Once the explanation of the permissions in `folder/subfolder2` makes sense to you, take a look at `testfile2` as seen in Figure 5.7. Note that there isn't any *rob* icon with a D. This is because files don't inherit the default directory ACL. Because there isn't any current support for a default access ACL, *rob* doesn't inherit any permissions at all from either the directory or subdirectory and is subject to the same permissions as any other user. Again, the way to modify this is to modify the mask (remember, it represents the maximum possible permissions) and double-check that the new mask value doesn't give other users more permissions than you intend.

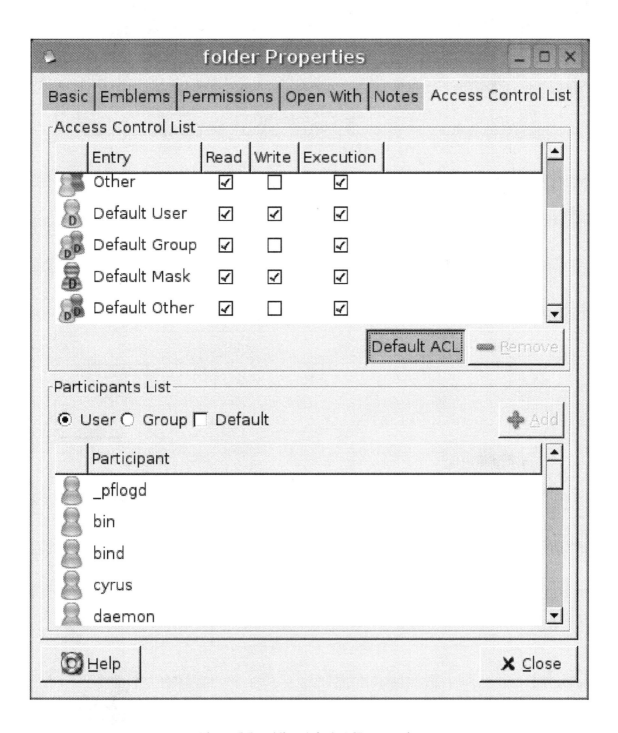

Figure 5.5: Adding default ACL properties

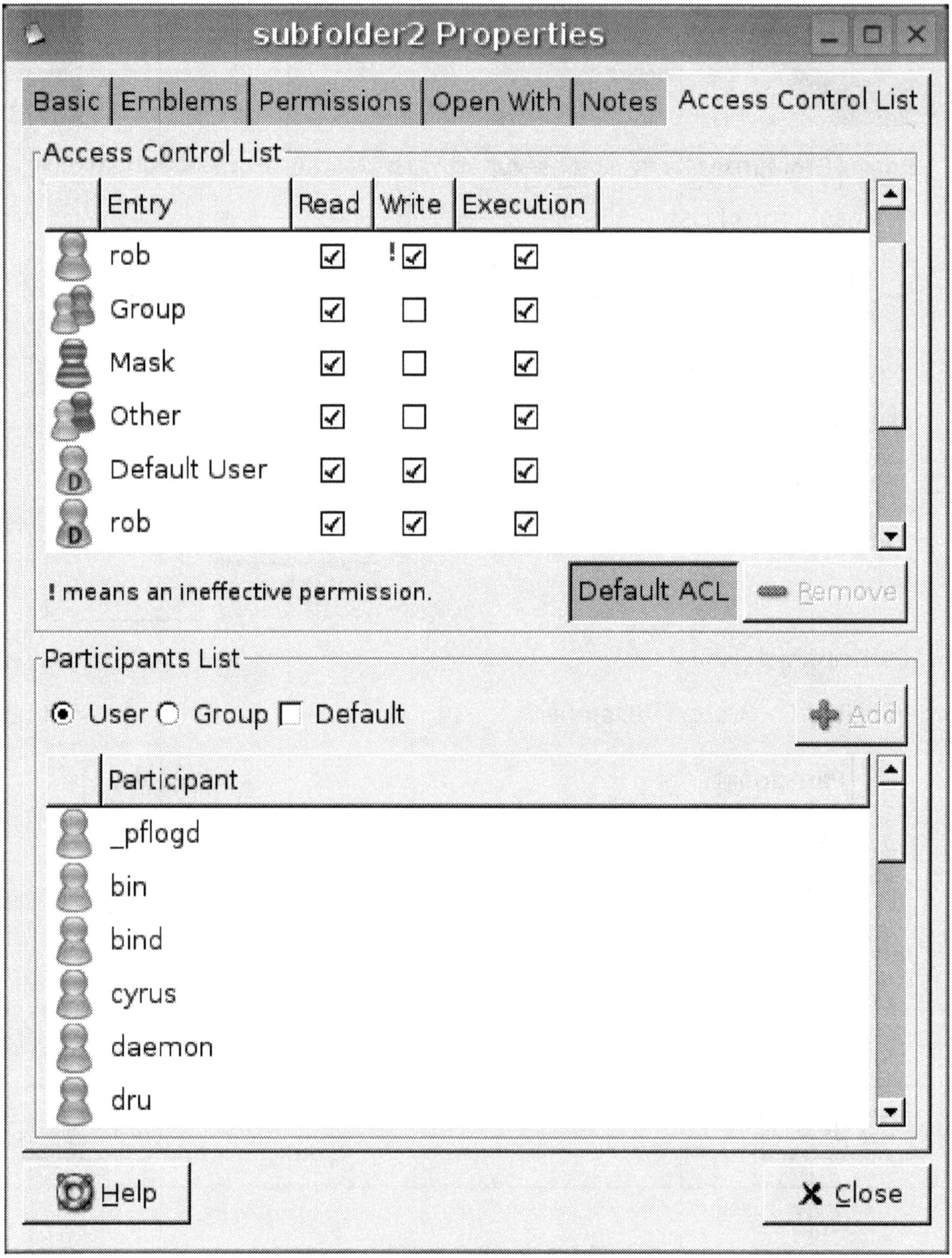

Figure 5.6: Effective ACLs

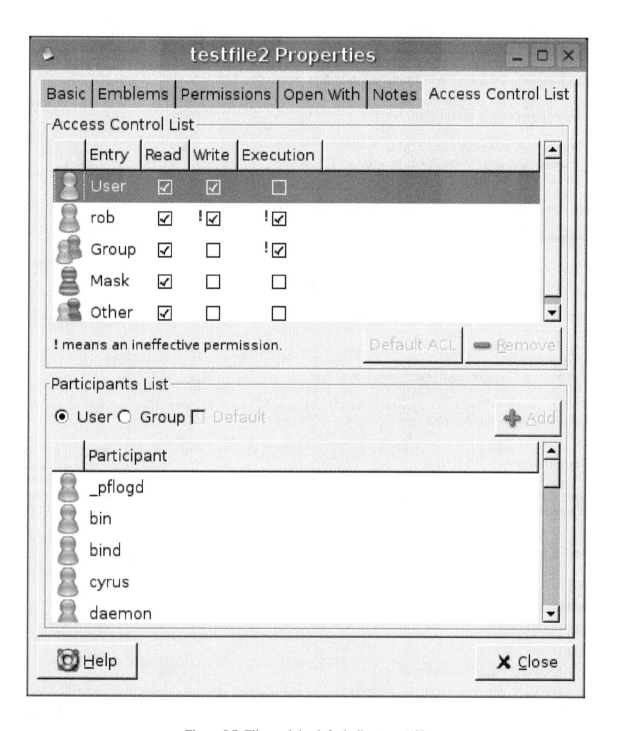

Figure 5.7: Files and the default directory ACL

Backing Up ACLs

One of the things you need to be aware of if you plan to use ACLs is that most backup utilities will correctly backup files containing ACLs, and even restore those files, but not their ACLs. A good solution to this is to install /usr/ports/archivers/star from the ports collection. If you've ever used **tar**, it won't take long to train yourself to add a few extra switches to catch all of those ACLs.

In this example, the superuser has made a backup directory for *dru* outside of her home directory so she can store backups of her home directory.

```
# mkdir -p /usr/backups/dru
# chmod dru:dru /usr/backups/dru
# exit
```

Next, *dru* backs up her home directory, which contains files with ACLs:

```
% whoami
dru
% cd
% star -cv -Hexustar -acl -f /usr/backups/dru/home.tar .
```

Next, *dru* will try a test restore in a temporary directory in her home directory:

```
% mkdir ~/tmp
% cd ~/tmp
% star -xv -Hexustar -acl -f home.tgz
```

Note: If you try to restore to a filesystem that doesn't have ACLs enabled, **star** will complain but will still restore the files minus the ACLs.

Conclusion

Many users either haven't yet heard of the benefits of ACLs or believe them to be difficult to use. Spend a half an hour showing your users how to use **eiciel** and **star**, and they'll wonder how they ever lived without ACLs.

Additional Resources

Original Article:

http://www.onlamp.com/pub/a/bsd/2005/09/22/FreeBSD_Basics.html

TrustedBSD Project:

http://www.trustedbsd.org/

ACL Section of FreeBSD Handbook:

http://www.freebsd.org/doc/en_US.ISO8859-1/books/handbook/fs-acl.html

Working With ACLs in FreeBSD 5.x:

http://ezine.daemonnews.org/200310/acl.html

eiciel Website:

http://rofi.roger-ferrer.org/eiciel/

6 Backups and RAID

6.1 Using Software RAID-1 with FreeBSD

Have you ever needed a software RAID solution for a low-end server install? Perhaps you've wanted your workstation to take advantage of the redundancy provided by a disk mirror without investing in a hardware RAID controller. Has a prior painful configuration experience turned you off software RAID altogether on Unix systems?

Since 5.3-Release, FreeBSD comes with **gmirror**, which allows you to easily configure a software RAID 1 solution. While tutorials on **gmirror** exist, I found them to require either manual calculations of partition sizes with **bsdlabel** or the use of a fix-it floppy on an existing system.

It made more sense to me to configure RAID during the install of the operating system. I also wanted a procedure that was easy to follow and didn't introduce human error in the form of a math miscalculation. After cobbling together the available documentation and experimenting my way through various configurations, I came across a procedure that has worked well for me on several different systems. I also received valuable feedback from Pawel Jakub Dawidek, the author of **gmirror**, who gave some insight into some of the not yet documented features of **gmirror**.

Some GEOM Background

Before demonstrating the configuration, it is useful to understand a bit about GEOM. GEOM is the modular disk framework introduced in FreeBSD 5.0. This modularity allows the creation of programs to manipulate disks. The best examples are the software RAID programs introduced with FreeBSD 5.3:

- **gstripe** provides a stripe set or RAID 0
- **gmirror** provides a mirror/duplex or RAID 1
- **graid3** provides a stripe with parity or RAID 3

The initial *g* indicates that each of these programs takes advantage of GEOM.

man 4 geom describes the terms it uses to refer to disks, some of which you'll see when setting up **gmirror**. These terms include the following:

provider – This GEOM entity appears in /dev. This section shows how to create a provider known as /dev/mirror/gm0, which represents the disk mirror/duplex.

consumer – This entity receives I/O requests. In the example of a mirror/duplex, it is the two physical drives. I use two IDE drives on separate cables; they are /dev/ad0 and /dev/ad2.

metadata – When referring to any RAID level, metadata includes the array members, their sizes and locations, descriptions of logical disks and partitions, and the current state of the disk array.

mirror/duplex – RAID 1 maintains the same data on two separate drives. In other words, it mirrors the data on one drive to another drive. If those two drives are attached to the same IDE cable, they are a mirror; if they are attached to separate cables, they are a duplex. Because a single cable introduces a single point of failure, most mirrors are actually duplexes.

Configuring the Mirror/Duplex During the Install

If you're going to use RAID 1, make your life easy and purchase two identical disks (of the same model and size). You can complicate things by insisting on different disks with different sizes, but in the end you just end up with a harder configuration that wastes the extra disk space on the larger disk. Cable the identical drives so that one is the primary master and the other is the secondary master. Before installing the operating system, double-check that your CMOS recognizes both disks.

Using your favorite installation method, start a FreeBSD install of any version (5.3 or higher). When you get to the Select Drives menu, it should show ad0 and ad2. Select ad0, as you will be installing the operating system on the primary master.

Within the **fdisk** utility, remove any existing partitions and then select "Use entire disk." When asked about the boot menu, choose "Standard MBR."

In the **disklabel** editor, set up the partitions on ad0 according to your requirements. If in doubt, choose a for automatic. Then choose your install sets and your install media, and let the operating system install as usual.

When finished, go through the postinstall configurations and set your time zone, create a user account, set the *root* password, and so on.

However, don't reboot when you end up back at the **sysinstall** main menu. Instead, press **Alt-F4**, which will take you to a command prompt. The first command I type is **csh** so I can get a shell with history (the default shell is Bourne).

Creating a mirror/duplex is as simple as typing:

```
# gmirror label -v -b round-robin gm0 /dev/ad0
```

where **gmirror label** creates the mirror; **-v** enables verbose mode; **-b round-robin** chooses a balance algorithm (at the moment, round-robin is the algorithm with the best performance); gm0 is the name of mirror/duplex (this name represents the first GEOM mirror); and /dev/ad0 represents the disk containing the data to be mirrored.

However, you'll be disappointed if you try the command now:

```
# gmirror label -v -b round-robin gm0 /dev/ad0
Can't store metadata on /dev/ad0: Operation not permitted
```

This is a security feature that indicates that the disk is currently mounted for writing and therefore is unavailable. However, you can get around this chicken-and-egg problem and temporarily force **gmirror** to bypass this measure in order to create the mirror/duplex by setting a sysctl value:

```
# sysctl kern.geom.debugflags=16
kern.geom.debugflags: 0 -> 16
```

Don't worry; this value will return to 0 when you reboot (which I'll have you do in just a few minutes). Try again:

```
# gmirror label -v -b round-robin gm0 /dev/ad0
Metadata value stored on /dev/ad0
```

That's it; you now have a RAID 1 system.

It is, however, useful to tell the operating system to load it whenever you boot. This requires edits to two files. The first one is currently empty, so just echo over the required line:

```
# echo geom_mirror_load="YES" > /boot/loader.conf
```

However, /etc/fstab is not empty, so I recommend making a backup copy before editing it:

```
# cp /etc/fstab /etc/fstab.orig
# vi /etc/fstab
```

Change each ad to a gm, and insert a mirror after /dev. For example, /dev/ad0s1a becomes /dev/mirror/gm0s1a. Unless you've made extra partitions, you'll have ad0s1 devices ending in *a*, *b*, *d*, *e*, and *f* and will need to edit each of those lines.

When finished, triple-check your changes to both /etc/fstab and /boot/loader.conf. While it is fixable, it sucks not being able to boot into a new system because of a typo.

Note: Some tutorials indicate you also need to add a swapoff option to /etc/rc.conf. This is no longer necessary, and neither is using **shutdown -r now** instead of **reboot**.

Once you're sure you don't have any typos, return to **Alt-F1** and exit the installation menu after removing your installation media.

Booting into the Mirror/Duplex

If you watch your boot-up messages, you should see this in bold white text right after the disks are probed:

```
GEOM_MIRROR: Device gm0 created (id=2125638583).
GEOM_MIRROR: Device gm0: provider ad0 detected.
GEOM_MIRROR: Device gm0: provider ad0 activated.
GEOM_MIRROR: Device gm0: provider mirror/gm0 launched.
GEOM_MIRROR: Device gm0 already configured.
Mounting root from ufs:/dev/mirror/gm0s1a
```

and the system will continue to boot. However, if you have a typo in /etc/fstab, the boot will stop at this point and wait for you to type something meaningful. In this example, I forgot to insert mirror when I edited /etc/fstab, meaning /dev/gm0s1a should have been /dev/mirror/gm0s1a so that FreeBSD could find my root filesystem:

```
Mounting root from ufs:/dev/gm0s1a
setrootbyname failed
ffs_mountroot: can't find rootvp
Root mount failed: 6
Manual root filesystem specification:
```

```
  <fstype>:<device>  Mount <device> using filesystem <fstype>
           e.g. ufs:da0s1a
  ?               List valid disk boot devices
  <empty line>       Abort manual input
mountroot>
```

Fortunately, that's not as scary as it looks. Start by listing your valid disk boot devices:

```
mountroot> ?
List of GEOM managed disk devices:
  mirror/gm0s1f mirror/gm0s1e mirror/gm0s1d mirror/gm0s1c mirror/gm0s1b
mirror/gm0s1a mirror/gm0s1 ad2s1 mirror/gm0 ad0s1 ad2 acd0 ad0 fd0
```

If you type in the correct location of the / filesystem, the system will continue to reboot:

```
mountroot> ufs:/dev/mirror/gm0s1a
Mounting root from /dev/mirror/gm0s1a
```

After logging in, be sure to edit the offending line in /etc/fstab and try rebooting again. When you can boot up and log in successfully, verify that each partition on the mirror mounted successfully with:

```
% df -h
Filesystem            Size    Used    Avail   Capacity    Mounted on
/dev/mirror/gm0s1a    248M    35M     193M    15%         /
devfs                 1.0K    1.0K    0B      100%        /dev
/dev/mirror/gm0s1e    248M    12K     228M    0%          /tmp
/dev/mirror/gm0s1f    7.3G    99M     6.7G    1%          /usr
/dev/mirror/gm0s1d    248M    196K    228M    0%          /var
```

df won't show your swap partition; you can verify it with:

```
% swapinfo
Device              1K-blocks   Used    Avail    Capacity
/dev/mirror/gm0s1b   629544     0       629544    0%
```

Synchronizing the Mirror/Duplex

The only thing left to do is to synchronize the data on both hard drives. This will happen automatically as soon as you issue the command to insert the second drive into the mirror:

```
# gmirror insert gm0 /dev/ad2
GEOM_MIRROR: Device gm0: provider ad2 detected.
GEOM_MIRROR: Device gm0: rebuilding provider ad2.
```

To see what's happening:

```
# gmirror list | more
Geom name: gm0
State: DEGRADED
Components: 2
Balance: round-robin
Slice: 4096
Flags: NONE
GenID: 0
SyncID: 1
ID: 2125638583
Providers:
1. Name: mirror/gm0
   Mediasize: 10262568448 (9.6G)
   Sectorsize: 512
   Mode: r6w5e2
Consumers:
1. Name: ad0
   Mediasize: 10262568448 (9.6G)
   Sectorsize: 512
   Mode: r1w1e1
   State: ACTIVE
   Priority: 0
   Flags: DIRTY
   GenID: 0
   SyncID: 1
   ID: 3986018406
2. Name: ad2
   Mediasize: 10262568448 (9.6G)
   Sectorsize: 512
   Mode: r1w1e1
   State: SYNCHRONIZING
   Priority: 0
   Flags: DIRTY, SYNCHRONIZING
   GenID: 0
   SyncID: 1
   Synchronized: 1%
   ID: 1946262342
```

Note the SYNCHRONIZING on the Flags line. It will take a while for these two drives to synchronize, as it is currently at 1 percent. I've seen times ranging from about 30 minutes for a 10GB drive to about two and a half hours for a 75GB drive. If you're curious, check the progress with:

```
# gmirror status
      Name     Status  Components
mirror/gm0   DEGRADED  ad0
                       ad2 (2%)
```

You'll see a status message in bold white text when the synchronization finishes:

```
GEOM_MIRROR: Device gm0: rebuilding provider ad2 finished.
GEOM_MIRROR: Device gm0: provider ad2 activated.
```

If you repeat **gmirror list**, you'll note that the State has changed from DEGRADED to COMPLETE and the Synchronized line is now gone. Don't worry if you see DIRTY on the Flags line, as it simply indicates that the system has written new data to the disk but hasn't mirrored it yet. If you were to wait a few seconds on a quiet disk, you would see the Flags line change to NONE.

For the final test, reboot the system. This time your startup messages should include:

```
GEOM_MIRROR: Device gm0 created (id=2125638583).
GEOM_MIRROR: Device gm0: provider ad0 detected.
GEOM_MIRROR: Device gm0: provider ad2 detected.
GEOM_MIRROR: Device gm0: provider ad0 activated.
GEOM_MIRROR: Device gm0: provider ad2 activated.
GEOM_MIRROR: Device gm0: provider mirror/gm0 launched.
Mounting root from ufs:/dev/mirror/gm0s1a
```

Final Notes

GEOM utilities are works in progress, and the developers constantly add new features and updates to the man pages. It's well worth your while to keep your favorite version of FreeBSD up-to-date using **csup** or to choose a newer release when deciding which version of FreeBSD to install.

If you wish to gather performance statistics on your mirror/duplex, try **gstat**. A good read through the **gmirror** manpage is also in order, especially if you want an overview of the procedure for replacing a failed disk.

Additional Resources

Original Article:

```
http://www.onlamp.com/pub/a/bsd/2005/11/10/FreeBSD_Basics.html
```

RAID Terminology:

```
http://www.webopedia.com/TERM/R/RAID.html
```

6.2 Understanding Archivers

In the next few sections, I'd like to take a look at backups and archiving utilities.

If you're like I was when I started using Unix, I was intimidated by the words **tar**, **cpio** and **dump**, and a quick peek at their respective man pages did not alleviate my fears.

So I quickly convinced myself that I really didn't need to learn how those utilities worked. After all, I didn't even own a tape drive on my home FreeBSD system. Yes, I knew that backups were really, really important, but surely I could just copy the files I needed as I needed them.

I've since learned that copying files is actually the hard way to do a backup and is not particularly conducive to me backing up everything I should on a regular basis. In this section, I'd like to introduce the concept of archiving, which archiving utilities are available, and some of the differences between the archiving utilities. In the next few sections, I'll continue by demonstrating the usage of each of these archiving utilities.

Recursive Copies

I'm currently logged in as the user *dru*. I'll **cd** into my home directory and take a look at its contents:

```
% cd
% ls
.                 .xinitrc             perlscripts
..                articles            this
.cshrc            ip.c                tricks
.history          jpegs               unix
.mailrc           lynx_bookmarks.html
.ssh2             pdfs
```

Let's say I want to backup the contents of my `perlscripts` directory to another directory I'll call `backup`. If I try:

```
% cp perlscripts backup
cp: perlscripts/ is a directory (not copied).
```

I'll see that the copy operation fails, since `perlscripts` is a directory. However, if I remember to use the **-r** or recursive switch:

```
% cp -r perlscripts backup
```

the copy command will be successful. A new directory named `backup` will be created for me and the contents of `perlscripts` will be copied to it.

That seemed easy enough, but it may not be the best way to do a backup. For starters, let's do a long listing of the original directory and the new backup directory:

```
% ls -l perlscripts
total 6
drwxr-xr-x    2 dru   wheel    512 Oct  4 07:29 .
drwxr-xr-x   22 dru   wheel   4096 Mar 24 07:07 ..
-rwxr-xr-x    1 dru   wheel    801 Feb 16 12:32 time.pl
% ls -l backup
total 3
drwxr-xr-x   3 dru   wheel   512 Mar 24 08:49 .
drwxr-xr-x   8 dru   wheel   512 Mar 24 08:49 ..
-rwxr-xr-x   1 dru   wheel   801 Mar 24 08:49 time.pl
```

You'll note that the last modified time for the file `time.pl` has been changed to the time I made the recursive copy, rather than the last time this file was actually modified, which was back in February.

This may or may not be a big deal to you if you are only interested in backing up some files in your own home directory. However, this could certainly cause confusion if this was the backup solution for larger portions of your FreeBSD system.

There are other considerations when using **cp -r** to backup files. What if I wanted to backup files for several users? I would probably do the backup as the superuser. Let's see what happens if I repeat that copy, but this time as the superuser:

```
% rm -r backup
% su
Password:
# cp -r perlscripts backup
# ls -l backup
total 3
drwxr-xr-x  3 root  wheel  512 Mar 24 09:20 ./
drwxr-xr-x  8 dru   wheel  512 Mar 24 09:20 ../
-rwxr-xr-x  1 root  wheel  801 Mar 24 09:20 time.pl
```

You'll note that both the backup directory and the time.pl file are owned by the user who did the copy, in this case *root*. This situation could have been avoided if I had remembered to include the **-p** switch to preserve the original permissions.

Just imagine the nightmare if I had backed up each user's home directory as the superuser using **cp -r**; I would have to readjust the ownership and possibly the permissions of any file that needed to be restored, plus the original file modification times would still be unknown.

If that's still not a big deal to you, consider how I would backup my entire home directory using **cp -r**. I do not want to do it this way, even though it seems logical enough:

```
% cd
% cp -r . backup
```

If I do try to do this, my hard drive will churn for an eerily long period of time before giving me an error message that includes several screens worth of the word backup and something about the name being too long. This is because the **cp** command will go into an endless loop if your destination happens to be in the same directory or a subdirectory of the source you are backing up. It will copy backup to backup/backup to backup/backup/backup and so on until it runs out of space.

So how would I backup my entire home directory? This is where things start to involve a bit more work and I start to get the gnawing suspicion that there has to be an easier way to accomplish this. This will work:

```
% mkdir backup
% cp -r .cshrc .history .mailrc .ssh2 .xinitrc articles file \
  ip.c jpegs lynx_bookmarks.html pdfs perlscripts tricks unix \
  backup/
```

but will quickly become time-consuming and inconvenient as the number of files in my home directory continues to grow. I could get a bit fancier by coming up with wildcard expressions that represent all of the files and directories in my home directory, but I would still be doing things the hard way.

Archivers

This is where the concept of archiving and utilities that were designed to do archiving come into play. So what exactly is an archive? It is a file containing a collection of other files in a structure that preserves the contents, permissions, timestamp, owner, group, and pathnames of the original files so they can be reconstructed at a later time. In other words, archiving utilities can copy all of the files and subdirectories within a directory and then recreate that original directory structure without losing any permissions or modification times along the way.

This is actually even more interesting once you realize that there are devices that don't even know what a filesystem is or how to read a filesystem hierarchy. We are used to thinking of our files living in a filesystem hierarchy. For example, my `time.pl` file is a file that lives in the `perlscripts` directory which is a subdirectory of my home directory `dru` which is a subdirectory of the `home` directory which is a subdirectory of the `/usr` filesystem. In other words: `/usr/home/dru/perlscripts/time.pl`.

Any device that can contain a filesystem and therefore understand a filesystem hierarchy is known as a block device. The hard drive that contains your FreeBSD operating system is an example of a block device.

However, there are devices that do not understand what a filesystem hierarchy is. Consider how a tape device works. When you write data to a tape, your characters are simply passed to the tape one after the other, or sequentially. There is no filesystem, or any concept that the file `time.pl` belongs within the `perlscripts` directory. Such devices are known as character devices and are often called raw.

Archiving utilities can backup to either a block or character device. The archive file itself contains all of the information required to recreate the original file hierarchy; that information is saved along with your data. This means you can backup your data to a character device such as a tape drive, and then later restore your data to a block device such as your hard drive.

There are several archiving utilities that come with your FreeBSD system. I will be covering **tar**, **cpio**, **pax**, **dd**, **dump** and **restore**. Let's see what the **whatis** command has to say about each of these utilities:

```
% whatis tar cpio pax dd dump
tar(1)                 - manipulate tape archives
cpio(1)                - copy files to and from archives
pax(1)                 - read and write file archives and copy directory hierarchies
dd(1)                  - convert and copy a file
dump(8), rdump(8)      - file system backup
```

Note that **tar**, **cpio**, and **pax** are considered to be archivers. We'll see that **tar** is easiest to use when you want to backup entire directory structures. In contrast, the **cpio** utility is the easiest command to use when you want to pick and choose which files to backup. And the **pax** command is a combination of both these commands with a bit of added functionality thrown in.

The **dd** utility is interesting as it can actually convert files as it backs them up. We'll see that this can be invaluable, say, when backing up files from a PC to a SPARC. Finally, the **dump** command is designed to backup an entire filesystem, not just a directory structure.

Tape Devices and Pathnames

I want to discuss a few more items, though, before we start using each of these commands. Most of these commands assume that you will be backing up to a SCSI tape drive but will let you change this default with a switch. On a FreeBSD system, **man 4 sa** describes the SCSI tape driver. The necessary entries in `/dev` will be created by `devfs` for you once the SCSI tape hardware is installed on the system. These entries will include:

`/dev/sa0` — once the backup is complete, this device will rewind, meaning your backup will be overwritten if you perform another backp to that tape

`/dev/nsa0` — this device will not rewind so use this device if you wish to store multiple backups to the same tape

/dev/esa0 — this device, when present, is capable of ejecting the tape once the backup is complete

The last thing I want to mention is the difference between absolute and relative pathnames. Since an archiving utility will save the pathname of a file and use that pathname information when recreating the file, it is important to know the difference between the two types of pathnames.

If a pathname begins with a / (slash) it means it is an absolute pathname. This is usually considered to be a bad thing in a backup as you will only be able to restore that file to the original directory it came from, meaning you will lose any changes you've made to that file since you backed it up. Even if you are in a different directory when you restore that file, it will still restore that file to its original location.

If a pathname begins with ./ (dot slash) or no / at all it means it is a relative pathname. This is usually considered to be a good thing in a backup as the file can be restored anywhere. You simply **cd** to the directory you want to restore the file to, and the archiver will add the current directory to the pathname as it restores the file.

Additional Resources

Original Article:

```
http://www.onlamp.com/pub/a/bsd/2002/05/02/FreeBSD_Basics.html
```

6.3 Backing up Files with Tar

Now that I have introduced the concept of archivers, I would like to demonstrate the usage of the **tar** archiver.

Preparing the Test Directory

Since we'll be backing up and restoring files, I recommend that you create a test user account to practice with until you are comfortable using the **tar** utility. On my system, I became the superuser and followed the prompts issued by the **adduser** command to create a test account named *test*.

I then wanted to quickly add a lot of subdirectories and files to this *test* user's home directory. Since I had the ports collection installed on my system, I copied over one of its subdirectories then changed the ownership of these files so they belonged to the *test* user:

```
# cp -r /usr/ports/www/ ~test/
# chown -R test ~test/www/*
```

I now had a lot of files in a test directory to practice with. I then logged in as the *test* user and checked out the contents of my home directory:

```
% ls -l
total 16
drwxr-xr-x  375 test  wheel  9728 May 11 09:53 www/
% du -h | tail -2
 28M    ./www
 28M    .
```

It looks like I have 28M worth of data to work with in my test directory.

Creating a Backup

In theory, **tar** can be as easy to use as this command:

```
% tar c .
```

where the c means "create an archive" and the "." means "of the current directory." However, if you try this, you will probably get the same error message I did:

```
% tar c .
tar: can't open /dev/sa0 : Permission denied
```

Aha, you may think; I'll try as the superuser:

```
% su
Password:
# tar c .
tar: can't open /dev/sa0 : Device not configured
```

Remember the previous section when I talked about tape devices? By default, the tar utility assumes that you want to backup to your first SCSI tape drive (/dev/sa0) which is great, if you happen to have one attached to your PC. If you don't, all is not lost. In Unix, a tape device is simply a file. So it is very easy to tell **tar** to create a backup to another file, whether that file be a different type of tape device, a floppy, another hard drive, another PC on the network, or an actual file somewhere on your system.

I'll start simple, by telling **tar** to create (c) a backup of my current directory (.) to a file I'll call /tmp/backup. tar. Since this is not the default backup location, I'll use the **f** switch to indicate the name of the file I'd like the backup sent to:

```
% tar cf /tmp/backup.tar .
```

When I ran this command, my prompt disappeared for a moment and I heard my hard drive churning away. When my prompt reappeared, I had a new file in the /tmp directory named **backup.tar**. If you don't want to just wait in silent anticipation, use the **v** switch and **tar** will tell you what it is doing while it is doing it. I'll remove that backup and try again with the **v** switch:

```
% rm /tmp/backup.tar
% tar cvf /tmp/backup.tar .
```

You'll understand the difference when you try this for yourself. Now, let's see what type of file **tar** created:

```
% file /tmp/backup.tar
/tmp/backup.tar: tar archive
```

This is not an ASCII text file, so I won't be able to view its contents with a pager or an editor. However, **tar** understands this file and I can ask it to read it for me using the **t** switch:

```
% tar t /tmp/backup.tar
tar: can't open /dev/sa0 : Device not configured
```

Oops, I forgot that **tar** expects to read that SCSI tape device unless I tell it to look somewhere else. I'll try again, this time including the **f** switch:

```
% tar tf /tmp/backup.tar
```

This time, a whole bunch of files and directories fly by very quickly; it looks like I've successfully made a backup. If I wanted to verify the file list, I'd send the output to a pager so I could read it one page at a time:

```
% tar tf /tmp/backup.tar | more
```

Compressed Backups

It is also possible to create a compressed backup by including the **z** switch when using **tar**. Let's take a look at the size of that backup we just created:

```
% ls -l /tmp/backup.tar
-rw-r--r--  1 root  wheel  25722880 May 11 16:41 /tmp/backup.tar
```

I'll now remove that backup, tell **tar** to create a compressed backup using the **gzip** utility, then view the difference in size and type:

```
% rm /tmp/backup.tar
% tar cvzf /tmp/backup.tar.gz .
% ls /tmp/backup.tar.gz
-rw-r--r--  1 root  wheel  5899840 May 11 16:45 /tmp/backup.tar.gz
% file /tmp/backup.tar.gz
/tmp/backup.tar.gz: gzip compressed data, from Unix
```

To list the files in a compressed archive, don't forget to include the **z** switch. Depending upon your version of **tar** you may get a strange error if you don't:

```
% tar tf /tmp/backup.tar.gz
tar: Hmm, this doesn't look like a tar archive.
tar: Skipping to next file header...
```

You'll note that when I created my backups, I gave the archives I created with the **z** switch the extension of *tar.gz*. I can call my archive whatever I want; I just used that convention to remind me that I'm dealing with a compressed **tar** archive file. It is always a good idea to use the **file** utility on an archive to verify whether or not it has been compressed.

Also, when listing the contents of an archive, you can include the **v**, or verbose, switch. Here is an example of the difference in the output:

```
% tar tzf /tmp/backup.tar.gz | tail -2
www/mod_tsunami/pkg-plist
www/Makefile
% tar tzvf /tmp/backup.tar.gz | tail -2
-rw-r--r-- test/wheel       116 May 11 09:53 2002 www/mod_tsunami/pkg-plist
-rw-r--r-- test/wheel      9713 May 11 09:53 2002 www/Makefile
```

Notice that long listing of the files in the backup and compare that to a long listing of the backup file itself:

```
% ls -l /tmp/backup.tar.gz
-rw-r--r--  1 root  wheel  15098016 May 11 17:31 /tmp/backup.tar.gz
```

The backup was created by the superuser at 17:31, yet the files in the backup still belong to the *test* user and those files were created at 9:53 (when I set up the test directory). This is what I was talking about in the last section when I said that archivers preserve the permissions and ownership of the files that are backed up.

tar Gotchas

It is also possible to tell **tar** to backup multiple directories:

```
% tar cvzf /tmp/partial.tar.gz www/apache2 www/chimera www/zope
```

The above command will create (c) a gzipped (z) file (f) named `partial.tar.gz` by archiving the contents of the directories `apache2`, `chimera`, and `zope`. Remember, tell **tar** which file you want to send the backup to first; everything after that name will be what **tar** will back up for you. It is important to ensure that the backup itself isn't in the same directory being backed up (in my examples it is in `/tmp`) to prevent the backup from looping until it exhausts disk space.

One last thing about creating archives with **tar**: **tar** was designed to back up everything in the specified directory. This means that every single file and subdirectory that exists beneath the specified directory will be backed up. It is possible to specify which files you don't want backed up using the **X** switch.

Let's say I want to backup everything in the `www` directory except for the `apache2` and `zope` subdirectories. In order to use the **X** switch, I have to create a file containing the names of the files I wish to exclude. I've found that if you try to create this file using a text editor, it doesn't always work. However, If you create the file using **echo**, it does. So I'll make a file called `exclude`:

```
% echo apache2 > exclude
% echo zope >> exclude
```

Here, I used the **echo** command to redirect (>) the word *apache2* to a new file called `exclude`. I then asked it to append (>>) the word *zope* to that same file. If I had forgotten to use two >'s, I would have overwritten the word *apache2* with the word *zope*. When making your own exclude file, put the name of each file you wish to exclude on its own line.

Now that I have a file to use with the **X** switch, I can make that backup:

```
% tar cvfX /tmp/backup.tar exclude www
```

This is the first backup I've demonstrated where the order of the switches is important. I need to tell **tar** that the **f** switch belongs with /tmp/backup.tar and the **X** switch belongs with the *exclude*. So if I decide to place the **f** switch before the **X** switch, I need to have the /tmp/backup.tar before the *exclude*. This command will also work as the right switch is still associated with the right word:

```
% tar cvXf exclude /tmp/backup.tar www
```

But this command would not work the way I want it to:

```
% tar cvfX exclude /tmp/backup.tar www
tar: can't open /tmp/backup.tar : No such file or directory
```

Here you'll note that the **X** switch told **tar** to look for a file called /tmp/backup.tar to tell it which files to exclude, which isn't what I meant to tell **tar**.

Let's return to the command that did work. To test that it didn't back up the file called apache2, I used **grep** to sort through **tar**'s listing:

```
% tar tf /tmp/backup.tar | grep apache2
%
```

Since I just received my prompt back, I know my exclude file worked. It is interesting to note that since apache2 was really a subdirectory of www, all of the files in the apache2 subdirectory were also excluded from the backup. I then tested to see if the zope subdirectory was also excluded in the backup:

```
% tar tf /tmp/backup.tar | grep zope
www/zope-zpt/
www/zope-zpt/Makefile
www/zope-zpt/distinfo
www/zope-zpt/pkg-comment
<output snipped>
```

This time I got some information back, as there were other subdirectories that started with the term zope, but the subdirectory that was just called zope was excluded from the backup.

Restoring Backups

Now that we know how to make backups, let's see how we can restore data from a backup. Remember the difference between a relative and an absolute pathname, as this has an impact when you are restoring data. Relative pathnames are considered a good thing in a backup. Fortunately, the **tar** utility that comes with your FreeBSD system strips the leading slash, so it will always use a relative pathname — unless you specifically override this default by using the **P** switch.

It's always a good idea to do a listing of the data in an archive before you try to restore it, especially if you receive a **tar** archive from someone else. You want to make sure that the listed files do not begin with a slash as that indicates an absolute pathname. I'll check the first few lines in my backup:

```
% tar tf /tmp/backup.tar | head
www/
www/mod_trigger/
www/mod_trigger/Makefile
www/mod_trigger/distinfo
www/mod_trigger/pkg-comment
www/mod_trigger/pkg-descr
www/mod_trigger/pkg-plist
www/Mosaic/
www/Mosaic/files/
www/Mosaic/files/patch-ai
```

None of these files begin with a slash, so I'll be able to restore this backup anywhere I would like. I'll practice a restore by making a directory I'll call testing, and then I'll restore the entire backup to that directory:

```
% mkdir testing
% cd testing
% tar xvf /tmp/backup.tar
```

You'll note that I **cd**'ed into the directory to contain the restored files, then told **tar** to restore or extract the entire /tmp/backup.tar file using the **x** or extract switch. Once the restore was complete, I did a listing of the testing directory:

```
% ls
www
```

I then did a listing of that new www directory and saw that I had successfully restored the entire www directory structure, including all of its subdirectories and files.

It's also possible to just restore a specific file from the archive. Let's say I only need to restore one file from the www/chimera directory. First, I'll need to know the name of the file, so I'll get a listing from **tar** and use **grep** to search for the files in the chimera subdirectory:

```
% tar tf /tmp/backup.tar | grep chimera
www/chimera/
www/chimera/files/
www/chimera/files/patch-aa
www/chimera/scripts/
www/chimera/scripts/configure
www/chimera/pkg-comment
www/chimera/Makefile
<snip>
```

I'd like to just restore the file www/chimera/Makefile, and I'd like to restore it to the home directory of the user named *genisis*. First, I'll **cd** to the directory to which I want that file restored, and then I'll tell **tar** just to restore that one file. Note that you have to be the superuser in order to restore to a directory owned by someone else:

```
# cd ~genisis
# tar xvf /tmp/backup.tar www/chimera/Makefile
```

You'll note some interesting things if you try this at home. When I did a listing of *genisis'* home directory, I didn't see a file called Makefile, but I did see a directory called www. This directory contained a subdirectory called chimera, which contained a file called Makefile. Remember, when you make an archive, you are including a directory structure, and when you restore from an archive, you recreate that directory structure.

You'll also note that the original ownership, permissions, and file creation time were also restored with that file:

```
# ls -l ~genisis/www/chimera/Makefile
-rw-r--r--  1 test  wheel  406 May 11 09:52 www/chimera/Makefile
```

Additional Resources

Original Article:

```
http://www.onlamp.com/pub/a/bsd/2002/05/23/FreeBSD_Basics.html
```

6.4 Understanding CPIO

While both **tar** and **cpio** will achieve the same results, the **cpio** utility approaches things a little bit differently. The **tar** utility assumes that you want to recursively archive everything under the specified directory or directories, meaning that you have to explicitly tell **tar** if you want to exclude certain portions of that directory structure.

In contrast, the **cpio** utility expects to be explicitly told which files or directories you wish to archive; this behavior is commonly referred to as "receiving from standard input." In other words, **cpio** expects to receive a list that contains one file per line, which is exactly the type of list that the **find** utility creates. The **ls** utility can also create this type of list, meaning that you will see either the **ls** or the **find** utility used in conjunction with **cpio**. And since **cpio** archives a list of files it receives from standard input, you usually use a pipe (|) whenever you create an archive with the cpio utility.

Creating cpio Archives

The **tar** utility also assumes that you want to write the archive to your first SCSI tape drive, unless you explicitly specify a file using the **f** switch. In contrast, the **cpio** utility writes to what is known as standard output. This means that you will be using either a redirector (either < or >) or a switch to specify a filename whenever you are creating, listing, or extracting a **cpio** archive file. Again, that file may be an actual file, or it may be your floppy, or it may be a tape device, since in Unix everything is a file.

This may sound a bit more complicated at first, but a few examples should convince you that it really isn't.

Let's start by creating a **cpio** archive. In the last section, I created a *test* user account and created a directory structure named www in this user's home directory so I would have some files on which to practice using the archiving utilities. I'll log in as the *test* user, **cd** into the **www** directory, and see what happens if I use the **ls** command with the **cpio** utility:

```
% cd www
% ls | cpio -ov > backup.cpio
```

You'll note that I first **cd**'d into the directory that contained the files I wished to archive. I used the **ls** utility to make a list of the files in the current directory and used a pipe (|) to send that list to the **cpio** utility. The **-o** switch invokes what is known as "copy out mode," which tells **cpio** to create an archive. The **-v** switch tells **cpio** to be verbose, meaning it will list each file as it archives it. Finally, I used the > redirector to write the results (the archive) to a file called `backup.cpio`. I can call this file anything I like; I chose to give it a *cpio* extension to remind me that it is a **cpio** backup file. I can verify the file type using the **file** utility:

```
% file backup.cpio
backup.cpio: cpio archive
```

Instead of using the redirector, I could have also used the **-F** switch to specify which file to write the archive to. So the following command will achieve the same results:

```
% ls | cpio -ovF backup.cpio
```

Once the archive was created, **cpio** told me how many blocks it wrote to the archive; in my case, it was 48 blocks.

So to create an archive, use the **-o** switch or copy-out mode. To either view or extract the contents of the archive, use what is known as "copy-in mode." You invoke this mode by using the **-i** switch. If you just want to view the contents of the archive, also include the **-t** switch, which will list the contents of the archive without extracting them:

```
% cpio -it < backup.cpio
```

You'll note that this time I used the other redirector (<), as I wanted the contents of the `backup.cpio` file to be sent to the **cpio** utility. I can also include the **-v** switch, if I want to see a verbose listing of the backup.

Restoring the Archive

Remember that it is important to view the contents of an archive before attempting to restore it, as you want to ensure that the files don't begin with a slash.

To restore this archive, I simply **cd** into the directory to which I'd like to restore the archive, and repeat the above command without the **-t** switch. I'll **cd** back into my home directory and create a directory named `backup` and do the restore there:

```
% cd
% mkdir backup
% cd backup
% cpio -iv < ~/www/backup.cpio
```

You'll note something interesting if you try this exercise yourself; if you use the **ls -F** command, you'll see that you did indeed restore all of the files and directories that were in the www directory. But if you **cd** into any of those subdirectories, you'll note that they are empty. Even more interestingly, if you try to remove any of those subdirectories, you have to use the **R** switch, as they are valid directories.

What happened here? Since the **cpio** utility received its file list from the **ls** utility (and the **ls** utility only listed the files in the current directory), **cpio** was unaware of all of the files that existed below the current directory. Remember, **cpio** will only archive the files that are sent to it in a list. This may seem odd at first, but it is an ideal way to archive just the files in the current directory. In order to do this with the **tar** utility, you would have to create an exclude file, as **tar** wants to recursively copy everything in and below the current directory.

This doesn't mean that **cpio** can't archive recursively; it simply means that if you want to just archive the current directory, you use **ls** and if you want to archive recursively, you use **find** instead.

Using find

Let's try that backup and restore again, this time using the **find** utility. First, I'll remove the old backup and empty out the backup directory:

```
% rm www/backup.cpio
% rm -R backup/*
```

Then I'll **cd** into the directory I wish to back up (www) and archive its contents:

```
% cd www
% find -d . -print | cpio -ov > backup.cpio
```

When using the **find** utility with **cpio**, it is always a good idea to include the **-d** (depth) switch as this switch prevents permissions from interfering with a backup.[1] When using this switch, either put **-d** right after the **find** and before the directory to search (in this case, "."), or put the word **-depth** after the directory to search, like so:

```
% find . -depth -print | cpio -ov > backup.cpio
```

So as a recap on the **find** command, I told **find** to search the current directory (".") and to print its contents; the | was used to send those contents to the **cpio** utility, which created an archive (**-o**) and wrote that archive to a file called backup.cpio. When I created this archive, I noted that **cpio** wrote 43097 blocks, which is many more than the 48 I received with the **ls** command.

Now let's see what happens when I try to restore this archive:

```
% cd ../backup
% cpio -iv < ~/www/backup.cpio
```

I received an interesting message on my screen when I did this restore:

---

[1] It will handle the file entries of a directory before the directory itself.

```
<snip>
cpio: mod_tsunami/Makefile: No such file or directory
cpio: mod_tsunami/distinfo: No such file or directory
cpio: mod_tsunami/pkg-comment: No such file or directory
cpio: mod_tsunami/pkg-descr: No such file or directory
cpio: mod_tsunami/pkg-plist: No such file or directory
mod_tsunami
Makefile
.
43097 blocks
```

It looks like **cpio** read all 43097 blocks but complained about missing files or directories. Indeed, if I do an **ls** on any of the restored subdirectories, I'll discover that they are once again empty! Don't worry, all of those files and directories are in that archive file; I've simply demonstrated the default extraction behavior of **cpio**. Unlike **tar**, the **cpio** utility does not recreate any directories during the restore unless you specifically ask it to with the **-d** switch. And, unlike **tar**, the **cpio** utility will not overwrite any existing files unless you specifically ask it to with the **-u** switch.

So let's try that restore again, this time using the **-d** switch to create the directories and the **-u** switch to overwrite the files I've already restored:

```
% cpio -ivdu < ~www/backup.cpio
```

This time I don't receive any error messages and I've successfully restored all of the subdirectories and their files.

Additional Switches

There're a few more switches you may consider using when backing up and restoring with **cpio**. If I compare the modification times of a file before it was archived and after it was restored, I will see this:

```
% ls -l www/zope/Makefile
-rw-r--r--  1 test  wheel  4308 May 11 09:53 www/zope/Makefile
% ls -l backup/zope/Makefile
-rw-r--r--  1 test  wheel  4308 Jun  2 11:38 backup/zope/Makefile
% ls -l www/backup.cpio
-rw-r--r--  1 test  wheel  22065664 Jun  2 10:39 www/backup.cpio
```

You'll note that the original file was created on May 11, that it was backed up on June 2 at 10:39, and that it was restored on June 2 at 11:38. If you want to preserve the file's original access time, include the **-a** switch when creating the archive, and the **-m** switch when restoring the archive:

```
% cd www
% find -d . -print | cpio -ova > backup.cpio
% cd ../backup
% cpio -ivdm < ~/www/backup.cpio
```

If you try this and repeat the **ls -l** commands, you'll see that the original times of the archived files were kept intact.

The nice thing about using the **find** utility with **cpio** is that you have all of **find**'s switches available to you, to fine-tune which files you would like to backup. For example, if you'd like to do an incremental backup, use find's **-newer** switch. In this example, I'll back up all of the files in my home directory that have changed since 11 PM on June 1st:

```
% cd
% touch -t 06012300 June1
% find -d . -newer June1 -print | cpio -ova > backup.cpio
```

Here I used the **touch** utility to create an empty file with a timestamp of month 06 day 01 time 2300, then I told **find** to use the time on that file as the reference point when searching the current directory. Alternatively, if I wasn't concerned so much about the time as the date, I could have used **find**'s **-atime**, **-ctime**, or **-mtime** switches. And if I only want to archive files of a certain size, I can use **find**'s **-size** switch.

I'd also like to demonstrate **cpio**'s third mode, which is known as "copy-pass mode." This is an interesting mode, as it archives and extracts in the same command, making it ideal for copying one directory structure and recreating it in another location.

Let's say I want to copy the www directory structure from the home directory of the *test* user to the home directory of the user *genisis*. I'll have to become the superuser, as I'll be creating the archive in one user's home directory and recreating it in another user's home directory:

```
% su
Password:
# cd ~test/www
# find -d . -print | cpio -pvd ~genisis/www
```

Note that I first **cd**'d into the directory I wanted to archive, in this case the www subdirectory of the *test* user's home directory. Then, with the **cpio** command, I invoked copy-pass mode with the **-p** switch and specified that I wanted the archive recreated in the www subdirectory of the home directory of the user *genisis*.

If I run this command and then do an **ls -l** of *genisis*' home directory, I'll see that I've successfully recreated the entire www directory structure. However, I'll want to fine-tune that above command as those restored files still belong to the user *test*. I'll repeat that command using the **-u** switch so it will overwrite that last restore, and I'll include the **-R** switch, which tells **cpio** to change the ownership of the files as it recreates them:

```
# find -d . -print | cpio -pvdu -R genisis ~genisis/www
```

When using the **-R** switch, follow it by the name of the user you wish to become the owner of the files, then follow that by the name of the directory to restore the files to.

Finally, if I want to keep the original times of the files instead of having them changed to the time the files were restored, I'd also add the **-a** and **-m** switches:

```
# find -d . -print | cpio -pvduam -R genisis ~genisis/www
```

This should get you started with the **cpio** command. If you're planning on using **cpio** to copy between different computers, you'll want to read its manpage first, as there may be considerations, especially if the computers are running different versions of Unix or different architectures.

Additional Resources

Original Article:

`http://www.onlamp.com/pub/a/bsd/2002/07/11/FreeBSD_Basics.html`

6.5 Archiving with Pax

It's unfortunate that the **pax** utility never seems to get the coverage that **tar** and **cpio** do. I've found that it combines the best qualities of both utilities into one easy-to-use and fairly intuitive utility.

The name of the utility stands for "portable archive exchange," as it was designed specifically to allow portability between different versions of Unix. There's also a bit of wry humor in the name, as **pax** attempts to bring some "peace" to the long-standing battle over which is better: **tar** or **cpio**. The **pax** utility can be used to create either type of archive, and during a restore, it automagically detects the type of archive for you. And it doesn't matter what type of Unix that archive happened to be created on, meaning you can back up files from your FreeBSD system and restore them to, say, a SCO system.

Basic Usage

Let's start with some examples of basic **pax** usage, then move on to some fancier stuff. To back up the contents of your home directory, invoke write mode using the **-w** switch:

```
% cd
% pax -wf /tmp/home.pax .
```

In this example, I went to my home directory with **cd**, then told **pax** to write (w) to a file (f) named /tmp/home.pax the contents of the current directory ("."). When you use **pax**, it's very important to remember to include that **-f** switch to indicate the name of the archive you'd like to create. If you forget the **f**, weird characters will be sent to your screen, accompanied by horrible, pained noises. Also, if you want to watch as **pax** does its thing, simply add the **-v**, or verbose, switch to the switch portion of the command.

To see what type of file you've just created, use the **file** command:

```
% file /tmp/home.pax
home.pax: tar archive
```

To see the contents of that archive, tell **pax** which archive file you'd like to view, using the **-f** switch:

```
% pax -f /tmp/home.pax | more
```

Since my archive file is rather large, I piped this output to the **more** command so I could read the contents of the archive one page at a time. If you also include the **-v** switch, you'll get an **ls -l** type output of the archive contents. Again, don't forget to specify the name of the archive with the **-f** switch, or nothing will happen, except that you'll lose your prompt until you press **Ctrl-C**.

The **pax** utility does support compression, so I could have performed a compressed backup by including the **-z** switch:

```
% pax -wzf /tmp/home.pax .
```

Let's do another example. This time I'll back up the /etc directory to a floppy:

```
% cd /etc
% su
Password:
# pax -wf /dev/fd0 .
```

You'll note that I became the superuser in this example. This was necessary for two reasons. First, the files in /etc are owned by *root*, since they are the configuration files for the system. Second, by default, only the superuser has permission to back up to a floppy drive. Also notice that I specified the floppy as the name of the archive file (/dev/fd0).

A couple of notes about backing up to a floppy: the **pax** utility is intelligent enough to realize when it fills up a floppy, and will prompt for another one if the archive file is too large to fit onto one floppy. However, **pax** does not support compression to a floppy; if you try adding the **-z** switch to the above example, you'll receive this error message:

```
gzip: stdout: Invalid argument
```

You should also be aware that, by default, when you back up to a floppy, you will lose any previous data stored on that floppy. If you would like to append to a previous archive, use the **-a** switch:[2]

```
% cd
% pax -wvf /dev/fd0 jpegs
% pax -wavf /dev/fd0 pdfs
% pax -f /dev/fd0
```

The above example will back up the jpegs directory to a floppy, then append the pdfs directory to the backup. When I list the archive, the contents of both directories will be on the floppy.

Restoring Archives

To restore (or use read mode on) an archive, first **cd** into the destination directory, then use the **-r** switch. For example, I'll restore the backup named /tmp/home.pax into the test subdirectory of my home directory:

```
% cd test
% pax -rvf /tmp/home.pax
```

The **pax** utility can also restore **tar** and **cpio** archives. It is able to automatically detect the correct format for you; however, you should use the **file** utility before attempting the restore to determine whether or not the archive is compressed. If it is, you'll need to include the **-z** switch.

As an example, I have a file called backup.old located in my home directory (~). I'll first use the **file** utility:

---

[2]The output is not shown in this example.

```
% file backup.old
```
backup: gzip compressed data, deflated, last modified: Sat Aug 17
14:21:12 2002, os: Unix

Since this backup is compressed, I'll use this command to restore it to the test directory:

```
% cd test
% pax -rvzf ~/backup.old
```

I have another file in my home directory called backup:

```
% file ~/backup
```
backup: cpio archive

This file isn't compressed, so I'll restore it, like so:

```
% pax -rvf ~/backup
```

The fact that the first backup happened to be a **tar** archive and the second a **cpio** archive didn't confuse **pax**; however, I would have received some strange error messages if I had forgotten to inform **pax** that the first archive was compressed.

You can do some pretty funky things when restoring with **pax**. For example, you can do an interactive rename/restore by including the **-i** switch. Issuing the following command:

```
% pax -rif ~/backup
```

will start an interactive restore of the archive named backup into the current directory. In interactive mode, **pax** will display the name of each file, one at a time, and prompt you to either rename it as it's restored, restore it with the original name, or to skip it and not restore it:

```
ATTENTION: pax interactive file rename operation.
drwxr-xr-x Aug 17 15:08 .
Input new name, or a "." to keep the old name, or a "return" to skip this file.
Input >
Skipping file.
```

Here, I pressed **Enter** as I didn't want to change the name of "." or the current directory.

```
ATTENTION: pax interactive file rename operation.
drwxr-xr-x Jul 26 16:10 file1
Input new name, or a "." to keep the old name, or a "return" to skip this file.
Input > old
Processing continues, name changed to: old
ATTENTION: pax interactive file rename operation.
-rw-r--r-- Jun 11 00:20 file2
Input new name, or a "." to keep the old name, or a "return" to skip this file.
Input > .
Processing continues, name unchanged.
```

You'll note that I changed the name of file1 to old and kept file2 as is. A listing of the restored directory will show two files: one named old and one named file2.

Copy Mode

One of the most powerful features of **pax** is that it is able to very quickly copy a complete directory structure to another portion of your hard drive, using copy mode. To use copy mode:

- **cd** into the source directory.

- Ensure the destination directory exists; if it doesn't, use **mkdir** to create it.

- Issue this command:

```
% pax -rw . destination_directory
```

Note that you don't include the **-f** switch in copy mode, as an archive file doesn't get created. Instead, the old directory structure is directly recreated into the new directory structure.

Also note that *you never want to do this*:

```
% cd
% mkdir test
% pax -rw . test
```

In the above example, I **cd**'d into my home directory, made a subdirectory named `test`, then invoked copy mode. In doing so, I ended up in an endless loop of test subdirectories, each containing the contents of my home directory. If I hadn't interrupted this cycle with a **Ctrl-C**, **pax** would have continued ad infinitum, where infinitum is defined as the point where I run out of disk space.

That's what this section of **man pax** refers to:

> Warning: The destination directory must not be one of the file operands or a member of a file hierarchy rooted at one of the file operands. The result of a copy under these conditions is unpredictable.

However, this works beautifully and almost instantaneously:

```
% su
Password:
# cd ~user1/big_project
# mkdir ~user2/big_project
# chown user2 ~user2/big_project
# pax -rw . ~user2/big_project
```

Voila, the entire `big_project` directory structure is now also in the second user's home directory. When using copy mode, you'll have to become the superuser as you'll be copying out of your home directory, so you can avoid the endless loop situation. If you have to make the new directory, it will be owned by *root*; if need be, use the **chown** command like I did to ensure that it has the desired ownership before doing the copy operation. You'll also want to take a look at **man pax**, specifically the **-p** switch followed by the letter **e**, to see how you want to handle the permissions of the copied directory structure.

It is also possible to interactively copy a directory structure by including the **-i** switch:

```
# pax -rwi . ~user2/big_project
```

Similarly to the previous interactive example, **pax** will display each filename, one at a time, so you can decide which files to copy over and which files to rename as you do so.

Incremental Backups

Now, let's do something useful with the **pax** command. I'll demonstrate how to create an incremental backup system. In this example, the user *genisis* would like to back up any changes she made to her home directory on a daily basis.

First, I'll become the superuser to create a directory to hold the backups:

```
% su
Password:
# mkdir /usr/backups
```

I'll then create a subdirectory and give the user *genisis* ownership of that subdirectory:

```
# mkdir /usr/backups/genisis
# chown genisis /usr/backups/genisis
```

I'll then **exit** the superuser account and as the user *genisis*, **cd** into my home directory. I'll then do a full backup of my home directory and save it to an archive file called Monday:

```
% pax -wvf /usr/backups/genisis/Monday .
```

Now that I have a full backup, I can take daily incremental backups to just back up each day's changes. So when I'm finished with my work on Tuesday, I'll issue this command:

```
% pax -wv -T 0000 -f /usr/backups/genisis/Tuesday .
```

Notice that I included the time (**-T**) switch and specified a time of midnight (*0000*). This tells **pax** to only back up the files that have changed since midnight, so it will catch all of the files that changed today. On Wednesday, I'll repeat that command but will change the archive name to Wednesday.

If you have the disk space and want to keep backups for longer than a week, modify your archive names to something like: Aug01, Aug02, etc. It's still a good idea to do a full backup once a week, followed by incremental backups the other days of that week. If disk space is an issue, include the **-z** switch so the backups will be compressed. Also note that the **-T** switch can be much pickier than I've demonstrated; see **man pax** for the details.

You have to be a bit careful when restoring an archive. By default, **pax** will overwrite any existing files. If you don't want it to overwrite any files, include the **-k** switch. If you want to be picky about which files are overwritten, use the **-i** switch.

You don't have to restore every file in an archive. If you're going to be selective, it's a good idea to list the archive first to see what you want and don't want. For example:

```
% pax -f /tmp/backup
./file1
./file2
./file3
```

To restore all of the files except `file3`, use this command:

```
% pax -rvf /tmp/backup -c './file3'
```

The **-c** switch is the exception switch. Note that your exception pattern (in my case, `file3`) needs to be enclosed in single quotes (the key next to your **Enter** key). Either use the literal pattern like I did (to **pax**, this file is known as `./file3`, not `file3`) or use a wildcard, like so:

```
% pax -rvf /tmp/backup -c '*file3'
```

If you use a wildcard (*) at the beginning of your pattern as in the above example, you will exclude all files that end with `file3` — for example: `file3`, `myfile3`, and `thatfile3`.

You can also specify which file to restore by using the **-n**, or pattern matching, switch. The following will just restore `file2`:

```
% pax -rvf /tmp/backup -n './file2'
```

The **-n** switch differs from the **-c** switch in that it will only restore the first file that matches the pattern. This means the following command will not restore `file3`, `myfile3`, and `thatfile3`:

```
% pax -rvf /tmp/backup -n '*file3'
```

Since `file3` is the first file to match the expression, it will be the only file that will be restored.

The **-c** and **-n** switches are also useful when creating an archive; use them to specify which file you'd like to back up, or which file(s) you don't want to back up.

Hopefully, this archiving chapter has taken some of the mystique out of Unix backups, so that you can choose the utility that works best for you and implement a regular backup schedule for the files on your FreeBSD system. Hopefully, you'll never need to restore a backup, but if you do, you'll be glad that you took the time to master and use your favorite archiving utility.

Additional Resources

Original Article:

```
http://www.onlamp.com/pub/a/bsd/2002/08/22/FreeBSD_Basics.html
```

7 Networking

7.1 Connecting to the Internet Using PPP or a DSL Modem

One of the first things every new FreeBSD user wishes to do is set up a connection to the Internet. Depending upon how you connect to your ISP, the Internet may "just work" when you boot into your new FreeBSD system. If you are using a dialup modem, it should "just work" once you tell FreeBSD the phone number to your ISP and the username and password you use to authenticate.

This section will go a bit deeper and describe what is happening behind the scenes during a PPP connection which can be quite useful on the rare occasions where things don't just work. I'll start with some definitions of common terms and explain how these terms interrelate when you connect to the Internet. Then I'll show you how easy it is to do a basic Internet connection with FreeBSD, and leave you with some references should you wish to try more complicated configurations.

Some Terminology

In order for two computers to exchange information, they need a connection between them, a physical device to handle the connection, and a protocol to package the data in a format both computers understand.

If the computers are physically located near each other, they will most likely be cabled together with either CAT-5 or coaxial cable to produce a LAN (Local Area Network). CAT-5 cable looks like the wire that plugs into your telephone jack, except that the connection at the end is bigger. Coaxial cable looks like cable-TV wiring. Both types of wiring will be attached to a NIC (Network Interface Card) at the back of each computer in the LAN. The NIC is responsible for transmitting electrical signals onto the wiring; these signals represent the data that the computers wish to exchange. As long as both computers are using the same protocol (rules of communication), they will be able to correctly translate the electrical signals back into the original data.

However, when you're connected to the Internet, you are really accessing other computers over a WAN (Wide Area Network). There is no way of knowing whether your data is travelling over CAT-5 cable, fiber optic cable, or transmissions from satellite links. Major telecommunications companies (e.g., MCI) control these links; you need an access point into this global network of telecommunication links. The most common way of gaining this access is through an account with either an ISP or a cable provider.

ISPs (Internet Service Providers) sell monthly access to the Internet; you access an ISP by dialing into their POP (Point of Presence) using a dial-up modem and your existing phone line or the PSTN (Public Switched Telephone Network). A modem is required to translate the digital signals used by your computer into the analog signals the telephone cabling in your home understands. Because you are dialing into another modem at the ISP using a temporary point to point connection, you need to configure the point to point protocol (PPP).

You don't need to configure PPP if you are using a cable modem, as you already have a constant connection to your cable provider. In essence, the cable modem is a virtual NIC connected to a very big virtual LAN. The cable modem does the necessary translation to make this work.

Testing the Modem

Before configuring PPP, you need to know the following:

- the COM (communications) port your modem is physically attached to
- the phone number of your ISP's POP
- the username and password the ISP provided you

Note, not all modems are created equal. Some modems require built-in software to work; unfortunately, this software only works on Windows computers, hence the nickname Winmodems.

Let's see if we can get the modem to dial out. As *root*, type:

```
# ppp
Working in interactive mode
Using interface tun0
ppp on hostname>
```

which will invoke the **ppp** utility; note that you will lose your prompt when using **ppp** and it will only accept **ppp** commands. If you wish to use a regular command prompt, switch to another terminal using the **Alt-Fx** keys.

To talk to the modem directly, we can use terminal mode, replacing # in the command line below with the number of your COM port minus one:

```
ppp on hostname> term /dev/cuad#
deflink: Entering terminal mode on /dev/cuad#
Type  ? for help.
```

Modems use something called AT commands to talk with each other; AT commands always start with the letters AT followed by at least two other letters that represent the command. Since we wish to tell the modem to dial a phone number, we use this AT command (replace 1234567 with the phone number to dial):

```
ppp on hostname> atdt1234567
```

You should hear your modem dial and try to connect, followed by a connect message and then by a Login prompt. Enter your username for the ISP, then your password when prompted. You should see something like this:

```
    Entering PPP Mode.
        IP address is xxx.xxx.xxx.xxx
        MTU is 1524.
ppp
PPp
PPP
```

If you get the line PPP in all caps, you've been successfully authenticated and are now connected to your ISP. To disconnect from your ISP, type the word **bye**.

This will disconnect your modem from the ISP, end the **ppp** program, and you will receive your regular prompt back.

Automating the PPP connection

You don't need to enter terminal mode every time you wish to dial your ISP. **ppp** has a configuration file, `ppp.conf`, that it reads whenever you start it. This file is almost ready to use as-is. You will need to double-check that it matches the COM port used by your modem as the default points to COM2 or `/dev/cuad1`:

```
# grep dev /etc/ppp/ppp.conf
# Ensure that "device" references the correct serial port
set device /dev/cuad1
```

That's pretty straightforward; doublecheck that the **set device** line has the correct COM port for your modem and change it if it doesn't.

You definitely will have to change these lines towards the bottom of the file:

```
# edit the next three lines and replace the items in caps with
# the values which have been assigned by your ISP.
#
set phone PHONE_NUM
set authname USERNAME
set authkey PASSWORD
```

Follow the instructions and replace the words in caps with the actual phone number, username, and password to your ISP. Save your changes and check whether the configuration file is successful by typing:

```
# ppp
ppp on hostname> dial papchap
```

You should hear your modem dial out and connect, and your prompt should automatically change from ppp to Ppp to PPp to PPP. Let's see if we received the necessary information we need to access the Internet from our ISP:

```
# netstat -rn
Destination       Gateway         Flags   Netif    Expire
default           xxx.xxx.xxx.xxx  UGSc    tun0
xxx.xxx.xxx.xxx   xxx.xxx.xxx.xxx  UH      tun0
```

This command allows you to view your IPV4 routing table; `tun0` is the tunnel device driver your modem uses with PPP. Flags of UG indicate that you have a gateway that is up. The IP address associated with this entry is the address of your default gateway.

You also need at least one DNS server entry to access the Internet, so let's verify you also received one of these from your ISP by typing:

```
# more /etc/resolv.conf
nameserver  xxx.xxx.xxx.xxx
```

If you have at least one entry, you're in business. For one more test, type:

```
# traceroute www.freebsd.org
```

You should receive back a numbered list of all the routers between you and *www.freebsd.org*.

Giving users permission to use PPP

Now let's fine-tune our system for **ppp**. By default, only *root* can use **ppp**, but you don't want to be *root* just to access the Internet. Let's look at the error message, and then fix it. Open up a terminal and log in as a regular user.

```
% ppp
/usr/sbin/ppp: Permission denied
```

If you look at a long listing of ppp, you'll see that only *root* and members of the *network* group have permission to use ppp:

```
% ls -l /usr/sbin/ppp
-r-sr-x--  1 root  network  324256 Jan 16  2007 /usr/sbin/ppp*
```

You can add your user to the *network* group by using your favorite editor to open the file /etc/group. Change the *network:* line to:

```
network:*:69:username1,username2
```

where *username1,username2* is a comma-separated list of the users you wish to give **ppp** access to. Save this file, switch to a terminal one of these users is logged into, and try again:

```
% ppp
default: User access denied
```

What happened? We put the user in the correct group to use **ppp**, but we didn't tell **ppp**. Let's edit the /etc/ppp/ppp.conf file as *root*. At the end of the *default:* section, add the following line:

```
allow users username1 username2
```

Again, substitute the actual usernames and save the file. Now your users should be able to connect to the Internet using **ppp**.

Configuring for a *DSL modem

If you connect to your ISP using *DSL, you don't need to input a phone number into /etc/ppp/ppp.conf as your connection is always on. You do need to know what type of PPP your ISP uses: it should be either PPPoE or PPPoA.

Once you know the type of PPP, change the **set device** line so it points to the correct type of PPP and the name of your NIC instead of the COM port for your modem. For example, my ISP uses PPPoE and the FreeBSD name of my NIC is rl0 so my line looks like this:

```
set device PPPoE:rl0
```

If you don't know the name of your NIC, try this command which searches for Ethernet addresses (which are burnt into NICs):

```
# grep Ethernet /var/run/dmesg.boot
rl0:  Ethernet address:  00:11:d8:ea:16:d7
```

Additional Resources

Original Article:

`http://www.onlamp.com/pub/a/bsd/2000/06/14/FreeBSD_Basics.html`

Pedantic PPP Primer:

`http://jamesthornton.com/freebsd/books/ppp-primer/`

7.2 Networking with TCP/IP

When you install FreeBSD, you are plunged into the wonderful world of TCP/IP. You may have heard about DNS, ports, RFCs, private ranges, and subnet masks but may be foggy on what these are and why you should care. This section will be a primer on the TCP/IP protocol for the novice and a refresher with some interesting links for those more seasoned FreeBSD users.

Protocol Primer

First off, let's make sure you are clear on what a protocol is. By definition, a protocol is the rules of communication. If you are travelling in a foreign country, you need to be aware of the customs of that country. A gesture that may seem friendly or insignificant to you may actually be considered an insult in other parts of the world. Awareness of protocol can save you the embarrassment of miscommunication.

Protocols are even more important if two computers wish to exchange information. Amazingly, computers communicate by subtly changing millions of electrical pulses, light pulses, or radio waves per second. Both computers need to be using the same protocol, or set of rules, to correctly interpret which of these pulses represent the address of the computer to receive the data, the address of the computer that sent the data, the data itself, and confirmation that the data received was the same data that was sent.

TCP/IP is more than a protocol; it is a protocol suite, or collection of protocols. TCP/IP was designed to allow any operating system on any type of hardware to talk to any other computer in the world. This is something we take for granted in the age of the Internet, but before TCP/IP changed all of the rules, most operating systems, hardware, and protocols were proprietary. Proprietary means that in order to exchange information with another computer, it has to be running the same hardware and the same version of the same operating system, which was provided by the vendor of the hardware.

Because TCP/IP is a collection of protocols, new protocols can be added as the capabilities of networking evolve. The designers of TCP/IP left room for the creation of up to 65,535 application protocols. To keep track of all of these application protocols (or rules for how an application expects to receive data), each is assigned a number known as a port number. For example, the port number for SSH is 22 and the port number for HTTP is 80. If I wish to **ssh** into a computer, TCP/IP will send out packets that contain (among other information we'll ignore for the moment) the port number 22. The other computer will realize that I wish to use the rules for SSH, which are very different than, say, the rules for surfing or checking my email.

Since TCP/IP is non-proprietary, anyone can add new functionality to TCP/IP, pending a review process of their peers known as the RFC or or Request For Comments. RFCs were started before the actual development of TCP/IP and have become a fascinating record of each step in the evolution of TCP/IP and the Internet. Ever wonder about who invented DNS and why and all the nitty-gritty details of how DNS actually works? The answer lies in the associated RFCs, which are available for anyone to read via the Internet.

There are many good sites on the Internet where you can search for and read RFCs, though the main repository is at http://www.rfc-editor.org.

Perhaps you've been told that reading RFCs is as much fun as reading manpages. Admittedly, RFCs can be written by anyone, so writing styles will differ. Some good RFCs to start with are:

- RFCs 1000, 1251, 2235, and 2468 - if you're interested in hearing about the history of the Internet from some of the people who made it happen

- RFCs 968, 1121, and 1882 - just in case you thought computer geeks had no sense of humor. If you enjoy humorous RFCs, see the list at http://www.wyae.de/docs/joke-rfcs/

TCP/IP Terminology

TCP/IP applications always have two components: the server component, also called the daemon, listens for connection requests; the client component initiates connection requests. In order for two computers to share data using a TCP/IP application, one computer must use the client component and the other computer must provide the server component. Let's take a look at the snipped output of the following command:

```
% apropos ftp
ftp(1) - Internet file transfer program
ftpd(8) - Internet File Transfer Protocol server
```

Notice the two results: **ftp**(1) is the client portion while **ftpd**(8) is the server portion of the FTP application protocol. Often you'll see the letter *d* after an application name; the *d* represents the daemon so you know that it is the server component. If you read the manpage for **ftp**, you'll learn how to use the FTP client to transfer files to and from a remote site. However, if you read the manpage for **ftpd**, you'll learn how to configure server issues such as welcome screens, authentication methods, and logging.

In order for users to connect to your FreeBSD system over a network, they need to have the client component of the application they wish to use, and the matching server component must be listening for requests on your computer. For example, a user can use a SSH client to connect to your SSH daemon. However, if your SSH daemon is not listening for requests, a connection can not be created and the user will instead receive an error message.

It's important to know which of your daemons are listening for requests to ensure that network users aren't connecting to services you're not aware of, and users are able to connect to the services you wish them to connect to. One way of determining which of your daemons are waiting for connection requests from clients is to use the **sockstat** command:

```
% whatis sockstat
sockstat(1) - list open sockets
```

The **sockstat** utility will show which daemons will accept IPV4 requests, IPv6 requests, and local Unix requests. If you just type **sockstat**, it will show all three types of requests; to specify one type of request, use the **-4**, **-6**, or **-u** switches with the command. Let's see which daemons on my computer are waiting for connection requests from clients running IPV4:

```
% sockstat -4
USER       COMMAND      PID   FD PROTO  LOCAL ADDRESS         FOREIGN ADDRESS
dru        firefox-bi 46355 50 tcp4     192.168.2.49:50548    72.140.203.95:80
dru        gaim         682  6  tcp4     192.168.2.49:51199    16.155.193.138:5050
root       sshd         545  3  tcp4     *:22                  *:*
root       sendmail     508  4  tcp4     127.0.0.1:25          *:*
root       syslogd      394  6  udp4     *:514                 *:*
```

Let's pick apart this output. Notice that each listening daemon is a process as it has a PID (Process ID). Also, each daemon has the choice of using either the TCP or the UDP transport protocol and some may actually use both. The local address section shows either which port that daemon listens on, or the socket for a connection that has already been established.

Remember that there are thousands of TCP/IP application protocols, and each one has been assigned a port number. This number is used by the client to indicate which daemon it wishes to make a connection to. For example, the port number for SMTP is 25 and the port number for HTTP is 80. Since clients request connections by using a port number, the associated daemon listens for requests on that port number.

If you are unsure which application is associated with a certain port number, do a **grep** through the /etc/ services file. For example, to see which daemon is listening on the foreign address port number of 5050, we could issue this command:

```
% grep -w 5050 /etc/services
mmcc           5050/tcp    #multimedia conference control tool
mmcc           5050/udp    #multimedia conference control tool
```

Now let's concentrate on this line of **sockstat** output:

```
dru        firefox-bi 46355 50 tcp4    192.168.2.49:50548    72.140.203.95:80
```

This line represents an active TCP connection on my computer. You'll notice that both the local address and foreign address sections are filled in with an IP address followed by a colon followed by a port number. An IP address followed by a port number is called a socket, hence the name of the utility we are using. You may recognize the port number of 80 as belonging to HTTP; let's see what port 50548 is:

```
% grep -w 50548 /etc/services
%
```

If you try the above command, you won't receive any results, just your command prompt back. To understand why, we need to look at how TCP connections are established.

There are thousands of TCP/IP applications and each chooses its transport, or the protocol used to transport the data between the server and the client. UDP is the connectionless transport, meaning that it just sends out data without double-checking that the other computer is ready to receive the data. This is similar to you just showing up at a friend's house in the hope that he may be home. TCP is the connection-oriented transport; it will not send out any data until it has contacted the other computer to ensure that it is ready to receive data. This would be similar to you phoning your friend first to see if he is home and willing to have you come over for a visit.

To create the necessary connection, TCP uses a mechanism known as the three-way handshake, as three packets are required to fully establish the connection. The first packet is sent out by the client and indicates which port number or application it wishes to make a connection with. The second packet is sent out by the server and includes the socket. Since the server needs to keep the original port number open so it can continue to listen for requests from other clients, it will choose a random, high port number not being used by any other daemon. It will bind the IP address of the client to that port number to create the socket. The IP address of the client is important, as a daemon may actually be responding to several clients at a time; for example, an FTP server may have many clients logged in simultaneously and needs to ensure that it is sending the correct data to the correct client. Finally, the third packet is sent by the client; it contains information confirming that it knows what socket it is bound to and states that it is ready for data transfer to occur.

Returning to our example, the user *dru* used **firefox** (an HTTP client) to access the **httpd** or web server running on port 80 of a computer with the IP address of 72.140.203.95. The **httpd** responded by choosing to bind port number 50548 to my IP address of 192.168.2.49. The reason why port 50548 did not show up in our **grep** of /etc/services is because it represents a socket or open connection, not a listening service.

If the **sockstat** output had shown this instead:

```
LOCAL ADDRESS              FOREIGN ADDRESS
192.168.2.49:80            72.140.203.95:50548
```

it would indicate that a user on a computer with the IP address of 72.140.203.95 had made a connection to my web server using port 80. To summarize, if a port number in the LOCAL ADDRESS column is found in the /etc/services file, it either represents a daemon on your computer listening for requests or it will be bound to the IP address of a client that has already established a connection with one of your daemons. If a port number used in a socket under the LOCAL ADDRESS column does not appear in /etc/services, it probably means that your computer used a client application to connect to another computer running TCP/IP.

IP Addressing Primer

Once TCP/IP has determined which application you wish to use and how that application wishes to transport its data, it needs a mechanism to make sure the data makes it to the right computer. In other words, it needs an addressing scheme. The only type of address TCP/IP understands is an IP address; if your computer does not have an IP address, you can't use TCP/IP. Most operating systems use IPv4 (IP version 4) IP addresses, but this will be changing within the next few years as the Internet is slowly transitioned over to IPv6.

In IPv4, an IP address is divided into two parts: one part indicates the address of the network and the second part indicates the address of the host. (In TCP/IP, anything with an IP address is called a host, or sometimes a node.) All IPv4 addresses contain four numbers ranging from 0-255 separated by three periods; this is called dotted decimal notation. Each number is the decimal equivalent of eight binary bits, so it really represents an octet, or eight numbers. Which octets represent the default network and the host addresses depends upon the class of IP address, as seen in Table 7.1.

Table 7.1: IPv4 Classes

Class	Network ID	Host ID	Range
A	first octet	last three octets	1-126
B	first two octets	last two octets	128-191
C	first three octets	last octet	192-223

To determine the class of an IP address, compare the number in the first octet to the Range column of the table. For example, 163.48.92.47 is a Class B address, since the 163 in the first octet falls within the range of 128-191.

Because it is a Class B address, the first two octets, 163.48, represent the default network address, and the last two octets, 92.47, represent the host address.

TCP/IP was designed to use a globally unique addressing scheme. This means you can't just make up an IP address for your computer, because it may conflict with an IP address that someone paid money to use. Network portions of an IP address are purchased to guarantee they are unique; once you have a network address, you can do whatever you want with the host addresses as long as no two computers in your network have the same host address.

Fortunately, each class of IP address also has a reserved private range. Anyone can use a private range network address for their own network; the only caveat is that you'll need a real (or purchased) IP address if you want to leave your network: for example, if you want to access the Internet. Table 7.2 shows the private ranges.

Table 7.2: Reserved Private IP Range

Class	Private Range
A	10.x.x.x
B	172.16.x.x to 172.31.x.x
C	192.168.x.x

It is a good thing to use one of the private ranges on your network; which class you use is up to you. Most networks use a combination of private range IP addresses and NAT, or Network Address Translation. NAT is a software mechanism that allows a network of private addresses (which can't go on the Internet) to share a real IP address (which can go on the Internet).

Every IPv4 address must also have a subnet mask. You should be aware of the default subnet masks so you can use the correct subnet mask for your IP address. The default subnet masks are different for each class (Table 7.3).

Table 7.3: Default Subnet Masks

Class	Default Subnet Mask
A	255.0.0.0
B	255.255.0.0
C	255.255.255.0

In my test network, I have three computers. I've decided to use the private Class A network range, the default subnet mask, and to use host addresses of 1, 2, and 3. This translates into the following addresses:

Hostname	IP address	Subnet mask
alpha	10.0.0.1	255.0.0.0
beta	10.0.0.2	255.0.0.0
gamma	10.0.0.3	255.0.0.0

On the computer named *alpha*, I used the **ifconfig** utility to bind an IP address to its NIC. In order to do this, I first had to determine the device name of the NIC using the following command:

```
% grep Ethernet /var/run/dmesg.boot
rl0: Ethernet address: 00:00:b4:94:9d:3f
```

which shows that the device name of *alpha*'s NIC is `r10`. To see if there is an IP address bound to your NIC, use the following command:

```
% ifconfig r10 inet
r10: flags=8843<UP,BROADCAST,RUNNING,SIMPLEX,MULTICAST> mtu 1500
        options=8<VLAN_MTU>
```

This NIC does not have an IPv4 address; I'll use the **ifconfig** command like so to assign one:

```
% ifconfig r10 10.0.0.1 netmask 255.0.0.0
ifconfig: ioctl (SIOCAIFADDR): permission denied
```

Note that regular users have sufficient permission to view, but not to change, the IP address assigned to a NIC. Let's become the superuser and try again:

```
# su
Password:
# ifconfig r10 10.0.0.1 netmask 255.0.0.0
# exit
% ifconfig r10 inet
r10: flags=8843<UP,BROADCAST,RUNNING,SIMPLEX,MULTICAST> mtu 1500
        options=8<VLAN_MTU>
        inet 10.0.0.1 netmask 0xff000000 broadcast 10.255.255.255
```

Once you've bound an IP address to a NIC, you'll want to use the **ping** utility to ensure that the NIC can send and receive TCP/IP packets. Start with your loopback address (127.0.0.1), which will check that TCP/IP has been initialized on your system. If this test does not work, you can't use TCP/IP.

Note: To end the **ping**, press **Ctrl-C**.

Then, **ping** your IP address (in this case, 10.0.0.1) to check that your IP address is valid. If this test does not work, check that you have a valid IP address and subnet mask and that no other host is using the same IP address.[1]

If you have another host on your network, ping its IP address. If this last test works, you're in business. If not, double-check your network cabling and ensure that the other computer is turned on and that you are pinging the correct address.

Name Resolution

TCP/IP uses IP addresses, but humans like to use hostnames. Quick, what's the IP address of `http://www.yahoo.com`? Don't feel bad if you don't know, as you don't need to in order to access Yahoo's webpage. Hostname resolution was designed to map hostnames to the IP addresses that TCP/IP understands. If you have a small network, you can use the `/etc/hosts` file to provide hostname resolution. DNS databases provide the same function in larger networks and on the Internet.

Editing the `/etc/hosts` file is an easy matter. First, you need to know, and possibly set, your hostname using the **hostname** utility. Anyone can view the computer's hostname by typing **hostname**. Only *root* can change the computer's hostname. One way to change a computer's hostname is like so:

---

[1]See section 3.6 to learn about some subnetting utilities.

```
# hostname alpha
```

This will set the computer's hostname to *alpha*.

Once the computers in your network have hostnames, you should edit the /etc/hosts file so you can access resources by hostname instead of IP address. Again, only *root* can modify this file. Each of the computers in my network has an /etc/hosts file that looks like this:

```
% more /etc/hosts
127.0.0.1    localhost
10.0.0.1       alpha
10.0.0.2       beta
10.0.0.3       gamma
```

After you edit the /etc/hosts file, always try pinging the hostnames that you've added. For example:

```
% ping alpha
% ping beta
% ping gamma
```

If any of the pings fail, you either have a typo in your /etc/hosts file or the hostname has not been set on that computer.

Additional Resources

Original Articles:

http://www.onlamp.com/pub/a/bsd/2000/08/23/FreeBSD_Basics.html

http://www.onlamp.com/pub/a/bsd/2001/01/31/FreeBSD_Basics.html

Understanding IP Addressing:

http://www.3com.com/other/pdfs/infra/corpinfo/en_US/501302.pdf

7.3 FreeBSD Networking Basics

Beginners to Unix-like operating systems such as FreeBSD are often stymied by their network settings. Sure, the install process may have set up your NIC for you, but where do you go to view these settings, and how do you proceed if your NIC stops working? Since networking is such an integral part of computing, this section will demonstrate how to verify, configure, and optimize your network settings.

Verifying Your Interface Configuration

If you've come from a Microsoft background, you've probably used either **winipcfg** or **ipconfig /all** to verify your network settings at the command line. Unix comes with a similar utility, named **ifconfig** (for interface config). By entering this command, you'll see all of the system's interfaces and their settings. Some versions require you to include the **-a**, or all, switch.

```
% ifconfig
rl0: flags=8802<BROADCAST,SIMPLEX,MULTICAST> mtu 1500
    options=8<VLAN_MTU>
    ether 00:05:5d:d2:19:b7
    media: Ethernet autoselect (10baseT/UTP)
    status: no carrier
rl1: flags=8802<BROADCAST,SIMPLEX,MULTICAST> mtu 1500
    options=8<VLAN_MTU>
    ether 00:05:5d:d1:ff:9d
    media: Ethernet autoselect (10baseT/UTP)
    status: no carrier
ed0: flags=8843<UP,BROADCAST,RUNNING,SIMPLEX,MULTICAST> mtu 1500
    inet 192.168.2.12 netmask 0xffffff00 broadcast 192.168.2.255
    ether 00:50:ba:de:36:33
lo0: flags=8049<UP,LOOPBACK,RUNNING,MULTICAST> mtu 16384
    inet 127.0.0.1 netmask 0xff000000
```

Your output will vary from this, but will contain similarities. This particular system isn't running the default kernel. I've removed the default IPv6, `gif`, and `faith` devices from this kernel, so they don't show in the output.

This system does have three physical interfaces (`rl0`, `rl1`, and `ed0`) and the loopback virtual interface (`lo0`). Different versions of Unix differ in their interface naming convention. For example, Linux uses `eth` for Ethernet NICs, so would show their names as `eth0`, `eth1`, and `eth2`. BSD uses the driver name for each NIC, allowing you to differentiate between different chipsets and the features available for each driver. To see the documentation for your NIC's driver, read section 4 of its driver manual. Note that you don't include the number of the interface, so look up `rl` instead of `rl0`:

```
% man 4 rl
rl -- RealTek 8129/8139 Fast Ethernet device driver
% man 4 ed
ed -- NE-2000 and WD-80x3 Ethernet driver
```

While this system has three NICs, only `ed0` is *up* and *running*. The two RealTek NICs don't have cables attached, as indicated by the *status: no carrier* lines. Accordingly, only `ed0` has an IP address (192.168.2.12), a subnet mask (0xffffff00), and a broadcast address (192.168.2.255).

That subnet mask is written in hex, as indicated by the beginning 0x. This particular mask isn't too hard to translate into decimal, if you remember that each pair of f characters (ff) is equivalent to 255. Thus, the subnet mask here is 255.255.255.0. If you find a pair of hex numbers that aren't ff (255) or 00 (0), use **bc** or the built-in calculator to translate that hex pair into decimal for you. For example, if your mask is 0xffffe000:

```
% bc
bc 1.06
Copyright 1991-1994, 1997, 1998, 2000 Free Software Foundation, Inc.
This is free software with ABSOLUTELY NO WARRANTY.
For details type `warranty'.
ibase=16
E0
224
<Ctrl-D>
```

Here, I asked **bc** to translate a base 16, or hex, number as input (ibase=16). Remember to convert any letters to uppercase, or you won't get the correct answer. Since e0 is decimal 224, this example mask is 255.255.224.0.

Verifying Your Default Gateway

Note that **ifconfig** gives the applicable status, MTU, IP address, subnet mask, broadcast address, and Ethernet (or MAC) address of each interface. However, it doesn't give the address of the default gateway or the DNS servers.

To see your default gateway address, use the **netstat**, or network status, command. Include the **-r** (routing) switch. Including the **-n** switch speeds up the results by skipping name resolution:

```
% netstat -rn
Routing tables
Internet:
Destination        Gateway            Flags    Refs     Use    Netif  Expire
default            192.168.2.100      UGS      0      72664    ed0
127.0.0.1          127.0.0.1          UH       1         46    lo0
192.168.2          link#3             UC       0          0    ed0
192.168.2.12       127.0.0.1          UGHS     0          0    lo0
192.168.2.100      00:48:54:1e:2c:76  UHLW     1          0    ed0    1172
```

Note: Linux users can also use the **route** command to receive similar results. The BSD **route** command works differently; see **man route** for details. However, **netstat -rn** works on many operating systems, including Linux and Microsoft operating systems.

In your output, look for the line that begins with the word *default*. The associated IP address is that of your default gateway. Also look at the flags for that entry. Hopefully they indicate *U* for up and *G* for gateway. This indicates that you can communicate with your gateway. If the number in the Use field isn't 0, you've actually sent your gateway that number of packets.

Finally, the last line of this output shows the MAC address of the default gateway.

Verifying Your DNS Settings

The resolver configuration file should contain your DNS settings. You can view that file with:

```
% more resolv.conf
nameserver 209.226.175.236
nameserver 204.101.251.1
nameserver 204.101.251.2
```

This particular system contains the IP addresses of three DNS servers. It's a good idea to have the addresses of at least two servers, in case your primary DNS server becomes unavailable.

While you have Internet access, you should know how to query your ISP's DNS servers and to record the results in a book containing your network settings. This will be invaluable if you ever need to recreate these settings manually. If you don't keep such a notebook, you can gather those settings from a system that does have working Internet access.

To find out the IP addresses of your DNS servers, use **dig**, the domain information groper.[2] Here, I'll ask for the *ns*, or name server, entries for my ISP:

```
% dig ns sympatico.ca

; <<>> DiG 8.3 <<>> ns sympatico.ca
;; res options: init recurs defnam dnsrch
;; got answer:
;; ->>HEADER<<- opcode: QUERY, status: NOERROR, id: 44589
;; flags: qr rd ra; QUERY: 1, ANSWER: 4, AUTHORITY: 0, ADDITIONAL: 4

;; QUERY SECTION:
;;      sympatico.ca, type = NS, class = IN

;; ANSWER SECTION:
sympatico.ca.          6h12m33s IN NS  ns5.bellnexxia.net.
sympatico.ca.          6h12m33s IN NS  ns6.bellnexxia.net.
sympatico.ca.          6h12m33s IN NS  dns1.sympatico.ca.
sympatico.ca.          6h12m33s IN NS  dns2.sympatico.ca.

;; ADDITIONAL SECTION:
ns5.bellnexxia.net.    9m36s IN A      209.226.175.236
ns6.bellnexxia.net.    9m37s IN A      209.226.175.237
dns1.sympatico.ca.     14m7s IN A      204.101.251.1
dns2.sympatico.ca.     3m56s IN A      204.101.251.2

;; Total query time: 46 msec
;; FROM: dru.domain.org to SERVER: 209.226.175.236
;; WHEN: Sun Apr 11 14:30:14 2004
;; MSG SIZE  sent: 30  rcvd: 182
```

Your output will be divided into several SECTIONs. For now, concentrate on the ANSWER SECTION, which contains the answer to your **dig** query. My ISP uses four DNS name servers, as seen in my answer. Each name server uses an IN (IPv4) record and a NS (name server) record. However, the answer shows the names of the name servers. You don't want to use names for name resolution; you want the IP addresses of your name servers.

You'll find those names mapped to IP addresses in the ADDITIONAL SECTION.

dig is also handy if you ever forget the name or IP address of your ISP's SMTP or mail server. This time, query for the mx, or mail exchange record. Here, I've shown only the ANSWER SECTION for brevity:

```
% dig mx sympatico.ca
<snip>
;; ANSWER SECTION:
sympatico.ca.          20m34s IN MX    5 mta2.sympatico.ca.
sympatico.ca.          20m34s IN MX    5 mta3.sympatico.ca.
sympatico.ca.          20m34s IN MX    5 mta1.sympatico.ca.
<snip>
```

---

[2]The *BIND 9 DNS Administration Reference Book* covers **dig** in great detail.

My ISP has three SMTP servers. See that number between the MX and the name of the mail server? That's the priority number. My ISP's mail servers all have the same priority; however, some ISPs use different priorities. If yours does, choose the mail server with the lowest priority number, as it has the highest priority.

Adding an Interface

It's one thing to know how to verify your interface configuration, but what if you need to configure an interface? Let's say you've just added another NIC to your system. Once your computer reboots, you'll want to verify that the new NIC was recognized. You can use **ifconfig** and look for an additional interface. You could also search the boot probe messages for found Ethernet addresses. Remember to include a capital E in your search:

```
% grep Ethernet /var/run/dmesg.boot
rl0: Ethernet address: 00:05:5d:d2:19:b7
rl1: Ethernet address: 00:05:5d:d1:ff:9d
ed0: <NE2000 PCI Ethernet (RealTek 8029)> port 0x9800-0x981f irq 10 ⇓
at device 11.0 on pci0
```

If your new NIC is listed, it's ready to be configured — but what if the new NIC wasn't found at bootup? The first question to ask yourself is, "Have I created a custom kernel?" If so, check your kernel configuration file; you may have removed the driver required by the new NIC.

If that's not the issue, you may have to reboot and examine your CMOS settings. Have you disabled any IRQs? Do you have enabled onboard devices that you don't use? If so, they may be wasting an IRQ, and there aren't any left over for your new NIC. If you do decide to change a CMOS setting, record the original value on a piece of paper. Change one setting, boot up and see if it made a difference. Repeat as necessary.

If the NIC is PCI, check your CMOS PnP OS setting. Sometimes changing it from yes to no will resolve the issue. Also, sometimes seating the NIC in another PCI slot solves the problem. Finally, as a last resort, you can determine if it is an IRQ problem by removing all cards except the new NIC and your video card. If the NIC is recognized, you have more cards than you have IRQs.

Configuring IP Address Information

Once your NIC is recognized, decide whether to set the IP address information manually or to use a DHCP server. Either method requires a change to /etc/rc.conf. If you prefer, you can use **sysinstall**, which will edit this file for you. This is the same utility you used when you installed your FreeBSD system. Once the utility starts, choose Configure, then Networking, and then use your **Space** bar to select Interfaces.

Otherwise, edit /etc/rc.conf directly using your favorite text editor. For example, these lines statically assign an IP address and subnet mask to rl0, and set the default gateway:

```
ifconfig_rl0="inet 192.168.2.25 netmask 255.255.255.0"
defaultrouter="192.168.2.100"
```

Also, if you're using static IP addressing, don't forget to add the IP addresses of your DNS servers to /etc/resolv.conf.

If you instead use a DHCP server to receive your IP address information, you only need to add one line to /etc/rc.conf:

```
ifconfig_rl0="DHCP"
```

You don't need to add your default router or DNS server addresses, as the lease assigned by your DNS server should include this information.

When you've saved your changes to /etc/rc.conf, initialize your network settings:

/etc/netstart

Note: If you ever need to renew your DHCP lease, use this command, but substitute rl0 for the name of your NIC:

dhclient rl0

Verifying Your DHCP Lease

If your IP settings are assigned by a DHCP server, you can see all of your settings at once by viewing your current lease.

The lease itself is contained within curly brackets. If you have several leases, the one at the top of the file is your most recent lease.

```
% more /var/db/dhclient.leases
lease {
  interface "ed0";
  fixed-address 192.168.2.12;
  option subnet-mask 255.255.255.0;
  option time-offset -18000;
  option dhcp-lease-time 345600;
  option routers 192.168.2.100;
  option dhcp-message-type 5;
  option dhcp-server-identifier 192.168.2.100;
  option domain-name-servers 209.226.175.236,204.101.251.1,204.101.251.2;
  renew 2 2004/4/13 02:13:03;
  rebind 3 2004/4/14 23:34:37;
  expire 4 2004/4/15 11:34:37;
}
```

Optimizing Your Configuration

Unless you have an extremely old NIC, or you specifically purchased a 100Mbps NIC, your NIC is 10/100Mbps. This means it is capable of negotiating a speed of 10 or 100 Mbps. It most likely also negotiates either half-duplex (cannot send and receive simultaneously) or full-duplex (can send and receive simultaneously) operation. This negotiation process occurs between the NIC and the hub or switch at the other end of your networking cable.

Obviously, 100Mbps at full-duplex is much better than 10Mbps at half-duplex. The limiting factor will be the hub or switch; its documentation will indicate its speed and mode of operation. If it doesn't support 100Mbps or full-duplex, you're not getting the most out of your NIC and your networking experience will be much slower.

However, you should also be aware that even if the hub or switch supports 100Mbps and full-duplex mode, the NIC and the hub or switch still renegotiate these values on an ongoing basis. If your NIC is always plugged into the same hub or switch, it makes sense to set these values to save the overhead of negotiation.

Whether you can do this depends upon the driver for your NIC, so carefully read the **man 4** for your driver. In my example network, I would be better off unplugging my ed0 and instead using one of the RealTek interfaces. Why? **man 4 ed** indicates that this particular driver only supports 10Mbps at half-duplex mode (IEEE 802.3 CSMA). However, **man 4 rl** indicates that this driver can be configured to use 100Mbps and full-duplex operation.

Here is an example of the lines I would use in /etc/rc.conf:

```
ifconfig_rl0="DHCP"
ifconfig_rl0="100baseTX mediaopt full-duplex"
```

There are several things to make note of here. One, the manpage will indicate which options are available and how to set them. Two, don't try to add a setting that your NIC driver doesn't support, as indicated by its manpage. Third, don't change your speed and duplex mode to a value that your hub or switch doesn't support!

To see if my changes worked, I'll plug my network cable into rl0 and issue the command **/etc/netstart**. I'll then check out the results:

```
% ifconfig rl0
rl0: flags=8843<UP,BROADCAST,RUNNING,SIMPLEX,MULTICAST> mtu 1500
    options=8<VLAN_MTU>
    inet 192.168.2.87 netmask 0xffffff00 broadcast 192.168.2.255
    ether 00:05:5d:d2:19:b7
    media: Ethernet autoselect (100baseTX <full-duplex>)
    status: active
```

Additional Resources

Original Article:

http://www.onlamp.com/pub/a/bsd/2004/05/13/FreeBSD_Basics.html

Setting Up NICs Section of Handbook:

http://www.freebsd.org/doc/en_US.ISO8859-1/books/handbook/config-network-setup.html

7.4 Using Wireshark

One of my favorite utilities in the ports collection is the network analyzer, Wireshark, formerly known as Ethereal. I've used NT's Network Monitor and Novell's Lanalyzer, but I've found that neither matches the functionality of this Open Source network analyzer.

If you've never used a network analyzer before, you may wonder why you'd want to use such a utility. If a network administrator is experiencing slow network performance, a network analyzer can help him pinpoint which NICs, cable segments, and protocols are generating the most traffic. The results can be used to determine if he needs to upgrade his cabling, change a faulty NIC, install a bridge, reorder his network bindings, consider using less chatty protocols, etc.

A security engineer can use the results to determine if his firewall system is responding to requests according to his security policy.

And finally, the results of a network analyzer provide the best learning environment to gain a practical understanding of the OSI model and how protocols actually interact with each other.

One word of caution before firing up any network analyzer: these utilities are designed to capture and show the contents of every frame that passes through a cable segment. Don't monitor a cable segment that is not part of your LAN unless you have explicit permission to do so.

Installation and Sample Capture

Before you can use Wireshark, you'll need to configure your X Server and Window Manager.[3] Once you have these, as *root*, and while connected to the Internet:

```
# pkg_add -r wireshark
# which wireshark
/usr/local/bin/wireshark
```

Running a network analyzer is an administrative task, meaning you'll have to configure your Window Manager to open this application as another user (the superuser). Alternately, you can open up an **xterm**, **su** to *root*, and start **wireshark**. If you start **wireshark** as a regular user, the utility will launch but it won't display any interfaces to monitor, meaning you won't be able to capture any packets.

wireshark has the ability to use display and capture filters which I won't be covering in this section. **man wireshark-filter** has some examples to get you started if you wish to experiment on your own. **man wireshark** also provides a handy reference for all of the menu options available within the GUI.

Let's do some example captures. We'll start with a simple **ping**. I have a computer named *alpha* with an IP address of 10.0.0.1 and another computer named *gamma* at 10.0.0.3. I've fired up **wireshark** on *gamma*, clicked on the Capture menu, and pressed Options. Because I'm *root*, I'm presented with the list of interfaces on *gamma*; I choose the one attached to my LAN cable segment and click Start. To make things a little more interesting, I'll forget to power on the computer named *alpha*.

Don't be afraid to try this exercise yourself; just **ping** a host that is either down or non-existent. I open up an **xterm** and type:

```
% ping 10.0.0.1
```

and wait; not surprisingly, nothing happens. I press **Ctrl-C** to end the **ping** and my **xterm** now reads:

```
PING 10.0.0.1 (10.0.0.1): 56 data bytes
ping: sendto: Host is down
<Ctrl-C>
--- 10.0.0.1 ping statistics ---
7 packets transmitted, 0 packets received, 100% packet loss
```

---

[3]X configuration is introduced in section 1.1.

Going back to **wireshark**, I click on the icon to Stop the running live capture and look at the results. I do have seven packets listed, but they are all ARP (Address Resolution Protocol) packets, not the ICMP echo/reply packets you would expect with **ping**.

For those of you who never had the opportunity to yawn your way through a lecture on the OSI model, I've just demonstrated the first rule of transmission on a TCP/IP network. No unicast packets — that is packets addressed to a specific host — can enter the wire until the MAC address of the NIC who will receive the packets is known; this is the job of ARP, the address resolution protocol.

As you can see from your capture, ARP isn't that complicated a protocol. It sends out a broadcast (to MAC address ff:ff:ff:ff:ff:ff) onto the cable segment that asks "who has 10.0.0.1? tell 10.0.0.3". This is the equivalent of your four-year-old yelling into a crowded room, "Where is my Mommy?" It's not the most elegant way of accomplishing a task, but it's usually quite effective.

Because 10.0.0.1 wasn't available to answer, there was no MAC address to send packets to, and **ping** was unable to send out its ICMP packets.

Analyzing a Capture

Let's fire up *alpha*, start another capture, and try pinging 10.0.0.1 again.

```
% ping 10.0.0.1
PING 10.0.0.1 (10.0.0.1): 56 data bytes
64 bytes from 10.0.0.1: icmp_seq=0 ttl=255 time=0.675 ms
64 bytes from 10.0.0.1: icmp_seq=1 ttl=255 time=0.522 ms
64 bytes from 10.0.0.1: icmp_seq=2 ttl=255 time=0.508 ms
64 bytes from 10.0.0.1: icmp_seq=3 ttl=255 time=0.498 ms
<Ctrl-C>
--- 10.1.0.2 ping statistics ---
4 packets transmitted, 4 packets received, 0% packet loss
round-trip min/avg/max/stddev = 0.498/0.539/0.675/0.061 ms
```

If I end the capture, I'll see that ten packets were captured. Two of these will be ARP packets; the first of these asks "who has 10.0.0.1? Tell 10.0.0.3". The second is the reply from 10.0.0.1 with its MAC address. The other eight packets are ICMP packets; half of these are "Echo (ping) requests", the other half are "Echo (ping) replies".

If you repeat this capture again and transmit six packets, the capture will only show the 12 ICMP packets. What happened to the two ARP packets? To find out, from your **xterm** type:

```
% arp -a
alpha (10.0.0.1) at 0:0:b4:3c:56:40 on fxp0 [ethernet]
```

ARP utilizes a cache (area of memory) where it keeps a list of which MAC addresses it has recently resolved; this cuts down on the number of broadcasts. Since ARP already knew *alpha*'s MAC address, it didn't have to issue another request for it.

If as superuser you type **arp -da** you will remove all the entries in your ARP cache, meaning **arp -a** will just return you back to your prompt.

If you then repeat the capture and **ping**, you'll notice the two extra ARP entries will reappear. And repeating **arp -a** will show *alpha*'s MAC address again.

Capturing a 3-way Handshake

Now let's look at some FTP traffic. At *gamma*, I've started a capture. At *alpha*, I've typed:

```
% ftp 10.0.0.3
Connected to 10.0.0.3
220 gamma FTP server (Version 6.00LS) ready.
Name (10.0.0.0:genisis): anonymous
530 User anonymous unknown.
ftp: Login failed.
Remote system type is UNIX.
Using binary mode to transfer files.
ftp>
```

I haven't set up an anonymous FTP login account at *gamma*, so the login failed. When I stop the capture, I have a total of ten packets.

The first three packets used the TCP protocol and represent TCP's three-way handshake as the flags were set at [SYN] (step 1 of handshake), [SYN, ACK] (step 2 of handshake), and [ACK] (step 3 of handshake). No FTP packets were sent until the handshake process finished successfully.

The first FTP packet was sent to *alpha*, and contained the information that first appeared on *alpha*'s screen:

```
220 gamma FTP server (Version 6.00LS) ready.
```

This is actually the first packet we've captured that had a data payload attached to it. Highlight it in Wireshark and look at the second section of your Wireshark screen where it says:

```
+ Frame4
+ Ethernet II
+ Internet Protocol
+ Transmission Control Protocol
+ File Transfer Protocol
```

This section allows you to view the various encapsulations that each layer of the OSI model added to the original data packet, from the physical layer up to the application layer. If you click on the + (plus) next to a layer, you will expand all the gory details that that layer added to the IP header. If you highlight something interesting, note that a portion of the data in the third section of Wireshark will become darker. This section of Wireshark shows the actual 1s and 0s (written in hex) that were sent to the NIC. Keep in mind that your NIC is actually raising and lowering the voltages on the cable segment to transmit all these 1s and 0s. Isn't networking amazing?

The next two FTP packets are *alpha*'s login information and *gamma*'s response:

```
530 User anonymous unknown.
ftp: Login failed.
```

The last two FTP packets are *alpha*'s request for system information, and *gamma*'s response:

```
Remote system type is UNIX.
Using binary mode to transfer files.
```

Note that the FTP utility on *alpha* modified *gamma*'s actual response slightly when it displayed it on *alpha*'s screen.

The rest of the TCP packets are acknowledgements, as TCP is responsible for ensuring reliable delivery of data.

I've kept the FTP prompt at *alpha*, so let's start another capture:

```
ftp> quit
% ftp 10.0.0.3
Connected to 10.0.0.3.
220 gamma FTP server (Version 6.00LS) ready.
Name (10.0.0.3:genisis): genisis
331 Password required for genisis.
Password:
230 User genisis logged in.
Remote system type is UNIX.
Using binary mode to transfer files.
ftp>
```

If I end the capture and analyze the packets, the first two packets are the TCP packets that ended the failed FTP session. Note that *alpha* sent a [FIN, ACK] to request the connection be closed, and *gamma* responded with a [RST] to reset the connection to make it available to other potential TCP sessions.

This was followed by another three-way handshake involving three TCP packets. Take a close look at the FTP response/reply pairs. When the user genisis typed in the password at *alpha*, the FTP client did not display the password at the terminal. However, this information was sent in the clear to *gamma* and wasn't hidden from the packet analyzer — one of many reasons FTP is an insecure protocol and why you don't analyze the traffic on other people's networks.

These exercises should provide you with a starting point for using Wireshark. If you are interested in how various operating systems send and receive network traffic, here are some interesting exercises to try on your own:

- Start a capture on a cable segment with an Windows 2000 Server and a Windows XP workstation; power on the XP workstation and end your capture once it has successfully logged into the network.

- Start a capture on a cable segment with a Novell server and a Novell client. From the Novell client, attach to the server and map a network drive.

- Start a capture on a cable segment with an NFS server. Have an NFS client mount a filesystem being exported by the NFS server and copy data to and from the mountpoint.

More Wireshark details and examples are covered in section 10.3.

Additional Resources

Original Article:

http://www.onlamp.com/pub/a/bsd/2000/08/16/FreeBSD_Basics.html

Wireshark Website:

http://www.wireshark.org/

Protocols.com:

http://www.protocols.com

7.5 Accessing a Cisco Router

In this section, I'd like to take a look at accessing a Cisco router from a FreeBSD box using a rollover cable.

Normally, the only time you need to access a Cisco router is to view or change its configurations and you use a network access utility such as **telnet** to do so. However, when you first purchase a router, or if you accidently erase your configurations, you can't telnet into it as the interfaces will be down and they won't have any IP addresses set to telnet into. If this is the case, you'll need to access the router via its console interface from a serial interface on your computer.

In Microsoft land, the Hyperterminal utility is usually used to do this. While you don't get Hyperterminal on your FreeBSD computer, there are two built-in utilities and several programs in the ports collection that provide this functionality. I'd like to demonstrate the use of **cu** and **tip**. I'll also install and demonstrate **minicom**, **kermit**, and **seyon** in this section.

Initial Configuration of Router with cu

If you're setting up a Cisco router for the first time, find the long, flat, light blue rollover cable that came with the router. This cable is easy to recognize if you compare both ends of the cable. You'll also see why it's called a rollover cable as the pinouts are opposite to each other; in effect, the cable was rolled over when the second connection was crimped on.

Plug one end of the rollover cable into the connection at the back of the router that is marked console in the same light blue color as the cable. Don't plug the other end of the cable into your FreeBSD computer yet, as you need to use one of the serial adapters that came with the router. You should have a 9-pin and a 25-pin adapter. Take a look at the back of your FreeBSD computer to see which serial port you have available to use. On my system, *com1* was taken by my mouse, but *com2* was free. Accordingly, I plugged the rollover cable into the 25-pin adapter, then I connected it to *com2* on my computer. Once everything was connected, I turned my FreeBSD computer back on and turned on the power switch at the back of the Cisco router.

Note: Newer Cisco rollover cables don't require an adapter as it is built into one end of the cable.

The last thing we need to sort out before starting is the FreeBSD device names for the com ports on your computer. Com ports are /dev/cuad# where the numbering starts at 0. If you used *com1*, you're using cuad0; since I'm using *com2*, I'll be using cuad1. Also, because we will be directly accessing serial devices, all of the utilities mentioned require you to be the superuser to use them.

Let's start with the utilities that come with FreeBSD — **cu** and **tip**. To use **cu**, simply specify your com port using the **-l** or line switch and a speed of 9600 baud using the speed switch like so:

```
# cu -l /dev/cuad1 -s 9600
Connected.
```

I'll now press **Enter** and I've entered the setup utility on the Cisco router. Note that I'll be prompted to set IP addresses on the interfaces, the enable password, and the telnet (virtual terminal) password. These are the minimum configurations that will be required to be able to access a Cisco router without the rollover cable. You'll note that in Cisco, most questions have an answer in "[]" (brackets) meaning you can just press **Enter** if you're satisfied with that answer. If you aren't, type in your desired response. The setup process should look like this:

```
First, would you like to see the current interface summary?  [yes]:
Any interface listed with OK? value "NO" does not have a valid configuration

Interface  IP-Address   OK? Method Status  Protocol
Ethernet0  unassigned   NO  unset  up      down
Serial0    unassigned   NO  unset  down    down

Configuring global parameters:
Enter host name [Router]:
The enable secret is a one-way cryptographic secret used
instead of the enable password when it exists.
Enter enable secret:

The enable password is used when there is no enable secret
and when using older software and some boot images.
Enter enable password:
Enter virtual terminal password:
Configure SNMP Network Management?  [yes]: no
Configure IPX? [no]:
Configure IP? [yes]:
Configure IGRP routing?  [yes]: no
Configure RIP routing?  [no]:

Configuring interface parameters:
Configuring interface Ethernet0:
Is this interface in use?  [yes]:
Configure IP on this interface?  [yes]:
IP address for this interface:  10.0.0.100
Number of bits in subnet field [0]:
Class A network is 10.0.0.0, 0 subnet bits; mask is /8

Configuring interface Serial0:
Is this interface in use?  [yes] no
The following configuration command script was created:
<snip>
Use this configuration?  [yes/no]: yes
Building configuration...
Use the enable mode 'configure' command to modify this configuration.
```

```
Press RETURN to get started!
Router>
```

My configurations are now finished and I'm presented with the user mode prompt. If you're familiar with your Cisco IOS commands, you can proceed to use them as usual.

When you wish to disconnect from the Cisco router by closing the **cu** session, type the tilde key followed by period:

```
~.
```

then press the **Enter** key. You should receive a Disconnected message and get your FreeBSD prompt back.

Using tip

Now let's try re-accessing the router using the **tip** utility. With **tip**, you don't use line or speed switches as **tip** expects you to use an entry from the /etc/remote file. Let's take a quick look at the relevant section of that file:

```
% tail /etc/remote
# Finger friendly shortcuts
sio0|com1:dv=/dev/cuad0:br#9600:pa=none:
sio1|com2:dv=/dev/cuad1:br#9600:pa=none:
sio2|com3:dv=/dev/cuad2:br#9600:pa=none:
sio3|com4:dv=/dev/cuad3:br#9600:pa=none:
sio4|com5:dv=/dev/cuad4:br#9600:pa=none:
sio5|com6:dv=/dev/cuad5:br#9600:pa=none:
sio6|com7:dv=/dev/cuad6:br#9600:pa=none:
sio7|com8:dv=/dev/cuad7:br#9600:pa=none:
```

Thanks to these shortcuts, to use **tip** I simply have to type:

```
# tip com2
connected
```

When I press **Enter**, I'll again see my router> prompt meaning I'm back into Cisco's user mode prompt. When I'm finished my **tip** session, I disconnect from the router by typing:

```
~^D
[EOT]
```

You need a bit more finger coordination for that disconnect sequence. Hold down **Shift** while you press the ~ (tilde) key; keep your finger on the **Shift** key as you press the **Control** key, then the letter **D**.

Third Party Serial Communications

Let's install some applications that can be used to access the Cisco router. I'll start with **minicom**:

```
# pkg_add -r minicom
```

The first time you use **minicom**, you'll want to enter its setup mode by using the **-s** switch like so:

```
# minicom -s
```

This will bring up the minicom configuration menu. I'll arrow down to the Serial port setup and press **Enter**. I'll then press **A** to change the Serial Device from /dev/cuad0 to /dev/cuad1. I'll then press **E** to change the Bps/Par/Bits, then press **E** again to select 9600. Finally, I'll press **F** to turn off Hardware Flow Control. I'll press the **Escape** key to leave this configuration menu, arrow down to Save setup as.. and I'll save this entry as "cisco". Once my configuration is saved, I'll arrow down to Exit at which point **minicom** will connect to the Cisco router and I'll see my router> prompt.

When you're finished and wish to end the **minicom** session, press **Ctrl-A**, let go of the **Control** key, then press **Q**. You'll want to choose Yes to leave without reset. If you ever need to access the Cisco router again using **minicom**, simply type:

```
# minicom cisco
```

to initiate the connection.

Let's move on to **kermit**:

```
# pkg_add -r kermit
```

To use **kermit**, type the following:

```
# kermit
C-Kermit> set line /dev/cuad1
C-Kermit> set carrier-watch off
C-Kermit> connect
```

then press the **Enter** key to get the router> prompt. When you're finished with your **kermit** session, hold down the **Control** key while pressing the \ (backslash) key, then let go and press the **Shift** key while pressing **C**. You'll return to the prompt where you can:

```
C-Kermit>
C-Kermit> quit
Closing /dev/cuad1...OK
```

The last port we'll take a look at is the one that is used from an X Window session:

```
# pkg_add -r seyon
```

Once installed, start an X Window session and, as the superuser start **seyon** from an **xterm**:

```
# seyon -modems /dev/cuad1
```

Two windows will open; one of the windows shows your connection to the router, while the other window contains the **seyon** commands. When you're finished with the router, you can press the Exit option with your mouse to end your session.

If you've ever used any of these utilities before, or have followed along by installing them for yourself, you'll realize that each of the utilities discussed in this section has far greater capabilities than I've mentioned. Even though I've concentrated on using them to access a Cisco router, these utilities provide powerful serial port communications. If you want to explore their other possibilities, every utility I've demonstrated does have an extensive man page for your perusal.

For more examples for working with a Cisco router, see section 8.11.

Additional Resources

Original Article:

```
http://www.onlamp.com/pub/a/bsd/2001/10/11/FreeBSD_Basics.html
```

8 Configuring Services

8.1 Building a Unix Server

I found myself spending time installing servers for a small startup. As I did, I remembered the myriad details needed to create servers optimized for both performance and security. While it would easily take a book to explain all the details, this section can certainly cover some of the common pitfalls to watch out for and the logical approach necessary to do the job correctly. I'll demonstrate for a FreeBSD system, but the same logic applies to your operating system of choice.

Planning the Install

If you're like the typical open source user, you spend a lot of time experimenting by installing, reinstalling, and uninstalling software. In the beginning, that software usually includes the OS itself as you discover exactly what you can and can't do to a system! While this is a fantastic learning experience, it's a luxury you can't afford when you move on to servers in a working environment. Enter production systems, no downtime, and the raised eyebrows and disparaging looks (or worse) from your superiors when something doesn't work.

It's no exaggeration to think of a server install as 99% preparation and 1% configuration. Sure, you can finish quickly by installing the operating system and applications with their default settings. There isn't a sysadmin out there who hasn't had to fix the fallout from such an install usually done by someone else who left town without a forwarding number.

You can save yourself a lot of future grief if you start by clarifying your superiors' needs. Put all of the cards on the table so that you understand exactly what they want and they understand what is technically feasible. You don't want to spend a week configuring and testing Apache 2 only to find out that the web-mail program your manager has his heart set on only works with Apache 1.x. Or to hear, "What do you mean, I have to download all of my email?" after configuring a POP3 server even though you'd originally tried to sell management on the greater security provided by an IMAP server. Yes, there's often a wide gulf between management's software needs and the technical details a sysadmin concerns himself with; it may take all of your communication skills and patience to work through this preparation phase.

Finally, if your manager is the type who is always discovering new software and constantly asking you to install "just one more thing," make sure she understands that servers are special; once you've started, you'll only install what you've agreed on and written down.

The Install

After you've agreed on the software to install, you'll naturally progress to the design phase. Will you install all of the software on one server or will you spread different services out among different servers? The answer will depend upon the company's security policy, the available hardware, and the budget available for acquiring additional hardware.

For each server, go out and buy yourself a binder. You'll need thorough documentation that you create as you go along. I can hear you groaning now or at least thinking, "I'll write down what I did later when I have more time." You won't. Even if you do, you won't remember half the stuff you did, especially the stuff you did at 3 a.m. because something still wasn't working and the server needed to be live by 6 a.m.

Next, decide whether to install using a CD or the two floppies and an Internet connection. If the system is not behind a firewall, buy or burn yourself a CD. The Number One rule when installing any server operating system is *never* expose it to the Internet until you have secured the OS and applications. This means it needs a firewall. It also means that you don't start creating rules on the firewall to let connections in to the server until you're satisfied the server is secure. (Instead, start with temporary firewall rules that only allow connections in from a specific testing system.)

When you reach the partitioning portion of the **sysintsall**, pause to consider the purpose of the server you're installing. The default partition sizes are usually fine for a desktop but rarely so for a server. For example, when I chose **a** for automatic on my 6.2 desktop system, I received:

```
512 MB          /
2022 MB         swap
2035 MB         /var
512 MB          /tmp
144 GB          /usr
```

This is totally out of whack for a server. If you start installing web, ftp, or mail servers, you want to log their activities. Logs go in /var where 2035 MB of space probably won't cut it. Things are even worse on a mail server, with mail stored in /var/mail until the user picks it up. Depending upon the type of server, /usr may also need to be fairly big as this partition contains user directories and installed software.

Unless experience has taught you otherwise, a safer assumption is to keep /, swap, and /tmp as-is and divvy up the rest of your disk space between /usr and /var. I usually press **a** for automatic, then **d** to delete /usr and /var. I can then use **c** to create more reasonable sizes. Ideally, I like to use two hard disks where /usr is the rest of disk 1 and /var takes over disk 2.

The other thing to keep in the back of your mind is inodes, those entries the file system uses to keep track of your files. You have a limited number of inodes. If you run out, you can't create any more files on your file system unless you delete files or repartition. Running out of inodes usually isn't an issue unless your partition will store a huge amount of very small files. The periodic script /etc/periodic/daily/400.status-disks emails *root* each night with the output from the **df** (disk free) command. After the installation, edit that script to add the **-hi** switch after **df**. This will change the output to human-readable with inode information. That way you can monitor both disk and inode usage on a daily basis.[1]

Finally, the installer will ask you what to install. For servers, I fall into the "install the bare necessities then add what you need" group of folks as I find it easier than "installing more than you need than taking out what you don't." To me this means no docs, manpages, or games as I always have an Internet-attached system nearby should I need to look something up or take a break. I do, however, choose src so I can recompile the kernel and rebuild the world. (Yes, you'll be recompiling the kernel to optimize it for the needs of a server.)

I also believe that X does not belong on a server. Servers should be lean, mean, performance machines without the prettiness, bloat, or security implications provided by a GUI. If other admins or technical support staff will administer the server, I'll instead install Webmin or Usermin.[2] These applications have configuration options to

---

[1] See section 2.13 for more details on periodic tasks.
[2] Webmin and Usermin are introduced in sections 4.4 and 4.5.

allow each support staff to access only the services they need to administer, with the added bonus of providing a GUI interface they can access from the comfort of their web browser.

You will most likely be installing software on the server and will want to keep that software up-to-date. While I'm probably the biggest fan of the ports collection out there, I don't install it on my servers as I can make better use of the 500 MB or so of /usr real estate needed to maintain it. I'll demonstrate how to use **porteasy** to make a leaner equivalent to the full ports tree.

Post-Install Configuration

When the installer finishes, follow through the post-install configuration menus. When it asks to create a user, make sure to create an account for yourself with a good password. Create an excellent password for the superuser account. When asked to view the ports collection, I say "yes" so I can install **porteasy**.

One of the first tasks I do after rebooting into the new system — before I even begin installing the required server applications — is to **csup** all of the changes to the operating system that have occurred since its release.

However, the very first thing I do once the install is complete is to grab my server binder. Up to this point I've taken only rough notes on my network settings and partition sizes. Even I have trouble deciphering my handwriting, so it's time to create some printable documentation. This is where **scp** (secure copy) comes in handy. I make sure to have **sshd** running on another system with a configured printer, then copy over my hardware information:

```
% scp /var/run/dmesg.boot dru@192.168.1.10:/usr/home/dru
```

The above command will access the SSH daemon running on 192.168.1.10, login as the user *dru* and copy /var/run/dmesg.boot from this system to *dru*'s home directory on the other system. As you can see, **scp** works just like the **cp** command, but allows the source or destination file to be on another system.

I'll then send the output of my NIC, default gateway, DNS, and partition and swap settings:

```
% ifconfig > nic_settings && \
    scp nic_settings dru@192.168.1.10:/usr/home/dru
% netstat -rn > gateway && scp gateway dru@192.168.1.10:/usr/home/dru
% scp /etc/resolv.conf dru@192.168.1.10:/usr/home/dru
% df -h > disk_usage && scp disk_usage dru@192.168.1.10:/usr/home/dru
% swapinfo > swap_usage && scp swap_usage dru@192.168.1.10:/usr/home/dru
```

From the system running **sshd**, I can now print the copied files and add them to my binder.

Securing the OS

Now it's time to start securing the system. First, I create a cvs-supfile:

```
# more /root/cvs-supfile
*default host=cvsup.ca.freebsd.org
*default base=/usr/local/etc/cvsup
*default prefix=/usr
*default tag=RELENG_6_2
*default release=cvs delete use-rel-suffix compress
src-all
```

Choose a host= geographically close to you and make sure that the tag= matches your OS version so you can track security advisories and critical fixes.

I'll then create the base directory and download the changed source:

```
# mkdir /usr/local/etc/cvsup
# csup -L 2 /root/cvs-supfile
```

While the download continues, I start my hardening routine. I'll also create an SSH banner on the server and use the AllowUsers option to limit SSH access to myself and other authorized staff.[3]

When the download finishes, it's time to rebuild the world and the generic kernel:

```
# cd /usr/src
# make buildworld
# make buildkernel
# make installkernel
# make installworld
```

After rebooting into the up-to-date OS, it's time to strip the kernel. After copying /usr/src/sys/i386/conf/GENERIC to another file, I'll carefully review each line and remove the hardware and options that aren't relevant to the server. I'll then read through /usr/src/sys/i386/conf/NOTES to see if there are additional options that will increase the security or performance of the server.

Next, I install and reboot into the new kernel, printing out a copy of the kernel configuration file with comments explaining why I modified the options I did, for my server book. I then copy my kernel config file to another location such as /usr/local/etc. At this point, it's a design decision whether to remove /usr/src from the system. Removing it frees up about 400 MB of space; however, /usr/src is sometimes necessary to implement the solution to a security advisory.

Installing Software

Now that you have an up-to-date OS and an optimized kernel, it's time to start installing software. While using **pkg_add -r** to install pre-compiled binaries is quick and convenient, it isn't always the best choice for a server. The same goes for installing a port without first reading its Makefile and combing through the installation instructions at the application's web site. Many server applications come with **make** options which influence the application's behavior and performance. Be aware of these options before you compile the binary. This brings us back to the "99% preparation, 1% configuration" truism.

It also brings us back to your server documentation. As you install a service, carefully note the **make** options you used. For example, here are two entries from one of my server installs:

```
#installed from /usr/ports/www/apache2
#use "make show-options" to see available make options
#use "make show-modules" to see available modules
#use anon auth and disable SSI and autoindexing:
make -DWITHOUT_AUTH -DWITHOUT_MODULES="autoindex" \
     -DWITHOUT_MODULES="include" install clean
```

---

[3]SSH server configuration details are covered in section 10.14.

```
#installed from /usr/ports/ftp/pure-ftpd
#install as stand-alone server with privilege separation
make -DWITH-PRIVSEP -DWITHOUT-INETD install clean
```

Knowing what options you used to compile the binary will greatly assist in troubleshooting future configuration issues. You'll also be able to repeat these options when you eventually upgrade the software.

How did I get those port directories to **cd** into when I didn't install the ports collection? This is where **porteasy** comes into play: it downloads just the ports skeletons you need. To do so, first set up your environment:

```
# setenv CVSROOT :pserver:anoncvs@anoncvs.at.FreeBSD.org/home/ncvs
# touch /root/.cvspass
```

Then, as you need a ports skeleton, tell **porteasy** what you want:

```
# porteasy -u www/apache2
```

That's it — all the convenience of the ports collection without maintaining the entire collection.

Keeping Software Up-to-Date

porteasy will also assist in keeping your software up-to-date. I create a script like this:

```
echo "Updating installed ports skeletons"
porteasy -uI
echo "The following ports need upgrading:"
porteasy -s | grep "<"
```

Note that this script will keep my ports skeleton up-to-date and inform me of out-of-date ports; however, it won't upgrade them for me. This is actually ideal for a server as you never want to upgrade applications blindly. Instead, carefully plan the upgrade, research any changes to the new version and their impact on your current configurations, and schedule the upgrade for a time that will least impact users on the off-chance that the upgrade results in an unforeseen glitch. Yes, I'm talking about more preparation. Most major server applications have an upgrade section to their documentation; all applications have an UPDATING or README that comes with the new version. Read them all.

A Final Word on Configuration

The actual configuration of an application will definitely depend on the application. Fortunately, most of the major server products provide excellent documentation at their web sites. If anything, a poor sysadmin might suffer from information overload!

If it's your first time plunging into a product, especially something as complicated as a web or mail server, take the time to skim through all of the documentation before you install anything. Much of it won't apply, but it will give you a good idea of what options you have and what the configuration will entail. You'll probably also find sections that you'll want to print out and add to your server binder until you're more familiar with the product.

I always print out a copy of the original configuration file(s) that come with an application and store it in my server binder. I find it convenient to pencil in the changes that I made with comments to myself reminding me why I did so. An alternate approach is to carefully comment your changes as you make them and to print out the final result. Either way, you do want a hard copy to refer to. (It goes without saying that you'll have at least one software backup copy of both the original and modified configuration files.)

Additional Resources

Original Article:

`http://www.onlamp.com/pub/a/bsd/2004/08/26/FreeBSD_Basics.html`

Using Cvsup Section of Handbook:

`http://www.freebsd.org/doc/en_US.ISO8859-1/books/handbook/cvsup.html`

Tuning FreeBSD:

`http://silverwraith.com/papers/freebsd-tuning.php`

8.2 Unix Printing Basics

Somewhere there must be a theory stating that the amount of configuration knowledge required is directly proportional to the need for using said configured service. This is certainly often the case with printing.

True, the configuration interfaces have steadily improved in the past few years. However, administrators still need a fair bit of knowledge to understand which particular software bits they need to make the most of the features of a particular printer. Additionally, the vast array of software available often confuses new users. As an example, there are over 300 print applications available in the ports collection. Where exactly does one start?

In this section, I'll explain some basic printing terminology. I'll also discuss some of the available applications for each printing component and cover some of the pros and cons of each application. Throughout, I'll demonstrate applying this knowledge to an example printer.

If you haven't already, take some time and skim through the printing section of the FreeBSD Handbook. While you may not understand everything, that section will still give you a good overview of the printing process on a Unix system. If you're new to hardware, you'll also find the hardware setup and troubleshooting subsections very helpful if you're having problems physically setting up your printer.

The Spooler

Let's start with the various components available when setting up your printer. Regardless of the operating system, the main printing software component will always be the spooler. This piece of software receives your print request, known as a print job, and places it in a print queue. As the name suggests, a queue is a lineup of jobs waiting for their turn to receive access to the hardware printer. The spooler monitors both the queue and the printer. As the printer becomes available, the spooler sends the next job for printing. Once the print successfully completes, the spooler removes the job from the queue and moves on to the next job.

Your FreeBSD system comes with **lpd**, the original Unix spooler. Another popular spooler, LPRng (LPR new generation), is available in the ports collection.

Both spoolers use the printer capability database located in `/etc/printcap` for configuration. Did you notice that the bulk of the printing section of the Handbook deals with the proper configuration of this file? That's for good reason; all printing components rely on the spooler, which calls them based on their appearance in the spooler configuration file. Depending upon your particular printer, it may be easier to create this file manually or use a printer configuration tool to create the necessary `/etc/printcap` entries. I'll discuss both methods shortly.

Ghostscript

Technically, a configured spooler will allow you to access your printer. You'll often want additional components, though. After all, your printer isn't very useful if it can only print gobbledygook or unformatted text with all of the appeal of plain ASCII on a terminal. It's also rather disappointing if your particular printer model comes with a slew of features, none of which you can access.

One of the required components is usually Ghostscript, especially if your printer was created for the home market. Most Unix programs assume that your printer speaks the PostScript printing language found in PostScript (which usually means expensive) printers.

Ghostscript provides a collection of print drivers. A print driver provides the necessary translation between programs and the language spoken by your particular printer. It also includes the command set required to access the features provided by your printer. Additionally, a print driver often uses a *PPD* (PostScript Printer Description) file to understand the capabilities of a particular printer.

Magic Filters and Configuration Utilities

Another useful component is the magic, smart, or input filter. This software recognizes different print formats and sends a job first to a necessary conversion program. Such filters usually come with a configuration utility, allowing for a fairly easy setup. Example filters from the ports collection include Apsfilter, CUPS, and Magicfilter.

Finally, your window manager may also provide a printer subsystem that includes a printer setup utility. For example, KDE uses KDEPrint, and Gnome provides the Gnome Print Manager.

Researching Your Printer

OK, now that we're aware of the various pieces, where do we go from here? Let's start with a checklist:

- A spooler (FreeBSD comes with **lpd**).
- Ghostscript.
- A print driver specific to your printer.

Depending upon which ports you've installed on your system, you may or may not already have Ghostscript. To see if you do:

```
% gs -v
GNU Ghostscript 7.07 (2003-05-17)
Copyright (C) 2003 artofcode LLC, Benicia, CA. All rights reserved.
```

Note that the name of the Ghostscript executable is **gs**. If you receive similar output, you have Ghostscript. If for some reason you don't keep your ports up-to-date, double-check that your version of Ghostscript is the latest available from the ports collection. Since Ghostscript is a collection of drivers and the maintainers constantly add new drivers, you do want a recent version of Ghostscript.

If you instead receive an error message about a missing command, install Ghostscript:

```
# pkg_add -r ghostscript-gnu
```

During the install, you'll receive a menu asking which portions to install. If you want, deselect the drivers you don't need. If you're not sure, stick with the defaults.

Next, you need to research the availability of a print driver for your particular printer model. This will let you know if there is an available Unix print driver and provide clues regarding the best route for installing and configuring that driver. Start your search at the Un*x printer compatibility database at http://www. linuxprinting.org.

As an example, I have an HP OfficeJet 4110. Fortunately for me, there is an entry in the database for this printer. Hopefully, your particular model will be here as well. (If you're in the market for a printer, check out the Suggested Printers for Free Software Users section of the website for practical advice on choosing a printer).

Click on the hyperlink for your model to receive a detailed description of the features and quirks provided by the driver. Before proceeding, carefully read through the driver description to see if there's anything you need to know. I made note of the following:

- The **hpijs** driver is the recommended driver for my printer.

- The **hplip** driver will allow me to access my printer's scanning and maintenance features.

Armed with this information, my next stop is the http://www.freshports.org search engine to see if there are any related FreeBSD ports. A search for **hpijs** and **hplip** shows a port for each.

For now, I'll install the **hpijs** driver:

```
# pkg_add -r hpijs
```

Note: Always check the ports collection for your driver. The print drivers that come with Ghostscript are compiled into its binary. Sometimes you'll need an additional port as a Ghostscript add-on to access the printer's full feature set. In my case, **hpijs** is an add-on to the ijs driver compiled into Ghostscript. I don't need **hplip** for printing per se, only for accessing the additional features of my all-in-one printer.

Check Your Hardware

Once you have Ghostscript and any necessary drivers installed, double-check that your FreeBSD system sees your printer. The FreeBSD Handbook has explicit instructions for testing a printer connected to a parallel or serial port. However, my printer uses a USB interface. Since USB is hot swappable, I can plug my printer into an available USB port without having to first shutdown the system. As soon as I make the connection, my console (**Alt-F1**) shows this message:

```
ulpt0: Hewlett-Packard officejet 4100 series, rev 2.00/1.00,
 addr 2, iclass 7/1
ulpt0: using bi-directional mode
```

Which is an encouraging sign.

Note: If your message instead shows ugen0 (the generic USB driver) message, you probably removed ulpt support from your kernel configuration file. Rebuild your kernel with device ulpt.

Choosing a Configuration Tool

How you proceed is a matter of personal preference. My favorite configuration utility is **apsfilter**, as it provides an easy-to-use, lightweight text interface. If your recommended driver is compiled into Ghostscript, you'll find configuring and testing your printer a breeze with **apsfilter**. It will automagically create the correct entries in /etc/printcap for you.

How do you find out if Ghostscript includes your driver? Once you've installed Ghostscript, type **gs -h**. You'll receive a page of output, so you may want to **grep** for your particular driver name. In my case, searching for **hpijs** will fail but searching for **ijs** will succeed.

Unfortunately, Apsfilter isn't the best approach for this particular printer. My recommended driver is an add-on to Ghostscript and Apsfilter is a script that lets you choose from the drivers compiled into Ghostscript. It would take a lot of trial and error on my part to find the closest driver in that list. I'm not really into a lot of trial and error. Besides, I want to take full advantage of the correct driver.

Instead, I'll take a look at what came with that **hpijs** port I installed:

```
# pkg_info -Lx hpijs
```

I'll receive a lot of output which includes a **foomatic-rip** binary and several hundred PPD files.

What exactly is **foomatic-rip**? It is a script that understands a database of all known printer drivers, even those not compiled into Ghostscript.

Using foomatic-rip

While it may seem counterintuitive, it looks like my easiest course of action is to edit /etc/printcap manually, telling it to use **foomatic-rip** and my printer's PPD file. The location of the PPD for my 4110 series printer can be found with:

```
# pkg_info -Lx hpijs | grep 4110
/usr/local/share/ppd/HP/HP-OfficeJet_4110-hpijs.ppd.gz
```

I'll create a spooling directory called OfficeJet to hold the print jobs sent to my OfficeJet printer:

```
# mkdir /var/spool/lpd/OfficeJet
```

Now, I'm ready to add the following lines to /etc/printcap:

```
lp|OfficeJet:\
    :lp=/dev/ulpt0:\
    :af=/usr/local/share/ppd/HP/HP-OfficeJet_4110-hpijs.ppd.gz:\
    :if=/usr/local/bin/foomatic-rip:\
    :sd=/var/spool/lpd/OfficeJet:\
    :sh:
```

Even if you don't have to create your /etc/printcap file manually, it's important to understand the contents of this file so that you can troubleshoot your printing system. **man printcap** will always show you the meanings of the various capabilities (for example, af, if, and sd). Let's pick apart this file:

```
lp|OfficeJet:\
```

The default printer is always lp. It can have as many nicknames as you want to give it, as long as you separate them with the pipe character (|). Here, I've given the nickname OfficeJet. Note that every line in this file (except for the very last one) ends with a :\ and every line (except the very first one) begins with a : (colon).

lp in the second line refers to the physical device where the printer attaches. Since mine is a USB printer, it uses /dev/ulpt0.

af gives the full path to the accounting or PPD file.

if gives the full path to the input filter. Here, I use **foomatic-rip**. If you instead use **apsfilter**, the entry it creates for you will refer to **apsfilter**.

sd gives the full path to the spooling directory.

sh stands for suppress header, so the spooler will not create a header page with the print job.

Creating a Test Page

Once I've finished configuring /etc/printcap, I need to tell **lpd** that its configuration file has changed:

 # /etc/rc.d/lpd restart

I'm now ready to try printing a test page. From the command line as a regular user, I'll ask for a print out of my printer configuration file:

% lpr /etc/printcap

Excellent, my printer starts to make printing noises. My console (**Alt-F1**) also gives messages showing that **foomatic-rip** is doing its thing.

For my next test, I start an X session where I'm using KDE as the window manager. I open up the Firefox browser, click on the File menu –> Print Preview, and see that this function works. I then successfully print a web page from my browser.

I next try to print a specified page from an OpenOffice document. Again, success. See how the various programs on a system all rely on a properly configured /etc/printcap file? With this file setup correctly, you should be able to print from any application.

Additional Resources

Original Article:

`http://www.onlamp.com/pub/a/bsd/2004/07/08/FreeBSD_Basics.html`

Printing section of Handbook:

`http://www.freebsd.org/doc/en_US.ISO8859-1/books/handbook/printing.html`

Interaction of Ghostscript and Postscript:

`http://www.linuxprinting.org/kpfeifle/LinuxKongress2002/Tutorial/III.PostScript-and-PPDs/`
`III.PostScript-and-PPDs.html`

Printing for the Impatient:

`http://www.onlamp.com/pub/a/bsd/2003/11/06/Big_Scary_Daemons.html`

8.3 Setting up a Secure Subversion Server

A client hired a team of web developers to assist his overworked web administrator. They asked me to set up a revision-control system to ensure that no one on the team inadvertently overwrote another member's work and to give the administrator the flexibility of rolling back to any version of a file.

My first thought was Subversion, as it is the revisioning system I used with my editor when writing *BSD Hacks*.[4] A search for **subversion** in the Ports Collection indicated that there are several related ports. For example, **esvn** looked like an excellent match for the client, as this GUI front end works from Unix, Mac OS X, and Windows. That's perfect for a web development team short on Unix skills who would be accessing data stored on a FreeBSD server from non-FreeBSD operating systems.

This section demonstrates how to create a secure repository using Subversion. The next will show how to train your users to access the repository using a GUI client.

Preparing the System

In my scenario, it was important that only the members of the development team have access to the repository. We also chose to have the repository on a system separate from the actual web server and left it up to the web administrator to copy over files from the repository to the web server as he saw fit.

To accomplish this, start by creating a backup of the existing directory structure you wish to put under revision control, and send it securely to the repository server. In my case, I backed up www/data on the web server to an internal server at 192.168.2.2:

```
# tar czvf - /usr/local/etc/www/data | \
    ssh dru@192.168.2.2 "cat > www.tar.gz"
```

Next, on the repository system, create a new group called *svn* and add to it any existing user accounts that need access to the repository. For example, I added my existing web administrator as I created the group by adding this line to /etc/group:

---

[4]Subversion was also used by the author and editor with this book, *The Best of FreeBSD Basics*.

```
svn:*:3690:webadmin
```

Then, create a new user called *svn* and, if necessary, any missing user accounts that need access to the repository. Make sure each account is a member of the *svn* group and has a password and a valid shell. I used **sysinstall** to create user accounts for the new web developers. When I finished, I double-checked the membership of the *svn* group. It looked something like this:

 # grep svn /etc/group
```
svn:*:3690:webadmin,devel1,devel2
```

Dealing with umask

Before installing Subversion, take a close look at the existing **umask** for the *svn* user. On my FreeBSD system it was:

 # su -l svn
% umask
```
022
```

In Unix, the **umask** value determines the default permissions of a newly created directory or file. It does this by defining which permissions to disable. If you remember:

```
r = 4
w = 2
x = 1
```

you'll see that this umask doesn't turn off any (0) permissions for the user (*svn*); it turns off write (2) for the group (*svn*); and it turns off write (2) for world.

Because the members of the *svn* group should be able to write to the repository, change that group 2 to a 0. If you don't want nongroup members even to be aware of the existence of the repository, also change the world 2 to a 7.

The easy part is changing the **umask** for the *svn* user's shell. If it uses **csh**, open up ~svn/.cshrc, find the existing **umask** line and change it to either 002 or 007.

Once you've saved your changes to ~svn/.cshrc, don't forget to tell the shell:

% source ~svn/.cshrc

If your *svn* user has a shell other than **csh**, make your edit in your chosen shell's configuration file.

Repeat the **umask** command to verify that your changes have taken place.

Note: You don't have to change the umask in order to use Subversion. If you choose to use the default umask, you can skip the next section as you won't require the wrapper.

Installing Subversion with the correct umask

If you chose a **umask** of 002, you can compile a wrapper into Subversion when you build it from the ports collection. If you chose a **umask** of 007 or prefer to install the precompiled version of Subversion, create a wrapper script to ensure that the Subversion binaries use your **umask** value.

To compile in a wrapper that sets a **umask** of 002:

```
# cd /usr/ports/devel/subversion
# make -DWITH_SVNSERVE_WRAPPER install clean
```

Alternatively, to install the precompiled binary:

```
# pkg_add -r subversion
```

Note: Before installing by either method, finish reading the section. You may find some additional compile options that interest you.

If you didn't compile in your wrapper, move your existing binary and create your own wrapper script:

```
# mv /usr/local/bin/svn /usr/local/bin/svn.orig
# vi /usr/local/bin/svn
#!/bin/sh
# wrapper script to set umask to 007 on subversion binaries

umask 007
/usr/local/bin/svn.orig "$@"
```

Set your **umask** to either 002 or 007 so that it is the same as the **umask** for your *svn* user.

Don't forget to make your wrapper script executable:

```
# chmod +x /usr/local/bin/svn
```

Creating the Repository

Now that your environment is set up properly, you're ready to create the repository itself. Log in as the user *svn* to ensure that both the *svn* user and the *svn* group own the files you create in the repository. From /usr/home/svn/, type:

```
% svnadmin create repository
```

In this example, I've called my repository *repository*. You can choose any name that is useful to you.

svnadmin create simply creates the directory infrastructure required by the Subversion tools:

```
% ls -F repository
README.txt    dav/    format  locks/
conf/         db/     hooks/
```

Notice that db directory? By default, Subversion uses databases to track changes to the files that you place under revision control. This means that you must import your data into those databases.

At that point, I untarred my backup so that I had some data to import. If you do this, don't restore directly into the ~svn/repository directory. (It's a database, remember?) Instead, I first made a new directory structure:

```
% pwd
/usr/home/svn
% mkdir www && cd www
% mkdir branches tags trunk
% cd trunk
% tar xzvf /full/path/to/www.tar.gz .
% cd
```

That made the *svn* user's home directory look like:

```
% ls -F ~svn
repository/      www/
```

Importing the Data

Next, it's time to import the information from ~svn/www/ into the Subversion databases. To do so, use the **svn import** command:

```
% svn import www file:///usr/home/svn/repository/www -m "initial import"
```

svn import is one of many **svn** commands available to users. Type **svn help** to see the names of all the available commands. If you insert one of those commands between **svn** and **help**, as in **svn import help**, you'll receive help on the syntax for that specified command.

After **svn import**, specify the name of the directory containing the data to import (www). Your data doesn't have to be in the same directory; simply specify the full path to the data, but ensure that your *svn* user has permission to access the data you wish to import. Note: Once you've successfully imported your data, you don't have to keep an original copy on disk. In my case, I issued the command **rm -Rf www**.

Next, notice the syntax I used when specifying the full path to the repository. Subversion supports multiple URL schemas or Repository Access (RA) modules. Verify which schemas your **svn** supports with:

```
% svn --version
svn, version 1.4.3 (r23084)
   compiled Mar 18 2007, 08:06:15
Copyright (C) 2000-2006 CollabNet.
Subversion is open source software, see http://subversion.tigris.org/
This product includes software developed by CollabNet (http://www.Collab.Net/).
The following repository access (RA) modules are available:
* ra_dav : Module for accessing a repository via WebDAV (DeltaV) protocol.
  - handles 'http' schema
  - handles 'https' schema
* ra_local : Module for accessing a repository on local disk.
```

```
- handles 'file' schema
* ra_svn : Module for accessing a repository using the svn network protocol.
- handles svn schema
```

Because I wished to access the repository on the local disk, I used the `file:///` schema. I also appended *www* at the very end of the URL, as I wish that particular part of the repository to be available by that name. Yes, you can import multiple directory structures into the same Subversion repository, so give each one a name that is easy for you and your users to remember.

Finally, I used the **-m** message switch to append the comment *initial import* to the repository log. If I hadn't included this switch, **svn** would have opened the log for me in the user's default editor (**vi**) and asked me to add a comment before continuing.

This is a very important point. The whole reason to install a revision control system is to allow multiple users to modify files, possibly even simultaneously. It's up to each user to log clearly which changes they made to which files. It's your job to make your users aware of the importance of adding useful comments whenever an **svn** command prompts them to do so.

Deciding Upon a URL Schema

Congratulations! You now have a working repository. Now's the best time to take a closer look at the various URL schemas and choose the access method that best suits your needs.

The Server Configurations chapter of the ebook *Version Control with Subversion* gives details about the possible configurations. You can choose to install the book when you compile the FreeBSD port by adding **-DWITH_BOOK** to your **make** command.

If all of your users log in to the system either locally or through **ssh**, use the `file:///` schema. Because users are local to the repository, this scenario doesn't open a TCP/IP port to listen for Subversion connections. However, it does require an active shell account for each user and assumes that your users are comfortable logging in to a Unix server. As with any shell account, your security depends upon your users choosing good passwords and you setting up repository permissions and group memberships correctly. Having users **ssh** to the system does ensure that they have encrypted sessions.

Another possibility is to integrate Subversion into an existing Apache server. By default, the FreeBSD port of Subversion compiles in SSL support, meaning your users can have the ability to access your repository securely from their browsers using the `https://` schema. However, if you're running Apache 2.x instead of Apache 1.x, remember to pass the **-DWITH_MOD_DAV_SVN** option to make when you compile your FreeBSD port.

If you're considering giving browser access to your users, read carefully through the Apache httpd configuration section of the Subversion book first. You'll have to go through a fair bit of configuration; fortunately, the documentation is complete.

A third approach is to use **svnserve** to listen for network connections. The book suggests running this process either through **inetd** or as a stand-alone daemon. Both of these approaches allow either anonymous access or access once the system has authorized a user using CRAM-MD5. Clients connect to **svnserve** using the `svn://` schema.

Anonymous access wasn't appropriate in my scenario, so I followed the configuration options for CRAM-MD5. However, I quickly discovered that CRAM-MD5 wasn't on my FreeBSD system. When a Google search failed to find a technique for integrating CRAM-MD5 with my Subversion binary, I decided to try the last option.

This was to invoke **svnserve** in tunnel mode, which allows user authentication through the normal SSH mechanism as well as any restrictions you have placed in your `/etc/ssh/sshd_config` file. For example, I could use the `AllowUsers` keyword to control which users can authenticate to the system. Note that this schema uses `svn+ssh://`. The appeal of this method is that I could use an existing authentication scheme without forcing the user to actually be on the repository system.

If you decide to use the **svnserve** server and you compiled in the wrapper, it created a binary called **svnserve.bin**. Users won't be able to access the repository until you:

```
# cp /usr/local/bin/svnserve.bin /usr/local/bin/svnserve
```

Additional Resources

Original Article:

`http://www.onlamp.com/pub/a/bsd/2005/05/12/FreeBSD_Basics.html`

Subversion ebook:

`http://svnbook.red-bean.com/`

8.4 Accessing Secure Subversion Servers

This section shows how to access and use a Subversion repository using both the command line and a GUI.

Starting the Server

Because I use SSH for authentication, I first needed to start the **svn** server in tunnel (**-t**) mode on the system hosting the repository. I could simply type this as the user *svn*:

```
% svnserve -t
```

However, that user would lose his prompt. You might be thinking, "do this instead":

```
% svnserve -t &
```

to start the service in the background. That is better; however, the service is still attached to svn's shell, so the service will stop abruptly if that shell ever closes. In this case, it is better to write a small shell script owned by the user *svn*. I saved mine as `/usr/local/home/svn/repository/conf/svnserve.sh`:

```
#!/bin/sh

# script to start svn server in tunnel mode
# first, set correct umask
umask 007

# then, use nohup to prevent program from closing if starting shell closes,
# send standard output and error to the bit bucket,
# and start in the background (to get prompt back)
nohup /usr/local/sbin/svnserve -t 2>&1 > /dev/null&
```

Don't forget to make the script executable and to double-check the permissions and ownership:

```
% chmod u+x ~svn/repository/conf/svnserve.sh
% ls -l ~svn/repository/conf/svnserve.sh
-rwxr--r-- 1 svn svn 112 Apr 29 09:36 /usr/home/svn/repository/conf/svnserve.sh
```

Then, as the user *svn*, run the script to start the service:

```
% ~svn/repository/conf/svnserve.sh
```

Simplifying User Authentication

Unless you configure a mechanism to cache your users' credentials, they will receive authentication prompts every time they view or make a change to the repository. Constant reauthentication can become very irritating very quickly.

Because I'm using the svn+ssh access method, I chose to implement public key authentication and use **keychain** to prevent the user from having to constantly retype in their passphrase.

Here are the steps I used for the user *devel1* who uses FreeBSD as his desktop. First, I had him generate a public/private key pair using RSA as the type (**-t**) of algorithm.

```
% ssh-keygen -t rsa
Generating public/private rsa key pair.
Enter file in which to save the key
    (/home/devel1/.ssh/id_rsa):
Enter passphrase (empty for no passphrase): type something long but memorable
Enter same passphrase again:
Your identification has been saved in /home/devel1/.ssh/id_rsa.
Your public key has been saved in /home/devel1/.ssh/id_rsa.pub.
The key fingerprint is:
f6:c2:51:ae:5c:17:91:57:53:c4:58:86:3f:5f:9a devel1@hostname
```

I then had *devel1* copy over his new public key to his home directory on the system hosting the repository; in this case, 10.1.1.1:

```
% scp ~/.ssh/id_rsa.pub 10.1.1.1:/usr/home/devel1/.ssh
```

Note: When you do this, make sure you copy over the key with the *.pub* extension! And you should first double-check that the destination doesn't already contain a public key with that name.

Before you can use that key, you have to append it to a file called authorized_keys. This will require one last ssh into the repository system using *devel1*'s username and password:

```
% ssh 10.1.1.1
(login using password as usual)
% cd ~/.ssh
% cat id_rsa.pub >> authorized_keys
% exit
```

Finally, I had *devel1* verify that SSH was using his public key for authentication. This time, instead of prompting him for his password, it prompted for his passphrase:

```
% ssh 10.1.1.1
Enter passphrase for key '/home/devel1/.ssh/id_rsa':
% exit
```

Now that the public key works on the repository system, it's time to deal with the private key.

I set up **keychain** to cache the credentials. As superuser on *devel1*'s system:

```
# pkg_add -r keychain
```

Then, I had *devel1* add these lines to his ~/.cshrc file:

```
'eval ssh-agent'
/usr/local/bin/keychain /usr/home/devel1/.ssh/id_rsa
source /usr/home/devel1/.ssh-agent > /dev/null
```

and inform **csh** about the change:

```
% source ~/.cshrc
KeyChain 2.5.3.1; http://www.gentoo.org/proj/en/keychain/
Copyright 2002-2004 Gentoo Foundation; Distributed under the GPL
 * Initializing /home/devel1/.keychain/hostname.org-csh file...
 * Adding 1 ssh key(s)...
Enter passphrase for /usr/home/devel1/.ssh/id_rsa:
 * Identity added: /usr/home/devel1/.ssh/id_rsa (/usr/home/devel1/.ssh/id_rsa)
```

devel1 entered his passphrase. Now, he will see no prompts for any credentials for the entirety of his session as **keychain** will inform the SSH server that the identity has not changed.

Note: **keychain** isn't required but does ease the process as it allows you to have one long-running **ssh-agent** process per system rather than per login session.

Checking Out the Repository

Now that the server is running and authentication works, it's time to access the repository. Because *devel1* prefers to work at the command line, I'll demonstrate the **svn** commands he'll use most often. I'll then install a GUI for *devel2* and demonstrate that it is merely a front end for the same commands.

Before you can make any changes to the repository, you must download a working copy to your system. In Subversion terms, this is a checkout. If you always work from the same PC, you need to run this command only once. The syntax is:

```
% svn checkout svn+ssh://10.1.1.1/usr/home/svn/repository/www
A www/apache
A www/apache/index.html
<snip long output>
Checked out revision 1.
```

The above command copied the entire repository to a directory called www in *devel1*'s home directory. This is his working copy. If you wish to specify an alternate location for your working copy, place it at the end of the command. For example, this will create a working copy called mycopy:

```
% svn checkout svn+ssh://10.1.1.1/usr/home/svn/repository/www mycopy
```

Using your working copy

Once you've checked out your working copy, you can modify its files, add files, and remove files. In order to use any **svn** commands, your present working directory will have to be somewhere within your working copy. For example, if I try to view the log from *devel1*'s home directory, I'll receive this error:

```
% pwd
/usr/home/devel1
% svn log
svn: '.' is not a working copy
```

However, if I **cd** to the working copy, in this case www:

```
% cd www
% svn log
```

the **svn** command will work. If you get a working copy error, **cd** to your working copy and try again.

It is very important that you always run this command before making any changes to your working copy:

```
% svn update
At revision 1.
```

The **update** command checks your working copy against the repository to ensure that they are the same. Because I just checked out my working copy, there aren't any differences. However, if someone else had made any changes to the repository, that command would download those changes and merge them into my working copy.

Suppose that you want to add a file to a repository. After you have created the file somewhere in your working copy, use **svn add** to add it. Here, I wish to add a test file called ~devel1/www/test:

```
% pwd
/usr/home/devel1/www
% svn add test
A         test
```

This has added the file, but it didn't upload it to the main repository yet. That won't happen until I commit the change:

```
% svn commit -m "test file added by devel1"
Adding  test
Transmitting file data .
Committed revision 2.
```

Note that I used the **-m** switch to add a message to the log and that the revision number has incremented.

You don't have to commit after every change, as **svn** will queue up your changes and commit everything when you issue **svn commit**. However, if you're the forgetful sort or if many people work on the repository simultaneously, it doesn't do any harm to commit often. If you do queue up a lot of changes, don't forget to mention them all when you add your message to the log.

Note that the main repository is now at revision 2, but my working copy is still at revision 1. For example, if I type **svn log**, I won't see my comment. However, if I update, I will:

```
% svn update
At revision 2.
% svn log
------------------------------------------------------------------
r2 | devel1 | 2005-05-02 11:37:02 -0400 (Mon, 02 May 2005) | 1 line
test file added by devel1
------------------------------------------------------------------
r1 | svn | 2005-04-29 08:31:47 -0400 (Fri, 29 Apr 2005) | 1 line
initial import
------------------------------------------------------------------
```

More svn commands

You can also delete files. However, don't use **rm** to do so. The proper method is **svn delete**:

```
% ls
apache   default.php     en      test
% svn delete test
D       test
% ls
apache   default.php     en
```

See how **svn** removed that file from my working copy? The D also indicates that issuing a commit will delete the file from the repository:

```
% svn commit -m "removed test file"
Deleting        test
Committed revision 4.
```

Why is it showing revision 4 when I'm at revision 2? Because someone else has committed a change since the last time I ran **svn update**. Let's see what it is:

```
% svn update
U frameset.html
Updated to revision 4.
```

Note that a new (added) file starts with A, a deleted file starts with D, and a modified (updated) file starts with U. Someone else modified the file `frameset.html` before I committed my change. **svn log** would tell me who, and I would see that my change was revision 4 and the other person's change was revision 3.

I could get exact details on the file's modifications by issuing a diff on revision 3:

```
% svn diff -r 3
Index: en/frameset.html
================================================================
--- en/frameset.html (revision 3)
+++ en/frameset.html (working copy)
@@ -2,10 +2,10 @@
<snip>
-<frameset rows="21%, 79%" border="0">
+<frameset rows=27%,73%" border="0">
<snip other changes>
```

You'll see that this is like any **diff -u** output. In this snippet, a single line has changed from its original values of 21 percent and 79 percent to new values of 27 percent and 73 percent.

If you wish to modify an existing file, simply make your edits. You don't have to **svn add**, as the file already exists. When you issue your next **svn commit**, your modifications will upload to the repository. Do remember to add a useful message to remind yourself and others of the edits you made.

Summary of svn commands

Here are the commands you'll use most often:

svn update — Always do this before changing your working copy or if a commit indicates a higher revision number than you were expecting.

svn add — Whenever you create a file; you have to create the file before you can add it.

svn delete — When you wish to delete a file. (Don't use **rm** in your working copy!)

svn commit — To upload your changes. Include **-m** with a message; otherwise, **svn** will open the **vi** editor so you can add your comments to the log.

svn log — To view the log of changes. Use the **-v** switch to list the filenames too.

svn diff -r # — To see details of the changes made by the specified revision (where # indicates version number). **svn diff** without specifying a revision will let you know if any changes have been made since your last update.

The Subversion Complete Reference chapter of the Subversion book gives details and examples for all of the **svn** commands.

Installing and Using a GUI

I originally planned to use **esvn** as the GUI, but found that the current version truncated the name of the repository, which made it impossible to use any **svn** commands. However, I had good luck with **rapidsvn**.

Installing on FreeBSD was a simple matter of:

```
# pkg_add -r rapidsvn
```

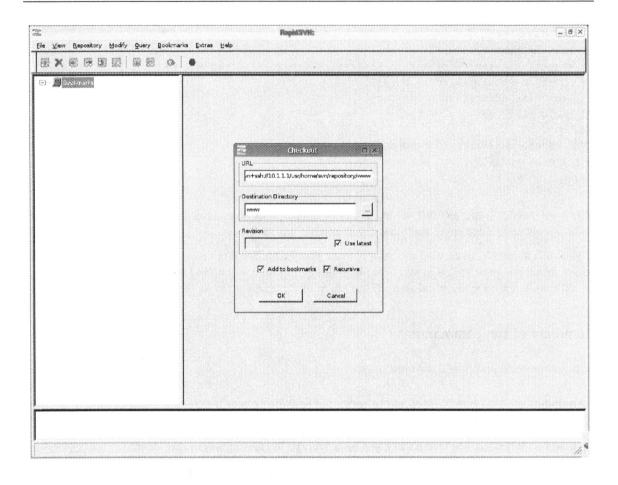

Figure 8.1: Checking out with rapidsvn

There are also binaries available as a Debian *.deb*, a Red Hat RPM, and a Windows installer.

Once *devel2* had **keychain** set up and working, I had him open up **rapidsvn** and choose Checkout from the Repository menu. (See Figure 8.1). He typed the same URL that *devel1* had used at the command line, and chose to save his working copy as www. Selecting Add to Bookmarks ensures that the copy will show up as a tree in the left pane.

Once he had a working copy, *devel2* went into the View menu and chose Preferences, then Programs. Here he defined his favorite editor and file explorer. That made it very easy for him to navigate between existing files on his system and his working copy.

The Modify menu contains the most often used **svn** commands. Each has either a **Ctrl-***letter* or a **Function** key shortcut for quick access. Once *devel2* learned how to use the various **svn** commands, he quickly became comfortable with the interface and was able to return to his real work of web development.

Summary

Subversion provides a feature-rich yet easy-to-learn method for sharing a project's files between users. Edits are simple to track, and if need be, users can revert any file to an earlier revision. While I've covered the most used commands in this section, refer to the Subversion web site for more information on how to get the most out of your repository.

Additional Resources

Original Article:

`http://www.onlamp.com/pub/a/bsd/2005/08/11/FreeBSD_Basics.html`

Introducing keychain:

`http://www.ibm.com/developerworks/linux/library/l-keyc2/`

Version Control with Subversion Book:

`http://svnbook.red-bean.com/`

RapidSVN Documentation:

`http://www.rapidsvn.org/index.php/Documentation`

8.5 Understanding Email

One of the first things every FreeBSD user wishes to configure on his computer is email access. However, a look in the mail section of the ports collection yields an amazing 650 applications dealing with email. To make matters worse, some claim to be MUAs, MTAs, POP3 clients, or IMAP4 servers. These descriptions are not helpful if you are unfamiliar with these terms and just want to be able to send and receive email.

In this section, I'll give a Readers Digest version of some important email concepts, with references to additional information. Then I'll walk you through the steps of configuring your FreeBSD system to send and retrieve email, as well as configuring Pine.

Email 101

Ever since networks were invented, people have wanted a method of sending messages to each other. This led to the development of many messaging programs, most of which were proprietary, meaning you could only send a message to someone who used the same messaging system. Early messaging systems allowed you to send a message directly to another person's computer. However, this method doesn't work if the other computer is turned off or there is a problem with the physical connection between the two computers.

Most messaging systems prefer to have all users send their messages to a centralized server for storage; since this server is always available, it can act like a post office. If a user has a mailbox on that server, he can periodically check his mailbox to see if he has received any messages.

As the need for messaging grew, standards were developed to allow users to send messages to any user, regardless of the messaging system they used. One of these standards was X.400; another was SMTP, which became the standard used on the Internet.

Unless you work at a company that uses an internal X.400 messaging system, you probably use SMTP to send email. The email addresses you are used to seeing are actually SMTP addresses and look like this: *anyuser@anycompany.com*. You'll note that an SMTP address looks similar to a web address, except it has a @ instead of the first period. The Internet already uses DNS (the Domain Name System) to locate a computer's

IP address. When an administrator sets up a mail server, he will create an MX (Mail eXchange) record in his DNS database to indicate which computer in his network is the mail server.[5] The name to the left of the @ indicates the name of a user's mailbox on that mail server.

When the Internet messaging standard was being developed, it was decided to use the centralized server (post office) approach where users would check their mailboxes. The Internet uses TCP/IP, so new TCP/IP protocols needed to be created. Remember that protocols define the rules of communication and that each TCP/IP protocol has an associated port number and at least one RFC which describes its operation.

SMTP (Simple Mail Transfer Protocol) describes the communications between mail servers. Its port number is 25, and its behavior is described in RFC 2821.

As its name implies, SMTP merely transfers mail from one server to another until it reaches the correct mail server. Once the mail is stored on the correct mail server, users can use the POP3 (Post Office Protocol 3) protocol to download their mail. POP3 uses port number 110 and is defined by RFCs 1734, 1957, 2449, and STD0053 (standard 53).

POP3 is also responsible for the management of the mailboxes on a mail server. POP3 will not let a user retrieve the messages in their mailbox until they have been authenticated.

If you are unfamiliar with the commands used by POP3 and SMTP, try the SMTP with Telnet tutorial at `http://ezine.daemonnews.org/199905/telnet.html`. This tutorial shows how you yourself can issue SMTP and POP3 commands to send and receive email. These are the same commands that are usually issued by messaging systems and email programs.

One other term you may come across is IMAP4 (Internet Message Access Protocol version 4). IMAP4 is similar to POP3, but with extra features. POP3 assumes that a user will download all of the mail in their mailbox so the copy on the mail server can be deleted; the user will then disconnect from the mail server to read his email offline. With IMAP4, a user can download just the headers of his email so he can decide which messages he wants to retrieve at this time; he can also delete messages directly at the mail server without having to download them first.

Messaging software is usually divided into two separate components: the MTA (Message Transfer Agent) and the MUA (Message User Agent). The MTA runs on the mail server and is able to send messages to other SMTP mail servers, receive messages from other SMTP mail servers, and store messages in the appropriate user mailboxes. Sendmail is the most common MTA in use on the Internet and comes bundled and ready to go on your FreeBSD system. Exim, Postfix, and Qmail are examples of other MTAs that you can build using FreeBSD's ports collection.

The MUA is used by users to compose and read email messages. Some MUAs have a POP3 client built-in, meaning you can check for new mail using the MUA; some do not, and will only display email you've retrieved using a separate POP3 client. MUAs differ widely in their features; which MUA to use is a matter of personal preference. There are dozens of MUAs in the ports collection; some of the most popular are Mutt, Pine, Evolution, and Thunderbird.

So, how do all these components work together when you send an email message? You use your MUA (for example, Pine) to create an email message; Pine will pass the message to the MTA (Sendmail), who will query DNS to find the address of the SMTP server hosting the mailbox of the user you are sending the message to. Sendmail will then use SMTP commands to transfer the message to that mail server. That mail server will put the message in the correct mailbox. Your recipient will use POP3 commands to retrieve the message and will use their favorite MUA to read the message and possibly compose a reply to it.

---

[5]You can see MX examples in section 7.3.

Getting Started with Pine

Let's look at the configuration of a FreeBSD system that will be using Sendmail (the MTA), fetchmail (the POP3 client), and Pine (the MUA). Let's assume a very quick and dirty scenario in which I have one user on a single FreeBSD computer who wishes to use email.

Like any MTA, Sendmail is a highly configurable and complex program capable of providing messaging for large companies and even ISPs. However, you don't want to start messing with the default Sendmail configuration files unless you know what you're doing. Fortunately, the default Sendmail configuration on your FreeBSD system will issue SMTP commands so you can send out email to the world.

You will need to install an MUA and perhaps a POP3 client. I'll demonstrate Pine and fetchmail:

```
# pkg_add -r pine
# pkg_add -r fetchmail
```

Now that we have the necessary software, we need to create a user account to use when sending and receiving email. You can either create a user with the same name as the mailbox portion of your email address, or you can create an alias to map an existing user to the mailbox name. Since my email address is *genisis@istar.ca*, to keep my life simple on my home FreeBSD box, I create a user called *genisis*. When I wish to access my email, I log in to my FreeBSD system as the user *genisis*. This trick is useful on small systems as it saves you editing an alias file.

If you need to create a new user, become the superuser and type **sysinstall** and select Configure, then User Management, then User. The login ID should be the same as the name of the mailbox, so in my case it is *genisis*. Input a password you'll remember and tab over to OK. Arrow over to Cancel twice, then arrow over to Exit Install.

Leave the superuser account and log in as the new user. Now type **pine** — you should see the following message:

```
Creating subdirectory /home/yourusername/mail where Pine will store
its mail folders.
```

This will be followed by Pine's greeting text. You'll notice that Pine's commands are always listed at the bottom of your screen. The ˆ (carat) symbol means use your **Control** key along with the letter next to the ˆ. Once you've read the greeting, use **ˆE** (Exit This Greeting). This will bring you to Pine's main menu.

Since this is the first time you are running Pine as this user, you'll need to press **S** to enter Setup, then **C** to enter Config. The first three items should be edited as follows:

personal-name — Press **C** to change its value and type in what you want the world to see when you send an email; for example, mine is set to Dru.

user-domain — Change this so it's the same value as the text to the right of the @ in your email address; for example, mine is set to *istar.ca*.

smtp-server — This should be the value you received from your ISP. For example, mine is set to *mail.istar.ca*.

You'll notice that Pine supports a lot of configuration values; if you find one that sounds interesting, highlight it and press the **?** key. This will give a short, and usually helpful, description of what this configuration parameter does. I usually change the following on mine:

- Under Viewer Preferences, I use the **Enter** key to put an [X] in `enable-msg-view-urls` and `enable-msg-vie` this will highlight URLs and email addresses so I can go directly to a web site or add an address to my address book.

- I receive a lot of email, so I constantly change the value of the `sort-key`. If I'm expecting an email from a particular person, I'll change it to "From"; if I'm sorting through mailing lists, I'll change it to "Subject."

- The very last configuration parameter in Pine is `url-viewers`. I change this to `/usr/local/bin/lynx`. Since Pine will highlight URLs in my email messages (because I told it to with the `enable-msg-view-urls` value), it will invoke **lynx** to open the site for me.

Once you've finished your configurations, press **E** to exit Setup and **Y** to commit changes. This will return you to the main menu where you can press **A** to edit the address book. The @ key will let you add an email address; when you're finished, type **^X** and the address should now show in your address book.

Highlight a user you've added to your address book and press **C** to compose an email message to them. Arrow down to Cc and input your email address so you'll be sent a copy of the message. Once you've composed your message, make sure you are connected to your ISP and press **^X** to send your message. Type **y** when Pine asks you if you want to send the message. It should say "Sending Mail", then "Message sent and copied to 'sent-mail'." Use your **<** key to return to the main menu, then **L** to enter the folder list. If you arrow over to `sent-mail` and press enter, you should be able to view and read the message that you sent.

One last point on Pine: it contains a built-in editor called Pico. Pico is a very easy editor to learn as its commands are always listed on the bottom of the screen. You don't have to run Pine to use Pico; if you want to edit a file with Pico, do this:

```
% pico filename
```

Picking up email with Fetchmail

Now that you've sent your first email with Pine, you'll want to check that you received your copy of the email by using the **fetchmail** program. Open up another virtual terminal, and log in as your user. I use **fetchmail** like so:

```
% fetchmail istar.ca
Enter password for genisis@istar.ca:
fetchmail: IMAP connection to istar.ca failed: Connection refused
1 message for genisis at istar.ca (868 octets).
reading message 1 of 1 (868 octets)   flushed
```

I can now return to the terminal where Pine is running and navigate to my inbox to read the downloaded email message.

Note that **fetchmail** added *genisis* to my email address for me because I am logged in as *genisis*. If I happened to be logged in as another user, say *biko*, it would use the address *biko@istar.ca* instead.

The fetchmail command would then fail as I don't have a mailbox called *biko* on Istar's mail server. However, if I'm logged in as *biko* and invoke **fetchmail** like so:

```
% fetchmail -u genisis istar.ca
```

This will tell **fetchmail** to use the mailbox name of *genisis* instead of my login name of *biko* so I can retrieve *genisis'* email.

Fetchmail also has a verbose mode which can be used to view the various POP3 commands between fetchmail and the mail server. You can invoke verbose mode with **-v** and very verbose mode with **-vv**. Here is a portion of a session with **fetchmail** in verbose mode:

```
% fetchmail -v istar.ca
Enter password for genisis@istar.ca:
fetchmail: 5.3.0 querying istar.ca (protocol auto) at Mon, 31 Jul 2000 11:16:28 -0400 (EDT)
fetchmail: 5.3.0 querying istar.ca (protocol IMAP) at Mon, 31 Jul 2000 11:16:28 -0400 (EDT)
fetchmail: IMAP connection to istar.ca failed:  Connection refused
fetchmail: 5.3.0 querying istar.ca (protocol POP3) at Mon, 31 Jul 2000 11:16:28 -0400 (EDT)
fetchmail: POP3< +OK iSTAR POP3 Server at istar.ca Ready v1.13 12.2.1996 ⇓
<398597cc398597cc@istar.ca
fetchmail: POP3> USER genisis
fetchmail: POP3< +OK Complete authentication with the PASS command for genisis@istar.ca
fetchmail: POP3> PASS *
fetchmail: POP3< +OK Authentication successful.
fetchmail: POP3> STAT
fetchmail: POP3< +OK 5 29820
fetchmail: POP3> LAST
fetchmail: POP3< +OK 0
5 messages for genisis at istar.ca (29820 octets).
fetchmail: POP3> LIST
fetchmail: POP3< +OK 5 messages (29820 octets)
fetchmail: POP3< 1 8777
fetchmail: POP3< 2 8961
fetchmail: POP3< 3 4837
fetchmail: POP3< 4 2806
fetchmail: POP3< 5 4439
```

You should be able to recognize the USER, PASS, and LIST commands if you have tried the "SMTP over Telnet tutorial."

Fetchmail is highly configurable through its use of switches; its manpage is well worth reading.

Additional Resources

Original Article:

http://www.onlamp.com/pub/a/bsd/2000/08/30/FreeBSD_Basics.html

Sendmail, 3rd Edition:

http://www.oreilly.com/catalog/sendmail3/

SMTP (and POP3) with telnet Tutorial

http://ezine.daemonnews.org/199905/telnet.html

8.6 Procmail Basics

If you receive more than a few email messages a day, you've probably discovered that it becomes increasingly difficult to sort and prioritize your email. Messages you want to read immediately can get lost in a sea of less-important messages. Worse, your inbox can become cluttered with spam, virus-infected messages, and other disagreeables. Fortunately, the **procmail** program has been designed to help you sort through this mess.

By creating your own customized recipes, you can organize the messages you do want to receive and deal with the messages you don't want to receive.

In this section, I'll install and configure **procmail** and get you started on a few basic recipes. In the next section, I'll continue with some more complicated recipes and look at **procmail**'s logging features.

Getting Started

To install **procmail** as the superuser:

```
# pkg_add -r procmail
```

Let's start off simple and configure **procmail** for one user. Once you've finished installing, you can leave the superuser account. I'll be working as the regular user *genisis* and will set up that user's **procmail** configuration. I'll start by copying over the example configuration files:

```
% cp /usr/local/share/examples/procmail/forward ~/.forward
% cp /usr/local/share/examples/procmail/1procmailrc ~/.procmailrc
```

I'll then reset the permissions on those files:

```
% chmod 644 ~/.forward
% chmod 644 ~/.procmailrc
```

Since I use the **fetchmail** program to regularly poll my ISP's mail server to check for new mail, I'll kill the **fetchmail** process until I'm finished configuring **procmail**:

```
% killall fetchmail
```

The **procmail** utility reads a configuration file known as procmailrc. The superuser can create a global configuration file in /usr/local/etc/procmail that will affect all users on that system. However, it is recommended that each user instead create their own .procmailrc in their home directory. This way, users can create their own filtering recipes without affecting any other users.

The .procmailrc file has two sections. The first section contains your path and environment variables; the second section contains your filtering recipes. Once you've copied the default .procmailrc into your home directory, immediately edit the first section before you try to download any email. I'll open up my .procmailrc with my favorite text editor to demonstrate:

```
# Please check if all the paths in PATH are reachable,
# remove the ones that are not.

PATH=$HOME/bin:/usr/bin:/usr/ucb:/bin:/usr/local/bin:.
```

FreeBSD doesn't have a /usr/ucb, so remove that bit, along with the extra colon, so the line looks like this:

```
PATH=$HOME/bin:/usr/bin:/bin:/usr/local/bin:.

MAILDIR=$HOME/Mail # You'd better make sure it exists
```

Because I use **pine**, my mail goes to a directory called mail, so I'll change that capital *M* to a small *m*. If you don't use **pine** as your email reader, do an **ls -F** of your home directory. Somewhere in the output you should have a directory where you store your email; it is usually called mail or Mail. If you do an **ls** of that directory, you should be able to recognize your mail folders (e.g. sent, saved, etc.) It is very important that your MAILDIR line reflects the correct directory.

The next three environment variables can be left as is. The DEFAULT variable tells **procmail** to create a directory called mbox, where it will store all messages that don't match any of your recipes. The LOGFILE variable creates a directory called from, where your **procmail** logs will be stored.

After the environment variables is the section containing some sample recipes:

```
:0                      # Anything from thf
* ^From.*thf@somewhere.someplace
todd                    # will go to $MAILDIR/todd
:0                      # Anything from people at uunet
* ^From.*@uunet
uunetbox                # will go to $MAILDIR/uunetbox
:0                      # Anything from Henry
* ^From.*henry
henries                 # will go to $MAILDIR/henries
# Anything that has not been delivered by now will go to $DEFAULT
# using LOCKFILE=$DEFAULT$LOCKEXT
```

Creating Recipes

Once you've edited your path and environment variables, the **procmail** utility has enough information to run correctly; until you customize those recipes, it will simply place all of your email in a folder called mbox. For now, I'll remove the sample recipes. I'll also test to make sure that I haven't broken anything by restarting **fetchmail** and opening up **pine**. I notice that I have a new folder in my folder list called mbox, and after a few moments, there's some new mail in it. So far so good.

Now the fun part begins, as I devise recipes to organize my email. I'll start by taking a look at the mailing lists I'm subscribed to, as they represent the biggest chunk of my email. I'm subscribed to freebsd-questions, several mailing lists from securityfocus.com, and the Internet drafts list. So I'll start by making three recipes to sort those three general topics.

Every recipe has the same basic syntax and requires a minimum of three lines. The recipe can be as simple or as complicated as you want to make it; there is no right or wrong way to create a recipe, as long as it follows the correct syntax and gets the job done. Let's start by looking at that three line syntax:

```
:0                  #first line
*                   #second line
file                #third line
```

You'll note that comments are allowed (and recommended, so you remember why you created that recipe) and are indicated by a #.

The first line indicates the beginning of a recipe and is easy for me to remember, as it sort of looks like my expression when I'm in the kitchen. You'll sometimes see more characters in the first line if someone is doing something a bit more complicated, but we'll save complicated for later.

The second line is the condition. In simple recipes, it will start with an * (asterisk) and go on from there; this is the part of the recipe that can be as complicated as you want. You can also make as many conditions as you want in a recipe.

The third line is the action, which usually indicates the folder in which you want **procmail** to put the email message that met your condition.

Now, let's translate all this into three recipes to organize my mailing lists. Recipes to sort mailing lists are the simplest to create, as we can use procmail's built-in ^TO_ expression. This expression will scan the To: and Cc: lines of an email message's header. This is ideal for finding mailing lists, as a person either sends a message "to" the mailing list, or they reply to the original posting, which will send a cc back to the mailing list.

Before I create the actual recipes, it's helpful to know what **procmail** does when it reads my recipes. By default, it will scan the headers of incoming email messages for the conditions I've created in my recipes. And, by default, it will stop reading when it finds a matching condition. This means that order is important for two reasons. One, **procmail** will work much faster if I put the recipes that will generate the most matches at the top of the recipe section; for example, most of my email comes from the freebsd questions mailing list, so that recipe should be near the top. Second, if I want a recipe that scans for virii, it should be placed before any other recipes, so it will scan every message as it arrives.

One last thing before creating those recipes: since **procmail** scans headers by default and most of your recipes will reflect this, it is helpful to understand what an email header is and what type of information one would expect to see in the various header fields. If you're rusty on this subject, there is an excellent tutorial at http://www.stopspam.org/email/headers.html.

OK, on with the first three recipes. Since most of my messages come from freebsd-questions, followed by the security lists, followed by the Internet drafts, my recipes look like this:

```
:0                      # Anything from questions@freebsd.org
* ^TO_*questions@freebsd.org
questions               # will go to $MAILDIR/questions
:0                      # Anything from a security mailing list
* ^TO_*security
security                # will go to $MAILDIR/security
:0                      # Anything regarding Internet drafts
* ^TO_*ietf
drafts                  # will go to $MAILDIR/drafts
```

I've used the same logic in each of the recipes. The only semi-complicated bit is the syntax of that expression in the condition line; it should look like this:

```
* ^TO_*
```

and be immediately followed by the expression you want **procmail** to search for in the To: or Cc: fields of a message's header. When you're creating your own recipes, take a look at those fields in your email messages and look for the common expression. For example, if I had told the first recipe to search for the expression "freebsd" instead of *questions@freebsd.org*, it would catch all messages from any FreeBSD mailing list (e.g. newbies, advocacy, security, etc.). I was a bit more particular and specified that I just wanted it to catch messages from the questions list at freebsd.org.

I kept my second recipe more general. It actually catches every message from *securityfocus.com*, *security@freebsd.org*, and even my daily security output, since they all share the common expression "security".

For the Internet drafts, I noticed that they always came from *ietf.org*. Since the expression "ietf" is fairly unique, I used that as my condition.

Each action specifies a folder for the messages to be placed in. The **procmail** utility automagically created the folders `questions`, `security`, and `drafts` for me the first time it came across a message that required that action. Any message that didn't match those three recipes was put in the default folder of `mbox`. This is handy when you're creating your recipes, as you'll be able to see which messages don't match a recipe and see if there is a need to lump them together and create a recipe to do that for you.

Useful Recipes

There're a few other recipes you may want to include to get you started. The first is out of **man procmailex** and deals with duplicate messages. It should be the very first recipe, and looks like this:

```
:0 Whc: msgid.lock
| formail -D 8192 msgid.cache    #prevent duplicate messages
:0 a:
duplicates                       #but store them instead of deleting them
```

This variant of the recipe will send all duplicate messages to a folder called `duplicates`. That manpage also gives an alternate recipe that will instead delete any duplicate messages, but also warns that you might lose other email messages if you have a scripting issue in a complicated recipe. You may want to stick with the above recipe until you reach **procmail** guru status.

The last recipe I'll demonstrate is an example of a virus-scanning recipe. The week I originally wrote this, the Badtrans virus was rampant and was becoming a bit of an irritation. I borrowed the following recipe from the freebsd-questions mailing list and placed it right below my duplicate recipe:

```
# Stupid BadTrans virus
:0:
* ^From: .+ \<_.*\>$
garbage
:0:
* ^From: _.+ \(.+\)$
garbage
```

This is an example of a more complicated expression. Don't despair if you don't understand the expressions in those condition lines; the important thing is that this recipe works. Remember, when you want to create a recipe, you don't have to reinvent the wheel. There's a good chance that someone else has already created a recipe that does what you want to do. This is especially true when new virii are released, as **procmail** users will post their recipes to the Procmail mailing list.

If I do a search for "badtrans", I'll come across several recipes which vary in their complexity, but which all get the job done.

Additional Resources

Original Article:

```
http://www.onlamp.com/pub/a/bsd/2001/12/06/FreeBSD_Basics.html
```

Procmail FAQ:

```
http://mirror.ncsa.uiuc.edu/procmail-faq/mini-faq.html
```

8.7 Filtering Spam with Procmail

This section starts by looking at **procmail**'s built-in logging mechanism. We'll then take a look at some other available resources that build on **procmail**'s capabilities.

Using mailstat

On your FreeBSD system, there is a utility called **mailstats** that gives you statistics on how many messages were handled by the **sendmail** program:

```
% mailstats
Statistics from Mon Dec 24 08:17:21 2001
 M    msgsfr  bytes_from   msgsto   bytes_to  msgsrej msgsdis  Mailer
 0        0          0K        7       10K        0       0  prog
 8        8         30K        1        3K        0       0  relay
=============================================================
 T        8         30K        8       13K        0       0
 C        8                     8                 0
```

When you installed **procmail**, it installed its own mail statistics program known as **mailstat**; notice the lack of the *s* at the end. Its syntax is also slightly different than the built-in FreeBSD command; I enjoyed the error message I received the first time I ran **procmail**'s **mailstat** program:

```
% mailstat
Most people don't type their own logfiles; but, what do I care?
```

This program then sat there waiting for me to create a logfile; instead, I did a **Ctrl-C** to end the program and tried again, this time giving the location of the log file that I specified when I created my .procmailrc:

```
% mailstat ~/mail/from
  Total  Number Folder
  -----  ------ ------
   5911       1 questions
  -----  ------
   5911       1
```

This utility is handy if you've created **procmail** recipes that place your email into several different folders; you'll be able to quickly see how many messages went into each folder since the last time you checked your mail. Once you've run the **mailstat** utility, it saves that set of statistics in a file called `from.old` and starts counting new email from scratch. So if I immediately rerun **mailstat**:

```
% mailstat
No mail arrived since Dec 24 10:32
```

I'll see that I haven't received any new mail since the last time I ran the **mailstat** program.

Using junkfilter

The previous section (8.6) demonstrated how to create some basic recipes that will sort your desired messages into their appropriate folders. After a bit of fine tuning, you'll find that the bulk of the messages that don't match a recipe, and therefore end up in your default folder, will be spam.

There are basically three options for dealing with the spam. The first is to become a **procmail** guru by figuring out how to create recipes that will catch spam without catching your non-spam messages. This is time-consuming, difficult, and a never-ending process — definitely, the hard way, so I won't demonstrate it. The second is to install one of the spam solutions that works with **procmail**. If you choose this method, you can take advantage of the expertise of **procmail** gurus who have honed their recipes and decided to share them. I'll be demonstrating two of these solutions in the rest of this section. The third is the easiest way and, depending upon your psychological makeup, either the least or the most gratifying method: simply use your delete key and move on to the next message.

spambnc and **junkfilter** are both available in the FreeBSD ports collection, making their installation painless. You'll find, though, it will take some trial and error on your part to tweak any spam filter to suit your needs. Also, no spam filter can be 100% accurate, as there will always be legitimate users that have email accounts with blocked domains and spammers are always trying to find new ways to bypass spam filters.

Keeping this in mind, let's start by installing and configuring **junkfilter** as the superuser:

```
# pkg_add -r junkfilter
# exit
```

You'll note that I became the superuser to install the package, but exited back to a regular user account so I could configure **junkfilter** for this user only. I then followed the instructions in `/usr/local/etc/junkfilter/` README to configure **junkfilter**.

The instructions first suggested that I move my `.procmailrc` to a new directory, then create a link back to my home directory like so:

```
% mkdir -m 755 $HOME/.procmail
% mv -i $HOME/.procmailrc $HOME/.procmail/procmailrc
% ln -s $HOME/.procmail/procmailrc $HOME/.procmailrc
```

Then, I added these lines to the variable section of `procmailrc` so **procmail** can find and use **junkfilter**:

```
PMDIR=$HOME/.procmail
JFDIR=/usr/local/etc/junkfilter/
INCLUDERC=$JFDIR/junkfilter
```

I also had to edit my path line so it looks like this:

```
PATH=$HOME/bin:/usr/bin:/bin:/usr/local/bin:/usr/local/etc:.
```

Finally, to tell **junkfilter** where to put the spam, the author suggests putting this recipe immediately after the INCLUDERC line:

```
:0
* JFEXP ?? .
{
        :0 f
        * JFSTATUS ?? 1
        | formail -i "X-junkfilter: $JFVERSION" \
                -i "X-Spammer: $JFEXP"
        :0 E :
        | formail -i "X-junkfilter: $JFVERSION" \
                -i "X-Spammer: $JFEXP" >> junkmail
}
```

At this point, **junkfilter** is ready to do its thing. You can fine tune what it does by becoming the superuser and tweaking the global configuration file `/usr/local/etc/junkfilter/junkfilter.config`. The nice thing about tweaking **junkfilter** is its simplicity. The configuration file itself contains straight-forward comments and you can toggle functions on and off by changing their values to 0 or 1. If you find that the filter is still catching legitimate mail instead of spam, you can also try putting your own filtering recipes before the **junkfilter** recipe. I'll leave it up to you to experiment with your own setup.

Using spambnc

I'd also like to show how to configure **spambnc** (aka SpamBouncer). Since I tested both of these programs on a single-user machine, I removed the lines from my `.procmailrc` that I had added to configure **junkfilter** before I installed **spambnc**. I then became the superuser and proceeded with the installation:

```
# pkg_add -r spambnc
# exit
```

At the very end of the install, you'll receive a message telling you that the rules were installed into `/usr/local/share/spambnc` and that you should read `/usr/local/share/doc/spambnc/documentation.html`. Unlike **junkfilter**, this utility doesn't have a global configuration file; instead, you add configuration options to your `.procmailrc`. You really should read that suggested documentation file to see which options are available to you as I won't cover them all here.

I found that **spambnc** had a few additional filtering features that I liked. For example, by default, it will filter out all emails written in Chinese, Japanese, Korean, Russian and Turkish. If you don't use these languages, any correspondence in them will probably be spam. However, if you happen to use one of those languages, don't forget to change the default no to yes for your particular language so **spambnc** won't filter out all of your email.

If you want to be more aggressive in your filtering of spam, you can configure **spambnc** to check a variety of Internet sites that keep lists of known spammers and relays. By default, these checks are turned off. Before enabling these checks, visit the relevant sites to ensure they are still in operation and to register if it is required. You'll find the current list of blocked sites at http://www.spambouncer.org/reference/blocklists.shtml.

To configure **spambnc**, you'll have to add these two lines to your .procmailrc:

```
SBDIR=/usr/local/share/spambnc
INCLUDERC=${SBDIR}/sb.rc
```

Note that the INCLUDERC line should be the very last line in your variable section, meaning it should be just before your own filtering recipes.

You'll also need to tell **spambnc** where to put the messages it filters out. There are two variables for this: the first tells **spambnc** where to put messages that might be spam, and the second tells it where to put messages that are pretty well guaranteed to be spam. I set up my two variables like this:

```
BLOCKFOLDER=$MAILDIR/garbage
SPAMFOLDER=$MAILDIR/spam
```

and placed them just before the INCLUDERC line.

Once you've set those four required variables, **spambnc** is ready to roll. There are several dozen other variables I haven't mentioned that might pique your interest enough to include in your own .procmailrc file; see that documentation file for details.

If you're subscribed to any mailing lists, you'll soon find that some mailing lists are caught and flagged by **spambnc**, while others survive the checks and make it to your own filtering recipes. For example, all the mail from the freebsd-questions list was being placed in my garbage folder instead of my questions folder, yet the messages from most (not all) of the securityfocus mailing lists made it to my security folder.

To tell **spambnc** not to filter a message just because it came from a mailing list, create a file in your home directory called legitlists. In that file, put the address of each mailing list you're subscribed to on one line; mine looks like this:

```
questions@freebsd.org
freebsd-questions@freebsd.org
security@freebsd.org
advocacy@freebsd.org
newbies@freebsd.org
sectools@securityfocus.com
newsscan@newsscan.com
```

After about a week or so of adding rogue lists to this file as you discover them, you shouldn't have any more trouble with mailing lists messages being blocked just because they came from a mailing list. However, virii and spam sent to those mailing lists will continue to be filtered out, which is probably what you were aiming for.

Another file you may want to create in your home directory is called `.nobounce`. If you have friends that send email from known spammer domains such as hotmail.com, put their addresses in this file, one address per line. This will tell **spambnc** that you trust that particular email address to not send you any spam.

Additional Resources

Original Article:

`http://www.onlamp.com/pub/a/bsd/2002/01/10/FreeBSD_Basics.html`

Procmail Spam Resources:

`http://partmaps.org/era/procmail/links.html#antispam`

8.8 Proxy Terminology 101

If you've ever accessed the Internet from an office environment, chances are your communications passed through a proxy. In the next few sections, I'll discuss the advantages of using a proxy and demonstrate the configuration of several proxies available from FreeBSD's ports collection.

You may not already know what a proxy does. Take a moment and go to `http://www.freebsd.org/ports/`, and in the "Search for:" box type in the word "proxy". You may be surprised at the number of proxies available, perhaps even a bit dismayed by all of the terms found in the descriptions: reverse proxy, arp proxy, transparent proxy, etc. Bear with me while I go through the most common proxy terms. Then we can start making sense of the terminology by looking at concrete examples.

Proxy Basics

In its simplest form, a proxy is a piece of software that acts on behalf of a network client. Keep in mind that in a network, a client is an entity that makes a network request and a server is an entity that responds to the request. For example, your web browser is a client which requests web content from a web server.

Depending upon the proxy, there are several ways it can act on behalf of the client. The first is to take the place of the client, meaning the client never communicates directly with the server. Instead, the client makes a connection to the proxy and the proxy makes the connection to the server, receives any responses from the server, and relays them back to the client. This is often done with web browsers and looks like this:

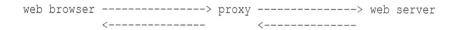

```
web browser ---------------> proxy ---------------> web server
             <---------------        <---------------
```

The next time you go to a web site, look at the bottom of your GUI web browser. If it says "Waiting for www.google.ca", your web browser is connecting directly to the specified web server. However, if it says something like "Connecting to 192.168.1.1", your request is going through a proxy located at that address.

Using a proxy offers several advantages to a network. First, the only computer in the network that requires a public IP address is the one hosting the proxy software. This means that an entire network can have access to the Internet, even if you're only able to get one IP address from your Internet Service Provider. Besides saving on cost, this also adds a bit of a security benefit as it hides your network from the Internet. The only IP address an Internet host is aware of is the IP address of the proxy.

There are further security advantages to using a proxy. Since all Internet requests pass through the proxy, most proxies allow you to configure which requests are allowed and which are banned. In fact, the amount and ease of configurability is usually what you are looking for when you are evaluating which particular proxy application is most suited for your network.

A proxy will also typically have a cache of previous requests which can save bandwidth. This is similar to your web browser's cache, except that an entire network can take advantage of the cached content. If one user has already requested an URL, the proxy will copy the content to its cache. When the next request for that URL arrives at the proxy, it will return the cached content rather than going back out on the Internet to retrieve the requested web page. Keep in mind that secure content won't be cached. For example, if you give your credit card information at a site whose URL starts with "https://", that information is not cached by the proxy.

A proxy that does caching will use an algorithm to determine how often to refresh the contents of its cache. A cache is great for saving Internet bandwidth, but users don't want to receive a page which has been stored in cache for over a month, especially if the original page has changed since then. Also, some pages are more dynamic than others. For example, Slashdot changes its contents often during the day whereas IANA rarely changes. The algorithm contains criteria to help the proxy determine when to refresh its cache and which pages to refresh first.

The most commonly used algorithms are ICP (Internet Cache Protocol), CARP (Cache Array Routing Protocol), and HTCP (HyperText Caching Protocol). These protocols have an additional advantage in that they allow multiple proxies to share their cache information. This allows a larger network to have a distributed cache and Internet requests can be load balanced.

There is a disadvantage to using a proxy: the client must be preconfigured to use it. This process is known as client modification. In the example of a web browser, it requires the user to go into the Preferences or Options portion of their web browser, locate the Proxy section, and input the IP address of the proxy and the port number the proxy application is listening on. Other applications may require that special proxy client software be installed and configured on each machine that needs access to the proxy.

This brings us to the other way a proxy may act on behalf of a client: as a transparent proxy. Transparent means that nothing is preconfigured on the client; in fact, the user may have no idea that their request is going through a proxy. A transparent proxy will intercept the client request, ensure that it is allowed, and then forward it on to the server. This type of proxy is often integrated into a firewall which allows you to configure the proxy as part of the network's security policy.

Application-specific Proxies

Now is a good time to mention that most proxies are considered to be application-specific. Take a closer look at your search results from the FreeBSD ports list. Notice that there are RealAudio proxies, IRC proxies, HTTP proxies, FTP proxies, SMTP proxies, and so on. For many Internet applications, there is a separate software proxy. This is an important point; it suggests the true power and configurability of proxy software.

Imagine for a moment a typical network protected by a firewall. Users behind the firewall wish to surf the Internet and send and receive email. The firewall has been configured to allow outbound ports 25 (SMTP), 80 (HTTP), and 110 (POP3) and to allow the responses to those packets back into the network. As a packet arrives at the firewall, its headers will be compared to the firewall's rules to ensure the port number and source/destination IP addresses are allowed.

That sounds pretty secure, doesn't it? As long as the data contained in the packet is what it claims to be, it is secure. One of the limitations of a firewall's rulebase is that it is restricted to the information contained in the packet's headers. In order for a firewall to inspect the data portion of a packet, it must understand that data. This is known as content inspection and requires additional software that understands the content being inspected. As you may have guessed, that additional software could be an application proxy.

Let's use an HTTP packet as an example. One of the network's users sends out a packet destined for port 80. It reaches the firewall which allows the packet, since the rulebase allows port 80 outbound. However, that packet didn't contain HTTP data. Instead, the user had configured his p2p application to use port 80, knowing that that port was open on the firewall. File sharing was probably the last thing the network administrator wanted to allow in her security policy, yet the firewall rulebase was unable to stop the unwanted packet.

Even if the packet contained legitimate HTTP data, how would the firewall know if it also included a virus, a malicious ActiveX component or JavaScript? Or a ton of annoying pop-up ads? A firewall won't know, but a good HTTP proxy will.

Finally, there is the authentication issue. A firewall can only make authentication decisions based on IP addresses, but IP addresses can be spoofed and more than one user can sit at the same computer. You can't write a firewall rule that says "Gwendolyn can surf from 10.0.0.1 but Martin can't". However, a proxy can be configured to force a user to authenticate before they are allowed Internet access as well as to keep a list of allowed users and their permitted locations.

A proxy sounds great, but why do you need a separate proxy for every application? For the simple reason that every application uses different commands. If you're connected to an SMTP server and try to use the LIST command, you'll receive an error. That's because LIST is a POP3 command, not an SMTP command. Similarly, a packet containing SMTP data will contain an SMTP command. An SMTP proxy can look for valid SMTP commands in the data portion of the packet. If it doesn't find any, the packet probably doesn't contain SMTP data.

If you're ever tasked with configuring an application proxy, it's handy to know where to find the commands used by each application, along with an explanation of what each command does. The best source of information is the RFC for that particular protocol. Here I've included the references for the most commonly used applications; as you skim through each RFC, look for the Commands section. You'll note that HTTP commands are instead referred to as Methods.

HTTP — RFC 2616

FTP — RFC 959

SMTP — RFC 2821

POP3 — RFC 1939

IMAP4 — RFC 2060

IRC — RFC 2812

We'll be revisiting application command sets as we build and configure some of the application proxies available in the ports collection.

Advanced Proxy Terms

There's a few other proxy terms I'd like to discuss before wrapping up this section. The first is a reverse proxy. Think back to the definition of a proxy: a software application that acts on behalf of a network client. A reverse proxy is the reverse of that: it acts on behalf of a network server. The most common usage of a reverse proxy is to protect a web server. When a user on the Internet requests data from a web server protected by a reverse proxy, the reverse proxy intercepts the request and ensures that the data contained in the request is acceptable. For example, that the data doesn't contain any non-HTTP data or any malicious HTTP commands. If the data is acceptable, the reverse proxy will receive the requested content from the web server and forward it on to the original user. In this way, users on the Internet never directly access your web server.

Another type of proxy is an ARP proxy. ARP is used whenever a TCP/IP host needs to send a packet. Before the host's interface can create a frame which will be sent to the network, it needs to know the hardware address of the host that will receive the frame. Since the packet itself only contains the IP address, ARP is used to determine which hardware address is associated with that IP address.

There are times, though, that ARP won't be able to find the hardware address. Let's take a look at a simple example:

```
web server ----- firewall/NAT device ------ Internet router ----- web browser
|-----DMZ-------|                      |-----------Internet-----------------|
|--- 10.0.0.0 --|                      |- 1.2.3.0 -|
```

Here a web server is located in a DMZ which is protected by a firewall. The web server has been assigned the private address of 10.0.0.1. The NAT device has also statically associated that private address with the real address 1.2.3.4. The DNS server has a record pointing to 1.2.3.4 so the world can find the real IP associated with the web server. The firewall/NAT device also has a public IP of 1.2.3.100.

What happens when a web browser wants to access the content on that web server? The web browser will query DNS to resolve the web server's address to 1.2.3.4. It will then send the web request out onto the Internet where routers will route the packet to the 1.2.3.0 network. The Internet router attached to network 1.2.3.0 will send out an ARP request looking for the hardware address of 1.2.3.4.

But there really isn't a physical interface associated with 1.2.3.4. Instead that address is just a logical association that tells the firewall that any packets destined for that address are really to be sent to the web server located at 10.0.0.1. Because there isn't a physical interface, there is no physical address and no host will respond to the router's ARP request. Without a response, the router will be unable to transmit the packet onto the network.

Enter an ARP proxy. This is where a host (in this case, the firewall) answers an ARP request with its own hardware address. The assumption is that once it receives the frame, it knows what to do with it. Your FreeBSD system has a builtin ARP proxy (the **arp** command). Let's pretend for a moment that the hardware address of the firewall is AA:BB:CC:11:22:33. To configure that firewall to receive frames for both its own IP address and for the web server's IP address, use this command as the superuser:

```
# arp -s 1.2.3.4 AA:BB:CC:11:22:33 pub
```

The **pub** (published) keyword is what invokes the ARP proxy. To verify it worked:

```
# arp -a
(1.2.3.100) at aa:bb:cc:11:22:33 on ed0 [ethernet]
(1.2.3.4.) at aa:bb:cc:11:22:33 on ed0 permanent published [ethernet]
```

Additional Resources

Original Article:

`http://www.onlamp.com/pub/a/bsd/2003/06/19/FreeBSD_Basics.html`

Documentation on Caching Protocols:

`http://icp.ircache.net/`

8.9 HTTP Proxies

Now that I've introduced some of the benefits to be gained by using a proxy, let's concentrate on HTTP proxies. We'll take a look at some of the HTTP proxies available in the ports collection and which proxies are suited for which needs.

If you have any familiarity with HTTP proxies, your first thought is probably Squid, the excellent HTTP proxy. Since there are already many fine articles and tutorials on using and configuring Squid, I won't cover that product in this series. Squid is an example of a very configurable HTTP proxy that can scale into very large networks. This is great if you are an administrator of a very large network, but overkill if you simply want to surf safely from your FreeBSD box or enforce a policy on a small home network. Thinking as a user, what are some of the irritants that go along with web browsing? The following quickly come to mind:

- Pop-up windows

- Flashing advertisements

- Cookies

- Webbugs

- Java applets

- Shockwave intros

- Speed, or the lack thereof

Depending upon the web browser you use, some of these irritants can be dealt with directly. Others require you to install additional proxy software. Let's start by taking a look at some common browsers, then move onto complementary proxies.

Web Browser Features

Keep in mind that new features are added with new versions, so features that are missing now may appear in later versions. Also, every web browser has a Preferences section, so if your browser isn't listed here, check it out to see what features are available.

The Preferences section is found under the Edit menu of Firefox, and under the Tools menu of Opera. Both browsers have an appropriately named setting that allows you to deal with cookies. Each also allows you to enable or disable Java and JavaScript. Finally, if you have a slow Internet connection and plenty of disk space, you may find a speed improvement by tweaking each browser's cache settings.

To deal with popup windows in Opera, click on General to find the setting to disallow popups. Firefox takes this a step further by either disabling popups entirely or on a site-by-site basis. You'll find the setting to disable popups all together under Content. Alternately, as you encounter a site with an irritating popup, simply right-click the page and choose to "Reject popup windows from this site."

bfilter

Now, let's see what some of the applications in the ports collection can do to augment the features already provided by your favorite web browser. I'll start with **bfilter**. This HTTP proxy not only controls popup windows, it also stops those annoying flashing ads and promises to disable webbugs. To install this application, become the superuser and:

```
# pkg_add -r bfilter
```

The application will be installed to `/usr/local/bin/bfilter` and its configuration file to `/usr/local/etc/bfilter/config`. Once the install is finished, leave the superuser account and type **bfilter** in order to start the proxy. Then verify that the proxy is listening for requests:

```
% sockstat -4
USER      COMMAND    PID    FD PROTO  LOCAL ADDRESS        FOREIGN ADDRESS
dlavigne  bfilter    20336   3 tcp4    127.0.0.1:8080       *:*
```

You'll note that **bfilter** listens on port 8080 on the loopback address. If you read the comments in its configuration file, you'll see that 127.0.0.1 means to listen for HTTP requests on the local computer. If you wish to listen only on one interface, specify its IP address in the configuration file.

bfilter is not a transparent proxy, meaning you will have to configure your web browser to use the proxy. Go into the Preferences section of your browser and you should find a setting that deals with Proxies. Type in the IP address and port number used by **bfilter**. In my example, **bfilter** is running on the same machine as my web browser, so I use 127.0.0.1 as the IP address and 8080 as the port number. If you are running **bfilter** on a separate computer, input that computer's IP address into the Proxies section of your browser.

man bfilter describes how to create URL patterns and content filters. However, I found that the default configuration worked flawlessly at catching popup windows and flashing ads. If you're looking for an easy-to-use proxy that works out of the box, **bfilter** is a very nice solution.

middleman

Another HTTP proxy I enjoy using is **middleman**. Like **bfilter**, it works as is, but what makes this proxy interesting are the additional features that provide an enticing way to learn more about HTTP and what is happening behind the scenes every time you visit a web site.

First, let's install the application:

```
# pkg_add -r middleman
```

Note that the name of the installed application will be `/usr/local/bin/mman`. You also need to know the name of the default configuration file in order to start the application. If you just type **mman**, you'll receive the help file. Instead, use the **-c** switch to specify the config file and start the proxy:

```
# mman -c /usr/local/etc/mman.xml.dist
```

I found that the proxy needs to be started as the superuser. Don't forget to check the port **mman** is listening on and set the Proxies section of your browser accordingly:

```
% sockstat -4
USER      COMMAND    PID   FD PROTO  LOCAL ADDRESS       FOREIGN ADDRESS
root      mman       575    0 tcp4   127.0.0.1:8080      *:*
```

If you plan on using **middleman**, take the time to read /usr/local/share/doc/middleman/README.html. This is the only documentation on the product, but it is very thorough and full of interesting ideas on how to use a proxy.

Although the default configuration will probably suit your needs, you should check out the included web interface by typing **mman** into your browser. This will allow you to view:

- Active connections

- Log entries

- Config

- Cache entries

- DNS cache

- Headers

- Connection pool

- Prefetch queue

A Bit About HTTP

If you've never managed an HTTP server or HTTP proxy before, you may be amazed at the amount of interaction that occurs whenever a web browser connects to a web server. I mentioned in the last section that we would be referring to the HTTP RFC (2616). Let's do a very quick rundown on how the HTTP protocol works; I'll leave it to you to refer to the RFC to fill in the details that interest you.

Whenever you browse a web site, your browser must make a separate request for every item on that page. For example, if I type slashdot.org into my browser, I'll see the following entries in my **mman** cache:

- http://images.slashdot.org:80/topics/topicgamesrts.gif

- http://images.slashdot.org:80/topics/topicinternet.gif

- http://images.slashdot.org:80/title.gif

- http://slashdot.org:80/

- http://images.slashdot.org:80/topics/topicaposx.gif

- http://images.slashdot.org:80/topics/topicms.gif

- `http://images.slashdot.org:80/topics/topiccomdex.gif`

- `http://images.slashdot.org:80/slc.gif`

- `http://images.slashdot.org:80/pix.gif`

- `http://images.slashdot.org:80/topics/topicscience.gif`

- `http://images.slashdot.org:80/greendot.gif`

- `http://slashdot.org:80/favicon.ico`

- `http://images.slashdot.org:80/topics/topichardware.gif`

Note that every GIF or image is a separate request, as each is stored as a separate file on the web server. In order for my web browser to display the main page of Slashdot's site, it had to individually request each of the 11 GIFs, the one .ico, and the HTML page that explained how to format everything together.

In HTTP, there are two types of packets: request packets and response packets. The request packet always comes from the web browser. This makes sense, as a web browser is a client and the job of a client is to make requests. Not surprisingly, the response packets always come from the web server.

A web browser's request packet has three components:

- Method

- Header

- Body

The method indicates what the client is requesting. The methods are all listed and explained in the RFC and typically are written in uppercase. The most common method is the GET method, as typically your web browser wants to get a particular page or image from the web browser. If you take a look at your **mman** log, or for that matter, the log from any HTTP proxy or HTTP server, you'll see GET requests:

```
Sat 21 16:04:43 [575] request: GET http://images.slashdot.org:80/greendot.gif
Sat 21 16:04:43 [575] cache: create: http://images.slashdot.org:80/greendot.gif
Sat 21 16:04:43 [575] request: GET http://images.slashdot.org:80/pix.gif
Sat 21 16:04:43 [575] cache: create: http://images.slashdot.org:80/pix.gif
Sat 21 16:04:43 [575] request: GET http://images.slashdot.org:80/topics/topicgamesrts.gif
Sat 21 16:04:43 [575] cache: create: http://images.slashdot.org:80/topics/topicgamesrts.gif
Sat 21 16:04:43 [575] request: GET http://images.slashdot.org:80/topics/topiccomdex.gif
Sat 21 16:04:43 [575] cache: create: http://images.slashdot.org:80/topics/topiccomdex.gif
<snip>
```

Here, **mman** issued the GET request on behalf of my browser, then placed a copy of the requested item into its cache.

A web server's response packet also has three components:

- Status

- Headers

- Body

That is, the request packet sends a method, and the web server responds with a status message. Status messages are numerical, and again are listed in the RFC. You've probably run across a "404 error," as 404 is the status number representing "not found." The most common status is 200 or OK. If a web browser issues a GET request and the server finds the requested resource, it will send it back along with a status of 200. If it can't find the requested file, it will instead send a status of 404.

You probably noticed that both request and response packets contain headers and a body. The body usually contains the requested page or image. So, when my web browser made a GET request for `http://images.slashdot.org:80/greendot.gif`, the web server found the GIF and sent a response packet with a status of 200 and the GIF itself in the body of that packet.

Displaying Headers with mman

Headers are the interesting part of HTTP packets. They contain useful information that help the web browser and web server to communicate effectively. They also contain sensitive information about both the web server and web browser. Here are the results of my clicking on Show Headers in **mman**'s web interface:

```
Unfiltered
Type            Value
Host            mman
User-Agent      Mozilla/5.0 (X11; U; FreeBSD i386; en-US; rv:1.3.1)Gecko/20030619
Accept          text/xml,application/xml,application/xhtml+xml,text/html;
        q=0.9,text/plain;q=0.8,video/x-mng,image/png,image/jpeg,image/gif;
        q=0.2,*/*;q=0.1
Accept-Language en-us,en;q=0.5
Accept-Encoding gzip,deflate,compress;q=0.9
Accept-Charset  ISO-8859-1,utf-8;q=0.7,*;q=0.7
Keep-Alive      300
Proxy-Connection keep-alive
Referer         http://mman/headers
Filtered
Type            Value
Host            mman
Accept          text/xml,application/xml,application/xhtml+xml,text/html;
        q=0.9,text/plain;q=0.8,video/x-mng,image/png,image/jpeg,image/gif;
        q=0.2,*/*;q=0.1
Accept-Language en-us,en;q=0.5
Accept-Encoding gzip,deflate,compress;q=0.9
Accept-Charset  ISO-8859-1,utf-8;q=0.7,*;q=0.7
Referer         http://mman/headers
User-Agent      Mozilla/4.0 (compatible; MSIE 6.0; Windows NT 5.0; Q312461)
```

Remember, every HTTP packet includes headers. Here you are seeing the values that are sent by my web browser. The Unfiltered section contains the defaults used by my web browser. It clearly shows my operating system and the version and type of web browser I am using. The Filtered section shows that **mman** changed some of those headers before sending them to the web server. If I don't like those new values, I can simply click on Config, Select Header, and edit, say, the User-Agent. This configuration section is quite powerful, as you can add, delete, and modify the contents of headers. Don't do this just for kicks, however. Make sure you've read the RFC and understand the ramifications of the particular header value you have the urge to muck about with.

It's also interesting to see the headers being sent by a web server. If I type this URL into my browser and remember to use two periods between the word "headers" and the URL:

```
headers..www.mp3.com
```

I'll see this:

```
*Server header:*
HTTP/1.1 200 OK
Date: Sat, 21 Jun 2003 21:17:43 GMT
Server: Apache/1.3.12m1 (Unix) yasl/2.25 sw/1.7 mod_rdbcookie/1.2
        mod_mp3idver/0.12 rwh/1.1 bw/3.37 rewrite/3.3 include/3.6
Connection: close
Transfer-Encoding: chunked
Content-Type: text/html
```

Notice that there aren't any secrets on the server end either. The header clearly indicates the type and version of web server software in use. If you are responsible for maintaining a web server, remember that by default every HTTP packet leaving your server reveals whether or not you've kept up with your web server patches!

Controlling Access

mman also supports features that can be very useful in a networked environment. One, it can force users to authenticate before they are allowed to use the Internet. I'll click on Config then select Access and add a policy. I'll then be presented with a form.

If I leave the IP address section empty, the access policy will affect every IP address that connects to the proxy. I can then set values in the username and password fields. Before saving the policy, I need to configure what access users will be allowed once they input the correct username and password. My choices are:

Web interface: This will allow users to configure the proxy, so I will leave this option unchecked.

Proxy requests: If I check this option, the proxy will accept requests from web browsers that have been manually configured to use the IP address and port number of the proxy.

CONNECT requests: CONNECT is an HTTP method that is often disabled due to its associated security risks.

HTTP requests: I want to remember to select this option, or users won't be able to access HTTP servers.

Transparent proxying: If I check this option, the proxy will intercept web requests, even if the web browser hasn't been configured to use the proxy. This is generally a good thing in a network, as it ensures users won't be able to bypass your proxy server.

Allow bypassing: **mman** has keywords that can be included with an URL to bypass restrictions for a particular site. For example, if I wanted to see the popups for a site, I could type this in my browser: **bypass[f]..www.mp3.com**. If you don't want users bypassing your filters, don't select this option.

If you decide to create your own policy, remember to create a second policy that will allow you as an administrator to configure **mman**. If you plan on configuring **mman** on the same computer that is running the proxy software, keep the default policy, but place it below your new policy that affects your users.

Now, when users open up their web browsers, the browser itself will prompt them for the username and password you created in your policy. If they type it in correctly, they will be able to access the Internet, according to the parameters you set in your policy.

The last feature I wish to mention is limits. This configuration allows you to control Internet access according to month, day, and time. For example, you could configure a policy that limits Internet access to the hours of 9:00 to 17:00 on Monday to Friday.

It seems that I've barely scratched the surface of the **middleman** proxy server. Perhaps I've piqued your interest and you will try this application for yourself.

Additional Resources

Original Article:

```
http://www.onlamp.com/pub/a/bsd/2003/07/03/FreeBSD_Basics.html
```

8.10 SMTP Proxies

Similar to an HTTP proxy, an SMTP proxy is used to add to the feature set already provided by your MTA, or mail server. Again, the amount of available configurable features will vary, depending upon the specific mail server software you've chosen to use in your environment.

The advantage of an SMTP proxy may lie in its ability to simplify your configuration. A web browser's configuration isn't that hard to figure out; simply play around with the available options in the Preferences menu. An SMTP server is a much more complicated piece of software. Finding and making configuration changes can involve reading reams of documentation and dealing with databases, macros, and multiple configuration files.

When dealing with email, one is usually concerned with controlling spam and viruses. Due to the prevalence of both email and the nasties associated with it, it's not surprising that there are myriad supporting applications available to a mail server administrator. This further increases the complexity. For example, one could install and configure a virus scanner, a separate application to tell the SMTP server to use the virus scanner, and yet another application to check for the possibility of spam.

A good SMTP proxy simplifies this configuration process. Remember, an application proxy scans the data portion of a packet. What better time to look for viruses and spam?

Building and Installing messagewall

I've chosen to demonstrate **messagewall**. I like this SMTP proxy, as it has many configurable features with a straightforward and very user-friendly configuration. Without further ado, let's become the superuser and install this application:

```
# pkg_add -r messagewall
```

Once the install is finished, you'll see a post-install message. If you missed it, you can read it again with **pkg_info -Dx messagewall**. Post install messages usually contain configuration information, so it's always a good idea to read them.

I'll go through **messagewall**'s message, as some of the commands work on a Linux box instead of your FreeBSD box. **messagewall** requires you to create two user accounts, two group accounts, and the directories to be used by the chroot. Let's take a look at the message and follow the instructions:

```
# pkg_info -Dx messagewall
Messagewall has been installed, now create the chroot environment:
mkdir /home/mwall
```

The next instruction says to create a group using **groupadd** and a user using **useradd**. Since FreeBSD doesn't use those commands, use **pw** instead:

```
# pw groupadd mwall
# pw useradd mwall -g mwall
```

Next, follow along and create two directories:

```
# mkdir /home/mwall/pids
# chown mwall:mwall /home/mwall/pids
# mkdir /home/mwalla
```

Substitute the **pw** command for the next user and group:

```
# pw groupadd mwalla
# pw useradd mwalla -g mwalla
```

One more directory:

```
# mkdir /home/mwalla/pids
# chown mwalla:mwalla /home/mwalla/pids
```

Finally, copy the included virus patterns into your chroot environment:

```
# cp /usr/local/etc/messagewall/virus.patterns /home/mwall
```

The final instruction is:

```
and don't forget to edit your configfile!
```

One way to find out the name of that installed configfile is to search for it in the port's package listing:

```
# pkg_info -Lx | grep conf
/usr/local/etc/messagewall.conf.sample
```

Since this is a sample configuration file, we'll start by copying it to the real configuration file we'll edit:

```
% cp /usr/local/etc/messagewall.conf.sample /usr/local/etc/messagewall.conf
```

Configuring messagewall

Now use your favorite editor to open up the configuration file. You'll note that everything is commented out, so the message wasn't kidding when it told you to edit the file first. The nice thing about this configuration file is the clear, readable comments. Every option is commented, and optional options are clearly labeled as OPTIONAL.

I'll walk through the configuration file with you, pointing out things to be aware of.

```
# This is the MessageWall sample configuration file.  All
# variables in this file must be uncommented and defined before
# MessageWall will start.
```

This comment is fairly clear. Since most of the defaults are reasonable, I will simply uncomment the following:

```
processes=1
max_clients=10
max_backends=5
max_per_ip=5
max_message_size=10485760
max_rcpt=25
max_errors=3
max_idle=60
max_parts=25
max_depth=5
```

As you go through your configuration file, read each comment and decide for yourself if your particular situation requires different values than the defaults. When in doubt, stick with the default value.

Now come some values that need to be customized for your installation. First, give the IP address of the machine running messagewall:

```
# The IP address, in dotted quad notation, that MessageWall should
# listen on. As MessageWall will bind to port 25 on this address, it
# will need to be run as root.
listen_ip=1.2.3.4
```

Next, the IP address of the SMTP server. This may or may not be the same machine as the one running messagewall:

```
# The IP address, in dotted quad notation, that MessageWall should
# connect to in order to deliver messages that have passed filtering.
# MessageWall will connect to this IP address on port 25 and speak
# ESMTP or SMTP.  The server running on this IP should support ESMTP,
# PIPELINING and 8BITMIME, but does not need to.  You may chain
# MessageWall installations in order to spread filtering across
# different systems, although this is highly inefficient.
backend_ip=127.0.0.1
```

Next, the name of your company. Typically, this is the name used in the MX record of your DNS database.

```
# The primary domain name that MessageWall is serving.  This is used
# in several SMTP responses.
domain=example.com
```

This is followed by several other options that you may wish to leave at the default values as you uncomment them, unless you're a real SMTP guru:

```
path_charset="abcdefghijklmnopqrstuvwxyzABCDEFGHIJKLMNOPQRSTUVWXYZ0123456789.-_+=@"
dnsbl_timeout=5
dnsbl_domain_timeout=5
dnsdcc_timeout=5
rmx_timeout=10
rdns_timeout=10
```

The next value needs to be changed, as it is incorrect. It should look like this:

```
profile_dir=/usr/local/etc/messagewall/profiles/
```

We'll look at that directory and the concept of profiles once we're finished with this file. The next path is correct and can simply be uncommented:

```
pid_dir=/pids/
```

For now, uncomment the next two profiles until we've had a chance to discuss profiles.

```
relay_profile=Relay
default_profile=Medium
```

Next come the options, meaning you don't have to uncomment these if they aren't pertinent to your situation:

```
# OPTIONAL
#local_domains=local_domains
#relay_ips=relay_ips
#special_users=special_users
#relay_auth=relay_auth
```

Hang in there, we're almost finished. Uncomment the lines for the user accounts you created and their home directories:

```
root=/home/mwall
user=mwall
group=mwall
auth_root=/home/mwalla
auth_user=mwalla
auth_group=mwalla
```

Finally, a few more options:

```
# OPTIONAL
#certificate=/usr/local/etc/cert.pem
#backend_certificate=/usr/local/etc/cert.pem
```

Once you're finished uncommenting your configuration file, save your changes.

Profiles and Viruses

Now, let's take a look at that profile directory that was mentioned in the configuration file:

```
# ls /usr/local/etc/messagewall/profiles/
Extreme        Medium        Reject        Strong Plus
Light          Medium Plus   Relay         Warning
Light Plus     None          Strong
```

Each profile is an ASCII text file that contains a set of rules indicating what **messagewall** should look for when it is reading the data portion of a packet. The configuration file uses the *Medium* profile by default, which looks like this:

```
# more /usr/local/etc/messagewall/profiles/Medium
reject_score=1
dnsbl=1,list.dsbl.org
dnsbl=1,bl.spamcop.net
rmx_required=1,1
filename_reject=1,.exe
filename_reject=1,.pif
filename_reject=1,.scr
filename_reject=1,.vbs
filename_reject=1,.bat
filename_reject=1,.com
filename_reject=1,.shs
filename_reject=1,.wsc
header_rejecti=1,Precedence:junk
header_rejecti=1,X-Mailer:Microsoft CDO
header_rejecti=1,X-Mailer:eGroups Message Poster
header_rejecti=1,X-Mailer:Delphi Mailing System
header_rejecti=1,X-Mailer:diffondi
header_rejecti=1,X-Mailer:RoryMAILER
header_rejecti=1,X-Mailer:GreenRider
header_rejecti=1,X-Mailer:GoldMine
header_rejecti=1,X-Mailer:MailPro
header_rejecti=1,X-Mailer:charset(89)
header_rejecti=1,X-Mailer:MailWorkZ
header_rejecti=1,X-Mailer:bulk
virus_scan=1,virus.patterns
```

Note that the file is composed of variables followed by values. Explanations of each variable and examples of possible values are given in **man messagewall_profiles**. Most of the values are straightforward. For example, the `filename_reject` variable indicates which attachments should be discarded. In this profile, any attachment with an extension of exe, pif, scr, vbs, bat, com, shs, or wsc will be rejected. One could easily follow the format and add his or her own lines for extensions that should also be rejected.

If you've ever configured a spam filter such as **procmail**[6], you'll recognize the `header_rejecti` variable. The values indicate what to look for in an email message's header. If that value is found, the message will be rejected as spam.

Unsurprisingly, the `virus_scan` variable tells **messagewall** to scan for viruses as long as this value is turned on or set to 1. You should note that, like most SMTP proxies, **messagewall** relies upon a separate virus-scanning product and follows the Open AntiVirus format.

Remember copying the default virus patterns earlier? These virus definitions will get you started, but you will still want to download the latest virus definitions. If you're the curious type, the format is in ASCII text, meaning you can take a look at the virus definition file.

Simply save the downloaded file to `/usr/local/etc/messagewall/virus.patterns`. Alternately, you can use any antivirus product that supports the Open AntiVirus format. Keep in mind when choosing an antivirus product that most are free for personal use, but cost for business or commercial use.

Before we leave the default profile, you should take the time to check out the settings in the other available profiles. If you find a profile that is better suited to your network's needs, don't forget to edit `messagewall.conf` to reflect the desired profile.

OK, you've chosen a profile, you've selected an antivirus product and downloaded its latest definitions. To start **messagewall**, simply type:

```
# messagewall
```

messagewall must be started as *root* in order to bind to the specified address on port 25. However, once the port is bound, it will enter the chroot and assume the identity of the *mwall* user. Note that you'll lose your prompt when you start **messagewall** and will see a series of messages:

```
STARTUP/STATUS: loaded profile Extreme
STARTUP/STATUS: loaded profile Medium Plus
STARTUP/STATUS: loaded profile Light
STARTUP/STATUS: loaded profile Relay
STARTUP/STATUS: loaded profile Warning
STARTUP/STATUS: loaded profile Medium
STARTUP/STATUS: loaded profile Reject
STARTUP/STATUS: loaded profile Strong
STARTUP/STATUS: loaded profile Light Plus
STARTUP/STATUS: loaded profile Strong Plus
STARTUP/STATUS: loaded profile None
{0} PROCESS/STATUS: start
{0} [0] BACKEND/STATUS: connect to 127.0.0.1 started
{0} [1] BACKEND/STATUS: connect to 127.0.0.1 started
{0} [2] BACKEND/STATUS: connect to 127.0.0.1 started
```

---

[6]See sections 8.6 and 8.7 for details about **procmail**.

```
{0} [3] BACKEND/STATUS: connect to 127.0.0.1 started
{0} [4] BACKEND/STATUS: connect to 127.0.0.1 started
{0} [0] BACKEND/STATUS: connection established
{0} [1] BACKEND/STATUS: connection established
{0} [2] BACKEND/STATUS: connection established
{0} [3] BACKEND/STATUS: connection established
{0} [4] BACKEND/STATUS: connection established
```

You can further verify that **messagewall** is listening for connections by telnetting to port 25 using the IP address you specified in your configuration file:

```
# telnet 1.2.3.4 25
Trying 1.2.3.4...
Connected to 1.2.3.4.
Escape character is '^]'.
220 example.com MessageWall 1.0.8 (You may not relay)
```

Other Utilities

Finally, there are two other utilities that were installed with **messagewall**. **messagewallctl** is used to interact with **messagewall** once it is running. It has its own manpage; type **messagewallctl** to receive its list of possible commands.

Virus definitions are usually updated on a daily basis. You'll need to make **messagewall** aware that the definitions have changed, but you don't want to stop the service in order to do so. Instead, simply type:

```
# messagewallctl reload-virus
```

This is the most common usage of **messagewallctl**. Refer to its manpage to see its other usages.

The other utility is **messagewallstats**. To use this handy utility, first create an empty file to hold the statistics. I've decided to create one in the chroot:

```
# touch ~mwall/messagewallstats
```

Then start **messagewall**, telling it to redirect its statistical output to this file:

```
# messagewall > ~mwall/messagewallstats
```

Now, whenever you want to view the statistics:

```
# messagewallstats ~mwall/messagewallstats | more
```

As you can see, I was pretty anxious and viewed my stats before any email actually arrived and had a chance to be acted upon by messagewall:

```
Client Connections: 0
QUIT: 0
Disconnect: 0
Disconnect inside DATA: 0
Bare LF: 0
Idle Timeout: 0
Too many errors: 0
Client TLS Attempts: 0
Success: 0
Overflows: 0
Per-IP Overflows: 0
Backend Overflows: 0
Backend Rejection Overflows: 0
Backend connection attempts: 0
Success: 0
TLS: 0
Invalid MAIL characters: 0
Invalid RCPT characters: 0
Client Messages: 0
Bare LF inside DATA: 0
8bit inside DATA: 0
Rejected by Profile: 0
Completely Received: 0
Sent to Backend: 0
Accepted by Backend: 0
Messages Rejected by Filter: 0
Failed To/CC: 0
Failed From: 0
Matched DNSBL: 0
Matched Domain DNSBL: 0
Matched DNSDCC: 0
Reverse Path MX/A lookup timed out: 0
Reverse DNS lookup timed out: 0
Failed Reverse Path MX/A: 0
Failed Reverse DNS: 0
Failed Body check: 0
Failed Header check: 0
Illegal attachment filename: 0
Virus: 0
No accepted MIME parts: 0
Missing MIME boundary: 0
Too many parts: 0
Illegal multipart encoding: 0
Unknown MIME encoding: 0
Invalid QP encoding: 0
Invalid base64 encoding: 0
Mail Traffic
Bytes received: 0
Bytes rejected: 0
```

```
Bytes accepted: 0
```

Additional Resources

Original Article:

```
http://www.onlamp.com/pub/a/bsd/2003/07/24/FreeBSD_Basics.html
```

Open AntiVirus:

```
http://www.openantivirus.org/
```

8.11 Configuring a TFTP Server

In section 7.5, I demonstrated how to configure a Cisco router using a FreeBSD computer and its built-in serial communications utilities. In this section, I'll show you how to set up a TFTP server so you can back up and upgrade a hardware appliance such as a Cisco router.

If you've ever had the opportunity to work with any hardware-based routers, security appliances, or intelligent switches, you're aware that these devices typically don't have hard disks for permanent storage of their configurations and underlying operating systems. Instead, they use a combination of volatile and non-volatile RAM and an EEPROM chip.

Since chips have far less storage capacity than hard drives, things get a bit more interesting when you want to install or upgrade the operating system. The operating system itself and the utilities that come with it will be optimized to fit into a small space. Most of the utilities you're used to finding on a computer's operating system will be missing. You won't find any browsers or download utilities here! You also won't find any backup utilities, even though you know the first rule in computing land is "backup, backup, backup".

The most common utility used to accomplish device backups and upgrades is TFTP, the Trivial File Transfer Protocol. This utility is similar to FTP, except that it has been stripped down in functionality in order to fit onto a chip; hence, the trivial. Hardware devices, such as a Cisco router or switch, contain a TFTP client. It is up to you to create a TFTP server somewhere in your network. The TFTP server will store a backup copy of your configurations and the images (or operating systems) of the hardware devices within your network.

Enabling a TFTP Server

Your FreeBSD system already contains a TFTP server, meaning you don't have to install any additional software. You only have to enable the TFTP service and properly configure a directory. Unlike most services, the TFTP server does not have it's own configuration file — instead it uses **inetd** or the Internet Super Server. **inetd** was originally created to save resources on Unix systems. Rather than creating processes for daemons that may not be used that often, this one daemon will listen on behalf of other daemons. If a client requests a connection on a port that is monitored by **inetd**, **inetd** will start a process for the daemon normally associated with that port so it can respond to the client's request. The configuration file /etc/inetd.conf tells **inetd** which ports to listen on; in other words, to enable TFTP we have to edit this file to tell **inetd** to listen for connections on port 69.

Let's take a look at **inetd**'s configuration file:

```
# head -30 /etc/inetd.conf
# $FreeBSD: src/etc/inetd.conf,v 1.70.2.1 2006/03/28 15:51:44 ceri Exp $
#
# Internet server configuration database
#
# Define *both* IPv4 and IPv6 entries for dual-stack support.
# To disable a service, comment it out by prefixing the line with '#'.
# To enable a service, remove the '#' at the beginning of the line.
#
#ftp    stream  tcp     nowait  root    /usr/libexec/ftpd       ftpd -l
#ftp    stream  tcp6    nowait  root    /usr/libexec/ftpd       ftpd -l
#ssh    stream  tcp     nowait  root    /usr/sbin/sshd          sshd -i -4
#ssh    stream  tcp6    nowait  root    /usr/sbin/sshd          sshd -i -6
#telnet stream tcp      nowait  root    /usr/libexec/telnetd    telnetd
#telnet stream tcp6     nowait  root    /usr/libexec/telnetd    telnetd
#shell stream  tcp      nowait  root    /usr/libexec/rshd       rshd
#shell stream  tcp6     nowait  root    /usr/libexec/rshd       rshd
#login stream  tcp      nowait  root    /usr/libexec/rlogind    rlogind
#login stream  tcp6     nowait  root    /usr/libexec/rlogind    rlogind
#finger stream tcp      nowait/3/10 nobody /usr/libexec/fingerd fingerd -s
#finger stream tcp6     nowait/3/10 nobody /usr/libexec/fingerd fingerd -s
#
# run comsat as root to be able to print partial mailbox contents w/ biff,
# or use the safer tty:tty to just print that new mail has been received.
#comsat dgram  udp     wait    tty:tty /usr/libexec/comsat      comsat
#
# ntalk is required for the 'talk' utility to work correctly
#ntalk dgram    udp     wait    tty:tty /usr/libexec/ntalkd     ntalkd
#tftp  dgram    udp     wait    root    /usr/libexec/tftpd      tftpd -l
-s /tftpboot
#tftp  dgram    udp6    wait    root    /usr/libexec/tftpd      tftpd -l
-s /tftpboot
#bootps dgram   udp     wait    root    /usr/libexec/bootpd     bootpd
```

Note: Even though it is possible to do so, it is rare to use this file to enable SSH or FTP as these services now come with their own startup scripts.

You'll notice that this file contains a line for every daemon that **inetd** can listen on behalf of. If a line begins with the comment character #, **inetd** will not listen on the port associated with that daemon. For the lines that have not been commented out, **inetd** needs the following information in this order:

1. the name of the service, so it can look it up in /etc/services and know which port number to listen on

2. whether this daemon understands streams of data or datagrams

3. whether this daemon uses TCP or UDP as its transport

4. whether **inetd** should wait for the daemon to finish transferring data to the client or not bother waiting before listening for more client requests on the port number

5. the name of the user account to start the daemon under

6. the full path to the daemon to start

7. any arguments that need to be passed to the daemon when starting it (starting with the name of the program)

In order to tell **inetd** to listen for TFTP requests, find the two lines that start with `#tftp` and remove the comment from the first line so it looks like this:

```
tftp   dgram  udp   wait  root  /usr/libexec/tftpd  tftpd -l -s /tftpboot
#tftp  dgram  udp6  wait  root  /usr/libexec/tftpd  tftpd -l -s /tftpboot
```

You'll note that FreeBSD supports both IPv4 and IPv6, so its **inetd** is capable of listening for both types of requests. Also note that TFTP uses UDP as its transport. This means it is not as reliable as FTP (which uses TCP). It also means that TFTP supports broadcasts, meaning you don't have to configure the TFTP client with the IP address of a particular TFTP server.

Once you've removed the #, save your changes. You now need to tell **inetd** that you've made some changes to its configuration file:

/etc/rc.d/inetd reload

Note: Use the **start** keyword instead if **inetd** is not already running. If you just get your prompt back rather than a starting message, you are missing the required **rc** variable which can be fixed by adding this line to `/etc/rc.conf`:

```
inetd_enable="YES"
```

This will also ensure **inetd** starts if the TFTP server reboots.

Next, ensure **inetd** is listening for UDP connections on port 69, the TFTP port:

netstat | grep 69
```
USER   COMMAND  PID   FD PROTO  LOCAL ADDRESS   FOREIGN ADDRESS
root   inetd    1713  4  udp4   *:69            *:*
```

Serving Files with TFTP

Now that the server is functional, you need to create a directory that will be used by the TFTP server to store the backups of your hardware devices' configurations and operating systems. This directory must be called `/tftpboot`:

mkdir /tftpboot

Next, populate this directory with the files you wish to download to your hardware devices. For example, if you wish to upgrade your Cisco IOS, download the desired image from the Cisco web site and save it to `/tftpboot`. Most software images have rather complicated names, such as `c1600-ny-mz.112-11.P.bin`. If you'll be serving many images, you should document which devices are using which images.

You'll also want to create empty files for the files you'll upload from the hardware devices themselves. These files can be called anything that is useful to you. For example, if I wish to save the configurations from a 1602 router, a PIX 501 firewall, and a 1924 switch, I could create the following files:

```
# touch 1602_config PIX_config 1924_config
```

Finally, since TFTP is a stripped-down version of FTP, it does not support authentication. For this reason, this directory and its contents must be accessible to your TFTP clients. Typically, this is accomplished by setting the permissions like so:

```
# chmod -R 777 /tftpboot
```

Depending upon the TFTP client built into the hardware device you are using, you may be able to successfully use stricter permissions. Unfortunately, with a Cisco device, it will fail unless the permissions are set this way. When you're finished, verify the permissions in the directory:

```
# ls -l /tftpboot
total 0
-rwxrwxrwx  1 root   wheel   0 May 18 15:24 1602_config
-rwxrwxrwx  1 root   wheel   0 May 18 15:24 1924_config
-rwxrwxrwx  1 root   wheel   0 May 18 15:24 PIX_config
-rwxrwxrwx  1 root   wheel   4194172 May 18 15:33 c1600-ny-mz.112-11.P.bin
```

Note: You may want to consider configuring a packet filter for restricting access to your TFTP service.

Speaking TFTP to the Server

You should now have an operational TFTP server. Since your FreeBSD system also has a TFTP client, you can test that the server is set up to properly transfer files. First, **tftp** to the address of your TFTP server as a regular user. If the server responds, your prompt will change. Here, I will use the **tftp** client from the same computer that is the TFTP server:

```
% tftp 127.0.0.1
tftp>
```

If you type **?**, you'll see that the **tftp** client supports few commands. The ones you'll use most often are **get** to download a file, **put** to upload a file, and **quit** to exit the utility. If you're used to using the **ftp** client, you'll notice the absence of **cd**, **ls**, **mget**, **mput**, and several dozen other supported FTP commands.

Now, try to get one of the files; your transfer will be more exciting if you pick a non-empty file. Here, I'll transfer an image file:

```
tftp> get c1600-ny-mz.112-11.P.bin
Received 4194172 bytes in 1.6 seconds
```

I'll then quit the utility:

```
tftp> quit
```

There's a couple of important points regarding this file transfer. First, it won't work if the file you want to transfer is not in /tftpboot. Notice when I used the **get** command that I didn't specify the path to the file, simply the filename. If I had tried this command instead, I would have received the following error message:

```
tftp> get /tftpboot/c1600-ny-mz.112-11.P.bin
Error code 1: File not found
```

Remember, **tftp** assumes that the file you want to transfer already exists and that it is located in /tftpboot. Second, make sure you spell the filename correctly. This is especially important with those long image filenames. If you're a terrible typist, you'll miss filename completion, as it's not supported by **tftp**. This is another reason why it is a good idea to document the files stored in /tftpboot and to check your spelling when you use the **get** command. Otherwise, you'll end up getting frustrated by "Error code 1" messages.

You may have noticed that I didn't specify where to put the file that was transferred using **get**. This is because it is automatically copied to the current working directory. Typically, this isn't a problem on a hardware device, but it is something to keep in mind should you ever initiate a **tftp** session using your FreeBSD computer.

Finally, you should use **ls -l** to verify that the number of bytes received matches the number of bytes in the file stored on the TFTP server. This is also a handy bit of information to have documented. If you have a printer attached to your FreeBSD system, you can easily print out the contents of /tftpboot once you've finished configuring the TFTP server:

```
$ ls -l /tftpboot | lpr
```

Uploading Images via TFTP

Now that I'm satisfied the TFTP server is operational, I'll demonstrate uploading that image file to a Cisco 1602 router. Once I'm connected to the router, I'll input the password required to enter privileged mode:

```
1602> enable
  Password:
1602#
```

Before starting the TFTP client, you should always verify connectivity to the TFTP server by pinging its IP address:

```
1602# ping 10.0.0.100
     !!!!!
```

On a Cisco router, ! indicates a successful **ping**. If you instead receive a series of dots the **ping** is timing out, which indicates a connectivity problem.

I'll then invoke the router's built-in TFTP client by using the following command:

```
1602# copy tftp flash
^^^^NOTICE^^^^
Flash load helper v1.0
This process will accept the copy options and then terminate the
current system image to use the ROM based image for the copy. Routing
functionality will not be available during that time. If you are logged
in via telnet, this connection will terminate. Users with console
access can see the results of the copy operation.
---- ^^^^^^^^ ----
Proceed? [confirm]
```

After reading the warning message, press **Return** to confirm the operation. You'll then be presented with the name of the current operating system on the router and the amount of memory available on the EEPROM chip:

```
System flash directory:
File Length Name/status
  1 3612396 c1600-ny-mz.110-8.P
[3612396 bytes used, 13164756 available, 16777216 total]
```

The client will then prompt for some information:

```
Address or name of remote host [255.255.255.255]
```

If you press **Enter** here, you'll receive the default value enclosed in square brackets, or the broadcast address. This means the TFTP client will send a broadcast onto the network looking for a TFTP server. If there are any intervening routers between this hardware device and the TFTP server, they will most likely discard the broadcast. To prevent that from happening, type in the IP address of your TFTP server.

Next, you'll be prompted for the source filename. That is, the filename of the image that you would like to download from the TFTP server. Remember, it's important not to mistype the name of the file in order for the transfer to succeed. I'll type in the name of my image:

```
Source file name? c1600-ny-mz.112-11.P.bin
```

Next, you'll be prompted for the destination filename. That is, what you would like the file to be called when it is copied to the router's EEPROM chip. Technically, you could change the filename to anything you want, but usually you keep the original image name, like I have done here:

```
Destination file name? c1600-ny-mz.112-11.P.bin
```

Now comes the moment of truth:

```
Accessing file 'c1600-ny-mz.112-11.P.bin' on 10.0.0.100...
```

If you get an "Error code 1," the command will abort and return you to the command prompt. This means you have a typo in the source file name, so repeat the command and try again. If you're sure you spelled the image name correctly, it's time to go to the TFTP server and ensure the file still exists in /tftpboot and is indeed spelled the way you are typing it.

If you receive a permissions problem, double-check the permissions of the image on the TFTP server. Chances are, you forgot to set them to 777.

If all goes well, the TFTP client will continue and give you output similar to this:

```
Loading c1600-ny-mz.112-11.P.bin from 10.0.0.100 (via Ethernet0): ! [OK]
```

You'll then be asked to confirm the operation three times to make sure you're really, really sure that you want to replace the current operating system with the new image:

```
Erase flash device before writing? [confirm]
Flash contains files. Are you sure you want to erase? [confirm]
Copy 'c1600-ny-mz.112-11.P.bin' from server
  as 'c1600-ny-mz.112-11.P.bin' into Flash WITH erase? [yes/no] yes
```

Once you've confirmed, you'll see a series of e's go by as the current operating system is erased:

```
Erasing device...eeeeeeeeeeeeeeeeeeeeeeeeeeeeeeeeeeeeeee...erased
```

and the new image is copied over; in this case, !s indicate success:

```
Loading c1600-ny-mz.112-11.P.bin from 10.0.0.100 (via Ethernet0):
!!!!!!!!!!!!!!!!!!!!!!!!!!!!!!!!!!!!!!!!!!!!!!!!!!!!!!!!!!!!!!
[OK - 4194172 bytes/16777216 bytes]
Verifying checksum... OK (0x5FDE)
Flash copy took 0:02:16 [hh:mm:ss]
```

You should double-check that the bytes transferred over match up with the number of bytes in the image file on the server. In my case, the 4194172 matches up and the checksum indicates that it is OK. If you received many dots or timeouts during the transfer, you should check your network connectivity and consider redoing the transfer. Finally, before rebooting the router into the new operating system, double-check that the correct image is indeed in the EEPROM chip:

```
1602# show flash
PCMCIA flash directory:
File Length Name/status
1 4194172 c1600-ny-mz.112-11.P.bin
```

Then, reboot the router:

```
1602# reload
```

Conclusion

Let's recap the steps necessary to configure your FreeBSD system as a TFTP server:

1. Remove comment from /etc/inetd.conf.

2. Reload **inetd**.

3. Create the /tftpboot directory.

4. Populate the /tftpboot directory.

5. Set permissions on the /tftpboot directory and its contents to 777.

I demonstrated one use of a TFTP server: upgrading the image file on a Cisco router. If you have any hardware devices in your network, read their documentation to see the syntax of the command each uses in order to access the files you have stored on your TFTP server.

There are additional uses for a TFTP server. You may find some of the following URLs useful as launching points into your own experiments:

- http://matt.simerson.net/computing/freebsd.netboot.shtml

- http://ezine.daemonnews.org/200301/sparc64-nfsroot.html

Just keep in mind that TFTP is designed for transferring files to and from chips on hardware devices. If you want to transfer files from one computer to another, TFTP is not the answer. There are many other options available that offer far more functionality and usually, more security.

Additional Resources

Original Articles:

http://www.onlamp.com/pub/a/bsd/2003/06/05/FreeBSD_Basics.html

http://www.onlamp.com/pub/a/bsd/2001/01/31/FreeBSD_Basics.html

8.12 Introducing DHCP

In the next few sections, I'll be covering the DHCP protocol: how it works and how to configure a DHCP client and a DHCP server using FreeBSD. If you've ever connected a computer to a network, you've probably heard of DHCP, the Dynamic Host Configuration Protocol. As its name suggests, this protocol is designed to configure a host dynamically with the TCP/IP information it needs in order to communicate on a network.

The alternative to dynamic addressing is static addressing. Static addressing occurs when you manually type in an IP address, subnet mask, and default gateway address. FreeBSD systems support both static and dynamic addressing. Typically, you would use static addressing to set up a small home network and dynamic addressing when you connect to the Internet.

Knowing Your Interfaces

Before using any type of addressing, you need to determine the FreeBSD name for your network interface card. To do that, use the **ifconfig** command like so:

```
% ifconfig -a
rl0: flags=8802<BROADCAST,SIMPLEX,MULTICAST> mtu 1500
    ether 00:05:5d:d2:19:b7
    media: Ethernet autoselect
ed0: flags=8843<UP,BROADCAST,SIMPLEX,MULTICAST> mtu 1500
    ether 00:50:ba:de:36:33
    media: Ethernet autoselect
lp0: flags=8810<POINTOPOINT,SIMPLEX,MULTICAST> mtu 1500
lo0: flags=8049<UP,LOOPBACK,RUNNING,MULTICAST> mtu 16384
    inet 127.0.0.1 netmask 0xff000000
```

The **ifconfig** command will display both physical and virtual interfaces. You can recognize the Ethernet interfaces as they will have an ether (MAC) address. The FreeBSD name for the adapter will have two or three letters followed by a number. In this example, there are two Ethernet NICs; one is named rl0 and the other ed0. There are also two virtual interfaces, lp0 and lo0. You may recognize 127.0.0.1 as the loopback address, meaning lo0 is the name of the loopback virtual interface.

Most interfaces have an entry in section 4 of the manual. In my case, I could try **man 4 rl**, **man 4 ed**, **man 4 lp**, and **man 4 lo** for more information about each interface. Note that you don't include the number when specifying the interface name with **man**. Instead, the interface number indicates how many interfaces of that type are installed; the count starts at 0. For example, if I had had two realtek NICs, they would be called rl0 and rl1. (That's "arr-ell", not "arr-one".)

Static Addresses

To assign a static IP address and subnet mask to the rl0 interface, I'll become the superuser and use **ifconfig** like so:

```
# ifconfig rl0 192.168.10.1 255.255.255.0
```

When you try this command, don't forget to specify the correct interface name for your system or you will receive an error message. To see if your command was successful, ask **ifconfig** to limit its information to one particular interface, rather than using the **-a** switch to see all the interfaces:

```
# ifconfig rl0
rl0: flags=8802<BROADCAST,SIMPLEX,MULTICAST> mtu 1500
        inet 192.168.10.1 netmask 0xffffff00 broadcast 255.255.255.0
        ether 00:05:5d:d2:19:b7
```

If your computer also requires a default gateway address, use the **route** command like so:

```
# route add default 192.168.10.25
```

To confirm your change:

```
# netstat -rn | grep G
Destination       Gateway           Flags    Refs       Use  Netif Expire
default           192.168.10.25     UGSc        5         0   rl0
192.168.10.1      127.0.0.1         UGHS        0         2   lo0
```

You'll note that I used **grep** to search the routing table for the G flag, which represents the gateway. The other flag to notice is U, which indicates that the gateway is up. This is always a good thing in a gateway.

This host is now configured, but none of those configurations will survive a reboot. It's inconvenient to retype in your static configurations every time you reboot a computer. Fortunately, you can tell your FreeBSD system to keep these configurations by including them in the system startup configuration file. On this host, I'll add the following lines to /etc/rc.conf:

```
ifconfig_rl0="inet 192.168.10.1 netmask 255.255.255.0"
defaultrouter="192.168.10.25"
```

Be careful when making changes to this file, including getting the required quotation marks right. To test your change, make sure this command does not result in any errors:

/etc/netstart

Dynamic Addresses

It's not a big deal to edit a few files if you only have one computer or a small network with just a few computers. However, if you are an administrator of a larger network, it is more convenient to use DHCP for two reasons. First, as the number of files you edit increases, so does the chance of typos and the possibility of two computers mistakenly being assigned the same IP address. Second, the more computers you have, the more inconvenient it is to have to sit down at each to enter their IP addressing information manually.

If your system is attached to a network that uses DHCP — the Internet, for example — you can take advantage of FreeBSD's built-in DHCP client. In my example, my second NIC (ed0) is attached to my cable modem. To receive an IP address from my ISP's DHCP server, I can use this command:

dhclient ed0

To see if it worked:

ifconfig ed0
```
ed0: flags=8843<UP,BROADCAST,SIMPLEX,MULTICAST> mtu 1500
        inet 2.2.2.2 netmask 0xffffff00 broadcast 255.255.255.255
        ether 00:50:ba:de:36:33
```

To configure this system to always use dynamic addressing, I can add the following line to /etc/rc.conf:

```
ifconfig_ed0="DHCP"
```

DHCP Terminology

You need to know some DHCP terminology if you're going to be able to troubleshoot **dhclient** or to create your own DHCP server to use on your network.

When a DHCP client receives configuration information from a DHCP server, it is in the form of a lease. This means that the client configuration remains valid for a limited period of time, configured on the DHCP server. The information contained in that lease was also configured on the server. A DHCP server can give out much more than just a host's IP address, subnet mask, and default gateway. It can inform the client of the IP addresses for dozens of types of servers in a network including:

- DNS servers
- finger servers

- font servers

- IRC servers

- log servers

- lpr servers

- NDS servers

- WINS servers

- NIS servers

- NNTP servers

- NTP servers

- POP servers

- SMTP servers

Whew, that's a lot of servers. In addition, DHCP can also set the client's MTU, TTL, hostname, and a few dozen other parameters. To see the complete list, check out **man dhcp-options**.

Once a DHCP client has a lease, it stores it in /var/db/dhclient.leases.int#, where *int* is the interface name and # is the interface number. Here is an example /var/db/dhclient.leases.ed0 lease file:

```
lease {
  interface "ed0";
  fixed-address 2.2.2.2;
  option subnet-mask 255.255.240.0;
  option routers 2.2.2.1;
  option domain-name-servers 2.2.2.94,2.2.2.93,2.2.2.46;
  option broadcast-address 255.255.255.255;
  option dhcp-server-identifier 2.2.2.21
  option host-name "thishost";
  option domain-name "thisdomain.com";
  renew 3 2007/4/2 00:22:38;
  rebind 6 2007/4/5 02:50:06;
  expire 6 2007/4/5 23:50:06;
}
```

If you've been running **dhclient** for a while, you'll note that your lease file will have many such sections which start with lease { and end with the closing curly brace }. The information between the curly braces is the lease itself. Since leases don't last forever, each new lease assigned to the DHCP client is added to the end of the file. Your current lease will be at the very end of the file.

How does this whole lease process work? Let's assume for a moment that somewhere on your network is a properly configured DHCP server. This server will listen on UDP port 67, waiting for lease requests from DHCP clients. Let's also assume you have a brand new DHCP client with an empty leases file. Remember, you made that host a DHCP client by adding this line to /etc/rc.conf:

```
ifconfig_ed0="DHCP"
```

Nothing in that line indicates the IP address of the DHCP server. This is just as well because at this moment ed0 doesn't even have an IP address; if it did, it wouldn't need to contact a DHCP server.

In order to contact the DHCP server, this host will send out a special packet known as a DHCPDISCOVER message. Since the host doesn't know the IP address of its DHCP server, it sends the packet to the broadcast address, 255.255.255.255, in the hopes that a DHCP server will see it and respond. If you're familiar with networking, you know that broadcast packets are processed by all hosts that see the packet. However, only a DHCP server will understand the message in the packet as it is destined for UDP port 67.

You might also be aware that routers drop broadcast packets. This has a very big ramification for DHCP: if there isn't a DHCP server on your subnet or cable segment, the DHCP server on another subnet will never receive that broadcast. Does this mean that you need to have a DHCP server on every subnet in your network? Fortunately, no. Instead, you use something known as a bootp relay agent to deliver that message to a DHCP server. I'll talk more about these relay agents in the next few sections.

Ideally a DHCP server will receive the DHCPDISCOVER message. When it does, it will check its database of available leases, setting one aside pending confirmation from the host. It will then send out a DHCPOFFER message containing the details of the lease. This message is sent to the DHCP client port, UDP 68. You should note that DHCP uses two different port numbers, one for the client and one for the server. You will need to know both those port numbers if there are any firewalls between the client and the server.

Once the client receives the DHCPOFFER, it will confirm the lease by sending out a DHCPREQUEST. Again, this is sent as a broadcast. It is possible that multiple DHCP servers saw the original request and each responded with a separate lease offer. This broadcast allows all of the servers to see which lease the client is willing to accept, so any extra servers will stop holding a lease for the client. The server with the successful lease will mark the lease as leased. It will also send a DHCPACK which indicates the client now has the lease and is allowed to use those configuration parameters.

Once the client receives the DHCPACK, it writes the particulars of the lease to /var/db/dhclient.leases. int# and uses the leased information to participate in a TCP/IP network.

DHCP Time Periods

The client knows it can't use that configuration forever. A lease expiry is clearly marked in the lease. Take a look at the last three lines before the closing curly brace in my example lease:

```
renew 3 2007/4/2 00:22:38;
rebind 6 2007/4/5 02:50:06;
expire 6 2007/4/5 23:50:06;
```

You'll note there are actually three time periods: renew, rebind, and expire. The syntax for each line is: day year/month/day hour:minute:second, where 0 means Sunday. In this example, this lease is ready to renew on April 2, 2007 at 12:22:38 in the morning.

What is the difference between renew, rebind, and expire? Renew is also known as T1 or when the leased time is at 50%. When T1 occurs, the DHCP client will send a DHCPREQUEST to the DHCP server which assigned the lease. Note that the lease itself indicates the address of the DHCP server in this line:

```
option dhcp-server-identifier 2.2.2.21
```

Since the client knows the address of the server, it doesn't have to send a broadcast. If all goes well, the server will receive the DHCPREQUEST and give the client permission to renew the lease. Basically, the client is allowed to reuse the configuration for the original lease time and all three times are bumped up to reflect the new lease period.

If the client doesn't hear back from the DHCP server, it will wait for T2 or when the lease is at 87.5%. This is also known as the rebind period. The client will again send a DHCPREQUEST, but this time it will be a broadcast. Basically, the client is starting to get a bit worried and just wants to get its lease period renewed before it expires. Hopefully, some DHCP server will respond, and again all three time periods will be bumped up to reflect the new lease period.

If things don't go well, the poor DHCP client won't hear back from any DHCP servers. When the expire time occurs, the client is no longer allowed to use its leased configurations and is basically back at square one. The only way to get a lease will be to start from scratch with a DHCPDISCOVER broadcast.

Things work a little bit differently if you reboot your computer before any of the three time periods arrive. At bootup, your FreeBSD system will look for the address of the DHCP server in its `/var/db/dhclient.leases.int#` file. It will then try to contact the server in order to renew its lease. However, if the DHCP server happens to be unavailable, the client will check to see if it has a non-expired lease. If it does, it will **ping** the default router from the leased address to see if it still appears to work. If the router responds, it will boot up with the address, and will try contacting the DHCP server in 5 minutes in order to validate the lease.

There are two other possible DHCP messages which you might come across. The first is a DHCPNACK or negative acknowledgement. This message will be sent from a DHCP server if a client requests an address which is no longer valid. This usually occurs when you physically move a computer between subnets.

This is all probably more than you thought you'd be learning about DHCP for one day. In the next section, I'll concentrate on the DHCP server and the configuration information it needs in order to assign leases to DHCP clients.

Additional Resources

Original Article:

`http://www.onlamp.com/pub/a/bsd/2003/04/17/FreeBSD_Basics.html`

8.13 Configuring a DHCP Server

Unlike the built-in **dhclient**, your FreeBSD system does not come with DHCP server software. This is because you only need to configure a DHCP server if you want to lease out IP configuration for your own network.

However, there are two ports that allow you to create your own DHCP server. The first is known as WIDE, or Widely Integrated Distributed Environment. As the name suggests, it has been optimized for very large networks, so I won't cover it in this series. The second is from the ISC, or Internet Software Consortium.

Note: Earlier versions of FreeBSD shipped with the ISC version of **dhclient**, but starting with FreeBSD 6.0 the OpenBSD **dhclient** is used instead.

Before building the DHCP server port, ensure that the `bpf` device is built into your kernel. It should be unless you removed it when creating a custom kernel. Once you have the `bpf` device, install the DHCP server package and make note of the post-install messages:

```
# pkg_add -r isc-dhcp3-server
```

This will install several files. Let's take a quick overview. First, you'll get two executables:

- **/usr/local/sbin/dhcpd** is the actual DHCP server application. Like most servers, or daemons, it ends in "d".

- **/usr/local/bin/omshell** is the OMAPI command shell. This application allows you to make changes to the DHCP server while it is running. You don't have to stop and restart DHCP in order for the changes to take effect.

You'll also get a startup script and a sample configuration script to get started with your own configurations:

- `/usr/local/etc/rc.d/isc-dhcpd` is the startup script for the DHCP server.

- `/usr/local/etc/dhcpd.conf.sample` is the sample configuration script for the DHCP server.

To aid in your configuration, several manpages are installed. You can see which by **grep**ing for man from a **pkg_info** listing:

```
# pkg_info -Lx dhcp | grep man
```

And finally, a documents directory was installed to `/usr/local/share/doc/isc-dhcp3-server/`.

The Configuration File

Let's start by taking a look at the configuration file for the DHCP server. You should leave the sample as is, and copy it over to the file that you will edit:

```
# cp /usr/local/etc/dhcpd.conf.sample /usr/local/etc/dhcpd.conf
```

Let's go through each line of this file to make sure you understand all of the options; then we'll customize it for a sample network. As you're reading through this configuration file, any line that starts with a # is a comment.

```
# more /usr/local/etc/dhcpd.conf
```

```
# dhcpd.conf
# Sample configuration file for ISC dhcpd

# option definitions common to all supported networks...
option domain-name "example.org";
option domain-name-servers ns1.example.org, ns2.example.org;
```

Each bit of information a DHCP server leases to a client is known as an option. Some options are considered to be global, meaning that every DHCP client in the network will receive that option as part of their lease. Some options are considered to be local to a specific subnet. For example, the option for the IP address of the default gateway will always be local, as a default gateway must live on the same subnet as the client. However, the two above options are considered to be global, as every computer in your network will share the same domain name and will use the same DNS servers.

```
default-lease-time 600;
max-lease-time 7200;
```

Some DHCP client software requests a lease time. If the client doesn't, the server will assign the lease with the `default-lease-time` value. If the client does, the server will honor the request, but only up to the `max-lease-time` value. Both values are in seconds.

```
# If this DHCP server is the official DHCP server for the local
# network, the authoritative directive should be uncommented.
#authoritative;
```

This line should be uncommented, as it allows your DHCP server to send a DHCPNACK to misconfigured clients. An example of a misconfigured client would be a computer that was physically moved to another subnet without releasing its old lease.

```
# ad-hoc DNS update scheme - set to "none" to disable dynamic DNS updates.
ddns-update-style ad-hoc;
```

The `ddns-update-style` parameter has three possible values. `ad hoc` has been deprecated and shouldn't be used. `interim` allows your DHCP server to update a DNS server whenever it hands out a lease. This way, your DNS server will know which IP addresses are associated with which computers in your network. In order for this to work, your DNS server must support DDNS (Dynamic DNS). If your DNS server doesn't support DDNS, or you don't want to take advantage of dynamic DNS, you should change this value to `none`.

```
# Use this to send dhcp log messages to a different log file (you also
# have to hack syslog.conf to complete the redirection).
#log-facility local7;
```

How you handle this option will affect where the DHCP server will send its logging information. `local7` refers to a locally defined log file. Until you define that log file, the DHCP server will write all of its events to the system log file, or `/var/log/messages`.

```
# No service will be given on this subnet, but declaring it helps the
# DHCP server to understand the network topology.

subnet 10.152.187.0 netmask 255.255.255.0 {
}
```

Now we get to the meat of this file, the subnet declarations. A DHCP server needs to know which network or subnet IDs your network contains. Additionally, for each network or subnet, it needs to know which pool of addresses it is allowed to lease out to the devices on that segment of the network. It is helpful to sketch out your network ahead of time, so you know which addresses are available for DHCP clients and which addresses are unavailable because they are already statically assigned. I'll walk through such a sketch with you in the next section, when I demonstrate a more complex network configuration.

In the meantime, it is important to declare each segment of your network, even if a segment does not contain any DHCP clients. This is the case in the above declaration for the subnet ID 10.152.187.0. Notice that the declaration includes the mask that matches the network ID, and is then followed by a pair of curly braces ({ }). Let's compare this declaration to the next subnet declaration:

```
# This is a very basic subnet declaration.
subnet 10.254.239.0 netmask 255.255.255.224 {
    range 10.254.239.10 10.254.239.20;
    option routers rtr-239-0-1.example.org, rtr-239-0-2.example.org;
}
```

This declaration is for the subnet 10.254.239.0. Within the curly braces is the range of IP addresses available to be leased. If you're familiar with classful subnet masking, you know that every IP address in your network must share the portion of the IP address that is masked by 255. In this example, there are three 255s in the mask, so every IP address in this network must start with the same three numbers: 10.254.239. The mask also contains a 224 in the last octet, which leaves a range of 30 possible valid addresses for each subnet represented by that octet. In this example, the DHCP server has been instructed to give out 11 of those possible valid addresses: 10 to 20.

The DHCP server has also been instructed to lease out two default gateway addresses. The closing curly brace indicates the end of the information to be leased out to each client.

The default configuration file continues on with several more examples of subnet declarations. I won't rehash them here; you'll notice as you read through them on your own that the examples vary in which options are to be leased to clients on each declared subnet.

A Sample Network

Now that we've had a chance to look through the default configuration file, let's configure a DHCP server for a simple network scenario. This sample network includes the following:

- A network ID of 192.168.10.0 255.255.255.0

- A domain name of mynetwork.com

- 10 DHCP clients on one network segment

- One default gateway with the address 192.168.10.1

- One DHCP server with the address 192.168.10.2

- Two DNS servers: 192.168.10.3 and 192.168.10.4

Note that the default gateway, DHCP server, and two DNS servers each have their own statically assigned address. It is important that the DHCP server is configured not to assign any of those addresses to the DHCP clients.

I'll now create the following file:

```
# vi /usr/local/etc/dhcpd.conf
#my dhcp server configuration file
#first, the global options

option domain-name "mynetwork.com";
option domain-name-servers 192.168.10.3, 192.168.10.4;
```

```
default-lease-time 86400;
max-lease-time 86400;

authoritative;
ddns-update-style none;

#next, my one and only subnet

subnet 192.168.10.0 netmask 255.255.255.0 {
    range 192.168.10.5 192.168.10.20;
    option routers 192.168.10.1;
}
```

You'll note that I changed the lease time to 86400 seconds, or 24 hours. I kept the default logging facility and disabled DDNS. I also defined a range of addresses: 5-20. This bypasses the statically assigned addresses (1-4) and leaves room for more computers, should this network segment ever experience growth. When you make your own configuration file, remember to place a semicolon at the end of each statement and to enclose your subnet declaration between opening and closing curly braces.

Now, let's see if the configuration file works. First, I'll start the daemon and watch for any error messages:

```
# /usr/local/etc/rc.d/isc-dhcpd onestart
Internet Software Consortium DHCP Server V3.0.5
Copyright 2004-2006 Internet Software Consortium.
All rights reserved.
For info, please visit http://http://www.isc.org/sw/DHCP
Wrote 0 leases to leases file.

Listening on BPF/de0/00:80:c8:3a:b8:46/192.168.10.0/24
Sending on   BPF/de0/00:80:c8:3a:b8:46/192.168.10.0/24
Sending on   Socket/fallback/fallback-net
```

While I'm at it, I should add the necessary `/etc/rc.conf` entries as suggested by the post-install message so the DHCP server will restart, should I ever reboot:

```
dhcpd_enable="YES"
dhcpd_flags="-q"
dhcpd_conf="/usr/local/etc/dhcpd.conf"
dhcpd_ifaces=""
dhcpd_withumask="022"
```

You can also run the startup script manually if you give it one of the following options: **start**, **stop**, **restart**, or **status**. For example:

```
# /etc/rc.d/isc-dhcpd status
root    1830  0.0  0.5  1784 1392  ??  Is  5:00PM  0:00.00 dhcpd
```

The **restart** option is very handy if you make a change to your configuration file. DHCP is one service that won't change its configuration if you simply **reload** it.

OK, let's see if the DHCP server is actually handing out leases. I'll boot one of the machines on the network which has already been pre-configured as a DHCP client. Once it finishes booting, I'll check its lease file, knowing that this computer's interface name is ed0:

```
# more /var/db/client.leases.ed0
lease {
  interface "ed0";
  fixed-address 192.168.10.20;
  option subnet-mask 255.255.255.0;
  option routers 192.168.10.1;
  option dhcp-lease-time 86400;
  option dhcp-message-type 5;
  option domain-name-servers 192.168.10.3,192.168.10.4;
  option dhcp-server-identifier 192.168.10.1;
  option domain-name "mynetwork.com";
  renew 1 2007/4/21 08:50:05;
  rebind 1 2007/4/21 18:38:59;
  expire 1 2007/4/21 21:38:59;
}
```

Excellent. It looks like this DHCP client successfully received a lease from the server. I'll also take a look at the leases file on the DHCP server to see which addresses it has leased out:

```
# more /var/db/dhcpd/dhcpd.leases
# All times in this file are in UTC (GMT), not your local timezone.
# This is  not a bug, so please don't ask about it.   There is no
# portable way to store leases in the local timezone, so please don't
# request this as a feature.   If this is inconvenient or confusing
# to you, we sincerely apologize.   Seriously, though - don't ask.
# The format of this file is documented in the dhcpd.leases(5) manual page.
# This lease file was written by isc-dhcp-V3.0.5

lease 192.168.10.20 {
  starts 0 2007/04/20 21:49:28;
  ends 1 2007/04/21 21:49:28;
  binding state active;
  next binding state free;
  hardware ethernet 00:50:ba:de:36:33;
}
```

Changing the Logging File

The last configuration I would like to demonstrate is changing the default logging file. First, I'll uncomment the logging line in /usr/local/etc/dhcpd.conf so that it looks like this:

```
log-facility local7;
```

Next, I'll create an empty log file called dhcpd.log:

```
# touch /var/log/dhcpd.log
```

Then, I'll create an entry for this logfile in /etc/syslog.conf by adding this line:[7]

```
local7.*                    /var/log/dhcpd.log
```

Let's take a look at that entry for a moment. By default, you're given eight logging facilities to use for local applications; these are called local0 to local7. You can use whichever local facility you wish, as long as it isn't being used by another application. I've decided to use local7, which is why I also referred to it by that name in the DHCP server configuration file.

Once you've chosen a facility, you follow it by a period and a logging level. I've chosen the logging level of *, which will log all events, regardless of their level. I then gave the location of the log file to which to write events.

Once I've saved the changes to /etc/syslog.conf, I need to restart **syslogd** so it is aware of the changes:

```
# /etc/rc.d/syslogd restart
```

I also need to make the DHCP server aware of the change:

```
# /usr/local/etc/rc.d/isc-dhcpd restart
```

Finally, I'll see if it worked:

```
# more /var/log/dhcpd.log
Apr 20 19:32:22 fubar dhcpd: Internet Software Consortium DHCP Server V3.0.5
Apr 20 19:32:22 fubar dhcpd: Copyright 2004-2006 Internet Software Consortium.
Apr 20 19:32:22 fubar dhcpd: All rights reserved.
Apr 20 19:32:22 fubar dhcpd: For info, please
        visit http://http://www.isc.org/sw/DHCP
Apr 20 19:32:22 fubar dhcpd: Wrote 1 leases to leases file.
<snip>
```

Additional Resources

Original Article:

http://www.onlamp.com/pub/a/bsd/2003/05/01/FreeBSD_Basics.html

ISC Website:

http://www.isc.org/index.pl?/sw/dhcp/

---

[7]See section 2.11 for more details about syslog configurations.

8.14 DHCP on a Multi-Segment Network

So far in this series about DHCP I have demonstrated how to configure DHCP clients and a DHCP server for a single segment network. In this section I'd like to finish the series by explaining how to use DHCP in a multi-segment network.

While I happen to be concentrating on the ISC software on a FreeBSD system, DHCP is a standard protocol: regardless of your particular mix of operating systems and the software you use to provide DHCP, the logic behind configuring DHCP remains the same.

What needs to be considered when using DHCP in a network that contains more than one segment? I'll discuss the following:

1. the addressing and subnetting scheme

2. dealing with broadcasts over multiple segments

3. configuring any intervening firewalls or router access lists

IP Addressing

Before you can successfully configure a network for DHCP, you need to know the physical and logical layout of the network. If you are fortunate, this information has already been recorded, is kept up-to-date, and you can actually find the necessary documentation. If so, immediately track down the responsible administrator and buy her or him lunch.

If you're not so fortunate, grab a pen and notepad and start walking through the network. Make note of every hub or switch and how many devices are plugged into each. Work your way toward the server closet and record the number of routers or LAN router interfaces. Find the locations of any DNS servers, WINS servers, and any other servers that may require static addresses. When you're finished, sketch out your results.

Next, determine which IP addressing scheme, if any, is currently in use on the network and add it to your sketch. If you are responsible for creating the addressing scheme, you will most likely be using one of the private range addresses:

- 10.0.0.0/8

- 172.16.0.0/12

- 192.168.0.0/16

Here is an example of a small office with four network segments:

```
network ID:   192.168.10.0
subnet mask:    255.255.255.224
front office:
available addresses:    192.168.10.33 - 61
subnet ID               192.168.10.32
broadcast ID            192.168.10.63
default gateway         192.168.10.62
6 workstations
```

server closet:
```
available addresses:    192.168.10.68 - 93
subnet ID               192.168.10.64
broadcast ID            192.168.10.95
default gateway         192.168.10.94
DNS server              192.168.10.65
WINS server             192.168.10.66
file server             192.168.10.67
```
lab1:
```
available addresses:    192.168.10.98 - 125
subnet ID               192.168.10.96
broadcast ID            192.168.10.127
default gateway         192.168.10.126
WINS server             192.168.10.97
25 workstations
```
lab2:
```
available addresses:    192.168.10.129 - 157
subnet ID               192.168.10.128
broadcast ID            192.168.10.159
default gateway         192.168.10.158
15 workstations
```

It's important to record the subnet ID and broadcast ID of each network segment, as those two addresses are unavailable for use as host IDs. Each segment will have a unique default gateway address which must be a valid host ID for that segment. If you're rusty on subnet masking or don't understand the subnet IDs and broadcast IDs in the above chart, you may find the following URLs helpful:

- http://www.3com.com/other/pdfs/infra/corpinfo/en_US/501302.pdf

- http://www.cisco.com/warp/public/701/3.html

Now let's see how the sketch of a network translates into a DHCP server configuration file. Remember that you will need a subnet declaration for each network segment. For the example above, I would need four subnet declarations or something like this:

```
# more /usr/local/etc/dhcpd.conf
#global options
option domain-name "smallcompany.com";
option domain-name-servers 192.168.10.65;
option netbios-name-servers 192.168.10.66, 192.168.10.97;
option netbios-node-type 2;
default-lease-time 86400;
max-lease-time 86400;
authoritative;
ddns-update-style none;
#front office
subnet 192.168.10.32 netmask 255.255.255.224 {
        range 192.168.10.33 192.168.10.61;
        option routers 192.168.10.62;
```

```
        }
#server closet
subnet 192.168.10.64 netmask 255.255.255.224 {
        range 192.168.10.68 192.168.10.93;
        option routers 192.168.10.94;
        }
#lab1
subnet 192.168.10.96 netmask 255.255.255.224 {
        range 192.168.10.98 192.168.10.125;
        option routers 192.168.10.126;
        }
#lab2
subnet 192.168.10.128 netmask 255.255.255.224 {
        range 192.168.10.129 192.168.10.157;
        option routers 192.168.10.158;
        }
```

See how straightforward the subnet declarations are once you know the layout of your network? You may have noticed that I've included two additional options in the global options section. The option `netbios-name-servers` refers to WINS, so it includes the IP addresses of the two WINS servers. It is followed by the option `netbios-node-type` which I have set to 2. There are four possible node types listed in Table 8.1.

Table 8.1: NetBIOS Node Types

Value	Type	Description
1	b-node	uses broadcasts instead of a WINS server
2	p-node	only uses a WINS server
4	m-node	tries a broadcast first, then a WINS server
8	h-node	tries a WINS server first, then a broadcast

The node type tells a computer running a Microsoft OS how to deal with NetBIOS name resolution. This type of name resolution is required whenever a computer needs to access a resource on a Microsoft network. In networking land, broadcasts are considered to be a bad thing and are discouraged when there are alternative ways to get the job done. The alternative in a Microsoft network is to use a WINS server.

The two WINS server options don't have to be global options. For example, if only *lab1* contains Microsoft operating systems, I could remove those two options from the global section and instead insert them into *lab1*'s subnet declaration:

```
#lab1
subnet 192.168.10.96 netmask 255.255.255.224 {
        range 192.168.10.98 192.168.10.125;
        option routers 192.168.10.126;
        option netbios-name-servers 192.168.10.66, 192.168.10.97;
```

```
        option netbios-node-type 2;
        }
```

Dealing with Broadcasts

You may be thinking that creating a DHCP server configuration file isn't all that hard. It isn't, but we're not finished yet. We still have to deal with broadcasts and ensure that DHCP clients will receive a lease that is suited to their network segment. Since DHCP uses broadcasts and a multi-segment network contains routers that will drop those broadcasts, you have a few choices on how to deal with dropped DHCP broadcasts. I'll discuss two possible options:

- place a DHCP server on every segment

- ensure every segment has either a DHCP server or a DHCP relay (but not both)

Either method will allow DHCP to run smoothly. Which one you choose will be a matter of configuration preference for the software which you have available.

If you decide to use option one, add a DHCP server to each segment in your sketch. Assign each one a static IP and ensure those addresses aren't in your pools of available addresses. Install the DHCP server software on each PC and create its configuration file.

In my example network, should I use the same DHCP server configuration file on each DHCP server on each of the four network segments? If I do, the DHCP servers won't know which subnet they are responsible for. For example, I want the DHCP server on the front office segment to just use the subnet declaration for the front office. Remember from the last section (8.13) that you could use empty subnet declarations? This is where they come into play. I should modify the configuration file for the front office DHCP server so it looks like this:

```
# more /usr/local/etc/dhcpd.conf
#global options
option domain-name "smallcompany.com";
option domain-name-servers 192.168.10.65;
option netbios-name-servers 192.168.10.66, 192.168.10.97;
option netbios-node-type 2;
default-lease-time 86400;
max-lease-time 86400;
authoritative;
ddns-update-style none;
#front office
subnet 192.168.10.32 netmask 255.255.255.224 {
        range 192.168.10.33 192.168.10.61;
        option routers 192.168.10.62;
        }
#server closet
subnet 192.168.10.64 netmask 255.255.255.224 {
        }
#lab1
subnet 192.168.10.96 netmask 255.255.255.224 {
        }
```

```
#lab2
subnet 192.168.10.128 netmask 255.255.255.224 {
        }
```

Now this DHCP server has lease information for the front office segment. It is aware that there are three other segments on the network, but it is not responsible for leasing out information to the DHCP clients on those segments.

The other three DHCP servers would have similar configuration files. The DHCP server on the server closet segment would have lease information for that segment and empty subnet declarations for the remaining three. The same idea would apply to the DHCP server on the *lab1* segment and the DHCP server on the *lab2* segment.

Using a relay agent

For option two, decide which segments will use a DHCP server and which will use a relay agent, and label your sketch accordingly. The DHCP relay agents don't have to use a static address, but they should be reliable machines that will be up whenever a client needs to contact a DHCP server. A relay agent isn't of much use when it is powered down.

If you are using a FreeBSD system for your relay agent, install the relay software with:

pkg_add -r isc-dhcp3-relay

After the install, add the /etc/rc.conf lines as suggested by the package message:

```
dhcrelay_enable="YES"
dhcrelay_flags="-a"
dhcrelay_servers=""
dhcrelay_ifaces=""
```

The modifications you'll make to those lines for your custom network will be fairly straightforward once you understand how a DHCP relay agent operates. When a segment contains a relay agent instead of a DHCP server, the relay agent will intercept a client's DHCP broadcast and convert it to a unicast. This means that it readdresses the packet so it is destined for the IP address of a DHCP server. Since routers pass unicast packets, the DHCP server will receive the request and respond with a lease.

There is one caveat: somehow the DHCP server needs to know which network segment the original client broadcast came from so that it can offer a lease that is appropriate for the client. This information is provided by setting the flags line to **-a**. This tells the relay agent to add an option to the DHCP request informing the DHCP server which interface on the relay agent the client request came from. This information is important: it allows the DHCP server to calculate which network segment the client resides on so it can offer it a suitable lease.

Let's see how this translates into my example network. I'll have one DHCP server in the server closet and three DHCP relay agents: one in the front office, one in *lab1*, and the third in *lab2*.

Since there is only one DHCP server, it will be responsible for assigning leases to all four subnets. Accordingly, its configuration file will contain the full lease information and no empty subnet declarations.

Each relay agent will indicate the name of its interface and the IP address of the DHCP server in its /etc/rc. conf file as in this example:

```
dhcrelay_servers="192.168.10.68"
dhcrelay_ifaces="ed0"
```

When configuring your own `dhcrelay_ifaces` line, use the interface name for that FreeBSD system. When configuring your `dhcrelay_servers` line, use the DHCP server address for your network. Once you've made your changes, try starting the agent:

/usr/local/etc/rc.d/isc-dhcrelay start
```
Internet Software Consortium DHCP Relay Agent V3.0.5
Copyright 2004-2006 Internet Software Consortium.
All rights reserved.
For info, please visit http://www.isc.org/sw/dhcp/
Listening on BPF/ed0/00:d0:09:ef:25:38
Sending on   BPF/ed0/00:d0:09:ef:25:38
Sending on   Socket/fallback
```

A **sockstat** should also show the relay agent is listening for DHCP requests:

sockstat | grep dhcrelay
```
root    dhcrelay  1664  4 udp4  *:67          *:*
root    dhcrelay  1664  3 dgram -             /var/run/logpriv
```

The DHCP relay startup script is similar to the DHCP server script in that it supports the options **start**, **stop**, **restart**, and **status**. If you ever need to stop the agent or check its status, use the appropriate option with the script.

Firewalls and DHCP

Once you have your DHCP server(s) and relay agent(s) configured, you'll want to ensure that the DHCP packets aren't being dropped by any intervening firewalls or routers. Depending upon the layout of your network, this may or may not be an issue. Some networks allow internal LAN traffic to flow freely and only inspect packets that are leaving for or entering from the Internet.

However, if your network does filter internal packets, check the rules on the firewall or the router access list. `/usr/local/share/doc/isc-dhcp3-server/README` explains what you're looking for in your rulebase:

> "If you are running the DHCP server or client on a computer that's also acting as a firewall, you must be sure to allow DHCP packets through the firewall. In particular, your firewall rules _must_ allow packets from IP address 0.0.0.0 to IP address 255.255.255.255 from UDP port 68 to UDP port 67 through. They must also allow packets from your local firewall's IP address and UDP port 67 through to any address your DHCP server might serve on UDP port 68. Finally, packets from relay agents on port 67 to the DHCP server on port 67, and vice versa, must be permitted.

> We have noticed that on some systems where we are using a packet filter, if you set up a firewall that blocks UDP port 67 and 68 entirely, packets sent through the packet filter will not be blocked. However, unicast packets will be blocked. This can result in strange behavior, particularly on DHCP clients, where the initial packet exchange is broadcast, but renewals are unicast - the client will appear to be unable to renew until it starts broadcasting its renewals, and then suddenly it'll work. The fix is to fix the firewall rules as described above."

Obviously, the syntax you use to achieve this will vary greatly depending upon the firewall or router in use. See section 10.7 for some IPFW examples for DHCP.

Additional Resources

Original Article:

```
http://www.onlamp.com/pub/a/bsd/2003/05/15/FreeBSD_Basics.html
```

8.15 Configuring and Using NFS

In order to manipulate data using Unix, a file system that contains the data must first be mounted. If the data is located on a hard drive, floppy, or CD-ROM drive physically cabled to that computer, you can mount that device directly using the **mount** command to specify the device, the filesystem, and a local mountpoint. To automate this process, you can add the correct entry to your /etc/fstab file.

If you wish to access data that is physically located on another Unix computer, you can use NFS, the Network File System. The computer where the data is physically located must be running **nfsd**, the NFS daemon. It must also have a properly configured configuration file which is read by **mountd**; this file is called /etc/exports. The computer that wishes to access the remote data must be running the NFS client and must be mentioned in the /etc/exports of the computer running **nfsd**.

Getting Started with NFS

The easiest way to install **nfsd** and the NFS client is through **sysinstall**. Let's pretend I want a computer named *alpha* that has an IP address of 10.0.0.1 to access the /usr directory on a computer named *gamma* that has an IP address of 10.0.0.3. Gamma needs the **nfsd**, and *alpha* needs the NFS client. Let's start by running **sysinstall** as *root* at *gamma*. When prompted, select Configure and then Networking. Press the space bar on the option NFS Server to select it. You will receive a message that it will invoke the **vi** editor to edit /etc/exports.

The examples given in the default /etc/exports are straightforward enough to get NFS up and running. If you want to fine-tune NFS and gain a better understanding of it, read **man exports**.

For now, let's just see if we can get NFS to work. Arrow down to the # in the line:

```
#/usr              huey louie dewie
```

press **x** to remove the #, arrow over to the h in huey and continue to press **x** to remove huey louie dewie. Press **i** for insert mode and type **alpha** — the line should now look like this:

```
/usr          alpha
```

Then press **Escape** and then **:wq** to save your changes and quit the editor. Exit out of **sysinstall**.

Next, ensure there is an entry for *alpha* in *gamma*'s /etc/hosts:

```
10.0.0.1     alpha
```

Let's also test that connectivity by both IP address and hostname is successful:

```
# ping 10.0.0.1
# ping alpha
```

If the pings are successful, start **nfsd** and verify its status:

```
# /etc/rc.d/nfsd start
Starting mountd.
Starting nfsd.
# /etc/rc.d/nfsd status
nfsd is running as pid 977 978 979 980.
```

Now that the server is configured, run **sysinstall** as *root* at *alpha*. Again, select Configure, then Networking; use your spacebar to select the NFS client and press OK, then exit out of **sysinstall**.

Accessing the Exported Data

Before we try mounting *gamma*'s /usr directory at *alpha*, let's create a mountpoint on *alpha*:

```
# mkdir /share
```

Now issue the **mount** command:

```
# mount 10.0.0.3:/usr /share
```

If you issued this as *root*, you should receive your command prompt back without any error messages. To see if it mounted:

```
# df | grep share
10.0.0.3:/usr  5996471   1069259   4447495      19%      /share
```

If you list the mountpoint, you should be able to see the contents of *gamma*'s /usr directory:

```
# ls /share
```

When you are finished, you can unmount /share like any other mounted file system:

```
# umount /share
```

Congratulations, you've just created your first NFS server; now let's fine-tune it a bit.

Normally, you won't want to export your entire /usr directory structure. Even if permissions are set correctly, you don't want remote users poking about your home and bin directories. Instead, create a subdirectory of /usr to contain the information you want remote users to access. As a practical example, I export /usr/ports, so my /etc/exports looks like this:

```
/usr/ports    10.0.0.1
```

The new **mount** command at *alpha* is:

```
# mount 10.0.0.3:/usr/ports /share
# ls /share
```

The above command will only show the ports collection stored on *gamma*.

NFS's behavior is a little weird if you want to share your CD-ROM over the network. If I edit /etc/exports on *gamma* to add the following line:

```
/cdrom      -alldirs        10.0.0.1
```

I would expect *alpha* to be able to access the contents of a data CD-ROM located on *gamma*. If I put a data CD-ROM in *gamma*'s CD-ROM drive, and at *alpha* type:

```
# mount 10.0.0.3:/cdrom /share
nfs: can't access /cdrom: Permission denied
```

So what happened? Let's take a look at /etc/fstab:

```
# grep cdrom /etc/fstab
/dev/cd0                /cdrom          cd9660  ro,noauto       0       0
```

And there's one problem: I tried to export a filesystem that is not set to mount automatically when I reboot. I can't export a filesystem that isn't mounted locally. To complicate matters further, I can't export a directory I've created, unless I create it as a subdirectory of /usr. This is where NFS gets a bit weird. Try this at *gamma*:

```
# mkdir /usr/cdrom
```

and modify that /etc/exports line to read:

```
/usr/cdrom  -alldirs        10.0.0.1
```

Save the change and restart **nfsd**:

```
# /etc/rc.d/nfsd restart
# df | grep cdrom
/dev/cd0      470754    470754        0   100%    /usr/cdrom
```

Note that /usr/cdrom was mounted for you; you will get an error if you try to **mount** it yourself:

```
# mount /cdrom
cd9660: Device busy
```

However, you should be able to list the contents of the cdrom:

```
# ls /usr/cdrom
```

Now, at *alpha*,

```
# mount 10.0.0.3:/usr/cdrom /share
# ls /share
```

should also show the contents of *gamma*'s CD-ROM.

You will have to be extra careful if you decide to export CD-ROMs; you don't want to inadvertently eject a mounted CD-ROM or reboot without a CD-ROM in your CD-ROM drive. I usually leave the cdrom reference commented out in /etc/exports and uncomment it and restart **nfsd** when I actually want to share my CD-ROM.

This should get you started with NFS; read the **man nfsd** to learn how to give read-only access, group access, and user access.

Whenever you edit /etc/exports, always test your changes at the client. **mount** the newly exported data to ensure that you haven't given the client access to more data then you intended.

One final note on NFS: it can be a security risk on computers attached to insecure networks such as the Internet. Usually, in a networked environment, there is only one computer with the Internet connection as it controls Internet access for the rest of the network. Don't run the **nfsd** on that computer.

Additional Resources

Original Article:

http://www.onlamp.com/pub/a/bsd/2000/07/26/FreeBSD_Basics.html

9 Security

9.1 Securing FreeBSD

I've been sorting through my piles of notes and organizing the security tips I've gathered from various resources over the years. I thought some of them might interest you, so I'll write a bit about securing your FreeBSD system.

Obviously, I won't be able to give a thorough coverage of such a broad topic in the confines of one short article. Which is just as well, since it is impossible to create a one-size-fits-all list that will guarantee the security of any system.

As I sort through my notes, I notice that most are geared toward tightening the security of a FreeBSD system that acts as some sort of server (e.g. Web server, mail server). Which isn't so great, if you are instead using your FreeBSD system as your personal system, and desire full desktop functionality. You would be a very unhappy camper if a security setting broke some functionality that took you a week of struggle to learn how to get working in the first place.

For this reason, you'll note that, unlike most security tutorials, this section will not address changing any of the permissions on your FreeBSD system. This is intentional. Unless you're securing a production server and you know what you're doing, don't change the file permissions. (If you must practice with permissions, stick to the files in your home directory). Otherwise, things might stop working; things you might miss like email, X, sound, etc. Strange things will happen at strange times, making it harder to clue in that they are related to the permission setting you played with a week ago Tuesday.

Closing Unused Ports

We all know that the Internet isn't always a friendly place and that you probably don't want to give the rest of the world the same access to your system as you give yourself. This means you don't want to be on the Internet without being protected by some sort of firewall. Fortunately, your FreeBSD system supports three firewalls: **ipfw**, **ipf**, and **pf**. Even better, the amount of easy-to-follow documentation has steadily improved over the last few years. If you're not behind a firewall, dedicate a Saturday afternoon to do some reading and configure firewall functionality on your system. You'll be glad you did.

Good security is always defense in depth, meaning that if one mechanism fails, there is a backup mechanism. Even though your system is now protected by a firewall, you should also disable all services except for those you absolutely need. On a desktop system, you need very few services.

To see which services are listening for connection attempts on your system, use the command **sockstat -l**. Your output will vary, depending upon what settings you selected during the final installation phase of FreeBSD and what ports and packages you have built since then.

Typically port 25 will show as open; you may or may not need to leave this default, depending upon which program you use to send and read your email. On newer versions of FreeBSD, the `sendmail` line in your output shows it is listening on the loopback address of 127.0.0.1, meaning noone can connect to your **sendmail** daemon but you can use **sendmail** to send emails. If your older system instead shows sendmail listening on * (all interfaces), put this line in /etc/rc.conf to force it to just listen on the loopback address:

```
sendmail_enable="NO"
```

Don't forget to run the **/etc/rc.d/sendmail reload** command to inform **sendmail** of the change and rerun **sockstat** to confirm port 25 is only listening on the loopback address.

If port 111 (portmap) shows up in your **sockstat** output, remove it by adding the following lines to /etc/rc. conf (or, if a line already exists in that file, change the YES to a NO):

```
nfs_server_enable="NO"
nfs_client_enable="NO"
portmap_enable="NO"
```

Portmap is only needed if you are running NFS, which you won't be on a stand-alone FreeBSD desktop. It also has a long history of security issues, so if you don't absolutely need it, disable it.

syslog (port 514) will probably also show in your output. You don't want to disable syslog completely, as you do want to receive logging messages. However, you don't need to have this port open to do so. In your /etc/rc.conf file, make sure syslog is enabled and add a second line with some flags:

```
syslogd_enable="YES"
syslogd_flags="-ss"
```

Those two ss'es (make sure you have two, not just one) in the flags will disable logging from remote hosts and close that port, but still allow your localhost to keep its logging capabilities. You will need to run the command **/etc/syslogd restart** before your change will take effect.

Next, make sure inetd_enable is not set to YES in /etc/rc.conf. In addition, if inetd is showing up in your **sockstat** output, something has been uncommented out in /etc/inetd.conf. If you don't need it, put a # back in front of that line, and stop **inetd** by typing **/etc/rc.d/inetd stop**.

If you find anything else in your **sockstat** output, skim through **man rc.conf** to see if there is an option to disable it. If there isn't, it was most likely started with a startup script that was installed with a package or a port. If this is the case, browse through /usr/local/etc/rc.d to see which startup scripts have been added to your system. Some packages/ports will install a sample script with a sample extension. As long as it ends in sample, that script will not run at startup. Other packages/ports install a working script that is read at bootup and you will find the culprit in this directory. The easiest way to disable the script is to rename it with a sample extension, and then kill the daemon so that its port number no longer shows up in **sockstat -l**.

Additional rc.conf Parameters

You might also want to consider adding the following options to /etc/rc.conf:

```
tcp_drop_synfin="YES"
```

This option prevents something known as OS fingerprinting, which is a scan technique used to determine the type of operating system running on a host. If you decide to enable this option, you will also have to rebuild your kernel with the following option included in your kernel configuration file:

```
options TCP_DROP_SYNFIN
```

Two related `rc.conf` options are:

```
icmp_drop_redirect="YES"
icmp_log_redirect="YES"
```

ICMP redirects can be used to launch a DOS attack.

Be very careful if you decide to include the `icmp_log_redirect` option, as it will log every ICMP redirect, which has the potential of filling up your logging directory if you ever are the victim of this type of attack.

When you configured your firewall, you probably included this `rc.conf` option:

```
log_in_vain="YES"
```

If you didn't, it is a good option to include, as it logs all attempts to closed ports.

An interesting option is:

```
accounting_enable="YES"
```

This will enable system accounting. If you're new to system accounting, read **man sa** and **man lastcomm** to decide whether this option would be useful to you or not.

Finally, this is a good option to include:

```
clear_tmp_enable="YES"
```

as it will clear `/tmp` at startup, which is always a good thing.

Configuring Blowfish Hashes

Let's leave `/etc/rc.conf` and see what else we can do to tighten up your system. I like to change the default algorithm used when encrypting a user's password to the Blowfish algorithm, as it provides the highest security at the greatest speed.

To implement Blowfish hashes, edit `/etc/login.conf` and change the `passwd_format` line so that it looks like this:

```
:passwd_format=blf:\
```

Save your change, then rebuild the login database with this command:

```
# cap_mkdb /etc/login.conf
```

You'll then have to change all of your user's passwords so they will get a new Blowfish hash. You can do this by typing **passwd username** for each username as the superuser. Whatever username you use, that will be the user whose password will be updated. Repeat for all of your users, including the *root* account.

Once you're finished, double-check that it worked and you didn't forget any users:

```
# more /etc/master.passwd
```

All of the passwords for your users should begin with $2.[1]

Finally, configure your FreeBSD system to use Blowfish whenever you create a new user by editing /etc/auth.conf. Change the crypt_default line so that it looks like this:

```
crypt_default=blf
```

Restricting Logins

You've probably noticed when you log in to your FreeBSD system that your login prompt reminds you that you are running FreeBSD. And that after you log in, you receive the FreeBSD copyright information, which is followed by the version of FreeBSD and the name of your kernel, and finally, a useful (but rather boring) motd (message of the day) which again reminds you that you are running FreeBSD. You probably already know what version of FreeBSD you are running and might not want to share that information with the rest of the world. And the motd is a good place to remind the rest of the world that they shouldn't be messing with your system anyways.

You can edit /etc/motd to say whatever suits your purposes, be it anything from your favorite sci-fi excerpt to all the nasty things that will happen to someone if they continue to try to log in to your system.

Next, to remove the copyright information, create an empty copyright file:

```
# touch /etc/COPYRIGHT
```

Then to change the text that appears at the login prompt, edit /etc/gettytab. Find the line in the default:\ section that starts with:

```
:cb:ce:ck:lc
```

Carefully, change the text between \r\n and \r\n\r\n: (for the im= initial banner message) to whatever text you wish to appear. Double-check that you have the right amount of \r's and \n's and save your change. For example, my login prompt looks like this:

```
I'm a node in cyberspace. Who are you?
login:
```

You can test your changes by going to another terminal and logging in.

Finally, even if you've edited your motd to remove your version and kernel information, by default FreeBSD will still re-add it to /etc/motd every time you log in. To prevent this behavior, add the following line to /etc/rc.conf:

---

[1]See section 9.9 for more details about password hashes.

```
update_motd="NO"
```

To have this change take affect immediately for new logins, type:

/etc/rc.d/motd restart

There are a few edits that will also restrict logins to your system in the first place. Since these changes modify the behavior of the **login** program, you'll want to carefully test your changes. Keep one terminal open and go to another terminal to log out and ensure that you can still log in. If for some reason you're unable to log in (this shouldn't happen, but you can't be too careful), you can return to the other terminal and look for typos in the file you just edited.

No one (including you) should ever log in to your system using the *root* account. To prevent this from happening, edit /etc/ttys.[2] Once you get past a page's worth of comments, you'll notice a section that goes from ttyv0 to ttyv8. Change the word secure on each of those lines to insecure. This is a file you don't want a typo in, so double-check your changes carefully. Tell **init** to reload /etc/ttys with:

init q

Test your change by trying to log in as *root* on one of your terminals. You should receive a Login incorrect message.

Personally, I tend to use all nine terminals on my desktop. If you don't, you can also change the word on to off on some of the ttys in /etc/ttys. Remember to leave at least one terminal on, or else you won't be able to log in, which will severely hamper the usefulness of your system. You'll also note that ttyv8 is off by default, which means you have to manually start an X Window session. If you'd like X to start automatically at bootup, change that off to on. See section 2.10 for more details about **init**.

You can also restrict who can log in to your system and from where. This is done by editing /etc/login. access.

If you want to prevent all remote logins (meaning you can only log in if you are physically sitting at your system), remove the # from this line:

```
#-:wheel:ALL EXCEPT LOCAL .win.tue.nl
```

and remove the .win.tue.nl so that the line now looks like this:

```
-:wheel:ALL EXCEPT LOCAL
```

If you plan on accessing your system remotely, replace .win.tue.nl with the IP address(es) or hostname(s) of the system(s) you'll be logging in from. If there are multiple addresses, separate them with a single space.

If you have only one or two user accounts that you wish to be able to log in to your system, you can prevent all other logins like so:

```
-:ALL EXCEPT user1 user2:ttyv0 ttyv1 ttyv2 ttyv3 ttyv4
```

---

[2]See section 2.10 for more details out /etc/ttys.

Replace `user1 user2` with the names of the user accounts to which you wish to give access. Put in as many ttys as you wish to restrict.

Alternatively, you can place the users in a group and give login access to that group. This example adds the users *genisis*, *biko*, and *dlavigne6* to a group called *mygroup* and allows only the members of that group to log in to my FreeBSD system. First, I'll edit `/etc/group` and carefully add this line:

```
mygroup:*:100:genisis,dlavigne6,biko
```

Note: When using groups, the group name should not match a user name.

When you add your own group, make sure you use a GID (in my case, 100) that is not being used by any other lines in your `/etc/group` file.

Then, change `/etc/login.access` to:

```
-:ALL EXCEPT mygroup:ttyv0 ttyv1 ttyv2 ttyv3 ttyv4 ttyv5
```

It is very important you test this change. Leave one terminal logged in, just in case something goes wrong. Go to another terminal and try to log in as each of the users in your group. That should work. Then try to log in as another user; if need be, create a test account and try to log in as that test account. That login attempt should result in a Permission denied message.

Configuring TCP Wrappers

Unless you are protected by a firewall, your default FreeBSD system is willing to accept connection requests from any client for any port that remains open on your system. An alternative to learning a firewall is to add a layer of security by telling FreeBSD to refuse any incoming connection requests that do not come from a client you trust.

This is where TCP Wrappers comes into play. It is already built into your system and is just waiting for you to configure which clients you are willing to accept connection requests from. The TCP Wrappers access control is for programs that are started by **tcpd** or use libwrap (like **inetd**). The name of its configuration file is `/etc/hosts.allow`, but you'll find the syntax of the file under **man 5 hosts_access** and additional options under **man 5 hosts_options**.

There are two things to keep in mind when editing this file:

- the first rule found that matches the client for a particular service is used to determine if the client is allowed or denied access to that service;

- if there are no rules that match the client, access is allowed.

The syntax itself is fairly straightforward; each rule has the following two fields and can use an optional third field:

```
daemon: client  :command
```

If your rule doesn't fit on one line, use the \ character at the end of the line to indicate that the rule continues to the next line.

There are a few useful wildcards and operators that you should be aware of.

- `ALL` matches all; it can be used in the daemon or client field

- `LOCAL` is used in the client field and matches hostnames that don't contain a dot in them; for example, it would match *genisis*, but not *genisis.istar.ca*

- `EXCEPT` is used in the client field; it allows you to allow some clients but not others

- `ALLOW` is used in the last field to allow the service

- `DENY` is used in the last field to deny the service

As you create your rules, you'll want to use the **tcpdmatch** utility to ensure that your rules are actually creating the access control you intend. Before I start creating access rules for the **telnet** daemon, let's see what happens if I try to **telnet** into my FreeBSD box withou any access restrictions.

Note: *telnet* is an insecure service and you should use SSH instead to access your system. This example is only to demonstrate the use of the **tcpdmatch** utility.

```
telnet localhost
Trying localhost...
Connected to genisis.
Escape character is '^]'.

FreeBSD/i386 (genisis) (ttyp1)

login: genisis
Password:
Last login: Thu Jan 18 17:44:29 on ttyv4
Copyright (c) 1980, 1983, 1986, 1988, 1990, 1991, 1993, 1994
     The Regents of the University of California.  All rights reserved.

FreeBSD 4.2-RELEASE (SOUND) #0: Tue Dec 12 20:01:29 EST 2000

You have mail.

genisis@ logout
Connection closed by foreign host.
```

Notice that this system is accepting telnet connections and responds by giving a login prompt on terminal `ttyp1`. It would appear that **inetd** did its job properly. Now, let's see what the default `/etc/hosts.allow` file looks like.

```
# more /etc/hosts.allow
# hosts.allow access control file for "tcp wrapped" applications.
# $FreeBSD: src/etc/hosts.allow,v 1.19.8.1 2006/02/19 14:57:01 ume Exp $
# NOTE: The hosts.deny file is deprecated.
#       Place both 'allow' and 'deny' rules in the hosts.allow file.
#       See hosts_options(5) for the format of this file.
#       hosts_access(5) no longer fully applies.
#       _____                    _    _
```

```
#        | ___| _   _    _ _    _ _ _    _ _    | |   _   | |
#        |  _|  \ \/ / / _` | | '_ ` _ \ | '_ \  | |  / _ \ | |
#        | |__   >  < | (_| | | | | | | | | |_) | | | |  __/ |_|
#        |____| /_/\_\ \__,_| |_| |_| |_| | .__/  |_| \___| (_)
#                                         |_|
# !!! This is an example! You will need to modify it for your specific
# !!! requirements!
# Start by allowing everything (this prevents the rest of the file
# from working, so remove it when you need protection).
# The rules here work on a "First match wins" basis.
ALL : ALL : allow
```

Let's stop right here to see if we can determine why that first rule prevents the rest of the file from working. It basically says: for all daemons, from all clients, allow access. Because this rule matches all clients, and it's the first match, it will always be used. Let's see what happens if I comment out that first rule, save the change and try the **telnet** command again:

```
telnet localhost
Trying localhost...
Connected to genisis.
Escape character is '^]'.
You are not welcome to use telnetd from localhost.
Connection closed by foreign host.
```

Looks like I've effectively blocked all telnet connections to my system. If I read through the rest of /etc/ hosts.allow, I'll discover sections which deal with **sshd**, DNS, IPv6 addresses, Sendmail, Exim, **rpcbind**, NIS, **ftpd**, and **fingerd**. However, there wont be any rules that specifically mention **telnetd**.

Instead, the last rule in the file is intended to cover all the left over daemons that didn't match earlier rules:

```
# The rest of the daemons are protected.
ALL : ALL
        :   severity auth.info
        :   twist /bin/echo "You are not welcome to use %d from %h."
```

Notice that the last rule allowed the connection, but closed it after echoing a message, which is what we saw when I attempted the telnet connection. The %d was replaced by the name of the daemon (telnetd), and the %h was replaced by the hostname of the client trying to connect (localhost).

We could have predicted this outcome if we had used the **tcpdmatch** utility. The syntax to use this utility is very simple:

```
tcpdmatch daemon_name host_name_of_client
```

You do not have to be the superuser to run this utility. Let's see what it says will happen if the host *biko* tries to connect to the **telnetd** on my FreeBSD system:

```
% tcpdmatch telnetd biko
client:   hostname biko
client:   address  10.0.0.1
server:   process  telnetd
matched:  /etc/hosts.allow line 77
option:   severity auth.info
option:   twist /bin/echo "You are not welcome to use telnetd from biko."
access:   delegated
```

This is very useful output as it tells us which line number in /etc/hosts.allow contains the matching rule and what the result of that rule will be for that client.

Let's modify /etc/hosts.allow to allow **telnetd** to accept connections from the hosts *genisis* and *biko*, but to disallow connections from any other clients. I'll become the superuser and add the following lines; it doesn't matter where in the file I add the lines as long as they appear before that last rule:

```
telnetd: biko,genisis :ALLOW
telnetd: ALL :DENY
```

I'll then check that my rules work by running **tcpdmatch** on *biko*, *genisis*, and a third host called *creed*:

```
% tcpdmatch telnetd biko
client:   hostname biko
client:   address  10.0.0.1
server:   process  telnetd
matched:  /etc/hosts.allow line 74
option:   ALLOW
access:   granted
% tcpdmatch telnetd genisis
client:   hostname genisis
client:   address  10.0.0.2
server:   process  telnetd
matched:  /etc/hosts.allow line 74
option:   ALLOW
access:   granted
% tcpdmatch telnetd creed
client:   hostname creed
client:   address  10.0.0.3
server:   process  telnetd
matched:  /etc/hosts.allow line 75
option:   DENY
access:   denied
```

Let's see what happens when the host *creed* tries to **telnet** into my FreeBSD system:

```
% telnet 10.0.0.2
Trying 10.0.0.2...
Connected to genisis.
Escape character is '^]'.
Connection closed by foreign host.
```

Notice that I didn't receive any message, as the rule on line 75 was the first match, not the rule on line 77.

Additional Resources

Original Articles:

http://www.onlamp.com/pub/a/bsd/2002/08/08/FreeBSD_Basics.html

http://www.onlamp.com/pub/a/bsd/2001/01/31/FreeBSD_Basics.html

9.2 Avoiding Trojans and Rootkits

Trojans, rootkits, and DDoS agents are a sad reality. It's a little disheartening to think that software exists which, given a chance, can install unwanted files on your system, overwrite or destroy your own files, send your data or user input elsewhere, or use your computer to attack another system.

The more advanced among you may be smiling and smugly thinking "that's why I run a Unix system". True, there are fewer nasties out there which target Unix systems, but they do exist. Further, as the Unix user base increases, so will the amount and frequency of exploits against Unix systems. Fortunately, as a FreeBSD user, there are many utilities available to you, as well as many good habits that you can teach yourself. The next few sections will discuss these utilities and habits.

First Things First

The first habit, as I've stressed many times in this book, is to be behind a firewall. It doesn't matter what type of firewall, as long as you choose something you are comfortable configuring. If you're intimidated at the prospect of learning the syntax of **ipf**, **ipfw**, of **pf**, invest in an inexpensive, preconfigured hardware firewall. If you're already running a free firewall on your Windows system, place your FreeBSD system behind it until you're ready to tackle a Unix firewall configuration.

Why the big deal about a firewall? Rootkits. These automated kits scan a portion of the Internet looking for open ports. Once a rootkit discovers a port it can attack, it tries to get into that system. A properly configured home firewall won't show any ports open, so a rootkit will pass you by and look for another victim.

What if you haven't been behind a firewall? How do you know if your system contains unwanted software? Sometimes it is hard to tell without doing a lot of investigative work. The best advice, unfortunately, is to back up your data files, reinstall, and set up a firewall before you reconnect to the Internet.

Assuming you are behind a firewall, you should test it to ensure that it is indeed hiding all of your ports. First, take an inventory of the open ports on all of the machines behind the firewall. On each machine, regardless of the operating system, run this command at a command prompt:

```
% netstat -an
```

For each line that begins with tcp or udp, record the port number or name that shows up in the "Local Address" section. If you run this command on your FreeBSD system, ignore the ugly looking lines after the "Active UNIX domain sockets" as those don't deal with port numbers.

FreeBSD systems come with the **sockstat** command which also shows open ports. I prefer the layout of its output to that of the **netstat** command. Since FreeBSD supports both IPv4 and IPv6 by default, and I'm not interested in the Unix domain sockets, I usually run the command like so:

```
% sockstat -46
```

Record the results of your **netstat** or **sockstat** command for each machine in your home network and repeat the command periodically. This way, you know which ports you expect to be open and will recognize if an extra port suddenly appears on your system.

Once you've recorded which ports are open on your computers, you want to see if your firewall is advertising any of them to the Internet. The best utility for this purpose is **nmap**.

It is very important that you double- and triple-check the address of your firewall before you launch your scan. You don't want to scan the wrong address inadvertently and have to explain to your ISP why they shouldn't ban you from further Internet access. A thorough scan of all TCP and UDP ports will take a long time. This command will launch such a scan:

```
# nmap -v -P0 -sU -p 1-65535 IP_ADDRESS
```

where *IP_ADDRESS* is the address of your firewall. Again, check for typos in that address before you press enter and launch the scan. If all goes well, the scan shouldn't find any open ports.

Checksums

Open ports aren't the only entry point for unwanted software. Whenever you download software you are really trusting that the software only does what it purports to do, and that the file you just downloaded is the same file that was originally placed on the FTP site, not a trojaned version of the original file.

Fortunately, most FTP sites that provide Unix software protect each downloadable file with an MD5 checksum. MD5 is used to verify the integrity of a file by ensuring none of the bits in the file have been tampered with. If an attacker were to replace a file on an FTP site with a trojan, the MD5 checksum would not match the trojaned file.

Note: Assuming the attacker doesn't also replace the original MD5 checksum with one that now matches the trojaned file. Compare with the original checksums as provided in the release announcement email.

As an example, navigate to `ftp://ftp.freebsd.org/pub/FreeBSD/ISO-IMAGES-i386/6.2`. Next to the four possible *.iso* files, there is a file called `CHECKSUM.MD5` which gives the checksum for each file. If I download `6.2-RELEASE-i386-disc1.iso`, I should use the **md5** command to verify the checksum before I burn the ISO to a CD:

```
% md5 6.2-RELEASE-i386-disc1.iso
MD5 (6.2-RELEASE-i386-disc1.iso) = 3d27214700687c0b5390e8b6dd3706e3
```

The number I receive back should be identical to the number in the `CHECKSUM.MD5` file on the FTP site. If I'm really paranoid, I can also compare the contents of `CHECKSUM.SHA256` by running the **sha256** utility against the ISO file.

It's good to make a habit of always checking the checksum(s) of any file you download from the Internet, refusing to download files that lack checksums. If you use the FreeBSD ports collection, the **make** command will do this automagically for you. This is the easiest and safest way to install software on your FreeBSD system.

If you are ever building a port and it stops to complain about a checksum mismatch, do not override the error and carry on with the build. One of two things just occurred and you need to rectify the situation. The first possibility is that your ports tree is out of date. If that is the case, **csup** to the latest version of the ports tree. The second possibility is that the file has been changed on the FTP site since the checksum was calculated. If this is the case, you should email the maintainer of the port so he can ensure the original file was not trojaned. You will find the email address of the maintainer in the `Makefile`. For example, if I were building the doom port, I would be in the `/usr/ports/games/doom` directory, and could run this command: (Note the mix of upper and lower case.)

```
# grep MAINTAINER /usr/ports/games/doom/Makefile
MAINTAINER =    jmz@FreeBSD.org
```

If you email the maintainer, remember to include the output of **uname -a** so he knows the version of FreeBSD you are using.

File Integrity Utilities

MD5 checksums can also be used to ensure that the files on your own system are untampered. One of the first things a trojan program will do is change some of your binaries so you won't notice that something nasty has just been installed on your system. For example, your **ps** command could be replaced with another **ps** that doesn't show any processes used by the trojan. Your **ls** command could be altered to hide directories created by the trojan. Fortunately, there are several file integrity utilities that automate the process of creating a database of checksums for the important files on your FreeBSD system. The most common and well known of these utilities is **tripwire**.

tripwire is available as a free, Open Source version and as a commercial version. I'll walk you through an installation of the Open Source version of **tripwire** on your FreeBSD system. There is no package for this utility as it requires you to build a local database, so we will install the port:

```
# cd /usr/ports/security/tripwire
# make install clean
```

This will trudge along for several minutes, so go grab a drink and wait until the install stops and presents you with this screen:

```
Installer program for:
Tripwire(R) 2.3 Open Source
Copyright (C) 1998-2000 Tripwire (R) Security Systems, Inc.  Tripwire (R)
is a registered trademark of the Purdue Research Foundation and is
licensed exclusively to Tripwire (R) Security Systems, Inc.
LICENSE AGREEMENT for Tripwire(R) 2.3 Open Source
Please read the following license agreement.  You must accept the
agreement to continue installing Tripwire.
Press ENTER to view the License Agreement.
```

At this point, you'll be presented with many pages worth of licensing information as it displays the full GNU General Public License followed by the Tripwire Trademark Information. Use your spacebar to read your way through it until you get to this line:

```
Please type "accept" to indicate your acceptance of this
license agreement. [do not accept] accept
```

Make sure you type the word **accept**; if you inadvertently press Return instead, the build will abort. Simply repeat **make install clean** and be careful to type **accept** next time you are prompted. At this point, the build will carry on, but don't go too far away as it will prompt for more user input. You'll see another pages worth of output which ends with:

```
Continue with installation? [y/n] y
```

Next, the installation will create several directories and copy some files. Note that some documents are created for you in /usr/local/share/doc/tripwire as well as manpages in section 5 and 8 of the manual.

You will then be prompted to create a passphrase which will be used whenever keys are used. Remember the passphrase or you will be unable to access the **tripwire** database. You'll be prompted for this passphrase several times as the installation creates and signs the **tripwire** configuration file, policy file, and database.

At one point, you may get several more errors complaining that Kerberos or other files are missing from your system. Don't worry, the installation will continue and when it is finished you'll receive your prompt back.

In the next section, I'll start with what to do with your newly installed **tripwire** database. Then I'll move on to some alternatives to **tripwire** as well as other ports that are designed to look for rootkits. In the meantime, take a peek at **man tripwire**.

Additional Resources

Original Article:

http://www.onlamp.com/pub/a/bsd/2003/03/06/FreeBSD_Basics.html

9.3 Checking System Integrity with tripwire

Tripwire comes with several utilities and documents which are used to create and maintain the **tripwire** database, configuration file and policy file:

- **tripwire**(8): used for the creation of the Tripwire database, and checking the integrity of the filesystem against that database.

- **twadmin**(8): used to create, encode, and sign Tripwire policy, configuration, and key files, and for various administrative functions.

- **twprint**(8): prints Tripwire database and report files in a plain text format.

- **siggen**(8): displays hash values for files.

- twfiles(5): provides an overview of the various files created and used by Tripwire, including default locations and settings.

- twconfig(4): explains the configuration file which is used to set system-specific information that affects Tripwire operation.

- twpolicy(4): explains the policy file, which specifies the files and directories Tripwire should check, and how they should be scanned.

Generating Tripwire Reports

The install process (covered in section 9.2) created a default database for you in the /var/db/tripwire directory. Let's see what type of files it contains:

```
% file /var/db/tripwire/*
/var/db/tripwire/hostname.twd:              data
/var/db/tripwire/report:                    directory
```

Your actual database name will reflect your system's hostname. Note that the tripwire database (the *.twd* file)
is not in ASCII text. You won't be able to view it in an editor or a pager. Instead, use the **tripwire** utilities to
manipulate that database. You'll also find that the report directory will be empty by default.

The premise behind **tripwire** is that a database is initialized using the parameters contained in a policy file.
This initialization takes a snapshot or baseline of the files on the system. You then periodically do an integrity
check to see which files have changed, investigating why any files have changed.

During the install, the database was initialized for you using the default policy parameters. It's up to you to use
the **tripwire** command to check the integrity of the database:

```
# tripwire --check
```

This will check your current system against the snapshot contained in the **tripwire** database. If it finds
any inconsistencies, they will be printed to your screen. In addition, a data file with the naming format
hostname-date-time.twr will be placed in /var/db/tripwire/report. Again, this file isn't in ASCII
text. View this report file with the **twprint** utility:

```
# cd /var/db/tripwire/report
# twprint --print-report -r reporthostname-20030309-104231.twr | more
```

Note that the name of your report file will depend upon your hostname and the date and time you generated the
report. Also, don't forget to include **-r** to specify the name of the particular report file you would like to view.

Let's take a look at a sample tripwire report:

```
*****

Note: Report is not encrypted.  Tripwire(R) 2.4.0 Integrity Check Report

Report generated by:        root
Report created on:          Sun Mar  11 10:42:31 2007
Database last updated on:   Never


=======================================================================
Report Summary:
=======================================================================


Host name:                  hostname
Host IP address:            1.2.3.4
```

```
Host ID:                    None
Policy file used:           /usr/local/etc/tripwire/tw.pol
Configuration file used:    /usr/local/etc/tripwire/tw.cfg
Database file used:         /var/db/tripwire/hostname.twd
Command line used:          tripwire --check


======================================================================
Rule Summary:
======================================================================


----------------------------------------------------------------------
  Section: Unix File System
----------------------------------------------------------------------

  Rule Name                   Severity Level   Added   Removed  Modified
  ---------                   --------------   -----   -------  --------
  Invariant Directories            66            0        0        0
  Sources                         100            0        0        0
  Temporary directories            33            0        0        0
* Tripwire Data Files            100            1        0        0
  Local files                      66            0        0        0
  Tripwire Binaries               100            0        0        0
  Libraries, include files, and other system files
                                  100            0        0        0
  System Administration Programs  100            0        0        0
  User Utilities                  100            0        0        0
  X11R6                           100            0        0        0
  NIS                             100            0        0        0
  (/var/yp)
  /etc                            100            0        0        0
  Security Control                100            0        0        0
* Root's home                    100            0        0        1
  FreeBSD Kernel                  100            0        0        0
  FreeBSD Modules                 100            0        0        0
  /dev                            100            0        0        0
  Linux Compatibility             100            0        0        0
  (/compat)

Total objects scanned:  102111
Total violations found:   2


*****
```

Note that the report gives a summary of how many files have been added, removed, and modified since the last check of the database. In my case, a **tripwire** file was added and a file in *root*'s home directory was modified. The summary is then followed by details regarding the changed files:

```
======================================================================
Object Detail:
```

```
==========================================================================
  Added Objects: 1

Added object name:  /var/db/tripwire/hostname.twd.bak


--------------------------------------------------------------------------
  Modified Objects: 1

Modified object name:  /root

  Property:          Expected                   Observed
* Modify Time        Sun Mar  11 09:54:01 2007   Sun Mar  11 10:42:34 2007
* Change Time        Sun Mar  11 09:54:01 2007   Sun Mar  11 10:42:34 2007
```

Finally, the report will indicate any errors. In my case, it repeated the Kerberos errors I encountered when I initially installed **tripwire**.

The above report is an example of a report that doesn't show any anomalies. As another example, I'll repeat the check after

- creating a new user on the system

- deleting the binary file **tip**

As you'd probably expect, this report will show the above changes; however, you may be surprised to see how the changes are reported. Here are the relevant bits of the report:

```
  Rule Name                 Severity Level   Added    Removed  Modified
* Tripwire Data Files       100              1        0        0
* User Utilities            100              0        1        1
* /etc                      100              0        0        6
* Root's home               100              0        0        1


==========================================================================
Object Detail:
==========================================================================

  Removed Objects: 1

Removed object name:  /usr/bin/tip


  -----------------------------------
  Modified Objects: 1

Modified object name:  /usr/bin

  Property:          Expected                   Observed
* Modify Time        Tue Mar   6 19:36:47 2007   Sun Mar  11 16:11:57 2007
* Change Time        Tue Mar   6 19:36:47 2007   Sun Mar  11 16:11:57 2007
```

Nothing surprising here. It clearly indicates that `/usr/bin/tip` was removed from the system at 16:11:57 on March 11th.

```
   Modified Objects: 6
Modified object name:  /etc
   Property:             Expected                 Observed
*  Modify Time           Sat Feb 17 10:48:13 2007  Sun Mar  11 16:02:39 2007
*  Change Time           Sat Feb 17 10:48:13 2007  Sun Mar  11 16:02:39 2007

Modified object name:  /etc/group.bak
   Property:             Expected                 Observed
*  Inode Number          961                       1297
*  Size                  404                       461
*  Modify Time           Wed Sep 20 13:28:27 2006  Sun Feb  11 13:07:19 2007
*  Change Time           Sat Nov  11 14:35:21 2006  Sun Mar  11 16:02:39 2007
*  CRC32                 A676qQ                    CqOlUf
*  MD5                   DyxBdqQBLU5dTDXG4sGHwl    BRoZrUEyVXd6aCYc0TsG/M

Modified object name:  /etc/master.passwd
   Property:             Expected                 Observed
*  Size                  2042                      2150
*  Modify Time           Sat Feb 17 10:48:13 2007  Sun Mar  11 16:02:39 2007
*  Change Time           Sat Feb 17 10:48:13 2007  Sun Mar  11 16:02:39 2007
*  Blocks                4                         8
*  CRC32                 DDJ4Ig                    BF6+V2
*  MD5                   DuVzv0gdyUQffuRQnHbKrC    CxQW2V/pqjJlep5vzunMG5

Modified object name:  /etc/passwd
   Property:             Expected                 Observed
*  Inode Number          1956                      1953
*  Size                  1499                      1543
*  Modify Time           Sat Feb 17 10:48:13 2007  Sun Mar  11 16:02:39 2007
*  Change Time           Sat Feb 17 10:48:13 2007  Sun Mar  11 16:02:39 2007
*  CRC32                 AEOtzi                    CF+noG
*  MD5                   DTYQyRBwdY/bsHG3TzCDS0    A35b+lMv45SAzp25IoUmVW

Modified object name:  /etc/pwd.db
   Property:             Expected                 Observed
*  Inode Number          1906                      1012
*  Modify Time           Sat Feb 17 10:48:13 2007  Sun Mar  11 16:02:39 2007
*  Change Time           Sat Feb 17 10:48:13 2007  Sun Mar  11 16:02:39 2007
*  CRC32                 B4ufr3                    Du5vQF
*  MD5                   A5cw0I8QyfWE76jhIupjbx    Aw92gyYFa0DPEx+eGFG1MM

Modified object name:  /etc/spwd.db
   Property:             Expected                 Observed
*  Inode Number          1955                      1837
*  Modify Time           Sat Feb 17 10:48:13 2007  Sun Mar  11 16:02:39 2007
*  Change Time           Sat Feb 17 10:48:13 2007  Sun Mar  11 16:02:39 2007
*  CRC32                 B1+c6t                    BnB5nm
```

```
* MD5                    BeDTKuET4SYQH9UgLdsv5i      BCU119GuWEYDvMd00+8LnP


------------------------------------------------------------------------
Rule Name: Security Control (/etc/group)
Severity Level: 100
------------------------------------------------------------------------
   Modified Objects: 1

Modified object name:  /etc/group

   Property:            Expected               Observed
* Inode Number          1297                   961
* Size                  461                    475
* Modify Time           Sun Feb  11 13:07:19 2007   Sun Mar  11 16:02:39 2007
* Change Time           Sun Feb  11 13:07:19 2007   Sun Mar  11 16:02:39 2007
* CRC32                 CqOlUf                 AdqVt7
* MD5                   BRoZrUEyVXd6aCYc0TsG/M  AFcDFbm7SEtHIYfQ7jy+KS
```

Notice how much happens behind the scenes when you add a user account. Both password files (`passwd` and `master.passwd`) are updated, the `group` database and its backup are updated, and both password databases (`pwd.db` and `spwd.db`) are updated.

Since I added that user and deleted that file, I can easily interpret the report. However, alarm bells would go off in my head if I were reading this report on a system where I knew I hadn't made those changes. Since the report includes the time of the change, I have a reference point for any necessary investigation: I can start looking at the logs for that time period or question other users who may have been on the system during that time period.

Notice also that tripwire continues to include the changes from previous reports. In my example, I still have the added **tripwire** file and the modified file in *root*'s home directory. Normally after you've analyzed the report and have accounted for any changes, you merge those changes back into the database so you don't have to review them again. To accomplish this, use the **update** switch and specify the name of the report file you wish to merge with the database:

tripwire --update -r *hostname-date-time*.twr

After a moment, the report will open up in an editor (**vi** by default). Toward the end of the report, you'll see some boxes like this:

```
Remove the "x" from the adjacent box to prevent updating the database with the new
values for this object.

Removed:
[x] "/usr/bin/tip"
```

By default, all your changes have the x, meaning if you leave them as is, the changes won't be repeated the next time you generate a new report.

So, I'll type **:wq** to write and quit the **vi** editor. I'll then be prompted for the passphrase so the database can be updated.

Customized Policies

Up to this point, we've used the default policy file. Next, I'll demonstrate a simple change to the policy file in order to resolve the error report section of the **tripwire** report.

When you installed **tripwire**, the default policy file was saved to `/usr/local/etc/tripwire/tw.pol`. This file is used by **tripwire** whenever you do a check on the database. However, you can't edit this file directly as it has been encoded and signed. Fortunately, there is an ASCII text version of the file called `/usr/local/etc/tripwire/twpol.txt`. Edit that file then use the **tripwire** utility to incorporate your changes into the encoded policy file.

Let's start by examining the contents of `/usr/local/etc/tripwire`:

```
# file /usr/local/etc/tripwire/*
hostname-local.key:              data
site.key:                        data
tw.cfg:                          data
tw.pol:                          data
twcfg.txt:                       ASCII text
twpol.txt:                       ASCII English text
twpol.txt.bak:                   ASCII English text
```

Note that the actual policy file (`tw.pol`) and configuration file (`tw.cfg`) are data files. However, each has an ASCII text equivalent; in addition, the ASCII equivalent of the policy file may also have a backup (`twpol.txt.bak`).

The first time you look at a **tripwire** policy file, you'll probably feel a bit intimidated by the ugly looking syntax. It's not that bad, especially if you stick with the basics. The FreeBSD port makes a policy file that should cover anything found in a FreeBSD install. Note that some lines begin with a #. This means that line is commented out (not used during the **tripwire** check). If you want **tripwire** to check for that file or directory, simply remove the #. Alternately, if you find something you don't want **tripwire** to check, place a # in front of it.

In my case, I want to comment all of the lines that deal with Kerberos in `twpol.txt` so I won't continue to receive Kerberos errors in my **tripwire** reports. Once I've saved my changes, I'll run this command to incorporate the changes into the encoded policy file:

```
# tripwire --update-policy /usr/local/etc/tripwire/twpol.txt
Parsing policy file /usr/local/etc/tripwire/twpol.txt
Please enter your local passphrase:
Please enter your site passphrase:
```

Note that you will be prompted for both passphrases. The best time to merge in a new policy is just after you do a **tripwire --update**. If you try to change a policy file and there are inconsistencies in the **tripwire** database (i.e. some files have changed since the last check), the policy merge will fail. While inconvenient, this is a safety feature as it forces you to be aware of any changes to the files on your system before you change the policy. So if your policy fails to update, do a **tripwire --check**, resolve your changes with **tripwire --update**, then try your **tripwire --update-policy** command again.

Commenting and uncommenting lines in the **tripwire** policy file is the easiest way to control which files **tripwire** monitors. If you're an advanced user who wants more control over the policy file, read **man twpolicy** thoroughly before starting your own experiments.

The configuration file has a much more user-friendly syntax which is covered in **man twconfig**. For example, if you're allergic to **vi**, change this line in `twcfg.txt` to reflect the full path to your favorite editor:

```
EDITOR          =/usr/bin/vi
```

Remember, if you make a change in the ASCII configuration file, use this command to merge your changes into the encoded configuration file:

```
# twadmin --create-cfgfile -S site.key twcfg.txt
Please enter your site passphrase:
```

Note that you'll receive a syntax error if you forget to include the **-S site.key** switch.

Now that you have an idea of how to use the **tripwire** utility, how often should you use it? This will depend upon the security policy of your network; or, if you're a home user, how often you're willing to read your **tripwire** reports and investigate the changed files on your system. Ideally, your **tripwire** check should be a part of your daily routine, something you do after reading the daily output and security emails that are sent to the superuser. If you do the **tripwire** check less often, you will have more changes to investigate and it will be harder to remember if you did something on that day that changed a file on your system.

You should also consider what to do with the ASCII versions of your configuration and policy files, as well as the **tripwire** reports themselves. It is an added security measure to backup these files to a removable media such as a floppy drive or backup tape, then remove them from the hard drive. However, don't remove your keys or your data files as they are needed for the proper operation of **tripwire**.

Additional Resources

Original Article:

`http://www.onlamp.com/pub/a/bsd/2003/03/20/FreeBSD_Basics.html`

9.4 File Integrity and Anti-DDoS Utilities

While **tripwire** is the most well-known of the file integrity utilities, it is not the only utility available for this purpose.

All file integrity utilities create a database of hashes representing a baseline of the files on a system. For this reason, the best time to create the database is just after installing and configuring the system and before connecting it to the Internet. When deciding upon which utility to use, the following factors come into play:

- The license

- The algorithm(s) used to create the hashes

- Ease of use

- Complexity of configuration file(s)

I've summarized the license and algorithms for three utilities in Table 9.1.

Table 9.1: File Integrity Utilities

Utility	License	Algorithms
tripwire	GPL, tripwire	MD5, SHA, HAVAL, CRC32
aide	GPL	MD5, SHA-1, RMD160, TIGER, HAVAL
yafic	BSD	SHA-1

aide

As for the ease of use and complexity of the configuration files, let's check out **aide** and **yafic** and see how they compare to **tripwire**. I'll start with **aide**:

```
# pkg_add -r aide
```

You'll note that both this and the **yafic** install will be much quicker than **tripwire**, and you won't be prompted to agree to any licenses. Unlike **tripwire**, you also won't be prompted to create any keys. This is an important distinction, as it affects how you actually use the file-integrity utility.

tripwire introduced the ability to sign its databases several years ago with version 2.3.1. Before then, it was up to the administrator to place all **tripwire** files onto removable media, such as a floppy, and to ensure that media was actually removed from the computer. If you didn't remove the **tripwire** database, an intruder could simply update the database after modifying your files. You'll remember from the previous section that the new system requires you to know both the local and the site passphrases to update the **tripwire** database. This means that you should be safe storing the database on the hard drive, if you choose secure passphrases.

This is where ease of use becomes a matter of preference, and your level of paranoia. With **tripwire**, you must generate keys and remember your passphrases. With other utilities, you instead must remember to move your database to a floppy, and then insert the floppy when you check the database and remove it when you are finished.

Let's return to **aide**. There are three main sources of documentation for this utility: **man aide**, **man aide.conf**, and http://www.cs.tut.fi/~rammer/aide/manual.html.

The install will create a /var/db/aide directory; by default, it only contains an empty databases/ subdirectory.

Unlike the **tripwire** install, an initial database is not initialized for you. To initialize the database using the default configuration file, follow the instructions you saw at the end of the package's installation. How long it takes will depend upon the size of your hard drive:

```
# cd /var/db/aide
# aide --init
AIDE, version 0.9.7.1
AIDE database at /var/db/aide/databases/aide.db.new initialized.
# mv databases/aide.db.new databases/aide.db
```

Unlike **tripwire**, which has separate policy and configuration files, **aide** only has one configuration file, /usr/ local/etc/aide.conf. The above command creates an ASCII text file called /var/db/aide/databases/ aide.db.new. It is important to note the distinction between this database and a **tripwire** database. A **tripwire** database is not ASCII text and it can only be understood by the **tripwire** utilities. Furthermore, it is signed, meaning you have to know the correct passphrase in order to modify the database. An **aide** database is ASCII text and is unsigned; in short, anyone can modify this database. It is important that you move this database to a floppy and remove the floppy from your floppy drive. When you move the database, ensure it does not end in a *new* extension:

```
# mount -t msdos /dev/fd0 /mnt
# mv databases/aide.db.new /mnt/aide.db
# umount /mnt
```

To make your life easier when you use the database, you should also edit the configuration file to point to the floppy. Open /usr/local/etc/aide.conf in your favorite editor and look for these two lines:

```
database=file:///var/db/aide/databases/aide.db
database_out=file:///var/db/aide/databases/aide.db.new
```

Change them to:

```
database=file:///mnt/aide.db
database_out=file:///mnt/aide.db.new
database_new=file:///mnt/aide.db.new
```

Now, whenever you want to check the database:

```
# mount -t msdos /dev/fd0 /mnt
# aide --check
```

aide will display any changes it finds. If you're not a speed reader, you can use the compare switch to go through the changes:

```
# aide --compare
```

You'll find the output to be very different from a **tripwire** report.

Once you've resolved any changes, you can update the database with:

```
# aide --update
```

When you're finished, don't forget to unmount the floppy and remove it from the floppy drive:

```
# umount /mnt
```

I found that the default configuration file worked well without any changes, other than the edit to point to the floppy. Unlike **tripwire**, I didn't have to resolve any errors. I also found the syntax of the file a little more logical. Both **tripwire** and **aide** allow you to get as complex as you like in your configuration file; I'll leave it up to you to decide which file you consider to be easier to work with. On the plus side, I found the **aide** command-line utility much easier to use than **tripwire**.

Yet Another File Integrity Checker

Now, let's move on to **yafic**, or "yet another file integrity checker":

```
# pkg_add -r yafic
```

Once installed, your documentation choices are **man yafic**, **man yafic.conf**, **man yafic.sign** and **man yafic-check**.

A sample configuration file is created for you at `/usr/local/share/examples/yafic/yafic.conf.sample`.

Copy and rename that file so it doesn't have the sample extension. Here, I've copied it to *root*'s home directory:

```
# cp /usr/local/share/examples/yafic/yafic.conf.sample /root/yafic.conf
```

Now, I'll see what happens when I type **yafic**:

```
# yafic
nothing done; use -c, -u, -d, or -l options
```

OK, it wants one of four options. From **man yafic**, those options do the following:

- **-c** checks the state of the filesystem against a known-database.

- **-u** examine the current state of the filesystem and save it to a new-database.

- **-d** compare a known-database with an exist-database.

- **-l** lists entries in the database.

So, I'll mount a floppy and try again:

```
# mount -t msdos /dev/fd0 /mnt
$ yafic -u /mnt/yafic.db
```

When using **yafic**, make sure you are in the directory containing `yafic.conf` and that you specify the name of the database you wish to create or check.

Note: Depending upon the size of your hard drive, `yafic.db` may not fit onto a floppy. In that case, use another type of removable media or use **-k** to specify an RSA or DSA key to be used to sign the database so it can remain stored on your hard drive.

Once you've created the initial database, unmount the floppy and remove it from the floppy drive. Whenever you want to check the database, remount the floppy, **cd** to the directory containing `yafic.conf`, and use the **-c** (check) switch:

```
# yafic -c /mnt/yafic.db
```

Again, any changes will be displayed to your screen. If you prefer to read the changes at a slower pace, pipe the output to a pager:

```
# yafic -c /mnt/yafic.db | more
```

Once you've resolved your changes, use the **-u** switch to update the database. If you are using a removable media, don't forget to unmount and remove it from the system when you are finished.

File Integrity Utilities Summary

You've probably noticed that all of these file integrity utilities follow the same routine:

- Initialize a database.

- Check the database.

- Update resolved changes into the original database.

- Repeat on a regular basis.

Ultimately, since it is you who will have to follow the routine, choose the utility whose switches and configuration file make the most sense to you. I encourage you to try all three utilities and choose the one that most fits your personality.

Note: Since originally writing this, I've settled on the built-in **mtree** utility as my favorite method for creating a file integrity database due to its ease-of-use, flexibility, and the added bonus of not requiring any extra software. I like it so much I included it as Hack #58 in BSD Hacks which is available from `http://www.oreilly.com/catalog/bsdhks/`.

DDoS Testing Utilities

As promised, I also want to take a look at DDoS testing utilities. If you're unfamiliar with the term DDoS, it stands for Distributed Denial of Service. Basically, this type of attack looks for vulnerable hosts. Once a host is infected, it will in turn look for other vulnerable hosts to infect. Once enough hosts are infected (potentially hundreds of thousands), they are used to launch a collective attack against a target.

Several utilities in the ports collection can determine if your FreeBSD computer or the computers in your network have been infected by a DDoS agent. The three most common Unix DDoS agents and the types of packets they use are listed in Table 9.2.

Table 9.2: Common Unix DDoS Agents

trinoo	UDP 27444, UDP 27665
tfn	uses ICMP
stacheldraht	TCP 16660, TCP 65000, ICMP

Let's start with **ddos_scan**, the utility created by Dave Dittrich:

```
# pkg_add -r ddos_scan
```

This will install an executable at `/usr/local/sbin/dds` and a file at `/usr/local/share/doc/ddos_scan/README`. That file contains a lot of useful information regarding DDoS, and I highly recommend that you take the time to read it.

This utility is designed to scan an entire network, looking for infected hosts. Its syntax is:

dds *A.B.C.D/mask*

For example, if your network has a network ID of 192.168.10, specify your network and mask as follows:

dds 192.168.10.0/24

If you only want to scan your own machine, simply give the IP address with no mask:

dds 192.168.10.1
No mask passed, assuming host scan (/32)

When running this utility, it's good to just receive your prompt back. That means the utility didn't find any infected hosts. The README file shows examples of what the output will be and what to do about it, if an infected host is found.

This is a good utility to run as a **cron** job. Remember to give the full path to **dds** in your crontab entry.

The Department of Homeland Security has released a similar utility. This utility was designed to scan only the local machine for DDoS agents, so it is suitable if you only have one FreeBSD computer. To install this package:

pkg_add -r find_ddos

It will install an executable at /usr/local/sbin/find_ddos and a document at /usr/local/share/doc/find_ddos/README.

To run this utility, simply type:

find_ddos
Running with the following default options:
find_ddos -g files -l LOG -p /tmp /
This material and tool is furnished on an "as is" basis. There are no
warranties of any kind, either expressed or implied as to any matter
including, but not limited to, warranty of fitness for a particular purpose
or merchantability, exclusivity or results obtained from use of the
material. There is no warranty of any kind with respect to freedom from
patent, trademark, or copyright infringement.
If the program "find_ddos" generates a log file revealing unlawful access
of a tested system, system administrators are encouraged to contact their
local FBI field office or the NIPC.
Please review the README file before continuing.
Do you accept these terms? **yes**
In the future, you can run this tool with the "-y" option from the
command line to acknowledge these terms
Logging output to: LOG
WARNING: Unable to scan running processes.
This will happen if the /proc directory is not a procfs.
Scanning "/tmp"...
Scanning "/"...
No DDOS tools found.

The output of this utility clearly indicates whether or not a DDoS agent was found. Note that if you want to include this check in a **cron** job, you'll need to include the **-y** switch to indicate acceptance of the license. However, if you just try this command:

```
# /usr/local/sbin/find_ddos -y
```

you'll receive this error:

```
Usage: find_ddos [-g grabdir] [-l logfile] [-p] [-v] [-V]
[-x exclude1] directory
If no parameters are given, the following defaults are used:
find_ddos -g files -l LOG -p /tmp /
If any parameters are given, the defaults are not used. In that
case, you must specify a directory to scan, or you can just use '-p' to
scan memory only.
```

This will work and will scan memory, /tmp, and /:

```
# /usr/local/sbin/find_ddos -y -g files -l LOG -p /tmp /
```

Cleaning a DDoS Agent

The final utility I'd like to cover is meant to be used if you find a DDoS agent running on your network:

```
# pkg_add -r zombiezapper
```

The install will create an executable at /usr/local/bin/zz and a directory, /usr/local/share/doc/zz/ containing the files USAGE and tekpaper.txt. USAGE gives detailed instructions on how to use the utility. Read it if you are ever unfortunate enough to have infected computers in your network.

In addition to trinoo, tfn, and stacheldraht, **zz** recognizes trinoo for Windows and shaft. It works over a network and was designed to stop infected machines from continuing to flood the network.

It is important to realize that all three DDoS tools are only effective as long as the attacker has not changed the default ports used by the DDoS attacks.

Additional Resources

Original Article:

http://www.onlamp.com/pub/a/bsd/2003/04/03/FreeBSD_Basics.html

Dave Dittrich's DDoS Resources Website:

http://staff.washington.edu/dittrich/misc/ddos/

9.5 One-Time Passwords

It can be challenging to create a password policy that balances ease of use with effectiveness. Also, utilities exist which are capable of cracking even the most hard to guess passwords. In this section, I'd like to demonstrate an alternative authentication system which is available on your FreeBSD system.

By default, when you login to your FreeBSD system, you are prompted for a password. This is known as a reusable password because you can input the same password whenever you login, until you either change the password on your own or are forced to change an expired password. This provides a measure of security: someone who doesn't know your password won't be able to access the resources on your system. However, this security is jeopardized if another user discovers your password.

There is another authentication system known as One Time Passwords (OTP). As the name suggests, you can only use a password once; you aren't allowed to reuse it. An OTP system ensures that a discovered password is useless to the person who discovers it. This can provide a bit more security in a world that contains password crackers, packet sniffers, and keyloggers.

Introducing OTP

OTP was developed at Bellcore (now Telcordia). Originally, it was a freely available software program known as S/Key. Bellcore went on to trademark the term S/Key in order to develop a commercial product. Software development continued elsewhere under the name One-time Passwords In Everything (OPIE). OTP eventually evolved into hardware products as well.

I won't show you how to integrate hardware OTP with your FreeBSD system as I'll assume that, like me, you don't have the budget to go out and purchase hardware tokens and proprietary authentication servers.

Fortunately, software OTP comes with your FreeBSD system and is easily configured. If you're using FreeBSD 4.x or lower, you already have both S/KEY and OPIE installed. OPIE is considered to be more secure as it uses MD5, whereas S/KEY uses the less secure MD4. Starting with FreeBSD 5.0, S/KEY was phased out and only OPIE is supported. I will cover the configuration of OPIE in this section.

Starting OTP

Before you can begin to use OPIE, you must add yourself to the database in /etc/opiekeys. By default this database is empty:

```
% more /etc/opiekeys
%
```

To add yourself to the database, use the **opiepasswd** command with the console switch:

```
% opiepasswd -c
Adding dlavigne6:
Only use this method from the console; NEVER from remote. If you are using
telnet, xterm, or a dial-in, type ^C now or exit with no password.
Then run opiepasswd without the -c parameter.
Using MD5 to compute responses.
Enter new secret pass phrase:
```

```
Secret pass phrases must be between 10 and 127 characters long.
Enter new secret pass phrase:
Again new secret pass phrase:
ID dlavigne6 OTP key is 499 dh0391
CHUG ROSA HIRE MALT DEBT EBEN
```

Let's take a closer look at what happened when I ran this command. Notice the warning at the beginning. When you run **opiepasswd -c** you want to be either physically sitting at the machine you normally login to or connected to the machine via **ssh**. Otherwise, your secret passphrase and resulting one-time password will be sent over the network in clear text, defeating the purpose of the exercise.

I was then prompted for a secret passphrase, and received a warning because my original passphrase was too short. This passphrase isn't used as a password per se; instead, it is used to prove that I am the person who added the *dlavigne6* account to the database and the rightful owner of the resulting response or one-time password. That response is comprised of those six uppercase nonsense words.

At this point, I can verify that I am indeed in the OPIE database:

```
% more /etc/opiekeys
dlavigne6 0499 dh0391        669a4a62db6714f3  Jan 18,2007 15:25:44
```

Notice that there is one entry in the database which contains my username, followed by a counter (499), followed by a seed (dh0391), followed by a key (669a4a62db6714f3), followed by the date and time the entry was added to the database. The counter and the seed are very important as they are used whenever I need to generate a one-time password.

If I ever need to verify my counter and seed, I should use this command:

```
% opieinfo
498 dh0391
```

The **opieinfo** command displays the count that will be used the next time I login. Note that it is expecting the response associated with 498, but I only know the response for 499. To figure out what response is expected, I use an OTP calculator, which is really the **opiekey** command.

Logging In

At this point I also have a choice: I can either use the calculator from a separate terminal every time I login, or I can print myself a list of responses and regenerate a new list whenever I run out of responses. Let's try both methods, starting with the first:

```
login: dlavigne6
otp-md5 498 dh0391 ext
Password:
```

Notice that when I login, I receive an OTP challenge. OPIE is waiting for the response, or one-time password, associated with counter 498. By default, users can decide whether or not to use OTP when they login. If I decide instead to type in my reusable password, it will be accepted and I'll login as usual.

If I decide to login using OTP, I'll first need to calculate the correct response. It doesn't matter where I use the calculator, *as long as I don't use it over a non-encrypted network connection.* I could use the calculator from another virtual terminal; for example, I could press **Alt-F3**, login locally and run the calculator. Alternately, if I have access to another computer in the room, or even a Palm Pilot running the calculator software, I could calculate the response there.

In order to use the calculator I need to know three things:

- the current counter

- my seed

- my secret passphrase

The current counter and seed are displayed in the challenge. However, it is important that only I know my secret passphrase; otherwise, anyone could calculate the response and login as if they were me.

When I use the calculator, I include the count I need the response for as well as my seed:

```
% opiekey 498 dh0391
Using the MD5 algorithm to compute response.
Reminder: Don't use opiekey from telnet or dial-in sessions.
Enter secret pass phrase:
MASK BALM COL HER RIFT TERM
```

Note that I was prompted for my secret passphrase, then given the response associated with counter 498: MASK BALM COL HER RIFT TERM.

Now that I know the correct response, I can return to my login prompt:

```
login: dlavigne6
otp-md5 498 dh0391 ext
Password: (here I pressed enter)
otp-md5 498 dh0391 ext
Password [echo on]: mask balm col her rift term
```

This time, instead of typing my reusable password, I pressed Return which turned on echo. This allowed me to see the response as I typed it. Echo is a bad thing with reusable passwords which is why it is always off. However, with a one-time password, it doesn't matter if anyone sees me typing it as it can't be reused. Also, unlike a reusable password, the response is not case sensitive so it doesn't matter if I type it in upper or lower case.

Now if I do an **opieinfo**, I'll see that the next expected response will be for counter 497. That is, every time I use a one-time password, the counter is decreased by one. I can merrily continue to calculate and use up my responses; I need only be careful that I never let my counter decrease to 0.

Generating Multiple Keys

It may not always be convenient to use the calculator every time you want to login. Let's demonstrate the second method, where a list of responses is generated.

This time, I'll use the number or **-n** switch with the calculator, to indicate how many responses I'd like to calculate. Here, I'll generate a list of 10 responses, starting at the next expected count of 497:

```
% opiekey -n 10 497 dh0391
Using the MD5 algorithm to compute response.
Reminder: Don't use opiekey from telnet or dial-in sessions.
Enter secret pass phrase:
488: COIN LO DOG GOLF ACTA FULL
489: SOD STUN SINK DRAW LAWN TILT
490: MALT STAY MASH CAR DEBT WAST
491: HOWE DRY WALL TOO BUDD SWIM
492: ROOT SPY BOND JEST HAIL SCAR
493: MEAN ADD NEON CAIN LION LAUD
494: LYLE HOLD HIGH HOME ITEM MEL
495: WICK BALI MAY EGO INK TOOK
496: RENT ARM WARN ARC LICE DOME
497: LEAD JAG MUCH MADE NONE WRIT
```

I now know what my next ten passwords will be. At this point, I could copy them to a piece of paper and store them in a safe place such as my wallet. Alternately, when you generate your own list, you could send the output to a file like so:

```
% opiekey -n 10 497 dh0391 > secretlist
```

and print the list. Be careful to remove that file from your hard drive once you've printed it as you don't want to keep a copy of your next ten passwords on your hard drive.

If my counter gets dangerously low, say around 10, I should reset it using the **opiepasswd** command. Once you're in the password database, use the **-n** or number switch in combination with the **-s** or seed switch instead of the **-c** switch. In the next example, I'll reset the counter back to 499 and change my seed to dh1357. When I do so, I'll be prompted for the response associated with my current counter, which happens to be 8:

```
% opiepasswd -n 499 -s dh1357
Updating dlavigne6:
You need the response from an OTP generator.
Old secret pass phrase:
        otp-md5 8 dh0391 ext
        Response: loot omit safe eric jolt dark
New secret pass phrase:
        otp-md5 499 dh1357
        Response: hewn as dot mel mali mann
```

Finishing Up

At this point, you may be wondering when would be the best time to actually use OTP, since you have a choice of using either OTP or a reusable password whenever you receive a login prompt. You probably won't use OTP when you login to a remote computer as you should use SSH for that purpose. Since SSH ensures that all of your information is encrypted, it has no need for OTP and hence does not support OTP. However, OTP can be appropriate when you need to login to your computer and you are concerned about shoulder surfing or someone else noticing your password as you type it in. For example, you may be in a crowded area with your laptop. Or your computer may happen to be located in a high traffic area, which increases the possibility of someone noticing what password you use to login.

It is convenient to leave users with the choice of using or not using OTP depending upon the likelihood of someone else noticing their password when they need to login. It is also possible to change this default and configure your FreeBSD system to force users to always use OTP. The original way to do this was to create a file called /etc/opieaccess. However, this method is considered to be a security hole and is even cautioned against in **man opieaccess**.

The preferred method is to use Pluggable Authentication Modules (PAM). Since I want to spend a fair bit of time on PAM, I'll introduce PAM in the next section, then carry on by configuring OTP as an example.

Additional Resources

Original Article:

http://www.onlamp.com/pub/a/bsd/2003/02/06/FreeBSD_Basics.html

9.6 PAM

Your FreeBSD system supports several types of authentication methods; you can choose which type your users are subject to by configuring something known as PAM, or Pluggable Authentication Modules.

As the name suggests, PAM consists of many modules. You can see which modules were installed with your system by issuing this command:

```
% ls /usr/lib/pam*
```

Note that each module ends in so and has a name that gives some indication of what that module is responsible for.

Pluggable means you have great flexibility. The entire framework already exists; you merely choose which portions of the framework you wish to implement. It also implies that one can plug in the desired module. Each module can be added or removed by simply adding or deleting a remark or changing a keyword in a configuration file.

If you are new to PAM, you will find excellent information regarding FreeBSD's implementation, written by the very person in charge of the implementation. Alternatively, if you installed the docs/ directory when you installed FreeBSD, you'll find the same information on your hard drive:

```
$ more /usr/share/doc/en_US.ISO8859-1/articles/pam/article.txt
```

PAM uses some terminology that I've summarized into the following tables. First, PAM has been divided into four groups known as facilities. Each group provides at least one function, known as a primitive. Table 9.3 matches each primitive to its facility and includes a brief description of the functionality provided by that primitive.

Next, PAM uses control flags to determine which authentication scheme or schemes to apply to a user. For now, I've summarized these flags in Table 9.4. Don't worry if this doesn't make sense; it will become more clear when we work through a configuration example.

443

Table 9.3: Four PAM facilities divided into six primitives

Facility	Primitive	Description
auth	pam_authenticate	Authenticates user.
	pam_setcred	Establishes UID, GID, resource limits.
account	pam_acct_mgmt	Time of day, server load.
session	pam_open_session	Record entry in utmp/wtmp, start SSH agent.
	pam_close_session	Same as above, but when session closes.
password	pam_chauthtok	Check for password expiry, easily-guessable password.

Table 9.4: PAM's Control Flags

Control Flags	Behavior
binding	Request is immediately allowed if this line succeeds but eventually is denied if this line fails.
required	This line must succeed.
requisite	Request is immediately denied if this line fails.
sufficient	Request is immediately allowed if this line succeeds.
optional	It's OK if this line fails.

Configuring Linux-PAM

Now that we're aware of the terminology used by PAM, we're ready to take a closer look at its configuration. Beginning with FreeBSD 5.0 is greatly-improved PAM support. For one, the type of PAM has changed from Linux-PAM to OpenPAM.

I'll start by showing you how to configure Linux-PAM on a FreeBSD 4.x system, then move on to show you the changes that came with OpenPAM.

In FreeBSD 4.x, the PAM configuration file is /etc/pam.conf. I won't display the entire file here, as it starts off with about two pages of comments. Even though the comments repeat the information in the above tables, they are well worth reading on your own. Once you get past the comments, you'll see this section:

```
# If the user can authenticate with S/Key, that's sufficient;
# allow clear password. Try kerberos, then try plain unix password.
login     auth       sufficient    pam_skey.so
login     auth       sufficient    pam_opie.so              no_fake_prompts
#login    auth       required      pam_opieaccess.so
login     auth       requisite     pam_cleartext_pass_ok.so
#login    auth       sufficient    pam_kerberosIV.so        try_first_pass
```

```
#login   auth      sufficient  pam_krb5.so       try_first_pass
login    auth      required    pam_unix.so       try_first_pass
login    account   required    pam_unix.so
login    password  required    pam_permit.so
login    session   required    pam_permit.so
```

Each line in this section starts with the word `login`, as this section affects the **login** service. This section configures how a person will authenticate when they receive a login prompt. Let's see if we can work out the syntax.

First, three of those lines are commented out, as they begin with a #. This means that *opieaccess* and both versions of Kerberos aren't used by default. Second, each line in the `pam.conf` file is divided up as follows:

```
service   facility   control flag   module name   module arguments
```

Notice that the service is `login`, which supports four facilities: `auth`, `account`, `password`, and `session`. Let's concentrate on the `auth` facility for a moment. There are seven listed ways a user can be authenticated: with s/key, OPIE, opie_access, a cleartext password, Kerberos IV, Kerberos 5, and the traditional Unix password authentication system.

The control flags determine which of the seven authentication methods a user is subject to. It's important to understand how these control flags interact with each other before you start editing this file. The lines are read in order, but some control flags tell PAM to read on to the next line, while other control flags tell PAM to stop reading.

For example, in the default configuration, `pam_unix.so` is `required` and `pam_cleartext_pass_ok.so` is `requisite`. Notice from the chart that authentication will fail if a user doesn't meet `requisite`. That is, if a user types in the incorrect cleartext password, the login will fail. However, if the user types in the correct cleartext password, PAM will continue reading. Since there aren't any other `requisite` lines and Unix password authentication is `required`, the correct cleartext password will be accepted as the user's authentication method.

Now, note the lines that use `sufficient`. If a user chooses to use an authentication method labeled as `sufficient` and their login attempt succeeds, PAM will stop reading and accept the authentication. However, a user is not required to authenticate using a method marked as `sufficient`. Since `pam_opie.so` is sufficient, the user can log in with their OTP, if they choose to do so. If they give the correct challenge, the login will be successful and they won't be prompted for any further login information. If the user instead decides not to use OTP, she will be prompted to input the `requisite` cleartext password.[3]

Now move down to the last four lines in this section. Notice there is a line for each facility and each line is `required`. If you ever change a line in a PAM configuration file, double check that the last line for each listed facility is `required`.

If you take a quick peek through the rest of /etc/pam.conf, you'll see sections for various services: **ftpd**, **sshd**, **telnetd**, `xserver`, **xdm**, **gdm**, `imap`, `pop3`, and `other`. This gives you the flexibility of specifying different authentication schemes for different services. If a user happens to connect to a FreeBSD system using a service not mentioned in the file, they will be subject to the `other` section, which by default requires a Unix password:

```
# If we don't match anything else, default to using getpwnam().
other    auth      required    pam_unix.so       try_first_pass
other    account   required    pam_unix.so       try_first_pass
```

---

[3]One Time Passwords are introduced in section 9.5.

Configuring OpenPAM

The OpenPAM available since FreeBSD 5.x follows the same logic, but adds more modules and lays out the configuration slightly differently. While OpenPAM supports /etc/pam.conf for backwards compatibility, this file isn't included for you. Instead, you should use the new layout:

```
# ls /etc/pam.d
README    imap     passwd    su
ftp       kde      pop3      system
ftpd      login    rsh       telnetd
gdm       other    sshd      xdm
```

Notice that each service in the old style /etc/pam.conf is now a separate file in the pam.d directory. The README file is the former comment section, and it has changed slightly, so yes, you should read it. In addition to the many new modules, more services have been added. The files themselves are identical to /etc/pam.conf, except the service name is missing as it is now the name of the file. For example, this line in /etc/pam.conf:

```
login    auth    sufficient    pam_opie.so    no_fake_prompts
```

is now this line in /etc/pam.d/login:

```
auth    sufficient    pam_opie.so    no_warn no_fake_prompts
```

Before you go about changing the default files for either type of PAM, I would highly recommend that you create a test account and be prepared for some experimentation. From one virtual terminal, make a change to the configuration file as the superuser. Then try to log in to another virtual terminal as the test user to see if your changes yield the intended result. This way if you come across any unexpected behavior, you can simply go back to the terminal where you changed the configuration file and undo the change.

As an example, let's see how one would go about always forcing users to use their OTP password at the login prompt. **man pam_opieaccess** gives a hint on how to take away a user's choice and force them to log in using OTP:

> To properly use this module, pam_opie(8) should be marked ''sufficient'', and pam_opieaccess should be listed right below it and marked ''requisite''.

It also indicates how this change will affect your users:

> The authentication component (pam_sm_authenticate()), returns PAM_SUCCESS in two cases:
>
> 1. The user does not have OPIE enabled.
>
> 2. The user has OPIE enabled, and the remote host is listed as a trusted host in /etc/opieaccess, and the user does not have a file named .opiealways in his home directory.
>
> Otherwise, it returns PAM_AUTH_ERR.

Let's compare those manpage hints to the relevant lines in /etc/pam.conf on a FreeBSD 4.7 system:

```
login    auth    sufficient    pam_skey.so
login    auth    sufficient    pam_opie.so                 no_fake_prompts
#login   auth    required      pam_opieaccess.so
login    auth    requisite     pam_cleartext_pass_ok.so
login    auth    required      pam_unix.so                 try_first_pass
```

Depending upon when you installed FreeBSD, your `pam_opieaccess.so` line may say `required` instead of `requisite`. This is a typo in `pam.conf`, as the manpage is correct. I'll change that line so it now looks like this:

```
login    auth    requisite    pam_opieaccess.so
```

Now, from another terminal, I'll try to log in as the test user. Instead of giving the OTP password, I'll try to give the reusable password for this account:

```
login: test
otp-md5 497 dh0908 ext
Password: (here I typed in the reusable password)
$
```

Hmmmm. At first glance, it looks like the configuration change failed to enforce OTP passwords, as the user successfully logged in using a reusable password. Better take another look at that section of the manpage:

> 2. The user has OPIE enabled, and the remote host is listed as a trusted host in /etc/opieaccess,
> and the user does not have a file named .opiealways in his home directory.

I wonder if it has something to do with that file `.opiealways`? There's no manpage for it, so I went to my good friend Google where I found the diary of OpenPAM's implementer which explained that the presence of this file will always force a user to use OTP. So, as the test user, I created that hidden file in my home directory. Then I logged out and tried to log back in without using OTP:

```
% touch .opiealways
% exit
login: test
otp-md5 497 dh0908 ext
Password: (here I typed in the reusable password)
pam_opieaccess: pam_sm_authenticate: Refused;
               remote host is not in opieaccess
Login incorrect
```

Voila, by simply removing a remark in the PAM configuration file and instructing the user to **touch .opiealways**, that user will now always be forced to use OTP.

Being the paranoid type, I also tested that the configuration change didn't adversely affect users who don't use OTP. I logged in as a regular user, received the regular login prompt, and successfully logged in after inputting the correct reusable password. I carried the test one step further by creating a `.opiealways` file in a regular user's home directory. Since the user wasn't in the OTP database, that file did not affect the user's login. However, should the user in the future add themselves to the OTP database, the presence of that file will force them to use OTP.

This behavior can simplify things, if you plan on creating new user accounts that may decide to use OTP. Create the following file:

```
# touch /usr/share/skel/dot.opiealways
```

Note that this skeleton file will only be inherited by new users you create. It won't affect existing user accounts.

Additional Resources

Original Article:

```
http://www.onlamp.com/pub/a/bsd/2003/02/20/FreeBSD_Basics.html
```

FreeBSD PAM:

```
http://www.freebsd.org/doc/en_US.ISO8859-1/articles/pam/
```

OpenPAM Website:

```
http://trac.des.no/openpam
```

9.7 Establishing Good Password Policies

In this section, I'd like to take a look at how to create a policy for reusable passwords on your FreeBSD system.

Policy Considerations

By default, in order for a user to log in to a FreeBSD system, they need to have a previously created user account and know the password associated with that user account. One of the responsibilities of the system administrator is to create a password policy that is appropriate for the users of the network. When creating the password policy, you need to consider the following points:

- What is the minimum required length of passwords? For example, are blank passwords (a bad idea) allowed, or do passwords have to be at least so many characters in length?

- What characters are allowed in a password? That is, can a password contain all lowercase letters, or must they contain some combination of upper and lowercase letters, numbers, and symbols?

- What is the password expiration date, meaning, how often are users forced to change their password?

- Do you want the system to enforce password history? This means that when a user changes their password, they can't change it back to their old password or a password they've used before. This is also sometimes called password uniqueness.

- Do you want to enforce lockout, and if so, after how many bad password attempts? Lockout means that a user will no longer receive the login prompt if they mistype the password so many times during a login attempt.

Often, administrators will have a password policy for regular user accounts and a separate policy for the *root* user account. For example, it is common to have a password length of six characters for regular users, but require a password length of 11 characters for the *root* user account. You may decide that it is too difficult to force users to use a password that requires both uppercase characters and symbols, but may want to keep this as a requirement on the *root* password so it will be much more difficult to guess.

There are additional considerations when creating a password policy. When a user account is created, the password is also created by the administrator. It is recommended that users immediately change this password the first time they log in; this ensures that no one knows the user's password except that user. Users should be taught not to give their password to anyone for any reason; remember, if worst comes to worst and a user forgets their password or a user leaves and access to their resources is required, the superuser has the ability to change the user's password.

Since users are responsible for creating their own passwords, it is up to the system administrator to educate users on what does and does not constitute a good password. Being human, it is far easier to remember a password that is the same as my username, my real name, my nickname, my dog's name, etc. Unfortunately, these are all examples of bad passwords. Many articles have been written that give examples of both good and bad passwords and the reasons why creating a good password is important.

Login Class Capability Database

Password policies were traditionally implemented by editing the `/etc/login.conf` file; however some can now be implemented with PAM, and others may require the installation of a utility or the use of a script. Let's start by seeing which parts of a password policy we can implement with the `/etc/login.conf` file:

```
% whatis login.conf
login.conf(5) - login class capability database
```

As you can see, `/etc/login.conf` is a database; as such, it has some pretty picky syntax concerning the entries it contains. Also, since it is a database, it is not enough for the superuser to just edit this file with an editor. If any changes are made to this file, the database must be updated using the **cap_mkdb** utility:

```
% whatis cap_mkdb
cap_mkdb(1) - create capability database
```

Let's take a look at some of the syntax this database uses. Because it is a class database, each record contains the information for one class. The bits of information are called fields, every field contains a value, and all the fields are separated by colons. To make the file a bit easier to read and edit, each field is on its own indented line; however, since all the fields are logically lumped together for each record, a slash is used to indicate that there is more information regarding the record on the next line. So, the syntax of each record ends up looking like this:

```
classname:\
        :field_1=value:\
        :field_2=value:\
        :last_field=value:
```

Note that every field is enclosed by two colons, and the last field does not have a trailing slash, as it is the last entry for that record.

Your FreeBSD system comes with several predefined classes, and each of these classes has predefined fields in the `/etc/login.conf` database. The first class, `default`, is used by all users unless you assigned them to a different class when you created their user account. The second class, root, is used by all user accounts that have a UID of 0.

The other predefined classes are standard, xuser, staff, daemon, news, and dialer. Each of these records has one field that is the same for each of these records. Let's look at the record for xuser as an example; I've snipped the output to show only the lines we're interested in:

```
xuser:\
        :tc=default:
```

Notice that since there is only one field, it does not end with a slash. The tc= tells the database to substitute the fields found in the default class. That is, by default, if you put a user in the xuser class, they will receive all the same information as a user in the default class. If you are going to put users into different classes, you will want to first change the information available to each class.

So, what type of information belongs in the fields? There are many predefined fields and they have been divided into the four major functions provided by this database: resource limits, environment, authentication, and reserved limits. Table 9.5 shows the possible fields.

Table 9.5: User Class Capabilities

Resource Limits		
Name	**Type**	**Notes/Description**
cputime	time	CPU usage limit.
filesize	size	Maximum file size limit.
datasize	size	Maximum data size limit.
stacksize	size	Maximum stack size limit.
coredumpsize	size	Maximum coredump size limit.
memoryuse	size	Max. size limit of core memory use.
vmemoryuse	size	Maximum permitted total virtual memory usage per process.
memorylocked	size	Maximum locked-in core memory size limit.
maxproc	number	Maximum number of processes.
openfiles	number	Maximum number of open files per process.
sbsize	size	Maximum permitted socketbuffer size.
Environment		
Name	**Type**	**Notes/Description**
charset	string	Set $MM_CHARSET environment variable to the specified value.

ftp-chroot	bool (false)	Limit ftp access to the home directory of the user.
hushlogin	bool (false)	Same as having a ~/.hushlogin file.
ignorenologin	bool (false)	Login not prevented by nologin.
label	string	Default MAC policy.
lang	string	Set $LANG environment variable to the specified value.
manpath	path	Default search path for manpages.
nocheckmail	boolean (false)	Display mail status at login.
nologin	file	If the file exists, it will be displayed and the login session will be terminated.
path	path (/bin /usr/bin)	Default search path.
priority	number	Initial priority (nice) level.
requirehome	bool (false)	Require a valid home directory to log in.
setenv	list	A comma-separated list of environment variables and values to which they are to be set.
shell	prog	Session shell to execute rather than the shell specified in the password file. The SHELL environment variable will contain the shell specified in the password file.
term	string	Default terminal type if not able to determine from other means.
timezone	string	Default value of $TZ environment variable.
umask	number (022)	Initial umask. Should always have a leading 0 to ensure octal interpretation.
welcome	file (/etc/motd)	File containing welcome message.

Authentication		
Name	**Type**	**Notes/Description**
copyright	file	File containing additional copyright information
host.allow	list	List of remote host wildcards that users in the class may access.
host.deny	list	List of remote host wildcards that users in the class may not access.
login_prompt	string	The login prompt.
login_backoff	number (3)	Number of login attempts before backoff delay.
login-retries	number (10)	Number of attempts before login fails.

passwd_format	string (md5)	The encryption format that new or changed passwords will use. Valid values include "md5" and "des." NIS clients using a non-FreeBSD NIS server should probably use "des."
passwd_prompt	string	The password prompt presented at login.
times.allow	list	List of time periods during which logins are allowed.
times.deny	list	List of time periods during which logins are disallowed.
ttys.allow	list	List of ttys and ttygroups that users in the class may use for access.
ttys.deny	list	List of ttys and ttygroups that users in the class may not use for access.
warn_expire	time	Advance notice of pending account expiry.
warnpassword	time	Advance notice of pending password expiry.

Reserved Capabilities		
These are not implemented in the base system		
Name	**Type**	**Notes/Description**
accounted	bool (false)	Enable session-time accounting for all users in this class.
auth	list (passwd)	Allowed authentication styles.
auth-type	list	Allowed authentication styles for the authentication type.
autodelete	time	Time after expiry when account is auto-deleted.
bootfull	bool (false)	Enable "boot only if ttygroup is full" strategy when terminating sessions.
daytime	time	Maximum login time per day.
expireperiod	time	Time for expiry allocation.
graceexpire	time	Grace days for expired account.
gracetime	time	Additional grace login time allowed.
host.accounted	list	List of remote host wildcards from which login sessions will be accounted.
host.exempt	list	List of remote host wildcards from which login session accounting is exempted.
idletime	time	Maximum idle time before logout.
minpasswordlen	number (6)	Minimum password length.

minpassword case	boolean (true)	Whether passwd will warn of an all lowercase password.
monthtime	time	Maximum login time per month.
passwordtime	time	Used by passwd(1) to set next password expiry date.
refreshtime	time	New time allowed on account refresh.
refreshperiod	str	How often account time is refreshed.
sessiontime	time	Maximum login time per session.
sessionlimit	number	Maximum number of concurrent login sessions on ttys in any group.
ttys.accounted	list	List of ttys and ttygroups for which login accounting is active.
ttys.exempt	list	List of ttys and ttygroups for which login accounting is exempt.
warntime	time	Advance notice for pending out-of-time.
weektime	time	Maximum login time per week.

Using the passwdqc PAM Module

From the table it looks like many fields which would be useful in implementing a password policy are reserved fields, meaning they are not available in the base system. Fortunately, most of their functionality is now available through the passwdqc (password quality-control) PAM module. From **man pam_passwdqc**, this module allows you to set:

- minimum password length

- maximum password length

- passphrase support and number of words required in passphrase

- matching algorithm to look for strings in password

- if similar passwords are allowed

- the ability to require a random password

- the number of tries allowed when choosing a strong new password

To use this PAM module, modify /etc/pam.d/passwd according to your needs. This file by default looks like this:

```
# more /etc/pam.d/passwd
# $FreeBSD: src/etc/pam.d/passwd,v 1.3 2003/04/24 12:22:42 des Exp $
# PAM configuration for the "passwd" service
# passwd(1) does not use the auth, account or session services.
# password
#password requisite pam_passwdqc.so enforce=users
password required pam_unix.so no_warn try_first_pass nullok
```

Obviously, we'll have to remove the comment from the line containing pam_passwdqc.so and to then input our desired options. Notice that the default option is to enforce=users, which according to the manpage forces users (but not superuser) to use a strong password. This is a good time to point out than any changes you make to this file will only be seen when a user uses the **passwd** command to change their password — hence the reason why this file is called /etc/pam.d/passwd.

In my policy, I'll change =users to =everyone which will also force the superuser to choose strong passwords. I'd also like to set a minimum password length of eight characters. I can do that by adding another option; let's take a look at a sample setting:

```
min=disabled,8,20,8,8
```

You'll note that five different types of passwords are defined by this module and that I must specify the minimum password length for each. The types are:

- passwords containing one character class only: e.g. all uppercase, all lowercase, all numbers, all symbols. I have chosen to disable this type of password.

- passwords containing a mix of two character classes: e.g. a mix of upper and lowercase, a mix of lowercase and numbers, etc. I have set a minimum password length of 8.

- this type defines the minimum passphrase length.

- passwords containing a mix of three character classes.

- passwords containing a mix of four character classes.

I'll also add the similar=deny option which will prevent users from choosing passwords similar to their old password. When I'm finished, my line looks like this:

```
password  requisite  pam_passwdqc.so  enforce=everyone min=disabled,8,8,8,8 similar=deny
```

Let's see what happens if the user *genisis* tries to change her password:

```
% passwd
Changing local password for genisis.
Old password:
You can now choose the new password or passphrase.
A valid password should be a mix of upper and lower case letters,
digits and other characters.  You can use an 8 character long
```

```
password with characters from at least 3 of these 4 classes.
Characters that form a common pattern are discarded by the check.
A passphrase whould be of at least 3 words, 8 to 40 characters
long and contain enough different characters.
Alternatively, if noone else can see your terminal now, you can
pick this as your password:  "dog_ramp,aloft".
Enter new password:
```

I'll find that I can't change my password if I choose a weak password, a password that is too short, the same password, or a new password that is too similar to my old password. It looks like the policy has been successfully implemented.

Additional Resources

Original Article:

```
http://www.onlamp.com/pub/a/bsd/2001/01/17/FreeBSD_Basics.html
```

9.8 Improving User Passwords with apg

In this section, I'll demonstrate an application from the ports collection that can assist users in choosing complex yet memorable passwords.

The **apg**, or automatic password generator, intrigued me, since it supports the pwdgen protocol, defined by RFC 972. Yes, I know I need to get out more often, but I find it interesting that this protocol has been available since 1986, yet most people have never heard of it or had the opportunity to use it in a network.

Let's install this application and see how useful it is:

```
# pkg_add -r apg
```

This will actually install three utilities: the **apg** client, the **apgd** server, and the Bloom filter manager, **apgbfm**. Each utility has an associated manpage, all chock-full of examples and useful URLs for additional reading.

Using the Client

In its simplest use, **apg** will generate six random passwords, in the hopes that one of them will appeal to you as a password choice. The passwords will be complex, meaning they won't be found by a dictionary cracker. To help make the passwords memorable, include the **-t** switch, which will show you how to pronounce the generated passwords. Here's an example:

```
% apg -t
UlmIrrors1 (Ulm-Irr-ors-ONE)
ziadrotAw (zia-drot-Aw)
FoacodCurt (Foac-od-Curt)
wroztAm1 (wrozt-Am-ONE)
HeudIfpyd9 (Heud-If-pyd-NINE)
BeshDaftem (Besh-Daft-em)
```

By default, **apg** creates passwords of eight to ten alphanumeric characters, using both upper and lower case. However, you can use additional switches to conform to any password policy. For example, to force the inclusion of symbols:

```
% apg -MS -t
loce>fruo (loc-e-GREATER_THAN-fruo)
afmisbol: (af-mis-bol-COLON)
pamob(ocon (pam-ob-LEFT_PARENTHESIS-oc-on)
swotbuad# (swot-bu-ad-CROSSHATCH)
naynalwak) (nayn-al-wak-RIGHT_PARENTHESIS)
cravser- (crav-ser-HYPHEN)
```

To ensure that each password is 14 characters long, specify 14 as both the minimum (**-m**) and maximum (**-x**) length:

```
% apg -MS -m14 -x14 -t
```

If your password policy insists on truly random passwords that aren't pronounceable, use **-a1** instead of **-MS**:

```
% apg -a1 -m14 -x14
V/u|X@/qO%y;`r
ux:S};"JRCf]I8
LLV5lb!WY5qH!9
-vUY&x6Lj+:IO^
m(X2R.I`C2["Mi
jO%H3w1ZMRnZTj
```

Hmmm. I think I'd better stick with the pronounceable passwords.

apg also supports the ability to check the randomly generated passwords against either a dictionary file or a Bloom filter file. If it happens to create a random password that is found in either file, it will scrap it and generate another password.

Your FreeBSD system provides the dictionary file /usr/share/dicts/words. If this file isn't on your particular system, you can install it by going into **sysinstall**, choosing Configure, and then Distributions, and selecting dict. This file is alphabetical and in ASCII text, meaning you can add your own words. It's common to add words like:

```
R00t
r00t
r00T
```

and so on, since the words are case-sensitive. It is recommended that you spend some time adding the words you don't want showing up as passwords in your network. Once you're finished, configure **apg** to double-check against your dictionary file by using the **-r** switch and specifying the name of the file:

```
% apg -MS -m14 -x14 -t -r /usr/share/dict/words
```

Even better, take the time to create a Bloom file as it will speed up things considerably. This will require you to specify both the name of the dictionary and the desired name of the generated Bloom file:

```
% apgbfm -d /usr/share/dict/words -f ~/bloomfile
Counting words in dictionary. Please wait...
```

This command can be run as a regular user. In this instance, I chose to create the Bloom file in my home directory. Once the file is generated, use the **-b** switch to tell **apg** where the Bloom file is located:

```
% apg -MS -m14 -x14 -t -b ~/bloom
```

If you try both the **-r** switch and the **-b** switch with **apg**, you'll find that the Bloom file is much quicker, as it uses an algorithm to determine whether or not the password would be found in the dictionary file.

The last switch I'll mention is the **-s**, or seed, switch. This switch is recommended, as it gives the random number generator a seed to work with:

```
% apg -MS -m14 -x14 -t -b ~/bloom -s
Please enter some random data (only first eight are significant)
(eg. your old password):>
jasvafwabvoud, (jas-vaf-wab-voud-COMMA)
rhylpoj:oruch~ (rhylp-oj-COLON-or-uch-TILDE)
dibogcewbowug{ (dib-og-cewb-ow-ug-LEFT_BRACE)
abun'frelfoksi (ab-un-GRAVE-frelf-oks-i)
dircunittanas" (dirc-un-itt-an-as-QUOTATION_MARK)
rhaph"drockeet (rhaph-QUOTATION_MARK-droc-keet)
```

Notice that these passwords are quite complicated, but still fairly pronounceable.

Simplifying the Client

For those of you who prefer GUI-based utilities, the **apg** author has also released the tkAPG front end. There isn't a port for this utility, but it is easy enough to install on your FreeBSD system. Once you've downloaded the source file from http://www.adel.nursat.kz/tkapg/download.shtml, untar it and **cd** to the newly created directory:

```
# tar xzvf tkapg-0.0.2a.tar.gz
# cd tkapg-0.0.2a
```

This directory contains a README and a script file called tkapg. Open the script in your favorite editor, and change this line:

```
exec wish "$0" "$@"
```

to:

```
exec /usr/local/bin/wish8.4 "$0" "$@"
```

Note: If `/usr/local/bin/wish8.4` doesn't exist on your system, you can install it with **pkg_add -r tk84**.

Once you've saved the changes, run that script from an X window session. A little GUI will pop up, allowing you to generate random passwords. I found the GUI to be a bit slower than the command line. It also didn't offer each switch possibility. However, take the time to check it out, as it may meet your password generation needs.

If you decide to stick with the command line, you may want to create a shell script so you don't have to remember to type in all of your options. Here, I've modified the suggestion from **man apg** to include my desired options:

```
% vi ~dlavigne6/bin/pwgen.sh
#!/bin/sh
apg -MS -m14 -x14 -t -b /usr/home/dlavigne6/bloom -s
```

Once I save this file, I need to make it executable:

```
% chmod +x ~dlavigne6/bin/pwgen.sh
```

When I want to generate random passwords, I simply type:

```
% pwgen.sh
```

If you want to test your script right away and you use the C shell, type **rehash** so it will find your new executable.

Another alternative is to create an alias. Since I only plan on using **apg** from one machine and I'm always in the C shell, I added this line to ~/.cshrc:

```
alias apg /usr/local/bin/apg -MS -m14 -x14 -t \
     -b /usr/home/dlavigne6/bloom -s
```

Now, whenever I type **apg**, it automagically uses all of my desired switches. Again, if you want to test your alias right away, tell the C shell to reread its configuration file:

```
% source ~dlavigne6/.cshrc
```

Using the pwdgen Server

Up to this point, we've concentrated on the **apg** client, meaning we haven't actually used the pwdgen protocol yet. Like any TCP/IP protocol, pwdgen requires both a client component and a server component. The job of the server component is to listen for client requests on its well-known port. To determine what port that is:

```
% grep pwdgen /etc/services
pwdgen          129/tcp     #Password Generator Protocol
pwdgen          129/udp     #Password Generator Protocol
```

This service is started by the **inetd** daemon, meaning you'll need to edit `/etc/inetd.conf` as the superuser so that it includes this line:

```
pwdgen       stream tcp      nowait  root     /usr/local/sbin/apgd    apgd
```

Once you've saved your change, simply type **inetd** to start the service. Alternatively, if you already have **inetd** listening for other services, inform it of your changes by typing:

/etc/rc.d/inetd reload

This command should show **inetd** listening on TCP port 129:

```
% sockstat -41
USER       COMMAND      PID    FD PROTO  LOCAL ADDRESS        FOREIGN ADDRESS
root       inetd        92412 4  tcp4    *:129                *:*
```

The advantage of using **apgd** is that you don't have to install the **apg** application on each user's computer. As users need to generate random passwords, they simply connect to port 129 on the **apgd** server. In this example, **apgd** is running on an internal server with an IP address of 10.0.0.1:

```
% telnet 10.0.0.1 129
Trying 10.0.0.1...
Connected to 10.0.0.1.
Escape character is '^]'.
AilEjmacGa
yotgakki
DrehojOird
yejBabif
albEifia
jolnapt6
Connection closed by foreign host.
```

Notice a few things here. One, don't panic over the *telnet* word. The insecure telnet service isn't running on 10.0.0.1. Instead, I've used the **telnet** client to make a direct connection to the pwdgen port of 129. In essence, **telnet** is acting as the **apg** client.

Second, using this method, the user has no control over the options used by **apg**, as they are pre-configured on the server. Depending upon your security policy, this may be seen as a bonus, as users won't be able to generate non-compliant passwords.

Let's take a closer look at that generated output. Remember, when I added my line to **inetd.conf**, I didn't include any switches to **apgd**. This means that I received the default of eight to 10 alphanumeric characters with no symbols. Also note the lack of the pronunciation guide, since I didn't include **-t** in my **inetd** entry.

I should probably change that entry to include the switches applicable to my network's password policy:

```
pwdgen       stream tcp      nowait  root     /usr/local/sbin/apgd    ⇓
        apgd -MS -m14 -x14 -t -b /usr/local/etc/bloom
```

Notice that that is now one very long line (wrapped for the sake of this book). Make sure you don't use an editor that tries to turn it into two lines. I've also created a Bloom file in a directory that is accessible to all users, rather than in one particular user's home directory. Notice also the lack of the **-s** switch; unfortunately, this option is not available with **apgd**.

Finally, I also have to remember to inform **inetd** of the changes:

```
# /etc/rc.d/inetd reload
```

Now, when a user connects to the **apgd** server:

```
% telnet 10.0.0.1 129
Trying 10.0.0.1...
Connected to 10.0.0.1.
Escape character is '^]'.
yeog-flaysdok: (ye-og-HYPHEN-flays-dok-COLON)
caijpyfratcef| (caij-py-frat-cef-VERTICAL_BAR)
ajyafdiwubaig] (aj-yaf-di-wub-aig-RIGHT_BRACKET)
nohoktegrogib( (no-hok-te-grog-ib-LEFT_PARENTHESIS)
nobkarcyonnip= (nob-karc-yonn-ip-EQUAL_SIGN)
hirkadlarjiaf[ (hirk-ad-larj-iaf-LEFT_BRACKET)
Connection closed by foreign host.
```

If you decide to use the **apgd** server, you can also modify /etc/syslog.conf so it will keep track of when users use this service. Let's see what happens if I add these lines to the bottom of /etc/syslog.conf:

```
!apgd
*.info                          /var/log/apgd.log
```

To inform **syslogd** of these changes:

```
# /etc/rc.d/syslogd reload
Oct 19 12:40:36  syslogd: /var/log/apgd.log: No such file or directory
```

Oops. I forgot to make that log file:

```
# touch /var/log/apgd.log
# /etc/rc.d/syslogd reload
```

Next, I'll reconnect to the **apgd** using **telnet** and then check out the entry in the log:

```
# more /var/log/apgd.log
Oct 19 12:43:01 genisis apgd[92692]:  password generation request from 127.0.0.1.49334
```

While not the most descriptive log entry, I do have a record of which IP address, in this case the localhost, used the pwdgen protocol and at what time.

This should get you started on generating random passwords. If you plan on trying this on your own system or in a very small network, you may prefer to install the **apg** port on each computer. For a larger network, install and configure **apgd** on one of your internal servers and instruct your users how to connect to port 129.

Note: Traffic sent on port 129 is in clear text, meaning it is possible for someone running a packet sniffer to capture the suggested passwords. If this is a concern, you can encrypt the traffic using /usr/ports/security/ stunnel or SSH.

Additional Resources

Original Article:

`http://www.onlamp.com/pub/a/bsd/2003/10/30/FreeBSD_Basics.html`

tkAPG:

`http://www.adel.nursat.kz/tkapg/index.shtml`

9.9 Cracking Passwords to Enhance Security

One way to enforce a password policy is to make users aware of the policy, then regularly run a utility that will tell you if that policy still allows for poor password selection.

But how can any utility view passwords since passwords are not stored anywhere on your FreeBSD system? Instead, a hash is stored in the password database, and these hashes are in an encrypted format. Let's take a minute to define what a hash is and how it is created.

Password Cracking Basics

A hash is a string of characters, like a password, that has been scrambled by an encryption algorithm. That is, some form of complicated math was done on the string of characters to make it very hard to guess what the original string of characters was. As an example, one could apply an algorithm to the word "password" and end up with something like 1hnH/w50a$tPdv5HZRsDP46FtsW8eXH.

Good hashes contain something called a salt. A salt is a set of random characters that are added to the original string of characters before they are encrypted. A simple example of a salt would be to add the time of day; for example, if I log in at 8:45 using the password "password," the string that would be encrypted could be "8pass45word." By adding this bit of randomness to the password, my hash will actually be different every time I log in, unless the only time I ever log in is at 8:45.

Whether a salt is used and what the salt actually is depends upon the operating system and the encryption algorithm being used. On your FreeBSD system, there is a function called `crypt` that uses either the DES or the MD5 encryption algorithms to encrypt passwords. If you're curious to see the technical details on how `crypt` works, read **man 3 crypt**. Don't be dismayed if you can't understand everything in this manpage; encryption is supposed to be cryptic. Also, don't confuse the utility **crypt(1)** with the function `crypt(3)`. The utility is a very primitive way to encrypt data files, while the function is an elaborate mechanism used to create password hashes.

By definition, password hashes are one-way. This means that if I apply the same encryption algorithm to the hash, I won't end up with the original password; instead, I'll just end up with a more scrambled hash. The only way to find the original password is to type in a password, encrypt it with the same algorithm, and compare the resultant hash. If the hash is different, I must have used the wrong password; if the hash is the same, I can assume that I've typed in the correct password.

Which brings us to password crackers. These are utilities that encrypt hundreds of thousands of passwords in order to compare the resulting hashes with the hashes in your password database. Password crackers do follow a certain logic as they'll try the most common passwords first; for example, they'll try the user's name forwards, backwards, and with a number, they'll try information in the user's GECOS field, and they'll try a list of common passwords such as password and pass. Then they'll go through all of the words in the dictionary.

Not surprisingly, these types of crackers are called dictionary password crackers. Some password crackers are called brute-force password crackers as they add a third step: they'll patiently try every keystroke combination possible until all the passwords have been cracked.

Using a Dictionary Cracker

Let's demonstrate using a dictionary password cracker to determine if the passwords your users are selecting conform to your password policy. We'll install and use the port called **crack**. As the superuser and while connected to the Internet, type:

```
# pkg_add -r crack
```

Once installed, remain as the superuser; cracking the contents of the password database is definitely an exercise that requires superuser privileges.

```
# cd /usr/local/crack
```

If you do a long listing in this directory you'll notice a restrictive set of permissions on its contents; regular users won't be able to even **cd** into or view the contents of this directory.

To run the password cracker, type:

```
# ./Crack -fmt bsd /etc/master.passwd
```

You'll receive a screen's worth of output followed by the word Done just before receiving your prompt back. Note that the word Done is a bit of a misnomer. The preparation is finished but the cracker process is still running in the background:

```
# top | grep crack
61162 root      129 0  9516K  8824K RUN   1:00 45.37% cracker
```

Now, let's take a look at the results thus far:

```
# ./Reporter -quiet
---- passwords cracked as of Sun Jan 14 12:17:41 EST 2007 ----

979492604:Guessed dlavigne [dlavigne] Dru Lavigne,,123-4567 [/etc/master.passwd
/bin/tcsh]
979492611:Guessed genisis [genisisgenisis] User & [/etc/master.passwd /bin/csh]

---- done ----
```

Hmmmm. Looks like I'll be having a talk with the users *dlavigne* and *genisis* to remind them of our password policy. The password for *dlavigne* is the same as the username *[dlavigne]*. The user *genisis* picked a nice long password, but it is only the username twice: *[genisisgenisis]*. However, the *root* user's password hasn't been cracked yet. I can either rerun the **Reporter** script periodically to watch the cracking progress or keep an eye on the **top** output to see when the cracker process is finished.

I'll have the user *dlavigne* change her password. One method of creating nonsense passwords is to use the first letter of each word in a song and throw some symbols or numbers into the mix; just remember not to hum the song while you are typing it in. Using the song "We All Live in a Yellow Submarine," *dlavigne* created the password "waliays87." Let's see what happens when I rerun the **Crack** utility:

```
# ./Crack -fmt bsd /etc/master.passwd
```

And use the **Reporter** utility once the cracker process is finished:

```
# ./Reporter -quiet
---- passwords cracked as of Sun Jan 14 19:23:42 EST 2007 ----

979492611:Guessed genisis [genisisgenisis] User & [/etc/master.passwd /bin/csh]

---- done ----
```

It looks like the new password for *dlavigne* survived the dictionary crack, as it no longer shows up in the output. If you run the **Crack** utility and don't receive any output in the report, you can assume that your users are choosing passwords that aren't simply some combination of their name or a word that can be found in a dictionary; that is, they must be choosing some random combination of numbers, letters, and symbols.

When **Crack** is run, it places its working files in the run directory; these files will end with an extension that was the PID of the **Crack** process. After you are finished using **Crack**, you should clean up by typing:

```
# make tidy
```

from the /usr/local/crack directory. It is also a good idea to manually delete the run/F-merged file, as it contains the results that were read by the **Reporter** utility:

```
# more run/F-merged
F:$1$ZQQGAmIW$jCPUT9KjRGbXR/IpFOM/E0:genisisgenisis
F:pZV8Ju.2sEqsY:dlavigne
# rm run/F-merged
```

Notice that it shows the encrypted hash followed by the cracked password, which is pretty sensitive information to leave on hard disk.

One last note on running **Crack**: Never run any type of password cracker on any computer that is not in a network that you are responsible for. It is perfectly acceptable to enforce password policy on your network; it is illegal to try to discover the passwords in use on another person's network.

Using a Brute Force Cracker

Let's compare the dictionary cracker to a brute-force cracker. As the superuser and while connected to the Internet, type:

```
# pkg_add -r john
```

Once it's installed:

```
# cd /usr/local/share/john
# unshadow /etc/passwd /etc/master.passwd > passwd.1
# john passwd.1
```

At this point, you'll lose your prompt for a long period of time; if you use the **top** command to see what your CPU is doing, you'll notice that most of your cpu cycles are being used by the brute-force cracker. Given enough time, **john** will be able to crack every single hash in the password database.

We've stumbled upon some interesting points in this exercise. First, there is no ethical reason to run a brute-force cracker on your FreeBSD machine. The administrator's job is to enforce sensible passwords, not to know the passwords used by his users. A utility such as **Crack** is sufficient to let the administrator know which users are using passwords that can be guessed within a short period of time by a dictionary password cracker.

However, the administrator does need to be aware that brute-force crackers are easily and freely available on the Internet. Fortunately, before a user can use a brute-force cracker, they need to have physical access to the password databases; notice that we had to unshadow both password databases into a file before we could run the **john** utility. It is the responsibility of the system administrator to ensure that only authorized, trusted users have access to the actual password database files and any backups that contain the password databases.

Let's summarize what we've learned so far about password policies. Ensuring that users use a lengthy password containing a random mix of characters should prevent other users from guessing each other's passwords and gaining access to resources they shouldn't have access to. Physically securing access to the password databases should prevent unauthorized users from using a brute-force cracking utility to obtain the passwords in use on your FreeBSD system.

Additional Resources

Original Article:

```
http://www.onlamp.com/pub/a/bsd/2001/01/24/FreeBSD_Basics.html
```

9.10 Hiding Secrets with Steganography

I've always been fascinated by algorithms and the whole concept that a bit of mathematics can be used to compress an image or a sound or a video. Or keep track of where it put the files on my hard drive. Or perhaps scramble the contents of one of those files so that only my intended recipient is capable of descrambling it. Granted, I don't even pretend to understand the mathematics behind algorithms. But I'm somewhat comforted that there are people in this world who do, and that their efforts help to keep the computers of this world computing.

In this section, I'll introduce the science of steganography by demonstrating two applications from the ports collection. Along the way, we'll also discover some interesting features of compression algorithms.

What is Steganography, Anyway?

The term steganography comes from the Greek words for covered writing. If, as a child, you ever wrote an invisible message in lemon juice and had your friend hold it next to a light bulb in order to watch the message magically appear, you've used steganography.

When using steganography on a computer, you actually hide a message within another file. That resulting file is called a *stego* file. The trick to computer steganography is to choose a file capable of hiding a message. A picture, audio, or video file is ideal for several reasons:

- These types of files are already compressed by an algorithm. For example, *.jpeg*, *.mp3*, *.mp4*, and *.wav* formats are all examples of compression algorithms.

- These files tend to be large, making it easier to find spots capable of hiding some text.

- These files make excellent distractors. That is, few people expect a text message to be hidden within a picture or an audio clip. If the steganographic utility does its job well, a user shouldn't notice a difference in the quality of the image or sound, even though some of the bits have been changed in order to make room for the hidden message.

Before we install the applications, you should be aware that steganography is also capable of encrypting a message before it is hidden in a file. Depending upon your geographic location, you may be limited by legal restrictions regarding the strength of encryption protocols, or even if you're allowed to use encryption in the first place.

jpeg and outguess

Let's start by installing the **jpeg** package which provides a suite of *.jpeg* manipulation utilities:

```
# pkg_add -r jpeg
```

This will install /usr/local/share/doc/jpeg/README, as well as manpages for the following utilities: **cjpeg**, **djpeg**, **jpegtran**, **rdjpgcom**, and **wrjpgcom**. I'll start with the **rdjpgcom** and **wrjpgcom** utilities. Did you know that the JPEG standard allows COM, or comment, blocks to be inserted into a *.jpeg* image? Being the curious type, when I first learned this, I was dying to know if the .jpegs on my hard drive had any interesting hidden comments. Fortunately, I had the **rdjpgcom** tool, so I could ReaD my JPG COMments:

```
% cd ~/images
% rdjpgcom pic1.jpg
% rdjpgcom pic2.jpg
```

I was sort of disappointed to learn that most of my *.jpegs* had no messages at all. One indicated that it had been created using "VT-Compress (tm) Xing Technology Corp." and another indicated it had been "Created with The GIMP."

Fortunately, I could change this situation by using the **wrjpgcom** utility to WRite in my own JPG COMments:

```
% wrjpgcom -comment \
    "This picture was taken on my June 2003 canoeing trip" \
    pic1.jpg > pic1a.jpg
```

Make sure that you give the newly commented file a different name, or you'll end up with an empty original file.

Now, if I check out the results:

```
% rdjpgcom pic1a.jpg
Created with the GIMP.
This picture was taken on my June 2003 canoeing trip
```

It's interesting to note that if I use the **file** command, it will pick up the original comment inserted by the GIMP, but not the comment I added myself. If I had instead wanted to delete the previous GIMP comment, I would have used the **-replace** switch instead of the **-comment** switch.

If I visually view both files, say with gimp, I won't recognize any differences between the two. Let's see if there are any differences:

```
% ls -l pic1*
-rw-r--r--  1 dlavigne6  wheel  6817 Nov 15 14:36 pic1.jpg
-rw-r--r--  1 dlavigne6  wheel  6873 Nov 15 14:36 pic1a.jpg
```

OK, the file with the comments is a little bit bigger than the original file. However, the **file** utility doesn't indicate any difference:

```
% file pic1*
pic1.jpg:  JPEG image data, JFIF standard 1.01, resolution (DPI),
        "Created with The GIMP", 72 x 72
pic1a.jpg: JPEG image data, JFIF standard 1.01, resolution (DPI),
        "Created with The GIMP", 72 x 72
```

Hiding More Data

Let's carry this idea a bit further and hide a complete text file within a *.jpeg* file. For example, I may want to protect my great grandmother's chocolate chip cookie recipe. Right now, it's stored in cookie.txt:

```
% ls -l cookie.txt
-rw-r--r--  1 dlavigne6  wheel  296 Nov 15 14:56 cookie.txt
```

I also have a picture of my grandmother, who entrusted that recipe to me when I was much younger:

```
% ls -l gramma.jpg
-rw-r--r--  1 dlavigne6  wheel   50873 Sep  5 09:13 gramma.jpg
```

Let's see what happens if I hide the recipe in that picture:

```
# pkg_add -r outguess
# exit
% rehash
% outguess -k "don't worry, the recipe is safe" \
    -d cookie.txt gramma.jpg grandma.jpg
Reading gramma.jpg....
JPEG compression quality set to 75
Extracting usable bits:   55365 bits
```

```
Correctable message size: 25855 bits, 46.70%
Encoded 'cookie.txt': 2368 bits, 296 bytes
Finding best embedding...
    0:  1219(50.8%)[51.5%], bias  1301(1.07), saved:   -4, total:  2.20%
    1:  1215(50.6%)[51.3%], bias  1235(1.02), saved:   -3, total:  2.19%
    5:  1192(49.7%)[50.3%], bias  1241(1.04), saved:   -1, total:  2.15%
    7:  1164(48.5%)[49.2%], bias  1217(1.05), saved:    2, total:  2.10%
   13:  1155(48.1%)[48.8%], bias  1176(1.02), saved:    3, total:  2.09%
   25:  1163(48.5%)[49.1%], bias  1156(0.99), saved:    2, total:  2.10%
   28:  1141(47.5%)[48.2%], bias  1145(1.00), saved:    5, total:  2.06%
28, 2286: Embedding data: 2368 in 55365
Bits embedded: 2400, changed: 1141(47.5%)[48.2%], bias: 1145, tot: 55200, skip: 52800
Foiling statistics: corrections: 499, failed: 0, offset: 46.129114 +- 142.525859
Total bits changed: 2286 (change 1141 + bias 1145)
Storing bitmap into data...
Writing grandma.jpg....
```

Let's take a look at that syntax. The **-k** or key switch is followed by a passphrase enclosed within double quotes. I need to remember that passphrase, in case I ever want to extract that secret recipe. I then used the **-d** switch to specify the name of the file to hide (cookie.txt), followed by the name of the file to hide it in (gramma.jpg) and the name of the new *stego* file (grandma.jpg).

If I now open both the original and new *.jpeg* files and examine them side by side, I'm hard pressed to see any differences between the two. This is to be expected, as the file to hide was very small (296 bytes) compared to the image file (50873 bytes). Interestingly, the new image file is slightly smaller than the original:

```
% ls -l grandma.jpg
-rw-r--r--   1 dlavigne6   wheel   50415 Nov 15 15:04 grandma.jpg
```

Retrieving The Hidden File

To retrieve the hidden file, I need to use the **-r** switch:

```
% outguess -k "don't worry, the recipe is safe" -r grandma.jpg test.txt
Reading grandma.jpg....
Extracting usable bits:  55365 bits
Steg retrieve: seed: 28, len: 296
```

I had to use the same key or passphrase I used to hide the message. If I read the resulting test.txt file, I'll see that the cookie recipe is still intact.

The **outguess** utility is capable of hiding messages in *.jpeg*, *.ppm*, and *.pnm* files. If you currently have a *.bmp* file that you'd like to hide a file in, use the **cjpeg**, or Convert JPEG, utility:

```
% cjpeg santa.bmp > test.jpeg
```

To my untrained eye, both files look the same in **gimp**. I can now use that new *.jpeg* file with the **outguess** utility.

Not surprisingly, **djpeg** converts the other way around; that is, from a *.jpeg* to the specified format:

```
% djpeg -bmp frosty.jpeg > icicle.bmp
% djpeg -gif frosty.jpeg > icicle.gif
```

Both of these utilities have several switches to control the quality of the images. See their respective manpages for details.

The final utility in the **jpeg** suite is **jpegtran** which can transform a *.jpeg* from, say, landscape to portrait. For example, the **-flip** horizontal switch will create a mirror image. That is, whatever is on the left will now be on the right:

```
% jpegtran -flip horizontal family.jpeg > reverse.jpeg
```

The manpage contains other switches to flip and rotate *.jpeg* images.

steghide

Let's move on to the next application, the **steghide** utility:

```
# pkg_add -r steghide
```

This utility will install **man steghide** as well as some informative information to /usr/local/share/doc/steghide/README.

I liked **steghide** as its syntax is a bit more sensible, it supports more file formats (*.jpeg*, *.bmp*, *.wav*, and *.au*), and it allows you to specify an encryption algorithm.

Hiding The Cookie Recipe Again

Let's see what happens if I embed that cookie recipe into a *.wav* file:

```
% steghide embed -cf hohoho.wav -ef cookie.txt -sf new.wav
Enter passphrase:
Re-Enter passphrase:
embedding "cookie.txt" in "hohoho.wav"... done%
writing stego file "new.wav"... done
```

Those switches make a lot of sense if you remember the three types of files you're using:

-cf *coverfile*, or the file you want to cover/hide

-ef *embedded file*

-sf *stegofile*

If I listen to both the embedded file and the stegofile in **xmms**, I can't tell a difference in the audio quality, which, granted, I've never found that great for *.wav* files anyway.

Extracting the Recipe Again

When I wish to extract my cookie recipe, I'll extract from the *stego* file like so:

```
% steghide extract -sf new.wav
Enter passphrase:
wrote extracted data to "cookie.txt".
```

Or like this:

```
% steghide extract -sf new.wav -xf secret.txt
Enter passphrase:
wrote extracted data to "secret.txt".
```

The first invocation will extract the recipe into the same file name as the original cover file. The second invocation allows me to specify the name of the newly extracted file.

Miscellaneous steghide Extras

The **steghide info** command is quite useful. It will tell me if a file contains hidden data (however, only from steghide-created files, as far as I know):

```
% steghide info new.wav
"new.wav":
  format: wave audio, PCM encoding
  capacity: 1.9 KB
Try to get information about embedded data ? (y/n) y
Enter passphrase:
  embedded file "cookie.txt":
    size: 296.0 Byte
    encrypted: rijndael-128, cbc
    compressed: yes
```

Notice that the default encryption algorithm is Rijndael, also called AES, at 128 bits. To see what other encryption algorithms are available:

```
% steghide encinfo
encryption algorithms:
<algorithm>: <supported modes>...
cast-128: cbc cfb ctr ecb ncfb nofb ofb
gost: cbc cfb ctr ecb ncfb nofb ofb
rijndael-128: cbc cfb ctr ecb ncfb nofb ofb
twofish: cbc cfb ctr ecb ncfb nofb ofb
arcfour: stream
cast-256: cbc cfb ctr ecb ncfb nofb ofb
loki97: cbc cfb ctr ecb ncfb nofb ofb
rijndael-192: cbc cfb ctr ecb ncfb nofb ofb
```

```
saferplus: cbc cfb ctr ecb ncfb nofb ofb
wake: stream
des: cbc cfb ctr ecb ncfb nofb ofb
rijndael-256: cbc cfb ctr ecb ncfb nofb ofb
serpent: cbc cfb ctr ecb ncfb nofb ofb
xtea: cbc cfb ctr ecb ncfb nofb ofb
blowfish: cbc cfb ctr ecb ncfb nofb ofb
enigma: stream
rc2: cbc cfb ctr ecb ncfb nofb ofb
tripledes: cbc cfb ctr ecb ncfb nofb ofb
```

Wow, that's a lot of supported algorithms. To use a different algorithm, simply include the **-e** or encryption switch at the end of your embed command. In this example, I'll choose blowfish:

% **steghide embed -cf hohoho.wav -ef cookie.txt -sf new.wav -e blowfish**

Once the *stego* file is created, I'll double-check that it worked:

% **steghide info new.wav**
```
"new.wav":
  format: wave audio, PCM encoding
  capacity: 1.9 KB
Try to get information about embedded data ? (y/n) y
Enter passphrase:
  embedded file "cookie.txt":
    size: 296.0 Byte
    encrypted: blowfish, cbc
    compressed: yes
```

Conclusion

This should get you started on using steganography utilities. The only question you may be asking yourself is "why use such a utility?" Probably the most common use is to safeguard passwords. We all know that we should use different passwords for various tasks. For example, you should use a different password to log into your computer, another to retrieve email, another for online banking, and yet another for when you create an account on a web server. It can be very handy to make a text file of each password and its usage, and to safeguard that file by hiding it in a place no one would suspect to look.

Until now, had you ever thought of looking in a picture or a sound file?

Additional Resources

Original Article:

http://www.onlamp.com/pub/a/bsd/2003/12/04/FreeBSD_Basics.html

Steganography & Digital Watermarking Website:

http://www.jjtc.com/Steganography/

outguess Website:

http://www.outguess.org/

10 Firewalls and VPNs

10.1 TCP Protocol Layers Explained

In the next few sections, I'd like to concentrate on IP packets and the information that can be found within the headers of an IP packet. This section will cover the various fields in the Layer 3 and 4 headers in preparation for the next where we'll capture and view this information using the **tcpdump** utility. We'll then be in good shape to see how this information relates to packet filter rules and firewalls.

Your FreeBSD system uses TCP/IP as its networking protocol. The best definition I've seen for a protocol is from http://www.whatis.com, and I quote it here:[1]

> "In information technology, a protocol (pronounced PROH-tuh-cahl, from the Greek protocollon, which was a leaf of paper glued to a manuscript volume, describing its contents) is the special set of rules that end points in a telecommunication connection use when they communicate. Protocols exist at several levels in a telecommunication connection. There are hardware telephone protocols. There are protocols between each of several functional layers and the corresponding layers at the other end of a communication. Both end points must recognize and observe a protocol. Protocols are often described in an industry or international standard."

The IP Header

Before your FreeBSD system can send data over a network connection, the TCP/IP protocol must first package that data into IP packets. An IP packet is simply a chunk of data that has had labelling information appended to the beginning of the data; like the Greek protocollon, this labelling information, called a header, is used to describe the data that follows the header.

All IP packets have at least one header, which is known as the IP header; sometimes this header is also called a Layer 3 or network header. The IP header is simply a series of bits which have been grouped into fields of a set size. All IP headers have the same structure; the only difference will be which bits have been set to 1 to either turn on a field's value or to represent a binary number within a field. Let's take a closer look at the fields in an IP header as shown in Table 10.1.

An IP packet has 14 fields; let's go through these fields one at a time.

Version: This is a 4-bit field that indicates the IP version, written in binary. For example if you are using IPv4, the bits will be set to 0100; if you are using IPv6, the bits will be set to 0110.

IHL or header length: This 4-bit field indicates how long the IP packet header is; this value is used to distinguish which part of the IP packet is the header, and which part is the actual data. If you take a look at the picture of the IP packet, you'll notice that it is 32 bits wide. Now take a look at the length of the packet: the data is not part of the header, the options are optional, but all other fields are required. This means that the

---

[1]This definition is republished with permission from WhatIs.com and TechTarget Inc.

Table 10.1: IP Header

Bits	00-03	04-07	08-15	16-18	19-31
Word 1	**Version**	**IHL**	**TOS**	**Total length**	
2	**Identification**			**Flags**	**Fragment offset**
3	**TTL**		**Protocol**	**Header checksum**	
4	**Source IP address**				
5	**Destination IP address**				
6	**Options and padding ...**				
	Data ...				

minimum header length is five 32-bit words, or binary 0101. You'll sometimes see these words translated into bytes; that is, five words multiplied by 4 bytes (32 bits divided by 8 bits to make a byte) equals a header length of 20 bytes. If the options are used, the header length will be at least six 32-bit words. Since this is a 4-bit field, the maximum length will be 2 to the power of 4 minus 1, or 15. This effectively limits the size of an IP header to 60 bytes (15 words multiplied by 4 bytes).

Type of Service (sometimes called TOS) flags: This field is 8 bits long; the first 3 bits are called precedence bits and the last 5 bits represent the type of service flags. These flags were originally created to prioritize which packets should be delivered and which packets could be dropped if a router became congested. Since then, other protocols have been invented to prioritize traffic and most routers ignore these flags even if they have been set.

Total length; also called packet length or datagram length: This 16-bit field represents the total length of the IP packet, meaning both the data and the header. The minimum size is 21 bytes (default header size plus one byte of data). Since this field is 16 bits long, the maximum packet size is 2 to the power of 16 minus one, or 65,535 bytes. (The minus one represents the illegal length value of 0.)

Identification: Every IP packet is given an identification number when it is created; that number is contained within this 16-bit field. It is possible for an IP packet to be separated into smaller fragments before it reaches its final destination; each fragment still belongs to the original IP packet, so each fragment will have the same identification number.

Flags: This field contains three flags as follows:

- reserved flag: must always be 0

- don't fragment flag: if set to 0, this flag is off, meaning you can fragment the IP packet; if set to 1, this flag is on, meaning you don't fragment this IP packet

- more fragments flag: if set to 0, there are no more fragments; if set to 1, there are more fragments of this IP packet yet to arrive

Fragment offset: If an IP packet has been fragmented, each fragment will have a value in this 13-bit field indicating where this fragment's data fits into the original IP packet. For example, let's pretend an IP packet containing 128 bytes of data was fragmented into two fragments each containing 64 bytes of data. The fragment containing the first 64 bytes of data would have a fragment offset of 0 as its data belongs at the very beginning of the original IP packet. The fragment containing the last 64 bytes of data needs to indicate that its data starts after the first 64 bytes. Since the number in this field represents an 8-byte multiple, its fragment offset will be 8 (8 multiplied by 8 = 64 bytes).

Time to Live (often called TTL): Whenever an IP packet passes through a router, the router will decrease the TTL by one; if the TTL ever reaches 0, the packet will be thrown away under the assumption that it must be undeliverable as it hasn't been delivered by now. The original TTL value depends upon the operating system; your FreeBSD system uses a default TTL of 64. Since this is an 8-bit field, the maximum allowable TTL is 255 (2 to the power of 8 minus 1; the minus 1 is for the non-allowable TTL of 0).

Protocol: This 8-bit value specifies which protocol's data is contained within the IP packet and gives a good indication of what type of information will be contained within the data portion of the packet. The protocol numbers that appear in this field are found in the /etc/protocols file on your FreeBSD system.

For example, the protocol number 1 represents the ICMP protocol. This means that this IP packet does not contain any data from an application; instead, it contains a small amount of ICMP data. We'll be taking an in-depth look at ICMP and how it affects your firewall in section 10.4.

A protocol number of 6 indicates the TCP protocol which is a connection-oriented transport. This IP packet will have an additional header known as a TCP header that will be located just after the IP header and before the beginning of the actual data that is being delivered.

A protocol number of 17 indicates the UDP protocol, which is the connectionless transport. This IP packet will have a UDP header located just after the IP header and before the beginning of the data that is being delivered.

Header Checksum: Whenever an IP header is created or modified, a CRC (Cyclic Redundancy Check) is run on the bits contained within the IP header. Basically, some math (the CRC algorithm) is done which results in an answer known as the checksum. When the IP packet is received, the same CRC is repeated on the header; if this results in the same answer (checksum), all of the bits of the IP header must have arrived in the correct order. If the CRC results in a different checksum, some of the bits in the header didn't arrive, meaning the IP packet was somehow damaged during transit.

Source Address: This will be the IP address of the host that sent the IP packet.

Destination Address: This will be the IP address of the host that is to receive the data contained within the IP packet.

Options and Padding: This is the only field in an IP packet which is optional, as all other fields are mandatory. This field is used to provide special delivery instructions not covered by the other fields in an IP header. It can allow for up to 40 bytes worth of extra instructions; these instructions must be in 32-bit words. If an instruction doesn't quite fill up a 32-bit word, the missing bits will be filled in with padding bits.

Data: The last field in an IP packet is called the data field. This will be the actual data that is being sent from one host to another. The data field may start with a Layer 4 header, which will give additional instructions to the application that will be receiving the data; alternately, it may be an ICMP header and not contain any user data at all.

The TCP Header

Now that we've examined what is contained in a Layer 3 (IP) header, let's move on to the Layer 4 header. A Layer 4 header occurs at the very beginning of the IP data field and can be either a TCP header or a UDP header. Let's start with the fields that will be found in a Layer 4 TCP header as shown in Table 10.2.

Note that a TCP header is also composed of 32-bit words; like an IP header, the default size is 20 bytes if the option field is not used. Let's summarize the fields that are available in a TCP header:

Table 10.2: TCP Header

Bits	00-03	04-07	08-09	10-15	16-31
Word 1	Source Port				Destination Port
2	Sequence Number				
3	Acknowledgement Number				
4	Data Offset	reserved	ECN	Control Bits	Window
5	Checksum				Urgent Pointer
6	Options and padding ...				
	Data ...				

Source Port: This 16-bit number represents the name of the application that sent the data in the IP packet. On your FreeBSD system, the file /etc/services lists which applications use which port numbers. There are 65,535 possible port numbers (2 to the power of 16 minus 1).

Destination Port: This 16-bit number represents the name of the application that is to receive the data contained within the IP packet. This is one of the major differences between a Layer 3 and a Layer 4 header: the Layer 3 header contains the IP address of the computer that is to receive the IP packet; once that packet has been received, the port address in the Layer 4 header ensures that the data contained within that IP packet is passed to the correct application on that computer.

Sequence Number: TCP is responsible for ensuring that all IP packets sent are actually received. When an application's data is packaged into IP packets, TCP will give each IP packet a sequence number. Once all the packets have arrived at the receiving computer, TCP uses the number in this 32-bit field to ensure that all of the packets actually arrived and are in the correct sequence.

Acknowledgement Number: This number is used by the receiving computer to acknowledge which packets have successfully arrived. This number will be the sequence number of the next packet the receiver is ready to receive.

Header Length or Offset: This is identical in concept to the header length in an IP packet, except this time it indicates the length of the TCP header.

Reserved: These 6 bits are unused and are always set to 0.

Control Flags: TCP uses six control flags with each flag being a unique bit. If the bit is set to 1, the flag is on; if the bit is set to 0, the flag is off. The order of the flags is:

- URGent
- ACKnowledgement
- PuSH
- ReSeT
- SYNchronize
- FINish

We'll be seeing these flags again when we run **tcpdump** and when we take a look at creating packet filter rules.

Window Size: Every TCP packet contains this 16-bit value that indicates how many octets it can receive at once. When IP packets are received, they are placed in a temporary area of RAM known as a buffer until the receiving computer has a chance to process them; this value represents how big a buffer the receiving host has made available for this temporary storage of IP packets.

Checksum: Unlike IP, TCP is responsible for ensuring that the entire IP packet arrived intact. TCP will run a CRC on the entire IP packet (not just the header) and place the resulting checksum in this field. When the IP packet is received, TCP re-runs the CRC on the entire packet to ensure the checksum is the same.

Urgent Pointer: If the Urgent flag was set to on, this value will indicate where the urgent data is located.

Options and Padding: Like IP options, this field is optional and represents additional instructions not covered in the other TCP fields. Again, if an option does not fill up a 32-bit word, it will be filled in with padding bits.

Data: This will be the actual data being sent and will not include any additional headers.

The UDP Header

Finally, let's take a look at a Layer 4 UDP header as seen in Table 10.3. Unlike TCP, UDP does not create a connection or guarantee the delivery of data. Accordingly, a UDP header has very few fields as compared to a TCP header:

Table 10.3: UDP Header

	Bits 00-15	16-31
Word 1	**Source Port**	**Destination Port**
2	**Length**	**Checksum**
3	**Data ...**	

A UDP header is always 8 bytes as it does not contain any options. The UDP header fields are as follows:

Source Port: Like TCP, this field indicates which application sent the data contained within the IP packet.

Destination Port: Again, indicates which application is to receive the data contained within the IP packet.

Length: Indicates the length (in bytes) of the UDP header and the data. Since all UDP headers are 8 bytes long, if you subtract 8 from this number you'll find out the size of the data being sent.

Checksum: Since UDP is not responsible for ensuring that the data actually arrives, a checksum is optional; if it is not used, this field will be set to 0.

Data: Again, this will be the actual data being sent and will not include any additional headers.

We've actually made it through all of the fields in the Layer 3 and Layer 4 headers of an IP packet. These fields should make more sense when we examine a dump file created by the **tcpdump** utility (as covered in the next section).

Additional Resources

Original Article:

`http://www.onlamp.com/pub/a/bsd/2001/03/14/FreeBSD_Basics.html`

10.2 Capturing TCP Packets

In the last section, we went through the various fields found in the Layer 3 and Layer 4 headers of an IP packet. While these fields may seem mind-numbingly technical at first, there is a good reason to be aware of the possible values for each field.

The values found in an IP packet's headers provide all of the information necessary to successfully send data from one computer running TCP/IP to another computer running TCP/IP; it doesn't matter if the two computers are cabled onto the same LAN or if they are physically separated by large geographic distances, the data will still arrive intact. Unfortunately, this robustness is a double-edged sword. If someone is so inclined, they can exploit the values found in an IP packet's headers in order to break into a computer running TCP/IP so they can steal or tamper with its data.

Your FreeBSD system provides many mechanisms to help protect your data from such exploits; these include **ipfw**, **natd**, **ipf**, and **pf**. In order to successfully configure these mechanisms and ensure that they are blocking unwanted IP packets but are still allowing the delivery of wanted IP packets, you need to be aware of the differences in the values in the IP headers of a wanted and unwanted IP packet.

In this section, I'd like to demonstrate the use of the **tcpdump** utility. This utility captures packets so you can examine the data and the headers within each packet. For this reason, you only run this utility on your own network; I repeat, don't run this utility on someone else's network unless they have given you explicit permission to do so.

The tcpdump Utility

When you run **tcpdump**, it will put your NIC into what is known as promiscuous mode. Normally, when a NIC sees a packet being transmitted on the media, it only monitors the signal long enough to determine if that packet is destined for its MAC address. If it is addressed to its MAC address, it will load the entire packet into RAM until the TCP/IP protocol has a chance to process the packet. If it is not addressed to its MAC address, it will simply ignore the rest of the packet and wait to monitor the next packet that is transmitted.

When a NIC is placed into promiscuous mode, it will load and process all packets, regardless of whom the packets are destined for. This doesn't mean that the original recipient won't receive its packet; instead, it means that the packet will be received by both the intended recipient and the NIC that is running in promiscuous mode.

When you put a NIC into promiscuous mode on a FreeBSD system, the Berkeley Packet filter or `bpf` device is loaded. Unless you have created a custom kernel, the `bpf` device is already in your kernel.

There is one last thing we need to be aware of before we run the **tcpdump** utility. Before an IP packet can be transmitted over a media, it must first be placed into a frame; this process is known as encapsulation. Encapsulation occurs at what is known as Layer 2, and it is the job of the interface that will transmit the packet to first encapsulate that packet into a frame. Just as there are many types of interfaces capable of transmitting packets, there are many types of frames. Instead of a NIC and Ethernet frames, you may use a dial-up modem to connect to a network; in this case, your modem uses PPP, which in turn uses a protocol known as HDLC to create the PPP frames.

In my home network, I have a computer named *genisis* with an IP address of 10.0.0.1; it is connected using an Ethernet topology to a computer named *biko* whose IP address is 10.0.0.2. I'll use the **tcpdump** utility to capture the packets that are used to establish and disconnect a **telnet** session between these two computers.

Only the superuser can run the **tcpdump** utility; regular users will receive this warning message instead:

```
% tcpdump
tcpdump: no suitable device found
```

On the computer *genisis*, I'll become the superuser and start the **tcpdump** utility like so:

```
% su
Password:
# tcpdump -s 1518 -i ed0 -w dump
tcpdump: listening on ed0, link-type EN10MB (Ethernet), capture size 1518 bytes
```

A note on the switches I used: I specified the maximum number of bytes to capture per frame with **-s 1518**, which is the maximum size of an Ethernet frame. I specified which interface to monitor with **-i ed0**, and I told **tcpdump** to send its output to a file named dump instead of to my screen with **-w dump**.

If I now press **Alt-F1**, I'll also see the following console message:

```
Mar 4 10:25:24 genisis /kernel:  ed0:  promiscuous mode enabled
```

Now, at the computer named *biko*, I'll **telnet** into the computer *genisis*; once I've successfully logged in, I'll immediately **exit** from the telnet connection:

Note: This exercise is used to demonstrate why telnet is an insecure way to access another system. For this reason, telnet is disabled on your FreeBSD system by default.

```
% telnet 10.0.0.1
Trying 10.0.0.1...
Connected to genisis.
Escape character is '^]'.

FreeBSD/i386 (istar.ca) (ttyp0)

login: genisis
Password:
Warning: your password expires on Thu Mar  8 17:31:47 2007
Last login: Sun Mar 4 10:23:04 from 127.0.0.1
Copyright (c) 1980, 1983, 1986, 1988, 1990, 1991, 1993, 1994
        The Regents of the University of California.  All rights reserved.

FreeBSD 6.2-RELEASE (SOUND) #0 Tue Dec 12 20:01P29 EST 2007

                Welcome to FreeBSD 6.2!!!

You have mail.
```

```
Everybody is somebody else's weirdo.
        Dykstra
```

```
% exit
logout
Connection closed by foreign host.
```

I then return to the keyboard on *genisis* and end the **tcpdump** by pressing **Ctrl-C** like so:

```
^C
88 packets received by filter
0 packets dropped by kernel
```

And if I double-check the console:

```
Mar 4 10:25:44 genisis /kernel: ed0: promiscuous mode disabled
```

Analyzing a Dump

Since there aren't any other computers on this network, all of those 88 packets captured during that 20-second interval dealt with establishing and ending that telnet session.

There are several ways to analyze the output of my newly created dump file. I'll demonstrate several ways to view this file so you can see that different utilities vary in the amount of detail they show you regarding the contents of each captured frame.

Let's start by seeing what type of file **tcpdump** created:

```
# file dump
dump:  tcpdump capture file (little-endian) - version 2.4 (Ethernet, capture length
1518)
```

The dump file is not a text file, so we won't be using an editor or a pager to view its contents. We can use the **tcpdump** utility with the **-r** (read) switch to analyze the contents of this file; however, this output is not exactly novice friendly. I'll show some snipped output to demonstrate; at the very least, you may recognize some fields from the last section:

```
# tcpdump -r dump
```

<snipped to just show packets 10-12>

```
10:25:36.854420 10.0.0.2.blackjack > 10.0.0.1.telnet: S 3205630181:3205630181(0) ⇓
 win 16384 <mss 1460> (DF) [tos 0x10]
10:25:36.854653 10.0.0.1.telnet > 10.0.0.2.blackjack: S 1746119590:1746119590(0) ⇓
 ack 3205630182 win 17520 <mss 1460> (DF)
10:25:36.854996 10.0.0.2.blackjack > 10.0.0.1.telnet: . ack 1 win 17520 (DF) ⇓
 [tos 0x10]
```

The FreeBSD ports collection contains a utility known as **tcpshow** that can be used to display dump files created by **tcpdump**. Let's install this utility as the superuser and try it out:

```
# pkg_add -r tcpshow
# rehash
# tcpshow < dump | more
```

I won't analyze every packet with you, but I would like to look at some of the highlights of packets 10 to 12. TCP uses a three-way handshake before any data is actually transmitted. Let's take a look at packet number 10:

```
-------------------------------------------------------------------
Packet 10
TIME:   10:25:36.854420 (6.232947)
LINK:   00:00:B4:3C:56:40 -> 00:50:BA:DE:36:33 type=IP
  IP:   biko -> genisis hlen=20 TOS=10 dgramlen=44 id=0013
        MF/DF=0/1 frag=0 TTL=64 proto=TCP cksum=26A7
 TCP:   port blackjack -> telnet seq=3205630181 ack=0000000000
        hlen=24 (data=0) UAPRSF=000010 wnd=16384 cksum=7814 urg=0
DATA:   <No data>
-------------------------------------------------------------------
```

Not counting the TIME heading, there are four parts to this packet. The LINK heading represents the Layer 2 frame. Normally, this is the portion of the packet that is monitored by the NIC; you'll note that it contains the MAC address of the sending computer and the MAC address of the destination computer. There are several different types of Ethernet frames; I can tell this is an Ethernet_II frame since it contains a type field.

The IP heading represents the Layer 3 IP header; all of the fields mentioned in the previous section are here except for the version field and the optional options field. You'll note that **tcpshow** resolved the IP addresses for *genisis* and *biko* for you; from the arrow, we can tell that this packet was sent by *biko* and is destined for *genisis*. Notice that the header length (hlen) has been interpreted as 20 bytes and the length of the entire IP packet (dgramlen) is 44 bytes. The MF/DF field represents the flags May Fragment and Don't Fragment; in this packet, the don't fragment flag has been turned on as it has been set to 1. Finally, the protocol (proto) indicates TCP; not surprisingly, the next column is labeled TCP, as it represents the Layer 4 TCP header.

In the TCP header, the source and destination port numbers have been resolved for you; not surprisingly, *biko* is trying to access the telnet port on the host *genisis*. This packet has a sequence number; since it is the first TCP packet, the acknowledgement has been set to 0 as there aren't any packets to acknowledge having been received yet. The TCP header length is 24 bytes; if you add these 24 bytes to the IP header length of 20 bytes, you'll receive the IP packet length of 44 bytes, so it looks like this packet arrived intact.

Now we get to the most interesting part of this IP packet. Note that the only TCP flag (UAPRSF) to be set to 1 is the S or the synchronize flag. This packet represents step one of the three-way handshake required to establish the TCP connection. Not surprisingly, there is no actual data being sent with this packet, and the DATA column contains no data. Remember, no data can be sent between applications that use TCP as their transport until the three-way handshake has been successful. Lastly, note that the Layer 4 header has indicated the window size *biko* is willing to use and has calculated the checksum on the contents of the IP packet.

Let's take a look at packet 11 to see how the computer *genisis* responded to this packet:

```
-------------------------------------------------------------------
```

```
Packet 11
TIME:   10:25:36.854653 (0.000233)
LINK:   00:50:BA:DE:36:33 -> 00:00:B4:3C:56:40 type=IP
  IP:   genisis -> biko hlen=20 TOS=00 dgramlen=44 id=9554
        MF/DF=0/1 frag=0 TTL=64 proto=TCP cksum=9175
 TCP:   port telnet -> blackjack seq=1746119590 ack=3205630182
        hlen=24 (data=0) UAPRSF=010010 wnd=17520 cksum=5FD9 urg=0
DATA:   <No data>
```

The TCP header contains the more interesting bits of *genisis'* response packet. Note that *genisis* responded with its own unique sequence number. Now compare the ack number in packet 11 with the original sequence number from packet 10; it is one more than the original sequence number of 3205630181. This indicates that the computer *genisis* successfully processed the IP packet containing that sequence number and is now ready to receive the packet that is next in sequence. When we look at *biko*'s response to this IP packet, we'll expect to see an ack number that is one higher than this packet's sequence number of 1746119590.

Also notice that an additional flag has been set on this packet, since it is the second packet involved in the three-way handshake. You can always recognize this type of packet because both the A (acknowledgement) and S (synchronize) flags will be set. Again, this packet should not contain any actual data.

Now, let's see if packet number 12 contains the last step of the three-way handshake:

```
Packet 12
TIME:   10:25:36.854996 (0.000343)
LINK:   00:00:B4:3C:56:40 -> 00:50:BA:DE:36:33 type=IP
  IP:   biko -> genisis hlen=20 TOS=10 dgramlen=40 id=0014
        MF/DF=0/1 frag=0 TTL=64 proto=TCP cksum=26AA
 TCP:   port blackjack -> telnet seq=3205630182 ack=1746119591
        hlen=20 (data=0) UAPRSF=010000 wnd=17520 cksum=7796 urg=0
DATA:   <No data>
```

It looks like we received the acknowledgement number that we were expecting; also note that *biko* responded to *genisis'* acknowledgement by sending the next packet in its sequence. This is the last packet involved in the three-way handshake; we can recognize it as such because the only flag that has been set is the A (acknowledgement) flag and there is no data contained within this IP packet.

Using Wireshark

Before we leave these three packets involved in the three-way handshake, I'd like to show you how **wireshark** (available from the ports collection) views these same three packets.[2] If I open up **wireshark** from the GUI, I can go to the File Menu and open up the dump file to view its contents. Once I've opened up this file, I can save it to a text file by again going to the File Menu and choosing Print. When the print screen is displayed, I choose to print to a file; the resulting file can then be viewed using an editor or a pager. On my system, I used this method to create a file called `etherdump` which reads like this:

---
[2]See section 7.4 for an introduction to Wireshark.

```
# more etherdump
<snip to just show packets 10-12>
Frame 10 (60 on wire, 60 captured)
Arrival Time:  Mar 4, 2001 10:25:36.8544
Time delta from previous packet:  6.232947 seconds
Frame Number:  10
Packet Length:  60 bytes
Capture Length:  60 bytes
Ethernet II
Destination:  00:50:ba:de:36:33 (genisis)
Source:  00:00:b4:3c:56:40 (biko)
Type:  IP (0x0800)
Trailer:  1011
Internet Protocol
Version:  4
Header length:  20 bytes
Differentiated Services Field:  0x10 (DSCP 0x04:  Unknown DSCP; ECN: 0x00)
0001 00..  = Differentiated Services Codepoint:  Unknown (0x04)
.... ..0.  = ECN-Capable Transport (ECT): 0
.... ...0 = ECN-CE: 0
Total Length:  44
Identification:  0x0013
Flags:  0x04
.1..  = Don't fragment:  Set
..0.  = More fragments:  Not set
Fragment offset:  0
Time to live:  64
Protocol:  TCP (0x06)
Header checksum:  0x26a7 (correct)
Source:  biko (10.0.0.2)
Destination:  genisis (10.0.0.1)
Transmission Control Protocol, Src Port:  blackjack (1025), Dst Port:  telnet (23),
Seq:  3205630181, Ack:  0
Source port:  blackjack (1025)
Destination port:  telnet (23)
Sequence number:  3205630181
Header length:  24 bytes
Flags:  0x0002 (SYN)
0... ....  = Congestion Window Reduced (CWR): Not set
.0.. ....  = ECN-Echo:  Not set
..0. ....  = Urgent:  Not set
...0 ....  = Acknowledgment:  Not set
.... 0...  = Push:  Not set
.... .0..  = Reset:  Not set
.... ..1.  = Syn:  Set
.... ...0 = Fin:  Not set
Window size:  16384
Checksum:  0x7814
Options:  (4 bytes)
```

```
Maximum segment size:  1460 bytes


Frame 11 (58 on wire, 58 captured)
Arrival Time:  Mar 4, 2001 10:25:36.8546
Time delta from previous packet:  0.000233 seconds
Frame Number:  11
Packet Length:  58 bytes
Capture Length:  58 bytes
Ethernet II
Destination:  00:00:b4:3c:56:40 (biko)
Source:  00:50:ba:de:36:33 (genisis)
Type:  IP (0x0800)
Internet Protocol
Version:  4
Header length:  20 bytes
Differentiated Services Field:  0x00 (DSCP 0x00:  Default; ECN: 0x00)
0000 00.. = Differentiated Services Codepoint:  Default (0x00)
.... ..0. = ECN-Capable Transport (ECT): 0
.... ...0 = ECN-CE: 0
Total Length:  44
Identification:  0x9554
Flags:  0x04
.1.. = Don't fragment:  Set
..0. = More fragments:  Not set
Fragment offset:  0
Time to live:  64
Protocol:  TCP (0x06)
Header checksum:  0x9175 (correct)
Source:  genisis (10.0.0.1)
Destination:  biko (10.0.0.2)
Transmission Control Protocol, Src Port:  telnet (23), Dst Port:  blackjack (1025),
Seq:  1746119590, Ack:  3205630182
Source port:  telnet (23)
Destination port:  blackjack (1025)
Sequence number:  1746119590
Acknowledgement number:  3205630182
Header length:  24 bytes
Flags:  0x0012 (SYN, ACK)
0... .... = Congestion Window Reduced (CWR): Not set
.0.. .... = ECN-Echo:  Not set
..0. .... = Urgent:  Not set
...1 .... = Acknowledgment:  Set
.... 0... = Push:  Not set
.... .0.. = Reset:  Not set
.... ..1. = Syn:  Set
.... ...0 = Fin:  Not set
Window size:  17520
Checksum:  0x5fd9
Options:  (4 bytes)
```

```
Maximum segment size:  1460 bytes

Frame 12 (60 on wire, 60 captured)
Arrival Time:  Mar 4, 2001 10:25:36.8549
Time delta from previous packet:  0.000343 seconds
Frame Number:  12
Packet Length:  60 bytes
Capture Length:  60 bytes
Ethernet II
Destination:  00:50:ba:de:36:33 (genisis)
Source:  00:00:b4:3c:56:40 (biko)
Type:  IP (0x0800)
Trailer:  0C0D0E0F1011
Internet Protocol
Version:  4
Header length:  20 bytes
Differentiated Services Field:  0x10 (DSCP 0x04:  Unknown DSCP; ECN: 0x00)
0001 00.. = Differentiated Services Codepoint:  Unknown (0x04)
.... ..0. = ECN-Capable Transport (ECT): 0
.... ...0 = ECN-CE: 0
Total Length:  40
Identification:  0x0014
Flags:  0x04
.1.. = Don't fragment:  Set
..0. = More fragments:  Not set
Fragment offset:  0
Time to live:  64
Protocol:  TCP (0x06) Header checksum:  0x26aa (correct)
Source:  biko (10.0.0.2)
Destination:  genisis (10.0.0.1)
Transmission Control Protocol, Src Port:  blackjack (1025), Dst Port:  telnet (23),
Seq:  3205630182, Ack:  1746119591
Source port:  blackjack (1025)
Destination port:  telnet (23)
Sequence number:  3205630182
Acknowledgement number:  1746119591
Header length:  20 bytes Flags:  0x0010 (ACK)
0... .... = Congestion Window Reduced (CWR): Not set
.0.. .... = ECN-Echo:  Not set
..0. .... = Urgent:  Not set
...1 .... = Acknowledgment:  Set
.... 0... = Push:  Not set
.... .0.. = Reset:  Not set
.... ..0. = Syn:  Not set
.... ...0 = Fin:  Not set
Window size:  17520
Checksum:  0x7796
```

You'll notice that **wireshark** shows every field in great detail. It's interesting to see how one dump file can be interpreted in varying degrees by three different utilities. We'll continue our analysis of this dump file in the next section.

Additional Resources

Original Article:

```
http://www.onlamp.com/pub/a/bsd/2001/03/21/FreeBSD_Basics.html
```

10.3 IP Packets Revealed

In the last section, we used the **tcpdump** utility to capture the packets involved in a **telnet** session and then examined the resulting dump file. Let's continue through the output of this file to see what else we can discover regarding a typical TCP connection.

Starting and Ending TCP Sessions

When we looked at the packets involved in the TCP 3-way handshake, we paid particular attention to the flags field in the TCP header. The only time a packet's SYN flag is set is if it is one of the first two packets involved in the 3-way handshake. This means that whenever a packet arrives with its SYN flag set, someone is trying to create a TCP connection. Notice in the output that every TCP header has an acknowledgement number and the ACK flag is set; the only exception to this rule is found in the very first packet involved in the 3-way handshake. That is, if a packet arrives with the SYN flag set but not the ACK flag, that packet is trying to initiate a connection to one of your network services; the destination port field will tell you which service they are trying to connect to.

Let's take one last look at that first packet in the 3-way handshake from section 10.2:

```
# tcpshow < dump
<snip to just show this one packet>
----------------------------------------------------------------
Packet 10
TIME:   10:25:36.854420 (6.232947)
LINK:   00:00:B4:3C:56:40 -> 00:50:BA:DE:36:33 type=IP
  IP:   10.0.0.2 -> 10.0.0.1 hlen=20 TOS=10 dgramlen=44 id=0013
        MF/DF=0/1 frag=0 TTL=64 proto=TCP cksum=26A7
 TCP:   port blackjack -> telnet seq=3205630181 ack=0000000000
        hlen=24 (data=0) UAPRSF=000010 wnd=16384 cksum=7814 urg=0
DATA:   <No data>
----------------------------------------------------------------
```

Note that this packet has no acknowledgement (ack=0000000000) and the only TCP flag that has been set (UAPRSF=000010) to 1 is the S or SYN flag. This packet came from 10.0.0.2 and it is trying to establish a connection to (->) the telnet port on 10.0.0.1.

TCP also has an established procedure for gracefully ending a TCP connection. As you may have guessed, it involves the use of the FIN flag. Either end of a TCP connection can ask to close the connection at any time. In our example, I typed the word **exit** as soon as I had established the **telnet** connection and had successfully logged in. Let's see what packets were involved in this transaction. Again, I've snipped the output of the **tcpshow** command to just show these packets:

```
------------------------------------------------------------------------
Packet 72
TIME:   10:25:43.153131 (1.174173)
LINK:   00:00:B4:3C:56:40 -> 00:50:BA:DE:36:33 type=IP
  IP:   10.0.0.2 -> 10.0.0.1 hlen=20 TOS=10 dgramlen=41 id=0037
        MF/DF=0/1 frag=0 TTL=64 proto=TCP cksum=2686
 TCP:   port blackjack -> telnet seq=3205630360 ack=1746120351
        hlen=20 (data=1) UAPRSF=011000 wnd=17520 cksum=0EE3 urg=0
DATA:   e
------------------------------------------------------------------------
```

This is the first packet we've seen that actually contains some data. Even though I typed the word **exit** from the computer 10.0.0.2, each character I typed was sent in a separate packet. The first packet contained the letter e.

```
------------------------------------------------------------------------
Packet 73
TIME:   10:25:43.153685 (0.000554)
LINK:   00:50:BA:DE:36:33 -> 00:00:B4:3C:56:40 type=IP
  IP:   10.0.0.1 -> 10.0.0.2 hlen=20 TOS=10 dgramlen=41 id=956E
        MF/DF=0/1 frag=0 TTL=64 proto=TCP cksum=914E
 TCP:   port telnet -> blackjack seq=1746120351 ack=3205630361
        hlen=20 (data=1) UAPRSF=011000 wnd=17520 cksum=0EE2 urg=0
DATA:   e
------------------------------------------------------------------------
```

This is the response from 10.0.0.1. Note that it acknowledged receipt of my packet as it incremented my sequence number by one. Strangely, it also returned the same data; this told the **telnet** client to echo the letter e onto my terminal.

If I look at the next two packets I'll see that they both came from 10.0.0.2. First, I acknowledged receipt of the packet from 10.0.0.1, then I sent the letter **x** in its own packet. I won't bore you with the outputs of packets 76 to 84 as they simply repeat this process of individually sending and echoing the letters x, i, and t, and acknowledging that each packet was received.

Packet 85 contains data from the telnet application running on 10.0.0.1. This application is now aware that I typed the word **exit**. It responds by sending me the entire word logout to be echoed to my terminal. In this packet the FIN flag has also been set. In other words, not only did the **telnet** application echo the word logout to my screen, it also indicated that it would finish up this TCP connection. At this point, my machine responded with two packets. The first acknowledged receipt of this packet, and the second agreed to the closing of the TCP connection by setting its own FIN flag.

The final packet in our dump file was the very last acknowledgement from 10.0.0.1.

Behind the Scenes of a telnet Session

We've looked at the very beginning and very end of the TCP connection. Now let's take a look at some of the stuff that happened in between. Once the TCP connection had been established, the rest of the packets either contained data from the **telnet** application or were acknowledgements that the data had been received. For example, packet 21 shows the terminal type being used for this telnet connection:

```
--------------------------------------------------------------------
Packet 21
TIME:   10:25:36.917010 (0.021554)
LINK:   00:00:B4:3C:56:40 -> 00:50:BA:DE:36:33 type=IP
  IP:   10.0.0.2 -> 10.0.0.1 hlen=20 TOS=10 dgramlen=77 id=0019
        MF/DF=0/1 frag=0 TTL=64 proto=TCP cksum=2680
 TCP:   port blackjack -> telnet seq=3205630297 ack=1746119656
        hlen=20 (data=37) UAPRSF=011000 wnd=17520 cksum=5F8D urg=0
DATA:   .. .115200,115200....'.......CONS25..
--------------------------------------------------------------------
```

The **wireshark** utility shows even more detail regarding the data that was passed between the telnet daemon and the **telnet** client.[3] Let's see how this same packet is viewed by **wireshark**. I've snipped the output of the packet to just show the telnet data:

```
Telnet
    Suboption Begin: Terminal Speed
        Here's my Terminal Speed
        Value: 115200,115200
    Command: Suboption End
    Suboption Begin: New Environment Option
        Here's my New Environment Option
        Value:
    Command: Suboption End
    Suboption Begin: Terminal Type
        Here's my Terminal Type
        Value: CONS25
    Command: Suboption End
```

Several other packets were sent between the telnet daemon and the **telnet** application before the login prompt appeared. This data was used to negotiate the various telnet options, window size, terminal type, and terminal speed. Even though this data was never displayed on my screen, it is interesting to note that what was happening behind the scenes was still captured by the **tcpdump** utility. The **tcpshow** utility didn't bother to interpret this data, but the **wireshark** utility did. I've snipped the output of the pertinent packets to indicate who sent the packet and the data that was sent in each packet:

```
Frame 13 (84 on wire, 84 captured)
    Source: biko (10.0.0.2)
    Destination: genisis (10.0.0.1)
Telnet
    Command: Do Encryption Option
    Command: Will Encryption Option
    Command: Do Suppress Go Ahead
    Command: Will Terminal Type
    Command: Will Negotiate About Window Size
    Command: Will Terminal Speed
    Command: Will Remote Flow Control
```

---

[3]Wireshark is introduced in section 7.4.

```
        Command: Will Linemode
        Command: Will New Environment Option
        Command: Do Status
```
Frame 14 (57 on wire, 57 captured)
```
        Source: genisis (10.0.0.1)
        Destination: biko (10.0.0.2)
Telnet
        Command: Do Authentication Option
```
Frame 15 (60 on wire, 60 captured)
```
        Source: biko (10.0.0.2)
        Destination: genisis (10.0.0.1)
Telnet
        Command: Won't Authentication Option
```
Frame 16 (92 on wire, 92 captured)
```
        Source: genisis (10.0.0.1)
        Destination: biko (10.0.0.2)
Telnet
        Command: Will Encryption Option
        Command: Do Encryption Option
        Suboption Begin: Encryption Option
            Send your Encryption Option
        Command: Suboption End
        Command: Will Suppress Go Ahead
        Command: Do Terminal Type
        Command: Do Negotiate About Window Size
        Command: Do Terminal Speed
        Command: Do Remote Flow Control
        Command: Do Linemode
        Command: Do New Environment Option
        Command: Will Status
```
Frame 17 (130 on wire, 130 captured)
```
        Source: biko (10.0.0.2)
        Destination: genisis (10.0.0.1)
Telnet
        Suboption Begin: Encryption Option
            Send your Encryption Option
        Command: Suboption End
        Suboption Begin: Negotiate About Window Size
            Here's my Negotiate About Window Size
            Value: P\000\031
        Command: Suboption End
        Suboption Begin: Linemode
            Send your Linemode
        Data: \022\000
        Command: Suboption End
        Command: Do Suppress Go Ahead
```
Frame 18 (60 on wire, 60 captured)
```
        Source: genisis (10.0.0.1)
        Destination: biko (10.0.0.2)
```

```
Telnet
    Command: Do X Display Location
    Command: Do Environment Option
Frame 19 (60 on wire, 60 captured)
    Source: biko (10.0.0.2)
    Destination: genisis (10.0.0.1)
Telnet
    Command: Won't X Display Location
    Command: Won't Environment Option
Frame 20 (72 on wire, 72 captured)
    Source: genisis (10.0.0.1)
    Destination: biko (10.0.0.2)
Telnet
    Suboption Begin: Terminal Speed
        Send your Terminal Speed
    Command: Suboption End
    Suboption Begin: New Environment Option
        Send your New Environment Option
    Command: Suboption End
    Suboption Begin: Terminal Type
        Send your Terminal Type
    Command: Suboption End
Frame 22 (57 on wire, 57 captured)
    Source: genisis (10.0.0.1)
    Destination: biko (10.0.0.2)
Telnet
    Command: Do Echo
Frame 23 (60 on wire, 60 captured)
    Source: biko (10.0.0.2)
    Destination: genisis (10.0.0.1)
Telnet
    Command: Won't Echo
Frame 24 (72 on wire, 72 captured)
    Source: genisis (10.0.0.1)
    Destination: biko (10.0.0.2)
Telnet
    Command: Will Echo
    Suboption Begin: Remote Flow Control
        Here's my Remote Flow Control
        Value:
    Command: Suboption End
    Suboption Begin: Remote Flow Control
        Send your Remote Flow Control
    Command: Suboption End
    Command: Don't Linemode
Frame 25 (60 on wire, 60 captured)
    Source: biko (10.0.0.2)
    Destination: genisis (10.0.0.1)
Telnet
```

```
      Command: Do Echo
      Command: Won't Linemode
Frame 26 (110 on wire, 110 captured)
      Source: genisis (10.0.0.1)
      Destination: biko (10.0.0.2)
Telnet
      Suboption Begin: Linemode
          Send your Linemode
      Data: \022\200
      Command: Suboption End
```

You'll remember that when I demonstrated the telnet session, several bits of information were displayed on my screen. Those bits of information came from the **telnet** application on 10.0.0.1 and we can use the **tcpshow** utility to see it being sent in the data fields of the following packets:

```
----------------------------------------------------------------------
Packet 28
TIME:   10:25:37.040099 (0.000144)
LINK:   00:50:BA:DE:36:33 -> 00:00:B4:3C:56:40 type=IP
  IP:   10.0.0.1 -> 10.0.0.2 hlen=20 TOS=10 dgramlen=90 id=955C
        MF/DF=0/1 frag=0 TTL=64 proto=TCP cksum=912F
 TCP:   port telnet -> blackjack seq=1746119733 ack=3205630343
        hlen=20 (data=50) UAPRSF=011000 wnd=17520 cksum=2DFE urg=0
DATA:   ...
        FreeBSD/i386 (istar.ca) (ttyp0)...          ...           login:
----------------------------------------------------------------------
Packet 51
TIME:   10:25:39.140175 (0.012092)
LINK:   00:50:BA:DE:36:33 -> 00:00:B4:3C:56:40 type=IP
  IP:   10.0.0.1 -> 10.0.0.2 hlen=20 TOS=10 dgramlen=51 id=9564
        MF/DF=0/1 frag=0 TTL=64 proto=TCP cksum=914E
 TCP:   port telnet -> blackjack seq=1746119790 ack=3205630352
        hlen=20 (data=11) UAPRSF=011000 wnd=17520 cksum=815F urg=0
DATA:   .
        Password:
----------------------------------------------------------------------
Packet 66
TIME:   10:25:41.680125 (0.020455)
LINK:   00:50:BA:DE:36:33 -> 00:00:B4:3C:56:40 type=IP
  IP:   10.0.0.1 -> 10.0.0.2 hlen=20 TOS=10 dgramlen=150 id=956B
        MF/DF=0/1 frag=0 TTL=64 proto=TCP cksum=90E4
 TCP:   port telnet -> blackjack seq=1746119801 ack=3205630360
        hlen=20 (data=110) UAPRSF=011000 wnd=17520 cksum=AE21 urg=0
DATA:   .
        Warning: your password expires on Thu Mar  8 17:31:47 2007.
        Last login: Sun Mar  4 10:23:04 from 127.0.0.1.
----------------------------------------------------------------------
Packet 68
TIME:   10:25:41.779159 (0.000175)
```

```
LINK:    00:50:BA:DE:36:33 -> 00:00:B4:3C:56:40 type=IP
  IP:    10.0.0.1 -> 10.0.0.2 hlen=20 TOS=10 dgramlen=283 id=956C
         MF/DF=0/1 frag=0 TTL=64 proto=TCP cksum=905E
 TCP:    port telnet -> blackjack seq=1746119911 ack=3205630360
         hlen=20 (data=243) UAPRSF=011000 wnd=17520 cksum=30D1 urg=0
DATA:    Copyright (c) 1980, 1983, 1986, 1988, 1990, 1991, 1993, 1994   .
         The Regents of the University of California.  All rights reserved...
         FreeBSD 6.2-RELEASE (SOUND) #0: Tue Dec 12 20:01:29 EST 2007.
                  Welcome to FreeBSD 6.2!!!.
         You have mail..
--------------------------------------------------------------------
Packet 70
TIME:    10:25:41.879117 (0.000163)
LINK:    00:50:BA:DE:36:33 -> 00:00:B4:3C:56:40 type=IP
  IP:    10.0.0.1 -> 10.0.0.2 hlen=20 TOS=10 dgramlen=237 id=956D
         MF/DF=0/1 frag=0 TTL=64 proto=TCP cksum=908B
 TCP:    port telnet -> blackjack seq=1746120154 ack=3205630360
         hlen=20 (data=197) UAPRSF=011000 wnd=17520 cksum=DDC6 urg=0
DATA:    .
         Everybody is somebody else's weirdo..
                  -- Dykstra.
         .[1mgenisis@ .[m:
--------------------------------------------------------------------
```

You may have noticed there were many packets that I snipped out between Packet 28, which echoed the login prompt; and Packet 51, which echoed the password prompt. These packets required sending the login name of *genisis* one character at a time. Again, each of these characters needed to be individually acknowledged and echoed to my screen.

The packets between Packet 51 and Packet 66 contained my password — again sent one character at a time. These packets were acknowledged but the characters were not echoed to my terminal. This is one of the reasons why you don't use telnet. If someone happens to be running **tcpdump** over the network, they will be able to capture and view the packets which contain the login and password prompts followed by the user's login name and password. At that point, it won't matter how good the password policy is on that network.

Finally, Packets 66, 68, and 70 showed the rest of the data from the **telnet** application that was echoed to my terminal during the session.

ARP Packets

So far, we've only examined the packets that contained TCP headers. However, TCP was not the only protocol involved during this telnet session; ARP also played a role.

Let's start with ARP or the Address Resolution Protocol. Before we can send an IP packet, it must first be encapsulated into a frame, in our case, an Ethernet frame. To create an Ethernet frame, the MAC (Media Access Control) address of the destination NIC must first be determined. A special packet known as an ARP packet is used to determine this MAC address. Since ARP knows the IP address of the destination, it can send out a broadcast packet, meaning all nodes must read the packet, asking for the MAC address associated with that IP address. **tcpdump** summarizes this procedure nicely:

```
# tcpdump -r dump
<snip output to just show packets 2 and 3>
10:25:28.608173 arp who-has 10.0.0.1 tell 10.0.0.2
10:25:28.608285 arp reply 10.0.0.1 is-at 0:50:ba:de:36:33
```

Because 10.0.0.2 wished to initiate a TCP connection with 10.0.0.1, it sent out an ARP request asking who was using that IP address. You'll notice that it received a reply that included the MAC address associated with 10.0.0.1.

Let's look at a more detailed view of these two packets using **tcpshow**:

```
# tcpshow < dump
<snip to just show packets 2 and 3>
-----------------------------------------------------------------
Packet 2
TIME:   10:25:28.608173 (4.305875)
LINK:   00:00:B4:3C:56:40 -> FF:FF:FF:FF:FF:FF type=ARP
 ARP:   htype=Ethernet ptype=IP hlen=6 plen=4 op=request
        sender-MAC-addr=00:00:B4:3C:56:40 sender-IP-address=10.0.0.2
        target-MAC-addr=00:00:00:00:00:00 target-IP-address=10.0.0.1
-----------------------------------------------------------------
Packet 3
TIME:   10:25:28.608285 (0.000112)
LINK:   00:50:BA:DE:36:33 -> 00:00:B4:3C:56:40 type=ARP
 ARP:   htype=Ethernet ptype=IP hlen=6 plen=4 op=response
        sender-MAC-addr=00:50:BA:DE:36:33 sender-IP-address=10.0.0.1
        target-MAC-addr=00:00:B4:3C:56:40 target-IP-address=10.0.0.2
-----------------------------------------------------------------
```

Notice the MAC addresses used in the LINK section of Packet 2. The source address is the MAC address of 10.0.0.2. This is needed so the response can make it back to the correct NIC. Since 10.0.0.2 does not know the MAC address of 10.0.0.1 (finding that MAC address is the whole point of this ARP packet), it uses a MAC address of FF:FF:FF:FF:FF:FF. A MAC address of all Fs indicates a broadcast packet, meaning all NICs must process the packet, but only the NIC the data pertains to should respond.

Also note that an ARP packet is different than an IP packet. It only contains one header and no data. Table 10.4 shows the ARP header structure.

The hardware type (htype) indicates this ARP request is looking for an Ethernet hardware address, that is, a MAC address. The protocol type (ptype) indicates the protocol address in use is an IP address. The hardware address length (hlen) is 6 bytes and protocol address length (plen) is 4 bytes. The operation (op) field indicates this is an ARP request. It then contains the known MAC and IP addresses. Because the target MAC address is the unknown value, it has been set to all zeros.

Packet 3 contains the response to Packet 2. Its op field indicates that it is a response, and it contains all of the necessary MAC addresses.

Additional Resources

Original Article:

http://www.onlamp.com/pub/a/bsd/2001/03/26/FreeBSD_Basics.html

Table 10.4: ARP Header

	Bits 00-07	08-15	16-31
Word 1	Hardware Type = 1		Protocol Type = 0x800
2	HLen = 6	PLen = 4	Operation Code
3	Source Hardware (MAC) Address		
4	Source Hardware Address cont.		Source Protocol (IP) Address
5	Source Protocol Address cont.		Destination Hardware (MAC) Address
6	Destination Hardware Address cont.		
7	Destination Protocol (IP) Address		

10.4 Examining ICMP Packets

Let's do a brief overview of the ICMP protocol, then look at a packet dump of ICMP packets.

ICMP stands for the Internet Control Message Protocol, and it was designed to send control messages between routers and hosts. For example, an ICMP packet may be sent when a router is experiencing congestion or when a destination host is unavailable.

ICMP Types and Codes

An ICMP packet has a slightly different structure than we've seen before.[4] An ICMP header follows the IP header in an IP packet, but it is not considered to be a Layer 4 header like TCP or UDP. Instead, ICMP is considered to be an integral part of IP; in fact, every vendor's implementation of IP is required to include ICMP. Table 10.5 shows the fields an ICMP header adds to an IP packet.

Table 10.5: ICMP Header

	Bits 00-07	08-15	16-31
Word 1	Type	Code	ICMP Header Checksum
2	Identifier		Sequence Number
3	Data ...		

An ICMP header is composed of six fields. Interestingly, the Data field does not contain the actual ICMP message. Instead, the Type and the Code fields contain numeric values, and each numeric value represents a specific ICMP message. Every ICMP packet must have a Type value, but only some ICMP types have an associated non-zero Code value.

http://www.iana.org/assignments/icmp-parameters contains the possible values for each ICMP type and code; I've summarized some of these into Table 10.6.

---

[4]See section 10.1 for details about IP headers.

Table 10.6: ICMP Codes

Type	Name	Code(s)	
0	Echo reply	0	None
3	Destination unreachable	0	Net unreachable
		1	Host unreachable
		2	Protocol unreachable
		3	Port unreachable
		4	Fragmentation needed and DF bit set
		5	Source route failed
		6	Destination network unknown
		7	Destination host unknown
		9	Communication with destination network is administratively prohibited
		10	Communication with destination host is administratively prohibited
4	Source quench	0	None
8	Echo	0	None
11	Time Exceeded	0	Time to live exceeded in transit
30	Traceroute	0	Outbound Packet successfully forwarded
		1	No route for Outbound Packet; packet discarded

You'll note that the ICMP types that do have associated codes use the Code field to further explain the message value in the Type field. For example, ICMP Type 3 represents destination unreachable. There can be many reasons why a destination is unreachable; accordingly, every ICMP Type 3 packet will also use one of the codes to explain why the destination was unreachable.

Analyzing ICMP Packets

In our previous dump file (in section 10.2), packets 4-9 contained ICMP information. These packets were created right after ARP had determined the destination MAC address and just before the TCP 3-way handshake. Let's take a look at packets 4 and 5:

```
# tcpshow < dump
<snipped to just show packets 4 and 5>
-------------------------------------------------------------------
Packet 4
```

```
TIME:    10:25:28.608640 (0.000355)
LINK:    00:00:B4:3C:56:40 -> 00:50:BA:DE:36:33 type=IP
  IP:    10.0.0.2 -> 10.0.0.1 hlen=20 TOS=00 dgramlen=84 id=0010
         MF/DF=0/0 frag=0 TTL=255 proto=ICMP cksum=A796
ICMP:    echo-request cksum=169F
DATA:    ....:_.:6....
                           ...... !"#$%&'()*+,-./01234567
-------------------------------------------------------------------
Packet 5
TIME:    10:25:28.608722 (0.000082)
LINK:    00:50:BA:DE:36:33 -> 00:00:B4:3C:56:40 type=IP
  IP:    10.0.0.1 -> 10.0.0.2 hlen=20 TOS=00 dgramlen=84 id=9551
         MF/DF=0/0 frag=0 TTL=255 proto=ICMP cksum=1255
ICMP:    echo-reply cksum=1E9F
DATA:    ....:_.:6....
                           ...... !"#$%&'()*+,-./01234567
-------------------------------------------------------------------
```

Notice that these are normal IP packets with the expected IP header fields. Immediately following the IP header is the ICMP header which is followed by some strange-looking data. The **tcpshow** utility did not show all of the ICMP fields, but you can see that Packet No. 4 was an echo-request and Packet No. 5 was an echo-reply. If we look up these names in the chart, we'll see that Packet 4 contains an ICMP Type 8 Code 0 message, and Packet 5 contains an ICMP Type 0 Code 0 message.

Let's look at these same packets using **wireshark**.[5] Because **wireshark** is so verbose, I'll just show the frame number and the ICMP header:

```
# more etherdump
<snipped to just show relevant header in packets 4 and 5>
Frame 4 (98 on wire, 98 captured)
Internet Control Message Protocol
    Type: 8 (Echo (ping) request)
    Code: 0
    Checksum: 0x169f (correct)
    Identifier: 0xdd00
    Sequence number: 00:00
    Data (56 bytes)
   0  3a5f a23a 36c3 0600 0809 0a0b 0c0d 0e0f    :_.:6..........
  10  1011 1213 1415 1617 1819 1a1b 1c1d 1e1f    ................
  20  2021 2223 2425 2627 2829 2a2b 2c2d 2e2f    !"#$%&'()*+,-./
  30  3031 3233 3435 3637                        01234567
Frame 5 (98 on wire, 98 captured)
Internet Control Message Protocol
    Type: 0 (Echo (ping) reply)
    Code: 0
    Checksum: 0x1e9f (correct)
    Identifier: 0xdd00
    Sequence number: 00:00
```

---

[5]Wireshark is introduced in section 7.4.

```
  Data (56 bytes)
  0   3a5f a23a 36c3 0600 0809 0a0b 0c0d 0e0f    :_.:6..........
 10   1011 1213 1415 1617 1819 1a1b 1c1d 1e1f    ...............
 20   2021 2223 2425 2627 2829 2a2b 2c2d 2e2f    !"#$%&'()*+,-./
 30   3031 3233 3435 3637                        01234567
```

Notice that **wireshark** interprets all of the ICMP fields, including the Type and Code numbers. It also indicates the name of the utility that issued these ICMP packets — before TCP initiated its 3-way handshake, three **ping** packets were sent out to verify connectivity between my **telnet** client and the telnet server. The first ping packet contained the echo-request and it was followed by the desired echo-reply.

Packets 6 and 7 contained the next echo-request/echo-reply pair. These packets were identical, except they both contained a sequence number of 01:00, instead of the sequence number of 00:00 you saw in Packets 4 and 5. Packets 8 and 9 contained the last echo-request/echo-reply pair and both shared a sequence number of 02:00. However, all six packets contained the same Identifier value of 0xdd00; this means that they were all issued from the same **ping** command.

To summarize, the **ping** utility sends out ICMP Type 8 Code 0 packets. Each packet will have the same identifier, but every packet's sequence number will be increased by 1. If you have connectivity to the other host, you should receive back ICMP Type 0 Code 0 packets with the same identifier. If you don't receive all the packets back in sequence, you don't have a very reliable connection.

traceroute

The **traceroute** utility is another utility that uses ICMP messages, but its usage is different from that of the **ping** utility. When you type **traceroute hostname**, three UDP packets are sent out with a TTL (time to live) value of 1. These three packets will arrive at the router closest to you which will decrease the TTL by one, meaning the TTL will now be 0. When routers notice a TTL of 0, they respond by sending an ICMP packet of Type 11 Code 0, or "time exceeded as time to live exceeded in transit". The **traceroute** utility will make note of the IP address of the router that sent back the three ICMP packets, calculate the time it took to receive each of the packets, then send out three more UDP packets, this time with a TTL of 2.

Because these packets have a TTL of 2, ICMP packets should be returned by the router that is two hops away from you. Once these packets are received and noted, **traceroute** sends out three more packets with a TTL of 3. The **traceroute** utility will continue this pattern until you either reach your final destination or you've gone through the default maximum of 30 routers. The results will be sent to your screen like so:

```
% traceroute www.freebsd.org
traceroute to freefall.freebsd.org (216.136.204.21), 30 hops max, 40 byte packets
 1 10.69.4.1 (10.69.4.1) 33.137 ms 110.654 ms 52.307 ms
 2 d226-12-1.home.cgocable.net (24.226.12.1) 15.413 ms 36.285 ms 12.538 ms
 3 cgowave-0-158.cgocable.net (24.226.0.158) 13.857 ms 14.130 ms 16.433 ms
<snip packets 4 through 18>
19 freefall.freebsd.org (216.136.204.21) 91.146 ms 88.509 ms 91.049 ms
```

Note that the **traceroute** utility numbered each hop, gave the name and IP address of the associated router, and recorded the time it took to receive an ICMP response to each of the three UDP packets that were sent to each router.

Path MTU Discovery

The **ping** and **traceroute** utilities are the most common utilities used by users that involve the ICMP protocol. However, there is another ICMP type that you should be aware of as it can affect network performance if there are routers between you and your final destination.

When I captured the packets involved in the telnet session, both the **telnet** client and the telnet server were cabled onto the same LAN and none of the packets had to pass through a router. During the TCP 3-way handshake, each host indicated the maximum segment size (MSS) it was capable of receiving. The **tcpshow** utility did not interpret this data, but it can be seen using **wireshark**:

```
# more etherdump
<snipped to show relevant data in TCP header of packets 10 and 11>
Frame 10 (60 on wire, 60 captured)
Internet Protocol
Source:  biko (10.0.0.2)
Destination:  genisis (10.0.0.1)
Transmission Control Protocol, Src Port:  blackjack (1025), Dst Port:  telnet (23),
Seq:  3205630181, Ack:  0
Source port:  blackjack (1025)
Destination port:  telnet (23)
Sequence number:  3205630181
Header length:  24 bytes
Flags:  0x0002 (SYN)
Window size:  16384
Checksum:  0x7814
Options:  (4 bytes)
  Maximum segment size:  1460 bytes


Frame 11 (58 on wire, 58 captured)
Internet Protocol
Source:  genisis (10.0.0.1)
Destination:  biko (10.0.0.2)
Transmission Control Protocol, Src Port:  telnet (23), Dst Port:  blackjack (1025),
Seq:  1746119590, Ack:  3205630182
Source port:  telnet (23)
Destination port:  blackjack (1025)
Sequence number:  1746119590
Acknowledgement number:  3205630182
Header length:  24 bytes
Flags:  0x0012 (SYN, ACK)
Window size:  17520
Checksum:  0x5fd9
Options:  (4 bytes)
  Maximum segment size:  1460 bytes
```

Because both computers were cabled onto the same LAN, they both understood and agreed upon a MSS of 1,460 bytes. Note that this is a maximum segment size, meaning a segment of data without including the extra bytes needed for the headers and frame. In this example, both hosts agreed that they wouldn't send a segment of data that was bigger than a 1,460-byte chunk.

What would happen if these two same hosts were not on the same LAN and their packets had to pass through a network that could only accept frames with a maximum transmission unit (MTU) size of 576 bytes? Because the two end hosts had already agreed upon a segment size of 1,460 bytes, they would be creating their IP packets accordingly. When these IP packets arrive at the router, which is cabled to the network with the smaller MTU, it will have to re-package every packet into smaller segments that will fit into the smaller size frames of that network. The destination host will then have to reassemble all of the fragmented packets back into the original agreed-upon sized segment. This creates more work and definitely slows things down.

To help prevent this, TCP uses something called Path-MTU Discovery. TCP will send out IP packets using the agreed MSS size, but will set the DF (don't fragment) bit to 1. If this packet is received by a router that needs to fragment the packet so that it will fit over a network that uses smaller-sized frames, the router will respond with an ICMP Type 3 Code 4 packet which translates to "destination unreachable as fragmentation needed DF bit set." When the host receives this ICMP packet, it knows that it needs to start sending smaller packets.

Source Quench Messages

The last ICMP type I'd like to cover is Source Quench, or ICMP Type 4 Code 0. This message is sent whenever a router is being overwhelmed by packets. It basically tells the host to slow down the rate it is sending packets so it can have a chance to deal with the packets it has already received. This is an important message — if the host does not slow down its transmission rate, the router will run out of buffer space to store packets and will have to start throwing packets away. Every packet that is thrown away will have to be re-transmitted which will make the original situation worse.

The ICMP types we've covered do have implications when you start creating packet filter rules on your FreeBSD system. Table 10.7 is a summary of the ICMP types and codes that we'll need to be mindful.

Table 10.7: ICMP Uses

ICMP Type	Code	Used By
0	0	Ping
3	4	Path-MTU Discovery
4	0	Source Quench
8	0	Ping
11	0	traceroute

Additional Resources

Original Article:

http://www.onlamp.com/pub/a/bsd/2001/04/04/FreeBSD_Basics.html

The Story of the **ping** Program

http://ftp.arl.mil/~mike/ping.html

Path MTU Discovery

http://www.znep.com/~marcs/mtu/

10.5 Scanning Your Network

In the last few sections, we've spent a fair bit of time examining IP packets and TCP/IP connections. In the next few sections, I'd like to demonstrate putting some of this knowledge together in order to increase the security of your FreeBSD system.

In my home network, I have a computer running FreeBSD 6.2; it has a constant connection to the Internet using a cable modem. Since I have a constant Internet presence, I should be aware of the information my FreeBSD system is willing to give to anyone who tries to find out. Once I know this, I can decide which IP packets from the Internet I am willing to allow into my machine.

Connect Scan

The ports collection includes the **nmap** utility, which is a valuable tool for determining which services your FreeBSD system is advertising to other TCP/IP hosts. However, like most useful utilities, it should only be used to test the computers in your own network. You should also be aware that it is very common for unscrupulous users to use this utility to scan for insecure hosts on the Internet. It is preferable for you to find out first what they'll be able to discover about your system so you can take measures to ensure they'll only be able to see what you want them to see.

I'll become the superuser, connect to the Internet, and install **nmap**; once the install is finished, I'll leave the superuser account:

```
% su
Password:
# pkg_add -r nmap
# exit
```

The **nmap** utility comes with several different scan types so you can test your network daemons for several different behaviors. Since I'll be running **nmap** on the same machine that I wish to scan, I'll run my scans against the localhost. If you wish to scan another host in your network, substitute that host's IP address for the word localhost.

Let's start by not specifying a scan type; this will tell the **nmap** utility to determine which daemons are listening for TCP connections:

```
% nmap -v localhost
Starting Nmap 4.20 ( http://insecure.org ) at 2007-06-12 18:42 EDT
Initiating Connect() Scan at 18:42
Scanning localhost (127.0.0.1) [1697 ports]
Discovered open port 22/tcp on 127.0.0.1
Discovered open port 25/tcp on 127.0.0.1
Increasing send delay for 127.0.0.1 from 0 to 5 due to max_successful_tryno ⇓
 increase to 4
Completed Connect() Scan at 18:43, 9.56s elapsed (1697 total ports)
Host localhost (127.0.0.1) appears to be up ... good.
Interesting ports on localhost (127.0.0.1):
Not shown:  1695 closed ports
PORT STATE SERVICE
```

```
22/tcp open ssh
25/tcp open smtp
Nmap finished:  1 IP address (1 host up) scanned in 9.669 seconds
```

If I now use **Alt-F1** to look at the console, I'll see something interesting:

```
Limiting closed port RST response from 253 to 200 packets/sec
Limiting closed port RST response from 233 to 200 packets/sec
Limiting closed port RST response from 256 to 200 packets/sec
Limiting closed port RST response from 275 to 200 packets/sec
```

If you ever see this type of message at your console and you weren't running the **nmap** utility, someone else was scanning your machine looking for open ports. When **nmap** scanned my ports, it tried to connect to 1697 of my ports, and my FreeBSD system responded by sending out an ICMP Type 3 Code 3 response for each non-listening port.[6] By default, FreeBSD limits itself to only sending 200 of these types of packets per second; this limit is a good thing, as it prevents your kernel from trying to respond to more packets than it can handle.

Now, what do I want to do with the results from this **nmap** scan? A good rule of thumb is to disable all the ports that you don't use. Since you can't disable the ports you do want to use, you'll need to secure those ports.

In my example, I don't want to disable SSH or SMTP since I do use these services, so I'll have to keep these in mind when I create my firewall rules so only appropriate hosts will have access.

Let's return for a moment to that original **nmap** scan. This connect() scan read a file called /usr/local/share/nmap/nmap-services and then attempted to reach the connect system call for every port listed in that file. The connect request failed for every port that wasn't listening for TCP connections and succeeded for the ports that were listening. However, this scan does not check for daemons that might be listening for UDP requests.

UDP Scan

All of the other scan types require superuser privileges; I'll become the superuser and use the **-sU** switch to scan for the daemons that are willing to accept UDP connections:

```
# su
Password:
# nmap -sU localhost
Starting Nmap 4.20 ( http://insecure.org ) at 2007-06-12 18:57 EDT
Interesting ports on localhost (127.0.0.1):
PORT STATE SERVICE
514/udp open|filtered syslog
Nmap finished:  1 IP address (1 host up) scanned in 200.011 seconds
```

Before we go any farther, let's run the **sockstat** utility and compare the results to the **nmap** scan:

```
% sockstat -4
USER     COMMAND    PID   FD   PROTO  LOCAL ADDRESS   FOREIGN ADDRESS
root     sshd       539   3    tcp4   *:22            *:*
root     sendmail   502   4    tcp4   127.0.0.1:25    *:*
root     syslogd    388   6    udp4   *:514           *:*
```

---

[6]See section 10.4 for details on ICMP types and codes.

You'll note that both utilities show the same port information: my machine is willing to accept TCP connections on ports 22 and 25, and UDP connections on port 514. Why would someone use **nmap** instead of **sockstat**? If you only need to secure one machine and you are sitting at it, it's easier to use the built-in **sockstat** utility. However, if you need to test the security of your entire network, you can scan every host at once using the **nmap** utility; you can even save your results to a file and have a record of which ports are enabled on each machine. It also saves you sitting down at every machine in order to run the **sockstat** utility. Finally, once you've built a firewall, you can test its reactions to your firewall rules by using the other types of **nmap** scans.

Planning the Firewall Rules

Now that I know which ports are open on my computer, I can start sketching out how I'll give appropriate access to each listening service. Before I start creating any type of firewall or packet filtering rules, there are a few points I should consider.

The first thing I need to decide is what types of packets I wish to allow in to my system. Since this is a stand-alone computer that is only connected to the Internet, any packets coming in will be one of two types.

The first type is packets from users on the Internet trying to connect to one of my daemons. Remember, if these packets are trying to make a TCP connection, they will have the SYN flag set but not the ACK flag.

Since I now know which of my ports are willing to accept connections, I should carefully re-examine each and see if I really want someone from the Internet trying to connect to these daemons. Let's look at each one at a time:

port 22 or ssh: The only person I'd want to use a secure shell into my machine would be me, and I don't plan on doing this over the Internet. Therefore, I don't want to let in these types of packets.

port 25 or smtp: While I do use smtp to send email out of my system, I'm not running an email server that accepts mail from other smtp servers, so I don't want to let in these types of packets.

UDP port 514 or syslogd: I should actually close this port to network connections as my system is not acting as a centralized logging server.

OK, now for the second type of incoming packets: responses from the Internet for packets I sent out. There's not much sense in me sending out packets to the Internet unless I remember to tell the firewall to allow back in the responses to my packets. For example, it would be very frustrating to send out an HTTP request to a web server but never receive a response back that could be displayed in my web browser.

If I don't want to restrict myself to the types of packets I'm allowed to send out to the Internet, I can still tell the firewall to not let in packets that aren't a response to my request. There are several ways to do this, and I'll demonstrate how when we make the actual firewall rules.

The last thing I should do is sketch out a list of activities I do over the Internet. This list will prove useful when I create my rules, as some applications require extra considerations so they will continue to work properly through a firewall. This is a good time to do some free association; creating a list will invariably remind me of related applications and possibly some tidbits of information that will be helpful in my firewall rules. Here's a rough sketch of my list:

- HTTP because I like to surf; that reminds me that I'll also need DNS.

- POP3 so I can pick up my email.

- FTP in case I want to download something; I'll have to look at my bookmarks, as I've heard that FTP is difficult to do through a firewall.

- DHCP, as I receive my IP address from my service provider's DHCP server.

- ICMP so I can do path-MTU discovery; I'll also have to review my ICMP types and codes.

I'm sure I'll think of more when I actually start creating the firewall rules, but this should get me started.

Additional Resources

Original Article:

`http://www.onlamp.com/pub/a/bsd/2001/04/18/FreeBSD_Basics.html`

10.6 IPFW Firewall

Your FreeBSD system comes with three built-in mechanisms for inspecting IP packets: **ipfw**, **ipf** and **pf**. Each have their own syntax for creating rulesets to determine which packets to allow and which packets to discard. In the next few sections I'll demonstrate the **ipfw** firewall.

Getting Started

Before you can use **ipfw**, check to see if the kernel module is loaded.

```
# kldstat | grep ipfw
#
```

No output means the **ipfw** kernel module is not loaded. Load it if it is not:

```
# kldload ipfw
ipfw2 (+ipv6) initialized, divert loadable, rule-based forwarding disabled
default to deny, logging disabled
```

See that status message? At the moment the firewall is up and running but it is denying all of your packets. We'll instead want it to read a custom ruleset so we'll temporarily stop the firewall while we create the ruleset — this way you'll still have Internet access while you're working on your rules:

```
# /etc/rc.d/ipfw stop
net.inet.ip.fw.enable:  1 -> 0
```

Note that the default is for **ipfw** to throw away all IP packets except those you've specifically allowed in your ruleset. While inconvenient, I prefer this default as it gives a finer control over which packets are being accepted; I'd hate to think my kernel was accepting packets I wasn't aware of. I will definitely notice if packets I want aren't being accepted and can change my ruleset to allow them; I'll never know the difference if packets I hadn't thought of are slipping through my firewall because I didn't make a rule to explicitly deny them.

You need to add the following lines to `/etc/rc.conf` so the firewall and its logging mechanism will start automatically should you reboot:

```
ipfw_enable="YES"
firewall_enable="YES"
firewall_logging="YES"
```

The following /etc/rc.conf settings are optional. This one specifies the name of your firewall ruleset, rather than loading the default ruleset:

```
firewall_type="/etc/ipfw.rules"
```

This one will show connection attempts to non-listening ports:

```
log_in_vain="YES"
```

This one will ignore ICMP redirect packets which are often used in exploits:

```
icmp_drop_redirect="YES"
```

Creating a Custom Ruleset

Creating a good ruleset is a bit of a fine art; if you're creating a firewall for the first time, wait until you have the time to experiment until everything works. You may find that the logic used by **ipfw** will not necessarily be the same logic you use.

Also, a firewall isn't something you just install and then forget about. Plan on spending some time tweaking it and scratching your head when it doesn't seem to do things the way you expected it would. You'll want to plan on completing the following three tasks:

1. Methodically add rules to your ruleset and test each new rule to ensure that you have indeed allowed only the packets you wish to allow.

2. Decide what you wish to log and watch the resulting log. You'll probably end up modifying your rules as you discover that you have inadvertently allowed or denied some packets that you didn't wish to.

3. Once you're satisfied that your firewall is dropping and accepting the packets you want, test your firewall to ensure it is behaving as you would expect.

I'll add my rules directly to the file I specified in /etc/rc.conf so I'll be creating a file called /etc/ipfw. rules.

Since there is no correct way to create a ruleset, and I can't possibly demonstrate how to add rules that will cover every possible scenario, I'll instead demonstrate the logic one goes through when creating a ruleset.

When creating your own ruleset, keep in mind that **ipfw** rules are read in numbered order, and as soon as a packet matches a rule, **ipfw** stops reading the ruleset. This means that if you create two rules, say number 400 and number 800, that could apply to a specific IP packet, rule 400 would always be used and rule 800 would not be read. It's always a good idea to look at your current rules before adding another one to make sure an older rule won't override your new rule.

Unless you specify otherwise, rules apply to every interface on your computer, that is, anything you can see in the output of **ifconfig -a**. This isn't a problem if you only use one interface as I'm doing in my example, but can make a difference if you're using multiple interfaces. For example, if one interface is connected to the Internet and another interface is connected to your internal LAN, you'll probably want to apply different security restrictions to each interface and can do so by specifying the interface name in your **ipfw** rules.

Taking Advantage of State

Let's return to my firewall setup. This is a stand-alone computer running FreeBSD 6.2 that has one interface cabled to the Internet. Since this is my home computer, I've decided not to place any restrictions on the types of packets I send out to the Internet; however, I only want my computer to accept IP packets that are a valid response to the packets I've sent out.

A good way to accomplish this task is to take advantage of the dynamic or stateful feature of **ipfw**. If I use dynamic rules, when I send out a packet to the Internet, **ipfw** will add an entry to its state table. This entry will include the IP address of the computer I sent the packet to, and what port number I made a connection to on that computer. When packets come back from the Internet, they will be discarded if they do not come back from that IP address using that port number.

The EXAMPLES section from **man ipfw** gives the three rules that are used to create this dynamic packet filter. Since I've decided to create my ruleset in a separate file that I've called `/etc/ipfw.rules`, I'll become the superuser, and create that file now with the following lines:

```
#from man 8 ipfw:
#allow only outbound TCP connections I've created
add 00400 check-state
add 00401 deny tcp from any to any in established
add 00402 allow tcp from any to any out setup keep-state
```

Notice that I've decided to start numbering my rules at 400 since rules 100, 200 and 300 are pre-created in the system startup script `/etc/rc.firewall` — those lines read as follows:

```
#############
# Only in rare cases do you want to change these rules
#
${fwcmd} add 100 pass all from any to any via lo0
${fwcmd} add 200 deny all from any to 127.0.0.0/8
${fwcmd} add 300 deny ip from 127.0.0.1/8 to any
```

I like to number related rules together, so I've numbered my rules 400, 401, and 402. When I create more, unrelated rules, I'll jump up to 500. Remember, you can number your rules any way you wish as long as the number isn't already in use and an earlier numbered rule won't prevent your new rule from being read.

You'll notice that these three rules contain some keywords that are described in **man ipfw**, which I've quoted here:

check-state: Checks the packet against the dynamic ruleset. If a match is found execute the action associated with the rule which generated this dynamic rule, otherwise move to the next rule.

keep-state: Upon a match, the firewall will create a dynamic rule, whose default behavior is to matching bidirectional traffic between source and destination IP/port using the same protocol. The rule has a limited lifetime (controlled by a set of sysctl(8) variables), and the lifetime is refreshed every time a matching packet is found.

established: Matches TCP packets that have the RST or ACK bits set.

setup: Matches TCP packets that have the SYN bit set but no ACK bit.

In other words, when a packet arrives at one of my interfaces, **ipfw** will first check to see if there is a matching connection in the state table; if it is, the packet is allowed. (Rule 400 does check-state.) If it's not in the state table and the RST or ACK bits are set, it will deny the packet because it's not a valid response to a connection I've created. (Rule 401 checks for established.) If the ACK flag is not set (meaning it wants to initiate a TCP connection), it is allowed, but only if the packet is outbound; if a packet meets this rule, it will also be added to the state table. (Rule 402 does setup and keep-state.)

Let's see what happens if I instruct **ipfw** to read these rules — remember this startup script reads /etc/rc.conf for the required settings:

```
# /etc/rc.d/ipfw start
Starting divert daemons:Flushed all rules.
00400 check-state
00401 deny tcp from any to any in established
00402 allow tcp from any to any out setup keep-state
Firewall rules loaded.
net.inet.ip.fw.enable:  0 -> 1
```

Testing the Rulebase

Seeing that the rules successfully loaded, I'll check if I can send any IP packets out to the Internet and receive some replies back:

```
% ping www.freebsd.org
ping: cannot resolve www.freebsd.org: Host name lookup failure
% lynx www.freebsd.org
Alert!. Unable to access document.
```

Hmmmmm. I'm starting to think that I don't have DNS name resolution. Let's try that again, using an IP address instead:

```
% lynx 69.147.83.33
```

This time, I find myself at the home page of http://www.freebsd.org. Let's try pinging that IP address:

```
% ping 69.147.83.33
PING 69.147.83.33 (69.147.83.33): 56 data bytes
ping: sendto: Permission denied
ping: sendto: Permission denied
ping: sendto: Permission denied
^C
--- 69.147.83.33 ping statistics ---
3 packets transmitted, 0 packets received, 100% packet loss
```

Now, let's try to understand this odd behavior, as obviously some packets are going in and out of my computer and some are not. Let's start by picking apart which protocols I used in each of the examples above.

Name resolution is failing, as I was only able to access http://www.freebsd.org by using its IP address. When I use DNS, I send a name lookup request to my service provider's DNS server, which should send the response back to me. This seems to match our rules, as I make the request on port 53 and should receive a request back on port 53. It's time to look a bit deeper at how name resolution works. While DNS is capable of using both TCP and UDP packets, it typically uses TCP for zone transfers between DNS servers. Requests for name resolution rarely use TCP and instead use UDP packets. Since I haven't allowed for UDP packets in my ruleset, I'm not getting DNS name resolution.

Now that we've solved that one, let's see why **ping** isn't working, even with an IP address. The **ping** utility uses ICMP, not TCP in its packets. Again, since I've only allowed my own TCP connections in my ruleset, I'm not going to have any luck if I try to send out ICMP packets.

If I run the **ipfw show** command, I'll see that Rule 00402 allowed my setup packet out when I connected to www.freebsd.org's IP address. Now, any packets that are addressed to or from 69.147.83.33 on port 80 will be allowed to enter or leave my computer.

In the output, rule 00402 has a number next to it representing the number of packets followed by the number of bytes that met each rule.

Before I add any more rules to my ruleset, I'll use the **ipfw zero** command to reset these counters. This way, when I test my new rules, I'll be able to see which rules have new packet statistics next to them.

I'll now add some rules to allow for DNS name resolution. Since DNS is using UDP, and UDP doesn't make a connection, I can't specify to only allow in valid responses to my connections. However, I can limit packets by the port number used by DNS (port 53), and I can choose to only accept these packets from the IP addresses of my provider's DNS servers on the interface cabled to my provider. You can determine which IP addresses to use from the output of the **more /etc/resolv.conf** command. I'll add the following lines to my /etc/ipfw.rules file:

```
#allow DNS
add 00500 allow udp from 24.226.1.90 53 to any in recv ed0
add 00501 allow udp from 24.226.1.20 53 to any in recv ed0
add 00502 allow udp from 24.2.9.34 53 to any in recv ed0
```

I'll then reload my rules with **/etc/rc.d/ipfw restart** and see if name resolution now works:

```
% lynx www.freebsd.org
Alert!. Unable to access document.
```

Wait a minute, how come I'm still not getting name resolution when I've explicitly allowed in these UDP packets? Let's do an **ipfw show** to see which rule has a packet count next to it:

```
# ipfw show
00400 0 0 check-state
00401 0 0 deny tcp from any to any in established
00402 0 0 allow tcp from any to any keep-state setup
00500 0 0 allow udp from 24.226.1.90 53 to any in recv ed0
00501 0 0 allow udp from 24.226.1.20 53 to any in recv ed0
00502 0 0 allow udp from 24.2.9.34 53 to any in recv ed0
65535 30 2196 deny ip from any to any
## Dynamic rules:
```

The only rule that has any packet statistics associated with it is that last deny rule; note that none of my allow udp rules were used. Then it dawns on me, I've never allowed out any udp packets; no wonder there aren't any udp replies anxious to come back in. Let's try adding one more line to that ruleset:

```
add 00503 allow udp from any to any out
```

Here I've specified that I'm willing to allow out my own udp packets. I'll clear those statistics with **ipfw zero**, rerun the **/etc/rc.d/ipfw restart** command, and try to access that website more time.

The main page of FreeBSD's website never looked so good. If I become the superuser, I should have a more satisfactory **ipfw show** output:

```
# ipfw show
00100 0 0 allow ip from any to any via lo0
00200 0 0 deny ip from any to 127.0.0.0/8
00400 0 0 check-state
00401 0 0 deny tcp from any to any in established
00402 20 15061 allow tcp from any to any keep-state setup
00500 10 1882 allow udp from 24.226.1.90 53 to any in recv ed0
00501 0 0 allow udp from 24.226.1.20 53 to any in recv ed0
00502 0 0 allow udp from 24.2.9.34 53 to any in recv ed0
00503 10 591 allow udp from any to any out
65535 31 2577 deny ip from any to any
```

Note that rule 00503 let out my DNS request, rule 00500 let in the DNS reply, and rule 00402 set up the HTTP connection.

Note: A better way to achieve this is to create rules similar to 00400 through 00402, but with udp instead of tcp and without the setup keyword. This is because there is no connection to setup when using UDP; there really isn't a state to watch either but you can take advantage of the built-in timer. UDP packets will still be allowed back in, but only for a short period of time; depending upon your security requirements this may be preferable to allowing UDP all the time like rule 00503 does.

I now have a working network connection, but there is still lots of room for improvement to this ruleset. In the next section, we'll take a look at the additional rules which should be added to the ruleset, then we'll take a look at logging and console messages.

Additional Resources

Original Articles:

```
http://www.onlamp.com/pub/a/bsd/2001/04/25/FreeBSD_Basics.html
```

```
http://www.onlamp.com/pub/a/bsd/2001/05/09/FreeBSD_Basics.html
```

ipfw(8) manual page:

man ipfw

Internet Firewalls Frequently Asked Questions:

```
http://www.interhack.net/pubs/fwfaq/
```

ipfw - protect your subnet:

`http://www.freebsddiary.org/firewall.html`

Ipfw HowTo:

`http://www.freebsd-howto.com/HOWTO/Ipfw-HOWTO`

FreeBSD Handbook Firewalls chapter:

`http://www.freebsd.org/doc/en_US.ISO8859-1/books/handbook/firewalls-ipfw.html`

10.7 IPFW: Fine-Tuning Rulesets

So far you've created a ruleset that told **ipfw** to allow responses to the connection requests made to the Internet and to also allow for DNS name resolution. In this section, I'd like to start fine-tuning this ruleset and begin to test its behavior by using the built-in logging facilities available to **ipfw**.

DHCP Rules

As my ruleset now stands, I'll enjoy my Internet connection until my DHCP lease runs out. At that point, everything will stop as I haven't created any rules that will allow me to receive a new DHCP lease. To know which rules will accomplish this, it is helpful to have a basic understanding of how DHCP works.[7]

I will have to allow UDP packets between my machine and my provider's DHCP server. DHCP also uses two port numbers: My DHCP client uses port 68 and my provider's DHCP server uses port 67.

You may remember that a DHCP has three expiry timers. The renew timer tells my DHCP client when it should go out and try to renew its lease with a known DHCP server. When this timer kicks in, my computer will attempt to send out UDP packets to port 67 on the DHCP server 24.226.1.41, so I should add a rule that will allow these packets to go out. Assuming the DHCP server receives my packets, it should respond that it is willing to renew my lease, and will send this information in UDP packets to port 68 on my computer. Accordingly, I'll also want to add a rule so that **ipfw** will allow in the response packets.

If I don't add these rules to my **ipfw** ruleset, or if for some reason the DHCP server does not respond to my renewal request, the rebind timer will kick in at a later date. At this point my DHCP client is starting to get a bit worried about its upcoming lease expiration and will send out some more UDP packets destined for port 67. However, this time they will not be addressed to a particular DHCP server, but will instead be sent to the broadcast address of 255.255.255.255 in the hope that any DHCP server will respond.

If no DHCP server responds, my lease will expire at the expire timer time– meaning my DCHP client is no longer sure that it is allowed to continue to use its lease information. At this point, several things may occur. The client will still try to contact a DHCP server, so will continue to send out broadcasts to UDP port 67. It will also try **ping**ing the default gateway address to see if its IP address is still valid, meaning it will be sending out ICMP type 8 code 0 packets and hoping to receive back ICMP type 0 code 0 packets. If worst comes to worst, and my client actually ends up with an invalid IP address, any responses that come back from a DHCP server will have to be received as broadcasts, that is, be addressed to port 68 on 255.255.255.255.

Now, knowing all this, what should I add to my ruleset? Before I add anything, I should first double-check what rules I currently have as order is starting to become increasingly important. The more rules I add to my ruleset, the greater the possibility that an earlier rule will override my new rule. Also, the trick to a good ruleset is to

---

[7]DHCP is introduced in sections 8.12, 8.13, and 8.14.

only allow the traffic you wish using as few rules as possible. Your firewall may still work if you add too many rules, but you will end up putting an unnecessary burden on **ipfw** as it has to read more rules before it finds the one that applies to a packet, and you will also create more confusion for yourself when you can't figure out which of your many rules is preventing the behavior you expect.

As the superuser I'll issue the **ipfw show** command to check my current rules:

```
# ipfw show
00400 0 0 check-state
00401 0 0 deny tcp from any to any in established
00402 0 0 allow tcp from any to any out keep-state
00500 0 0 allow udp from 24.226.1.90 53 to any in recv ed0
00501 0 0 allow udp from 24.226.1.20 53 to any in recv ed0
00502 0 0 allow udp from 24.2.9.34 53 to any in recv ed0
00503 0 0 allow udp from any to any out
65535 0 0 deny ip from any to any
```

Because I need to allow UDP packets, I'll want to specify the DHCP port numbers and the IP address of my DHCP server. As the superuser, I'll consider adding the following lines to my /etc/ipfw.rules file:

```
# allow DHCP
add 00600 allow udp from any 68 to 24.226.1.41 67 out via ed0 keep-state
add 00601 allow udp from 24.226.1.41 67 to any 68 in via ed0 keep-state
```

These should be the bare minimum rules that will allow my DHCP client to renew its lease with the DHCP server 24.226.1.41. Whether more rules will be required will vary according to the dependability of that DHCP server. If the DHCP server always responds to my renewal requests, I won't have to resort to sending out UDP broadcasts, pinging my default gateway, or receiving UDP broadcasts. If my DHCP server is not so dependable, I might have to also add the following rules:

```
add 00602 allow udp from any 68 to 255.255.255.255 67 out via ed0 keep-state
add 00603 allow udp from any 67 to 255.255.255.255 68 in via ed0 keep-state
```

I won't immediately add rules 00602 and 00603, though, as up to this point, my DHCP server has been quite dependable. I have made a mental note to myself to remember to keep these rules in mind, just in case my provider ever has problems with this DHCP server or actually changes the IP address of my DHCP server.

Before I save my changes, I'll compare rules 00600 and 00601 to the rest of my ruleset to ensure there aren't any conflicts or overlaps. I immediately notice an overlap between rules 00503 and 00600:

```
add 00503 allow udp from any to any out
add 00600 allow udp from any 68 to 24.226.1.41 67 out via ed0 keep-state
```

Since rule 00503 already allows any UDP packet to go out of my computer, the more specific rule of only sending out UDP packets from port 68 will never be read. At this point, I need to make a choice between creating a minimum number of rules or using a maximum amount of paranoia and responsibility.

I originally added rule 00503 when I created the rules to allow DNS resolution. If I decide to remove rule 00503, I'll have to replace it with three more rules that will allow UDP packets to be sent out to the three DNS servers. Also, if I ever need to access any other type of server that requires me to send it a UDP packet, I'll have to create an extra rule to do so. This will result in adding extra rules, and thus extra overhead, to my **ipfw** ruleset, instead of using one all-encompassing rule.

This goes against the philosophy of using a minimum amount of rules, but I also need to look at the implications of keeping that one all-encompassing rule. There's no security risk to me if I send out UDP packets, as long as I restrict whom I'm willing to accept UDP packets from. For example, rule 00503 allows me to send out any UDP packet, but rules 00500, 00501, 00502, and 00601 ensure I'll only accept UDP packets from my provider's three DNS servers and one DHCP server. This seems to be an acceptable policy for my stand-alone FreeBSD computer.

However, I would have to rethink this policy if I ever put any clients behind my FreeBSD firewall. For example, some Microsoft clients send out an inordinate amount of UDP packets to advertise their shared resources. It would be both irresponsible of me and a security risk to allow those packets to leave my network by being allowed out through my firewall. In this case, I would have to use the overhead of extra rules to ensure that I was only sending out necessary UDP packets and I would have to remove the rule that allows any UDP packet to leave my firewall.

For now, I'll keep rule 00503 as I'm currently only protecting this stand-alone FreeBSD computer. I might as well delete rule 00600 as it will never be read. My change to this file now looks like this:

```
# allow DHCP
add 00601 allow udp from 24.226.1.41 67 to any 68 in via ed0 keep-state
```

I'll save my change, load it using **/etc/rc.d/ipfw reload**, try to renew my lease and see what happened:

```
# dhclient ed0
# more /var/db/dhclient.leases.ed0
<snip to just show bottom 3 lines>
  renew 3 2007/5/16 07:46:25;
  rebind 5 2007/5/18 08:50:46;
  expire 6 2007/5/19 01:12:14;
# ipfw show
00100  0     0 allow ip from any to any via lo0
00200  0     0 deny ip from any to 127.0.0.0/8
00400  0     0 check-state
00401  0     0 deny tcp from any to any in established
00402  0     0 allow tcp from any to any keep-state setup
00500  8 1322 allow udp from 24.226.1.90 53 to any in recv ed0
00501  0     0 allow udp from 24.226.1.20 53 to any in recv ed0
00502  0     0 allow udp from 24.2.9.34 53 to any in recv ed0
00503  8  469 allow udp from any to any out
00601  4 1592 allow udp from 24.226.1.41 67 to any 68 in recv ed0 keep-state
65535 29 8591 deny ip from any to any
```

It looks like I received eight UDP packets from the DNS server 24.226.1.90 and four UDP packets from the DHCP server 24.226.1.41. I also successfully contacted the DHCP server and renewed my lease, so it looks my DHCP rule is successful.

ICMP Rules

Now, let's take a look at allowing some ICMP, as my ruleset is currently denying all ICMP packets. Denying all ICMP is a bad thing as it will break Path-MTU Discovery and will prevent Source Quench messages. ICMP uses both types and codes to specify the actual ICMP message.

When creating an **ipfw** rule that refers to ICMP, you can only specify the ICMP type, not the associated code. As the superuser I'll add the following lines to my /etc/ipfw.rules file:

```
# allow some icmp types (codes not supported)
# allow path-mtu in both directions
add 00700 allow icmp from any to any icmptypes 3

# allow source quench in and out
add 00701 allow icmp from any to any icmptypes 4
```

While I'm at it, I should consider whether I want to be able to ping hosts outside of my network, or run the traceroute command. Because I want to be able to do both and receive responses, but I don't want anyone on the Internet to try to ping or traceroute me, I'll add these rules:

```
# allow me to ping out and receive response back
add 00702 allow icmp from any to any icmptypes 8 out
add 00703 allow icmp from any to any icmptypes 0 in
# allow me to run traceroute
add 00704 allow icmp from any to any icmptypes 11 in
```

Remember that ICMP type 8 is an echo request and ICMP type 0 is an echo reply. Since I've only allowed echo requests out and echo replies in, I can **ping** out but no one can ping me.

When I run traceroute, I send out UDP packets that I've already allowed using rule 00503. However, if I want to receive any responses back, I have to accept back in ICMP type 11 packets.

That looks pretty good so I'll save my changes and reset my **ipfw** counters using the **ipfw zero** command. I'll then restart **ipfw**, and try to do a **ping** and a **traceroute**:

```
# ipfw zero
# /etc/rc.d/ipfw restart
# ping www.freebsd.org
PING www.freebsd.org (69.147.83.33):  56 data bytes
64 bytes from 69.147.83.33:  icmp_seq=0 ttl=239 time=85.250 ms
64 bytes from 69.147.83.33:  icmp_seq=1 ttl=239 time=88.338 ms
64 bytes from 69.147.83.33:  icmp_seq=2 ttl=239 time=83.757 ms
 ^C
--- www.freebsd.org ping statistics ---
3 packets transmitted, 3 packets received, 0% packet loss
round-trip min/avg/max/stddev = 83.757/85.782/88.338/1.908 ms

# traceroute www.freebsd.org
traceroute to www.freebsd.org (69.147.83.33), 30 hops max, 40 byte packets
1 10.69.4.1 (10.69.4.1) 8.678 ms 8.739 ms 10.055 ms
```

```
2 d226-12-1.home.cgocable.net (24.226.12.1) 9.800 ms 10.642 ms 7.876 ms
3 cgowave-0-158.cgocable.net (24.226.0.158) 25.910 ms 15.288 ms 13.693 ms
(snip hops 4 through 18)
19 www.freebsd.org (69.147.83.33) 104.100 ms 95.821 ms 85.909 ms
```

So far, so good. I'll now doublecheck which rules were used:

```
# ipfw show | grep -wv 0
00500 29 5847 allow udp from 24.226.1.90 53 to any in recv ed0
00501 2 163 allow udp from 24.226.1.20 53 to any in recv ed0
00502 3 397 allow udp from 24.2.9.34 53 to any in recv ed0
00503 93 4712 allow udp from any to any out
00700 3 168 allow icmp from any to any icmptype 3
00702 3 252 allow icmp from any to any out icmptype 8
00703 3 252 allow icmp from any to any in icmptype 0
00704 53 2968 allow icmp from any to any in icmptype 11
65535 29 8591 deny ip from any to any
```

You can see those three echo request packets (rule 00702) and the three echo reply packets (rule 00703) used by the **ping** utility. You can also see that it took 53 ICMP type 11 packets to respond to the traceroute (rule 00704). It also looks like rule 00700 allowed three ICMP type 3 packets. However, I can't tell the exact reason why I received those three Destination Unreachable messages as I wasn't able to specify an associated code in my rule.

Additional Resources

Original Article:

```
http://www.onlamp.com/pub/a/bsd/2001/06/01/FreeBSD_Basics.html
```

10.8 IPFW Logging

Like creating rulesets, logging is a bit of a fine art. What you decide to log will depend upon your degree of curiosity, how important the data is that you're trying to protect with your firewall, the amount of disk space you have available to hold the logged information, and a realistic assessment of how much information you're willing to wade through to see if anything happened that you didn't want to happen.

Even if you don't explicitly add the `log` keyword to any of the rules in your **ipfw** ruleset, there are still several places that your FreeBSD kernel will record events as they occur. Let's spend some time examining the type of information that is recorded and the locations where that information is stored. Before we do so, let's take a look at my current ruleset as I've changed it slightly. Because I like to log denied packets, I've added the `log` keyword to rule 00401 and have added rule 00800 to log all packets that were not explicitly allowed by any of my rules:

```
# ipfw show
00100 135946  11920244 allow ip from any to any via lo0
00200     0         0 deny ip from any to 127.0.0.0/8
```

```
00400       0        0 deny ip from 127.0.0.0/8 to any
00400       0        0 check-state
00401     753   112227 deny log logamount 10 tcp from any to any in established
00402  233176 107186044 allow tcp from any to any keep-state out setup
00500   15823  2353615 allow udp from 24.226.1.90 53 to any in recv ed1
00501    2787   155141 allow udp from 24.226.1.20 53 to any in recv ed1
00502    2781   154266 allow udp from 24.2.9.34 53 to any in recv ed1
00503   21503  1222215 allow udp from any to any out
00601    1785   694722 allow udp from 24.226.1.41 67 to any 68 in recv ed1
00700     607    34028 allow icmp from any to any icmptype 3
00701       0        0 allow icmp from any to any icmptype 4
00702       4      336 allow icmp from any to any out icmptype 8
00703       4      336 allow icmp from any to any in icmptype 0
00704      63     3528 allow icmp from any to any in icmptype 11
00800     135     7452 deny log logamount 10 ip from any to any
65535       0        0 deny ip from any to any
```

Daily Security Output

If you are not already in the habit of doing so, you should read the *root* user's email on a daily basis as several important bits of information are recorded by the **periodic** scripts.[8] As you read these daily email messages, you'll become familiar with what is normal behavior for your FreeBSD system. When you read the daily run output email, take note of the disk status section. Pay attention to the capacity of /var as this is where logged information is stored. You should find that its capacity will grow at a fairly steady daily rate; for example, mine grows at about 4 percent per day. Knowing this, you'll have an idea of how often you should clean out your /var partition. You'll also be alerted if there is a significant increase in capacity used. For example, if I were to read my email tomorrow and the capacity on /var had jumped up to 85 percent, I'd immediately take a look at my logs to see why the kernel had logged so many events.

You'll also want to read the security check output that is sent by email to the *root* user. Here are some sample lines from one of mine:

```
Checking for passwordless accounts:

hostname denied packets:
> 00301     14      560 deny log logamount 10 tcp from any to any in established
> 00700     28     1580 deny log logamount 10 ip from any to any

ipfw log limit reached:
00301     14      560 deny log logamount 10 tcp from any to any in established
00700     28     1580 deny log logamount 10 ip from any to any

hostname kernel log messages:
> Connection attempt to TCP 127.0.0.1:113 from 127.0.0.1:3198
> Connection attempt to TCP 127.0.0.1:113 from 127.0.0.1:3198
> Connection attempt to UDP 127.0.0.1:512 from 127.0.0.1:1307
> Connection attempt to TCP 127.0.0.1:113 from 127.0.0.1:3231
```

---

[8]The **periodic** scripts are introduced in section 2.13.

```
> Connection attempt to TCP 127.0.0.1:113 from 127.0.0.1:3231
> Connection attempt to UDP 127.0.0.1:512 from 127.0.0.1:1340
<snip as it goes on for a while>
```

Let's pick apart the sections that deal with logged events. Note that you won't get any entries under `hostname denied packets` or `ipfw log limit reached` unless you add the `log` keyword to a rule in your ruleset. It looks like my firewall denied 14 packets that tried to make a TCP connection to my FreeBSD box (rule 00401), and it also denied 28 packets that didn't meet any of the allow rules in my ruleset (rule 00800).

Under `hostname kernel log messages`, I had a lot of entries. Not only did this make for a very large email, it also reflected the growing size of the file `/var/log/messages` as this section is really a copy of the changes made to that file within the last 24 hours. All of those changes are events that were recorded to the console found at **Alt-F1**.

When I originally read that email, I took a look at the console and sure enough, it was flooded with entries regarding ports 113 (*auth*) and 512 (*biff*). What was happening was that every time I received an email message, Sendmail did an auth lookup on my user account, then it tried to notify the **biff** client to advise it that a new mail message had been received for my user account. I receive a lot of email and have configured **fetchmail** to check my POP3 account every 5 minutes, thus I had an amazing amount of console entries.

I wanted to disable these console messages for two reasons. One, if I get used to hundreds of trivial messages showing up on my console, I might miss an important console message. Two, I don't want to waste disk space on these entries as I already know that I receive a lot of email and I don't need to be notified every time an email arrives.

Let's start by getting rid of the biff messages. I found the simplest way to do this was to add this line to the `.cshrc` file in my home directory:

```
/usr/bin/biff n
```

Now whenever I login, **biff** will be disabled and not used by Sendmail.

We'll be seeing auth again as we start to pick apart our logs as many mail servers use the auth daemon; we'll find that how we configure **ipfw** to treat auth may make a difference in mail delivery speed. But for now, I just want to suppress the console messages that tell me that my Sendmail program did an auth check as it delivered my email. To do so, I'll open up `/etc/inetd.conf`, and remove the # from this line:

```
#auth    stream  tcp    nowait  root    internal    auth -r -f -n -o UNKNOWN -t 30
```

Remember that changes to this file won't take effect until I notify **inetd**:

 # /etc/rc.d/inetd reload

Once I did this, those messages stopped appearing on the console and now when I read my security run output, I don't have to wade through all of those unnecessary entries.[9]

---

[9]Section 10.9 has an example of just sending a TCP reset (RST) instead.

Firewall Logs

Now let's take a look at /var/log to see which files contain information logged by the **ipfw** kernel. I'll do a long listing to see the size of the pertinent files in this directory:

```
# ls -l /var/log
total 520
-rw-r-----  1 root  wheel  11150 Jun 10 03:05 dmesg.today
-rw-r-----  1 root  wheel  10503 Jun  9 03:05 dmesg.yesterday
-rw-r-----  1 root  wheel    371 Jun 10 03:05 ipfw.today
-rw-r-----  1 root  wheel    359 Jun  9 03:05 ipfw.yesterday
-rw-r--r--  1 root  wheel  78371 Jun  9 21:45 messages
-rw-------  1 root  wheel   4870 Jun  9 19:50 security
```

Let's start by taking a look at ipfw.today:

```
# more /var/log/ipfw.today
00200 0 0 deny ip from any to 127.0.0.0/8
00400 0 0 deny ip from 127.0.0.0/8 to any
00401 751 112147 deny log logamount 10 tcp from any to any in established
00800 125 6520 deny log logamount 10 ip from any to any
65535 0 0 deny ip from any to any
```

You'll note that this is slightly different than the hostname denied packets section of the security check output as it shows all the rules that deny packets, not just the ones that have the log keyword. You can also compare it to ipfw.yesterday to get an indication of any anomalies in traffic. Again, if you do this consistently, you'll have a good idea of what is normal for your firewall and will more easily notice any strange behavior. These two logs are small, are over-written daily, and give a quick reference check on the number of packets that are being denied on a daily basis.

If I take a look at dmesg.today, I should recognize most of the entries from the hostname kernel log messages section of the security check output. Again, this is just today's portion of the much larger file messages. It is useful to be aware of both, as they do record the same information, but in slightly different formats. I'll display the last 10 lines of each file using the **tail** command to demonstrate; you'll note that I've blocked out my IP address.

```
# tail /var/log/dmesg.today
Connection attempt to UDP x.x.x.x:4780 from 24.226.1.20:53
Connection attempt to TCP x.x.x.x:2058 from 209.75.20.41:80
Connection attempt to TCP x.x.x.x:2059 from 209.75.20.41:80
Connection attempt to TCP x.x.x.x:2058 from 209.75.20.41:80
Connection attempt to TCP x.x.x.x:2059 from 209.75.20.41:80
Connection attempt to TCP x.x.x.x:2058 from 209.75.20.41:80
Connection attempt to TCP x.x.x.x:2059 from 209.75.20.41:80
Connection attempt to TCP x.x.x.x:2058 from 209.75.20.41:80
Connection attempt to TCP x.x.x.x:2059 from 209.75.20.41:80
sigreturn: eflags = 0x13216
```

```
# tail /var/log/messages
```

```
Jun 9 20:21:06 hostname /kernel:   Connection attempt to TCP x.x.x.x:2059 from
209.75.20.41:80
Jun 9 20:21:06 hostname /kernel:   Connection attempt to TCP x.x.x.x:2058 from
209.75.20.41:80
Jun 9 20:21:06 hostname /kernel:   Connection attempt to TCP x.x.x.x:2059 from
209.75.20.41:80
Jun 9 20:21:36 hostname /kernel:   Connection attempt to TCP x.x.x.x:2058 from
209.75.20.41:80
Jun 9 20:21:36 hostname /kernel:   Connection attempt to TCP x.x.x.x:2059 from
209.75.20.41:80
Jun 9 20:42:00 hostname gconfd (genisis-82257):  Failed to load source
'xml:readonly:/usr/X11R6/etc/gconf/gconf.xml.mandatory':  Failed:  Could not make
directory '/usr/X11R6/etc/gconf/gconf.xml.mandatory':  Permission denied
Jun 9 20:42:01 hostname gconfd (genisis-82257):  Failed to load source
'xml:readonly:/usr/X11R6/etc/gconf/gconf.xml.defaults':  Failed:  Could not make
directory '/usr/X11R6/etc/gconf/gconf.xml.defaults':  Permission denied
Jun 9 21:41:08 hostname /kernel:  sigreturn:  eflags = 0x13216
Jun 9 21:45:13 hostname gconfd (genisis-85334):  Failed to load source
'xml:readonly:/usr/X11R6/etc/gconf/gconf.xml.mandatory':  Failed:  Could not make
directory '/usr/X11R6/etc/gconf/gconf.xml.mandatory':  Permission denied
Jun 9 21:45:13 hostname gconfd (genisis-85334):  Failed to load source
'xml:readonly:/usr/X11R6/etc/gconf/gconf.xml.defaults':  Failed:  Could not make
directory '/usr/X11R6/etc/gconf/gconf.xml.defaults':  Permission denied
```

The log file dmesg.today is a little easier to read, but messages contains more details, such as the time the event was logged. Also, dmesg.today is overwritten on a daily basis, whereas messages is not. Because the **newsyslog** daemon is responsible for the growth of log files, let's take a look at its configuration file to see how large the messages log can become:

```
# more /etc/newsyslog.conf
<snip to just show entries for messages and security>
# logfilename [owner:group] mode count size when [ZB] [/pid_file] [sig_num]
/var/log/messages           644  5     100  *    JC
/var/log/security           600  10    100  *    JC
```

The 100 in the size column means this log will grow until it reaches 100 Kbytes in size. When it does, the J in the [ZB] column indicates that it will be compressed, renamed to messages.0.bz2, and a new messages log will be started. The count column indicates how many compressed logs will be kept before **newsyslog** will delete the oldest compressed log; in this case, there can be up to five.

You'll note that I also showed the entry for the security log, which is the last log that deals with **ipfw**. In the next section, I'd like to demonstrate what type of information to look for when reading the security log, and what you can do about the information you find in it.

Also see section 2.11 for more details about logging and rotating logs.

Additional Resources

Original Article:

http://www.onlamp.com/pub/a/bsd/2001/06/21/FreeBSD_Basics.html

10.9 Monitoring IPFW Logs

In the last section, we left off at `/var/log/security` which is the file I'd like to concentrate on in this section as it wraps up this series on **ipfw** nicely.

We had to learn a fair bit about IP packets and some of the more common TCP/IP applications in order to correctly set up the ipfw firewall. Now as we read through the security log, we'll get to see first-hand what sort of packets do try to make their way into your FreeBSD computer.

When I first set up a firewall on a system, I like to keep an eye on the `security` log for the first week or so to see the amount and type of traffic which is being logged. As the superuser, I'll open up a terminal other than the console, and run the following command:

```
# tail -f /var/log/security
```

This allows me to watch the log as it grows as any changes to the log will also be sent to this terminal.

As a demonstration of how to decipher what is being logged, let's take a tour of my most recent `security` log. You'll note that my log has been sanitized as my IP address has been replaced by x.x.x.x. There are several ways to replace text on your FreeBSD system, but my favorite is to use the following Perl one-liner:

```
# perl -pe 's/my_IP_address/x.x.x.x/g' /var/log/security > ~genisis/clean
```

I had to run this command as the superuser due to the permissions on the `/var/log/security` file. The syntax of this one-liner is fairly simple. The **perl -e** tells Perl to run this line directly from the command prompt instead of looking for a Perl script to read. Don't forget to include the **p** in your **-pe**, or else Perl won't print its output. The ′s tells Perl to look for the regular expression (regex) found between the first two slashes and replace it with the string of characters enclosed between the last two slashes. If you decide to use this command, replace `/my_IP_address/` with your real IP address. The `g′` tells Perl to replace every occurrence of `/my_IP_address/`, not just the first occurrence. Finally, I told Perl to run this operation on the file `/var/log/security` and to send the results to a file named `clean` which was to be created in the home directory of the user *genisis*.

As a reminder, the only rules I'm logging in my firewall are attempted TCP connections to my FreeBSD system (rule 00401) and any other packets that were denied because I didn't explicitly allow them (rule 00800).

Tracking Down Packet Senders

One of the first things I noticed when I started to read my firewall logs was that I was logging entries from the same host to port 119 (the news port) on a regular basis:

```
Jun  5 12:17:21 hostname /kernel:  ipfw:  700 Deny TCP 24.0.0.203:58668 x.x.x.x:119 in
via ed1
Jun  8 14:04:28 hostname /kernel:  ipfw:  301 Deny TCP 24.0.0.203:50849 x.x.x.x:119 in
via ed1
Jun  9 07:21:19 hostname /kernel:  ipfw:  301 Deny TCP 24.0.0.203:37248 x.x.x.x:119 in
via ed1
Jun 17 13:22:50 hostname /kernel:  ipfw:  301 Deny TCP 24.0.0.203:49221 x.x.x.x:119 in
via ed1
```

```
Jun 18 04:42:59 hostname /kernel:  ipfw:  301 Deny TCP 24.0.0.203:39324 x.x.x.x:119 in
via ed1
Jun 20 13:25:56 hostname /kernel:  ipfw:  301 Deny TCP 24.0.0.203:57611 x.x.x.x:119 in
via ed1
Jun 21 02:33:09 hostname /kernel:  ipfw:  301 Deny TCP 24.0.0.203:53902 x.x.x.x:119 in
via ed1
```

To find out who this mysterious host is, I'll use the **-x** option to the **dig** utility to perform a reverse DNS lookup. When I run this command, I'll receive about a page's worth of output; I'll find the portion that is useful for determining who this host is in the ANSWER section:

```
% dig -x 24.0.0.203
<snip>
;; ANSWER SECTION:
203.0.0.24.in-addr.arpa.  59m38s IN PTR authorized-scan1.security.home.net.
```

The host name in the answer section reminds me that my ISP routinely runs scans to see if any of its clients are running unauthorized news servers.

With that mystery solved, let's see if any other interesting ports are appearing in my log. I occasionally notice connection attempts to port 113 (the *auth* or **identd** port). Here is an example:

```
Jun  5 13:32:23 hostname /kernel:  ipfw:  301 Deny TCP 216.13.25.80:47892 x.x.x.x:113
in via ed1
Jun  5 13:32:23 hostname last message repeated 3 times
```

And here is the result of the reverse lookup on this host:

```
% dig -x 216.13.25.80
<snip>
;; ANSWER SECTION:
80.25.13.216.in-addr.arpa.  23h58m26s IN PTR atlas.ctsolutions.com.
```

The name ctsolutions.com rang a bell, and when I checked my mail reader's outbox, I saw that I had sent an email to that company about a minute before these entries appeared in my security log. It is common practice for some mail servers to do an **identd** lookup whenever you send them an email message. It is also common practice to make a special rule in your ruleset to respond with a TCP packet that has its reset flag set. This speeds up communications with the mail server as it doesn't have to wait for the **identd** request to timeout before it processes your email message.[10]

Because the mail server is initiating the request, I'll have to ensure this new rule is numbered before my keep-state rules. I'll show the first bit of my ruleset so you can see the syntax of this new rule and where it was placed:

```
# more /etc/ipfw.rules
#speed up email
add 00150 reset log tcp from any to any 113
```

---

[10]As an alternative, section 10.8 provides an example of running an "auth" service.

```
#from man 8 ipfw: allow only connections I've created
add 00400 check-state
add 00401 deny log tcp from any to any in established
add 00402 allow tcp from any to any out setup keep-state
<snip>
```

I decided to log this new rule to see if it made any difference in my security log; the next time I sent an email to this mail server, the following entries were logged:

```
Jun  8 13:29:57 hostname /kernel:  ipfw:  150 Reset TCP 216.13.25.80:37824 x.x.x.x:113
in via ed1
Jun  8 13:30:04 hostname last message repeated 4 times
```

Mail servers aren't the only types of servers that may do an **identd** lookup; FTP servers, POP3 servers and IRC servers may also try to send packets to port 113.

Unfortunately, not all packets sent to your computer are as benign as the examples I gave for ports 119 and 113. If someone was looking for a machine to compromise, they could in theory try to get in on any open port. Fortunately, they usually tend to use common exploits on a few notorious trojan ports. There will be times when you are reading your firewall log that you'll be glad you that you took the time necessary to create and maintain your firewall. What, if anything, can you do about these entries? You can send a polite email with a copy of the firewall entries to either the host's service provider or to the administrator of the network where the host resides. To find out who to send the email to, do a:

% **dig -x *IP_address_of_sender***

to get the host name of the machine that sent the undesirable packets. You can then try a **whois** query on the last portion (or TLD) of the host name to see who registered that TLD (top-level domain). For example, I received a lot of netbus (a common trojan) entries from a host whose name ended with home.com. When I ran the **whois** utility, I received the following response:

```
# whois home.com
Registrant:
Home Network (HOME-DOM)
   425 Broadway St.
   Redwood City, CA 94063
   US

   Domain Name:  HOME.COM

   Administrative Contact, Technical Contact:
      DNS Administration   (DA24627-OR)  abuse@HOME.COM
      @Home Network
      425 Broadway St
      Redwood City , CA 94063
      US
      650-556-5399
      Fax- 650-556-6666
<snip>
```

Because this is a service provider, I'm not surprised that the email address of the administrative contact is *abuse@home.com*. If this had been a small company who had not set up an abuse email account, I could instead send an email to the person listed in the Administrative Contact, Technical Contact section.

If you don't receive any results from your **whois** query, the host probably lives in a different portion of the globe and its TLD may be registered in a different database. The **whois** utility on your FreeBSD system has several switches to allow you to query the various **whois** databases. A quick read through **man whois** shows how to specify: the APNIC database which handles Asia, Australia, New Zealand, and the Pacific Islands; by country-code; the African database; the Korean database; the Latin American database; the European database; and the Russian database.

A common complaint from those who take the time to send polite email is that they never receive acknowledgement that their email was even received or that any satisfactory action against the offending host took place. As a result, many administrators now upload their firewall logs to a centralized database. There are several interesting initiatives available; even if you don't want to participate, you can still view the accumulated statistics to see which ports are being probed and by whom.

One initiative is at `http://www.mynetwatchman.com`. Its script allows you to upload your **ipfw** logs.

Another is at `http://aris.securityfocus.com`. They accept snort logs.

Yet another initiative is at `http://www.incidents.org` which is headed up by the SANS Institute. If you are interested in security issues, it sends out a weekly newsletter known as SANS Newbites. Subscription information or the RSS feed can be found on the website.

Additional Resources

Original Article:

`http://www.onlamp.com/pub/a/bsd/2001/07/05/FreeBSD_Basics.html`

10.10 Building a Desktop Firewall

Everyone knows that you should be behind a firewall whenever you go online. However, not everyone knows that it's easy to create a personal firewall for a FreeBSD (or PC-BSD or DesktopBSD) system. This section shows how even a casual home user can get a firewall up and running in about ten minutes.

The Software

Like all of the BSDs, FreeBSD has always been security conscious. It offers several built-in firewalls to choose from: **ipfw**, **ipf**, and **pf**. I use **pf** because it is built into all of the BSDs, including OpenBSD, NetBSD, and DragonFly BSD.

I also recommend using a GUI firewall editor called **fwbuilder**. While my examples will demonstrate this utility from a FreeBSD system, it is available for Linux, Mac OS X, and Windows XP and supports **iptables**, **ipf** (IP Filter), **pf** and **ipfw**.

pf comes with FreeBSD, but double-check that it is loaded on your system by typing the following as the superuser:

```
# kldload pf
```

If you get your prompt back, you just loaded it manually. If you're in the habit of turning off your computer, add a line to /etc/rc.conf to reload **pf** when your system boots:

```
pf_enable="YES"
```

If you instead get an error like:

```
kldload: can't load pf: File exists
```

it means that your system is already configured to load **pf** for you.

Installation

From the GUI, become the superuser and install and start **fwbuilder**:

```
# pkg_add -r fwbuilder
# rehash
# fwbuilder
```

The **fwbuilder** command will open up the "Welcome to Firewall Builder" screen. A prompt will ask if you want to open an existing project file or create a new one. Click on the Create new project file button and give it a filename; the program will add the *.fwb* extension. Click on the Next button to proceed.

The next screen offers two possibilities:

- Activate Revision Control system for this file (if you don't do this now, you can always activate it later)

- Let the program automatically open this file when you start it next time (you can activate this option later using Preferences dialog)

Revision control is a very good thing. Every time you start **fwbuilder**, it maintains a copy of your existing project file (i.e., your last session). This gives you a history of all of your sessions. More importantly, if you mess things up, you can go back to a previous working session. I recommend selecting both options, then pressing Finish.

Configuring the Firewall Object

This will take you to the **fwbuilder** GUI, which is divided into two main sections. The left frame contains an Object tree and the right frame contains your firewall rules (after you have defined some objects). Using objects is a very powerful visual aid, allowing you to quickly see your networks, computers, and services, and to cut and paste these objects into firewall rules.

The first object you create should represent your firewall. Click on the New Object icon (it looks like a sheet of paper) and select New Firewall from the drop-down menu. Give your firewall a name (I called mine my_ firewall), select PF from the drop-down menu of firewall software, and click Next. Keep the default to Configure interfaces manually, and press Next.

You should see a screen like Figure 10.1.

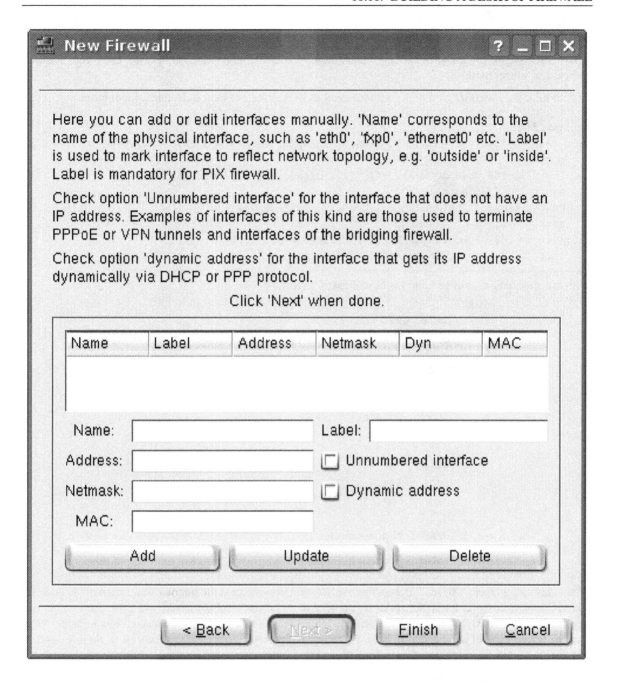

Figure 10.1: Your new firewall

Note: If your screen doesn't include the Netmask and MAC options, you didn't start **fwbuilder** as the superuser. Only the superuser can create firewall objects and firewall rules.

Be sure to Add the interface information for each NIC in your computer as well as the loopback. If your firewall will protect only your personal computer, you need only one physical NIC installed in your computer. If you wish your computer to provide NAT to other computer(s) on your home network, you need to have two NICs installed.

If your ISP assigns you a DHCP address, check the Dynamic address option. Otherwise, enter your static IP address and subnet mask.

To determine the FreeBSD names of your interfaces as well as the associated IP addressing information, type:

```
# ifconfig
xl0: flags=8843<UP,BROADCAST,RUNNING,SIMPLEX,MULTICAST> mtu 1500
    options=9<RXCSUM,VLAN_MTU>
    inet 192.168.2.49 netmask 0xffffff00 broadcast 192.168.2.255
    ether 00:04:75:ee:e0:21
    media: Ethernet autoselect (100baseTX <full-duplex>)
    status: active
lo0: flags=8049<UP,LOOPBACK,RUNNING,MULTICAST> mtu 16384
    inet 127.0.0.1 netmask 0xff000000
```

With my information, I entered into the New Firewall screen:

Name:	xl0
Address:	*(greyed out because I checked Dynamic address)*
Netmask:	*(greyed out because I checked Dynamic address)*
MAC:	00:04:75:ee:e0:21
Label:	external

Name:	lo0
Address:	127.0.0.1
Netmask:	255.0.0.0
MAC:	*(leave empty)*
Label:	loopback

When choosing a label, "external" is good for the NIC you use to access the internet, and "internal" is good for the NIC attached to your home network. If you need to add a static subnet mask, you must first convert that hex number (0xffffff00, for example) to decimal. Ignore the 0x, as that simply indicates a hex number. What remains is four pairs of numbers: ff ff ff 00. ff is easy; it represents 255; and 00 represents 0. So this mask is: 255.255.255.0. If you have a pair that isn't an ff or a 00, use the conversions in Table 10.8.

Note to users of modems: your interface name will be either ppp0 or tun0. Running **ifconfig** while connected to the Internet will make it easier to spot your IP address.

Once you've entered the information for a NIC, click Add and repeat for each of your NIC(s). When finished, click on the Finish button. The Firewall properties menu will stay open for you, but you can close it to keep the defaults. If you take a look at your Object tree, it now contains some new objects: one for your firewall and one for each interface you defined.

You have one last change to finish the firewall object — marking one of the interfaces as a Management interface. For a personal firewall, it should be the loopback. Double-click your loopback object and check the Management interface box, then close that screen.

Table 10.8: Hex Conversion Table

Hex	Decimal
80	128
c0	192
e0	224
f0	240
f8	248
fc	252
fe	254

Creating a Simple Firewall Ruleset

You now have everything you need to create a simple firewall ruleset that allows your personal computer to access the internet and prevents anyone on the internet from accessing your computer.

Click on the Rules menu and select Insert Rule (see Figure 10.2). Notice that the default rule denies any source from reaching any destination using any TCP/UDP service. To allow the system running the firewall, right-click your firewall object and select Copy. Right-click inside the Source box of the rule and Paste. Your firewall should now show as the source of packets. Next, right-click the Deny word under Action and change it to Accept. In the Options box, right-click and select Logging Off — you don't want to log every one of your successful packets.

You should always add a comment to remind yourself why you made a rule. If you double-click on the box, you can type in your comment. I wrote:

```
allow my computer to access the internet
```

That one rule is enough to give you a working firewall. If you want, you can add a second rule. Click on the Rules menu and select Add Rule Below. Add a comment:

```
deny all other traffic
```

If you don't plan on looking at your firewall logs, turn off logging in the Options box.

Note that this second rule isn't necessary for this setup, because the **pf** firewall assumes you want to deny any traffic you didn't explicitly accept. This is known as an implicit deny. You may find it useful to add the rule with a comment to remind you of this behavior.

Tip: A quick administrator's trick is to add this rule only when you are troubleshooting a problem and to leave the Logging option on.

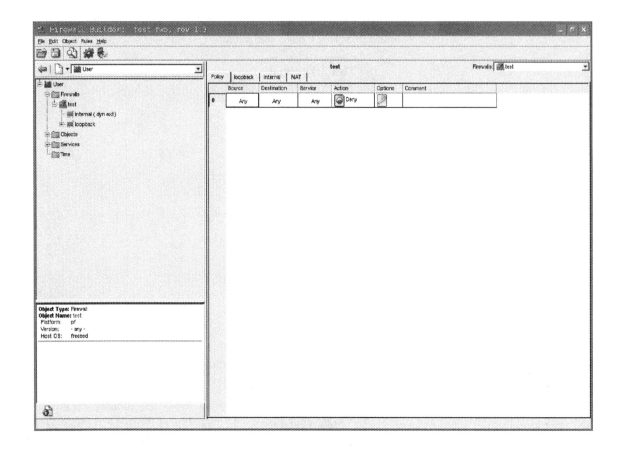

Figure 10.2: Inserting a rule

Installing your Firewall Rules

You've just created a firewall ruleset, but it won't start working until you install it.

First, you need to configure **sshd** to allow the superuser to connect and install the firewall rules. By default, FreeBSD doesn't allow superuser **ssh** sessions. Change this default by typing the next line very carefully and double-checking your upper- and lowercase and your **>>** before pressing enter:

```
# echo "PermitRootLogin yes" >> /etc/ssh/sshd_config
```

Don't worry; no one on the internet will be able to **ssh** to your computer once you install your firewall rules. Next, tell **sshd** about that change:

```
# /etc/rc.d/sshd reload
Reloading sshd config files.
```

If you see an error:

```
sshd not running? (check /var/run/sshd.pid).
```

use this command instead:

```
# /etc/rc.d/sshd start
Starting sshd.
```

Double-check that **sshd** is running with:

```
# /etc/rc.d/sshd status
sshd is running as pid 5467.
```

Next, select Install from the Rules menu. You'll receive this message:

> Some objects have been modified since you compiled the policy last time.
>
> Do you want to recompile it before you install?

You do, so click the Compile button. A text box should open and the last message should read "Policy compiled successfully." Click the Install button. Under authentication information, enter "root" for the username and type in the password for your superuser account, then press Next. You should receive a New RSA key message:

> You are connecting to the firewall 'my_firewall' for the first time. It has provided you its identification in a form of its host public key. The fingerprint of the host public key is: "b6:76:30:aa:01:27:64:48:3b:18:28:18:5b:c9:ae:e4" You can save the host key to the local database by pressing YES, or you can cancel connection by pressing NO. You should press YES only if you are sure you are really connected to the firewall 'my_firewall'.

It is safe to press Yes because you know you are connecting to your own firewall. However, it is good to know how to check a host's fingerprint in case you ever connect to a remote FreeBSD system:

```
# ssh-keygen -l -f /etc/ssh/ssh_host_dsa_key.pub
1024    b6:76:30:aa:01:27:64:48:3b:18:28:18:5b:c9:ae:e4
```

Note: You will only need to verify the fingerprint the very first time you install your firewall.

Once you click Yes, a text box will open (mine was minimized). You will get a message about "No ALTQ support in the kernel", but that's OK, as you aren't using it. Simply close the message box. Your firewall is now running.

Controlling the Firewall

Use the **pfctl** (pf control) command to see what's happening with your firewall and to stop and start the firewall. Use the show switch (**-s**) to view the rules currently running on the firewall:

```
# pfctl -s rules
No ALTQ support in kernel
ALTQ related functions disabled
pass out quick inet from (xl0) to any keep state label "RULE 0 -- ACCEPT "
block drop in quick inet all label "RULE 1 -- DROP "
block drop out quick inet all label "RULE 1 -- DROP "
block drop in quick inet all label "RULE 10000 -- DROP "
block drop out quick inet all label "RULE 10000 -- DROP "
```

If you compare that text to the rules you made in **fwbuilder**, you'll recognize rules 0 and 1. Rule 10000 is that implicit deny rule.

If you ever wish to stop your firewall, use the disable switch:

```
# pfctl -d
```

To restart the firewall, specify the name of your ruleset. It will be in `/etc` and have the same name as your firewall. In my case, it is in `/etc/my_firewall.conf`. To start this firewall, I use **pfctl** at the command line to load the rules and enable the packet filter:

```
# pfctl -e -f /etc/my_firewall.conf
```

Alternatively, I can right-click the firewall in the Objects tree and choose Install from the drop-down menu. (Note that this will fail for the current set of rules. It's easy to fix though.)

Note: If you added the line to `/etc/rc.conf` mentioned at the beginning of this section, add another line to load your ruleset if you reboot your computer:

```
pf_rules="/etc/my_firewall.conf"
```

where `my_firewall.conf` is the name of your ruleset. It is always a good idea to run **pfctl -s rules** after a reboot to double-check that your firewall is running.

Fine-Tuning the Rules

If you take a look at your first rule, it allows the firewall to go anywhere as a Source. However, nothing can connect to the firewall as a Destination. This includes the firewall making a connection to itself in order to install a policy, so if you were to add a rule you would get an error when you tried to install it. This is fine if you are happy with your firewall as is. Try it out — you should be able to surf, send/receive email, and do most of the things you normally do on the internet.

However, if you find you need to add more rules, you must start with a rule that allows the firewall to install a policy. Click on the number 0 in the first rule, go to the Rules menu, and select Insert Rule. Because the firewall needs to access the loopback management interface over **ssh**, it makes sense to have the rule look like this:

Source:	`my_firewall`
Destination:	`my_firewall:lo0:ip`
	You'll find this if you click the + (plus) by your loopback object.
Service:	`ssh`
Action:	`Accept`
Options:	`Logging On`
Comment:	`allow firewall to install policy`

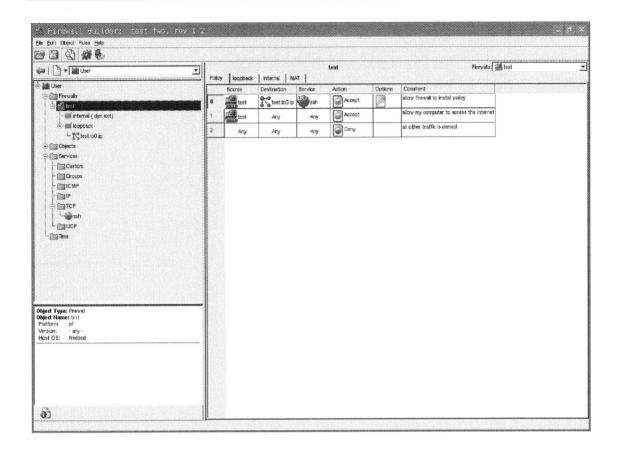

Figure 10.3: Firewall rules that allow ssh

You haven't made a ssh object yet, so do so now. Click + next to Services to expand its tree. Right-click TCP and select New TCP Service. Under Name:, enter "ssh". Under Destination Port Range Start, enter "22" and click the Apply Changes button. When finished, your firewall rules should resemble Figure 10.3.

Before you can install the new rule, you will have to temporarily stop the firewall — remember, it currently doesn't allow any connections to itself.

```
# pfctl -d
```

Install the rulebase as usual; it will restart the firewall for you. You should be able to see your new rule if you type:

```
# pfctl -s rules
```

My new rule looks like:

```
pass out log quick inet proto tcp from (x10) to 127.0.0.1 port = ssh ⇓
   keep state label "RULE 0 -- ACCEPT "
```

Conclusion

I've demonstrated how to make a personal firewall that protects your system while allowing you to access the internet. The next section will show you how to install a NAT policy with **fwbuilder** and explore some of its other features.

Additional Resources

Original Article:

`http://www.onlamp.com/pub/a/bsd/2006/08/03/FreeBSDBasics.html`

The OpenBSD PF Packet Filter Book: PF for NetBSD, FreeBSD, DragonFly, and OpenBSD:

`http://www.reedmedia.net/books/pf-book/`

10.11 Sharing Internet Connections

The previous section demonstrated how even novice BSD users can quickly create a working firewall to protect their own systems. I want to start with that base firewall and explore how to fine-tune rules, configure NAT so other PCs can share an Internet connection, and review firewall logs.

Adding Rules

The rulebase created in the previous section allows your computer to access the Internet, and allows **fwbuilder** to use SSH on the localhost to install firewall policies. This means you should be able to do most Internet-related activities including web browsing, sending email, using **pkg_add** to install software, using **csup** and **portupgrade** to keep your software up-to-date, and using most of the common internet applications such as Gaim for chat, Skype for free communications, XMMS to listen to music, and RSS feeders to keep abreast of the latest news.

Occasionally, you'll run across an application your firewall blocks. The reason is that the application needs to make a connection to you in order to send packets. Some Internet games do this; a Google search should tell you which ports you need to open on your firewall. Simply make a TCP or UDP object which contains the required port(s) and insert a rule that allows that service from any source.

Some other services, besides Internet games, may not work as you expect. As an example, I use **fetchmail** to download email from my ISP's POP3 server. After installing my firewall, I was surprised to discover that I could send email but not receive it. **fetchmail** had no problem connecting to the ISP to download the email; the problem was that **fetchmail** expected to contact Sendmail before it delivered that email into my inbox. The problem disappeared after I added this rule:

Source	Destination	Service	Action	Options	Comment
Any	test:lo0:ip	smtp	Accept		used by fetchmail

I created that smtp object by starting **fwbuilder**, right-clicking the TCP object in the Services tree, and choosing New TCP Service from the menu. I gave it the name "smtp" and a Destination Port Range Start of 25.

Notice that the destination is the loopback address, which only local mail delivery uses. Even if you don't use **fetchmail**, you should still add this rule so that your periodic scripts can successfully send mail to the superuser account.

You may be surprised to learn that **ping** won't work until you add another firewall rule. This is because **ping** uses two types of ICMP packets: one goes out from your machine (an echo request), but you'll never know your request made it to the destination unless your firewall allows an echo reply packet to come in. The current firewall rules only allow your packets to go out.[11]

To fix this, start by creating two ICMP objects. Right-click ICMP and select New ICMP Service from the menu. Name the first object "Echo Request", and enter an ICMP Type of 8 and an ICMP Code of 0. When you make the second ICMP object, name it "Echo Reply" and enter an ICMP type of 0 and an ICMP code of 0.

Note: If you're curious, the types and codes for ICMP packets are available from `http://www.iana.org/assignments/icmp-parameters`.

Next, decide if you just want the firewall to be able to **ping** out or if you also wish to allow others to ping your firewall. This rule will allow all pings:

Source	Destination	Service	Action	Options	Comment
Any	Any	echo request	Accept		Allow all pings
		echo reply			

Note: Technically, you don't need to add the echo request service, as the existing firewall rules already allow your outbound packets. I've included it because it makes more sense to me when I view the rule.

If you want to be more restrictive and only allow your firewall to ping out and not allow others to ping your firewall, modify the rule so it looks like:

Source	Destination	Service	Action	Options	Comment
Any	firewall	echo reply	Accept		Allow all my pings

Again, you don't have to allow your echo requests out, as they already fall under the rule that allows you to access the Internet. It is up to you whether to include that service in this rule.

Preparing Your Computers to Share an Internet Connection

Before creating the rules you need within **fwbuilder** to share your Internet connection, make sure that your network is properly set up. The computer running **fwbuilder** needs to have a NIC, which it uses to communicate with the other computers in your home network. This NIC is separate from the hardware you use to communicate with your ISP; that might also be a NIC (in the case of a cable or DSL connection) or it might be a modem (in the case of a dial-up PPP connection). Make sure the NIC you use to communicate with your other computers is plugged into the same hub or switch as your other computers.

You also need to decide on an addressing scheme to use on your home computers. The easiest method is to choose one of the addresses from the private address ranges. These addresses always start with either 10, 172.16 up to 172.31, or 192.168.

---

[11]Section 10.4 has more details about these ICMP types.

In my example, a FreeBSD system running **fwbuilder** will share its Internet connection with a Windows XP system. I've assigned the address 10.0.0.1 to the FreeBSD system and 10.0.0.2 to the XP system. Starting on the XP system:

- From Control Panel, select Network Connections (depending upon your view, Network Connections might be inside Network and Internet Connections).

- Double-click the icon that represents the NIC, then click Properties.

- Double-click Internet Protocol TCP/IP.

- Click the button for Use the Following IP Address, and input "10.0.0.2" for the address, "255.0.0.0" for the mask, and "10.0.0.1" for the gateway.

- Under preferred DNS server, enter the first address found in /etc/resolv.conf on the FreeBSD system, then keep clicking OK until you exit this utility.

On the FreeBSD system, become the superuser and type **ifconfig** to determine the name of the NIC you will use to communicate with the XP system. If you have multiple NICs and are currently connected to the Internet, choose the NIC that currently doesn't have an IP address. In my example, rl0 is connected to the XP system and xl0 is connected to the ISP.

Assigning the IP address is simple. (Replace rl0 with the FreeBSD name of your NIC):

```
# ifconfig rl0 10.0.0.1
```

Double-check that the connection is good with a **ping**:

```
# ping 10.0.0.2
```

(Press **Ctrl-C** to end.)

Configuring Shared Internet Connection on Firewall

Now that your computers are ready, it's time to add object(s) to your firewall to represent the computer(s) on your home network, recheck your rules to ensure all computers are allowed Internet access, and then add a NAT rule to enable the actual connection sharing.

There are several ways to represent the computers on your network: you can create host objects for each computer, or you can create a network object to represent all of the computers on your home network. Because I have only one other computer, I've chosen to add a host object to represent my XP computer.

Right-click Hosts and select New Host from the menu. Give the host a descriptive name; I called mine "XP". When asked to configure the interfaces manually, add the IP address and subnet mask for the computer; you can leave the rest of the parameters empty. Just make sure that you have added the address. In my case, I entered "10.0.0.2" and "255.0.0.0" with a label of "my_network".

Next, review your current firewall rules and ask yourself, should only the firewall computer be able to do this or should all my computers? For example, I should add the XP computer as a Source for the rule that allows access to the Internet, but I should leave the firewall loopback as the only Destination for the SSH rule that allows me to install a firewall policy. My complete rulebase resembles Figure 10.4.

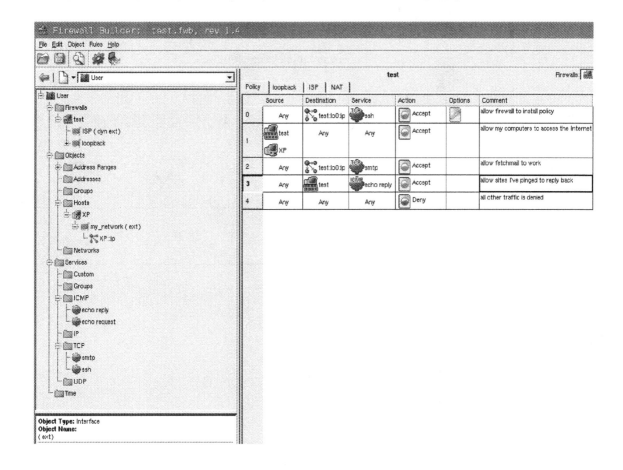

Figure 10.4: My complete rulebase

Creating the NAT rule is easy. In the right frame, click on the NAT tab. Your firewall rules should disappear (don't worry, they are still available from the Policy tab). You should see an empty frame, as you haven't created any NAT rules yet. Right-click and choose Insert Rule. Notice that NAT rules have different fields than regular firewall rules:

Original Src	default value of Any
Original Dst	default value of Any
Original Svr	default value of Any
Translated Src	default value of Original
Translated Dst	default value of Original
Translated Svr	default value of Original
Comment	empty by default

This is what you want to happen: when your other computer needs to access the Internet, it should go through the firewall and then out its other interface to the ISP. Create a rule that does that by changing two of the default values:

Original Src   *host object*

Translated Src   *external interface of firewall*

In my case, I called my host object XP and my external firewall interface ISP, so my rule looks like Figure 10.5.

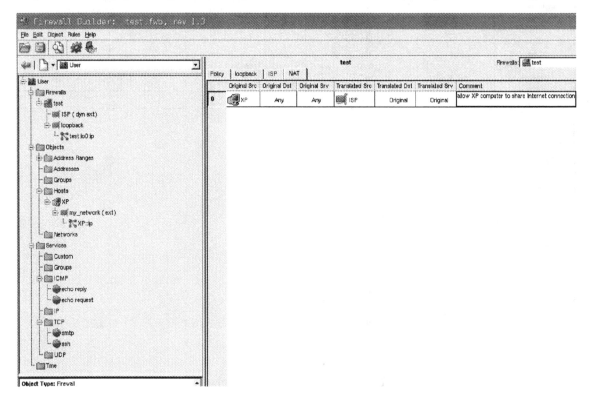

Figure 10.5: My NAT rule

Don't forget to install your policy when you finish creating your NAT rule. Then try to access a website from your other computer. Assuming you remembered to add that host to your Internet access rule, everything should just work.

Hint: if you'd like to see your NAT rules using **pfctl**, type **pfctl -s rules** as the superuser. To see your NAT translations or your current NAT connections, type **pfctl -s state**.

Fancy Stuff: Logging

There are several things you need to do if you'd like to view your firewall logs. First, make sure that you've chosen the Logging On Action in at least one of your firewall rules.

Hint: choose wisely when deciding which rules to log; if you log everything, you will have to wade through very large logfiles! If you only want to log when you think there is a problem — for example, one of your applications doesn't seem to work through the firewall — enable logging temporarily for your Internet access rule until you've figured out the problem.

Next, make sure that you have **pflog** loaded:

```
# kldstat | grep pflog
7    1 0xc52d4000 2000   pflog.ko
```

If you see this, **pflog** is good to go. If you only get your prompt back, load the module:

```
# kldload pflog
```

and add these lines to /etc/rc.conf to reload the module at boot time:

```
pflog_enable="YES"
pflog_logfile="/var/log/pflog"
pflog_flags=""
```

If that logfile doesn't already exist, create it:

```
# touch /var/log/pflog
```

You should now be able to start **pflog**:

```
# /etc/rc.d/pflog start
Starting pflog.
# /etc/rc.d/pflog status
pflog is running as pid 95363.
```

The logfile that this creates is not a text file, meaning you can't read it directly or use a utility such as **tail -f** to watch the log. Instead, use **tcpdump**:

```
# tcpdump -n -e -ttt -r /var/log/pflog
```

To view the file as it grows, use:

```
# tcpdump -n -e -ttt -i pflog0
```

Admittedly, those are some pretty long commands just to view a log. This is an excellent time to create some key bindings. These **tcsh** bindings work from a terminal, so I run them from **Alt-F2** instead of the GUI. The first command will bind **Ctrl-L** to the command that reads the logfile, and the second command will bind **Ctrl-g** to the command that watches the log as it grows:

```
# bindkey -s "^L" "tcpdump -n -e -ttt -r /var/log/pflog"
# bindkey -s "^g" "tcpdump pn -e -ttt -i pflog0"
```

I find that pressing **Ctrl-L** or **Ctrl-g** is much quicker. If you prefer to have your bindings work in your GUI, install and configure **xbindkeys_config** from the Ports collection.

Note: Select a letter which you don't normally use as a keybinding.

Fancier Stuff: Advanced Logging

Even with key bindings, **tcpdump** can still be a little inconvenient; it displays your log entries in pure text. There currently aren't any GUI **pflog** entry readers, but you can hack an HTML equivalent that will allow you to view your logs in a browser. Start by installing the **pflogx** utility:

```
# cd /usr/ports/sysutils/pflogx
# make install
```

Note that I've chosen to install the port, not the binary package, and that I didn't use the **clean** target to **make**. This is because I want to use an *.xsl* file that comes with but isn't installed by the package. Also, during the install, you'll see a menu asking if you want to use Expat; selecting this option will give you the ability to merge logfiles.

Once installed, check out the installed *.xsl* files:

```
# ls pflogx/work/xsl
export_csv.xsl      export_xhtml.xsl    last_date.xsl
export_html.xsl     first_date.xsl
```

The /usr/local/share/doc/pflogx/README holds directions for using **pflogx** and descriptions of each *.xsl* file.

Here is an example to get you started. Using the logfile as input (**-i**), create an XML file as output (**-o**):

```
# pflogx -i /var/log/pflog -o ~/log.xml
```

Copy export_html.xsl to your home directory:

```
# cp /usr/ports/sysutils/pflogx/work/pflogx/xsl/export_html.xsl ~
```

Open ~/log.xml in your favorite text editor. The first line should say:

```
<?xml version="1.0" encoding="UTF-8"?>
```

Right after that line, add:

```
<?xml-stylesheet type="text/xsl" href="export_html.xsl"?>
```

After you save your change, type the full path to log.xml into your browser. You should see something like Figure 10.6.

One last note for advanced **pf** users: if you right-click your firewall object and choose Edit, then Firewall Settings, you'll find many interesting tunables. If you wish to implement some **pf** features not currently supported by **fwbuilder**, such as ALTQ or CARP, experiment with adding the required lines to the Prolog/Epilog tab.

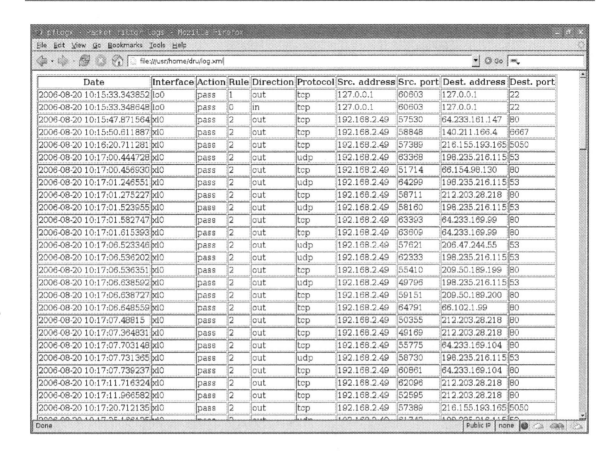

Figure 10.6: An HTML firewall log report

Additional Resources

Original Article:

http://www.onlamp.com/pub/a/bsd/2006/10/05/FreeBSD_Basics.html

fwbuilder User Guide:

http://www.fwbuilder.org/UsersGuide.pdf

The **pf** FAQ:

http://www.openbsd.org/faq/pf/

Firewalling with **pf**:

http://home.nuug.no/~peter/pf/en/

10.12 Cryptographic Terminology 101

In the next few sections, I'd like to concentrate on securing data as it travels over a network. Most network traffic is transmitted in clear text and can be decoded by a packet sniffing utility. This can be bad for transmissions containing usernames, passwords, or other sensitive data. Fortunately, other utilities known as cryptosystems can protect your network traffic from prying eyes.

To configure a cryptosystem properly, you need a good understanding of the various terms and algorithms it uses. This section is a crash course in Cryptographic Terminology 101. Following sections will demonstrate configuring some of the cryptosystems that are available to FreeBSD.

What is a cryptosystem and why would you want to use one? A cryptosystem is a utility that uses a combination of algorithms to provide the following three components: privacy, integrity, and authenticity. Different cryptosystems use different algorithms, but all cryptosystems provide those three components. Each is important, so let's take a look at each individually.

Table 10.9: Encryption Algorithms

Algorithm	Bit Size	Patented	Comment
DES	56		slow, easily cracked
3DES	168		slow
Blowfish	32 - 448	no	extremely fast
IDEA	128	yes	
CAST	40 - 128	yes	
Arcfour	40, 128		
AES (Rijndael)	128, 192, 256	no	fast
Twofish	128, 256	no	fast

Privacy

Privacy ensures that only the intended recipient understands the network transmission. Even if a packet sniffer captures the data, it won't be able to decode the contents of the message. The cryptosystem uses an encryption algorithm, or cipher, to encrypt the original clear text into cipher text before it is transmitted. The intended recipient uses a key to decrypt the cipher text back into the original clear text. This key is shared between the sender and the recipient, and it is used to both encrypt and decrypt the data. Obviously, to ensure the privacy of the data, it is crucial that only the intended recipient has the key, for anyone with the key can decrypt the data.

It is possible for someone without the key to decrypt the data by cracking or guessing the key that was used to encrypt the data. The strength of the encryption algorithm gives an indication of how difficult it is to crack the key. Normally, strengths are expressed in terms of bitsize. For example, it would take less time to crack a key created by an algorithm with a 56-bit size than it would for a key created by an algorithm with a 256-bit size.

Does this mean you should always choose the algorithm with the largest bit size? Not necessarily. Typically, as bit size increases, the longer it takes to encrypt and decrypt the data. In practical terms, this translates into more work for the CPU and slower network transmissions. Choose a bit size that is suited to the sensitivity of the data you are transmitting and the hardware you have. The increase in CPU power over the years has resulted in a double-edged sword. It has allowed the use of stronger encryption algorithms, but it has also reduced the time it takes to crack the key created by those algorithms. Because of this, you should change the key periodically, before it is cracked. Many cryptosystems automate this process for you.

There are some other considerations when choosing an encryption algorithm. Some encryption algorithms are patented and require licenses or restrict their usage. Some encryption algorithms have been successfully exploited or are easily cracked. Some algorithms are faster or slower than their bit size would indicate. For example, DES and 3DES are considered to be slow; Blowfish is considered to be very fast, despite its large bit size.

Legal considerations also vary from country to country. Some countries impose export restrictions. This means that it is OK to use the full strength of an encryption algorithm within the borders of the country, but there are restrictions for encrypting data that has a recipient outside of the country. The United States used to restrict the strength of any algorithm leaving the U.S. border to 40 bits, which is why some algorithms support the very short bit size of 40 bits.

There are still countries where it is illegal to even use encryption. If you are unsure if your particular country has any legal or export restrictions, do a bit of research before you configure your FreeBSD system to use encryption.

Table 10.9 compares the encryption algorithms you are most likely to come across.

How much of the original packet is encrypted depends upon the encryption mode. If a cryptosystem uses transport mode, only the data portion of the packet is encrypted, leaving the original headers in clear text. This means that a packet sniffer won't be able to read the actual data but will be able to determine the IP addresses of the sender and recipient and which port number (or application) sent the data.

If a cryptosystem uses tunnel mode, the entire packet, data and headers, is encrypted. Since the packet still needs to be routed to its final destination, a new Layer 3 header is created. This is known as encapsulation, and it is quite possible that the new header contains totally different IP addresses than the original IP header. We will see why in a later section when we configure your FreeBSD system for IPsec.

Table 10.10: Cryptographic Checksums

Checksum	Checksum length	Known flaws
MD4	128	yes
MD5	128	theoretical
SHA	160	theoretical
SHA-1	160	theoretical

Integrity

Integrity is the second component found in cryptosystems. This component ensures that the data received is indeed the data that was sent and that the data wasn't tampered with during transit. It requires a different class of algorithms, known as cryptographic checksums or cryptographic hashes. You may already be familiar with checksums as they are used to ensure that all of the bits in a frame or a header arrived in the order they were sent. However, frame and header checksums use a very simple algorithm, meaning that it is mathematically possible to change the bits and still use the same checksum. Cryptographic checksums need to be more tamper-resistant.

Like encryption algorithms, cryptographic checksums vary in their effectiveness. The longer the checksum, the harder it is to change the data and recreate the same checksum. Also, some checksums have known flaws. Table 10.10 summarizes the cryptographic checksums.

The order in the chart is intentional. When it comes to cryptographic checksums, MD4 is the least secure, and SHA-1 is the most secure. Always choose the most secure checksum available in your cryptosystem.

Another term to look for in a cryptographic checksum is HMAC or Hash-based Message Authentication Code. This indicates that the checksum algorithm uses a key as part of the checksum. This is good, as it's impossible to alter the checksum without access to the key. If a cryptographic checksum uses HMAC, you'll see that term before the name of the checksum. For example, HMAC-MD4 is more secure than MD4, HMAC-SHA is more secure than SHA. If we were to order the checksum algorithms from least secure to most secure, it would look like this:

- MD4

- MD5

- SHA

- SHA-1

- HMAC-MD4

- HMAC-MD5

- HMAC-SHA

- HMAC-SHA-1

Authenticity

So far, we've ensured that the data has been encrypted and that the data hasn't been altered during transit. However, all of that work would be for naught if the data, and more importantly, the key, were mistakenly sent to the wrong recipient. This is where the third component, or authenticity, comes into play.

Before any encryption can occur, a key has to be created and exchanged. Since the same key is used to encrypt and to decrypt the data during the session, it is known as a symmetric or session key. How do we safely exchange that key in the first place? How can we be sure that we just exchanged that key with the intended recipient and no one else?

This requires yet another class of algorithms known as asymmetric or public key algorithms. These algorithms are called asymmetric as the sender and recipient do not share the same key. Instead, both the sender and the recipient separately generate a key pair which consists of two mathematically related keys. One key, known as the public key, is exchanged. This means that the recipient has a copy of the sender's public key and vice versa. The other key, known as the private key, must be kept private. The security depends upon the fact that no one else has a copy of a user's private key. If a user suspects that his private key has been compromised, he should immediately revoke that key pair and generate a new key pair.

When a key pair is generated, it is associated with a unique string of short nonsense words known as a fingerprint. The fingerprint is used to ensure that you are viewing the correct public key. (Remember, you never get to see anyone else's private key.) In order to verify a recipient, they first need to send you a copy of their public key. You then need to double-check the fingerprint with the other person to ensure you did indeed get their

Table 10.11: Diffie Hellman Groups

Group Name	Bit Size
1	768
2	1024
5	1536
14	2048
15	3072
16	4096
17	6144
18	8192

public key. This will make more sense in the next section when we generate a key pair and you see a fingerprint for yourself.

The most common key generation algorithm is RSA. You'll often see the term RSA associated with digital certificates or certificate authorities, also known as CAs. A digital certificate is a signed file that contains a recipient's public key, some information about the recipient, and an expiration date. The X.509 or PKCS #9 standard dictates the information found in a digital certificate. You can read the standard for yourself at `http://www.rsasecurity.com/rsalabs/pkcs` or `http://ftp.isi.edu/in-notes/rfc2985.txt`.

Digital certificates are usually stored on a computer known as a Certificate Authority. This means that you don't have to exchange public keys with a recipient manually. Instead, your system will query the CA when it needs a copy of a recipient's public key. This provides for a scalable authentication system. A CA can store the digital certificates of many recipients, and those recipients can be either users or computers.

It is also possible to generate digital certificates using an algorithm known as DSA. However, this algorithm is patented and is slower than RSA.

There is one last point to make on the subject of digital certificates and CAs. A digital certificate contains an expiration date, and the certificate cannot be deleted from the CA before that date. What if a private key becomes compromised before that date? You'll obviously want to generate a new certificate containing the new public key. However, you can't delete the old certificate until it expires. To ensure that certificate won't inadvertently be used to authenticate a recipient, you can place it in the CRL or Certificate Revocation List. Whenever a certificate is requested, the CRL is read to ensure that the certificate is still valid.

Authenticating the recipient is one half of the authenticity component. The other half involves generating and exchanging the information that will be used to create the session key which in turn will be used to encrypt and decrypt the data. This again requires an asymmetric algorithm, but this time it is usually the Diffie Hellman, or DH, algorithm.

It is important to realize that Diffie Hellman doesn't make the actual session key itself, but the keying information used to generate that key. This involves a fair bit of fancy math which isn't for the faint of heart. The best explanation I've come across, in understandable language with diagrams, is at `http://www.netip.com/articles/keith/diffie-helman.htm`.

It is important that the keying information is kept as secure as possible, so the larger the bit size, the better. The possible Diffie Hellman bit sizes have been divided into groups. Table 10.11 summarizes the possible groups.

When configuring a cryptosystem, you should use the largest Diffie Hellman Group size that it supports.

The other term you'll see associated with the keying information is PFS, or Perfect Forward Secrecy, which Diffie Hellman supports. PFS ensures that the new keying information is not mathematically related to the old keying information. This means that if someone sniffs an old session key, they won't be able to use that key to guess the new session key. PFS is always a good thing and you should use it if the cryptosystem supports it.

Putting It All Together

Let's do a quick recap and summarize how a cryptosystem protects the data transmitted onto a network.

1. First, the recipient's public key is used to verify that you are sending the data to the correct recipient. That public key was created by the RSA algorithm and is typically stored in a digital certificate that resides on a CA.

2. Once the recipient is verified, the DH algorithm is used to create the information that will be used to create the session key.

3. Once the keying information is available, a key that is unique to that session is created. This key is used by both the sender and the receiver to encrypt and decrypt the data they send to each other. It is important that this key changes often.

4. Before the data is encrypted, a cryptographic checksum is calculated. Once the data is decrypted, the cryptographic checksum is recalculated to ensure that the recipient has received the original message.

In the next section, you'll have the opportunity to see many of these cryptographic terms in action as we'll be configuring a cryptosystem that comes built-in to your FreeBSD system: **ssh**.

Additional Resources

Original Article:

http://www.onlamp.com/pub/a/bsd/2002/10/31/FreeBSD_Basics.html

10.13 The SSH Cryptosystem

Your FreeBSD system uses OpenSSH and it is installed and ready to go. As the name implies, this is an Open Source implementation of the SSH cryptosystem.

In section 10.2, I demonstrated that the **telnet** utility can be used to login to a remote computer from another system. Once logged in, a user can do anything on that remote system as if he were physically sitting in front of it. That is, every keystroke is sent to the remote system and interpreted as if it had come from the keyboard attached to that remote system (even though that keyboard input first had to travel over a network). We also saw that every single keystroke and response was sent in clear text, meaning that a sniffer could watch the entire session.

A SSH cryptosystem will allow a user to login to a remote system and work just as if he were physically there. However, before the user is given a login prompt, a key will be generated to encrypt and decrypt all of the data that will be passed between the two computers. That is, more is happening behind the scenes.

Since SSH is used to access another computer, a user account must exist on the computer to be accessed. Additionally, the computer being accessed is known as the SSH server and must be running the SSH daemon; by default, this daemon listens on TCP port 22. The machine you are sitting at is known as the SSH client; it will contact the daemon on the other machine.

Your FreeBSD system has default configurations that allow you to use SSH as is. I'll demonstrate the default configuration first, then move on to some changes you may wish to make to increase the security of SSH.

Generating Server Keys

I'll be using two computers. 10.0.0.1 will be the SSH daemon, the computer I wish to access, and 10.0.0.2 will be the SSH client, the computer I'm sitting at. On both systems, I have created a user account called *genisis*. You'll note that the cryptosystem is called OpenSSH. It uses a protocol usually written as uppercase SSH, and the commands you type, **ssh** and **sshd**, are written in lowercase. Also, you can use the **ssh** command to access either an IP address or a hostname. In this section, I'll purposefully use IP addresses. In the next section I'll take a closer look at name resolution issues when using SSH.

First, I need to check if the host keys have been created on the system that will be the server. At 10.0.0.1, I'll run this command:

```
% ls /etc/ssh
moduli                  ssh_host_dsa_key.pub    ssh_host_rsa_key
ssh_config              ssh_host_key            ssh_host_rsa_key.pub
ssh_host_dsa_key        ssh_host_key.pub        sshd_config
```

This output shows I have the necessary keys. However, if I instead get this output:

```
moduli          ssh_config      sshd_config
```

there aren't any host keys and I will need to generate them before I can start the SSH daemon. The easiest way to ensure the necessary keys are generated and that SSH starts whenever the system reboots is to add the following line to /etc/rc.conf:

```
sshd_enable="YES"
```

Once I've saved my changes, I'll type:

```
# /etc/rc.d/sshd start
Generating public/private rsa1 key pair.
Your identification has been saved in /etc/ssh/ssh_host_key.
Your public key has been saved in /etc/ ssh/ssh_host_key.pub.
The key fingerprint is:
12:d9:3d:f3:95:92:0e:e7:6b:54:09:80:77:a0:3e:cf root@hostname
Generating public/private dsa key pair.
```

```
Your identification has been saved in /etc/ssh/ssh_host_dsa_key.
Your public key has been saved in /etc/ssh/ssh_host_dsa_key.pub.
The key fingerprint is:
22:69:d7:05:23:c6:db:d9:55:2a:20:a3:34:bd:f4:ef root@hostname
Generating public/private rsa key pair.
Your identification has been saved in /etc/ssh/ssh_host_rsa_key.
Your public key has been saved in /etc/ssh/ssh_host_rsa_key.pub.
The key fingerprint is:
4b:cf:7e:af:f1:a8:01:08:64:1b:c0:79:e3:a2:58:78 root@hostname
Starting sshd.
```

Let's take a look at that output. You'll note that three separate key pairs were generated: one for rsa1, one for rsa, and one for dsa. You should recognize the RSA and DSA acronyms from the last section on cryptographic terms. But why so many key pairs? There are two versions of the SSH protocol, and OpenSSH supports them both. Not surprisingly, the rsa1 keypair is used by SSH version 1. SSH version 2 supports both RSA and DSA.

Each key in a key pair is stored in a separate file. You can identify the public key files, as they have a *.pub* extension. Additionally, each public key has an associated fingerprint which is unique to that key. We'll see that fingerprint again.

Not only were the necessary keys generated, the SSH daemon was also started. This can be verified with the sockstat command:

```
% sockstat | grep ssh
root     sshd     69820   3 tcp4   *:22                *:*
root     sshd     69820   3 tcp6   *:22                *:*
```

Using SSH

OK, now that 10.0.0.1 is listening on port 22, let's see what happens when I use the **ssh** command from 10.0.0.2 as the user *genisis*:

```
% ssh 10.0.0.1
The authenticity of host '10.0.0.1 (10.0.0.1)' can't be established.
DSA key fingerprint is 22:69:d7:05:23:c6:db:d9:55:2a:20:a3:34:bd:f4:ef.
Are you sure you want to continue connecting (yes/no)? yes
Warning: Permanently added '10.0.0.1' (DSA) to the list of known hosts.
Password:
```

Once I type the correct password for the user *genisis*, I'll receive my motd and customized prompt. I'll then type **exit** to leave the session:

```
% exit
logout
Connection to 10.0.0.1 closed.
```

I'll now repeat a second time but this time won't be prompted to verify the fingerprint:

```
% ssh 10.0.0.1
Password:
```

Let's pick apart what happened here. The very first time I used SSH, I was asked to verify the fingerprint of the server's DSA public key. Once I doublechecked that it was correct and typed **yes**, a copy of the server's public key was placed on the client or 10.0.0.2:

```
% more ~genisis/.ssh/known_hosts
10.0.0.1 ssh-dss AAAAB3NzaC1kc3MAAACBAPiOFgV4PpsbXfkaxGD+hCr02Cv9P3OJDKfaXge059
cSohLN/n/kd2Nz/E1mDvT4Y8nSAQL7M667iMeqJ0WTpcdI59ktuPtvOsYBc7SNoJ6aPqqoKo682mAfC
NpUFZ3jirbWGFnaF3WpJsWFyeOY6vyD4hVT6CkunL2ovoYSJND7AAAAFQDjZ2TNBixZByXB+h00wxCN
tHZ8zQAAAIEA14lePs+e5v9f1H9312GLXtxXhXyasr+X42HnKgKQTMR+iLgxhtD0Eb/ftTMK+n2ECn9
3MwCNTgx5tdGX06dyBdK5xEfjV4tJnmnP42UweBwOHKpRkNLiMBN4onh7KKXjhXWmH0MpO5fhaHy6k0
f+yTTLckCKd2IO/TgGJitjlo4AAACBAM+3JMr8M+MQoa6D7BU0pNJVGoTmGdxrLotMNLmUdqM0xIFKr
3dBrgqY+gsDciQEG1CSqDDhusrkz3LRBmnuG68tE7WPPjzGZrT46ZYCmMeZume67xVN0dDd57BuxmhK
B7iKvmlM0v+EkvJ0XT1NCwBTWuU3cdTdhkWT7swxGhvf
```

The next time I used SSH, the server's public key was compared to the copy of that key on the client; since they were the same, SSH knew I was connecting to the correct server so I wasn't asked to re-verify a fingerprint. Instead, I simply received the login prompt on the server.

Let's recap what happens behind the scenes:

1. The SSH client contacts the SSH server on port 22.

2. The SSH server sends the SSH client a copy of its public key to prove its identity.

3. The SSH client compares the server's public key to its copy of the server's public key. If it does not have a copy of the server's key, it prompts the user to verify the fingerprint.

4. Once the server is authenticated, a key is created that will be used to encrypt and decrypt the data sent between the client and the server.

5. Now it is the user's turn to be authenticated; by default, the server will prompt for the user's password which will be sent encrypted.

6. Once the user authenticates, he will receive his shell on the other system, and all data sent between the two systems will be encrypted.

Generating User Keys

OpenSSH supports other authentication methods, but this is what happens in the default configuration on your FreeBSD system. You may have noticed that the server sent its DSA public key, meaning that it was using SSH version 2. This is a good default, as version 2 is much more secure than version 1.

You may have also noticed that the user doesn't require a key pair in the default configuration, only their password. Let's change that. First, I'll have to generate a key pair for the user *genisis* by using the **ssh-keygen** command at 10.0.0.2:

```
% ssh-keygen -t rsa
Generating public/private rsa key pair.
Enter file in which to save the key (/home/genisis/.ssh/id_rsa):
Enter passphrase (empty for no passphrase):
Enter same passphrase again:
Your identification has been saved in /home/genisis/.ssh/id_rsa.
Your public key has been saved in /home/genisis/.ssh/id_rsa.pub.
The key fingerprint is:
fd:5a:cc:cf:a9:f0:ea:9c:93:ea:1a:04:48:b1:47:14 genisis@hostname
```

When using **ssh-keygen**, use the **-t** switch to specify which type of key pair to create. Since SSH version 2 is more secure than version 1, and since RSA is more secure than DSA, I chose to create a SSH version 2 RSA keypair. I was also prompted for a passphrase which will be used in the future to prove that I am the owner of the key pair, or, more importantly, the private key. A passphrase is similar to a password, but should be longer yet memorable. Whenever I wish to use the private key, I will be prompted for the passphrase. If I ever forget the passphrase, I will need to generate a new key pair.

Remember that the public key in a key pair is meant to be public and it is up to you to ensure the private key is kept private. Let's take a look at the default permissions on those keys:

```
% ls ~genisis/.ssh
total 4
-rw-------   1 genisis   genisis   951 Nov   9 15:00 id_rsa
-rw-r--r--   1 genisis   genisis   247 Nov   9 15:00 id_rsa.pub
```

The private key, id_rsa, is only accessible by the user *genisis*. The public key, id_rsa.pub, is readable by anyone. If I use the **file** utility, I'll see that both files are ASCII text, meaning they can be viewed with a pager:

```
% more id_rsa.pub
ssh-rsa AAAAB3NzaC1yc2EAAAABIwAAAIEA1gfc4NRnq9K17TLqhhKT3L6feKUttHTJvM054k+WhjI
vsdt4YoeNa3m61plnOxwOh2w6o+xu+xuiHa/CQkvkAdxFU1ZGtnxtQWV06QJdodUEk55U/0y417TaDF
HlaYjsgPPSpjulKCLQv263C9KOSpjDrjZ74ZLOlQHtsJINY2c= genisis@hostname
```

Note that I only showed you my public key, not my private key.

Configuring Public Key Authentication

Creating the key pair is not enough. I still need to copy my public key into my home directory on the SSH server. Once the server has a copy of my public key, whenever I use SSH it will ask for my public key so it can compare it to its copy. If they match, I will be authenticated.

I'll use the **scp** or secure copy command to copy the key to the server. This utility comes with OpenSSH and allows you to transfer files over an encrypted session. Its syntax is similar to the regular old **cp** command; the only difference is that the either the source or the destination file starts with an IP address, followed by a full colon, followed by the path of the filename.

So, at 10.0.0.2, I'll issue this command to copy my public key to the server:

```
% scp ~/.ssh/id_rsa.pub 10.0.0.1:~/.ssh/authorized_keys
Password:
id_rsa.pub:      100% |************************|    247        00:00
```

Note that I was careful to copy over the public key, not the private key; that is, I chose the file with the *.pub* extension. I also had to change the name of the destination file to ~/.ssh/authorized_keys.[12] I was prompted for my password on the destination system before the actual copy occurred.

Now that my public key is copied over, I'll try another SSH:

```
% ssh 10.0.0.1
Enter passphrase for key '/home/genisis/.ssh/id_rsa':
```

This time, I wasn't prompted for a password but for my passphrase. While this may seem as inconvenient, it actually increases security as you have to know your username and passphrase as well as have a copy of the matching private key. Section 8.4 demonstrates how you can use **ssh-agent** to automate this process so you don't have to constantly reauthenticate.

Remember, the security of the system still depends upon you. Just like you don't give other users your password, don't give other users your private key or your passphrase. If you ever suspect that your private key has been compromised, generate a new key pair using a different passphrase and copy over the new public key to the SSH server.

When using **ssh**, you don't have to be logged in to the same account on the client machine as you want to access on the server machine. For example, if I'm currently logged in as *biko* but want to access *genisis* on the server machine, I can use the **-l** switch or login switch at the client:

```
% ssh -l genisis 10.0.0.1
```

I could also use this equivalent command:

```
% ssh genisis@10.0.0.1
```

Since there isn't a copy of *genisis'* public key in *biko*'s home directory, I'll be prompted for a password. I need to input the password for *genisis*, not for *biko*. While it's a little bit harder to remember who I am on each system, it does mean that I don't have to create a user account called *genisis* on both machines.

Let's see what happens if I try to use SSH from the superuser account:

```
# ssh 10.0.0.1
Password:
Password:
Password:
Permission denied (publickey,keyboard-interactive).
```

Even though I gave the correct password for the superuser account, access was denied. This is a very good default. Just like you should never login directly as *root*, you should never **ssh** into another system from the *root* account. If you need superuser access on the remote system, **ssh** using a regular user account which has permission to become the superuser once logged in to the remote system.[13]

---

[12] The authorized_keys file may contain multiple keys. Note: this **scp** example replaces any existing ~/.ssh/authorized_keys file on the remote server.

[13] Section 10.10 has an example of configuring SSH for *root* logins.

Additional Resources

Original Article:

```
http://www.onlamp.com/pub/a/bsd/2002/11/14/FreeBSD_Basics.html
```

OpenSSH website:

```
http://www.openssh.org/
```

The SSH FAQ:

```
http://www.employees.org/~satch/ssh/faq/ssh-faq.html
```

10.14 Configuring SSH

In this section I want to spend a bit of time in the SSH configuration files, then mention briefly other utilities that allow the integration of SSH between your FreeBSD system and other operating systems.

Since SSH is composed of a client and a server, there are two configuration files. Not surprisingly, one is called `ssh_config` and the other `sshd_config`. That extra *d*, for daemon or the SSH server, is significant. The very first time I changed an SSH configuration file, I mistakenly added a server line to the client configuration file and scratched my head in puzzlement when it had no effect on my system. Remember to keep in mind that the SSH client is where you are sitting, and the SSH server is the machine you want to access remotely.

Both of these files have manpages which explain all of the possible configuration options. Both are well worth a read as you might possibly be intrigued by an option that I didn't cover here. Let's start by taking a look at the default SSH client configuration file.

Configuring the SSH Client

If you **more /etc/ssh/ssh_config**, you'll notice that every line in this file starts with a # or remark character. This doesn't mean that the SSH client has no configurations. Instead, the defaults are listed here as a reference. If you want to change a default, you first remove the # on the appropriate line, then insert the new value. All of the possible values are listed in **man ssh_config**.

As you go through the manpage, you'll notice that some configuration options only apply to certain versions. Whenever possible, you should use SSH version 2. If you always use a FreeBSD client to connect to a FreeBSD server, the default configurations on both the client and the server will ensure you always use version 2. However, if you are using your FreeBSD system to access a non-FreeBSD system, you may be forced to use version 1 as that is all many systems support.

What are the differences between versions 1 and 2? If you do a search on the Internet, the most common answer you'll receive is that version 2 is a complete re-write that addressed many of the security issues that appeared in version 1. The two versions also differ in the algorithms that they support which I've summarized in Table 10.12.

You'll note that version 2 has support for stronger algorithms, and it provides protection against tampering. Remember, HMAC is a good acronym to find in a cryptosystem.[14]

Note this line in the client configuration file:

---

[14]Section 10.12 introduces HMAC.

Table 10.12: SSH Protocols

Version	Encryption Algorithms	Cryptographic Checksums
version 1	DES, 3DES, blowfish	none
version 2	AES-128, AES-192, AES-256, blowfish, CAST-128, ArcFour	HMAC-MD5, HMAC-SHA-1, HMAC-RIPEMD

```
#Protocol 2,1
```

This means that the client will try to use version 2; if the server only supports version 1, the client will use that instead. If you change the line to:

```
Protocol 2
```

the client will fail to connect to any servers that only support version 1. Remember that if you do make any changes, remove the # or your change will be ignored as it will still be commented.

Two lines deal with ciphers or encryption algorithms:

```
# Cipher 3des
# Ciphers aes128-cbc,3des-cbc,blowfish-cbc,cast128-cbc,arcfour, aes192-cbc,aes256-cbc
```

The first line is used during a version 1 session. The manpage indicates that you should not use DES unless you absolutely have to. Note that the default is 3DES instead of the stronger, more efficient blowfish. This is because many non-FreeBSD systems don't support blowfish. Unfortunately, there are systems who only support version 1 and also only support DES. If this is the case, the default client configuration will fail, meaning you will have to change the line to:

```
Cipher DES
```

Avoid this if possible. While this is still much, much better than using **telnet** to connect to the system and sending everything in clear text, it decreases the security provided by SSH.

The second line that deals with ciphers is used during a version 2 session. This line gives an ordered list of encryption algorithms. The first algorithm that matches the server will be used to encrypt the data.

Note that /etc/ssh/ssh_config is the global client configuration file. This means that the values in this file can be overridden by using switches with the **ssh** command. Also, if you are a lazy typist and always end up using the same switches, you can create a customized configuration file in your home directory. For example, instead of using the **-l** switch in order to login as the user *biko*, I could create a file called ~/.ssh/config and place this line in it:

```
HostName 10.0.0.1
User biko
```

All SSH parameters are case sensitive, so make sure to capitalize the U in User.

Now whenever I **ssh** to 10.0.0.1, I don't have to remember to include the **-l** switch and I'll still be prompted for *biko*'s password.

If you are using a hostname or FQDN instead of an IP when you use the **ssh** command, you may find that your client will hang for a moment or so while the name is resolved. You might find a speed difference if you add an entry for the SSH server in /etc/hosts on the SSH client.

SSH Server Configuration

Let's switch gears a bit and move on to the SSH server configuration file /etc/ssh/sshd_config. This file is similar to the SSH client file in that all lines begin with a # and all possible values are listed in its manpage.

Treat the SSH daemon with more care. After all, in order to run the daemon, you need to open port 22 on that system. If that system has Internet access, anyone in the world can attempt to connect to that computer on that port. If you are using password authentication and an unauthorized user is able to guess a username and password, they will be able to login to that system with all of the rights of that user. See why *root* SSH logins aren't allowed and why using a public key with a passphrase protected private key is a good thing?

It is important to verify that you are using a recent version of the SSH daemon. To check the SSH server version, telnet to port 22 of the machine running the SSH daemon. If you're sitting at the server, the following command works; otherwise, telnet to the IP of the server.

```
% telnet localhost 22
Trying ::1...
Connected to localhost.
Escape character is '^]'.
SSH-2.0-OpenSSH_4.5p1 FreeBSD-20061110
quit
Connection closed by foreign host.
```

There are several ways to control which hosts and users are allowed to access your SSH daemon. One is with a firewall. If you don't want anyone to access your SSH server over an Internet connection, place the SSH server behind a firewall with rules that deny access to port 22. If you do have users that will be accessing the SSH server over the Internet, you will need to add a rule that allows port 22. If your SSH clients have static IPs, you can allow just those addresses in your firewall rule.

Next, you can modify /etc/ssh/sshd_config. First, make a banner. While a banner itself offers no security, it does serve as a warning to unauthorized users and may make a bit of difference if you ever need to approach an ISP or legal authorities regarding unauthorized access. Here, I've made a simple banner:

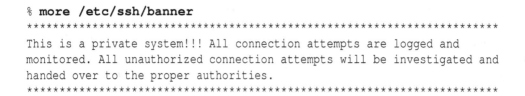

```
% more /etc/ssh/banner
***********************************************************************
This is a private system!!! All connection attempts are logged and
monitored. All unauthorized connection attempts will be investigated and
handed over to the proper authorities.
***********************************************************************
```

Then, to tell the daemon to display the banner, I'll change this line in /etc/ssh/sshd_config:

```
#Banner /some/path
```

to

```
Banner /etc/ssh/banner
```

The banner itself will be displayed before the password or passphrase prompt. Note that banners will only be displayed to clients using SSH version 2 as they are unsupported by version 1.

If your SSH clients don't have static IPs or don't always use the same computers to access the SSH server, it is difficult to specify source IPs in your firewall rule. Fortunately, you can specify which users are allowed to authenticate to the SSH server by adding the `AllowUsers` parameter to the SSH daemon configuration file. Here, I'll restrict access to the users *genisis* and *biko*:

```
AllowUsers genisis biko
```

Any user that is not in that list will still receive a password prompt when they attempt to connect to the SSH daemon. However, even if they give a correct username and password, they will receive a permission denied message and their connection attempt will fail. A message regarding the failed attempt will be printed to the console of the SSH daemon, copied to `/var/log/messages` and emailed to *root* as part of the daily security run output. As you can see, this is a very good line to add to the SSH daemon configuration file. To be even pickier, if your users always login from the same system, you can do this:

```
AllowUsers genisis@10.0.0.2 biko@10.0.0.2
```

However, don't be that picky if your users don't always sit at the same system or if those systems don't have static IPs. For example, if *genisis* tries to connect from 192.168.10.1, she will receive a connection denied message.

Depending upon your requirements, you might also want to add these lines:

```
ClientAliveInterval 120
ClientAliveCountMax 2
```

The first value indicates that if the client hasn't sent any data for more than 2 minutes (120 seconds), the server will send a message to the client asking for a response. The second line indicates that if the client doesn't respond after 4 minutes (120 times 2), the server will disconnect the client.

You can also consider changing the value in this line:

```
#Port 22
```

to another port number. If you do so, make sure your clients are aware of the port they must use to connect to the server so they can specify it either on the command line or in the `ssh_config` file. While this adds a bit of security by defeating random or scripted attempts to port 22, a knowledgable unauthorized user can simply use **telnet** to connect to your alternate port and discover that the SSH daemon is listening.

If you don't want the world in general to know that your SSH server is running FreeBSD, you can also change this parameter:

```
#VersionAddendum FreeBSD-20050903
```

You may remember seeing a similar line in the output when I **telnet**ted to port 22. If I change that to something like this:

```
VersionAddendum   For Authorized Users Only!!!!
```

it will change that line in the **telnet** output to:

```
SSH-2.-OpenSSH_4.5p1 For Authorized Users Only!!!!
```

Note that it will still indicate the version of OpenSSH in use. This is another reason why you always want to be running a recent, fully patched version as any user who knows how to use **telnet** can easily find out if your SSH server is patched against known exploits.

If your SSH server has multiple IPs, all of them will listen for port 22 connection attempts by default. If you only want one of the addresses to listen, change this line, replacing 0.0.0.0 with the desired IP address:

```
#ListenAddress 0.0.0.0
```

Remember, if you make any changes to the daemon's configuration file, you'll need to notify **sshd** of the changes:

 # /etc/rc.d/sshd reload

After informing **sshd** of the changes, always use a separate **ssh** session to test your changes. For example, if I add this line:

```
Allowusers genisis biko
```

yet find that user *dlavigne* is still able to connect, it is time to check that line for a typo. It is very easy to forget that parameters are case sensitive. In this case, AllowUsers would have worked but Allowusers was silently ignored and failed miserably. You don't want to find out six months later that anyone was allowed to connect when you thought you had restricted connections to two users.

10.14.1 Additional Resources

Original Article:

http://www.onlamp.com/pub/a/bsd/2002/11/28/FreeBSD_Basics.html

Top 10 SSH FAQs:

http://www.oreillynet.com/pub/a/oreilly/networking/news/sshtips_0101.html

10.15 VPNs and IPsec Demystified

A VPN, or Virtual Private Network, is a cryptosystem that allows you to secure your data as it travels over an insecure network such as the Internet. While this may sound similar to the SSH cryptosystem, VPNs have a different purpose. SSH was designed to allow a user to login securely to and remotely administer another computer. A VPN is designed to allow a user to access transparently the resources of a network. As far as the user is concerned, she will be able to do anything she normally would be able to do, even when she is away from the network. Because of this, VPNs are popular with telecommuters and with offices that need to share resources over physically separate locations.

VPN Tunnels

Before configuring a VPN, you should be aware of the terminology it uses and some of the configuration pitfalls. Let's start with some terminology. A VPN always consists of a point-to-point link known as a tunnel. The tunnel itself occurs over the insecure network which is usually an Internet connection. A point-to-point link means that it is always between two computers which are referred to as peers. Each peer is responsible for encrypting the data before it enters the tunnel and decrypting the data as it leaves the tunnel.

Even though the VPN tunnel is always between two peers, each peer can set up tunnels with other peers. For example, if three telecommuters were to establish a VPN to the same office, there would be three separate VPN tunnels to that office. However, each tunnel would share the same office peer. This can occur because it is possible for a peer to encrypt and decrypt data on behalf of an entire network as seen in Figure 10.7.

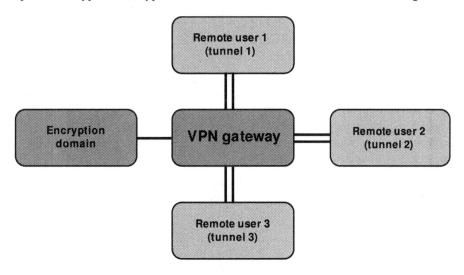

Figure 10.7: VPN gateway to a network

When this occurs, the VPN peer is also known as a VPN gateway, and the network behind the gateway is referred to as the encryption domain. It makes sense to use a gateway for several reasons. First, all users are required to go through the same device, which makes it easier to administer a security policy and control which traffic is allowed in and out of the network. Second, it would quickly become unworkable to set up separate tunnels for every PC a user wanted to access. (Remember, a tunnel is a point-to-point link). With a gateway, the user initiates a tunnel to the gateway and is then allowed access to the network, or encryption domain, behind that gateway.

It is interesting to note that no encryption occurs within the encryption domain. This is because that portion of the network is considered to be secure and under your administrative control while the Internet is considered to be insecure and beyond your control. This also makes sense when using two VPN gateways to connect two offices. It ensures all data is encrypted as it traverses the insecure link connecting the two offices. Figure 10.8 shows a VPN connecting two offices.

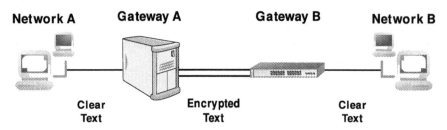

Figure 10.8: A secure network over an insecure network

Network A is considered to be the encryption domain of VPN Gateway A, and Network B is the encryption domain of VPN Gateway B. When a user on Network A wishes to send data to Network B, VPN Gateway A will encrypt the data and send it over the VPN tunnel. VPN Gateway B will decrypt the data and send it to the destination in Network B.

Remember the difference between transport mode and tunnel mode? Whenever two VPN gateways are used to connect two networks, they always use tunnel mode. This means that the entire IP packet is encrypted and a new IP header is added. That new IP header contains the IP addresses of the two VPN gateways. This adds an extra benefit in that a packet sniffer will only see the IP addresses of the gateways. There is no way to identify a source computer in the first encryption domain or a destination computer in the other encryption domain.

Compare this to Figure 10.7, which shows the other use of a VPN, allowing remote users with laptops and users who work from home to access the resources at the office network. In order for this to work, the user needs VPN client software installed on their PC to negotiate a VPN tunnel with the office VPN gateway. In this scenario, tunnel mode is still used as the remote user wants to access the resources within the encryption domain rather than the resources on the VPN gateway itself. The only time transport mode is used is when one computer wants to access another computer directly.

There are many options for VPN gateways and VPN clients. There are hardware VPN appliances and VPN software that can be installed on routers or PCs. Your FreeBSD system comes with software that allow you to set up either a VPN gateway or act as a VPN client. There are also additional applications in the ports collection, which allow interconnectivity with other VPN peers on non-FreeBSD systems.

Regardless of the VPN software being used, all VPNs share the following behaviors:

1. Both peers authenticate each other before establishing the tunnel to ensure the encrypted data will be sent to the expected peer.

2. Both peers require a pre-configured policy stating which protocols can be used to encrypt the data and provide data integrity.

3. The peers compare their policies to determine which algorithms will be used; if the peers are unable to agree upon the necessary algorithms, the tunnel is not established.

4. Once the policy is agreed upon, a key is created which will be used by the symmetric algorithm to encrypt and decrypt the data.

There are several standards which dictate how the above occurs. You may have heard of some of them: L2TP, PPTP, and IPsec. Since IPsec is the standard that most VPNs support, and it also has the most acronyms to wade through, I'll devote the rest of this section to IPsec.

IPsec

The IPsec standard was designed to add security to the IP protocol. It does this by using protocols which add additional headers, also called encapsulations, to an IP packet. Since IPsec is an Internet standard, there are RFCs (Request For Comments) for IPsec and the protocols it uses. If you are interested in the inner workings of IPsec, Table 10.13 lists RFCs that are useful references and can be found at `http://www.rfc-editor.org/`:

Table 10.13: IPsec RFCs

RFC 4301	IPsec
RFC 4302	AH
RFC 4303	ESP
RFC 4306	IKE

I'll give a brief overview of each, so you will have the necessary information to understand the next section when I demonstrate configuring an IPsec VPN using a FreeBSD system. Let's start with the acronyms and then see how they fit together to create an IPsec VPN.

AH is the Authentication Header protocol. It provides integrity by ensuring that none of the bits in the portion of the packet being protected were tampered with during transit. I won't get into the details of which portion of the packet is protected and where in the packet the AH header is added as that depends upon the encryption mode and is covered in detail, with diagrams, in the RFC. Additionally, using AH can be problematic, especially if the packet passes through a NAT device. NAT changes the IP address in an IP packet to allow a private source address to access the Internet. Since the packet changes, it won't match the AH checksum. Also, AH was designed only to provide integrity. It does not provide privacy by encrypting the contents of the packet.

ESP is the Encapsulating Security Protocol and it provides both integrity and privacy. In transport mode, the ESP header is placed between the original, clear text IP header and the TCP or UDP header. In tunnel mode, the ESP header is placed between the new IP header and the original, completely encrypted IP packet.

Since both AH and ESP add an additional header, they have an associated protocol ID so the IP header knows to look for an AH or an ESP header. You may remember that each type of header has a number associated with it. For example, TCP is 6 and UDP is 17. If you are using IPsec behind a firewall, you have to remember to create a rule allowing the AH and/or ESP protocol ID. AH has a protocol ID of 51, and ESP has a protocol ID of 50. When making your firewall rule, remember that a protocol ID is not the same as a port number.

The third protocol used by IPsec is IKE, or the Internet Key Exchange protocol.   As its name suggests, this protocol is used to manage the exchange of keys between the two VPN peers. While it is possible to generate the key manually, it is better and certainly much more scalable to allow the IKE protocol to do this for you automatically. Remember, you want the keys to change often, and you don't want to rely on yourself to remember to find time to do this manually on a regular basis. However, do remember to create a rule in your firewall to allow UDP port 500 as this is the port used by IKE.[15]

---

[15]Section 10.17 has an **ipfw** example.

The SA, or Security Association, is the IPsec term for a connection. When a VPN is established, one SA pair is created for each protocol used (i.e. one for AH and one for ESP). SAs are created in pairs as each SA is one directional, so two are required (one for each direction). These SA pairs are stored at each peer. If your peer has SAs, it means that a VPN tunnel has successfully been established.

Since each peer is capable of establishing multiple tunnels with multiple peers, the SAs have a unique number so you can tell which SAs belong to which peers. That number is called an SPI or Security Parameter Index.

SAs are stored in a database which is called, surprisingly enough, the SAD or Security Association Database. We will see this database again when we set up an IPsec VPN.

Each IPsec peer also has a second database, the SPD or Security Policy Database. This database contains the policy you have pre-configured on the peer. Most VPN implementations allow you to create multiple policies so you can choose the algorithm combinations which are suited to each peer with which you want to establish.

What sort of configuration goes into a policy?

1. The symmetric algorithm(s) you are willing to use to encrypt/decrypt the data.

2. The cryptographic checksum(s) you are willing to use to ensure the integrity of the data.

3. The type of authentication method you are willing to use to authenticate the peer. Pre-shared secrets or RSA digital certificates are the most common forms of authentication.

4. Whether to use tunnel mode or transport mode.

5. Which Diffie Hellman group to use.

6. How often to re-authenticate the peer.

7. How often to exchange the key used to encrypt/decrypt the data.

8. Whether or not to use PFS.

9. Whether to use AH, ESP, or both.

When creating the policy, it is usually possible to create an ordered list of algorithms and Diffie Hellman groups. The first to match on both peers will be used. Remember, it is very important to ensure that everything in the policy will allow for a match on the peer. Even if everything else in the policy matches but one portion does not match, the peers will be unable to negotiate the VPN. If you are configuring a VPN between two different types of systems, you should take the time to research which algorithms each system supports, so you can choose the most secure policy from what is available.

Phase One and Phase Two

Now, let's see how all of this works together. Establishing and maintaining an IPsec VPN tunnel occurs in two phases. In Phase One, the two peers negotiate an authentication method, encryption algorithm, hash algorithm, and Diffie Hellman group. They also authenticate each other. All of this can occur in either three clear text packets (known as aggressive mode) or in six clear text packets (known as main mode). Assuming this is successful, a Phase 1 SA (also called an IKE SA) is created and the peers move on to Phase Two.

In Phase Two, the keying material is generated, and the two peers agree upon the policy that will be used. This mode, which is called quick mode, differs from Phase One in that it can't occur until after Phase One is successful; also all of the Phase Two packets are encrypted. This makes troubleshooting a little more difficult as it is possible for Phase One to be successful but Phase Two to fail. If Phase Two is successful, it will result in a Phase 2 SA, also called an IPsec SA, and the tunnel will be fully established.

When does all of this occur? The very first time a packet arrives at a peer with a destination in another encryption domain, the peer will initiate Phase One with the peer associated with that other encryption domain. Assuming both peers successfully establish the tunnel, the tunnel will stay up, ready to receive packets. However, the peers will re-authenticate each other and re-compare their policies at a pre-configured time. This time is known as the Phase One or IKE SA lifetime.

The peers will also re-negotiate the key that is used to encrypt and decrypt the data at another pre-configured time known as the Phase Two or IPsec SA lifetime. The Phase Two lifetime is shorter than the Phase One lifetime as you do want to change the key often. A typical Phase Two lifetime is 60 minutes. A typical Phase One lifetime is 24 hours.

It is your job to ensure both peers are configured with the same lifetimes. If they are not, it is possible for the tunnel to be established initially, but then cease to work when one of the mis-matched lifetime periods arrives. You will also encounter strange problems if the Phase One lifetime is shorter than the Phase Two lifetime. If a previously working tunnel appears to hang, one of the first things to check is the two lifetime settings on each peer. Also, if you do change a policy on a peer, it won't take effect until the next time Phase One occurs. If you want your change to take effect immediately, you need to remove the SAs for that tunnel from the SAD. This will force a renegotiation using your new policy parameters.

We now have enough background information to create an IPsec VPN on your FreeBSD box. A demonstration of the required configurations is the subject of the next section.

Additional Resources

Original Article:

`http://www.onlamp.com/pub/a/bsd/2002/12/12/FreeBSD_Basics.html`

VPNLabs:

`http://www.vpnlabs.com/`

VPN Consortium:

`http://www.vpnc.org/`

10.16 Configuring IPsec

When I first started configuring VPNs, I quickly discovered two things. First, there is more than one way to configure a VPN correctly. Along with my demonstration configuration files, I'll be including URLs to other IPsec tutorials, and you'll see for yourself that the syntax will vary slightly from tutorial to tutorial. Don't let the discrepancies bother you; instead, choose a configuration style that makes sense to you and results in a working VPN. Second, I found that I was typically left to my own devices when a VPN didn't work. There are few things in life more frustrating than following a set of instructions, only to discover that they don't work for your specific situation. Accordingly, I've included error messages which I have run across and my resolutions in the hopes that they might aid you in troubleshooting.

I'll be demonstrating a tunnel between two FreeBSD machines acting as VPN gateways. While my demonstration is specific to FreeBSD, it's possible to successfully apply the logic underlying the configurations to allow any system to access any IPsec VPN gateway. If this is your first VPN configuration, try it between two FreeBSD systems first. Once you get a handle on how a working tunnel operates and how to resolve the pitfalls you may come across, you'll be in good shape to experiment with other systems. The success of your experiments will depend upon the VPN gateway you are connecting to and how far the vendor has deviated from the IPsec standard by adding extra features.

Getting the Necessary Software

In order for your FreeBSD system to use IPsec, you must first configure IPsec support into your kernel as it is not included in GENERIC. If you're unsure whether your custom kernel already has IPsec support, use this command:

```
% sysctl -a | grep ipsec
```

If you don't get anything back, you need to recompile your kernel. If your tunnel is between two FreeBSD machines, both machines need IPsec support. This is how I configured my kernels. First, as the superuser, I copied the GENERIC kernel configuration file to a file I called IPSEC:

```
# cp /usr/src/sys/i386/conf/GENERIC /usr/src/sys/i386/conf/IPSEC
```

Then, using my favorite editor, I added the following four lines to the options section of /usr/src/sys/i386/conf/IPSEC:

```
options         IPSEC
options         IPSEC_ESP
options         IPSEC_DEBUG
options         IPSEC_FILTERGIF
```

Once you've saved your changes:

```
# cd /usr/src
# make buildkernel KERNCONF=IPSEC && \
    make installkernel KERNCONF=IPSEC
```

Normally I would reboot after a kernel is installed, but in this instance I'll wait until I've finished the rest of my configurations.

When you install IPsec support, you are installing the ability to use AH and ESP and to understand SADs and SPDs. However, you still have to create the policy that will be stored in that SPD and the SAs that will be stored in the SAD. It is possible to do all of this manually using a command known as **setkey**. But you may remember that it's better to use a key negotiation protocol to create those SAs for you on a regular basis. IKE, also known as ISAKMP, is the key negotiation protocol used by IPsec.

Two possible ways to install IKE support on your FreeBSD can be found in ports collection. The first is called **racoon2** and the second is a port of OpenBSD's implementation called **isakmpd**. I've found that the syntax used by **isakmpd** is easier for a novice to understand so I'll demonstrate its usage.

To install **isakmpd**:

```
# pkg_add -r isakmpd
```

Creating the Policy

Once this is installed, I have the necessary ingredients for the VPN and can now concentrate on the VPN policy. That policy will be limited to the parameters supported by isakmpd, which can be found in **man isakmpd.conf**. I've summarized those parameters in Table 10.14.

Table 10.14: IKE Key Management Daemon Parameters

Feature	isakmpd
Authentication Methods	RSA, preshared-key, DSS
Encryption Algorithms	3DES, DES, Blowfish, CAST, AES
Integrity Algorithms	MD5, SHA1, RIPEMD, SHA2-256,384,512
Encryption Modes	transport, tunnel
DH Groups	1, 2, 5, 14
PFS	supported
Phase 1 default lifetime	one hour
Phase 2 default lifetime	20 minutes

Remember, it is important to ensure that the policy you configure will match up on both peers. If the other VPN gateway isn't running **isakmpd**, you'll have to research that vendor's documentation to see which parameters are supported to ensure you configure the most secure policy that will result in a match on both peers.

I've decided to use the policy in Table 10.15.

Table 10.15: My VPN Policy

Authentication method	pre-shared secret of "dontguessme"
Encryption algorithm	blowfish
Authentication algorithm	SHA1
Encryption mode	tunnel
DH group	5
PFS	yes
Phase 1 lifetime	24 hour
Phase 2 lifetime	60 min

Whenever I configure a VPN, I always write the policy parameters on a piece of paper which I can refer to as I configure the policy. Underneath the policy, I sketch out the two gateways I'll be configuring and clearly label their IP addresses in Figure 10.9.

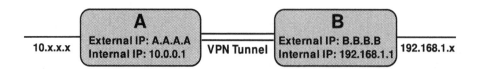

Figure 10.9: A logical VPN diagram

You'll note that each gateway has two interface cards and two IP addresses. The external IP is the address used to connect to the Internet. The internal IP will usually be a private range address. Notice that I haven't given you my real external addresses, but have labeled them as *A.A.A.A* and *B.B.B.B* for the purposes of this section.

It only takes a few minutes to sketch out your network, but it might save you hours of troubleshooting. It is very easy to inadvertently place the wrong IP in the wrong configuration file if you don't have a sketch to refer to.

Configuration on Gateway A

We're ready to start the configurations; I'll start with the configuration on Gateway A. The directory `/usr/local/share/examples/isakmpd/` contains several working VPN examples for which you simply replace the IP addresses and double-check that the parameters match your policy needs. In my example, Gateway A is on the "west side"; since **isakmpd** assumes the config file is `/usr/local/etc/isakmpd/isakmpd.conf` unless otherwise specified, I'll copy the west sample file to that location:

```
# mkdir /usr/local/etc/isakmpd
# cp /usr/local/share/examples/isakmpd/VPN-west.conf \
    /usr/local/etc/isakmpd/isakmpd.conf
```

Once I edit that file to match my IP addresses and policy it will look like this:

```
# 10.0.0.1 - west A.A.A.A - B.B.B.B east - 192.168.1.1
#
# "west" and "east" are the respective security gateways (aka VPN-nodes).

[Phase 1]
B.B.B.B= ISAKMP-peer-east
[Phase 2]
Connections= IPsec-west-east

[ISAKMP-peer-east]
Phase= 1
Transport= udp
Address= B.B.B.B
Configuration= Default-main-mode
Authentication= dontguessme

[IPsec-west-east]
Phase= 2
ISAKMP-peer= ISAKMP-peer-east
```

```
Configuration= Default-quick-mode
Local-ID= Net-west
Remote-ID= Net-east

[Net-west]
ID-type= IPV4_ADDR_SUBNET
Network= 10.0.0.0
Netmask= 255.0.0.0

[Net-east]
ID-type= IPV4_ADDR_SUBNET
Network= 192.168.1.0
Netmask= 255.255.255.0

[Default-main-mode]
DOI= IPSEC
EXCHANGE_TYPE= ID_PROT
Transforms= BLF-SHA

[Default-quick-mode]
DOI= IPSEC
EXCHANGE_TYPE= QUICK_MODE
Suites= QM-ESP-BLF-SHA-PFS-SUITE

[General]
Default-phase-1-lifetime= 86400
Default-phase-2-lifetime= 3600
```

Configuration on Gateway B

On Gateway B, I copied and edited `/usr/local/share/examples/isakmpd/VPN-east.conf` so that it matched from B's perspective. Here is the final result on Gateway B:

```
# 10.0.0.1 - west A.A.A.A - B.B.B.B east - 192.168.1.1
#
# "west" and "east" are the respective security gateways (aka VPN-nodes).

[Phase 1]
A.A.A.A= ISAKMP-peer-west

[Phase 2]
Connections= IPsec-east-west

[ISAKMP-peer-west]
Phase= 1
Transport= udp
Address= A.A.A.A
Configuration= Default-main-mode
```

```
Authentication= dontguessme

[IPsec-east-west]
Phase= 2
ISAKMP-peer= ISAKMP-peer-west
Configuration= Default-quick-mode
Local-ID= Net-east
Remote-ID= Net-west

[Net-west]
ID-type= IPV4_ADDR_SUBNET
Network= 10.0.0.0
Netmask= 255.0.0.0

[Net-east]
ID-type= IPV4_ADDR_SUBNET
Network= 192.168.1.0
Netmask= 255.255.255.0

[Default-main-mode]
DOI= IPSEC
EXCHANGE_TYPE= ID_PROT
Transforms= 3DES-SHA

[Default-quick-mode]
DOI= IPSEC
EXCHANGE_TYPE= QUICK_MODE
Suites= QM-ESP-AES-SHA-PFS-SUITE

[General]
Default-phase-1-lifetime= 86400
Default-phase-2-lifetime= 3600
```

Next I'll copy the file containing the pre-shared secret on both gateways:

```
# cp /usr/local/share/examples/isakmpd/policy \
    /usr/local/etc/isakmpd/isakmpd.policy
```

Note that this file already contains a pre-shared secret which does not match the one I wish to use. I simply have to edit the `Licensees` line so it matches:

```
Licensees:   "passphrase:dontguessme"
```

Make sure that edited file exists on both gateways. Doublecheck for typos in the password itself, especially if you use a hard to guess password, which you should.

At this point, **isakmpd** is configured and ready to go. I just need a few more configurations to tell FreeBSD about the VPN. To ensure that the included startup script is used, add this line to /etc/rc.conf:

```
isakmpd_enable="YES"
ipsec_enable="YES"
ipsec_file="/etc/ipsec.conf"
gif_interfaces="gif0"
ifconfig_gif0="10.0.0.1 netmask 255.0.0.0 192.168.1.1 netmask 255.255.255.0"
gifconfig_gif0="A.A.A.A netmask 255.255.240.0 B.B.B.B netmask 255.255.240.0"
```

The last two lines tell your FreeBSD system which addresses to use in the headers. Remember that in tunnel mode the original IP packet contains the IP addresses of the real source and destination, which are usually private range addresses within the two encryption domains. The new IP header created by ESP contains the external IP addresses of the two VPN gateways. The `ifconfig_gif0` configuration contains the internal IP addresses of the two gateways and the `gifconfig_gif0` configuration contains the external IP addresses of the two gateways. On Gateway A, you should place Gateway A's IP addresses first, followed by Gateway B's. On Gateway B, switch the order so Gateway B's addresses are first.

The `ipsec.conf` File

The last file we need to create is `ipsec.conf`. At first, this file seems redundant as it creates the policy stored in the SPD. You may be thinking, "I've already configured that policy in isakmpd.conf". Actually, you only told the IKE protocol what policy parameters it should use when negotiating the SAs which will be placed in the SAD. However, **isakmpd** can't place the policy in the SPD for you; that is the job of **setkey**. Creating `/etc/ipsec.conf` means you won't have to run **setkey** manually every time you reboot.

My file on Gateway A looks like this:

more /etc/ipsec.conf

```
#delete all existing entries from the SAD and SPD databases
flush;
spdflush;

#add the policy to the SPD database
spdadd 10.0.0.0/8 192.168.1.0/24 ipencap -P out ipsec
esp/tunnel/A.A.A.A-B.B.B.B/require;

spdadd 192.168.1.0/24 10.0.0.0/8 ipencap -P in ipsec
esp/tunnel/B.B.B.B-A.A.A.A/require;
```

The policy lines (the two lines that start with `spdadd`) aren't one long wrapped line, meaning you can press enter after the word `ipsec`. The first policy line says whenever packets from network 10.0.0.0 need to go out to network 192.168.1.0, they are required to be encrypted by ESP and to go through the tunnel that goes from Gateway A to Gateway B.

The second policy line says that whenever packets from network 192.168.1.0 need to come in to network 10.0.0.0, they are required to be encrypted by ESP and to go through the tunnel that goes from Gateway B to Gateway A.

The file on Gateway B will be similar, but the addresses will be reversed so in and out match up. See why it is handy to have a sketch of your network so you can remember which address belongs where?

The last thing to do is to change the permissions on the config files:

```
# chmod 600 /usr/local/etc/isakmpd/isakmpd.conf
# chmod 600 /usr/local/etc/isakmpd/isakmpd.policy
```

We've covered a lot in this section. The next one will show you what to watch out for when you reboot your computer after the configurations are complete. We'll then test the tunnel and work through some troubleshooting scenarios.

Additional Resources

Original Article:

```
http://www.onlamp.com/pub/a/bsd/2002/12/26/FreeBSD_Basics.html
```

IPsec Section of FreeBSD Handbook:

```
http://www.freebsd.org/doc/en_US.ISO8859-1/books/handbook/ipsec.html
```

Implementing OpenBSD's IPsec

```
http://www2.papamike.ca:8082/tutorials/pub/obsd_ipsec.html#scenario_4
```

10.17 Debugging IPsec

The one configuration I purposefully left out last time is the necessary changes to the firewall ruleset. You might remember that we need to allow UDP port 500 for IKE and protocol number 50 for ESP. The syntax for those rules will depend upon whether your system is protected by **ipfw**, **ipf**, **pf**, or is behind another type of firewall. It will also depend upon the order of the existing rules in your ruleset and the degree of paranoia dictated by your security policy.

For this demonstration, I'll create two rules near the top of a **ipfw** ruleset. I may have to tweak their placement later on when I start working with the negotiated tunnel. Here are the example **ipfw** rules:

```
#rules to allow IPsec VPN
add 00201 allow log esp from any to any
add 00203 allow log udp from any 500 to any
```

Until you are happy with your tunnel, you should log your temporary rules. If your security policy allows it, consider allowing all sources and destinations until your tunnel is successful. Afterwards, you can tighten up those rules by specifying particular sources, destinations, directions, and interfaces.

Post-Configuration Tests

Once I've added my firewall rules, I'll reboot both gateways into their new IPsec enabled kernels. I'll also watch the startup messages as they go by. In particular, I'm looking for error messages. If you see something interesting in your startup messages, press the scroll lock key and use your page up key to go back to the error. Make sure all of your firewall rules load successfully. If you have a typo, your startup message will indicate which rule prevented the rulebase from loading.

You should also see this message in your output:

```
ipsec: enabled
```

If you don't, doublecheck that `/etc/rc.conf` contains this line:

```
ipsec_enable="YES"
```

You should also see your route being added:

```
Starting local daemons:add net 192.168.1.0: gateway 10.0.0.1
```

Once you have resolved any error messages, login and verify that the `gif` was successfully created:

```
# ifconfig gif0
gif0: flags=8010<POINTOPOINT,MULTICAST> mtu 1280
        tunnel inet A.A.A.A --> B.B.B.B
```

You can also verify your route:

```
# netstat -rn
Routing tables
Internet:
Destination     Gateway         Flags   Refs    Use     Netif   Expire
<snip>
192.168.1       10.0.0.1        UGSc    0       0       ed0
```

Finally, verify that the SPD contains the correct policy:

```
# setkey -DP
192.168.1.0/24[any] 10.0.0.0/8[any] any
        in ipsec
        esp/tunnel/B.B.B.B-A.A.A.A/require
        spid=2 seq=1 pid=183
        refcnt=1
10.0.0.0/8[any] 192.168.1.0/24[any] any
        out ipsec
        esp/tunnel/A.A.A.A-B.B.B.B/require
        spid=1 seq=0 pid=183
        refcnt=1
```

If you don't have a policy, there is a problem with `/etc/ipsec.conf`. You either have a typo or you forgot to tell `/etc/rc.conf` to load that file at bootup. Once **isakmpd** is up at both peers, and both peers have a matching policy, you are ready to try tunnel negotiation.

Testing the Tunnel

Whenever I negotiate a tunnel for the first time, I run several tests and either take full advantage of my virtual terminals, or I use /usr/ports/sysutils/screen if I'm restricted to one terminal. First, I start the isakmp daemon in logging mode, then instruct **tcpdump** to read the logging file:

```
# isakmpd -L
# tcpdump -vs 1500 -r /var/run/isakmpd.pcap
```

Then, I open another terminal where I'll try to negotiate the tunnel. If your firewall rules allow you to **ping**, pinging the inside interface of the peer is a very good tunnel test. If all goes well, your ping will hang for a moment while the tunnel is negotiated, then you'll see your ping responses displayed to your terminal. You'll also see output in the first terminal which is running **tcpdump**.

Note that first the Phase 1, or ISAKMP, SA is established with a unique SPI. Then two Phase 2, or IPsec, SAs are established, one in each direction, and each with a unique SPI.

```
# tcpdump port 500
tcpdump: listening on ed0
13:04:31.067156 A.A.A.A.isakmp > B.B.B.B.isakmp: isakmp: phase 1 I agg:
[|sa]
13:04:31.067682 B.B.B.B.isakmp > A.A.A.A.isakmp: isakmp: phase 1 R agg:
[|sa]
13:04:31.680474 A.A.A.A.isakmp > B.B.B.B.isakmp: isakmp: phase 1 I agg:
(hash: len=20)
13:04:31.681046 A.A.A.A.isakmp > B.B.B.B.isakmp: isakmp: phase 2/others I
inf[E]: [encrypted hash]
13:04:31.697564 A.A.A.A.isakmp > B.B.B.B.isakmp: isakmp: phase 2/others I
oakley-quick[E]: [encrypted hash]
13:04:31.703306 B.B.B.B.isakmp > A.A.A.A.isakmp: isakmp: phase 2/others R
inf[E]: [encrypted hash]
13:04:31.770199 B.B.B.B.isakmp > A.A.A.A.isakmp: isakmp: phase 2/others R
oakley-quick[E]: [encrypted hash]
```

You may remember that Phase One aggressive mode uses 3 packets, which you can see from this **tcpdump**. This is followed by Phase Two. Note that all Phase Two packets are encrypted.

Finally, you know your tunnel is fully established when your SAD contains the SAs. You can confirm that with:

```
# setkey -D
A.A.A.A B.B.B.B
        esp mode=tunnel spi=63238165(0x03c4f015) reqid=0(0x00000000)
        E: blowfish-cbc  a24ac0e7 36f7e153 26f81300 43d0d333
        A: hmac-sha1  6bb84116 e90d2b1b 2ac95285 0dd394fb afa0c3d8
        seq=0x00000004 replay=4 flags=0x00000000 state=mature
        created: Dec 29 13:07:21 2002   current: Dec 29 13:15:32 2002
        diff: 491(s)    hard: 86400(s)  soft: 69120(s)
        last: Dec 29 13:07:35 2002      hard: 0(s)      soft: 0(s)
        current: 544(bytes)     hard: 0(bytes)  soft: 0(bytes)
```

```
        allocated: 4     hard: 0 soft: 0
        sadb_seq=1 pid=50830 refcnt=2
B.B.B.B A.A.A.A
        esp mode=tunnel spi=82702499(0x04edf0a3) reqid=0(0x00000000)
        E: blowfish-cbc  ece45b91 af659b1f 1031b8eb e6268c60
        A: hmac-sha1  eb46c7b6 12051da0 567ca3a6 1c889e72 3faa5553
        seq=0x00000004 replay=4 flags=0x00000000 state=mature
        created: Dec 29 13:07:21 2002   current: Dec 29 13:15:32 2002
        diff: 491(s)     hard: 86400(s)  soft: 69120(s)
        last: Dec 29 13:07:35 2002      hard: 0(s)       soft: 0(s)
        current: 336(bytes)    hard: 0(bytes)  soft: 0(bytes)
        allocated: 4     hard: 0 soft: 0
        sadb_seq=0 pid=50830 refcnt=1
```

If your tunnel successfully negotiates, give yourself a pat on the back, and do the happy dance. If it doesn't, take heart and follow along as I demonstrate some common errors.

Troubleshooting

If you don't receive any **tcpdump** output at all, there aren't any IKE packets being sent. This usually means that you forgot to allow UDP port 500 on your firewall, or forgot to tell your firewall about the changes to your ruleset, so your firewall is discarding those packets. However, it could also indicate a routing or policy misconfiguration. Remember, your policy tells **isakmpd** when it is required to negotiate a tunnel.

For example, part of my policy in /etc/ipsec.conf states:

```
spdadd 10.0.0.0/8 192.168.1.0/24  -P out ipsec
```

This means that if I try to send packets (from a **ping**, for example) to a host with an IP address starting with 192.168.1, those packets won't be sent until IKE has negotiated a tunnel. It also means that if I send packets to any other network, IKE does not come into play. If **tcpdump** shows that IKE isn't being used, double-check that your policy does require IPsec for the remote network.

Sometimes a **tcpdump** will show your packets going out, but no replies coming back. This usually indicates that the firewall at the peer is discarding the packets. Check the firewall rules at the peer to ensure they allow IKE and ESP.

Sometimes Phase One will fail, and you can't quite tell why from the log. When this happens, I bring out the big guns and use Wireshark. This allows me to analyze the policy negotiations in great detail, as it records each policy parameter as sent by each peer. If Phase One is failing, it will be because of a policy mismatch or a peer authentication failure. If it is a policy mismatch, you should find it in isakmpd.conf. However, if the policies are identical, you'll really need that packet sniff to pinpoint exactly what is happening.

Advanced Troubleshooting

Things get a lot more interesting if Phase One succeeds but Phase Two fails. Once Phase One is finished, all of the data is encrypted. A packet sniff won't help you in pinpointing which policy parameter is failing to match up. If both peers are running **isakmpd**, the culprit will most likely be a typo or mismatch in isakmpd.conf. However, if the other peer is not running **isakmpd**, you may have some detective work ahead of you.

Many commercial IPsec implementations include additional features. It's unfortunate that some of those features are only supported by that particular product and are usually enabled by default. If Phase One works, Phase Two hangs, and you know you've configured both peers with identical parameters, you've most likely stumbled upon such a feature. Scour that product's documentation and vendor's knowledge base looking for default configurations and how to disable them.

Failing that, you may be able to find working configs between **isakmpd** and the particular product you are struggling with. I've found the VPNC Interoperability Profiles at `http://www.vpnc.org/InteropProfiles/` to be useful.

Finally, if your blood, sweat, and tears results in a working tunnel, be kind and post your how-to somewhere on the Internet. You just might make a harried admin's day.

Interactions with Anti-Spoofing Rules

The last scenario I want to discuss in this section deals with VPNs and anti-spoofing rules. Depending upon the firewall(s) you are using to protect the gateways, this may or may not become an issue. This scenario can be the most frustrating as IKE is able to successfully establish the VPN. Unfortunately, all of the packets that enter the resulting tunnel end up being discarded by the firewall's anti-spoof rules.

If you're unfamiliar with anti-spoof rules, they are the set of rules that drop all traffic entering a network from a private address range. Normally, this is useful, as most legitimate traffic coming in from the Internet can't have a source address in the 10.x.x.x, 172.16.x.x-172.31.x.x, or 192.168.x.x ranges as Internet routers drop those addresses. A VPN tunnel operates differently. While in the tunnel, the packets have the Internet routable addresses of the peers' external interfaces. However, the data in the packet itself is destined for an internal address, which is usually within the private address range.

Whether or not this is a problem depends upon the firewall and the order in which packet processing occurs. Several factors are at play here: a packet needs to be encrypted or decrypted, it must be NATed, and it also needs to be compared to a firewall ruleset to see if the packet is allowed to pass. If the NATing occurs in the wrong place, it is quite possible that a legitimate packet will be mistaken for a malicious, spoofed packet.

How do you resolve the situation if your particular firewall's processing order is working against you? Sometimes trial and error in rule order will work. You've already created rules to allow the VPN to be established; those were the IKE and ESP rules. You'll still need rules allowing your users to access the services you wish to allow through the tunnel, otherwise you wouldn't have created a tunnel in the first place. Try placing those rules towards the top of a rulebase. Include the `quick` keyword in the case of an **ipf** or **pf** rulebase.

If that doesn't help, it may be time to reconsider the usefulness of the anti-spoof rules in regards to your particular security policy. Balance the need for the VPN against the benefits gained from the anti-spoof rules. If you log those rules for a week or two, you'll have an idea of how much those rules are used and how much protection they offer.

If your security policy requires the anti-spoof rules, there is some information that can be gleaned from the Internet, which might apply to your situation. As firewalls mature, they gain extra features. There may indeed be an extra switch or keyword that you can place in your rulebase that will resolve the anti-spoof problem. That extra knob may be in the works and available in another six months.

Additional Resources

Original Article:

`http://www.onlamp.com/pub/a/bsd/2003/01/09/FreeBSD_Basics.html`

Index

www.ingramcontent.com/pod-product-compliance
Lightning Source LLC
Chambersburg PA
CBHW080131060326
40689CB00018B/3742